a gift
film
war   4/17/70

Measurement and Evaluation
in the Modern School

Measurement and Evaluation in the Modern School

J. RAYMOND GERBERICH, Ph.D.

PROFESSOR OF EDUCATION

and

DIRECTOR, BUREAU OF EDUCATIONAL RESEARCH AND SERVICE

UNIVERSITY OF CONNECTICUT

HARRY A. GREENE, Ph.D.

PROFESSOR EMERITUS OF EDUCATION

STATE UNIVERSITY OF IOWA

ALBERT N. JORGENSEN, Ph.D.

PRESIDENT

UNIVERSITY OF CONNECTICUT

DAVID McKAY COMPANY, INC.

NEW YORK

MEASUREMENT AND EVALUATION IN THE MODERN SCHOOL

COPYRIGHT © 1962 BY DAVID MC KAY COMPANY, INC.

PUBLISHED SIMULTANEOUSLY IN THE DOMINION OF CANADA

LIBRARY OF CONGRESS CATALOG CARD NUMBER: 61-13537

MANUFACTURED IN THE UNITED STATES OF AMERICA

VAN REES PRESS • NEW YORK

Preface

This volume is a supplement to, but neither a revision of nor a replacement for, its 1953 and 1954 predecessors, the second editions of *Measurement and Evaluation in the Elementary School* and *Measurement and Evaluation in the Secondary School*. It is the eighth book in a series started by a single volume in 1929 and continued in separate books for the elementary and secondary levels in 1935 and 1936 by the two last-named authors of the present volume. Authorship was extended for the 1942 and 1943 first editions of the two titles previously listed by addition of the first-named author of the present book.

The third of a century since the first of these volumes appeared has been marked by significant changes in educational philosophy and psychology and by resultant adjustments in the curriculum, in teaching methods, and in instructional materials as well as in classroom measurement and evaluation. The continued and extensive interest on the part of teachers and students of education in the justifiably important place of measurement tools and techniques in education and the wide acceptance given the predecessors of this volume combine to encourage the authors now to present in this single volume a rather short and nontechnical discussion of the applications of measurement and evaluation to the problems of instruction in today's schools.

In this supplement to the two volumes published in 1953 and 1954, standardized tests and standardized techniques are expanded by the inclusion of two new areas—measures of socioeconomic status and measures of health and physical fitness. Attention to measurement in these areas augments the continued emphasis on tests of general and special mental abilities, on inventories and techniques for use in personality measurement, and on all kinds of achievement tests. It is possible to survey educationally important aspects of a pupil's traits and characteristics by measuring his home and socioeconomic background, his present level of physical fitness, and his present status in mental and personality characteristics and educational attainments. Instruments and techniques for making such a survey, and also for projecting an estimate of his probable future, are nontechnically but comprehensively presented in a section of this volume.

The authors have continued to stress the crucial and practical classroom problems of improving all types of teacher-made examinations, tests, and evaluative instruments. Oral and essay tests are supplemented by a brief treatment of short-answer tests. Techniques for measuring skills of various important types are dealt with in two ways—measuring the performance itself and evaluating the product resulting from the performance. Various evaluative tests and other instruments and a number of evaluative techniques are also treated briefly and simply. The construction, improvement, and use of informal objective tests are accorded a new and expanded treatment that includes numerous samples of major item types and specific suggestions for writing the most widely useful varieties of items. The section of this volume devoted to these classroom approaches to pupil evaluation shows how the teacher or prospective teacher can develop skill in devising his own achievement tests and evolve his own techniques for measuring the attainments of his pupils.

By principle and by example, the construction, improvement, and use of all types of evaluative devices are treated in detail for major subjects and subject areas as well as for all grade levels from the primary through the senior high school. Each of the ten chapters of this type consists of an integrated treatment of the various appropriate tests and techniques of pupil appraisal—aptitude and prognostic tests, paper-and-pencil and performance tests of achievement, attitude scales, interest inventories, and other evaluative instruments and techniques. These chapters and the final chapter on general achievement tests are intended to supply the type of attention to modern achievement measurement by subject areas that users of earlier volumes in this series of books have reported to be especially significant and helpful.

Any modern teacher or education student who wishes to analyze test results effectively for small groups of pupils has definite need for at least a few simple statistical skills and related understandings. The simplest level, involving estimates based on test scores arranged in descending order of size, requires nothing more difficult computationally than simple multiplication and long division. A second level entails the arrangement of scores in frequency distributions and slightly more demanding computational procedures. Methods for estimating or for computing the basically important statistical measures are both presented in a section of this volume—at the level of greatest simplicity for those students or teachers whose greatest concern is with the relatively small groups of pupils in individual classrooms and at the second level for those who prefer to use somewhat more precise methods for small pupil groups or who may have reason to analyze test results for large groups. Moreover, the reliability and validity of tests and such derived scores as percentile ranks, important in the interpretation of test results, are developed either by methods of estimation or of simple computation. The authors believe that the student and teacher will find outlined in this volume the most simple and nontechnical procedures available for obtaining the statistical measures that are needed in classroom measurement and evaluation.

The authors consider this volume most suitable as a first book in measurement and evaluation for those students who at the time of studying it know very little about measurement in education and its possibilities for the improvement of classroom instruction. However, it also provides ready sources of help for the experienced teacher who may wish to become more adept in selecting, constructing, and using modern tests and techniques of pupil appraisal in the classrooom. It is also believed that the volume provides a systematic and readily usable handbook for any serious student or teacher requiring a straightforward and understandable discussion of all of the fundamental ideas and techniques of evaluation in the classroom.

To their many colleagues and friends and the innumerable classroom teachers, students, and teachers of measurements who through their comments and suggestions have contributed directly or indirectly to selection of content and determination of emphasis in this volume, the authors wish to express their grateful acknowledgments and thanks. They are especially indebted to the many users of the seven preceding volumes who by their consistently friendly but sometimes critical comments have stimulated and encouraged the development of this volume. Teachers who prefer a somewhat longer and more technical treatment of pupil appraisal and who feel a need for separate volumes at the elementary and secondary levels may be pleased to know that the 1953 and 1954 publications in this series will continue to be available.

THE AUTHORS

January, 1962

Contents

Tables

Figures

PART 1

Acquiring Background for
Pupil Appraisal

The classroom teacher has recently come to occupy an increasingly responsible, challenging, and interesting place in the modern school program of pupil appraisal. The teacher today is naturally expected to take care of the usual problems involved in evaluating most classroom attainments of the pupils he teaches. He is often expected, also, to aid in the selection of tests for schoolwide use and perhaps to administer and even to score standardized tests of achievement, of intelligence, and sometimes of personality. Moreover, it is reasonable to assume that he knows enough about such tests and about test scores and other measurement results to be able to translate the results into effective classroom practices.

Teachers can with relatively little difficulty acquire the level of skills, knowledges, understandings, and other outcomes of learning necessary for fulfilling these responsibilities. The authors of this volume believe that teachers can do so most effectively after attaining an overview of modern methods of pupil appraisal and their historical backgrounds, after learning about the characteristics of good examinations, and after gaining understandings about the major ways in which pupil behavior is modified by instruction. The primary purpose of Part 1 is to supply this type of orientation.

1

EDUCATIONAL MEASUREMENT AND EVALUATION

FOR CLASSROOM TEACHERS

The purpose of this chapter is to introduce the reader to several general ideas concerning educational measurement and evaluation and to provide a brief preview of the contents and organization of this book, as follows:

A. Measurement in education not a new idea.
B. Meanings of testing, measuring, and evaluating.
C. Needs for testing in present-day schools.
D. Measurement of pupil background and status.
E. Objectives and outcomes of instruction.
F. Measurement of instructional and other learning outcomes.
G. Significance of measurement and evaluation in education.
H. Organization of this volume.

Teachers have always attempted to measure the growth and progress of their pupils toward desired educational goals. They have tried also to diagnose pupil deficiencies and to supply appropriate remedial treatment. Moreover, they have wanted to know why some pupils learn easily and rapidly while others are slow and dull in the classroom. Attempts to measure pupil progress, to diagnose learning difficulties, and to determine underlying reasons for individual differences in learning ability were largely matters of personal judgment on the part of the individual teacher over a period of many generations, but the present century has seen significant improvement in the situation.

1. DEVELOPMENT OF OBJECTIVE METHODS
IN EDUCATIONAL AND MENTAL MEASUREMENT

Studies of the reliability of such methods as are mentioned above gradually cast doubt on their accuracy, with the result that a continuous search for more dependable procedures was instituted. It is only recently, in actuality, that any high degree of accuracy has been introduced into classroom measurement. Today the testing movement has passed through the first stages of its development. Forty years ago it was necessary to popularize the idea. Now the advantages of objective tests are recognized by most educators and even by most laymen. Moreover, the tests themselves have been greatly improved in content and in structure as a result of the critical analysis and refinement to which they have been subjected. They are not now looked upon as mysterious instruments for the confusion of the uninitiated, but are viewed as useful devices for assisting the professionally minded educator to improve the conditions under which children learn and teachers teach. If they aid in the accomplishment of this, the primary purpose of the educative process, they are thoroughly justified.

Testing, Measuring, and Evaluating Instructional Outcomes

Several different attitudes toward the use of educational measurements in the school have held sway at various times since the objective approach to the measurement of pupil intelligence and achievement made its appearance shortly after the beginning of the twentieth century. These different attitudes or approaches fall under the following headings: (1) testing, (2) measuring, and (3) evaluating and appraising.

Testing. Chronologically, the first concept was that of testing, which considered the development of objective devices for testing intelligence and achievement of pupils to be of major importance. This attitude was doubtless the result of the early need for the development of objective instruments, for such instruments were not available in any significant quantity for some years after the concept of objectivity of tests first made its appearance in the field of education.

Measuring. When objective tests became fairly numerous and classroom teachers began to use objective methods in their own examinations, attention turned more toward the use of test results and toward the development of instruments for measuring certain of the more elusive types of instructional outcomes that do not lend themselves readily to objective measurement. This period may be characterized as one during which the major approach was that of measuring.

Evaluating and appraising. The development of the evaluation and appraisal concept was doubtless prompted by the increasing realization that paper-and-pencil tests can measure only a limited portion of the outcomes of instruction and types of pupil behavior about which the teacher and other school officers need information. Therefore, the present view is that objective tests constitute probably the major type of evaluative instruments but that such other means of measurement as the anecdotal record, the interview, the questionnaire, the rating scale, and such tools as the individual pupil profile, the class record, the cumulative record, and the case study also have a very significant place in the evaluation of pupil behavior and achievement. The evaluation concept has also doubtless been stimulated by the attention of educators and psychologists to the whole child and his behavior. This tendency to consider the child as a whole, rather than as an individual whose behavior and abilities can be catalogued into a number of different compartments, places definite responsibility on the user of tests and other instruments of evaluation for considering the child in this broad sense. It is through the application of the evaluation concept rather than of the narrower concepts of measuring and testing that this result is most effectively obtained.

Actually, then, the recent development of modern educational instruments of measurement and evaluation may be regarded as an extension and improvement of an old practice. The modern educational measuring instrument presents a quite accurate picture of the course objectives as well as an analysis of the underlying skills, knowledges, concepts, understandings, and other outcomes upon which accomplishment in different subject areas depends. Educational tests and the information resulting from their use in the classroom have come to be almost universally identified with good teaching practice. Today the professionally equipped teacher is expected to be well versed in their construction, selection, and use in the classroom.

Testing, Measuring, and Evaluating Mental Traits

A wide variety of tests that cannot be said to measure educational achievement but that have many educational uses have also come into existence rather recently as the result of a long process of study and development. Although their purposes and the names under which they go differ widely, they are designed in the main to discover aspects of pupil ability and personality that are related to learning and that seem in some pupils to hamper and in others to promote learning. Such instruments are usually referred to as mental tests.

Best known among instruments in these related areas are mental ability tests, which are to be distinguished from mental tests, and the closely similar instruments known as intelligence tests, scholastic aptitude tests, and psychological examinations. Other instruments for measuring such aspects of personality as interests, attitudes, and adjustments are also used in many modern schools. In any event, the tool kit of the present-day teacher is not complete unless he can select tests of these and still other more specialized types to serve his purposes and then make effective use of the results.

Modern Types of Classroom Needs for Tests

In most fields of human endeavor, the best results are obtained when the worker knows the material with which he has to work, knows what he is trying to accomplish, and knows how well he has succeeded in his efforts. He must know his material before he can make a judgment about what he can do with it. Then he must know what he desires and is expected to accomplish with his material. Finally he must know how well he has succeeded in accomplishing his purposes. If knowledge is lacking or inadequate at any stage in this process from raw material to finished product, the result is likely to be defective or not up to standard.

When the worker is a classroom teacher and the pupils are his material, closely similar conditions seem to apply. The teacher must know intimately the characteristics of his pupils if he is to teach them effectively. He must know what his instructional purposes and goals are if he is to work realistically toward their attainment. Furthermore, he must know the degree to which he has succeeded in bringing about the desired changes in his pupils. The next three sections of this chapter deal briefly with these three phases of a testing program—measurement of pupil background and status, instructional objectives and outcomes, and measurement of the results of instruction and learning. Many of the issues merely introduced in these three sections are discussed in considerable detail in other chapters of this volume.

2. MEASUREMENT OF PUPIL BACKGROUND AND STATUS

It seems feasible to distinguish three periods in considering a pupil's traits and characteristics at any given time—his status at that particular time; his preceding growth, development, and learning, as well as the environment in which these occurred; and, in anticipation, his subsequent growth, development, and learning. A major concern of educational measurement and evaluation is, of course, the pupil's present status. However, a second important concern is with the contributions of his past environment, growth, development, and learning to his present status. Information about both the present and the past can contribute greatly to the effective guidance of the pupil, not only in his present classroom and other school experiences but also in his later school and even postschool activities.

At least five measurable aspects of human traits and characteristics can be distinguished. These are home and social background and status, development and status in physical, in mental, and in personality characteristics, and behavioral changes resulting from learning. All five of these, and especially the changes resulting from learning, are treated extensively in Section 2 of this book for pupils in elementary and secondary schools.

Measurable Aspects of Home and Social Status

Increasingly during the last quarter century, teachers have been encouraged to look to the child's home, his father's occupation, his family's socioeconomic status, and other aspects of his background and present environment for partial explanations of his school behavior. The influences of the home, the community, and other primarily sociological agencies during the child's early and most formative years are later reflected in his educational attitudes, interests, and potentialities. A few of the ways in which the classroom teacher can take a careful look into this background, or at least use results obtained by others, are outlined in Chapter 4.

Measurable Aspects of Health and Physical Fitness

Students of educational measurement and evaluation are also much more concerned with the physical traits and characteristics and the physical fitness of pupils than was true even a decade or so ago. Pupil proficiencies not only in manual but also to a large degree in intellectual skills are dependent upon health, and physical and motor fitness. Among the variety of measurement tools in this area are medical and sensory tests, measures of body posture and body mechanics, cardiovascular tests, measures of strength and endurance, and the even more specific physical and motor fitness tests themselves. These areas, treated in Chapter 5, are distinguishable from the measures of achievement, or of instructional outcomes, in physical education and recreation discussed in Chapter 24.

Measurable Evidences of Mental Ability

Mental ability is a third important area in which pupil traits and characteristics are very influential in the determination of behavior. The three major distinctions among types of mental ability instruments are the general intelligence or mental ability tests, the tests of special mental abilities, and the multiaptitude test batteries. These, also involving important differences such as exist between individual and group tests and verbal and nonverbal tests, are the major concern of Chapter 6.

Measurable Characteristics of Personality

A pupil's personality is reflected in his attitudes, his interests, his modes of adjustment to life, and in all of his social behavior. It therefore becomes apparent that these aspects of personality are exceedingly important determiners of a pupil's reactions to his educational experiences in the school. The self-report inventories and scales filled out by the pupil himself and the more technical observational and projective techniques are presented in Chapter 7.

Measurable Aspects of Achievement

The changes brought about in pupils by their school and out-of-school learning are evidenced in their behavior. It is in the measurement of such behavior, known as educational outcomes, that achievement tests have their greatest significance. As the primary emphasis of this book is on educational measurement and evaluation, Chapter 8 is devoted to a treatment of standardized achievement testing in those aspects that should serve as a foundation for Part 3, on the construction and use of classroom tests and techniques, and Part 5, on measurement and evaluation in the school subjects.

3. INSTRUCTIONAL OBJECTIVES AND OUTCOMES

The second problem, that of determining what to measure, is a critical one in educational measurement and evaluation. It is here that the importance of the outcomes of instruction and of the related objectives becomes so apparent. Many lists of educational objectives are available, both for education conceived broadly and for specific school subjects and levels. Such lists often include statements that are too abstract, vague, ambiguous, and even visionary to serve appropriately as leads for constructing tests designed to measure related outcomes. Such words as *habits, ideals,*

ideas, and *qualities,* and such phrases as *ability to, apprehension of, awareness of, capability to, command over, comprehension of, desire to, disposition to, furtherance of, increase in, realization of,* and *sense of* are
representative of the vague and indefinite terminology often employed
by curriculum specialists.

The authors sincerely believe that instructional objectives and outcomes
must be stated in exact and meaningful terms if they are to be of optimum
value to the classroom teacher in his measurement of pupil achievement,
or, for that matter, to the test maker at any level of skill or proficiency.
This seems to be a necessity if the test maker is to distinguish pupil behaviors that indicate or represent the attainment of the desired outcomes,
and if he is to have a reasonable degree of assurance that he is actually
measuring what he sets out to measure.

General Outcomes of Elementary and Secondary Education

One of the most significant lists of general objectives or goals is found
in Kearney's report for the Mid-Century Committee on Outcomes in
Elementary Education.[1] The four types of behavioral changes—knowledge
and understanding, skill and competence, attitude and interest, and action
pattern—are extensively treated from the standpoint of the teacher and
student of educational measurement separately for the primary grades,
the intermediate grades, and the junior high school. Kearney outlined
realistic goals in these four areas at the three different educational levels
and in nine broad experience and curriculum areas: (1) physical development, health, and body care, (2) individual social and emotional development, (3) ethical behavior, standards, and values, (4) social relations,
(5) the social world, (6) the physical world, (7) esthetic development,
(8) communication, and (9) quantitative relationships.[2]

What is in effect a companion report [3] listed and elaborated on three
general directions of growth involved in achieving maturity—growth
toward self-realization, growth toward desirable interpersonal relations
in small groups, and growth toward effective membership or leadership
in large groups—in a somewhat more traditional pattern. Detailed illustrative behaviors are also given in four crosscutting areas of behavioral competence: (1) attaining maximum intellectual growth and development, (2)
becoming culturally oriented and integrated, (3) maintaining and im-

[1] Nolan C. Kearney, *Elementary School Objectives.* Russell Sage Foundation, New
York, 1953. p. 35-41.
[2] *Ibid.* p. 52-120.
[3] Will French and associates, *Behavioral Goals of General Education in High School.*
Russell Sage Foundation, New York, 1957. p. 88-89.

proving physical and mental health, and (4) becoming economically competent.[4]

Types of Instructional and Learning Outcomes

In a somewhat more specific sense, Gerberich [5] listed and discussed ten types of instructional or learning outcomes acquired by pupils as a result of their school and out-of-school learning: (1) skills, (2) knowledges, (3) concepts, (4) understandings, (5) applications, (6) activities, (7) appreciations, (8) attitudes, (9) interests, and (10) adjustments. If the behavioral changes are brought about rather directly even if not solely through the influence of the school, they are usually called instructional outcomes. Learning outcomes, more broadly, include changes in behavior resulting from experiences in which learning occurs even though there may have been no intent on the part of any person to teach or instruct.

Outcomes in achievement measurement. The first seven of the outcomes listed above refer to behaviors that range from tangible to intangible, from easily measurable to measurable only with considerable difficulty. Skills and knowledges are the most tangible and the most easily measured of all outcome types. At an intermediate level of tangibility but measurable without great difficulty are concepts, understandings, applications, and activities. The seventh outcome—appreciations—is in the area of personal tastes and preferences, as are the last three of the outcome types in the list.

Skills in physical and motor performances are definitely involved in many of the types of behavior considered under this heading, although this does not preclude the operation of mental processes in skill behavior. Reading skills, work-study skills, language skills, computational skills, shop and laboratory skills, typing skills, and athletic skills are representative of the variety and scope covered by this type of outcome.

Knowledges involve in their attainment the establishment of such mental associations as those between an object and its name, a date and an event, a term and the color or characteristic it represents, and a symbol and its meaning. Outcomes of this type are represented by knowledges concerning facts, principles, and laws, knowledges concerning processes and procedures, and knowledges concerning sources of information.

Concepts presuppose that meaning has been attached to what has been learned, whereas purely knowledge outcomes may be, but are not necessarily, organized at the conceptual level. Abilities to give the meanings of words, to discriminate types or qualities of color, and to use abstract words

---

[4] *Ibid.* p. 92-215.

[5] J. Raymond Gerberich, *Specimen Objective Test Items: A Guide to Achievement Test Construction.* Longmans, Green and Co., New York, 1956. p. 16-21.

in thinking, speaking, and writing demonstrate the attainment of concepts. The emphasis in modern schools on the development of meanings represents the attempt to develop this type of instructional outcome.

Understandings are complex and difficult to define or describe. Knowledge alone, embodied in the psychologically unsound truism that "knowledge is power," represents a much lower and less functional instructional outcome than that referred to in the psychologically sound statement that "understanding passeth knowledge." [6] Knowledge without power, or without understanding of its significance, is useless. Understandings are probably similar to, but at a higher level than, concepts. Understandings even more than concepts appear to be essential prerequisites to the functional use of what has been learned. Modern schools are increasingly stressing the development of understandings in pupils.

Applications, or abilities of pupils to apply the results of learning in logical thinking and in solving problems, represent an end product or an ultimate goal of teaching. Skills, knowledges, concepts, and understandings all contribute to the attainment of this outcome. The development of realistic tastes and preferences is also prerequisite to the effective use of what has been learned in a functional situation. Logical thinking and problem solving are not limited to mathematics, where the terms have perhaps most often been applied, but extend to any area, whether social, economic, political, or scientific, in which problems exist and decisions are to be made.

Activities are represented when a pupil willingly and usually of his own volition performs some informal and self-directed action. Not considered under this heading, however, are the school and even out-of-school experiences that are imposed on the pupil by others. The two salient characteristics deemed most important here are the self-direction represented by voluntary participation and the informality more often found in out-of-school than in school experiences.

Appreciations are the inner feelings of satisfaction which are obtained in varying degree from different experiences and which are difficult, perhaps even impossible, to convey to another person. Most widely recognized in art, music, drama, and literature, appreciations are by no means restricted to the fine arts. Appreciations of patterns in mathematical or quantitative formulas, of logical organization of ideas, and of projected plans for action represent other possibilities.

The seven outcomes discussed above are to a large degree direct out-

---

[6] Harl R. Douglass and Herbert F. Spitzer, "The Importance of Teaching for Understanding." *The Measurement of Understanding,* Forty-Fifth Yearbook of the National Society for the Study of Education, Part I. University of Chicago Press, Chicago, 1946. p. 7.

comes of instruction or at least of learning. As such, they are usually considered to represent the major outcomes achievement tests are designed to measure and evaluate. They are consequently accorded considerable attention in Parts 3 and 5 of this volume.

Outcomes in personality assessment. The last three outcomes listed above—attitudes, interests, and adjustments—are less tangible than the first seven. Their intangibility reflects not only the difficulties encountered in their measurement but also the problems encountered in the interpretation and use of evaluation results.

Attitudes indicate a state of readiness, mental and emotional, for reacting in a habitual manner to certain situations, persons, or things. More concretely, they indicate how a person feels about certain practices, issues, and persons or groups of persons. Attitudes are similar to beliefs, for both terms apply to issues or propositions on which no final evidence seems to be available. Opinions are verbal statements of attitudes, and morale reflects attitudinal states.

Interests, closely similar to attitudes, are allied with preferences, feelings, likes and dislikes, and should be considered in terms of the objects and activities which give the individual satisfactions. They involve highly personal expressions of feelings, whereas attitudes entail expressions of beliefs about issues where the person's own welfare may be only indirectly concerned.

Adjustments are effected when a person finds and adopts modes of behavior suitable to his environment or to changes occurring in his environment, when persons or groups of persons accept or compromise with nature, social forces, and one another. They imply an active rather than a passive process of adaptation to two worlds—of nature and of human beings.

All three of these behavioral outcomes result in part from instruction but they are also strongly influenced by growth and developmental changes in the area distinguished above as personality. Consequently they receive more extensive consideration in Chapter 7.

4. MEASUREMENT OF THE RESULTS
    OF INSTRUCTION AND LEARNING

This third stage in the three-phase process does not greatly differ from the achievement aspects considered in a foregoing section of this chapter when pupil background and status are under consideration. Assessment of final pupil status upon the completion of a course unit, a school term, a school year, or even a still larger unit of educational advancement consequently serves two purposes, one immediate and the other supplementary.

The first and central purpose is to determine how successfully the instructional objectives have been attained. This is done by measuring the degree to which pupils reflect the attainment of these objectives in the form of instructional outcomes, or acquired modifications in their behavior. The results of this appraisal have a second, and at this point incidental, value, i.e., to serve as an indication of pupil status in planning the next step up the educational ladder, whether that next step be another course unit or term under the same teacher, whether it be another school year under another teacher in the same school, or whether it be in a school at a higher level under quite different teaching personnel.

Pupil advancement is actually accomplished as a continuous process, of course, rather than as a spasmodic series of advances. Consequently the measurement of attainments at the conclusion of one instructional unit typically serves as the measurement of status for the subsequent course unit. Although this sequence is broken when school vacations occur, the pupil continues to move ahead and to learn as a result of his many and varied out-of-school experiences. It follows that his educational status is constantly changing, although the changes occur so gradually that needs for formal or extensive measurement of his attainments and at the same time of his educational status arise only periodically. In a more general sense, however, evaluation should be a continuous process.

5. SIGNIFICANCE OF EDUCATIONAL MEASUREMENT AND EVALUATION

There is reason to think that a pattern of measurement and evaluation such as the one outlined in the foregoing sections of this chapter satisfies needs of parents as well as requirements of teachers. For example, McConnell made a study of what parents in a large urban community want to know about their children's achievement.[7] He found that parents of pupils in the primary grades wanted information about their children primarily in the areas of personal and classroom behavior, academic progress, social behavior, aptitude or ability, and health and physical conditions. Three of these types of behavior are at least in part, and perhaps even best, evaluated by the kinds of tools and procedures dealt with in this chapter.

Scope of Testing in Present-Day Schools

It requires but a casual inspection of educational practices to discover the significance that is attached to tests and examinations by the school,

[7] Gaither McConnell, "What Do Parents Want to Know?" *Elementary School Journal,* 58:83-87; November 1957.

as well as by classroom teachers. Pupils spend a great deal of time in preparing for and writing examinations. The school spends considerable time and money setting up an organization for the preparation and administration of examinations. Teachers devote much effort to the preparation, scoring, and marking of quizzes and examinations.

Two recent reports show that testing is carried on widely in the schools. Traxler [8] noted that approximately 108,000,000 standardized tests, or more than two per pupil, were administered in the schools and colleges of the United States during 1957. A recent survey of testing in a number of large public high schools from which many graduates go on to college [9] found that pupils in the last two years of high school spend on the average about one day of time per school year in taking a wide variety of standardized tests. Since neither of these studies took into account the many quizzes, end-of-unit tests, and final examinations used by teachers in their classroom testing, the extent of the testing activities in present-day schools is not shown in its entirety by these results. However, the emphasis on testing seems not to be out of balance when it is realized that only a modest portion of classroom time is devoted to testing, measuring, and evaluating the pupil and his behavior and that by far the majority of class time is spent in instructing him.

Some Major Uses and Values of Tests

Examinations of the various types mentioned above play an important part in the public relations of the school. To a certain extent they carry to the parents in the community the educational purposes of the school, the aims of specific subjects and courses, and the various emphases held important by the instructional staff of the school. Examinations in part serve as a means of revealing to both parent and pupil the basis for a pupil's scholastic rating, his promotions, failures, conditions, awards, and preparation for further educational work.

For the teacher, achievement examinations focus attention on specific objectives and provide a means of determining his efficiency in achieving them. They also aid in revealing overemphasis or wrong emphasis in teaching method and make possible the experimental evaluation of subject-matter organization.

The emphasis on the use of the standardized test in many discussions of measurement problems often leads to the mistaken idea on the part of

[8] Arthur E. Traxler, "Ten Essential Steps in a Testing Program." *Education,* 79:357-62; February 1959.

[9] College Entrance Examination Board, *A Survey of the Use of Tests in the 11th and 12th Grades.* The Board, New York, 1960. p. 1-2.

the student that these more formal types of tests are the most important measures of achievement. In most subject fields this is distinctly not the case. The use of some form of testing procedure for instructional purposes probably constitutes nine-tenths of the teacher's measurement activity in the classroom. Accordingly, more attention can well be given to the improvement of the teacher's informal measures of achievement.

The informal objective examination has increased in popularity with great rapidity during the last three decades although it is well recognized that there are certain areas of educational accomplishment in which it does not measure adequately. The successful construction of objective examinations calls for the application of many of the principles of test construction that are involved in the development of standardized tests.

Teachers themselves must assume a larger share of the responsibility for the use of educational tests in the classroom, and for the interpretation and application of the results after the tests have been given. Only by so doing does the teacher receive an adequate return from the use of tests. If this responsibility is to be wisely exercised, the teacher must have an understanding of the possibilities and the weaknesses of tests. He must be trained in their use and the interpretation of their results. He must be willing to exchange a certain amount of personal effort for the information concerning his teaching problems that the tests can furnish him.

Training in the use of tests comes as a result of their use. Opportunity for this training may be afforded through the preparation and use of informal objective tests as substitutes for, and in addition to, the traditional examination.

6. ORGANIZATION OF THIS BOOK

The two following chapters round out the background aspects of educational measurement and evaluation introduced in the foregoing pages. Chapter 2 briefly outlines a few historically important steps in the development of mental and educational tests and also includes a discussion of the major types of tests and other procedures for pupil appraisal. Chapter 3, which discusses at some length the characteristics or criteria of a good examination, is exceedingly important. It can most advantageously be studied after a reasonable understanding of certain statistical techniques has been established. A comprehensive understanding of the three most important criteria of a good examination depends upon the ability to interpret correlation coefficients. It is believed that a brief study of selected sections of Chapters 13 and 14 will sufficiently acquaint the student with the meaning and uses of correlation for the immediate purposes of the discussion in Chapter 3.

Part 2 consists of a chapter on each of the five areas of standardized testing and appraising briefly set apart in a preceding section of this chapter. Preliminary to the final and in a sense culminating chapter of this part on standardized achievement tests there are four chapters on related areas in which appraisal of pupil characteristics often reveals important needs and abilities. Thus, Chapters 4 to 7 deal with socioeconomic and home-status scales, health and physical fitness tests, mental ability tests, and personality inventories and techniques.

In Part 3, methods of constructing and using the major varieties of teacher-made tests, and also of evaluative techniques, are presented in detail. Treated in this part of the book are oral, essay, and short-answer tests in Chapter 9, informal objective tests in Chapter 10, performance tests in Chapter 11, and evaluative tools and techniques in Chapter 12. These treatments supplement the broader consideration of achievement tests in Chapter 8 and lay the groundwork for the last part of this volume.

The two chapters of Part 4 give a somewhat condensed and nontechnical treatment of basic statistical terms and concepts. Although the modern teacher should be familiar with these terms and concepts and be able to use them intelligently in working with the results of testing, he can safely postpone attainment of proficiency in many of the computational skills and more technical understandings until such time as he may take a more advanced course in educational measurement and evaluation or even a course in statistical methods. Consequently, these chapters are designed primarily to develop functional understandings and meanings rather than to emphasize highly formal knowledges and computational skills. It is believed, however, that those readers who wish to acquire some proficiency in computation of statistical measures will find adequate guides in the rule-of-thumb procedures outlined and illustrated in these chapters.

Part 5 consists of eleven chapters developing briefly for ten subject areas and also for general educational achievement some of the most practical methods of testing, measuring, and evaluating, and for using the results in educationally constructive ways. These chapters depend considerably on the backgrounds supplied by the foregoing Parts 1 to 4. It is in these chapters that some of the most immediately functional presentations of educational measurement and evaluation occur, for the limited scope of particular subject areas of instruction makes treatments of this type feasible. This is accomplished by devoting considerable attention to appropriate learning outcomes in each subject area, as well as by discussing and illustrating various practicable techniques of pupil appraisal.

TOPICS FOR DISCUSSION

1. When in educational history did the idea of measurement in education first enter into the thinking of teachers?
2. What major distinctions are there between instructional outcomes and mental traits as the teacher observes them in pupils?
3. In what broad ways do the testing, the measuring, and the evaluating of learning outcomes differ?
4. What two major types of mental traits are usually distinguished?
5. What three major divisions of pupil background and status need to be considered in educational measurement and evaluation?
6. What are the five aspects of pupil background and status that receive attention in this book?
7. What are some of the general outcomes of elementary and of secondary education?
8. What are the distinctions among some major specific types of instructional and learning outcomes?
9. What are some evidences that educational measurement and evaluation in the modern school constitute a large and significant enterprise?

SELECTED REFERENCES

AMMONS, R. B., AND AMMONS, C. H. "Skills." *Encyclopedia of Educational Research.* Third edition. New York: Macmillan Co., 1960. p. 1282-87.

ANDERSON, SCARVIA B., KATZ, MARTIN R., AND SHIMBERG, BENJAMIN. *Meeting the Test.* New York: Scholastic Magazines, Inc., 1959.

CALIFORNIA TEST BUREAU. *A Glossary of Measurement Terms.* Los Angeles: California Test Bureau, 1959.

CROOK, FRANCES E. "The Classroom Teacher and Standardized Tests." *Teachers College Record,* 58:159-68; December 1956.

DOBBIN, JOHN E. "What Parents Need to Know about Tests and Testing." *National Elementary Principal,* 34:152-60; September 1954.

DOOLITTLE, NETTIE-ALICE. "Minimum Essentials of Measurement for the Classroom Teacher." *School and Society,* 69:403; June 4, 1949.

EDUCATIONAL TESTING SERVICE. *Essential Characteristics of a Testing Program.* Evaluation and Advisory Service Series, No. 2. Princeton, N. J.: Educational Testing Service, 1956.

ENGLISH, HORACE B., AND ENGLISH, AVA C. *A Comprehensive Dictionary of Psychological and Psychoanalytical Terms.* New York: Longmans, Green and Co., 1958.

GERBERICH, J. RAYMOND. *Specimen Objective Test Items: A Guide to Achievement Test Construction.* New York: Longmans, Green and Co., 1956. p. 16-21, 35-38, 56-59, 80-82, 97-100, 140-43, 154-57, 165-68, 179-82, 190-93, 199-202.

GOOD, CARTER V., editor. *Dictionary of Education.* Second edition. New York: McGraw-Hill Book Co., Inc., 1959.

HENSLEY, IVEN H., AND DAVIS, ROBERT A. "What High-School Teachers Think and Do about Their Examinations." *Educational Administration and Supervision,* 38:219-28; April 1952.

HUTT, MAX L. "Diagnosis." *Encyclopedia of Educational Research.* Third edition. New York: Macmillan Co., 1960. p. 376-81.

KING, JOSEPH E., JR. "Using Tests in the Modern Secondary School." *Bulletin of the National Association of Secondary School Principals,* 32:5-92; December 1948.

LENNON, ROGER T. *A Glossary of 100 Measurement Terms.* Test Service Notebook, No. 13. Yonkers, N. Y.: World Book Co.

RUSSELL, DAVID H. "Concepts." *Encyclopedia of Educational Research.* Third edition. New York: Macmillan Co., 1960. p. 323-33.

SIEVERS, FRANK L., AND OTHERS. "Testing Issue." *School Life,* 42:3-27; September 1959.

"Testing and Evaluation." *NEA Journal,* 48:15-31; November 1959.

THOMPSON, ANTON. "Test Giver's Self-Inventory." *California Journal of Educational Research,* 7:67-71; March 1956.

THUT, I. N., AND GERBERICH, J. RAYMOND. *Foundations of Method for Secondary Schools.* New York: McGraw-Hill Book Co., Inc., 1949. Chapters 5, 16.

2

DEVELOPMENT AND PRESENT STATUS

OF PUPIL APPRAISAL

This chapter deals both with the historical forerunners of present-day evaluation methods and with the various modern tests and techniques used in pupil appraisal, as follows:

A. Measurement prior to 1800.
B. Nineteenth-century developments in measurement.
C. Twentieth-century developments in pupil appraisal.
D. Present status of psychological and educational measurement.
E. Special types of mental and educational tests.
F. Major techniques of mental and aptitude measurement.
G. Important instruments and techniques for personality evaluation.
H. Basic tools and techniques used in educational measurement.

Measurement of human behavior with primary reference to the capacities and educational attainments of school children may well be divided roughly into three periods. During the first period, from the beginning of historical records down to about the nineteenth century, measurement in education was naturally quite crude. During the second period, embracing approximately the nineteenth century, educational measurement began to assimilate from various sources the ideas and the scientific and statistical techniques which were later to result in the modern objective testing movement. The shorter third period, dating from about 1900 to the present, has been characterized by tremendous advances in statistical techniques, in the measurement and evaluation of intelligence, personality, and achievement, and in the classroom use of test results.

The measurement and evaluation of the whole child involve the use of many tests and other devices that cannot properly be called tests. Most of the remaining chapters of this volume are devoted to treatments of the various types of tests, nontest tools, and techniques used in pupil appraisal. A few important distinctions are made in this chapter, however, to supplement the brief historical treatment and to supply background for the more detailed treatments to follow.

Five aspects of pupil background—home and social status, physical and motor fitness, mental ability, personality, and achievement—are set apart and briefly discussed in Chapter 1. Only the last three, those involving educational and closely related psychological aspects of the school child, are dealt with in this chapter. The sociological emphasis of socioeconomic class distinctions and the major responsibility of physical education for physical and motor fitness justify their omission here.

1. DEVELOPMENTS IN MEASUREMENT PRIOR TO 1800

For a number of centuries prior to 1800, the foundations of modern techniques of pupil appraisal were slowly being developed. Brief comments on a few early milestones at this point should enable the reader to approach later chapters of this book with some meaningful and helpful historical understandings.

Early Examinations

Probably the initiation ceremonies by which primitive tribes have tested the knowledge of tribal customs, endurance, and bravery of their young men prior to their admission to the ranks of adult males are among the earliest examinations employed by human beings. Use of a crude oral test was reported in the Old Testament, and Socrates is known to have employed searching types of oral quizzing. Elaborate and exhaustive written examinations were used by the Chinese as early as 2200 B.C. in the selection of their public officials. These illustrations [1] may be classified as crude historical antecedents of performance tests, oral examinations, and essay tests in the modern usage of those terms. In the sense that they

---

[1] Harry A. Greene, Albert N. Jorgensen, and J. Raymond Gerberich, *Measurement and Evaluation in the Elementary School,* Second edition. Longmans, Green and Co., New York, 1953. p. 20-21; and Harry A. Greene, Albert N. Jorgensen, and J. Raymond Gerberich, *Measurement and Evaluation in the Secondary School,* Second edition. Longmans, Green and Co., New York, 1954. p. 20-21.

measured outcomes of learning and instruction, however informal and opportunistic the learning situations may have been, they were informal achievement tests.

Early School Examinations

Somewhat more formal tests of physical prowess and stoicism in Sparta as early as 500 B.C. and of proficiency in athletic games and in the language and fine arts in ancient Greece were administered to the young men. Written tests were used in the University of Bologna by A.D. 1219, in the University of Paris during the thirteenth century, and at Cambridge University in 1702.[2] These tests were probably similar to some modern school achievement tests in many formal aspects.

2. DEVELOPMENTS IN MEASUREMENT FROM 1800 TO 1900

When human beings first recognized differences among themselves in mental abilities and other significant traits is unknown, but the scientific recognition of such differences and, later, their scientific measurement came about during the nineteenth century. These discoveries and the derivation of statistical methods needed for the summarization and analysis of these differences were necessary foundations for subsequent developments in measurement and evaluation.

Consequently, the earliest known examples of measurement prior to 1800 were supplemented during the nineteenth century by a number of first occasions when a certain tool or technique was used. Furthermore, the three broad areas for which relatively distinctive procedures are distinguished today—educational, mental, and personality—began to emerge during the past century.

Educational Testing in the Nineteenth Century

Three persons made outstanding contributions to nineteenth-century developments. The ideas of these men—Horace Mann, George Fisher, and J. M. Rice—appear to be forerunners of developments during the present century.

First notable educational tests. The first school examinations of note appear to be those instituted in the Boston schools of 1845 as substitutes for oral tests when enrollments became so large that the school committee

---

[2] *Ibid.* p. 21-22,

could not longer examine all pupils orally. These written examinations, in arithmetic, astronomy, geography, grammar, history, and natural philosophy, impressed Horace Mann,[3] then secretary of the Massachusetts Board of Education. As editor of the *Common School Journal*, he published extracts from them and concluded that the new written examination was superior to the old oral test in these respects: [4]

1. It is impartial.
2. It is just to the pupils.
3. It is more thorough than older forms of examination.
4. It prevents the "officious interference" of the teacher.
5. It "determines, beyond appeal or gainsaying, whether the pupils have been faithfully and competently taught."
6. It takes away "all possibility of favoritism."
7. It makes the information obtained available to all.
8. It enables all to appraise the ease or difficulty of the questions.

Although these ideas were apparently those represented by modern tests, the instruments themselves were inadequate. However, in successive issues of the *Common School Journal* Mann suggested most of the elements in examinations that are found in the modern measurement and evaluation movement.

First objective educational tests. To Reverend George Fisher, an English schoolmaster, goes the credit for devising and using what were probably the first objective measures of achievement. His "scale books," used in the Greenwich Hospital School as early as 1864, provided means for evaluating accomplishments in handwriting, spelling, mathematics, grammar and composition, and several other school subjects. Specimens of pupil work were compared with "standard specimens" to determine numerical ratings that, at least for spelling and a few other subjects, depended on errors in performance.[5] Although Fisher's "scale books" included the germ of many of the ideas that are incorporated in present-day educational scales, his work apparently had little or no effect on practices in measurement until some forty years later.

First objective educational tests in America. The real inventor of the comparative test in America was J. M. Rice, who, in 1894,[6] hit upon the idea

---

[3] Since Horace Mann doubtless exerted considerable influence, the examinations were probably strong reflections of his own ideas.
[4] Greene, Jorgensen, and Gerberich, *op. cit.* p. 23.
[5] *Ibid.* p. 23.
[6] Leonard P. Ayres, "History and Present Status of Educational Measurements." *The Measurement of Educational Products,* Seventeenth Yearbook of the National Society for the Study of Education, Part II. Public School Publishing Co., Bloomington, Ill., 1918. p. 11.

he developed so effectively that it became the foundation of objective measurement in education. Rice, having administered a list of spelling words to pupils in many school systems and analyzed the results, confounded the educators at the 1897 session of the Department of Superintendence of the National Education Association with the declaration that pupils who had studied spelling 30 minutes a day for eight years were not better spellers than children who had studied the subject 15 minutes a day for eight years.

Rice was attacked and reviled for this "heresy," and some educators even attacked the use of a measure of how well pupils could spell for evaluating the efficiency of spelling instruction. They contended that spelling was taught to develop the pupils' minds and not to teach them to spell. It was more than ten years later that Rice's pioneering resulted in significant attention to objective methods in educational testing.[7]

Mental Testing in the Nineteenth Century

The tremendous impact of Binet on the early history, as well as on the present status, of intelligence testing warrants a division here into the pre-Binet and the Binet periods. All of the directly significant developments in mental testing during the nineteenth century occurred during its last two decades.

Pre-Binet mental testing. Dr. E. S. Chaille, an American physician, is credited as early as 1887 with the development of standards and simple tests for judging the mental levels of children to the age of three and with having implied, although not definitely used, the concept of mental age [8] as an index of mental maturity.

Cattell apparently first used the term "mental test" [9] in 1890, almost at the beginning of the period during which scientific method was first applied to the measurement of mental ability. Attempts during the last decade of the nineteenth century by Cattell and others to measure intelligence by means of physical characteristics, sensory acuity, and motor skills tests gave, for the most part, negative results.[10]

First Binet mental testing. During the same period, Binet and his colleagues were experimenting in France with tests of a somewhat similar but less specific type. In 1895, Binet and Henri described tests of memory, imagination, attention, comprehension, suggestibility, and esthetic ap-

[7] *Ibid.* p. 12.
[8] Florence L. Goodenough, "An Early Intelligence Test." *Child Development*, 5:13-18; March 1934.
[9] J. McKeen Cattell, "Mental Tests and Measurements." *Mind*, 15:375-81; July 1890.
[10] Frank N. Freeman, *Mental Tests: Their History, Principles and Applications*, Revised edition. Houghton Mifflin Co., Boston, 1939. p. 58.

preciation that were forerunners of the Binet-Simon scales of the twentieth century.[11]

Personality Testing in the Nineteenth Century

Personality testing had its antecedents in the work of Kraepelin and Sommer on free association tests during the last decade of the nineteenth century. Although free association tests have persisted to the present day, the questionnaire and rating scale methods used by Galton and others at still earlier dates became the dominant early methods of personality measurement in America.[12]

3. TWENTIETH CENTURY DEVELOPMENTS IN MEASUREMENT

The modern era in mental and educational measurements was born soon after the dawn of the new century. Although the historical antecedents briefly sketched in the two preceding sections were essential prerequisites, developments first in mental testing and shortly thereafter in personality and educational testing opened new vistas and disclosed challenging new roads for further exploration by a new breed of educator just beginning to emerge—the measurement and evaluation specialist.

Developments in Intelligence Testing since 1900

Of the three areas of testing mentioned above, intelligence testing was the first to be accorded the type and quality of twentieth-century attention mainly responsible for its present status. For this reason primarily, measurement by the use of general intelligence tests, specific intelligence tests, and factored intelligence tests warrants attention at this point.

General intelligence tests. Attempts to measure general intelligence, or what will here be defined only as ability to learn or ability to adapt oneself to new situations, continued into the twentieth century both in America and in France. The results of these attempts to measure general intelligence or mental ability were that the first individual test was developed in France and that the first group test was developed some years later in America.

Individual intelligence scales were originated by Binet and Simon in 1905. Their first scale was devised primarily for the purpose of selecting

[11] Anne Anastasi, *Differential Psychology: Individual and Group Differences in Behavior,* Third edition. Macmillan Co., New York, 1958. p. 15.
[12] Greene, Jorgensen, and Gerberich, *op. cit.* p. 32.

mentally retarded pupils who required special instruction. This pioneer individual intelligence scale utilized the basic idea of interpreting the relative intelligence of different children at any given chronological age by the number of tests of varied types and increasing levels of difficulty they could pass. These characteristics were all re-embodied in the 1908 and 1911 revisions of the *Binet-Simon Scale* and also are basic to most individual intelligence scales even today. The 1908 Revision introduced the fundamentally important concept of mental age (MA) and provided means for obtaining it.[13]

Several American adaptations of these pioneer scales appeared during the period 1911 to 1916. One of the two individual scales most widely used today is formally known as a revision of the Binet-Simon, whereas the other, available both at adult and children's levels, shows a less direct but still material dependence on the same source. Both make use of the intelligence quotient (IQ), based on the relationship between the subject's mental age and his chronological age.[14]

Group intelligence tests first appeared in the form of *Army Alpha,* used for the measurement and placement of army recruits and draftees during World War I. Various psychologists had been working on group intelligence tests, and Otis was near the point of issuing such a test around 1917, when the United States entered the war. A major result of their collaboration was *Army Alpha.* This test, widely used for testing men who could read and understand English, was accompanied by *Army Beta,* a nonlanguage test for use with illiterates and men who, although perhaps literate in a foreign language, could not read English.[15]

Other group intelligence tests began to appear almost immediately following the end of World War I, and the period from 1918 to the middle twenties was marked both by the publication of many such tests and by an upsurge of interest in intelligence testing. Although testing techniques have been refined considerably since then, and there are now scores of commercially published group tests, the past forty years have brought no outstanding changes in the methods of measuring general intelligence. The *Army General Classification Test* and the *Army Individual Test of Mental Ability* served functions in World War II closely similar to those of *Army Alpha* and *Army Beta* in World War I.

Aptitude or specific intelligence tests. The measurement of aptitudes, or those potentialities for success in an area of performance that exist prior to direct acquaintance with that area, has been tied up with intelligence testing both fore and aft. Early attempts to measure general intelli-

[13] Freeman, *op. cit.* p. 86-88.
[14] *Ibid.* p. 101.
[15] *Ibid.* p. 113-35.

gence were by means of tests of many specific traits and aptitudes, but that approach was dropped when Binet showed that tests of more complex forms of behavior were superior. It was soon apparent, however, that general intelligence tests were not highly predictive of certain types of performance, especially in the trades and industries.

Münsterberg's aptitude tests for telephone girls and streetcar motormen in 1913 were followed by tests of mechanical aptitude, musical aptitude, art aptitude, clerical aptitude, and aptitude for various subjects of the high-school and college curricula prior to 1930.[16] Spearman's splitting of total mental ability into a general factor and many specific factors [17] had its influence on this movement, and accounted for the fact that aptitude tests are frequently called specific intelligence tests.

Factored intelligence tests. With the development of factor analysis methods, largely within the past two decades, certain group factors of intelligence thought to differ from the specific factors or aptitudes and also from general intelligence have emerged.[18] These group factors are in a sense midway between specific and general intelligence.

Developments in Personality Testing since 1900

The second type of psychological measurement to have its modern origins not long after the start of the twentieth century is personality measurement. The two major aspects of measurement in this area are projective techniques and personality inventories.

Projective methods. Jung in 1905 published a free association test designed to reveal emotional complexes.[19] Although the *Rorschach*, the first modern projective test, was introduced in 1921, it was not until some twenty-five years ago that projective techniques employing such unstructured situations as inkblots and pictures came into wide use in the study of personality.[20] An outgrowth of psychiatry and academic psychology, these unstructured methods of studying personality came to be termed projective methods only in 1939.[21]

---

[16] Goodwin Watson, "The Specific Techniques of Investigation: Testing Intelligence, Aptitudes, and Personality." *The Scientific Movement in Education,* Thirty-Seventh Yearbook of the National Society for the Study of Education, Part II. Public School Publishing Co., Bloomington, Ill., 1938. p. 365-66.

[17] Charles Spearman, " 'General Intelligence' Objectively Determined and Measured." *American Journal of Psychology,* 15:201-93; April 1904.

[18] Godfrey H. Thomson, *The Factorial Analysis of Human Ability.* Houghton Mifflin Co., Boston, 1939. p. 14.

[19] Watson, *op. cit.* p. 368.

[20] *Ibid.* p. 369.

[21] Helen Sargent, "Projective Methods: Their Origins, Theory, and Application in Personality Research." *Psychological Bulletin,* 42:257-93; May 1945.

Personality inventories. Woodworth devised a *Personal Data Sheet,* in reality an inventory of neurotic tendencies and emotional maladjustment, for use with American soldiers during World War I. This was probably the outstanding early contribution in this field.[22] A significant number of these structured personality inventories have been developed during the past forty years for the measurement of adjustment, attitudes, and vocational interests.

Developments in Achievement Testing since 1900

Modern achievement testing was stimulated by the issuance by Thorndike in 1904 of the first book dealing primarily with mental, social, and educational measurements.[23] Both through this book and his influence on his students, he more than any other person was responsible for the early development of standardized tests. Two other twentieth-century developments in this area are informal objective tests and evaluative tests and techniques.

First standardized achievement tests. Stone, a student of Thorndike's, published his arithmetic reasoning test, the first standardized instrument of this type to make its appearance, in 1908.[24] Thorndike in 1909 published his *Scale for Handwriting of Children*—the first standardized achievement scale.[25] During the period from 1909 to 1915, a series of arithmetic tests and five scales for measuring abilities in English composition, spelling, drawing, and handwriting were published.[26] It is interesting to note that only two of these pioneer instruments were tests, while the remaining five were scales. Literally thousands of standardized achievement tests have been published during the last half century. Generous samplings of them are discussed and illustrated later in this chapter, in Chapter 8, and in Part 5 of this volume.

Informal objective tests. The idea of the informal objective examination, referred to during its early days rather loosely as the "New-Type Test" and the "Objective Test," apparently was first publicly expressed by McCall,[27] whose article in 1920 first suggested that teachers do not

[22] Watson, *op. cit.* p. 368.

[23] Edward L. Thorndike, *An Introduction to the Theory of Mental and Social Measurements.* Teachers College, Columbia University, New York, 1904.

[24] Cliff W. Stone, *Arithmetical Abilities and Some Factors Determining Them.* Contributions to Education, No. 19. Teachers College, Columbia University, New York, 1908.

[25] Edward L. Thorndike, "Handwriting." *Teachers College Record,* 11:83-175; March 1910.

[26] C. W. Odell, *Educational Measurements in High School.* Century Co., New York, 1930. p. 34-35.

[27] William A. McCall, "A New Kind of School Examination." *Journal of Educational Research,* 1:33-46; January 1920.

need to depend solely upon standardized tests but that they can construct their own objective tests for classroom use. The pioneer book dealing almost entirely with this testing adaptation was published in 1924.[28] The informal objective test has since come into such wide use that probably a majority of elementary- and secondary-school teachers now make at least some use of these teacher-made or classroom instruments. Chapter 10 of this volume is devoted to the informal objective test.

Evaluative tests and techniques. The history of achievement measurement since the late twenties has been characterized mainly by increasing recognition of the fact that test results offer only one, although the major one, of the types of acceptable evidence on pupil achievement. The tendency toward evaluation, which is broader in scope than testing, has been accompanied by a strong trend toward more scientific use of measurement tools. Tyler, in 1931, outlined steps of procedure for test construction and validation which clearly pointed out the essential dependence of a program of achievement testing on the objectives of instruction and the recognition of forms of pupil behavior indicating attainment of the desired instructional outcomes.[29] Perhaps he more than any other single test specialist was responsible for the extension of achievement testing to the more intangible outcomes of instruction, for his contributions nearly thirty years ago doubtless did much to bring into being the broad modern conception of evaluation to replace the earlier and narrower concept of testing.

Evaluation instruments developed in the Eight-Year Study of member schools of the Progressive Education Association, completed some twenty years ago, affected measurement and evaluation practices markedly. The evaluation staff developed a series of instruments for measuring such outcomes as logical reasoning, ability to apply principles in the sciences, ability to interpret data, and ability to interpret literature. These and various tests of general educational development published more recently are designed to measure functional and relatively intangible outcomes in areas of behavior rather than more formal and tangible instructional outcomes in separate subjects or areas of the curriculum.

Evaluative tools and techniques for measuring procedures involved in and products resulting from certain types of skill performances and various other aspects of behavior of the whole child were developed in parallel with the paper-and-pencil evaluative tests. Prominent among such evaluative tools are the check list, the rating scale, the questionnaire,

[28] G. M. Ruch, *The Improvement of the Written Examination.* Scott, Foresman and Co., Chicago, 1924.
[29] Ralph W. Tyler, "A Generalized Technique for Constructing Achievement Tests." *Educational Research Bulletin,* 8:199-208; April 15, 1931.

the pupil profile, the class record sheet, and the cumulative record. Evaluative techniques are represented by the anecdotal report, the interview, the case study, the sociogram, and observational analyses of group dynamics.

Present Status of Mental and Educational Testing

Although measurement and evaluation, whether of intelligence, personality, or achievement, are still in a developmental stage, Monroe [30] stated that the movement, beyond its infancy in 1920, had reached early adulthood by 1945. He also commented that the fifty or more types of objective test items or item groups represented a marked extension and improvement in techniques of measurement and evaluation. Gerberich, more recently, distinguished and illustrated 227 subvarieties of achievement test items and classified them into 13 major varieties and four basic types.[31]

The measurement and evaluation aspects of the school program have markedly increased in scope and significance during the past score or so of years. Measurement and evaluation techniques now not only reflect developments in educational philosophy and psychology but also increasingly are furnishing evidence that aids school officials in charting the future course. Pupil guidance may be considered the central theme, for directly or indirectly all educational planning and procedures are designed to effect improvements in the education and in the guidance of the individual school child. The classroom teacher remains the key person in pupil measurement and evaluation. Measurement and evaluation specialists, subject-matter specialists, and specialists in areas of child behavior increasingly cooperate with and depend upon the classroom teacher in the development of new instruments, tools, and techniques for pupil appraisal.

4. SPECIAL TYPES OF MENTAL AND EDUCATIONAL TESTS

Modern tests are so varied in type and purpose that it is extremely difficult to classify them clearly. Tests can be classified in terms of their forms, their origins, their functions, and their content. In this chapter tests are first classified broadly by function—intelligence, personality, and educational—and within major divisions are classified by whatever pattern seems most likely to familiarize the student with their major characteristics.

[30] Walter S. Monroe, "Educational Measurement in 1920 and in 1945." *Journal of Educational Research,* 38:334-40; January 1945.
[31] J. Raymond Gerberich, *Specimen Objective Test Items: A Guide to Achievement Test Construction.* Longmans, Green and Co., New York, 1956.

Intelligence tests have as their purpose the measurement of pupil intelligence or mental ability in a large degree without reference to what the pupil has learned either in or out of school. *Personality tests* attempt to measure such intangible aspects of behavior as attitudes, interests, and emotional adjustment. *Educational tests* have as their primary function the measurement of the results or effects of instruction and learning.

There is not complete uniformity of terminology with respect to mental and educational tests. Although the latter have a commonly accepted meaning, the former are thought variously to include educational, intelligence, and personality tests, to include intelligence and personality but not educational tests, and even to mean the same thing as intelligence tests. Modern practice seems often to make use of the three-way classification —intelligence tests, personality inventories, and educational tests. As this distinction appears to be most satisfactory for the purposes of this book, it will be followed throughout this volume.

Tests, Scales, and Scaled Tests

Objective tests can be classified in a manner that cuts across the three fields of intelligence, personality, and educational testing—into tests and scales, and also scaled tests. This distinction is of some value, but at times it results in confusion since certain types of objective tests resemble scales or contain certain features of scales as an essential part of their construction.

In general terms, a *test* is an instrument designed for the measurement and evaluation of any knowledge, quality, or ability. It may measure degree or amount of achievement, mental abilities, or even such intangible qualities as personality and character traits. It may be made up of items of similar difficulty, items arranged in increasing order of difficulty, or items arranged in such other ways as by types of items or order of occurrence of topics in a course. Ordinarily the test is used in the classroom by the pupils.

A *scale* is a series of objective samples or products of different difficulty or quality that have been arranged in a definite order or position, usually in ascending order of difficulty or merit. The samples are equally spaced on a scale of value, of difficulty, or of quality. Usually the scale is employed by the teacher as an aid in the evaluation of a particular product.

A *scaled test* combines certain properties of the test and the scale. If the items in a test are arranged in order of increasing difficulty, the instrument is a scaled test. The process of determining the difficulty of test items and arranging them in an ascending order on that characteristic is called scaling.

The accompanying items from the *Metropolitan Achievement Tests* illustrate the increasing level of difficulty from the first to the last item of a scaled word discrimination test.

EXCERPT FROM *Metropolitan Achievement Tests* [32]

1 The cat likes to _____ the mouse.
- ☐ case   ☐ chase
- ☐ chose   ☐ close

25 Drop the tablet in water to _____ it.
- ☐ disclose ☐ disturb
- ☐ dispel   ☐ dissolve

12 Fill this _____ with cold water.
- ☐ picked   ☐ pitcher
- ☐ picture   ☐ picket

36 The winning team left the field in _____.
- ☐ triumph   ☐ triangle
- ☐ trumpet   ☐ tribute

Speed and Power Tests

Tests of speed or rate and of power are used both in intelligence and educational testing, although personality inventories seem to involve neither the speed nor the power concept.

A *speed test* usually consists of items approximately equal in difficulty. Ordinarily such a test contains so many items that no pupil is able to finish in the working time allowed. Usually the items are so easy that there is no question about the pupil's ability to answer them correctly. Thus, speed tests are measures of the speed and accuracy with which a pupil is able to respond to standardized items of a uniform degree of difficulty.

A *power test* consists of a series of items arranged in ascending order of difficulty, and hence is also a scaled test. It measures a pupil's ability to answer more and more difficult items within a given field. The time allowed is sufficient for nearly all pupils to complete as many of the items as they are able to answer. Theoretically, a pupil's score on a power test should represent the degree of difficulty of the most difficult item he is able to answer correctly, but such a score is so hard to obtain that the number of items answered correctly is generally taken as his score.

If a speed test may be compared to a race in which as many hurdles of uniform height as possible are to be cleared during a specified period of time, a power test may be compared to a contest in which the hurdles to be jumped regularly increase in height from very low at the start to such eventual height that no one is able to jump the next hurdle. In the first

---

[32] Harold H. Bixler and others, *Metropolitan Achievement Tests: Test 2, Word Discrimination.* Elementary Battery, Form B. Copyright 1959 by Harcourt, Brace and World, Inc., New York. All rights reserved. Quoted by special permission.

case, the score (speed) would be expressed in terms of the number of hurdles jumped during the specified time. In the second case, the score (power) would be expressed as the height of the last and highest hurdle the individual was able to clear.

Furthermore, certain multiple-attribute tests of achievement combine the measurement of power and speed in one test or performance although not in one score. Thus, accuracy and speed in typewriting, legibility and speed in handwriting, and comprehension and speed in reading are dual, although not necessarily equally important, characteristics of a good performance. Inasmuch as stress on speed usually reduces quality and stress on quality typically reduces speed of performance, an optimum balance between the two characteristics is ordinarily desired.

Verbal, Nonverbal, and Performance Tests

Another classification crosscutting intelligence, personality, and educational tests is that dependent on the degree to which words are used in test items and in pupil responses.

Verbal tests, by far the most common, are ordinarily of the pencil-and-paper variety although they may be oral or may even require identification of physical objects and materials presented. In any event, words are used by the pupils in attaching meaning to, in responding to, or both in comprehending and in responding to, the test items. A test unless qualified or further described is ordinarily considered to be a verbal test of the pencil-and-paper type.

Nonverbal tests, again of the pencil-and-paper or even oral variety, are those in which pupils do not use words in attaching meaning to or in responding to test items. Tests involving the use solely of numbers, of graphical representations, or of three-dimensional objects and materials are of this type.

Performance tests are also nonverbal but they may require use of pencil and paper by the pupils in responding, they may require solely the manipulation of physical objects and materials, or they may require paper-and-pencil responses to physical objects and materials presented in certain ways. Such tests are commonly used with persons having serious language handicaps and in situations where certain types of skills are of greater importance than is verbalization ability.

Teacher-Made and Standardized Tests

A distinction most fundamental in educational testing, also applicable to personality measurement but not pertinent in intelligence testing, is that between the teacher-made and the standardized test. The teacher often constructs educational achievement tests and sometimes develops informal inventories or questionnaires for measuring such personality characteristics as interests and attitudes. Standardized tests occur in all three major areas of measurement—intelligence, personality, and educational.

The most common types of *teacher-made tests* are the oral, essay, and informal objective. The *oral test* is typically developed by the teacher in the classroom as the occasion warrants and consists of asking individual pupils questions to be answered orally. The *essay test,* consisting of questions to which the pupils respond in writing, is also ordinarily used by a teacher in his own classes.

Informal objective examinations, most often prepared by a teacher for use in his own classes, may be constructed cooperatively by two or more teachers for use with their several classes in the same subject, or even by several persons for use throughout a large school system. Illustrations of a few item types commonly used in informal objective tests are given later in this chapter.

A *standardized test* is composed of test or inventory items selected in the light of the particular type of mental ability, personality trait, or achievement the instrument is designed to measure. The items have necessarily been subjected to a preliminary tryout with a representative pupil group so that it became possible to arrange them in the desired manner with respect to difficulty and the degree to which they effected certain types of discriminations among groups of pupils. Such a test is accompanied by the appropriate type of table for transforming resulting scores into meaningful characterizations of pupil mental ability, personality, or achievement.

Both the informal objective test and the standardized test come under the broader heading of *objective tests.* When used in measuring educational achievement, the informal objective and standardized tests typically make use of the same item types.

Tests, Nontest Tools, and Techniques

An important but perhaps fairly obvious distinction exists among tests, nontest instruments or tools, and techniques neither of a test nor of a tool nature. The distinction is important particularly in personality and educational measurement but also pertains in some degree to mental measurement.

Tests, discussed above, are used directly by the pupil. There are a number of *nontest tools,* such as the cumulative record, pupil profile, progress chart, class analysis chart, and report card, which are not used by the pupil who is being evaluated. In addition, there are a number of *techniques,* primarily observational in nature, such as the anecdote, the case study, the interview, sociometric methods, and techniques in the area of group dynamics.

5. COMMON TYPES OF MENTAL AND EDUCATIONAL TESTS

In addition to the special types of tests discussed in the preceding section, there are many tests belonging to one or another of the three best known types—intelligence tests, personality inventories, and educational tests. Some of the major types of instruments in each of these areas are characterized below.

Intelligence Tests

Intelligence tests measure what is perhaps most simply and most commonly described as ability to learn or ability to adapt oneself to new situations. Whereas achievement tests measure skills or abilities more or less directly, intelligence tests face the problem of measuring mental qualities indirectly in terms of the manner in which an individual's intelligence affects or conditions his behavior. It is sufficient here merely to comment upon this important distinction. Chapter 6 presents more fully the problems and techniques of intelligence testing.

General intelligence and scholastic aptitude tests. The most widely known tests of mental ability are usually referred to as general intelligence tests, although such other terms as general mental ability tests and scholastic aptitude examinations have almost identical meanings. General intelligence tests attempt to measure mental ability broadly enough, by the use of a wide variety of test situations in scaled order of difficulty, to obtain a measure representative of the individual's mental efficiency in general.

Individual intelligence scales can be administered to only one person at a time. Such tests require the full attention of a trained examiner. Although the techniques for administering these tests are highly standardized, the examiner modifies the procedure in various ways according to the age, ability, and even sex of the pupil being tested. Since these instruments are usually in scaled form, and are frequently devised to cover a wide age range, they are often called age scales.

Group intelligence tests or group tests of general mental ability are usually paper-and-pencil instruments that can be administered to a large number of persons at the same time. They usually have a number of different parts, each of which deals with a certain broad type of performance. In several of these tests two or more part scores are combined to obtain a verbal score and the remaining two or more part scores are combined to net a nonverbal score. In some of these instruments, also known as *bifactor tests,* the two part scores are called linguistic and quantitative or verbal and mathematical.

The accompanying sample items from the *Lorge-Thorndike Intelligence Tests* illustrate one of the techniques used in group intelligence tests.

EXCERPT FROM *Lorge-Thorndike Intelligence Tests* [33]

One word has been left out of each sentence on these two pages. Choose the word that will make the best, the truest, and the most sensible complete sentence. Look at sample sentence 0.

0. Hot weather comes in the ———.

    A fall   B night   C summer   D winter   E snow

|A|B|C|D|E|

The best answer is **summer.** The letter before **summer** is **C,** so you should make a heavy black pencil mark in the **C** answer space for sentence 0.

Now look at sentence 00.

00. ——— bark at cats.

    F Cows   G Mice   H Cats   J Hens   K Dogs

|F|G|H|J|K|

The best answer is **Dogs,** so you should make a heavy black pencil mark in the K answer space for sentence 00.

Do all the sentences on these two pages in the same way. Try every sentence.

1. Boys will become ———.

    A infants.   B little   C intelligent   D stupid   E men

|A|B|C|D|E|

2. We see ——— only at night.

    F children   G plants   H stars   J houses   K trees

|F|G|H|J|K|

3. Fred was six years old. There were six ——— on his birthday cake.

    L candles   M boys   N girls   P parties   Q children

|L|M|N|P|Q|

4. Not every cloud gives ———.

    R weather   S shade   T sky   U climate   V rain

|R|S|T|U|V|

Specific intelligence tests. In contrast to the general intelligence tests that attempt to measure broadly the ability to learn are the tests of specific intelligence that attempt to measure ability to learn in relatively narrow fields of subject matter or areas of performance.

Aptitude tests attempt to forecast an individual's future success in certain school subjects or certain areas of performance. They are designed for use with persons who may or may not have had previous experience in the achievement areas with which they deal. Such tests attempt to measure

---

[33] Irving Lorge and Robert L. Thorndike, *The Lorge-Thorndike Intelligence Tests, Verbal Battery.* Level 3, Form A. Houghton Mifflin Co., Boston, 1954.

the potentialities for success apart from those abilities resulting from specific training. They are found for such areas as English, foreign languages, music, art, mathematics, and the sciences, and for such specific subjects as algebra, geometry, physics, and chemistry.

Readiness tests have for some years been used with primary-school children in order to determine whether or not they have reached a level of maturity necessary for success in reading. Arithmetic readiness tests have been devised more recently for use in determining whether pupils have sufficient mental maturity to permit efficient learning of various arithmetic skills. Although there might be some question concerning the classification of readiness here, it seems that particularly for children entering school for the first time these tests more largely measure special mental abilities than the results of learning.

Multifactor tests. Tests of group factors of intelligence have evolved since general intelligence and specific aptitude tests first made their appearance, and have recently attained considerable growth in usage. Group factors of intelligence are in a sense midway between specific and general intelligence.

Multifactor tests are now available for measuring from six to ten or more group factors of intelligence. Perhaps the terms most often used to characterize these multiple group factors of intelligence are differential aptitudes or primary mental abilities. Representative of such factors are spatial, numerical, mechanical, abstract, memory, induction, and deduction.

Performance tests. Performance tests are of several types, which cut across the classifications of intelligence tests outlined above. Some are individual and others are group tests. Some measure general intelligence and others measure specific aptitudes. The term usually designates tests for which motor or manual responses rather than verbal or written responses are required of the pupil.

Personality Inventories and Evaluations

Although psychologists are in agreement that the common conception of personality is not psychologically sound, they are not in agreement concerning the real meaning of the term. They do, however, believe that personality has to do with the total behavior of the individual, both that which can and that which cannot be observed. In the discussion that follows, four of the types of behavior generally classified under personality which seem to be most useful concepts to the teacher are discussed. These, as well as some other types of behavior usually listed under personality, are discussed more completely in Chapter 7.

Attitude scales. The attention that has been directed toward attitudes by several nation-wide surveys of public opinion illustrates the educational importance of attitudes. Attitudes are formed, crystallized, and sometimes modified or changed in the home, the church, on the playground, and elsewhere, as well as in the school.

Attitude scales are of several types, but they frequently are based on a two-, three-, or five-point scale of agreement-disagreement with statements concerning controversial issues or at least issues on which opinions may readily differ. Some of these scales deal with a specific issue, such as attitude toward the Chinese. Others are generalized, and may deal equally well with attitudes toward any racial group or any vocation, for example.

Interest inventories. The interests of different individuals vary tremendously. Not only are the individual's fields of interest sometimes obscured intentionally or unintentionally by his behavior, but in some instances his real interests may be unknown to him. Interest questionnaires use techniques somewhat similar to those for attitude testing, and frequently request indications of the presence of interest or the degree of interest a person has in various occupations, modes of behavior, types of activity, kinds of reading, and types of recreation, to name only a few.

Adjustment inventories. Adjustment inventories attempt to measure emotional adjustment primarily. Known by a variety of names—personality tests, personality inventories, personality schedules, adjustment inventories, and in various other ways—they ask the pupil to respond objectively to items probing his behavior, his likes and dislikes, his environment, and many other aspects of his life. A major purpose of such instruments is to locate peculiarities of behavior and various other types of maladjustment.

An excerpt from the *California Psychological Inventory* is shown herewith to indicate types of questions in true-false form not uncommonly asked in adjustment inventories.

Projective techniques. Paper-and-pencil instruments are useful in measuring attitudes, interests, and even adjustment, but they cannot be used in measuring conduct in the many life and school situations where paper and a pencil are not natural parts of the environment. The most widely used but at the same time the most highly technical devices for evaluating total personality through the observation of complex behavior are known as projective techniques. Designed for administration by psychological examiners and other technically trained psychologists, projective techniques variously ask the child to interpret inkblots or pictures, to complete unfinished stories or pictures, and to use toys, dolls, blocks, paints, and other recreational materials in play. Although classroom teachers

EXCERPT FROM *California Psychological Inventory* [34]

1. I enjoy social gatherings just to be with people.

2. The only interesting part of the newspaper is the "funnies."

3. I looked up to my father as an ideal man.

4. A person needs to "show off" a little now and then.

5. Our thinking would be a lot better off if we would just forget about words like "probably," "approximately," and "perhaps."

6. I have a very strong desire to be a success in the world.

7. When in a group of people I usually do what the others want rather than make suggestions.

8. I liked "Alice in Wonderland" by Lewis Carroll.

may on occasion use results obtained by technicians, they are seldom qualified to administer and interpret projective techniques.

Educational Tests

Considered as educational here and throughout this book are all instruments and techniques designed to measure what the individual has learned both in and out of school. It is obviously impossible to be certain about the exact proportions of the attainments of a school pupil that are the result of direct classroom instruction, of the by-products of classroom and other school activities, and of the wide range of his out-of-school experiences. A rather wide variety of tests, of other instruments, and of techniques for measuring types of abilities not definitely taught in any classroom or even in the school should be considered educational, for the education of the child is not confined entirely to the hours he spends in school. Various aspects of educational testing are dealt with in greater detail in Chapters 8 through 12 and in the section of this book devoted to measurement and evaluation in various subject fields.

[34] Harrison G. Gough, *California Psychological Inventory*. Consulting Psychologists Press, Inc., Palo Alto, Calif., 1956.

When examinations, other tools, and techniques are classified in terms of their form or structure, five types may be distinguished: (1) oral examinations, (2) essay examinations, (3) objective examinations and scales, (4) performance tests and scales, and (5) other evaluative instruments and techniques.

Oral examinations. Oral questioning of pupil groups is used in the classroom for measuring recall of factual knowledges. Such questioning often constitutes a major part of the so-called recitation, in fact. It usually consists of asking pupils sequentially or in a somewhat random order to answer questions based on the assignment for the day and of attempting to evaluate the quality of their responses. Oral examining may take many forms, some of which are inappropriate but others of which are sound for measurement purposes. A section of Chapter 9 deals with the oral examination in some detail.

Essay examinations. In the essay examination, a limited number of questions are posed by the teacher as a basis for written answers by the pupils. Typically, the questions are selected by the teacher to elicit essay-type responses on the subject matter of the course the individual pupils have presumably learned. This type of examination frequently poses questions of the *who, when, where, what,* or *why* type, although it may ask pupils to name, to locate, to discuss, to evaluate, to distinguish between, to define or describe, to illustrate or explain, to give reasons for or causes of, or otherwise respond to more-or-less definite issues.

The essay type of examination is often used as a final examination or as a test over several weeks of course work. As such, it may be thought of as the essay examination proper. It is also often used in shorter form as a check on pupil preparation of assignments, in which situation it is usually known as a written quiz. A quite complete discussion of the essay examination appears in Chapter 9.

Objective examinations and scales. As was pointed out in a preceding section of this chapter, the distinction between informal objective tests and standardized tests of achievement is concerned with matters other than the types of test items employed. The item forms used in the informal objective test are limited only by the degree of ingenuity employed by the teacher or teachers who construct it. Similarly, the quality of the informal objective test and its appropriate uses are below those of the standardized test only if the constructors lack the ability and the desire to construct a good test. The principles of objective test construction are so closely similar for these two types of tests that they are treated here under the more general heading of objective tests.

A tremendous variety of item types has been developed, and new adaptations are quite common. However, all objective items may be classified either as the selection or the supplementation type. Selection types, of which the alternate-response and scaled-choice, multiple-choice, and matching forms are the most common, make only indirect demands upon the initiative of the pupil, inasmuch as the material basic to the issue in question is stated, or perhaps misstated, in the item. Supplementation types, however, of which the completion type is probably the most common, place demands upon the initiative and frequently the memory of the pupil by expecting him to supply or to state the correct answer.

The illustrations below show how a factual knowledge can be measured by the three of the above types that are most brief in form. The first two are selection and the third is supplementation in form.

1. The President of the United States in 1863 was Abraham
   Lincoln.   Ⓣ   F
2. The President of the United States in 1863 was: (*a*) Ulysses
   S. Grant, (*b*) Millard Fillmore, (*c*) Abraham Lincoln, (*d*)
   Andrew Johnson, (*e*) Zachary Taylor.   <u>(*c*)</u>
3. The President of the United States in 1863 was   <u>(*Abraham Lincoln*)</u>

The tremendous variety of objective examination item types and the complexity of some of them make impossible the presentation of more than a few of the most common forms here. A comprehensive treatment of this important type of examination is given in Chapters 8 and 10.

Survey and prognostic tests serve different purposes and are constructed on somewhat different lines, but both may be considered general tests in the sense that their functions demand resulting scores which have general significance rather than highly specific or analytic meaning.

Survey tests are instruments that measure general achievement in certain subjects or areas of knowledge. They are used to test skills and abilities of widely varying types. The accompanying excerpt from the science part of the *Essential High School Content Battery* illustrates multiple-choice items, probably the most widely used of all item types in survey tests.

Prognostic tests are intended for use in the prediction of future success in specific subjects of the school curriculum. As they usually test the background skills and abilities found to be prerequisite for success in the particular subject, prognostic tests are most common among subjects in which success can be rather well defined in terms of certain basic abilities. They also frequently test some of the aptitude factors that are not directly dependent upon previous training of a specific type. Therefore, prognostic tests are probably most closely related to aptitude tests. The accompanying illustration from the *Prognostic Test of Mechanical Abilities* shows how previous learning contributes to success on this type of test.

EXCERPT FROM *Essential High School Content Battery* [35]

1. The science which deals with the composition of substances
   is called —
   a. chemistry.
   b. ecology.
   c. physics.
   d. meteorology.
   e. physiology.

2. Substances are broken down into simpler substances by the
   process of —
   f. synthesis.
   g. assimilation.
   h. photosynthesis.
   i. precipitation.
   j. decomposition.

3. A substance composed of two or more elements that are
   united chemically and in definite proportions is called —
   a. an alloy.
   b. a compound.
   c. a mixture.
   d. an emulsion.
   e. a solution.

4. All living matter consists of —
   f. cytoplasm.
   g. nucleus.
   h. protoplasm.
   i. chromatin.
   j. plasma.

Diagnostic and analytic tests are both intended for the separate measurement of rather specific aspects of achievement in a single subject or
field. Diagnostic tests measure somewhat narrower aspects of achievement than do analytic tests, so they may be thought of as serving specific
and general diagnostic functions respectively.

Diagnostic tests yield measures of highly related abilities underlying
achievement in a subject. They are designed to identify particular
strengths and weaknesses on the part of the individual child, and within
reasonable limits to reveal the underlying causes.

Analytic tests may be considered as general diagnostic tests. Fundamentally, all tests may be considered diagnostic in the sense that they

[35] David P. Harry and Walter N. Durost, *Essential High School Content Battery:
Test 2, Science.* Form A. Copyright 1950 by Harcourt, Brace and World, Inc., New York.
All rights reserved. Quoted by special permission.

actually yield useful information about pupil achievement. However, the diagnosis afforded by many present-day tests is extremely general. Many so-called diagnostic tests are not diagnostic, but are merely analytic tests. Moreover, the content structure of certain subjects, as reading and language, is such that detailed diagnosis is not practicable.

EXCERPT FROM *Prognostic Test of Mechanical Abilities* [36]

TEST II. READING SIMPLE DRAWINGS AND BLUEPRINTS

16-30. DIRECTIONS: The following are exercises in reading simple drawings and blueprints. Read each statement, look at the drawing, and write the letter that appears before the best answer on the line to the right of the statement. Do not use a ruler or scale.

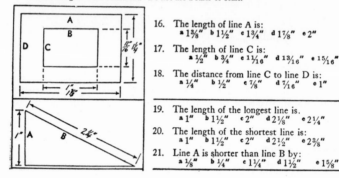

16. The length of line A is:
    a 1⅜" b 1½" c 1¾" d 1⅞" e 2" ____16

17. The length of line C is:
    a ½" b ¾" c 1¹⁄₁₆" d 1³⁄₁₆" e 1⁵⁄₁₆" ____17

18. The distance from line C to line D is:
    a ¼" b ½" c ⅞" d ⁷⁄₁₆" e 1" ____18

19. The length of the longest line is.
    a 1" b 1½" c 2" d 2½" e 2¼" ____19

20. The length of the shortest line is:
    a 1" b 1½" c 2" d 2½" e 2⅜" ____20

21. Line A is shorter than line B by:
    a ⅛" b ¼" c 1¼" d 1½" e 1⅝" ____21

Quizzes and mastery tests are most often teacher-made, for they are ordinarily used in particular courses when the teacher sees need for them. They differ from most objective tests in length and in function more than in form. By nature the scope of these tests is quite restricted.

Quizzes, typically consisting of ten to fifteen true-false or other objective items or eight to ten short-answer items or problems, are used by many teachers on occasion during a portion of a class period for the primary purpose of determining whether or not the pupils have read assigned materials. Although they may be announced in advance, they frequently are given without forewarning to the pupils.

Mastery tests are designed to measure only those fundamental skills and abilities that all pupils supposedly have acquired, so the tests are at a very low level of difficulty for most pupils. Perfect scores are therefore commonly made by a majority of the pupils. These tests are typically constructed by the teacher for use in his own classes.

Instructional and practice tests are sometimes constructed by the teacher, but they are also included in many of the workbooks provided particularly for elementary-school subjects and to some degree for high-

[36] J. Wayne Wrightstone and Charles E. O'Toole, *Prognostic Test of Mechanical Abilities.* Form A. California Test Bureau, Monterey, Calif., 1946.

school subjects. The scope of a test of this type is narrow, for typically only one aspect of a skill or one phase of a content area is covered.

It is in this area that teaching machines, perhaps first envisioned by Pressey[37] as early as 1926 and recently developed by Skinner[38] and others, may play a significant role in the future. If such machines come into widespread use or if the instructional values they are thought to possess are attained by simpler devices,[39] it may well be that classroom teachers will in the future be constructing instructional tests according to new and quite unusual patterns.

Source scales, confined almost solely to the field of spelling, are frequently referred to as product scales. The scales themselves are ordinarily not used by the pupils. Rather they provide the source materials for constructing tests. In spelling scales, the words of a given degree of spelling difficulty are either grouped together and placed on a scale ranging from easy to hard for each grade, or they are arranged in alphabetical order followed in each instance by the average percent of spelling accuracy. The teacher wishing to construct a spelling test of a given degree of difficulty for a certain grade can do so by selecting appropriate words from such a source scale.

The accompanying excerpt from *The New Iowa Spelling Scale* gives some of the words spelled correctly by 50 percent of the pupils in Grade 8.

EXCERPT FROM *The New Iowa Spelling Scale* [40]

absence	bargain	delicious	inferior	respectfully
affectionate	certificate	eventually	inhabitant	steadily
applying	characters	exceptional	multitude	stretch
appreciate	conceal	expenses	occasional	succeed
assistant	congratulate	fierce	officials	tailor
attitude	continually	ignorant	receiver	tremendous

Performance tests and scales. Tests of this type involve the manipulation or the production of two-dimensional and perhaps primarily of three-dimensional objects. Paper and a pencil are sometimes necessary for the pupil in taking such a test, but in other situations the pupil actually constructs or manipulates some physical materials in the attempt to demon-

[37] Sidney L. Pressey, "A Simple Apparatus Which Gives Tests and Scores—and Teaches." *School and Society,* 23:373-76; March 20, 1926.

[38] B. F. Skinner, "Teaching Machines." *Science,* 128:969-77; October 24, 1958.

[39] Paul B. Diederich, "Self-Correcting Homework in English." *Proceedings of the Invitational Conference on Testing Problems, 1959.* Educational Testing Service, Princeton, N. J., 1960. p. 70-86.

[40] Harry A. Greene, *The New Iowa Spelling Scale.* Bureau of Educational Research and Service, State University of Iowa, Iowa City, 1954.

strate his skill. Performance tests are dealt with in Chapter 11 of this volume.

Object tests entail the presentation of physical objects to the pupils for them to identify by name or type, for them to classify in some prescribed manner, or for them to use in identifying certain characteristics of the objects. Manipulation of the objects is not entailed unless handling is necessary in obtaining answers to the questions.

Quality and rating scales are useful in many school subjects, such as handwriting, composition, industrial arts, and the practical arts, where pupils produce results in some tangible form through the application of their skills to assigned tasks. Their products differ in quality and in speed of production. The teacher's problem becomes one of evaluating the product and perhaps of recording the time taken in its production.

Quality scales are used in judging the quality of work produced by pupils in handwriting, lettering, English composition, and a few other areas. In using such scales, the product resulting from the pupil's activity is compared by the teacher with specimens or standards provided in the quality scale and is then assigned the numerical value of the scale specimen it most nearly resembles.

Rating scales or score cards are used especially in the practical arts and industrial arts. Calibrated numerical ratings appear on the scale or score card for use by the teacher, after observing, measuring, or otherwise judging the product, in assigning quantitative values to work at various quality levels.

Check lists are most often used in evaluating the procedures employed by a pupil in the performance of some skill. Such check lists are useful in laboratory sciences and other performance areas in which certain tasks are most effectively performed by the use of sequences and techniques previously taught to the pupil. A check list of actions, both appropriate and inappropriate, is prepared in advance. The teacher observes each pupil separately as he attempts to perform the assigned task and keeps a running account of his procedures, both good and bad, in order of occurrence. The pupil's performance is then evaluated in terms of how closely it compares with the most efficient and direct procedures for reaching the goal he was seeking.

Other evaluative instruments and techniques. To be treated here are the tests, nontest instruments, and techniques that are used in evaluating learning outcomes not closely related to specific school subjects and used in the presentation and summarization of other measurement results. These instruments and techniques are discussed in Chapter 12.

Evaluative tests are difficult to distinguish from more formal tests, since there are at least several types of tests which in form or in mode of behavior measured probably should be considered evaluative in nature. In general, these evaluative tests are designed to measure some of the relatively intangible types of instructional outcomes.

Interpretive tests are represented by integrated units of test materials for the measurement of such relatively intangible outcomes as ability to interpret data, ability to interpret literature, ability to apply principles in the sciences, logical reasoning, and critical thinking. Tests of practices and activities, concerned with such out-of-school activities as health and safety practices and fiction reading, are also of this type. Certain tests of values in the areas of literature and reading, the fine arts, and recreations measure such intangible outcomes of school and out-of-school experiences as appreciations and satisfactions. In addition, some of the test batteries properly classified as a whole under survey tests have distinct evaluative features embodied in certain parts.

Other evaluative tools used in pupil evaluation are the participation schedule, the profile chart, the progress chart, the cumulative record, and the report card, all used with the individual pupil, and the class analysis chart, used both for an over-all evaluation of the group and for relating the status of the individual pupil to the over-all group picture.

Evaluative techniques include observation, the interview, and the questionnaire, frequently used informally in pupil evaluation. These are perhaps the most widely used techniques for evaluating educational outcomes. Both are, of course, used more formally for more specialized purposes. Two other techniques, the anecdotal record and the case study, may also be used to measure educational outcomes even though their typical use may be in the area of personality evaluation.

6. PLANNING A COMPREHENSIVE TESTING PROGRAM

Achievement testing done in his classroom under his immediate direction and planned by him should naturally and properly be the aspect of pupil appraisal most immediately of concern to the classroom teacher. However, the testing program of a modern school is likely to involve pupils in large numbers on frequent occasions and to go into mental ability and perhaps even personality areas of pupil behavior. This requires that needs for information about pupils be envisioned broadly and in terms of general and long-range educational objectives. The teacher's contribution to a program of this scope may well consist of some participation in the planning stage and of some part, even in some cases a minor one, when the tests are administered and scored. As one of the users of results from such tests, however, he should be as well informed and as much concerned as if he himself had planned and administered the tests.

TABLE 1

Suggested Program of Standardized Testing

Grade	Season	Small School		Medium School		Large School	
		8-4 or 6-2-4	6-6 or 6-3-3	8-4 or 6-2-4	6-6 or 6-3-3	8-4 or 6-2-4	6-6 or 6-3-3
1	Autumn	Readiness 1	Readiness 1	Readiness 1	Readiness 1	Readiness 1	Readiness 1
	Winter						
	Spring						
2	Autumn					Gen. Int. 1	Gen. Int. 1
	Winter						
	Spring		Gen. Ach. 1		Gen. Ach. 1		Gen. Ach. 1
3	Autumn	Gen. Int. 1		Gen. Int. 1		Gen. Ach. 1	
	Winter						
	Spring		Gen. Int. 1		Gen. Int. 1		
4	Autumn	Gen. Ach. 1		Gen. Ach. 1		Gen. Int. 2	Gen. Int. 2
	Winter						
	Spring						
5	Autumn			Reading 1	Reading 1	Reading 1	Reading 1
	Winter						
	Spring						
6	Autumn		Gen. Ach. 2	Gen. Ach. 2	Gen. Ach. 2	Gen. Ach. 2	Gen. Ach. 2
	Winter						
	Spring	Gen. Int. 2	Gen. Int. 2	Gen. Int. 2	Gen. Int. 2	Gen. Int. 3	Gen. Int. 3
7	Autumn						
	Winter						
	Spring	Gen. Ach. 2		Reading 2	Reading 2	Reading 2	Reading 2

Grade (Autumn / Winter / Spring)						
8	Gen. Int. 3		Gen. Ach. 3 Gen. Int. 3	Gen. Ach. 3 Scho. Apt. I	Gen. Ach. 3 Gen. Int. 4	Gen. Ach. 3 Scho. Apt. I
9	Gen. Ach. 3	Gen. Ach. 3 Scho. Apt. I	Gen. Ach. 3 Multiapt. I	Gen. Ach. 3	Gen. Ach. 4 Multiapt. I	Gen. Ach. 4
10	Gen. Ach. 3	Gen. Ach. 3	Gen. Ach. 4 Voc. Int. I	Multiapt. I Voc. Int. I Gen. Ach. 4	Gen. Ach. 5 Voc. Int. I Gen. Ach. 6	Gen. Ach. 5 Multiapt. I Voc. Int. I Gen. Ach. 6
11	Scho. Apt. I	Scho. Apt. 2	Scho. Apt. I	Scho. Apt. 2	Scho. Apt. I	Scho. Apt. 2
12	Gen. Ach. 4	Gen. Ach. 4	Gen. Ach. 5	Gen. Ach. 5	Gen. Ach. 7	Gen. Ach. 7

Recommended Supplements as Needed and When Feasible

Physical fitness tests
Individual intelligence tests
Standardized achievement tests in subject areas
Standardized achievement tests in specific subjects
Standardized adjustment inventories
Standardized attitude scales
Evaluative tools and techniques
Performance tests of achievement
Measures of socioeconomic and home status
Projective techniques

In planning a comprehensive testing program for an entire school system or for a division of it, such as the elementary school or the high school, many factors must be considered. Traxler dealt with some of them in his discussion of ten steps he believed to be essential in a testing program.[41] The first five of these, dealing with the planning stages, are pertinent here. He framed them as questions in essentially this form: (1) WHAT do we want to find out? (2) WHY are we developing a program? (3) WHEN should the tests be given? (4) WHERE in the grades and high school should the tests be given? (5) HOW should the program be carried on and the results be organized for effective use?

Whether considered as questions to be answered or areas in which decisions need to be made, program planning involves many factors and influences. Among these are the organization of the school, its size and financial ability, the level of teacher preparation, the attitudes of parents toward testing, and the existence of capable leadership in the technical aspects of a testing program. Table 1 presents suggestions for minimum testing programs for small, medium, and large schools and for four patterns of school organization: (a) the 8-grade elementary school and 4-year high school; (b) the somewhat similar 6-grade elementary school, 2-year grammar school, and 4-year high school; (c) the 6-grade elementary school and 6-year high school; and (d) the somewhat similar 6-grade elementary school, 3-year junior high school, and 3-year senior high school.

Only the most commonly used and fundamentally important types of standardized group tests of mental ability, achievement, and vocational interests are included in the table proper. Certain other types of tests and techniques are listed as desirable supplements to a basic program when needs for them are recognized and their inclusion is feasible. Informal objective and other teacher-made tests are not included in the table, inasmuch as any program planned for the school as a whole is in addition to, although not desirably apart from, the teacher's program based directly on the particularized needs of his pupils and on his personal planning.

The program outlined in the table is intended to point up a few important ideas but not to present a pattern prescribed for use in any school. Tests of certain types should doubtless be given at spaced intervals during a pupil's school career, so that reasonably up-to-date information may be available at all times and so that his background of growth and development may become more fully depicted as he advances in school. Some tests may well be given before rather than after a pupil moves from one level to another of the school, in order that the results be available to aid in orienting him to the new setup. Some tests are perhaps given more ad-

---

[41] Arthur E. Traxler, "Ten Essential Steps in a Testing Program." *Education,* 79:357-62; February 1959.

vantageously at one season of the school year than another. Tests of certain types have major values and uses at various grade levels, often in accordance with pupil growth and maturation and consequent needs for specialized information. A few other more detailed considerations lie behind certain aspects of the table, but these represent the most widely significant factors for planning a testing program to fit local needs, and, consequently, the teacher should be somewhat familiar with them.

SUGGESTED ACTIVITIES

1. Look into one of the following references in the chapter bibliography for interesting historical backgrounds: (1) Caldwell and Courtis for the Boston examinations; (2) Peterson for early attempts to measure intelligence; (3) Pintner for World War I intelligence testing.
2. Look up some historical personage, such as Horace Mann, Francis Galton, J. McKeen Cattell, J. M. Rice, Alfred Binet, Edward L. Thorndike, or Lewis M. Terman, in a standard encyclopedia or biographical dictionary to see what aspects of his background may help to explain his contribution to measurement.

TOPICS FOR DISCUSSION

1. Show how educational testing had its origins centuries before standardized and informal objective tests were developed.
2. List and evaluate the most important ideas concerning examinations expressed by Horace Mann.
3. Discuss the contributions of Binet and Simon to the intelligence testing movement.
4. What types of abilities are measured by general intelligence tests? By specific intelligence or aptitude tests? By tests of group factors of intelligence?
5. Discuss structured personality inventories and projective methods.
6. Who were the pioneers in the development of standardized educational tests? What was their influence on the measurement movement?
7. Indicate the part played by informal objective examinations in the development of educational measurement.
8. What influences contributed to the rise of evaluation instruments, tools, and techniques?
9. Comment upon the status of educational and mental measurement and evaluation today.
10. Distinguish the three general types of tests—educational, mental, and personality.
11. Distinguish between tests and scales. What are scaled tests?
12. Distinguish between verbal and nonverbal tests.

13. Briefly note some of the differences between individual and group tests of general intelligence.
14. What do aptitude and readiness tests measure? For what fields are they provided?
15. What do group-factor tests measure? In what areas are they provided?
16. Briefly characterize attitude scales, interest inventories, adjustment inventories, and a few of the projective techniques used in personality measurement.
17. Briefly characterize the four forms of educational tests—oral examination, essay examination, objective examination, and performance test.
18. Indicate the major characteristics of survey and prognostic tests. Of diagnostic and analytic tests.
19. Illustrate several types of items used in objective examinations.
20. For what achievement areas are source scales and quality scales provided? How are these scales related to tests?
21. What types of evaluative tests and techniques are used in educational measurement?
22. Comment on the similarities and differences of performance tests as they are used in mental and in educational measurement.

SELECTED REFERENCES

ANASTASI, ANNE. *Differential Psychology: Individual and Group Differences in Behavior.* Third edition. New York: Macmillan Co., 1958. Chapter 1.

ANASTASI, ANNE. *Psychological Testing.* Second edition. New York: Macmillan Co., 1961. Chapters 1-2.

AYRES, LEONARD P. "History and Present Status of Educational Measurements." *The Measurement of Educational Products.* Seventeenth Yearbook of the National Society for the Study of Education, Part II. Bloomington, Ill.: Public School Publishing Co., 1918. Chapter 1.

BELL, JOHN E. *Projective Techniques: A Dynamic Approach to the Study of Personality.* New York: Longmans, Green and Co., 1948. Chapters 1, 25.

BINGHAM, WALTER V. *Aptitudes and Aptitude Testing.* New York: Harper and Brothers, 1937. Chapters 4-5.

CALDWELL, OTIS W., AND COURTIS, STUART A. *Then and Now in Education, 1845-1923.* Yonkers, N. Y.: World Book Co., 1923. Chapters 3-6.

CRONBACH, LEE J. *Essentials of Psychological Testing.* Second edition. New York: Harper and Brothers, 1960. Chapters 2, 7.

EBEL, ROBERT L., AND DAMRIN, DORA E. "Tests and Examinations." *Encyclopedia of Educational Research.* Third edition. New York: Macmillan Co., 1960. p. 1502-17.

FERGUSON, LEONARD W. *Personality Measurement.* New York: McGraw-Hill Book Co., Inc., 1952. Chapters 2-9.

FREEMAN, FRANK N. *Mental Tests: Their History, Principles and Applications.* Revised edition. Boston: Houghton Mifflin Co., 1939. Chapters 1-8.

FRYER, DOUGLAS. *The Measurement of Interests.* New York: Henry Holt and Co., 1931. Chapter 10.

GARRETT, HENRY E. *Great Experiments in Psychology.* Third edition. New York: Appleton-Century-Crofts, Inc., 1951. Chapters 11-13, 15.

GERBERICH, J. RAYMOND. *Specimen Objective Test Items: A Guide to Achievement Test Construction.* New York: Longmans, Green and Co., 1956. Chapters 17-18.

GOODENOUGH, FLORENCE L. *Mental Testing: Its History, Principles, and Applications.* New York: Rinehart and Co., Inc., 1949. Chapters 3-6.

HULL, CLARK L. *Aptitude Testing.* Yonkers, N. Y.: World Book Co., 1928. Chapter 3.

MONROE, WALTER S. "Educational Measurement in 1920 and in 1945." *Journal of Educational Research,* 38:334-40; January 1945.

NUNNALLY, JUM C., JR. *Tests and Measurements: Assessments and Prediction.* New York: McGraw-Hill Book Co., Inc., 1959. Chapters 1-2.

PETERSON, JOSEPH. *Early Conceptions and Tests of Intelligence.* Yonkers, N. Y.: World Book Co., 1925. Chapters 1-2, 5-11.

PINTNER, RUDOLF. *Intelligence Testing.* New edition. New York: Henry Holt and Co., 1931. Chapters 1-3, 6-7.

REMMERS, H. H. *Introduction to Opinion and Attitude Measurement.* New York: Harper and Brothers, 1954. Chapter 3.

SARGENT, HELEN. "Projective Methods: Their Origin, Theory, and Applications in Personality Research." *Psychological Bulletin,* 42:257-93; May 1945.

SCATES, DOUGLAS E. "Fifty Years of Objective Measurement and Research in Education." *Journal of Educational Research,* 41:241-64; December 1947.

SYMONDS, PERCIVAL M. *Diagnosing Personality and Conduct.* New York: D. Appleton-Century Co., Inc., 1931. Chapters 5-9.

TABA, HILDA, AND OTHERS. *Diagnosing Human Relations Needs.* Washington, D. C.: American Council on Education, 1951.

TERMAN, LEWIS M., AND MERRILL, MAUD A. *Stanford-Binet Intelligence Scale: Manual for the Third Revision,* Form L-M. Boston: Houghton Mifflin Co., 1960.

THURSTONE, L. L., AND CHAVE, E. J. *The Measurement of Attitude.* Chicago: University of Chicago Press, 1929.

THUT, I. N., AND GERBERICH, J. RAYMOND. *Foundations of Method for Secondary Schools.* New York: McGraw-Hill Book Co., Inc., 1949. p. 162-90, 238-66, 323-47, 380-98.

TYLER, RALPH W. "The Specific Techniques of Investigation: Examining and Testing Acquired Knowledge, Skill, and Ability." *The Scientific Movement in Education.* Thirty-Seventh Yearbook of the National Society for the Study of Education, Part II. Bloomington, Ill.: Public School Publishing Co., 1938. Chapter 29.

WATSON, GOODWIN. "The Specific Techniques of Investigation: Testing Intelligence, Aptitudes, and Personality." *The Scientific Movement in Education.* Thirty-Seventh Yearbook of the National Society for the Study of Education, Part II. Bloomington, Ill.: Public School Publishing Co., 1938. Chapter 30.

WOODRUFF, ASAHEL D., AND PRITCHARD, MARALYN W. "Some Trends in the Development of Psychological Tests." *Educational and Psychological Measurement,* 9:105-8; Spring 1949.

WRIGHTSTONE, J. WAYNE. "Frontiers in Educational Research in the Measurement of Aptitudes and Achievement." *Journal of Educational Research,* 40:389-96; January 1947.

3

CHARACTERISTICS OF GOOD EDUCATIONAL

APPRAISAL

This chapter presents a discussion of the following character-istics of good educational appraisal devices and techniques:

A. Validity as an essential characteristic of good measurement.
B. Types of validity—content, concurrent, predictive, and construct.
C. Reliability as an essential aspect of validity.
D. Reliability coefficients—equivalence, internal consistency, and stability.
E. Adequacy and objectivity as important aspects of reliability.
F. Practicality—administrability, scorability, and economy.
G. Comparability of meaning in the results of appraisals.
H. Utility as an over-all characteristic of good measurement.

The selection of any standardized educational test, mental test, or personality inventory requires careful consideration of the characteristics of a good examination. Similarly, the construction of any test or nontest instrument and the preparation of any evaluative technique, whether educational, mental, or in the area of personality, require careful consideration of the characteristics of good measurement. Although the characteristics of a good examination, tool, or technique can be listed and classified in many different ways, test specialists are in general agreement concerning the aspects that should receive attention in selecting or constructing them. The criteria discussed below undoubtedly represent the most important considerations to be taken into account.[1]

[1] Although the discussion of this chapter is typically in terms of test or examination criteria, in order to avoid cumbersome wording, the reader should bear in mind the fact

It is recommended that the student refer frequently to the discussion of Chapter 14 on the statistical methods of determining test validity and reliability in connection with the study of these two exceedingly important criteria. An adequate understanding of these criteria depends on both their theoretical and their statistical aspects. The brief illustrations interspersed through this chapter of how the authors of certain standardized achievement tests have attempted to make sure that their tests satisfy these and other characteristics of a good examination are supplemented by occasional references to the treatment of achievement tests in Chapter 8.

1. VALIDITY

Validity is the most important characteristic of a good examination, for unless a test is valid it serves no useful function. *The validity of an examination depends on the degree to which it measures what it attempts to measure.* A test must, therefore, accomplish the purpose the user has in mind in order to satisfy this fundamental criterion for all testing. In fact, the uncritical acceptance of an invalid test by a teacher for performing a desired function might easily result in serious injustice to the pupils.

Teachers cannot be too careful in assuring themselves of the validity of the tests they use. For example, a teacher who used a test that measures only knowledge of facts in a course in American history would not be correct in drawing conclusions on the basis of the results about the abilities of his pupils to apply historical facts to the reasoned interpretation of events. It follows, also, that a test must be used with pupils who possess the proper intellectual maturity and background of experience for taking the test if it is to possess validity. For example, a standardized arithmetic survey test intended for use with pupils in Grades 6 to 9 might be invalid for use with most pupils in Grade 5 and probably with all pupils in the lower grades.

Thus, a test of high validity for ranking pupils in Grade 9 on algebraic problem solving would have lower and lower validities for testing college students in analytic geometry, for measuring the arithmetic skills of pupils in Grade 4, for predicting course marks in a high-school French course, for measuring general intelligence, and for measuring attitudes toward war and peace.

Validity is, therefore, a specific rather than a general criterion of a good examination. It is specific in the sense that a test may be highly

---

that the broad and general rather than the narrower, special use of the term is intended. The criteria should be interpreted as applying in only slightly modified form to nontest evaluative tools and to evaluative techniques as well as to tests and examinations.

valid for use in one situation and highly invalid for use in another manner. It is specific, also, in the sense that a test may be valid for use with one group of pupils but not for use with a different pupil group. Tests cannot correctly be described as valid in general terms, for they are valid only in connection with their intended use and at the intended ability level of the pupils.

Four types of test validity are distinguished here—content, concurrent, predictive, and construct.[2] The first is most widely applicable in achievement testing, but the last is particularly pertinent when some of the newer and less tangible outcomes measured by achievement tests are under consideration. The other two, concurrent and predictive validity, have greatest significance for intelligence and aptitude tests.

Content Validity

Achievement tests of the highly tangible knowledge and skill outcomes are most often based on content, or curricular, validity, although tests of such other cognitive outcomes as concepts, understandings, and perhaps applications may sometimes be similarly founded. A teacher who constructs an informal objective test or any other evaluation instrument, or who carefully selects a standardized test for his class, is attempting to insure content validity by making certain that the test (1) deals with the types of educational outcomes he is attempting to achieve and hence wishes to measure and (2) is at the proper level of difficulty for his pupils. There are various direct and indirect sources of evidence to guide the teacher in this consideration of content validity. Among these, in addition to his own formulations of instructional objectives and of resulting behavioral outcomes, are textbooks, courses of study, reports of committees, and writings of subject and test specialists.

Teacher-formulated objectives and outcomes. The sequence now most favored in classroom appraisal of achievement is to devise tests that measure the degree to which pupils have attained the instructional outcomes formulated by the teacher. In fact, the extent to which the outcomes can be evaluated objectively may well be a significant indication of their suitability. Content validity of a high degree can be obtained when instruc-

---

[2] (1) Committees on Test Standards, American Educational Research Association and National Council on Measurements Used in Education, *Technical Recommendations for Achievement Tests.* National Education Association, Washington, D. C., 1955. p. 15-27; (2) Joint Committees, American Psychological Association, American Educational Research Association, and National Council on Measurements Used in Education, *Technical Recommendations for Psychological Tests and Diagnostic Techniques.* American Psychological Association, Washington, D. C., 1954. p. 13-28. (Supplement to the *Psychological Bulletin,* Vol. 51, No. 2, Part 2; March 1954.)

tional outcomes are clearly stated and are real outgrowths of the teaching procedure.

Textbook and course of study analyses. The major weakness in the analysis of textbook and course of study content as a validation method is that it tends to perpetuate faulty and inadequate curricular content if such defects exist in the source materials. It does not look beyond present practices. On the other hand, the overlapping of instructional material that is common to a large number of textbooks and courses of study almost certainly represents important content.

Recommendations of committees and specialists. Reports of national committees and writings of subject and test specialists often serve as good guides to content in achievement test construction. Such reports and recommendations are usually based on statements of instructional objectives and of desired learning outcomes in terms of pupil behavior. These source materials often provide excellent foundations for standardized and informal objective test construction, and the use of modern reports and writings by recognized committees and specialists is unlikely to result in perpetuating the errors in past practices.

Social utility. The validation of content in terms of social utility assumes that the course of study itself is based on that point of view. An example of this approach to spelling test construction is the use of words that exhaustive word counts have shown to be most widely used in written language, and therefore words that the pupils need most to be able to spell correctly. Also, home mechanics tests are often based in part on the skills, such as fixing a leaking water tap, hanging a window weight, or wiring a buzzer, that activity analyses have shown to be most frequently required in the maintenance of household equipment.

An example of content validity is found in the *Nelson Biology Test,* in the construction of which analyses of eight widely used high-school biology textbooks and nearly as many workbooks were supplemented by analyses of expert opinion as found in various yearbooks, bulletins, proceedings, and journal articles.[3]

Concurrent Validity

The first of the two statistical procedures used in validating tests is based on the establishment of concurrent validity. This procedure usually involves determination of the degree to which the test scores can replace or be used as a substitute for scores or measures already existing. Basic to this method is the belief that the test is valid if a high correlation is ob-

[3] Clarence H. Nelson, *Nelson Biology Test: Manual of Directions.* World Book Co., Yonkers, N. Y., 1951. p. 2.

tained between scores on it and on such criterion measures as similar tests, teachers' marks, and ratings of expert judges. The implication of this procedure is that the criterion measure or measures can be accepted as measurement standards. Correlation coefficients obtained in such situations are known as *coefficients of concurrent validity.*

Correlation with other test scores. This method may be utilized in fields in which extensive critical work in test development has already been done. There would be reason to doubt the validity of a factual achievement test in American history that did not show some relationship to achievement of knowledge outcomes as measured by previously existing valid tests in this subject. This is particularly true in the content subjects as contrasted with the skill subjects. This method of test validation is most frequently used when an outstandingly superior test is available to serve as the criterion. For example, the individual intelligence test constitutes the best basis at present for the validation of group intelligence tests.

Correlation with previous school marks. The method of validation by correlation with course marks assumes that in the long run an achievement test has validity if the pupils' scores on it are closely related to their achievement in the subject as evaluated by the teacher. That is, a test in language must have considerable validity if pupils whose marks in the subject have been consistently high make the superior scores on the tests and if pupils whose marks in the subject have been low make the inferior scores on the test. In spite of the apparent unreliability of teachers' marks for refined measurements, an achievement test that consistently picks out the pupils who in the teacher's judgment of a specific ability are superior or inferior probably does have significant validity.

Correlation with ratings of expert judges. This procedure is related in many respects to the one discussed above. To the extent that teachers' marks are the judgments of experts, the two procedures are identical.

Concurrent validity is represented by the correlation coefficients between scores on the *California Study Methods Survey* and scholastic success of 231 pupils in Grade 10 as measured by grade-point averages. Carter reported such coefficients of concurrent validity of .47, .58, and .32 for three part scores and of .57 for total scores on the test.[4]

Predictive Validity

The second statistical technique of test validation involves the establishment of predictive validity. A high correlation between scores on a test and the related future outcomes the test is designed to predict is

[4] Harold D. Carter, *California Study Methods Survey: Manual.* California Test Bureau, Monterey, Calif., 1958. p. 6.

accepted as evidence of validity. This method of validation is used with tests of general intelligence and aptitude, several types of achievement tests, and interest inventories. Correlation coefficients between scores on such tests and measures of school success, of vocational or occupational success, and even of maladjustment are known as *coefficients of predictive validity*.

Prediction of scholastic success. General intelligence and specific aptitude tests, prognostic tests, and even general achievement tests are used in predicting the subsequent scholastic success of school and college students. Success both in terms of school marks in specific subjects and in terms of grade-point averages can be predicted sufficiently well to warrant use of results from such tests in pupil guidance, in the sectioning of classes, and in various other ways.

An illustration of a coefficient of predictive validity is found in the coefficient of correlation of .56 for 38 tenth-grade pupils in one school between scores on the *Modern Language Aptitude Test* and their first-term marks in a course in French.[5]

Prediction of vocational or occupational success. Postschool success of pupils in vocational and occupational areas can also be predicted by the use of test results. Multiaptitude tests and interest or preference scales for use with high-school pupils, and also with college students, are the most important instruments for what is called differential prediction. Such prediction is not limited to one vocation only but simultaneously affords predictions for the several occupational areas a pupil might enter or for the several vocational areas he might by further study prepare to enter. Guidance workers find predictions of vocational success useful in counseling students about their postschool careers, whether the careers may be in the trades or in the professions, whether they may be entered immediately or are open only after a training period, whether they may require no special preparation or may require extended periods of technical study.

Prediction of maladjustment. It is sometimes possible to anticipate maladjustment in pupils by the use of observational techniques, personality inventories, projective methods, and, subsequently, by the employment of various more technical diagnostic and clinical techniques. In such instances, it may be possible to prevent the development or intensification of maladjustment or at least to minimize its consequences. Although this type of prediction fortunately is limited in its major significance to a small proportion of pupils, its importance in the administration of the guidance program in the modern school is great.

5 John B. Carroll and Stanley M. Sapon, *Modern Language Aptitude Test: Manual.* Psychological Corporation, New York, 1959. p. 12.

Construct Validity

The fourth and most subtle, but perhaps the most important, type of validity is called construct validity. There are some areas, such as study skills, understandings, appreciations, and interests, in which it appears to be impossible to secure an objective or statistical basis of validation. In general, these areas are made up of many interrelated abilities as contrasted with those practical skill areas where the tested performance either is an exact representation of, or a very similar substitute for, the instructional outcome sought. Analysis both of the desired outcome and of the proposed test by psychological and logical methods may well reveal a sufficient degree of commonality or of similarity to justify the belief that the test constitutes a valid measure of the outcome. Such methods are also followed quite frequently in such complex fields as language and the reading-study skills. Two somewhat related methods, rise in percentage of success and performance of widely spaced groups, represent the most common means of establishing construct validity.

Rise in percentage of success. This method is based on the changes in the type and quality of pupil responses that education and maturation bring about. A valid reading test is expected to show significant increases in scores indicative of increased achievement as the tests are used in successive school grades. If twelve-year-old children do not demonstrate a higher level of mental maturity than eleven-year-old children on the same mental ability test, there is reason to question the validity of the instrument.

Accomplishment of widely spaced groups. One of the readily recognized evidences of validity in test content is the power of such material to reveal significant differences in the accomplishment of widely spaced groups. For example, a scale designed to measure interests in, but not familiarity with, classical art might be validated in terms of how well it discriminates between persons who prefer to visit the art galleries and persons who prefer to attend the opera when they are in New York or some other city affording both types of cultural facilities.

Carter's method of constructing the *California Study Methods Survey* also illustrates the use of construct validity.[6] He validated the test for predicting high-school achievement in part by selecting self-report items that discriminated between the 200 high achievers and the 200 low achievers among about a thousand high-school sophomores.

[6] Carter, *op. cit.* p. 5.

2. RELIABILITY

A test is said to be reliable when it functions consistently. *The reliability of an examination depends on the degree to which it measures what it does measure.* This statement may appear on the surface to conflict with, or to repeat, the statement in the preceding section concerning the validity of an examination. Such is not the case, however. A test may satisfactorily test what it does test without to any effective degree testing what its user attempts to test. However, it cannot efficiently measure what it attempts to measure unless it efficiently measures whatever it does measure. This is equivalent to the statement that a test may be reliable without being valid, but its validity cannot be established unless it is reliable. Therefore, reliability is really an aspect or a phase of validity.

When a reliable test is used with the type of pupils and for the purpose for which it is intended, it will also be valid. This concept is fundamentally a restatement of the fact brought out in the foregoing section—that validity is specific and that it depends not only on test content but also on the proper use of the test. Thus, reliability, even though it is an aspect of validity, is general in nature. Reliability, in turn, has two aspects, adequacy and objectivity. These are discussed later in this chapter.

Reliability is most frequently expressed by the use of the coefficient of correlation. Thus, as is true of a validity coefficient, a reliability coefficient is simply a special application of the coefficient of correlation. In each of the methods presented below for obtaining or estimating reliability coefficients, it is the internal consistency or self-consistency of the test that is being evaluated. Only the general methods of obtaining the various types of coefficients and discussions of their applications are given here. The statistical procedures involved in obtaining the various coefficients are presented in Chapter 13.

Four types of coefficients are dealt with here—the coefficient of equivalence, two types of coefficients of internal consistency, and the coefficient of stability.[7] The last of these is used rather infrequently.

Coefficient of Equivalence

A basic method of determining the reliability of a test is by means of correlating scores on two equivalent forms of the same test given successively by the same procedure to the same group of pupils. The resulting measure is called the *coefficient of equivalence.* Students interested in making a critical analysis of the reliabilities of standardized tests should

[7] (1) Committees on Test Standards, *op. cit.* p. 27-32; (2) Joint Committees, *op. cit.* p. 28-33.

doubtless do so in large degree on the basis of the correspondence of scores on two forms of the test. The resultant coefficient when properly applied is likely to be free from the factors making for artificially high relationships that sometimes result from the use of less critical methods.

Coefficients of equivalence are illustrated by the values .85, .92, and .87 reported between scores on Form A and Form B of the mathematics test of the *Essential High School Content Battery* for sample groups of pupils in Grades 10, 11, and 12 respectively.[8]

Coefficients of Internal Consistency

Two procedures are commonly used in estimating test reliability when two forms of the instrument cannot conveniently be given or when only one form is available. These procedures are therefore based on results from one administration of a test.

Chance-half coefficient. A common method of estimating the reliability of a test is by means of the chance-half coefficient. The test is given to a group of pupils and their scores are then obtained for two arbitrarily determined halves of the test. Usual methods of dividing a test into chance-halves are (1) obtaining separate scores on the odd-numbered and on the even-numbered items, or (2) obtaining separate scores on items 1, 4, 5, 8, 9, 12, 13, etc., and on items 2, 3, 6, 7, 10, 11, etc., to equalize difficulty of the two half-scores when the items are in a scaled order of difficulty. The correlation coefficient obtained between the two sets of scores indicates the degree of conformance between the two chance-halves of the test. The coefficient of equivalence which would be expected for a test as long as the two halves combined is then found by using the *Spearman-Brown Prophecy Formula*.

This method of estimating test reliability has been popular in the past, since it involves a relatively small amount of labor and expense. Lindquist pointed out that the reliability coefficients estimated by this method are less dependable than those obtained by correlating scores on two forms of a test and are also likely to be spuriously high.[9] Despite that fact this is one of the most feasible methods for use with informal objective examinations for which ordinarily no second or alternate form is available.

Internal consistency reliability coefficients of the chance-half type, corrected by use of the Spearman-Brown formula, were found by the authors

[8] David P. Harry and Walter N. Durost, *Essential High School Content Battery: Manual of Directions*. World Book Co., Yonkers, N. Y., 1951. p. 15.
[9] E. F. Lindquist, *A First Course in Statistics*, Revised edition. Houghton Mifflin Co., Boston, 1942. p. 219.

of the *Modern Language Aptitude Test* to be .92 and .94 respectively for 116 pupils in Grade 10 and 159 pupils in Grade 11.[10]

Kuder-Richardson "Footrule" Coefficient. A useful method of estimating test reliability is a footrule coefficient which may in some cases be an underestimate but which is never an overestimate of the reliability coefficient. Called a "footrule" coefficient because it admittedly is not the most accurate method, it requires the use of only three facts and measures from the test in a simple formula—the arithmetic mean and standard deviation of the scores and the number of items in the test.[11] Because of its simplicity and because it furnishes a result of sufficient accuracy for many purposes, this method is a possibility for use by teachers in estimating the reliability of their informal objective examinations. The method of computing this coefficient is presented in Chapter 13.

Wrightstone and his colleagues were reporting on this second type of internal consistency reliability when they listed Kuder-Richardson "Footrule" coefficients of .833 and .771 based on random samples of 200 pupils each for the *New York Test of Arithmetic Meanings*.[12]

Coefficient of Stability

A method of representing the consistency of test scores when two forms of the test are not available, or even in some instances when equivalent test forms are used, is the *coefficient of stability*. The test and retest, with an intervening period of time, are given to the group of pupils under similar testing conditions and the coefficient is obtained between the two sets of scores. Alternatively, equivalent forms of a test are given under similar conditions. The second administration of the test should not too closely follow the first, but neither should it be delayed until intervening learning or development complicates the meaning of the coefficient of stability. Lindquist pointed out that this method is in general unsatisfactory, especially for achievement tests, and that it results in a spuriously high coefficient.[13]

As an illustration of test-retest correlations, coefficients of stability of .78, .80, and .76 for the three part scores and of .86 for the total score were reported by Carter for 215 pupils in Grade 10 on the *California Study Methods Survey*.[14]

[10] Carroll and Sapon, *op. cit.* p. 17.

[11] G. F. Kuder and M. W. Richardson, "The Theory of the Estimation of Test Reliability," (Formula 21). *Psychometrika,* 2:151-60; September 1937.

[12] J. Wayne Wrightstone and others, *New York Test of Arithmetic Meanings: Examiner's Manual and Key.* World Book Co., Yonkers, N. Y., 1956. p. 11.

[13] Lindquist, *op. cit.* p. 219-20.

[14] Carter, *op. cit.* p. 4.

Standard Error of Measurement

As is indicated above, estimates of reliability coefficients often result in spuriously high or low statements of test reliability. The various types of reliability coefficients must be based on known and appropriate ranges of ages or grade placement of pupils if they are to mean what they purport to mean. Hence, a reliability coefficient is neither an entirely adequate device nor, for that matter, the only method of indicating the internal consistency of a test.

The other increasingly popular device by which test reliability can be estimated is the *standard error of measurement*. This standard error indicates the degree of accuracy existing in the test score obtained for each pupil on a test. Accuracy here does not relate to the type resulting from lack of errors in computing the scores but rather to the magnitude of sampling errors of the type discussed and illustrated in the following section of this chapter. Since the standard error of measurement is not affected by the range of talent of the pupil group on which it is based, as are reliability coefficients, it is coming to be recognized as a more concrete way of indicating test reliability than the coefficients. Methods of obtaining this measure of reliability are developed in Chapter 13.

An illustration of a standard error of measurement used as evidence of reliability is the 2.6 reported for the English test of the *Essential High School Content Battery* at the Grade 10 level.[15]

3. ADEQUACY

A test can be described as adequate when it is long enough or consists of enough items to serve its purpose. *The adequacy of an examination depends on the degree to which it is of sufficient length to sample widely the behavior it is designed to measure.* If it meets this requirement, the test should be reliable and valid as well as adequate, for adequacy contributes directly to reliability and, as is pointed out in the preceding section, reliability is an aspect of validity. Thus, adequacy is prerequisite to reliability and reliability in turn is prerequisite to validity.

The careful test maker never assumes that the instrument he has constructed is capable of measuring all of the knowledges or skills that a pupil has acquired in a course. There are too many by-products and incidental learnings to make this possible. When not only knowledges and skills but also concepts, understandings, applications, and tastes and preferences are considered, the task of measuring all of the outcomes from any

[15] Harry and Durost, *op. cit.* p. 15.

course, any instructional unit, or even any single class period becomes hopeless. At best, a test is a sample of certain portions of the total behavior which the examiner considers essential for pupil competency in the field. Just as a grain buyer samples a carload of wheat by taking samples from different places in the car and grading the samples in order to obtain a measure of quality for the whole carload, a test constructor measures the educational attainments of pupils by constructing items that represent widely the types of pupil outcomes expected and accepts the scores resulting from their use as representative of the pupils' relative achievements for the entire area sampled by the test items.

Although it is not easy to consider test adequacy separately, or apart from test reliability, the achievement battery authored by Thorpe, Lefever, and Naslund includes sufficient scoring points—464— and requires sufficient pupil working time—370 minutes—to suggest that it satisfies this characteristic of a good test.[16] As the battery provides ten separate scores in work-study skills, reading, language arts, and arithmetic, an average of 46.4 scoring points and of 37 minutes of pupil working time is allotted to each score.

4. OBJECTIVITY

A test is objective when the scorer's personal judgment does not affect either the scoring process or the results. *The objectivity of an examination depends on the degree to which the influence of personal opinions and subjective judgments is eliminated or controlled in the scoring process.* Objectivity, then, contributes directly to reliability, although it does so in an entirely different way from adequacy, discussed in the section above. So objectivity is a second prerequisite to reliability and reliability in its turn is prerequisite to validity. To summarize this important series of relationships, validity is dependent upon reliability and reliability is dependent upon adequacy and objectivity. In other words, a test cannot be valid unless it is reliable and a test cannot be reliable unless it is adequate and objective.

Recognition of the need for elimination of subjectivity in the marking of examinations was one of the major factors contributing to the development of standardized and informal objective tests. In general, objective test items are so worded that only one answer satisfies the requirements of the statement. The advantage of selecting highly objective items for use in educational tests is that there can be little or no disagreement on what is the correct answer. This means that outside of chance errors

[16] Louis P. Thorpe, D. Welty Lefever, and Robert A. Naslund, *SRA Achievement Series: Examiner Manual*, 6-9. Science Research Associates, Inc., Chicago, 1955. p. 4, 23.

there should be no variation in the scores assigned to a given test by different persons or by the same person on different occasions.

Objectivity, as well as validity and reliability, of a test may be expressed by the use of the correlation coefficient. The coefficient obtained between scores or marks assigned to a group of papers by the same individual at two different times is sometimes called the *coefficient of objectivity*. However, this coefficient is less widely used than are those for estimating validity and reliability, inasmuch as the fact is quite obvious that the best types of test items are relatively high in objectivity.

Objectivity in a test that is being evaluated is usually considered either from the standpoint of the test items themselves and the degree of subjectivity involved in scoring them or in terms of how objectivity is reflected in test reliability. However, when highly objective types of tests are occasionally checked for reader reliability by correlating marks assigned to a set of papers by a scorer on one occasion with marks assigned to the same papers by the same scorer on a second occasion, the result is essentially a correlation coefficient of 1.00.[17] In practice, then, most objective tests are tacitly accepted as satisfying this criterion; it is for the essay test, short-answer test, and completion type of objective test that serious deficiencies in objectivity sometimes occur.

5. PRACTICALITY

A good examination must also possess certain practical qualities. These characteristics of administrability, scorability, and economy are concerned with ease of administering the test and scoring the results and with the requirements in labor and financial outlay entailed in using the examination effectively. Although these are not major criteria of a good examination, their practical significance is great.

Administrability

An examination possesses administrability when it is suitable in format, when the materials for giving it are easy to assemble and to handle, when directions for the examiner and directions to the pupils are clear and unambiguous, and when the examiner can use the test without undue effort in the measurement of pupil behavior. Ease of administration must be evaluated from two distinct points of view—that of the test administrator and that of the pupils taking the test.

Specifications should be complete and precise both for advance prepara-

[17] Robert L. Ebel and Dora E. Damrin, "Tests and Examinations." *Encyclopedia of Educational Research,* Third edition. Macmillan Co., New York, 1960. p. 1504.

tions and for actual test administration. Definite provisions should be made for the preparation, distribution, and collection of test materials, for oral instructions by the examiner preceding, during, and at the end of the examination, for written directions to the pupils covering the test as a whole and for each separate part, for timing of the test or test parts, and for a variety of other factors.

Instructions to the pupils, whether they are written, oral, or both written and oral, should be simple, clear, and concise. Any unusual types of items or test elements of complex nature should be introduced by sample items and illustrated by practice exercises. The test format should be such that pupils will have no difficulties in reading the items, in recording their answers, in moving from one page to the next or from one part to the next, and in various other practical uses of the testing materials. Illustrations should be clear-cut and easily tied up with the appropriate test items. The page size, length of line, size and style of type, and other mechanical features should be such as to facilitate rather than hamper the administration of the test.

For a standardized test, provisions of these types should be made in the test booklet and manual. For informal objective tests, performance tests, essay tests, and other evaluation procedures and tools, great care should also be taken in standardizing the examination procedure by the advance preparation of specifications for administration. Assurance that a test possesses the characteristics of administrability discussed above is best given by adequate printed or written specifications which are made available to, and are followed strictly by, the test administrator.

Scorability

A test possesses scorability when provision for pupil answers on the test or a separate answer sheet is carefully prescribed, when scoring keys are well prepared and easy to use, and when the scorer can accurately and rapidly obtain the desired scores. It is important that tests be subject to accurate scoring by clerical workers or other persons not conversant with their content. Various methods of facilitating the scoring of tests, and thereby increasing their scorability, have been devised. Among these methods, discussed in Chapter 8 of this volume, are the use of prepared keys, the use of separate answer sheets to be scored by hand, and the use of separate answer sheets to be scored by machine.

A convenient form of answer key or stencil should be provided for standardized tests, and the manual of directions should carry complete instructions for scoring the instrument. The scoring keys should be arranged so that easy and accurate scoring of the tests can be accomplished. Properly spaced answers on scoring keys for informal objective examinations can be provided by filling in the correct answers on a copy of the test and converting it into a set of strip keys, cutout stencils, or a combination of the two, according to the nature of the test parts.

Economy

Real economy in testing cannot be achieved by indiscriminate use of cheap tests or testing methods. Nor is it necessarily true that the most costly instruments and methods are the best. *A test possesses economy when the outlay in time of school personnel and of money is reasonable in terms of the resulting values.*

There are many devices by which costs of testing can be kept low without reducing the effectiveness of a measurement program. Informal objective tests can be prepared by use of the mimeograph or gelatine plate, and some types can even be given by a chalkboard method or orally. The economies of time made possible through the use of some of the scoring devices mentioned in the preceding section result in real financial saving. Cooperative testing programs operating under institutional or public educational auspices in many of the states offer testing services to the schools at very low rates. Test booklets that are not necessarily destroyed by one use are now available for many standardized tests, whether machine-scoring or hand-scoring is used. Therefore, an effective testing program need not be dependent on great financial outlay.

An illustration of provision for administrability and scorability of tests, or for what are probably the two most important practical considerations, was developed for the *Sequential Tests of Educational Progress* [18] in a comprehensive 12-page set of directions accessory to the tests.

6. COMPARABILITY

A test possesses comparability when the results are given meaning in objective terms by the use of derived scores, norms, marks, ratings, or still other devices. There are two means whereby comparability of results is established for standardized tests: (1) availability of duplicate forms of the test, and (2) availability of adequate norms. A standardized test should be accompanied in the test manual or elsewhere by adequate tables of norms adapted in type to the age and grade levels for which the test is intended and to the types of abilities it measures. By the use of such norms, the performance of individual pupils or class groups can be com-

[18] Cooperative Test Division, Educational Testing Service, *STEP: Directions for Administering and Scoring.* Educational Testing Service, Princeton, N. J., 1957.

pared with the average performance of pupils of similar age or grade placement or with that of pupils taking the same course. By the use of duplicate forms of a test, results from testing before and after a period of instruction can be made comparable without the necessity of using the same test twice.

Comparability of results can be established for informal objective tests by the simple statistical procedures presented in Chapter 14. In a sense, a series of duplicate forms is established when different class groups are tested over a period of several years, even though the tests used from year to year may overlap considerably in content. In a sense, also, norms can be statistically established on the basis of results from any but very small classes, although such norms do not possess the reliability and wide significance of norms for standardized tests that are based on extensive pupil populations. The importance of comparability of test results is great, for without comparability of measures some of the major values resulting from the use of tests are lost.

The *Stanford Achievement Test* provides a grade score on each of the nine tests at the intermediate and advanced levels that has comparable meaning from test to test and for all five forms—J to N—of the battery. Derivable from these grade scores by the use of various tables of norms are such comparable results as two types of grade equivalents, two types of age equivalents, percentile ranks by grades, and special purpose K-scores.[19] These various derived scores are designed to serve several types of purposes.

7. UTILITY

A test may possess adequately all of the important characteristics of a good test discussed above and yet be of relatively little value for use in a particular school situation. *A test possesses utility to the degree that it satisfactorily serves a definite need in the situation in which it is used, i.e., when the results are employed effectively in the guidance of pupils and in the improvement of the school program.* Unless tests are selected or constructed for definitely conceived purposes and their scores used in an intelligent attempt to bring about the desired results, they are of little value and may even, in fact, be harmful. The modern teacher has a definite purpose in mind when he administers tests and makes as effective use as possible of the results in the guidance of his pupils.

If the test is standardized, illustrations of the methods of interpreting

[19] Truman L. Kelley and others, *Stanford Achievement Test: Directions for Administering, Intermediate and Advanced Study Skills Test.* World Book Co., Yonkers, N. Y., 1953. p. 4-7.

and using the results should be given in the manual. If the test is con-structed by the teacher himself, its utility depends largely upon the fore-sight of the teacher in so planning the test and its use that the results will serve the needs of the local classroom.

Utility may in a sense be considered a final master criterion. It is cer-tainly not entirely distinct from the other criteria, but it may be an effective final check on the value of the test.

Although utility depends more on the user's needs than on any other considerations, it also depends on the availability of such instructions for putting test results into use [20] and such detailed accessory materials [21] for facilitating their applicational values as were prepared by the authors and editors of the *Sequential Tests of Educational Progress*.

SUGGESTED ACTIVITIES

1. Read a review of a standardized achievement test in one of the Buros *Mental Measurements Yearbooks* and note what the author wrote about how well the test fulfills at least the major characteristics of a good examination in terms of its stated purposes.

2. Examine a copy of a standardized achievement test, the manual of direc-tions, and any accessory materials; note what the authors say about the purpose of the test; and decide how well you think the test fulfills the stated purpose.

TOPICS FOR DISCUSSION

1. What is meant by the validity of an examination? Define or explain in several ways. Is it a general or a specific concept?

2. What are the principal differences among the four major types of validity?

3. Discuss and illustrate the major methods by which validity is obtained in a test. What is the final or ultimate basis on which test validation depends?

4. What cautions should be observed in the formulation of instructional outcomes as a basis for test validation?

5. Define or explain reliability as a criterion of a good examination. Is it a general or a specific concept?

6. What are the outstanding differences among the three major types of reliability coefficients?

20 For example: Cooperative Test Division, Educational Testing Service, *STEP Manual for Interpreting Scores: Reading.* Educational Testing Service, Princeton, N. J., 1957. p. 10-22.

21 Cooperative Test Division, Educational Testing Service: (1) *STEP Student Profile,* (2) *STEP Class Record,* (3) *STEP Score Distribution Sheet,* and (4) *Student Report.* Educational Testing Service, Princeton, N. J., 1957 and 1958.

7. Briefly discuss the methods by which the reliability coefficient of a test can be obtained or estimated. Consider the relative merits of the several methods.
8. Is a valid test necessarily reliable? Explain. Is a reliable test necessarily valid? Explain.
9. Show how test adequacy is essential to reliability. How is adequacy assured?
10. Show how objectivity contributes to reliability. What are the specific features of an objective test?
11. By what means is administrability obtained in a test? Is this an important criterion of a good examination?
12. How may scorability be obtained in an examination?
13. What is the importance of economy as a criterion?
14. What is meant by comparability as a criterion of a good examination? What are the two major means of attaining comparability?
15. Explain how norms or their equivalent are essential to an examination that possesses comparability.
16. In what way is utility in a sense a master criterion of a good examination?
17. Give a few examples to show how authors and publishers of some standardized tests have attempted to make sure that their tests meet various criteria of a good examination.
18. Review the criteria of a good examination and show why a good test must be properly balanced in all respects if it is to serve its purpose efficiently.
19. How do the criteria of a good examination apply to other types of measuring instruments and techniques?

SELECTED REFERENCES

ADAMS, GEORGIA S., AND TORGERSON, THEODORE L. *Measurement and Evaluation for the Secondary-School Teacher.* New York: Dryden Press, 1956. Chapter 3.
BUROS, OSCAR K., editor. *The Fifth Mental Measurements Yearbook.* Highland Park, N. J.: Gryphon Press, 1959.
BUROS, OSCAR K., editor. *The Fourth Mental Measurements Yearbook.* Highland Park, N. J.: Gryphon Press, 1953.
BUROS, OSCAR K., editor. *The Third Mental Measurements Yearbook.* New Brunswick, N. J.: Rutgers University Press, 1949.
COMMITTEES ON TEST STANDARDS, AMERICAN EDUCATIONAL RESEARCH ASSOCIATION AND NATIONAL COUNCIL ON MEASUREMENTS USED IN EDUCATION. *Technical Recommendations for Achievement Tests.* Washington, D. C.: National Education Association, 1955.
CONRAD, HERBERT S. "Norms." *Encyclopedia of Educational Research.* Revised edition. New York: Macmillan Co., 1950. p. 795-802.
CRONBACH, LEE J. "Validity." *Encyclopedia of Educational Research.* Third edition. New York: Macmillan Co., 1960. p. 1551-55.

CURETON, EDWARD E. "Validity." *Educational Measurement.* Washington, D. C.: American Council on Education, 1951. Chapter 16.

GERBERICH, J. RAYMOND. *Specimen Objective Test Items: A Guide to Achievement Test Construction.* New York: Longmans, Green and Co., 1956. p. 23-29.

GERBERICH, J. RAYMOND, AND PETERS, CHARLES C. "Reliability." *Encyclopedia of Modern Education.* New York: Philosophical Library, 1943. p. 673-75.

GREENE, EDWARD B. *Measurements of Human Behavior.* Revised edition. New York: Odyssey Press, 1952. Chapter 3.

GREENE, HARRY A., JORGENSEN, ALBERT N., AND GERBERICH, J. RAYMOND. *Measurement and Evaluation in the Elementary School.* Second edition. New York: Longmans, Green and Co., 1953. Chapter 4.

GREENE, HARRY A., JORGENSEN, ALBERT N., AND GERBERICH, J. RAYMOND. *Measurement and Evaluation in the Secondary School.* Second edition. New York: Longmans, Green and Co., 1954. Chapter 4.

GUILFORD, J. P. "New Standards for Test Evaluation." *Educational and Psychological Measurement,* 6:427-38; Winter 1946.

HOYT, CYRIL J. "Reliability." *Encyclopedia of Educational Research.* Third edition. New York: Macmillan Co., 1960. p. 1144-47.

JOINT COMMITTEE, AMERICAN PSYCHOLOGICAL ASSOCIATION, AMERICAN EDUCATIONAL RESEARCH ASSOCIATION, AND NATIONAL COUNCIL ON MEASUREMENTS USED IN EDUCATION. *Technical Recommendations for Psychological Tests and Diagnostic Techniques.* Washington, D. C.: American Psychological Association, Inc., 1954. (Supplement to *Psychological Bulletin,* Vol. 51, No. 2, Part 2; March 1954.)

LENNON, ROGER T. "Assumptions Underlying the Use of Content Validity." *Educational and Psychological Measurement,* 16:294-304; Autumn 1956.

MICHEELS, WILLIAM J., AND KARNES, M. RAY. *Measuring Educational Achievement.* New York: McGraw-Hill Book Co., Inc., 1950. Chapter 4.

NOLL, VICTOR H. *Introduction to Educational Measurement.* Boston: Houghton Mifflin Co., 1957. Chapter 4.

SCHRADER, WILLIAM B. "Norms." *Encyclopedia of Educational Research.* Third edition. New York: Macmillan Co., 1960. p. 922-27.

THORNDIKE, ROBERT L. "Reliability." *Educational Measurement.* Washington, D. C.: American Council on Education, 1951. Chapter 15.

THORNDIKE, ROBERT L., AND HAGEN, ELIZABETH. *Measurement and Evaluation in Psychology and Education.* Second edition. New York: John Wiley and Sons, Inc., 1961. Chapter 7.

THUT, I. N., AND GERBERICH, J. RAYMOND. *Foundations of Method for Secondary Schools.* New York: McGraw-Hill Book Co., Inc., 1949. p. 101-7.

TORGERSON, THEODORE L., AND ADAMS, GEORGIA S. *Measurement and Evaluation for the Elementary-School Teacher.* New York: Dryden Press, 1954. Chapter 3.

TRAXLER, ARTHUR E. "Administering and Scoring the Objective Test." *Educational Measurement.* Washington, D. C.: American Council on Education, 1951. Chapter 10.

WESMAN, ALEXANDER G. *Expectancy Tables—A Way of Interpreting Test Validity.* Test Service Bulletin, No. 38. New York: Psychological Corporation, December 1949.

WRIGHTSTONE, J. WAYNE; JUSTMAN, JOSEPH; AND ROBBINS, IRVING. *Evaluation in Modern Education.* New York: American Book Co., 1956. p. 42-56.

PART 2

Using Standardized Tests and Techniques

Five types of standardized tests and techniques are distinguished in this discussion—socioeconomic and home-status scales, health and physical fitness tests, intelligence and aptitude tests, personality inventories and techniques, and achievement tests. The first four receive at this point the only direct and reasonably intensive treatment accorded them in this volume. However, only the foundations of standardized achievement tests, and less directly of other types of achievement tests and techniques, are presented here.

A teacher in the modern school is expected to be familiar with standardized approaches to pupil appraisal in all five of these areas. This means that he must be able to take part appropriately and variously in the chain of events leading from the recognition of need for a certain type of appraisal to the use of results in the classroom. It does not mean, however, that he should be capable of playing a major role in the appraisal of socioeconomic status, physical fitness, intelligence, and personality. His part in these areas is usually that of cooperating participant in most stages of the process but of informed and major user of results in the classroom. His most prominent and inclusive role is appropriately reserved for the area of achievement measurement.

The emphasis of this book is understandably most direct and extensive on the last of these areas, inasmuch as the direction of pupil learning, and hence the measurement of learning outcomes, is a central responsibility of the classroom teacher. Consequently, the many and various important aspects and areas of achievement measurement receive much attention in subsequent parts of this volume. Occasional references are later made to the four related areas of measurement at points where they are significant.

4

SOCIOECONOMIC AND HOME-STATUS SCALES

This chapter deals with the following educationally significant aspects of socioeconomic class and its measurement:

A. Scales for measuring characteristics of the home.
B. Measures of occupational status.
C. Broad measures of socioeconomic status.
D. Meaning of terms used in describing socioeconomic classes.
E. Some major factors related to socioeconomic status.

First and certainly not least important among the environmental factors affecting the child's early growth and development and even his status later in life are those related to social class. Among the many such factors, three that are perhaps most often recognized and distinguished are the primary concern of this chapter. These are home status, occupation of the father, and, more broadly, socioeconomic status.

Social stratification, according to Barber,[1] can be studied by the use either of objective or subjective approaches. Barber listed occupation, income, and influence or power as objective and rated ideologies, attitudes, and aspirations as subjective. Both objective and subjective procedures can be used scientifically, however, and the methods of stratification considered in this chapter are of both types.

1. MEASURES OF HOME STATUS

One group of instruments for evaluating socioeconomic status obtains evidence about the characteristics of the home as reported by the pupils

<hr />

[1] Bernard Barber, *Social Stratification: A Comparative Analysis of Structure and Process.* Harcourt, Brace and Co., New York, 1957. p. 58-59.

themselves or as rated by visitors to the home. Pupils in the upper elementary grades and above usually have sufficient knowledge and awareness of their home conditions to respond accurately to the questions of these instruments. The classroom teacher may very properly be the person who visits the homes of his pupils. Thus, whether the pupils supply the information, whether the teacher obtains the information by visitation, observation, and perhaps interview, or whether some combination of the two is employed, knowledge of home status is important in the increased insights into child behavior it often affords the school.

Home-Status Index

Leahy developed the *Minnesota Home Status Index,* a socioeconomic scale that involves brief interviews with the school child and with one of his parents, usually his mother, as a means of obtaining information.[2] Although the index might normally involve visits to the pupils' homes, the techniques of interviewing and of analyzing data are sufficiently non-technical, as is indicated below, to make its use by classroom teachers feasible.

Designed for use in urban communities, the index requires answers to 42 *yes–no* questions and nine questions of varied types having several possible answers each. The alternate-response questions are primarily of the *presence–absence* type (Does family have an automobile?), the *engaged in–not engaged in* sort (Has child had paid lessons in music outside of school?), and the *member–not a member* variety (Has father been a member of a civic or political club?). The less-structured questions deal with the number of children's and adult books in the home, the number of daily papers and the number and quality of magazines regularly taken, the highest level of education attained by the parents, and the father's usual occupation.

These questions are classified under six headings, each of which provides an index: (1) Children's Facilities Index, (2) Economic Status Index, (3) Cultural Status Index, (4) Sociality Index, (5) Occupational Status Index, and (6) Educational Status Index. The six indices for each pupil, easily obtained from a conversion table for translating total scores into comparable "sigma scores," can be represented on a Home-Status Profile to show graphically how the child's home compares with the average home in these six socioeconomic areas.

[2] Alice M. Leahy, *The Measurement of Urban Home Environment: Validation and Standardization of the Minnesota Home Status Index.* University of Minnesota Press, Minneapolis, Minn., 1936.

Home Index

Another instrument useful in measuring socioeconomic status by the questionnaire method is Gough's *Home Index*.[3] This unstandardized instrument consists of 20 *yes–no* questions of a *presence–absence* type (Do you have a fireplace in your home?), an *attended–not attended* species (Did your father go to high school?), and several miscellaneous varieties (Do you have your own room at home? Does your family take a daily newspaper?). One three-option question is concerned with the number of books in the home.

Home Scale

A third instrument designed primarily for use in urban communities as an index of socioeconomic status is the *American Home Scale*.[4] The scale, consisting of 50 items classified as cultural, aesthetic, economic, and miscellaneous, is designed for use with pupils in Grade 6 or above. Among the household items of the *presence–absence* type, but framed for yes or no answers, are a vacuum cleaner, bathtub or shower, and telephone.

2. MEASURES OF OCCUPATIONAL STATUS

Another approach to determination of socioeconomic class is through the occupation of the father. Many classification systems, ranging from concise to very extensive, have been evolved. Few of them are easy to apply, however. One of the best-known classifications, by Edwards for use in the 1940 U. S. Census,[5] listed six major classes of occupations: (1) professional persons; (2) proprietors, managers, and officials, including farm owners and tenants, and wholesale and retail dealers; (3) clerks and kindred workers; (4) skilled workers and foremen; (5) semiskilled workers; and (6) unskilled workers, including farm and other laborers and servants. Although this classification has been widely used in research studies and has been the basis for other indices of social class, it does not lend itself readily to use by persons not having technical training.

Sims is the author of a *Social Class Identification (SCI) Occupational*

[3] Harrison G. Gough, "A Short Social-Status Inventory." *Journal of Educational Psychology*, 40:52-56; January 1949.

[4] W. A. Kerr and H. H. Remmers, *American Home Scale*. Psychometric Affiliates, Chicago, 1942.

[5] Alba E. Edwards, *Population: Comparative Occupational Statistics for the United States, 1870 to 1940; Sixteenth Census of the United States, 1940.* U. S. Government Printing Office, Washington, D. C., 1943.

Rating Scale [6] that determines the socioeconomic level or the social class with which an individual indirectly identifies himself. This is accomplished by having the high-school pupil or older person specify for as many of 42 specific occupations as he has knowledge of whether they are at the same level as, or are at a higher or a lower level than, he and his family in the socioeconomic sense.

In the accompanying illustration of a few items from the scale, when people in a specified occupation are compared by the pupil with his family's social class, S = the same, H = higher, L = lower, and D = doubtful or uncertain. By a process of counting types of responses, the teacher can obtain two numerical values for a pupil that are easily converted to an SCI score. The score, in turn, leads directly to the classification of the pupil and his family in the upper, upper-middle, middle, middle-working, working, or lower-working class.

EXCERPT FROM *Sims SCI Occupational Rating Scale* [7]

10. Janitor _____S H L D
11. State supreme court judge_____S H L D
12. Corporation lawyer _____S H L D
13. Real estate salesman _____S H L D
14. Surgeon _____S H L D

3. INDEX OF STATUS CHARACTERISTICS

A third means of securing information about socioeconomic status involves the employment of several types of indices, including home and occupational characteristics of a type differing considerably from the status indices previously presented. Warner, Meeker, and Eells outlined six different methods of Evaluated Participation (EP) for measuring socioeconomic class membership by the use of time-consuming and quite highly specialized interview procedures. [8] They also presented procedures for evolving an Index of Status Characteristics (ISC) that gives similar results but that can be obtained through a relatively simple system of rating and assigning weights to four characteristics—occupation, source of income, house type, and dwelling area. Since the skills involved in obtaining

[6] Verner M. Sims, *Sims SCI Occupational Rating Scale.* World Book Co., Yonkers, N. Y., 1952.

[7] Verner M. Sims, *Sims SCI Occupational Rating Scale.* Copyright 1952 by Harcourt, Brace and World, Inc., New York. All rights reserved. Quoted by special permission.

[8] W. Lloyd Warner, Marchia Meeker, and Kenneth Eells, *Social Class in America: A Manual of Procedure for the Measurement of Social Status.* Science Research Associates, Inc., Chicago, 1949. Part 2.

this index are nontechnical and easily acquired, the three steps of procedure are briefly outlined below.[9]

(1) The first step is to obtain a rating for each of the four status characteristics on a seven-point scale, as follows:

Occupation (Original scale)
1. Professionals and proprietors of large businesses
2. Semi-professionals and smaller officials of large businesses
3. Clerks and kindred workers
4. Skilled workers
5. Proprietors of small businesses
6. Semi-skilled workers
7. Unskilled workers

Source of Income
1. Inherited wealth
2. Earned wealth
3. Profits and fees
4. Salary
5. Wages
6. Private relief
7. Public relief

House Type (Revised scale)
1. Excellent houses
2. Very good houses
3. Good houses
4. Average houses
5. Fair houses
6. Poor houses
7. Very poor houses

Dwelling Area
1. Very high—best houses; wide, clean streets; many trees
2. High—superior but less pretentious houses; fewer mansions; clean streets
3. Above average—nice, clean, but not pretentious houses; clean streets
4. Average—small, neat, but unpretentious workingmen's houses; clean streets
5. Below average—somewhat run-down houses; industrial or business section
6. Low—closely grouped, run-down houses; cluttered streets; semi-slums
7. Very low—shacks; unpleasant and unhealthy locality; slums

(2) After the four ratings have been assigned, the following weights are used in obtaining a composite or total: Occupation—4; Source of Income—3; House Type—3; and Dwelling Area—2.

(3) After the total of the weighted ratings is obtained, the following social-class equivalents are used in obtaining the Index of Social Status.

Total	Social Class Equivalents
12-22	Upper
23-24	Upper or Upper Middle
25-33	Upper Middle
34-37	Upper Middle or Lower Middle
38-50	Lower Middle
51-53	Lower Middle or Upper Lower
54-62	Upper Lower
63-66	Upper Lower or Lower Lower
67-84	Lower Lower

[9] *Ibid.* Part 3.

To illustrate the procedures, the computations should be carried through in this manner if the son of a salaried public-school teacher who with his family lives in an above-average dwelling area is to be classified on socioeconomic class.

Category	Rating	Weight	Product
Occupation	2	4	8
Source of Income	4	3	12
House Type	3	3	9
Dwelling Area	3	2	6
			35 (Weighted Total)

When the weighted total of 35 is interpreted by use of the scale for social-class equivalents, it is determined that the boy's father, and hence the boy himself and other members of his family, should be rated in the upper-middle or lower-middle class.

4. SOCIOECONOMIC CLASS CHARACTERISTICS AND DISTRIBUTIONS

Only approximate meanings attach to such socioeconomic class terms as appear in the foregoing sections of this chapter unless some means of interpreting them is provided. Although the terms used in different methods of classification have some similarities, there is no standard list available to simplify the problem of giving definite meaning to such designations as upper-middle class, working class, or even service workers. Consequently, brief consideration is given here to the meanings of results from one occupational index and one socioeconomic index discussed earlier in this chapter.

Table 2 shows percentages of high-school and of college students reported by Sims as falling into each of the seven occupational classes he distinguished in standardizing his SCI rating scale. Three characteristics of his results seem to merit mention—the concentration in occupations representing the middle and middle-working classes, the relatively higher occupational status of college students than of high-school pupils, and the infrequency of occurrence of the lowest and, particularly, the highest socioeconomic classes.

The percentages of Table 3 show how two samples of "Yankee City" residents studied by Warner and Lunt were found to be distributed among the six socioeconomic classes they set apart. These results seem to be notable particularly for the frequency with which persons are classified in the two lowest socioeconomic classes. Even though the percentages of the table are specifically applicable only to the community the authors studied intensively, they are often considered to be good representations of social-class status for the country as a whole. However, they cannot be expected to apply precisely in any local situations because of the fact that wide differences in social-class status often exist not only from community to community but also from state to state and from region to region.

TABLE 2

Typical Occupations at Various Social-Class Levels and Class Frequencies among High School and College Students on the *Sims SCI Occupational Rating Scale* [10]

Social-Class Level	Common Illustrations	Percentages of Students	
		HIGH SCHOOL	COLLEGE
Upper-upper	president of a university, bank, or large railroad; U. S. ambassador		
Upper	corporation lawyer; chain-store owner; large-city mayor; surgeon	1.1	4.2
Upper-middle	newspaper editor; minister; civil engineer; U.S. army colonel	5.6	26.2
Middle	real estate salesman; high-school teacher; druggist; owner-operator of large farm	25.3	40.8
Middle-working	railroad ticket agent; telegraph operator; store bookkeeper; owner-operator of small grocery	50.0	24.2
Working	factory worker; house-to-house brush salesman; automobile mechanic; telephone operator	16.2	3.7
Lower-working	garbage collector; farm hand; cook for a family; cotton-mill worker	1.6	0.1

No attempt should be made to compare the results shown here for the SCI scale and for "Yankee City" residents, primarily because the superficially similar terms used by Sims in his occupational ratings and by Warner and Lunt in their socioeconomic classes have quite different meanings. The purpose here is primarily to indicate the type of information by which reasonably precise meaning can be given to indices of occupational, socioeconomic, and even home status.

[10] Verner M. Sims, *Sims SCI Occupational Rating Scale: Manual of Directions.* Copyright 1952 by Harcourt, Brace and World, Inc., New York. p. 4. All rights reserved. Quoted by special permission.

TABLE 3

Illustrations of Various Socioeconomic Groups and Class
Frequencies for "Yankee City" Residents on the
Index of Status Characteristics

Social-Class Status	Common Illustrations	Percentages of Persons FIRST SAMPLE [11]	SECOND SAMPLE [12]
Upper-upper	wealthy people of old families; aristocrats; landed gentry	1.4	2.6
Lower-upper	wealthy but newly-rich people; prominent families	1.6	2.9
Upper-middle	business and professional people; prominent and substantial people; community leaders	10.2	13.5
Lower-middle	small tradesmen; white-collar workers; some skilled tradesmen	28.1	31.2
Upper-lower	semi-skilled and unskilled workers; hard-working people; poor but respectable people	32.6	32.3
Lower-lower	shiftless, dirty, and disorderly people; poor and unfortunate people	25.2	17.5

5. SOCIOECONOMIC FACTORS AND SCHOOL SUCCESS

It is a well-known fact that school success is significantly related to socioeconomic factors, as evidenced by the greater and more frequent scholastic success and the longer continuance in school and college of children from middle- and upper-class homes than of children from the lower classes. The school is usually thought to embody middle-class and upper-middle-class points of view and customs in the standards of conduct and of learning it sets for pupils. Perhaps this is because most teachers and other school officials themselves come from these same socioeconomic classes.

Some of the reasons for the relationship between socioeconomic factors and school success are known, but others are not well established or are highly complex. At least some part of this relationship is doubtless accounted for indirectly through the relationships existing between certain socioeconomic backgrounds and other characteristics of pupils.

[11] W. Lloyd Warner and Paul S. Lunt, *The Social Life of a Modern Community*. Yale University Press, New Haven, Conn., 1941. p. 203.
[12] W. Lloyd Warner and Paul S. Lunt, *The Status System of a Modern Community*. Yale University Press, New Haven, Conn., 1942. p. 68.

Socioeconomic Status and Mental Ability

Much evidence is available to show that socioeconomic class, home status, and occupational status are all significantly related to general mental ability. Anastasi summarized some of the most pertinent studies on this question by pointing out that relationships between intelligence test scores and three different social-status indices—of home status, of occupational level, and of social status broadly—are all positive and significant.[13] This is true of occupational level whether employed persons themselves or children classified according to paternal occupation are under consideration. A related issue, the effect of social-class status on the intelligence quotients obtained from group tests of mental ability, is dealt with in Chapter 6.

TABLE 4

Army General Classification Test Scores for Occupational Groups [14]

Occupation	No.	Median
Accountant	216	129
Teacher	360	124
Clerk-Typist	616	119
Stock Control Clerk	152	117
Photographer	70	114
Motion Picture Projectionist	111	110
Watch Repairman	51	109
Automotive Electrician	57	108
Railway Brakeman	182	105
Bricklayer	213	102
Tractor Driver	968	99
Cook	653	96
Lumberjack	236	85

One particular study, by Stewart, reports median scores on the *Army General Classification Test* for World War II draftees coming from 227 occupational areas. Table 4 shows the numbers of men represented and their median scores in a few selected occupations. The median scores decrease in size from the highest, for accountants, to the lowest, for lumberjacks, in approximate accordance with the prestige status of occupational groupings.

[13] Anne Anastasi, *Differential Psychology: Individual and Group Differences in Behavior,* Third edition. Macmillan Co., New York, 1958. p. 535.
[14] Naomi Stewart, "A.G.C.T. Scores of Army Personnel Grouped by Occupation." *Occupations,* 26:5-41; October 1947.

Socioeconomic Status and Personality

Various aspects of personality have been shown to be related to socio-economic and occupational status in a wide variety of studies. Here, however, the relationships are less consistent and uniform than those illustrated in the foregoing section for mental ability. Anastasi, summarizing results from a number of these studies,[15] reported that school children from the lower classes are emotionally less secure and have more worries than higher-level children, that persons from the lower classes are more radical in their attitudes than those higher in the social scale, and that interest patterns differ significantly for various occupational levels. These examples, selected to represent a wide variety of studies, illustrate relationships between socioeconomic or occupational factors and the three aspects of personality most often set apart—adjustments, attitudes, and interests.

SUGGESTED ACTIVITIES

1. Select two boys or two girls, preferably from the same school grade or class group, one pupil known to be high and the other known to be low in socioeconomic class; observe and compare them in such things as dress, manners, speech, associates, interests, and attitudes; and compare them, if feasible and appropriate, in intelligence quotients and school marks.
2. Observe pupils in a school grade or class group if possible and note whether nicknames, prestige status, cliques, and other pupil interactions seem to give clues to socioeconomic class memberships.

TOPICS FOR DISCUSSION

1. Which types of behaviors, those subject to study by objective or by subjective methods, are represented more fully in pupil activities?
2. Why should a teacher be interested in the socioeconomic and home backgrounds of his pupils?
3. In what major respects do techniques used for measurement of home and occupational status differ? In what ways are they similar?
4. What is the nature of the relationship between home status and father's occupation?
5. Why is an index of status characteristics likely to be a more reliable device for estimating socioeconomic level than a home-status or occupational-status scale?
6. Approximately what proportions of people belong to the higher, middle, and lower classes as those terms are commonly used?

[15] Anastasi, *op. cit.* p. 508-15.

7. Which type of approach to determination of socioeconomic class, objective or subjective, is represented most widely in the techniques discussed in this chapter?
8. What are some of the reasons underlying the relationship between socioeconomic status and mental ability?
9. What are some of the conditions that underlie the relationship between socioeconomic status and personality traits?

SELECTED REFERENCES

ANASTASI, ANNE. *Differential Psychology: Individual and Group Differences in Behavior.* Third edition. New York: Macmillan Co., 1958. Chapter 15.

BARBER, BERNARD. *Social Stratification: A Comparative Analysis of Structure and Process.* New York: Harcourt, Brace and Co., 1957.

CENTERS, RICHARD. *The Psychology of Social Classes: A Study of Class Consciousness.* Princeton, N. J.: Princeton University Press, 1949.

CHAPIN, FRANCIS S. *The Measurement of Social Status by the Use of the Social Status Scale.* Minneapolis, Minn.: University of Minnesota Press, 1933.

EMPEY, LaMar T. "Social Class and Occupational Aspiration: A Comparison of Absolute and Relative Measurement." *American Sociological Review,* 21:703-9; December 1956.

GOUGH, HARRISON G. "A Short Social Status Inventory." *Journal of Educational Psychology,* 40:52-56; January 1949.

HARRELL, THOMAS W., AND HARRELL, MARGARET S. "Army General Classification Test Scores for Civilian Occupations." *Educational and Psychological Measurement,* 5:229-39; Autumn 1945.

LEAHY, ALICE M. *The Measurement of Urban Home Environment.* Minneapolis, Minn.: University of Minnesota Press, 1936.

SIMS, VERNER M. "A Technique for Measuring Social Class Identification." *Educational and Psychological Measurement,* 11:541-48; Winter 1951.

SMITH, MAPHEUS. "An Empirical Scale of Prestige Status of Occupations." *American Sociological Review,* 8:185-92; April 1943.

STEWART, NAOMI. "A.G.C.T. Scores of Army Personnel Grouped by Occupation." *Occupations,* 26:5-41; October 1947.

TYLER, LEONA E. *The Psychology of Human Differences.* Second edition. New York: Appleton-Century-Crofts, Inc., 1956. Chapter 12.

WARNER, W. LLOYD, AND LUNT, PAUL S. *The Social Life of a Modern Community.* Yankee City Series, Vol. I. New Haven, Conn.: Yale University Press, 1941.

WARNER, W. LLOYD, AND LUNT, PAUL S. *The Status System of a Modern Community.* Yankee City Series, Vol. II. New Haven, Conn.: Yale University Press, 1942.

WARNER, W. LLOYD; MEEKER, MARCHIA; AND EELLS, KENNETH. *Social Class in America: A Manual of Procedure for the Measurement of Social Status.* Chicago: Science Research Associates, Inc., 1949.

WRIGHTSTONE, J. WAYNE; JUSTMAN, JOSEPH; AND ROBBINS, IRVING. *Evaluation in Modern Education.* New York: American Book Co., 1956. Chapter 22.

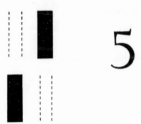

5

HEALTH AND PHYSICAL FITNESS TESTS

The measurement aspects of health and physical fitness dealt with in this chapter are as follows:

A. Significance of results from measurements of growth and development.
B. Measurement of health practices, attitudes, and knowledges.
C. Medical and sensory tests of physical fitness.
D. Cardiovascular and respiratory tests of physical fitness.
E. Measures of strength, power, and endurance.
F. Measures of body mechanics and body structure.
G. Significance of health and physical fitness testing.

An individual's health practices, attitudes, and knowledges at any given time reflect learning, both formal and informal. However, a person's health status at a given time also determines in part how effectively he can engage in the activities of living that are normal for him. Furthermore, health education is not an integral and formally recognized school subject, as are those treated in Part 5 of this volume; instead, it is variously the subject of units or segments of courses, particularly in physical education and science. Consequently, the ways in which health contributes to physical fitness are dealt with in this chapter.

Physical fitness may be considered both as an outcome of physical education and as a prerequisite to effective performance, not only in sports and athletics but also in such everyday skills as standing, walking, sitting, and engaging in the many other physical activities of normal living. It is in the second sense that physical fitness is considered here.

1. MEASUREMENT OF GROWTH AND DEVELOPMENT

When physical aspects of growth and development are under consideration, a rather wide variety of measures, and also of measurement techniques, are involved. The most obvious characteristics and those seemingly of most general interest and concern at all age levels are height and weight. A few of the concepts used to indicate physical growth status are the only aspects presented here.

Measurement of Height and Weight

Height and weight measures are by far the most widely used in assessing growth status and in analyzing growth progress in children. Moreover, despite the many problems involved in interpreting what appear to be simple results, these two types of measures are the most satisfactory now available for general purposes. Major problems arise not so much in how to take the measurements as in how to interpret the height and weight results in relation to each other.

Wood-Baldwin Age-Height-Weight Tables.[1] These are probably the best-known and most widely used tables relating height and weight for pupils at different age levels. However, such tables in their dependence upon average weights for pupils of known ages and heights fail to provide for individual deviations from the average.

Pryor's Width-Weight Tables.[2] These tables are based on the belief that not only age, sex, and height but also the body framework and body structure are important factors in measurement. Available separately for each age and sex and for persons with narrow, average, and wide chests, they are used in predicting a pupil's appropriate weight. The particular table relevant to the age, sex, and chest-width of a pupil is used to determine his normal weight in terms of his bi-iliac diameter, or pelvic width.

Measures of Physical Maturity

Results obtained from the use of the Wood-Baldwin and Pryor tables give weight norms, i.e., indications of the average weight of a group of pupils equivalent in age and height, or in age, sex, height, and pelvic width, to the person whose physical characteristics are under consideration. However, another method of measuring the pupil's status is available—the age

[1] Bird T. Baldwin, Thomas D. Wood, and R. M. Woodbury, *Height-Weight-Age Tables.* American Child Health Association, New York, 1923.
[2] Helen B. Pryor, *Width-Weight Tables,* Second edition. Stanford University Press, Stanford, Calif., 1940.

in years and months for which his development in any one of several characteristics is typical. For example, a pupil whose weight age is nine years and six months (9-6) is as heavy as the average child who is nine years and six months of age chronologically.

A rather wide variety of such ages have been distinguished. Several of them, in the areas of mental ability and achievement particularly, are treated later in this volume. Several others are more concerned with the primarily physical aspects of growth and development. Among them are weight age; height age; anatomical age, skeletal age, and carpal age, variously dependent on development of the bones; dental age, based on tooth development; physiological age, based on development of the internal organs; and grip age, based on strength of grip. The organismic age [3] is an over-all average of at least several of these ages and those for the mental and achievement aspects of growth treated later.

2. TESTS OF HEALTH PRACTICES, ATTITUDES, AND KNOWLEDGES

There are several aspects of health that seem not necessarily to be direct outcomes of education, or at least of health education in the schools. Health practices, health attitudes, health knowledges, and health statuį are mutually dependent in various ways, but they are sufficiently distinctive that standardized test makers have constructed tests or devised techniques for measurement in each of the four. The first three are usually measured by the use of paper-and-pencil tests of the types briefly treated here. The area of health status, however, is dealt with later in this chapter in a variety of ways under the general heading of physical fitness.

A few items from the Johns and Juhnke *Health Practice Inventory* are given here to show how pupil engagement in desirable or undesirable health practices can be measured by written tests. The five-option scaled-choice item type employed in the samples shown below is widely used for measuring practices, activities, and attitudes.

One other aspect of health testing is illustrated here by sample multiple-choice items from the *Kilander Health Knowledge Test*. This item type is unquestionably the most widely used in standardized tests designed for measuring knowledge outcomes in all subjects and subject areas.

Tests of health knowledges and attitudes do not necessarily give direct leads to health conditions in the pupil that should receive early attention.

---

[3] Willard C. Olson and Byron O. Hughes, "The Concept of Organismic Age." *Journal of Educational Research,* 35:525-27; March 1942.

EXCERPTS FROM *Health Practice Inventory* [4]

DO YOU

1. Plan your day to include time for work, physical activity, relaxation, and sleep?
   1 Never 2 Rarely 3 Sometimes 4 Usually 5 Always

2. Spend two to three minutes each day caring for your hair and scalp?
   1 Never 2 Rarely 3 Sometimes 4 Usually 5 Always

38. Use combs or lipsticks belonging to others?
   5 Never 4 Rarely 3 Sometimes 2 Usually 1 Always

39. Go to bed at once when you have a cold?
   1 Never 2 Rarely 3 Sometimes 4 Usually 5 Always

77. Use publicly advertised medicines without the advice of your physician?
   5 Never 4 Rarely 3 Sometimes 2 Usually 1 Always

78. Read the label on any container from which you are about to take medicine?
   1 Never 2 Rarely 3 Sometimes 4 Usually 5 Always

The knowledge tests fulfill general rather than more specific measurement purposes, and results from attitude scales are not necessarily indicative of health behavior. Health practice tests probably give more direct leads to conditions needing remediation, but even here the significance of results for preventative or alleviative action is doubtless not as great as exists for some of the methods treated in the next section of this chapter.

EXCERPTS FROM *Kilander Health Knowledge Test* [5]

31. An occupational disease resulting from breathing certain types of rock- or sand-dust over long periods of time is—
   1. pneumonia.
   2. the bends.
   3. silicosis.
   4. bursitis.

33. Which one of the following is probably most conducive to better posture in the schoolroom?
   1. having a chair and desk of the right height
   2. having the light come from the left side
   3. not carrying too many books to and from school
   4. wearing comfortable clothing that does not bind

3. TESTS OF PHYSICAL FITNESS ASPECTS

Physical fitness is often, perhaps most often, evaluated in terms of various components or aspects. However, the ability of the individual to

[4] Edward B. Johns and Warren L. Juhnke, *Health Practice Inventory*. Stanford University Press, Stanford, Calif., 1952.
[5] H. F. Kilander, *Kilander Health Knowledge Test*. Copyright 1950 by Harcourt, Brace and World, Inc., New York. All rights reserved. Quoted by special permission.

perform tasks requiring muscular effort is measured only in certain elements or phases when this approach is used. Among the measures of the components of physical fitness that are relatively distinguishable and that can be measured by at least some nontechnical procedures are (1) medical and sensory tests, (2) cardiovascular and respiratory tests, (3) measures of strength, power, and endurance, (4) measures of posture and body mechanics, and (5) measures of nutrition and body build.

Medical and Sensory Tests

The individual's physical fitness depends upon his organic and physiological efficiency in considerable degree. This is true not only of his muscular but also of his neurological bodily structures and their functional efficiency. The medical and dental examinations, necessarily performed by competent physicians and dentists, and the inspections and examinations conducted by school nurses are regularly provided for in many modern schools.

However, it is the classroom teacher who is most directly in contact with pupils and who has almost daily opportunities to observe them. A teacher who is alert to symptoms of disease and signs of disability can do much to anticipate illness and to safeguard the health and welfare of his pupils. He can also employ some relatively simple and nontechnical methods of measuring sensory acuity, particularly of sight and hearing.

Teachers can observe and informally measure the physical characteristics and sensory equipment of school children even though they do not possess the skills of medical technicians, nurses, or specialists in health and physical education. In doing so, they need only a few items of equipment—a measuring tape, a set of scales, a thermometer, a box of wooden tongue sticks, an eye chart, and a watch.[6] In the capacity of careful observer and nontechnical measurer, the teacher is an adjunct of the nursing, medical, and dental services, for many of the most important diagnoses a teacher can make should be followed up by referrals to specialists.

Appraisals of physical characteristics. Teachers can measure the height and weight of their pupils accurately and without any special training. They can also use simple tools and techniques, according to Rogers,[7] in appraising the condition of face and lips, hair and scalp, skin and nails, nose and throat, teeth and neck, chest and back, arms and legs, hands and feet. When the teacher combines daily inspections in the elementary

6 James F. Rogers, *What Every Teacher Should Know about the Physical Condition of Her Pupils*. U. S. Office of Education Pamphlet, No. 68. U. S. Government Printing Office, Washington, D. C., 1936. p. 3.

7 *Ibid.* p. 4-21.

grades and the use of health record cards with a discerning alertness to symptoms of disease and disability, he can make significant contributions to the health and physical fitness of his pupils.

Tests of vision. Two general tests and one special technique for testing vision can be used by the classroom teacher who has no background of technical training and to whom no expensive equipment is available. Moreover, the teacher can be alert to pupil complaints that are symbolic of visual discomfort and watch for such signs of abnormal vision as sleepiness, squinting, rapid blinking, tense facial expression, and holding a book abnormally close to or far away from the face in reading.

The *Snellen Chart*,[8] composed of several rows of letters in descending order of size from top to bottom, is widely used in testing general visual acuity. Its use in testing involves determination of the smallest size of letters the pupil can read from a distance of twenty feet with not more than two errors per line. The eyes should be tested separately, and a pupil who wears glasses should be tested both with and without these visual aids. When the pupil's distance from the chart is divided by the scale value of the smallest size of letters he can read, a measure of his visual acuity is obtained. Thus, 20/20 indicates normal vision and 20/40 means that the pupil can read twenty feet from the chart what a person with normal vision can read from a distance of forty feet.

The *Eames Eye Test* [9] is something of a compromise between the chart described immediately above and the more elaborate and costly instruments that require much technical knowledge for their administration. The Eames test consists of two parts, one designed for screening out pupils with eye trouble and the other likely to be of interest to school psychologists and remedial teachers. The five tests in Part I are the (1) Visual acuity test, similar to the Snellen chart, (2) Lens test, to detect farsightedness, (3) Astigmatic chart test, to detect astigmatism, (4) Coordination test, to detect muscular imbalance, and (5) Fusion test, to detect defects of binocular vision. The two tests of Part II are the (6) Fusion of type test and (7) Eye dominance test.

The *Dvorine Pseudo-Isochromatic Plates* [10] consist of 23 color plates for use in testing color blindness. In the 15 basic plates, the pupil whose vision is being tested is asked to read the numbers appearing as diffuse figures on a background. Three or more incorrect responses are indicative of a red-green visual deficiency. Eight additional plates, designed for use with young children or illiterates and in confirming basic results, entail tracing of a pathway by the pupil.

[8] Available from the National Society for the Prevention of Blindness, Inc., New York.
[9] Available from Harcourt, Brace and World, Inc., New York.
[10] Available from Western Psychological Services, Los Angeles.

Tests of hearing. Several simple tests of auditory acuity can be administered easily and without special equipment, although the results are unlikely to accomplish more than to disclose marked hearing losses. Such pupil behavior as asking for the repetition of statements or questions, failure to respond when called, failure to orient the source of a sound, certain types of spelling errors, and even some defects of speech may also indicate to the alert teacher that hearing deficiencies probably exist.

The *Watch-Tick Test* [11] is based on the very rough standard that the ticking of a watch can be heard at a distance of 36 inches by a person with normal hearing. The pupil is asked to close his eyes and to stop one ear with a finger. As the teacher varies the location and distance of the watch, he is expected to report when he can and when he cannot hear the watch ticks. A ratio between the distance in inches at which the pupil can just hear the watch ticks (numerator) and the "standard" distance (denominator) gives a rough index of his hearing acuity. Thus, an index of 36/36 indicates normal acuity, but an index of 28/36, for example, indicates a deficiency in hearing.

The *Forced-Whisper Test* [12] is based on the principle that an unaccentuated whisper can be heard at a distance of twenty feet by a person with normal hearing. Again with one ear stopped, and with the ear that is being tested turned toward the sound source, the pupil repeats the numbers or words whispered by the teacher when he can hear them. A ratio of 20/20 indicates normal hearing but one of 15/20, for example, is representative of a hearing loss.

Cardiovascular and Respiratory Tests

One type of physical fitness index is found in the cardiovascular tests, particularly of pulse rate and blood pressure, and occasionally in respiratory tests of vital capacity and breath-holding ability. These indices are variously based on measurements taken before, during, and after prescribed amounts of exercise. Inasmuch as most of the tests, and also those most easy to administer, involve pulse rate or blood pressure, one pulse rate test only is discussed here to represent its type.

The *Brouha Step Test,* having separate versions for boys [13] and for girls,[14] is based on the principle that the rate of heartbeat deceleration

[11] H. Harrison Clarke, *Application of Measurement to Health and Physical Education,* Third edition. Prentice-Hall, Inc., Englewood Cliffs, N. J., 1959. p. 88-89.

[12] *Ibid.* p. 88-89.

[13] J. Roswell Gallagher and Lucien Brouha, "A Simple Method of Testing the Physical Fitness of Boys." *Research Quarterly,* 14:23-30; March 1943.

[14] Lucien Brouha and J. Roswell Gallagher, "A Functional Fitness Test for High School Girls." *Journal of Health and Physical Education,* 14:517, 550; December 1943.

after a prescribed amount of exercise is a measure of physical fitness. The subject steps up on and down from a rigid platform of a specified height at a prescribed rate for a predetermined length of time. After cessation of this activity, the subject sits down and remains quiet. His pulse rate is determined at several specified intervals and a physical fitness score is determined by computing a quotient between the duration of exercise and the pulse counts. Such factors as height of the step, duration and rate of exercise, the specified quotient, and interpretation of results vary according to sex and also, for boys, surface area of the body.

Measures of Strength, Power, and Endurance

Tests of strength and endurance, particularly those involving the large muscles of the body, are used as a third type of physical fitness index. Such relatively simple instruments as the manuometer (hand grip), dynamometer (back and leg strength), tensiometer (pulling power), and spirometer (lung capacity) can be used by a teacher who possesses a minimum amount of technical skill. Furthermore, a few common items of gymnasium equipment are the only necessities for making some of the tests of strength, power, and endurance.

Kraus-Weber Strength Tests.[15] Six tests of muscular strength requiring no special equipment constitute the series for determining the strength and flexibility of those body parts on which demands are made daily. Three of the tests involve a supine starting position from which the pupil is asked to roll up to a sitting position in two versions and to lift his stiffened legs several inches. In the fourth and fifth tests, from a prone position and with a pillow under his abdomen, the pupil is asked to lift his chest, head, arms, and shoulders and to lift his stiffened legs. The sixth test consists of the pupil's attempt to bend at the waist with knees stiff and to touch the floor with his finger tips. No norms are available for these tests. Rather they are considered to represent minimum levels of fitness, so that pupils who are unable to succeed in them are rated as physically unfit.

PFI Tests.[16] A personal fitness index can be obtained from the use of a variety of tests. The various tests, useful with girls as well as boys, although in somewhat different ways, consist of pull-ups and push-ups as measures of arm strength, leg lift, back lift, hand grip, and lung capacity. The various results are combined in prescribed ways to obtain a strength index (SI) and a personal fitness index (PFI).

---

[15] Hans Kraus and Ruth P. Hirschland, "Minimum Muscular Fitness Tests in School Children." *Research Quarterly*, 25:178-88; May 1954.
[16] Clarke, *op. cit.* p. 183-209.

Measures of Posture and Body Mechanics

All parts of the human body must work harmoniously and in perfect synchronization if the total result is a balanced whole. The body must act against gravitational forces and other resistances; maximum effort at least cost in terms of energy expenditure is the goal sought. Not only the body mechanics, or physical principles, but also the posture of the pupil are indicative of his physical fitness.

Functional posture appraisal. Direct measurement of posture by means of silhouettes and various types of technical equipment can be supplanted for practical purposes by a functional appraisal involving use of a rating scale.[17] From a standing start, where he is observed from the front and side, the pupil is further observed as he walks, sits, rises, turns, stops, reaches upward, climbs and descends stairs, lowers and raises a weight, and, finally, skips rope in going through a prescribed routine. Four types of qualitative ratings ranging from excellent to poor are assigned by the observer on each of some thirty characteristics of his performance. Marked failures to attain satisfactory ratings justify the subsequent use of more technical means of appraisal or referral for medical or orthopedic diagnoses.

Detection of spinal curvature. Two techniques for discovering spinal curvature are relatively nontechnical.[18] One involves the use of a scoliometer of ruled transparent material that shows the nature and degree of any curvature when superimposed over the pupil's back. The other involves the placement of a taut string on the pupil's spine in a prescribed manner so that the string will be deflected sideward where curvature exists.

Measures of Nutrition and Body Build

Nutritional deficiencies frequently lead to interruptions in the growth and development of children, and a person's body type is related to his health, physical performance, and possibly even his personality characteristics. These premises underlie the methods presented here for the use of body measurements in diagnosing the pupil's nutritional deficiencies and in attaining improved understandings of his behavior through knowledge about his physical characteristics. The height-weight and related matters presented in a preceding section of this chapter are indirectly dependent on nutritional status, as well as on the measures presented here.

---

[17] Donald K. Mathews, *Measurement in Physical Education*. W. B. Saunders Co., Philadelphia, 1958. p. 256-59.
[18] Clarke, *op. cit.* p. 166-68.

A-C-H Index of Nutritional Status.[19] This index is useful in screening out those pupils between the ages of seven and twelve who should receive a thorough medical examination. The three measures in combination— upper arm girth (A), chest depth (C), and hip width (H)—give a measure of nutritional status as it is reflected in the relation between soft bodily tissue and skeletal build. After measurements are obtained by using a tape and wooden calipers, a table is employed in interpreting the results.

Somatotyping. Somatotypes are the categories of human body type set apart by Sheldon and his colleagues.[20] They specified three major components of body type—endomorphy, mesomorphy, and ectomorphy. The male endomorph is characterized by roundness and softness of body, prominence of the abdomen, high square shoulders and a short neck, smoothness of skin, little muscular relief, and little chest hair. The mesomorph, in contrast, has a square body, hard and prominent muscles, massive legs and arms, broad shoulders, a relatively slender waist, and a coarse skin. Lastly, the ectomorph is fragile and has small bones, thin muscles, drooping shoulders, and a flat abdomen.

Somatotyping consists of assigning a number from 1 to 7 to each of the three components, with 1 representing the lowest and 7 the highest degree of each type, and combining the results into a three-digit descriptive number. Thus, 711, 171, and 117 indicate extremes of endomorphy, mesomorphy, and ectomorphy respectively, whereas 444 represents a person having no pronounced tendency toward any of the three somatotypes. Close to ninety different types of body build, represented by as many number combinations, have been identified by rather elaborate procedures for analyzing front, rear, and side photographs of the person who is being typed.

Cureton [21] devised a simplified method of somatotyping that is based on three seven-point scales for gross aspects of body build—external fat, muscular development and condition, and skeletal development. This nontechnical method, based on careful observations of children, is satisfactory for practical purposes even though it is not as accurate as Sheldon's technique.

4. BROAD TESTS OF PHYSICAL FITNESS

Physical fitness, sometimes referred to as motor fitness, can be tested not only in terms of its aspects or components, by use of such techniques

[19] Raymond Franzen and George Palmer, *The ACH Index of Nutritional Status.* American Child Health Association, New York, 1934.
[20] W. H. Sheldon, S. S. Stevens, and W. B. Tucker, *The Varieties of Human Physique.* Harper and Brothers, New York, 1940.
[21] Thomas K. Cureton, *Physical Fitness Appraisal and Guidance.* C. V. Mosby Co., St. Louis, Mo., 1947.

as are presented in the preceding section, but also by a whole method. Presented here are two procedures for measuring the organic equipment of the body as it is affected by the total performance of the pupil.

Motor Fitness Testing of Boys

The *J-C-R Test* [22] measures the fundamental skills of running, jumping, and dodging in such manner as to involve power, strength, speed, agility, and endurance. The three test elements are (1) jumping from a standing start to touch the highest possible point on a wall in three trials, (2) chinning as many times as possible, and (3) running a short shuttle course five times for speed. A table is provided for converting the three resulting measures into an index of physical fitness.

Motor Fitness Testing of Girls

O'Connor and Cureton evolved a motor fitness test for girls [23] that employs tests of balance, flexibility, agility, strength, power, and endurance. Requiring only standard physical education equipment, the stunt-type tests are scored on a pass or fail basis that makes possible the screening out of the girls not possessing motor fitness.

5. PHYSICAL FITNESS AND BEHAVIOR

Individual differences in physical characteristics are among the most obvious of human differences. However, there are many aspects of health and physical fitness, particularly those that are not accompanied by un-usual physical traits, that are of even greater concern than gross bodily features. School success of pupils in physical education and in some types of motor skills is naturally dependent on health status and physical fitness. For success in other school subjects and areas, however, the relationship is far from direct. Moreover, relationships between physical fitness and intellectual and personality traits may even be reflected indirectly in school success.

A popular misconception is that bright children are physically unde-veloped, weak, and anemic. Instead, there is evidence to indicate a very low degree of positive relationship between physical size and mental ability for children of the same chronological age,[24] so that bright children are

---

[22] B. E. Phillips, "The J. C. R. Test." *Research Quarterly,* 18:12-29; March 1947.

[23] Mary E. O'Connor and Thomas K. Cureton, "Motor Fitness Tests for High School Girls." *Research Quarterly,* 16:302-14; December 1945.

[24] Leona E. Tyler, *The Psychology of Human Differences,* Second edition. Appleton-Century-Crofts, Inc., New York, 1956. p. 419-20.

more often found to be slightly superior to their duller schoolmates in physical characteristics as well as superior in mental traits and achievement status.

It has been established, however, that physical disabilities of two types, those attacking the central nervous system and those resulting in extreme sensory handicaps, adversely affect the educational success of pupils.[25] Birth injuries and abnormal brain conditions often result in types of mental deficiencies that in turn are reflected in marked educational disabilities. Such extreme sensory handicaps as blindness and deafness, and even less severe sensory defects of sight and hearing, are frequently accompanied by educational retardation, great or small. However, there is little evidence to support the belief that minor sensory deficiencies and ordinary ailments and diseases have any effects either upon mental ability or, in anything beyond the transitory effects of absence, upon school success.

Although many attempts have been made to relate physical appearance to personality and temperament, the social stereotypes growing out of them have little scientific foundation. It is possible, however, that acceptance of a stereotype, itself without scientific validity, may sometimes modify a person's behavior by inducing him to behave the way he thinks he is expected to behave.[26] There is some evidence that body types, such as the pyknic, athletic, leptosome, and dysplastic proposed by Kretschmer,[27] and the somatotypes of Sheldon discussed in a foregoing section of this chapter, are in minor degree related to temperament, as illustrated, perhaps, by the tendency in America to find mesomorphy in men associated with success and the type of dominance often reflected in leadership roles.[28]

SUGGESTED ACTIVITIES

1. Try out the watch-tick test and the forced-whisper test on some of your friends and estimate the reliability of the techniques as used by you in terms of the degree to which the two tests rank your friends in the same order between acute and defective hearing.
2. Try out on yourself or a few friends some of the simpler Kraus-Weber and J-C-R test elements in order to gain some understanding of how physical fitness tests can be administered.

[25] *Ibid.* p. 427-29.
[26] Anne Anastasi, *Differential Psychology: Individual and Group Differences in Behavior,* Third edition. Macmillan Co., New York, 1958. p. 125-26.
[27] Ernst Kretschmer, *Physique and Character.* Harcourt, Brace and Co., New York, 1925.
[28] Anastasi, *op. cit.* p. 183.

TOPICS FOR DISCUSSION

1. What major problems are involved in determining an optimum or desirable height-weight ratio? What attempts are made to solve them in available height-weight tables?

2. What are some of the major aspects of physical growth and development for which maturity levels are sometimes stated in years and months?

3. What in general terms is meant by organismic age?

4. How are health practices, attitudes, and knowledges related to physical fitness?

5. What are some of the ways in which the teacher's alertness to signs of illness and sensory deficiencies in pupil behavior can contribute significantly to the school's health and physical fitness program?

6. What sensory tests can a teacher use for detection or verification of deficiencies in pupils most seriously handicapped?

7. What major principle is embodied in most cardiovascular and respiratory tests?

8. On what grounds are strength, power, and endurance tests employed in the measurement of physical fitness?

9. How do measures of posture and body mechanics contribute to an understanding of physical fitness?

10. How is body build related to nutritional status and to physical fitness?

11. How can the classroom teacher employ some of the cardiovascular, strength or power, postural, and nutritional testing techniques with his pupils?

12. What kinds of physical behavior are involved in broad tests of physical fitness?

13. Is the popular belief that bright children are weak and anemic based on factual evidence?

14. How and to what extent does physical fitness appear to affect the school progress of pupils?

15. In what respects are social stereotypes about physical characteristics perhaps not entirely fallacious?

SELECTED REFERENCES

ANASTASI, ANNE. *Differential Psychology: Individual and Group Differences in Behavior*. Third edition. New York: Macmillan Co., 1958. Chapters 5-6.

BALDWIN, BIRD T., WOOD, THOMAS D., AND WOODBURY, R. M. *Height-Weight-Age Tables*. New York: American Child Health Association, 1923.

BOVARD, JOHN F., COZENS, FREDERICK W., AND HAGMAN, E. PATRICIA. *Tests and Measurements in Physical Education*. Third edition. Philadelphia: W. B. Saunders Co., 1949. Chapters 3-4, 7-9.

BROUHA, LUCIEN, AND GALLAGHER, J. ROSWELL. "A Functional Fitness Test for High School Girls." *Journal of Health and Physical Education*, 14:517, 550; December 1943.

CLARKE, H. HARRISON. *Application of Measurement to Health and Physical Education.* Third edition. Englewood Cliffs, N. J.: Prentice-Hall, Inc., 1959. Part 2.

CURETON, THOMAS K., AND OTHERS. *Endurance of Young Men: Analysis of Endurance Exercises and Methods of Evaluating Motor Fitness.* Monographs of the Society for Research in Child Development, Vol. 10, No. 1. Washington, D. C.: The Society, 1945.

CURETON, THOMAS K., AND OTHERS. *Physical Fitness Appraisal and Guidance.* St. Louis, Mo.: C. V. Mosby Co., 1947.

DEAVER, GEORGE G. *Fundamentals of Physical Examination.* Philadelphia: W. B. Saunders Co., 1939.

DEHAAN, ROBERT F., AND KOUGH, JACK. *Identifying Students with Special Needs.* Teacher's Guidance Handbook, Vol. I, Secondary School Edition. Chicago: Science Research Associates, Inc., 1956. Section 4.

DZENOWAGIS, JOSEPH G., AND IRWIN, LESLIE W. "Prevalence of Certain Harmful Health and Safety Misconceptions among Fifth- and Sixth-Grade Children." *Research Quarterly,* 25:150-63; May 1954.

JENSS, RACHEL M., AND SOUTHER, SUSAN P. *Methods of Assessing the Physical Fitness of Children.* Children's Bureau Publication, No. 263. Washington, D. C.: U. S. Government Printing Office, 1940.

KOUGH, JACK, AND DEHAAN, ROBERT F. *Identifying Children with Special Needs.* Teacher's Guidance Handbook, Vol. I, Elementary School Edition. Chicago: Science Research Associates, Inc., 1955. Section 4.

KRAUS, HANS, AND HIRSCHLAND, RUTH P. "Minimum Muscular Fitness Tests in School Children." *Research Quarterly,* 25:178-88; May 1954.

KROGMAN, WILTON M. *A Handbook of the Measurement and Interpretation of Height and Weight in the Growing Child.* Monographs of the Society for Research in Child Development, Vol. 13, No. 3. Evanston, Ill.: Child Development Publications, 1950.

LARSON, LEONARD A. "Defining Physical Fitness—With Procedures for Its Measurement." *Journal of Health and Physical Education,* 13:18-20, 50-51; January 1942.

LARSON, LEONARD A., coordinator. *Measurement and Evaluation Materials in Health, Physical Education, and Recreation.* Washington, D. C.: American Association for Health, Physical Education, and Recreation, 1950. Chapters 1-5.

LARSON, LEONARD A., AND YOCOM, RACHEL D. *Measurement and Evaluation in Physical, Health, and Recreation Education.* St. Louis, Mo.: C. V. Mosby Co., 1951. Parts 2-3.

MATHEWS, DONALD K. *Measurement in Physical Education.* Philadelphia: W. B. Saunders Co., 1958. Chapters 4-6, 8-10.

MAYSHARK, CYRUS. "A Health and Safety Attitude Scale for the Seventh Grade." *Research Quarterly,* 27:52-59; May 1956.

McCLOY, C. H. *Appraising Physical Status: Methods and Norms.* University of Iowa Studies in Child Welfare, Vol. XV, No. 2. Iowa City: University of Iowa, 1938.

McCLOY, C. H. *Appraising Physical Status: The Selection of Measurements.* University of Iowa Studies in Child Welfare, Vol. XII, No. 2. Iowa City: University of Iowa, 1936.

McCLOY, CHARLES H., AND YOUNG, N. D. *Tests and Measurements in Health and Physical Education.* Third edition. New York: Appleton-Century-Crofts, Inc., 1954. Chapters 8-12, 14-15, 18, 21, 23, 27-28.

MEREDITH, HOWARD V. "A 'Physical Growth Record' for Use in Elementary and High Schools." *American Journal of Public Health,* 39:878-85; July 1949.

METHENY, ELEANOR, chairman. "Physical Performance Levels for High School Girls." *Journal of Health and Physical Education,* 16:308-11, 354-57; June 1945.

O'CONNOR, MARY E., AND CURETON, THOMAS K., JR. "Motor Fitness Tests for High School Girls." *Research Quarterly,* 16:302-14; December 1945.

OLSON, WILLARD C., AND HUGHES, BYRON O. "The Concept of Organismic Age." *Journal of Educational Research,* 35:525-27; March 1942.

PHILLIPS, B. E. "The J. C. R. Test." *Research Quarterly,* 18:12-29; March 1947.

ROGERS, JAMES F. *What Every Teacher Should Know about the Physical Condition of Her Pupils.* U. S. Office of Education Pamphlet, No. 68. Washington, D. C.: U. S. Government Printing Office, 1936.

ROGERS, FREDERICK R. *Physical Capacity Tests.* New York: A. S. Barnes and Co., 1931.

SCOTT, M. GLADYS, AND FRENCH, ESTHER. *Evaluation in Physical Education.* St. Louis, Mo.: C. V. Mosby Co., 1950. Chapter 6.

SHELDON, W. H., STEVENS, S. S., AND TUCKER, W. B. *The Varieties of Human Physique.* New York: Harper and Brothers, 1946.

SOUTHWORTH, WARREN H., LATIMER, JEAN V., AND TURNER, CLAIR E. "A Study of the Health Practices, Knowledge, Attitudes, and Interests of Senior High School Pupils." *Research Quarterly,* 15:118-36; May 1944.

STRADTMAN, ALAN D., AND CURETON, THOMAS K. "A Physical Fitness Knowledge Test for Secondary School Boys and Girls." *Research Quarterly,* 21:53-57; March 1950.

TORGERSON, THEODORE L., AND ADAMS, GEORGIA S. *Measurement and Evaluation for the Elementary-School Teacher.* New York: Dryden Press, 1954. Chapter 5.

TUTTLE, W. W. "The Use of the Pulse-Ratio Test for Rating Physical Efficiency." *Research Quarterly,* 11:5-17; May 1931.

TYLER, LEONA E. *The Psychology of Human Differences.* Second edition. New York: Appleton-Century-Crofts, Inc., 1956. Chapter 16.

WILLGOOSE, CARL E. *Evaluation in Health Education and Physical Education.* New York: McGraw-Hill Book Co., Inc., 1961. Chapters 5-9, 13.

6

MENTAL ABILITY TESTS

The aspects of mental ability or intelligence, intelligence testing, and the use of mental ability test results that are given major attention in this chapter are as follows:

A. Nature of intelligence and scholastic aptitude.
B. Individual and group tests of mental ability.
C. Special and multifactor tests of mental abilities.
D. Performance tests of mental ability.
E. Scores derived from intelligence and scholastic aptitude tests.
F. Distribution of intelligence.
G. Major controversies about the intelligence quotient.
H. Classroom uses of mental ability test results.

It is important for the teacher to be conversant with the nature of intelligence and with techniques for its measurement. It is also imperative that he be able to obtain and use at least the major types of derived scores in furnishing guidance of various types to his pupils. This chapter discusses the theory and measurement of intelligence and the applied aspects of intelligence and intelligence testing.

Workers in the field of mental abilities are far from agreement both on the correct terminology to use in discussing mental abilities and on the exact nature of the ability or abilities to which the terms apply. It is therefore a formidable task to prepare a brief treatment of intelligence and intelligence testing. Cronbach distinguished two types of tests broadly—tests of mental ability, which seek to measure the maximum performance of which an individual is capable, and personality inventories, which attempt to measure a person's typical or habitual behavior.[1] This distinction and its corollary, that a pupil should score as high as he can in a mental ability test but that he should reflect typical or habitual methods of behavior on a personality test, are reflected in this chapter and in the treatment of personality measurement in Chapter 7.

The discussions of mental ability or intelligence in this chapter are based on what the authors believe to be the best modern terminology in this field. However, the reader will doubtless encounter instances in which test titles and references will not be completely in harmony with the usage that is followed.

1. MENTAL ABILITY AND ITS MEASUREMENT

The nature of the combination of abilities known as mental ability or intelligence is not known at all precisely even today. However, it is definitely known that individuals differ in the amount and probably the quality of it they possess and that within limits it can be measured.

Nature of Intelligence

Although intelligence and mental ability are used almost interchangeably in describing one of the major aspects of behavior, the former has been defined and particularized more often than the latter by psychologists. A number of definitions formulated forty years ago [2] are still acceptable in characterizing this combination of mental traits.

These definitions fall into at least three patterns: (1) the rather formal ones, stressing ability to reason, to engage in abstract thinking, and to use the higher mental powers, (2) those emphasizing ability to do the work of the school and to learn, and (3) those stressing ability to adapt to new situations. It is felt by the authors that intelligence is most meaningfully conceived as *the ability to adapt oneself to new situations*. The fact that ability to learn and ability to think in abstract terms are both evidences of intelligence should not be overlooked. Moreover, these activities themselves require adaptation to new situations. Stoddard, more recently, included two and perhaps all three of these concepts in his broad definition of intelligence as:

the ability to undertake activities that are characterized by (1) difficulty, (2) complexity, (3) abstractness, (4) economy, (5) adaptiveness to a goal,

---

[1] Lee J. Cronbach, *Essentials of Psychological Testing*, Second edition. Harper and Brothers, New York, 1960. p. 29-32.

[2] Symposium, "Intelligence and Its Measurement." *Journal of Educational Psychology*, 12:123-47, 195-216; March and April 1921.

(6) social value, and (7) the emergence of originals, and to maintain such activities under conditions that demand a concentration of energy and a resistance to emotional forces.[3]

Intelligence is sometimes defined, in still another way, as whatever it is that intelligence tests test. This circular approach, of defining intelligence in terms of how it is measured rather than in terms of what it is, actually has meaning. In this connection, it should be noted that the definitions discussed in the preceding paragraphs concur in considering intelligence in terms of what it does or what it makes possible—the ability to reason, the ability to learn, or the ability to adapt oneself to new situations, for example—rather than in terms of what it is. The statement implies, therefore, that a person's intelligence directly influences his behavior and that it can be estimated by measuring and observing his behavior even though the thing being measured has not been very precisely defined or described.

Factual Content of Intelligence Tests

The preceding definitions perhaps suggest that this type of ability is subject to evaluation in a rather direct manner. Such is not the case, however, for ability to learn can only be inferred from the fact that learning has occurred in a test situation. Since intelligence cannot be measured directly, test makers can only measure the performance of tasks the successful completion of which is generally believed to be dependent upon intelligence. The value of the intelligence test lies in the fact that it affords an objective basis for this inference. It samples widely from the fields of learning resulting from experiences assumed to be common to all persons subjected to the test. The pupil's capacity to learn or to adapt to new situations is determined by summing up his reactions to the items of the test.

Obviously, a test of ability to learn must have some type of content. Intelligence tests admittedly contain factual and skill materials. Such tests attempt to measure abilities to see relationships, to draw reasoned inferences, to manipulate, to compare, to contrast, and otherwise to handle materials which themselves are so commonly known and at such low difficulty levels that all persons who have had any but the most restricted environmental backgrounds should know the necessary facts and have the necessary skills for understanding and taking, although not necessarily for succeeding upon, the tests. To contend that intelligence tests have been completely successful in eliminating the significance of the factual

[3] George D. Stoddard, *The Meaning of Intelligence*. Macmillan Co., New York, 1943. p. 4.

and skill content would be foolhardy and contrary to available evidence, however.

Kelley,[4] many years ago, stated that general intelligence tests and achievement tests overlap to the degree indicated by a correlation coefficient of .90. Coefficients of .40 to .60 are typically found between tested intelligence and academic achievement when more recently published tests are employed, but even higher degrees of relationship sometimes occur. When such correlations approach .70 or .80, the intelligence test is looked upon with suspicion by some and may be considered a general scholastic achievement test rather than an intelligence test.[5]

Nature of Scholastic Aptitude

It seems inescapable, as is pointed out in the preceding paragraphs, that intelligence tests must be based in part on what has been learned and that intelligence tests and achievement tests are not so distinctively different as some persons have contended. In consequence, there has been a tendency of late to give new names to some of the recently published tests of general mental ability, such as scholastic aptitude tests, school ability tests, and even tests of educational ability. These tests admittedly measure what are described as developed abilities and even as cultural or educational learnings and make no pretense of holding factual and skill content to a minimum.

This type of distinction is not clear cut, so differences in this respect are of degree rather than of kind. Other types of differences dealt with below are more evident, such as those between general and special tests and between written and performance tests. A rough distinction is nevertheless made in the following sections of this chapter between intelligence tests and scholastic aptitude tests. Both types are considered to be tests of mental ability.

2. GENERAL MENTAL ABILITY TESTS

The two types of general mental ability tests—individual intelligence scales and group intelligence and scholastic aptitude tests—are discussed and a few samples of them are shown in the following pages. Brief consideration of the newly issued form of the most widely used individual scale is supplemented by attention to several of the best known group

---

[4] Truman L. Kelley, *Interpretation of Educational Measurements.* World Book Co., Yonkers, N. Y., 1927. p. 208.

[5] Paul L. Boynton, "Intelligence." *Encyclopedia of Educational Research.* Macmillan Co., New York, 1941. p. 630.

tests. These discussions and illustrations should aid the student in obtaining an adequate understanding of the characteristics and general content of these important instruments for the measurement of general mental ability.

Individual Scales of Intelligence

Individual intelligence examinations constitute the most accurate devices for the measurement of intelligence. The length of the test, the wide variety of reactions called for, the fact that the subject receives his instructions personally from the examiner, the fact that the examiner is afforded an opportunity to observe each reaction made by the subject, and the careful standardization of procedures for administering the test and scoring the subject's reactions all contribute to the high degree of accuracy. The full time of an examiner is required for each pupil tested. The examiner must be a person who is more capable and efficient in test administration than is the typical teacher. Furthermore, he must be one who has had extensive training and experience in giving individual intelligence tests.

Individual intelligence tests are largely patterned on the Binet-Simon tests brought out in France from 1905 to 1911, as is briefly discussed in Chapter 2. The newly published 1960 edition of the *Stanford-Binet Intelligence Scale,* by Terman and Merrill, is successor to the widely used 1916 and 1937 editions by these authors. Another widely used pair of scales that are dependent on the Binet tests somewhat less closely are the *Wechsler Adult Intelligence Scale* [6] and the *Wechsler Intelligence Scale for Children.*[6]

The general procedure in administering the *Stanford-Binet* is quite representative of that used in other individual scales. The type of performance tested varies considerably with the different exercises constituting the scale. These test elements are presented to the child by means of spoken directions. The test should be given in a quiet room where there is freedom from distraction. A friendly attitude between examiner and subject should be maintained. The examiner is expected to make sure that the subject understands what is to be done, and in all cases the burden of proof is with the examiner to show that the subject has responded in a way that is representative of his ability.

After rapport has been established, i.e., the child has been put at ease, the examiner starts the test with materials at a scale level on which the subject is likely to succeed with some effort. If he is successful on all tests at this level, the examiner, assuming that he could pass all tests at lower

[6] Published by Psychological Corporation, New York.

levels, passes on to the higher levels and continues on through the scale until the subject fails all tests at one age level. In effect the child has been tested over the entire scale, for his success on all tests at one age level makes almost certain that he could pass all tests at lower levels and his failure on all tests of another, and higher, age level indicates with essential certainty that he could go no higher on the scale. The child's mental age is determined by giving him credit for the number of years below the level on which he passes all tests and adding to this amount the years and months of credit assigned to the higher-level tests he succeeds in passing.

It is not feasible here to reproduce more than a few sample test elements, but the two samples from the *Stanford-Binet* give some idea of the nature of the test.

SAMPLE ITEMS FROM *Stanford-Binet Intelligence Scale*[7]

Year III-6; Item 5, Sorting Buttons [8]

Material: Twenty half-inch buttons, 10 black and 10 white. Small box.

Procedure: Empty the button box onto the table in front of the child and place the box cover beside the box ready for sorting the buttons. Take a button of each color from the mixed pile in front of the boxes, saying, as you illustrate: *"See, the black buttons go in this box, and the white buttons go in that box. Now you put all the black buttons in that box and all the white buttons in this box."* Time limit, 2 minutes.

Score: No error. Errors made in the process of sorting, if corrected spontaneously, are disregarded in scoring.

Year XIII; Item 3, Memory for Sentences III [9]

Procedure: Say before giving each sentence, *"Listen, and be sure to say exactly what I say."*

(*a*) *"The airplane made a careful landing in the space which had been prepared for it."*

(*b*) *"Tom Brown's dog ran quickly down the road with a huge bone in his mouth."*

Score: 1 plus. No error. Errors include omissions, substitutions, additions, changes in words or in order of words.

The lists of item titles [10] at several age and maturity levels of the Form L-M *Stanford-Binet* between Year II and Superior Adult III, which are at the bottom and top of the scale, indicate the variety of abilities

---

[7] Lewis M. Terman and Maud A. Merrill, *Stanford-Binet Intelligence Scale: Manual for the Third Revision*, Form L-M. Houghton Mifflin Co., Boston, 1960.
[8] *Ibid.* p. 75.
[9] *Ibid.* p. 103.
[10] *Ibid.* p. 67-121.

ested, the scalar arrangement of items from easy to difficult, and the duplication at different levels of similar types of test situations at varying levels of difficulty.

Year II

Three-Hole Form Board
Delayed Response
Identifying Parts of the Body
Block Building: Tower
Picture Vocabulary
Word Combinations

Year VII

Picture Absurdities I
Similarities: Two Things
Copying a Diamond
Comprehension IV
Opposite Analogies III
Repeating 5 Digits

Year XII

Vocabulary
Verbal Absurdities II
Picture Absurdities II
Repeating 5 Digits Reversed
Abstract Words I
Minkus Completion I

Superior Adult III

Vocabulary
Proverbs III
Opposite Analogies IV
Orientation: Direction III
Reasoning II
Repeating Thought of Passage II: Tests

Group Tests of Intelligence and Scholastic Aptitude

Written tests of intelligence for the simultaneous measurement of groups of persons were inaugurated with the development of *Army Alpha,* as is mentioned in Chapter 2. The *Army General Classification Test* and comparable instruments developed by other branches of the armed services during World War II are the modern counterparts. Scores of group intelligence tests were published during the second quarter of the present century and several new tests of the scholastic aptitude variety have made their appearance since mid-century. Space limitations prevent the use of illustrations from more than a few of these tests and permit only a brief treatment of the techniques used in their construction.

The accompanying reproduction of a few items each from two of the parts of the *Kuhlmann-Anderson Test* shows items that measure ability to select the three words in each list of five that are alike in some functional way and to identify the middle one of five quantitative terms when they are arranged in order of value from least to most. These parts are among the eight in the separate answer sheet edition of this recently revised test. Bases are provided for interpreting results in terms of the mental age (MA), intelligence quotient (IQ), and percentile scores, all of which are discussed later in this chapter.

EXCERPTS FROM *Kuhlmann-Anderson Test* [11]

Test G 3

EXAMPLES: X. walk   rest   hike   wait   tramp
              A   B   C   D   E

          Y. sob   smile   laugh   frown   grin
              A   B   C   D   E

1. feeble   capable   qualified   faulty   competent
    A   B   C   D   E

2. trickery loyalty   desertion   faithfulness   devotion
    A   B   C   D   E

3. amiable   friendly   wise   unkind   gracious
    A   B   C   D   E

4. skill   incompetence   aptitude   ability   reward
    A   B   C   D   E

Test G 7

EXAMPLES: X. quarter nickel dollar dime penny
              A   B   C   D   E

          Y. sprout bush blossom seed fruit
              A   B   C   D   E

1. one multitude few none many
    A   B   C   D   E

2. week fortnight year month decade
    A   B   C   D   E

3. solo quartette trio chorus duet
    A   B   C   D   E

4. 20%   60% $\frac{1}{4}$ 78% $\frac{3}{4}$
    A   B   C   D   E

[11] F. Kuhlmann and Rose G. Anderson, *Kuhlmann-Anderson Test*, Seventh edition. Booklet G. Personnel Press, Inc., Princeton, N. J., 1960.

The *Davis-Eells Games,* tests designed to measure general intelligence or problem-solving ability in the primary and elementary grades, are illustrated by an accompanying excerpt showing three boys trying to paint a chair. Pupils taking the test are asked orally by the examiner to mark the box numbered in agreement with the picture that shows the best way of painting the chair. Emphasis in the test is placed on practical problems keyed to the ability levels and experiences, but not to the formal learnings, of children in the attempt to avoid the abstractness, emphasis on reading skills, and other formal characteristics of many tests of general intelligence.[12] This type of emphasis is in harmony with the attempt of the authors to develop a test that does not reflect any influence of socioeconomic status in the test scores of pupils. Further comments on this test and its attempt to be culturally fair appear later in this chapter.

EXCERPT FROM *Davis-Eells Games* [13]

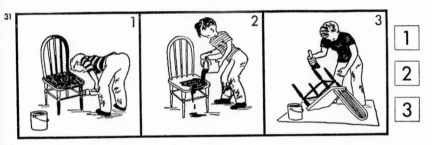

These two tests, together with the *Lorge-Thorndike Intelligence Tests* illustrated on page 35, are classified by Cronbach [14] as placing very close to the minimum dependence on learned behaviors, in contrast with the greater number of present-day tests that purposely and openly measure scholastic aptitude by placing considerable emphasis on the results of specific instruction. Two of the tests he classified as close to the other end of the scale, or as having greater dependence on subject-matter learnings, are illustrated herewith. A second characteristic found in many of the scholastic aptitude type of tests is also embodied in the samples shown— the provision of two part scores and a total mental score. Such instruments are sometimes called *bifactor tests.*

[12] Allison Davis and Kenneth Eells, *Davis-Eells Games: Manual.* World Book Co., Yonkers, N. Y., 1953. p. 1-6.

[13] Allison Davis and Kenneth Eells, *Davis-Eells Games* (Davis-Eells Test of General Intelligence or Problem-Solving Ability), Elementary. Form A. Copyright 1953 by Harcourt, Brace and World, Inc., New York. All rights reserved. Quoted by special permission.

[14] Cronbach, *op. cit.* p. 234-35.

Sample items from the "numerical-computation tasks" and the "sentence-completion tasks" of the *Cooperative School Ability Test* at the Grade 6 to 8 level are shown in an accompanying excerpt. The items are to be answered by selecting the lettered responses that give the correct computational results or that should be inserted in the blank spaces in the sentences for correct completions of meaning. The numerical items contribute to a quantitative score, the sentence-completion items contribute to a verbal score, and a total score is based on a combination of the two part scores. Percentile norms by grades are used in interpreting results.

EXCERPTS FROM *Cooperative School Ability Test* [15]

16 $0.3 \times 0.3 = (?)$

    F 0.009
    G 0.09
    H 0.6
    J 0.9
    K 9.0

19 $\frac{1}{4}$ of $0.24 = (?)$

    A 0.06
    B 0.6
    C 0.96
    D 9.6
    E None of these

23 $2\overline{)9 \text{ feet } 8 \text{ inches}}$

    A 3 feet 4 inches
    B 4 feet 4 inches
    C 4 feet 9 inches
    D 4 feet 10 inches
    E None of these

6 There is always dust in the air, and many other small (   ), known and unknown.

    F beings   G airplanes   H particles
    J diseases   K birds

13 The old glassmaker bent the strips of lead, which had been heated just enough to make them (   ).

    A glow   B stiff   C molten
    D elastic   E flexible

The second scholastic aptitude type of test illustrated in an accompanying excerpt is the *California Short-Form Test of Mental Maturity* for Grades 9 to 13. Test 2 and Test 7 are respectively from the nonlanguage and language portions of the instrument. Mental ages and intelligence quotients can be obtained separately for these two major parts as well as for a total measure of general intelligence.

3. TESTS OF SPECIAL MENTAL ABILITIES

The two types of special, or specific, intelligence tests—aptitude and readiness—differ primarily in the ages and maturity levels of the pupils to whom they are given. Whereas aptitude tests presuppose some ability to read, to compute, and to engage in other learned activities, readiness tests assume that even the most elementary of such learned behaviors have not yet been acquired. In most other respects, the two types of tests are quite similar.

[15] Cooperative Test Division, Educational Testing Service, *Cooperative School Ability Test,* Form 4A. Educational Testing Service, Princeton, N. J., 1956.

EXCERPTS FROM *California Test of Mental Maturity* [16]

TEST 3

DIRECTIONS: The first three pictures in each row are alike in some way. Decide how they are alike and then find the one picture among the four to the right of the dotted line that is most like them and mark its number.

TEST 7

DIRECTIONS: Mark as you are told the number of the word that means the same or about the same as the first word.

H. blossom	[1] tree	[2] vine		121. harbinger	[1] tractor	[2] flag
	[3] flower	[4] garden	H		[3] herald	[4] threat	121
96. wither	[1] fade	[2] admire		122. viand	[1] food	[2] route
	[3] perform	[4] bleach	96		[3] loot	[4] spike	122
97. organic	[1] musical	[2] pompous		123. rancor	[1] malice	[2] capacity
	[3] living	[4] smooth	97		[3] regard	[4] position	123
98. minute	[1] small	[2] wise		124. motley	[1] verbose	[2] plausible
	[3] special	[4] retarded	98		[3] spotted	[4] mixed	124
99. nauseate	[1] envy	[2] sicken		125. divest	[1] distract	[2] depress
	[3] drowse	[4] modify	99		[3] delude	[4] deprive	125

Aptitude Tests

Special tests of the aptitude type are available for many broad subject areas and a few specific school subjects. These various tests largely possess in common the characteristic of testing the individual's potentialities in terms of the specific abilities resulting from inheritance and general experience but of disregarding insofar as possible results of specific training or education. Thus these tests parallel intelligence tests, although they are narrower in scope. The earliest aptitude tests, primarily useful at the

[16] Willis W. Clark and Ernest W. Tiegs, *California Short-Form Test of Mental Maturity,* Grades 9 to 13. Form A. California Test Bureau, Monterey, Calif., 1957.

college level, were followed by other aptitude tests for algebra and geometry, English, the foreign languages, mathematics, and the sciences for secondary-school use.

The accompanying excerpt from the *Iowa Algebra Aptitude Test* illustrates the number series type of item rather common to aptitude tests in mathematics. It is apparent that some persons who could perform the necessary arithmetical operations for answering item 5, for example, would not do so because they failed to discover the "pattern" of the number series.

The variety of areas of behavior served by aptitude tests makes impracticable a comprehensive discussion of such instruments here. They receive consideration in Chapters 15 to 24 by subject fields, in parallel with prognostic tests, which, although frequently measuring the results of training, have somewhat similar uses. Aside from tests in the music and art fields aptitude tests are devised almost exclusively for use at the high-school and college levels.

EXCERPT FROM *Iowa Algebra Aptitude Test* [17]

Part 3.   NUMERICAL SERIES

Time allowance—12 minutes.

Directions: Each of the following number series is made up according to some rule. Addition, subtraction, multiplication, and division, and various combinations of these processes are used in forming the different series. Discover the rule for each example, decide what the next term would be, and write it on the blank line following the series. Then place a cross (X) in the circle directly over the answer that agrees with yours. If no answer agrees with yours place the X in the circle over "Not Given." You will receive no credit for a correct answer unless it is marked in the correct answer space. The sample is answered correctly.

							Answers			
Sample·	1	2	3	4	5	6	7 _8_	○ 7	⊗ 8	○ 9 ○ Not Given

							ANSWERS			
1. 2	4	6	8	10		1.	○ 11	○ 12	○ 13	○ Not Given
2. 9	8	7	6	5		2.	○ 5	○ 3	○ 2	○ Not Given
3. 1	1	5	5	9	9	3.	○ 11	○ 12	○ 13	○ Not Given
4. 2	4	8	16	32		4.	○ 48	○ 64	○ 96	○ Not Given
5. 5	8	11	14	17		5.	○ 20	○ 21	○ 23	○ Not Given

Readiness Tests

These special intelligence tests, found primarily in reading and arithmetic, measure the results of inheritance and general training rather than of direct instruction. As readiness tests imply by their general designation, they measure readiness to undertake a new type of activity that is depend-

[17] H. A. Greene and A. H. Piper, *Iowa Algebra Aptitude Test,* Revised edition. Bureau of Educational Research and Service, University of Iowa, Iowa City, 1942.

ent upon the maturation of various physical and mental abilities. They may in one sense be considered as aptitude tests at the elementary- and even the primary-school levels, where they almost entirely occur.

Tests of this type are usually restricted in applicability to a particular subject field. However, the *Metropolitan Readiness Tests* are devised for determining the readiness of a child to learn first-grade skills of all types, and consequently are briefly discussed and illustrated here. The six parts of the test seem to measure the types of abilities used primarily in reading and number work. Tests 4 and 5, for which the instructions are given orally by the examiner and which require few skills in pencil manipulation of any complexity, measure respectively ability in visual perception and knowledge of number.

EXCERPT FROM *Metropolitan Readiness Tests* [18]

TEST 4. MATCHING

TEST 5. NUMBERS

4. MULTIFACTOR TESTS OF MENTAL ABILITIES

The factor analysis movement gave rise some twenty or more years ago to the first use of group factors of intelligence in testing practice. The tests having two factors, such as those discussed in the preceding section of this chapter, made their appearance first, and it has been only during the past fifteen years or so that the multifactor tests have passed their experimental stage. These tests can be considered to measure intellectual abilities less broad than general mental ability but in major respects broader than the areas measured by special intelligence or mental ability tests. Some of the parts, or factors, variously represented in such tests are abstract, spatial, perceptual, numerical, reasoning, memory, deduction, and induction.

The accompanying illustration from four of the *Differential Aptitude Tests* shows some of the techniques used in multifactor tests. The verbal reasoning test employs an analogy type of item in which a numbered response is used to fill the first blank and a lettered response is required to complete the analogy. In the abstract reasoning test the appropriate lettered response is selected to carry on the progression established in the four left-hand figures. The problem in the space relations test is to select the lettered response that represents the three-dimensional figure resulting when the left-hand figure is folded and assembled. In the mechanical reasoning test the nature of the problem is self-evident.

5. PERFORMANCE TESTS OF MENTAL ABILITY

Performance tests require motor or manual rather than verbal responses. In their simplest form language is required neither in administering the tests nor in responding to them. With the exception of certain form board tests for measuring complex types of mechanical aptitude, they are devised mainly for use with very young children, with mental defectives, and with persons unable to use English with reasonable efficiency. Therefore, their primary purpose seems to be the measurement of abilities not requiring language proficiency, or the measurement of abilities in certain types of persons for whom tests demanding reading and writing are precluded by their language handicaps. Both illiterates and persons who can read, write, and speak a foreign language with fluency but who are deficient in the ability to use English are included in this last group.

Two types of performance tests may be distinguished—those requiring the use of a pencil for marking, but not for writing, and those requiring manipulations of various items of testing equipment.

Revisions of the *Army Beta Examination,* for use with adults who cannot read, write, or perhaps even understand English, illustrate the first type.

EXCERPTS FROM *Differential Aptitude Tests* [19]

VERBAL REASONING

1. . . .is to street as rd. is to....
   1. lo.   2. ma.   3. st.   4. aw.
   A. city   B. France   C. end   D. road

2. . . .is to cavalry as foot is to....
   1. horse   2. cemetery   3. votary   4. hiding
   A. yard   B. travel   C. armory   D. infantry

ABSTRACT REASONING

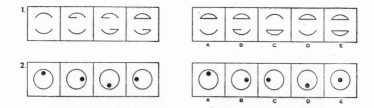

SPACE RELATIONS

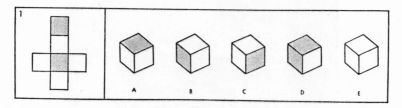

MECHANICAL REASONING

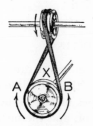

2

When the top pulley turns in the direction shown, which way will the lower pulley turn? (If either, mark C.)

Directions are usually given by pantomime, and the subjects respond by tracing mazes, indicating whether groups of numbers are alike or unlike, and supplying missing elements in pictures.

[19] George K. Bennett, Harold G. Seashore, and Alexander G. Wesman, *Differential Aptitude Tests,* Form A. Psychological Corporation, New York, 1947.

Another type of performance test, often requiring manipulation of apparatus, involves such materials as blocks, mazes, and form boards that are not unlike jigsaw puzzles. The accompanying picture of the materials comprising the *Arthur Point Scale of Performance Tests* shows the general nature of the second type of nonverbal test of mental ability. Directions are usually given orally by the examiner, and such factors as time, errors, moves, and other evidences of success or failure are taken into account in scoring the results. Five separate tests, four of them revised or devised by Arthur, are included in the scale—the *Knox Cube Test,* the *Seguin Form Board,* the *Arthur Stencil Design Test,* the *Healy Picture Completion Test II,* and the *Porteus Maze Test.* The scale is intended for use with children from five to fifteen years of age who are deaf, who have serious reading or speech disabilities, or who do not speak English.

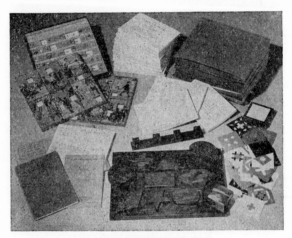

FIGURE 1. Tests of the *Arthur Point Scale of Performance* [20]

6. DERIVED RESULTS OF MENTAL ABILITY TESTING

A raw score from a test has little or no meaning unless it can be compared by the use of norms or in some other manner with similarly obtained raw scores. This general principle applies to all types of tests. Therefore, it is important that the teacher know the meaning of, and the method of obtaining, the most common types of derived measures used in the interpretation of mental ability test results. As the methods of obtaining the most important of the derived scores discussed below are given fully in Chapter 14, only general meanings are treated here.

[20] Grace Arthur, *Arthur Point Scale of Performance Tests,* Revised Form II. Copyright 1947, The Psychological Corporation, New York.

Mental Age

A person's mental age is his general mental ability or general intelligence expressed in terms of the chronological age of which his mental ability is typical. For example, a child has a mental age of ten years if his level of mental development is equal to that of the normal child who is exactly ten years of age. Thus if a representative group of pupils, all of whom are ten years of age, makes an average score of 45 on an intelligence test that is being standardized, any pupil who subsequently takes this test and earns a score of 45 is said to have a mental age of ten years. An average score for each age group is established in the same manner.

The mental age (MA) is a measure of mental level or of mental maturity of the individual. Taken alone it tells nothing of how relatively bright or dull the pupil may be, but it does give an indication of the level of ability at which the child potentially can work. For example, information to the effect that a certain pupil has a mental age of 7-6 does not enable a person to judge whether the pupil is bright, average, or dull. It is only when he knows or at least can estimate the child's chronological age that he can draw conclusions concerning his brightness.

Intelligence Quotient

When the chronological age (CA), i.e., life age in years and months, is known for a pupil, and his mental age (MA) has been determined from his score on an intelligence test, his intelligence quotient (IQ) can be computed. The intelligence quotient is a simple method of expressing the relationship between a pupil's mental age and his chronological age.

Quotient-type intelligence quotient. To obtain this type of IQ, a pupil's mental age (in months) is divided by his chronological age (in months), the result is multiplied by 100 to remove the decimal point, and the whole number nearest to the result is taken as his intelligence quotient. The formula is:

$$IQ = 100 \frac{MA}{CA}$$

If this formula is applied for a child who has a mental age (MA) of twelve years six months (150 months) when he has a chronological age (CA) of ten years five months (125 months), the following is the result:

$$IQ = 100 \frac{MA}{CA} = 100 \frac{12\text{-}6}{10\text{-}5} = 100 \frac{150 \ (months)}{125 \ (months)} = 120$$

Deviation-type intelligence quotient. A number of modern mental ability and intelligence tests provide for obtaining an IQ by the deviation method. When this is done, the difference between a pupil's test score and the normal score for his chronological age is determined by use of the test norms and the difference is added to 100 if his score is greater than the norm or subtracted from 100 if his score is smaller than the norm. Although some tests specify minor departures from this general practice in obtaining deviation IQs, the results are commonly referred to as intelligence quotients and are interpreted in the same manner as are quotient IQs.

The intelligence quotient, whether of the true quotient or the deviation type, is a measure of the pupil's relative brightness. If it is assumed that a typical child grows in mentality at the same rate as he ages chronologically, it then appears that children who have IQs over 100 are above average and children who have IQs below 100 are below average. This is in harmony with the usual indication of normal intelligence as being represented by IQs between 90 and 110, for people of normal intelligence center around but are not necessarily exactly at the average of intelligence. However, as this concept of the average is applicable only in terms of the population as a whole and as very few pupil groups are average in this sense, the teacher should not generalize this statement and make it apply to all pupil groups in the school. Furthermore the IQ alone tells nothing about the level of work of which a child is capable, for two children of age six and age twelve might both have IQs of 110 and yet the younger child would be entirely incapable at that time of types of performance commonplace to the older child.

Percentile Score

Percentile scores, occasionally called centile scores, are frequently used to indicate a pupil's status in mental ability or intelligence. This method is used particularly at the high-school and college levels, for the intelligence quotient is not as meaningful a measure for postadolescent and adult years as it is for periods of childhood and adolescence. The percentile score describes a pupil's placement in an age or grade group in terms of the percentage of the group scoring lower than he does. The *School and College Ability Tests* at both the high-school and college levels present norms for the interpretation of scores in terms of percentiles for different grade levels.

Standard Score

Another type of measure that indicates a pupil's intelligence level in terms of his position within a certain age or grade group is based on the arithmetic mean and the standard deviation. Most frequently called standard scores, these measures have advantages over such relative indications of placement as percentile scores.

The 1937 edition of the *Stanford-Binet Intelligence Scale* provided a table for translating intelligence quotients into standard scores.[21] For the 1960 edition, however, the authors stated that standard-score units of deviation were incorporated into the revised IQ tables provided with the scale and that the IQs obtained from their use have a mean of 100 and a standard deviation of 16.[22] Methods of computing and interpreting standard scores are presented in Chapter 14.

7. MAJOR CHARACTERISTICS OF THE INTELLIGENCE QUOTIENT

It is important for the teacher to know more about the intelligence quotient in at least two respects if he is to make effective use of mental test results in the classroom. First, he should know how the IQ is distributed among people in general. Second, he should know enough about two areas in which there is disagreement about the IQ to take the different points of view into consideration appropriately.

Distribution of the Intelligence Quotient

The many reports of the distribution of intelligence show that no single pattern of the distribution of intellectual ability can be expected to apply widely to different school situations. Typical groups of school children are not unselected, as might be supposed, but have been affected variously in their composition by many selective factors.

Intelligence can be conceived of both in terms of some such measure as the IQ and in terms of descriptions of the types of performance possible for persons of different intelligence levels. A distribution of intelligence quotients for an unselected group of children and the general descriptive terms used for different levels are presented here as an indication of the manner in which this measure of brightness is distributed.

Table 5 shows the distribution of intelligence quotients for a normal population. Figure 2 presents the same data graphically. It will be noted that about 45 percent of the population fall within ten IQ points of the average IQ of 100. On the average, one person in each 100 is in the genius

[21] Lewis M. Terman and Maud A. Merrill, *Measuring Intelligence*. Houghton Mifflin Co., Boston, 1937. p. 42.
[22] Lewis M. Terman and Maud A. Merrill, *Stanford-Binet Intelligence Scale: Manual for the Third Revision*, Form L-M. Houghton Mifflin Co., Boston, 1960. p. 27-28.

TABLE 5

Distribution of Intelligence Quotients in a Normal Population [23]

Classification	IQ	Percentages of All Persons
Near genius or genius	140 and above	1
Very superior	130-139	2.5
Superior	120-129	8
Above average	110-119	16
Normal or average	90-109	45
Below average	80-89	16
Dull or borderline	70-79	8
Feeble-minded: moron	60-69	2.5
imbecile, idiot	59 and below	1

or near-genius class and one person in each 100 is in the very low feeble-minded group. About 10 to 12 percent of the total may be considered as distinctly superior and 10 to 12 percent as distinctly inferior. Persons at the highest level of feeble-mindedness, i.e., morons, are not uncommon in the lower grades of the school.

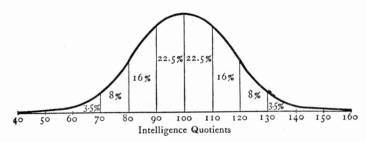

FIGURE 2. Percentages of Persons in a Normal Population at Different
Levels of Intelligence

Controversies about the Intelligence Quotient

Two major problem areas involve the intelligence quotient in such a way that a teacher using the IQ in the guidance of his pupils must either recognize them and face their implications in one way or another or deny their existence. The first issue, dealing with the constancy of the IQ, refers to the tendency of a person's intelligence quotient to vary only in minor degree or, contrariwise, in major degree over a period of some years. The other, and newer, issue deals with whether or not children from the lower

[23] Adapted from Terman and Merrill, *Measuring Intelligence, op. cit.* p. 38-41.

socioeconomic classes attain lower IQs than their abilities warrant as a result of their environmental handicaps.

Constancy of the IQ. A heated controversy over the constancy of the intelligence quotient has been waged during the last twenty-five years. Although it has long been recognized that the IQ obtained by the use of the best modern tests fluctuates within limits because the tests are not perfectly reliable, and that major environmental changes for an individual may well be reflected in his IQ, rather startling evidence was presented nearly thirty years ago [24] to show average gains of twenty IQ points for 600 children who had attended preschool for four years. Later and more startling evidence [25] showed that children of dull parentage who were placed in foster homes shortly after birth had mean intelligence quotients of 116 when they were tested a few years later. These and other studies supported the belief that the intelligence quotient is significantly influenced by very favorable environments.

Although such findings have not been uniformly obtained by experimenters,[26] they are supported by other types of experimental evidence revealing at least the possibility of marked changes in intelligence quotients as the result of improved environments.[27] Stoddard summed up the evidence on inconstancy of the IQ [28] and pointed out Binet's expression of the belief [29] that the IQ is subject to improvement under desirable conditions of stimulation.

The answer to this question may never be known for certain. In fact, the IQ itself is under attack and may in time be replaced by a more satisfactory measure. However, the majority of school children do not undergo such radical changes of environment during their school careers that the problem is of great practical significance to most teachers. Yet, as there are questions concerning motivation, emotional adjustment, optimum placement of pupils, and many others that bear significantly upon pupil performances not only on intelligence tests but also on achievement tests

---

[24] Beth L. Wellman, "The Effect of Pre-School Attendance on the IQ." *Journal of Experimental Education,* 1:48-69; September 1932.

[25] Harold M. Skeels, "Mental Development of Children in Foster Homes." *Journal of Consulting Psychology,* 2:33-43; March-April 1938.

[26] Florence L. Goodenough and Katharine M. Maurer, "The Mental Development of Nursery-School Children Compared with That of Non-Nursery-School Children." *Intelligence: Its Nature and Nurture,* Thirty-Ninth Yearbook of the National Society for the Study of Education, Part II. Public School Publishing Co., Bloomington, Ill., 1940. p. 161-78.

[27] Percival M. Symonds, "Psychological Tests and Their Uses: Review and Preview." *Review of Educational Research,* 8:217-20; June 1938.

[28] George D. Stoddard, "The IQ: Its Ups and Downs." *Educational Record,* 20:44-57; Supplement No. 12; January 1939.

[29] Alfred Binet, *Les Idées Modernes sur les Enfants.* Ernest Flammarion, Paris, 1909. p. 146.

and in scholarship, the teacher should at least be aware of this controversial issue and some of its implications.

Social class and the IQ. Results from group intelligence tests have
tended to show that children from certain socioeconomic groups attain
higher mean scores than do children from other, and lower, socioeconomic
groups. For example, rural children typically score lower than urban
children, southern white pupils regularly score lower than northern white
pupils, and children from working-class homes attain lower average scores
than do those from homes at the professional and managerial levels.

Warner, Meeker, and Eells [30] showed that the cultural patterns of
homes at different socioeconomic levels differ greatly. Davis, Havighurst,
and others [31] obtained evidence to show that standard intelligence tests
are not "culture fair" but that they reflect the cultural biases of the upper-
middle-class test constructors. Davis [32] indicated that differences of 8 to 12
IQ points for children from six to ten years of age and as high as 20 to 23
IQ points for children fourteen years of age between low and high socioeconomic groups reflect the cultural bias of the tests. He stated that
culturally fair tests used experimentally show pupils of low and high
socioeconomic status to be closely similar in "innate intelligence" or "real
intelligence."

These findings concerning the influence of culture, or home environment,
on the IQ as obtained from standard intelligence tests appear not to be
in disharmony with the evidence concerning the inconstancy of the IQ.
Although the implications of the findings are still not clear, intelligence
quotients doubtless warrant careful consideration in terms of the socioeconomic factors discussed in Chapter 4. The *Davis-Eells Games* test,
illustrated and discussed in a foregoing section of this chapter, is one
direct outgrowth of the issue.

The Intelligence Quotient and the Future

It is apparent from the above discussion that the intelligence quotient
is far from a perfect measure of brightness. Its constancy seems to be
somewhat in question. The influence of socioeconomic backgrounds may
be significant. These weaknesses and others of a more technical nature
raise logical questions concerning its continued and final acceptance as the
best measure of brightness, although it is still one of the most satisfactory

---

[30] W. Lloyd Warner, Marchia Meeker, and Kenneth Eells, *Social Class in America.*
Science Research Associates, Inc., Chicago, 1949.

[31] *Ibid.* p. 26.

[32] Allison Davis, "Socio-Economic Influences on Learning." *Phi Delta Kappan,* 32:253-
56; January 1951.

measures from which to predict success in school and is highly useful in pupil guidance.

Although the teacher should certainly understand the nature and proper uses of the IQ, he should also have some realization of its limitations, technical though they may be, and should be alert to the alternative methods for designating levels of intelligence which have been developed and which may be evolved in the future. Several of the less technical alternative methods of interpreting mental test results are presented in a foregoing section of this chapter.

8. CLASSROOM USES OF MENTAL ABILITY TESTS

Despite the controversial nature of the most widely used measure of mental ability, as pointed out above, intelligence quotients, mental ages, and percentile ranks and standard scores when applied to mental test results are all important tools of enlightened teaching procedure. They are likely to remain so until improved tools for mental testing or better procedures for interpreting mental test results are developed.

During the early years of the intelligence testing movement the classroom teacher was given little part in the testing procedures and frequently was even denied access to the results. However, as teachers have become more conversant with intelligence testing techniques and the use of results, they have been given more responsibility in the administration and scoring of group tests and in the use of results from group and also individual intelligence tests.

On the whole intelligence tests seem secure in the place they now hold as supporting tools for achievement tests. There are, however, a few dangers attached to their careless or indiscriminate use which the teacher and administrator should guard against. The more important of these dangers are probably social in their character. Problems may arise through giving publicity to the results of intelligence testing. In the long run, damage may be done by using intelligence test results for any other than local school purposes and they probably should be used cautiously for any purpose. The safest practice probably is to restrict information concerning results of intelligence testing to responsible school officers and teachers in the main, to make such information available to parents only in occasional and well-considered instances where need arises, and in most instances to withhold such information from pupils themselves. In no case does it seem justifiable to make intelligence quotients of individual pupils known to any persons other than their teachers and school officers, their parents, and themselves. This seems to represent the position taken by members of a symposium on use of test results in their consideration of intelligence tests.[33]

As tests of general intelligence, of aptitude and readiness, of group factors of intelligence, and of performance differ widely in type, mode of use, and nature of the resulting scores, it is inevitable that the situations in which they are most appropriately used must also differ. Some of these situations are commented upon here.

General Mental Ability Tests

There is wide use for the results of general intelligence tests in the classroom. Results from group tests must be interpreted cautiously, however, for these indirect measures of adaptability or of ability to learn are not always highly reliable. Results that may safely be used for group interpretations may well be too unreliable for individual pupil interpretations. The best safeguard is to administer group tests frequently—perhaps every two or three years—during the school career of the pupil and to judge pupil intelligence more in terms of average intelligence quotients than in terms of the results from any one test, even the most recent, alone. For pupils who have very low or very high IQs and for pupils who are poorly adjusted to school, the administration of an individual intelligence test by a school psychologist is desirable. It is for the maladjusted, dull or borderline, and superior pupils that group test results are most likely to be unreliable. Furthermore, it is for pupils of these types that the attainment of optimum adjustment in the school is the most difficult. Hence, the significance of results from individual intelligence tests in such cases is great.

Individual diagnosis. The general intelligence test may prove especially valuable to the classroom teacher in assisting him to solve problems relating to the unusual child. If a pupil is unusually bright, troublesome, dull, or in some other way quite out of the ordinary, the teacher may wish to know whether his typical responses are in line with his general ability, and whether or not the judgments of his former teachers and supervisors are correct. Intelligence tests will give information not obtainable in any other way.

The intelligence test, when given to an entire group, frequently uncovers a bright child who has been content to go on with the group without revealing his real ability or a dull child who has made excellent use of his limited abilities. In any case, the intelligence test will assist both in ex-

[33] Robert L. Ebel and others, "Eight Critical Questions about the Use of Tests in Education." *Education,* 81:67-99; October 1960.

plaining difficult cases and in revealing unsuspected general strengths and weaknesses.

Educational guidance. The use of general intelligence test results for educational guidance is similar to, but goes far beyond, their use for individual pupil diagnosis. Pupils can be much more effectively advised in their selection of courses and of curricula if information is available concerning their intellectual levels. Pupils may be better qualified for certain types of courses or curricula than for others, in terms of their levels of intelligence.

Vocational guidance. The dividing line between educational and vocational guidance cannot be clearly drawn, for the first merges gradually into the second. Whereas educational guidance is of primary concern in the elementary school, even there it has its vocational implications. Vocational aspects of guidance assume an increasingly prominent position as the pupil progresses through junior and senior high school and in many instances nears the end of his school career. Although general intelligence test results can be used with less confidence for vocational than for educational guidance, the information they furnish concerning the general intellectual abilities of pupils is of great value in vocational counseling.

Class analysis and diagnosis. Viewed from the standpoint of the teacher, achievement tests and intelligence tests are supplementary devices. After the teacher has given achievement tests and compared his class with the norms in a given subject, he is still in danger of making false assumptions about the significance of these results unless he has available further information such as is furnished by general intelligence tests. In avoiding this danger, he has a need for some means of determining approximately the intellectual ability of the class. General intelligence tests meet this need. By giving one or more such tests, the teacher can determine with a fair degree of accuracy whether his class is up to normal expectation in ability to do satisfactory schoolwork.

Finally, the bifactor or scholastic aptitude types of tests, most often supplying a verbal and a nonverbal score, doubtless distinguish two major factors of ability at any level from the intermediate grades to the college years. Boys regularly attain higher mean scores on the nonverbal sections than do girls, whereas the sex difference is typically in the opposite direction for verbal scores. Overlaps between the sexes are very great, however, so that many girls score far above the mean for boys on the nonverbal tests and many boys surpass the mean for girls on the verbal tests by a wide margin. The diagnostic significance of these part scores seems sufficiently well established to warrant their use in individual pupil guidance when supporting evidence of other types is at hand.

Tests of Special Mental Abilities

Much of what has been said concerning the uses of general intelligence tests applies also to aptitude and readiness tests. However, the specific nature of these types of tests limits their significance to certain uses that are correctly made of general intelligence tests.

Aptitude tests are valuable for educational and vocational guidance. However, they have minor significance for class analysis because they measure such specific abilities that individual pupil characteristics assume much greater importance than do characteristics of the class as a whole. Aptitude tests are primarily suited for use with pupils of the junior-high-school or higher levels, for the general and nonspecialized type of course in the elementary school is less well adapted to aptitude testing than are the more specialized courses of the high school and the college.

Readiness tests are useful for individual pupil guidance, particularly in the primary and lower elementary grades. Such tests also have specific rather than general significance, so that the results from their use should be interpreted for the pupil as an individual rather than on the basis of the class group.

Multifactor Tests of Mental Abilities

The group-factor tests, lying perhaps midway between general intelligence and aptitude tests in specificity, have uses similar to those outlined above. As these instruments have been developed comparatively recently, scores resulting from their use should be interpreted with caution and primarily by educational and vocational counselors until their validities for various purposes have become well established.

Multifactor tests of primary mental abilities and differential aptitudes have not yet resulted in a clear-cut and generally accepted list of ability factors, nor have the validities of the various part scores been established to the point where their predictive significance is well known. Somewhat more widely available for the high-school than for the intermediate-grade levels, their major uses appear to be in the areas of vocational and educational guidance. It seems desirable at the present time to use results from multifactor tests for pupil guidance only in conjunction with other data of well-established validity.

Performance Tests of Mental Ability

Performance tests are less frequently a tool of the classroom teacher than of the educational or vocational counselor. Pupils who have visual, language, or physical handicaps that preclude reliable testing of their abilities by group intelligence tests should be tested by individual intelligence scales or performance tests. The uses of results from performance tests do not differ significantly from the uses of group intelligence test results except that performance tests furnish less accurate measures of general intelligence than do group and individual intelligence tests and therefore should be employed with caution.

SUGGESTED ACTIVITIES

1. Obtain intelligence quotients for the three children whose chronological and mental ages are given below and compare them in brightness with one another and with people in general.

    Tom   CA = 9-2;   MA = 8-3
    Dick   CA = 9-2;   MA = 9-0
    Harry CA = 9-2;   MA = 11-0

2. Determine the mental ages of the three pupils whose chronological ages and intelligence quotients are given below and discuss the implications of their mental levels for selection of high-school programs.

    Sally CA = 12-6;   IQ = 80
    Irene CA = 12-6;   IQ = 100
    Mary   CA = 12-6;   IQ = 120

TOPICS FOR DISCUSSION

1. Indicate several of the ways in which intelligence has been defined or described. Which type of definition is most acceptable to you?
2. What is the nature of the distinction between intelligence tests and scholastic aptitude tests?
3. How is general mental ability measured by the use of individual intelligence scales? Group intelligence tests?
4. What is the distinction between aptitude tests and readiness tests?
5. What is the significance of multifactor tests of mental abilities?
6. For what purposes are performance tests of mental ability and aptitude ordinarily used?
7. How do mental ages and intelligence quotients differ as measures of general mental ability? In what different ways are they used?
8. How do quotient-type and deviation-type intelligence quotients differ?
9. Discuss the use of percentile scores and standard scores for the interpretation of mental ability test results.
10. Does a person's intelligence quotient remain constant throughout his life? Give evidence to support your answer.

11. What might a culturally fair intelligence test accomplish that standard intelligence tests do not accomplish?
12. How is intelligence distributed among the population as a whole?
13. List and discuss some of the ways in which mental ability test results are useful in the classroom.
14. Under what conditions, if any, do you think classroom teachers should be responsible for giving and scoring intelligence tests?

SELECTED REFERENCES

ANASTASI, ANNE. *Psychological Testing.* Second edition. New York: Macmillan Co., 1961. Parts 1-3.

BINGHAM, WALTER V. *Aptitudes and Aptitude Testing.* New York: Harper and Brothers, 1937.

BLAIR, GLENN M., AND JONES, R. STEWART. "Readiness." *Encyclopedia of Educational Research.* Third edition. New York: Macmillan Co., 1960. p. 1081-86.

BUROS, OSCAR K., editor. *The Fifth Mental Measurements Yearbook.* Highland Park, N. J.: Gryphon Press, 1959. p. 415-561, 667-721.

BUROS, OSCAR K., editor. *The Fourth Mental Measurements Yearbook.* Highland Park, N. J.: Gryphon Press, 1953. p. 371-483.

BUROS, OSCAR K., editor. *The Third Mental Measurements Yearbook.* New Brunswick, N. J.: Rutgers University Press, 1949. p. 293-399, 627-750.

COLLEGE ENTRANCE EXAMINATION BOARD. *A Description of the College Board Scholastic Aptitude Test.* Princeton, N. J.: The Board, 1958.

CRONBACH, LEE J. *Essentials of Psychological Testing.* Second edition. New York: Harper and Brothers, 1960. Chapters 7-10.

DeHAAN, ROBERT F., AND KOUGH, JACK. *Identifying Students with Special Needs.* Teacher's Guidance Handbook, Vol. I, Secondary School Edition. Chicago: Science Research Associates, Inc., 1956. Section 2.

DOPPELT, JEROME E. "Progress in the Measurement of Mental Abilities." *Educational and Psychological Measurement,* 14:261-64; Summer 1954.

EBEL, ROBERT L., AND OTHERS. "Eight Critical Questions about the Use of Tests." *Education,* 81:67-99; October 1960.

FREEMAN, FRANK N. *Mental Tests: Their History, Principles and Applications.* Revised edition. Boston: Houghton Mifflin Co., 1939. Chapters 1-7, 9-11, 13-16.

FREEMAN, FRANK S. *Theory and Practice of Psychological Testing.* Revised edition. New York: Henry Holt and Co., 1955. Chapters 3-13.

FROEHLICH, CLIFFORD P., AND HOYT, KENNETH B. *Guidance Testing.* Chicago: Science Research Associates, Inc., 1959. Chapters 5-6.

GERBERICH, J. RAYMOND. "How Is Intelligence Tested?" *NEA Journal,* 50:38-39; January 1961.

GOODENOUGH, FLORENCE L. *Mental Testing: Its History, Principles, and Applications.* New York: Rinehart and Co., Inc., 1949. Chapters 20-23, 29.

GREENE, EDWARD B. *Measurements of Human Behavior.* Revised edition. New York: Odyssey Press, 1952. Chapters 5-6, 8-11.

GREENE, HARRY A., JORGENSEN, ALBERT N., AND GERBERICH, J. RAYMOND. *Measurement and Evaluation in the Elementary School.* Second edition. New York: Longmans, Green and Co., 1953. Chapter 10.

GREENE, HARRY A., JORGENSEN, ALBERT N., AND GERBERICH, J. RAYMOND. *Measurement and Evaluation in the Secondary School.* Second edition. New York: Longmans, Green and Co., 1954. Chapter 10.

HARRIS, CHESTER W. "Intelligence." *Encyclopedia of Educational Research.* Third edition. New York: Macmillan Co., 1960. p. 715-18.

HAVIGHURST, ROBERT J. "Using the IQ Wisely." *NEA Journal,* 40:540-41; November 1951.

HOLZINGER, KARL J. "Factor Analysis." *Encyclopedia of Educational Research.* Revised edition. New York: Macmillan Co., 1950. p. 429-33.

HULL, CLARK L. *Aptitude Testing.* Yonkers, N. Y.: World Book Co., 1928.

HUMPHREYS, LLOYD G., AND BOYNTON, PAUL L. "Intelligence and Intelligence Tests." *Encyclopedia of Educational Research.* Revised edition. New York: Macmillan Co., 1950. p. 600-12.

KOUGH, JACK, AND DEHAAN, ROBERT F. *Identifying Children with Special Needs.* Teacher's Guidance Handbook, Vol. I, Elementary School Edition. Chicago: Science Research Associates, Inc., 1955. Section 2.

LINDQUIST, E. F., AND MCCARREL, TED. *ACT: The American College Testing Program.* Iowa City, Iowa: Measurement Research Center, Inc., 1959.

MICHAEL, WILLIAM B. "Aptitudes." *Encyclopedia of Educational Research.* Third edition. New York: Macmillan Co., 1960. p. 59-63.

MURSELL, JAMES L. *Psychological Testing.* Second edition. New York: Longmans, Green and Co., 1949. Chapters 3-7, 9-10.

STODDARD, GEORGE D. *The Meaning of Intelligence.* New York: Macmillan Co., 1943. Chapters 1, 11-12, 15-16.

SUPER, DONALD E. *Appraising Vocational Fitness by Means of Psychological Tests.* New York: Harper and Brothers, 1949. Chapters 4, 6, 8-11, 15.

TERMAN, LEWIS M., AND MERRILL, MAUD A. *Stanford-Binet Intelligence Scale: Manual for the Third Revision.* Boston: Houghton Mifflin Co., 1960.

7

PERSONALITY INVENTORIES AND TECHNIQUES

The following aspects of personality and its measurement are discussed in this chapter:

A. Nature of personality.
B. Methods of personality measurement.
C. Nature and measurement of attitudes.
D. Nature and measurement of interests.
E. Nature and measurement of adjustments.
F. Measurement of total personality.
G. Classroom uses of personality test results.

Teachers are expected to understand their pupils, and through this understanding to increase the efficiency of their teaching. The modern teacher should have a knowledge of child or adolescent psychology and the nature of individual differences in intelligence, achievement, and other important aspects of the pupil and of his behavior. Teachers have sometimes given too little attention to the personality aspects of the pupil, preferring to work with the more readily observable and more tangible behaviors such as those treated in the chapters on intelligence and achievement testing. In any event, attention is increasingly being directed toward the more effective adjustment of the pupil to life. Thus, efficient teaching demands much more than a chance and casual acquaintance with personality measurement procedures.

Cronbach differentiated between procedures used in personality measurement and those employed in mental ability testing in a manner that is worth noting here.[1] His distinction that personality inventories attempt to measure typical or habitual forms of behavior but that mental ability tests seek to measure the maximum performance of which pupils are capable is borne out in the discussion of this chapter and also in the treatment of mental ability tests in Chapter 6.

1. PERSONALITY AND ITS MEASUREMENT

For centuries, man has been aware of differences among individuals and has made attempts to classify human beings according to types of personality. However, the concept of personality types represented in the early attempts at classification and even in the later impressionistic theories based on physiognomy, glandular secretions, and even body build have largely been abandoned. Present-day personality testers find such type theories inconsistent with the normal distribution that has been found to apply to many personality traits as well as to characteristics of mental ability and achievement.

If personality characteristics are the result in significant degree of the environment, which seems a justifiable conclusion, it is important for the teacher to be alert to the influence of the school in shaping the personality of the child as well as to its potentialities for correcting the maladjustments that pupils may have acquired prior to school entrance. It is also important for the teacher to be familiar with the nature of personality and modern methods of measuring it.

Nature of Personality

Personality is the most inclusive term that can be used in the discussion of human behavior. Psychologists are not in complete agreement concerning the meaning of the term, but they recognize that personality describes more fundamental types of human behavior than the surface evidences by which the man on the street evaluates it. In general, psychological definitions of personality explain what personality is in terms of the types of human behavior thought to contribute to it. Psychologists agree roughly upon these components of personality, but they usually resort to indirect methods of defining the term.

Shaffer and Shoben defined personality of an individual as "his persistent tendencies to make certain qualities and kinds of adjustment." [2] Traxler

---

[1] Lee J. Cronbach, *Essentials of Psychological Testing*, Second edition. Harper and Brothers, New York, 1960. p. 29-32.

[2] Laurance F. Shaffer and Edward J. Shoben, Jr., *The Psychology of Adjustment*, Second edition. Houghton Mifflin Co., Boston, 1956. p. 310.

Measurement and Evaluation in the Modern School

considered the term to include the "sum total of an individual's behavior in social situations." [3] These statements perhaps represent the most meaningful view of personality for teachers and other persons who are not technical workers in the field of personality study. It should be kept in mind that the behavior of the individual is controlled by his personality and at the same time furnishes the evidence by which his personality can in part be evaluated.

Psychologists divide personality into many areas for study. However, the aspects of personality useful to the teacher can well be listed under fewer headings, although any classification must be largely arbitrary. The phases treated in this chapter are attitudes, interests, adjustment, and total personality. It is believed that these are the areas of greatest present significance to the teacher.

Although the preceding statements include intellectual and physical traits as components of personality, these traits are not generally considered when personality measurement is undertaken. Consequently, although the psychology of personality rightly deals with the contributions of intellectual and physical traits to an individual's development, these areas are not of direct concern here.

Techniques of Personality Measurement

Personality is measured by several different types of approaches. Among those most commonly used are (1) personal reports, (2) rating scales, (3) observational methods, and (4) free association methods. Although all of them can be used by an able classroom teacher, it is probable that personal reports and observation of behavior are the methods most practicable and useful in the typical classroom. Each of these methods is discussed briefly in this section of the chapter. In the later sections various methods of measurement are discussed in terms of their uses for the evaluation of attitudes, interests, emotional adjustment, and total personality.

Personal reports. The personal-report method makes use of what are variously called scales, questionnaires, blanks, and structured inventories. The responses are given, or the instruments are filled out, by the pupils themselves. As many of the items on these instruments request highly personal responses, the personal-report method of measuring personality suffers from the fact that pupils sometimes reply as they think they should reply rather than as they truly react to the various items. Most persons are hesitant in revealing their inner personalities to other persons freely.

[3] Arthur E. Traxler, *Techniques of Guidance: Tests, Records, and Counseling in a Guidance Program,* Revised edition. Harper and Brothers, New York, 1957. p. 102.

In fact, the customs of civilized society place something of a premium upon the ability to hide or disguise emotions, likes and dislikes, attitudes, and other reactions in many situations. Therefore, it is not surprising that pupils sometimes fail to answer personality inventory items truthfully. Despite this major weakness, personal-report instruments for the measurement of personality are usually thought to be of considerable value in the classroom.

Rating scales. Rating scales are widely used in the evaluation of pupil personality. In this procedure, the teacher or some other person intimately acquainted with the pupils rates them on personality traits in terms of the manner in which the individuals have impressed the rater. Obviously, the judges should know intimately the pupils they are rating. Most rating methods suffer in accuracy because some raters tend to be too lenient whereas others are too critical. They are least accurate for use with intangible traits, upon which observers usually vary rather widely in their evaluations.

Widely used among rating techniques are the graphic rating scale and variations of that form. In this procedure, the judge places a check mark at a certain position on a line to indicate his evaluation of the person he is rating. The line may be divided into five (or some other number of) sections designated superior, good, average, poor, and inferior, or meaning may be given to positions on the scale by other and more definitely descriptive terms. Again, there may be designations at occasional intervals beneath the line to indicate specifically for each trait varying evidences of its possession by the person being rated.

Observational methods. Several different methods based on the observation of individual pupil behavior have been suggested and successfully applied. They all probably require an ability that few teachers have but most can acquire. Untrained teachers make use of their own interpretations of events they observe, whereas objectivity is attained only by a rather rigid account of what actually occurred. The characteristics of objective observational methods, highly useful in the study of pupil personality, make it inadvisable for inexperienced teachers to attempt to make more than experimental use of them until some experience in observation has been acquired.

The two common observational procedures most applicable in the school are (1) directed observation and (2) the anecdotal method. The first, because the observation is directed toward a particular pupil or pupil group under specified conditions, is a laboratory rather than a classroom procedure. Some of the projective techniques also involve use of directed observation. The second, however, uses the results from observations of pupil behavior made at any time, and therefore is definitely a classroom method of evaluation.

Free-association methods. Two association methods are widely used in the study of personality: (1) verbal association techniques, and (2) visual stimulus techniques. Although word association methods were in use long before modern projective methods evolved, both types are now known as projective techniques.

Verbal associations are established when the person to whom a word is spoken responds with the first word that enters his mind. Other free-association procedures are based on completions given to incomplete sentences and to partly told stories.

The best-known visual stimulus methods are based on free responses to inkblots and pictures. In these situations the subject is to respond by telling what he is reminded of or what he sees in each. Both the nature of the responses and the manner in which they are given furnish considerable evidence to the experienced psychologist on which to base inferences concerning emotional disturbances in the subject.

2. MEASUREMENT OF ATTITUDES

Attitude formation is a process to which not only the school but also the home, religious and other groups, and such agencies as the movie, radio, and television contribute. Furthermore, lists of course objectives in many subject areas commonly include attitudes and beliefs the school seeks to develop or modify in pupils. Thus, as is pointed out in Chapter 1, attitudes are properly considered to be results of instruction, although not alone of school instruction, and also of informal and unplanned situations where learning occurs. Consequently, attitudes are dealt with briefly both in this chapter and in several other chapters where measurement in subject areas is under consideration.

Nature of Attitudes

Thurstone and Chave defined an attitude as "the sum total of a man's inclinations and feelings, prejudice or bias, preconceived notions, ideas, fears, threats and convictions about any specific topic." [4] An attitude is a state of readiness that exerts a directive, and sometimes a compulsive, influence upon an individual's behavior. Attitudes may be either general or specific. For example, a person who has a general attitude of liberalism may behave in a highly conservative manner in a particular situation in

[4] L. L. Thurstone and E. J. Chave, *The Measurement of Attitude.* University of Chicago Press, Chicago, 1929. p. 6-7.

which his personal welfare is threatened. An attitude of conservatism is general, but an attitude toward a certain person is specific.

Attitude Scales

The types of personal reports used in attitude measurement are commonly referred to as attitude scales. Although the interview technique, briefly treated in Chapter 12, can be used for this purpose, the teacher ordinarily has more use for attitude scales. The attention given to attitude measurement here is consequently restricted to these personal-report instruments.

Although attitudes are most often conceived as operating in those areas of human knowledge where controversial issues are prominent, they are by no means restricted to such areas. Attitudes are sometimes based on false or incomplete evidence and on wishful thinking. Measurement of attitudes is influenced by the absence of correct or right answers, such as are commonly available in the measurement of such tangible outcomes of learning as knowledges and certain skills. Three types are probably measured more often than others—social attitudes, scientific attitudes, and health attitudes.

The first two of these are treated briefly in Chapters 18 and 19, devoted to the sciences and social studies, so major distinctions only are made at this point. Scientific attitudes are probably most obviously represented in superstitions and closely similar unfounded beliefs. Social attitudes, probably more frequently measured and certainly more widely different in type, can be represented here by attitudes toward censorship and capital punishment, toward the movies and television, and toward school subjects and occupations.

Measurement of attitudes in the third area mentioned above is illustrated by the accompanying excerpt from the *Byrd Health Attitude Scale*.

EXCERPT FROM *Byrd Health Attitude Scale* [5]

13. Children should be allowed to stay up as late as they please.

   Strongly agree[1]   Agree[2]   Undecided[3]   Disagree[4]   Strongly disagree[5]

14. People should be vaccinated for smallpox about every seven years.

   Strongly agree[5]   Agree[4]   Undecided[3]   Disagree[2]   Strongly disagree[1]

15. Children should be allowed to attend the "second" (late) show.

   Strongly agree[1]   Agree[2]   Undecided[3]   Disagree[4]   Strongly disagree[5]

[5] Oliver E. Byrd, *Byrd Health Attitude Scale*. Stanford University Press, Stanford, Calif., 1940.

The scaled-choice items of the illustration allow the pupil to express his beliefs on a five-point scale ranging from strongly agree to strongly disagree. This item type finds wide use in the measurement of attitudes and certain other aspects of personality.

Another and somewhat broader scale for measuring attitudes is also represented here by an excerpt. The *Survey of Attitudes and Beliefs,* asking for responses of agree, uncertain, or disagree on scaled-choice items, provides scores on attitudes toward society, toward education and work, and toward sex, marriage, and family with separate norms for high-school boys and girls.

EXCERPT FROM *Survey of Attitudes and Beliefs* [6]

		A	U	D
76.	Going to school too much makes a person discontented with the rest of the world..	⊙	⊙	⊙
77.	A person should not be compelled to go to high school................	⊙	⊙	⊙
78.	Criticism is usually hard for people to take..........................	⊙	⊙	⊙
79.	Most things a person learns in school help him to meet the problems he encounters when out of school...	⊙	⊙	⊙
80.	For the most part life is composed of a series of disappointments.........	⊙	⊙	⊙
81.	A person should work on a job instead of going to high school for four years..	⊙	⊙	⊙

3. MEASUREMENT OF INTERESTS

Interests are similar to attitudes not only in their nature, as is indicated below, but also in the manner of their formation and the procedures used in their measurement. Interests appear in lists of instructional objectives in many subject areas for the guidance of classroom teachers, but they are influenced by widely varying types of informal experiences as well as by classroom instruction. Consequently, the measurement of interests, as well as of attitudes, receives brief attention in this chapter and occasional attention as seems appropriate in the subject chapters of Part 5.

Nature of Interests

Interests are most often classified today in terms of the objects and activities from which the individual obtains satisfaction.[7] Thus, a person is interested in football but cares very little for tennis, or he is interested in music but is not interested in the drama. It is in this nontechnical

[6] Leslie W. Nelson, *Survey of Attitudes and Beliefs.* Science Research Associates, Inc., Chicago, 1954.

[7] Douglas Fryer, *The Measurement of Interests.* Henry Holt and Co., New York, 1931. p. 15.

ıanner of considering interests that measurement in this field can be most
.irectly meaningful for the classroom teacher.

ınterest Inventories

Interests are subject to measurement by the use of standardized inven-
ories, informal check lists, and interviews. The first two, of the personal-
eport variety, are dealt with briefly here, but the interview is given con-
ideration in Chapter 12. Standardized interest inventories are available
ʼrimarily for the measurement of vocational interests, but the simpler,
eacher-constructed check lists are usually designed for measuring avoca-
ional and other recreational interests.

Probably the best-known measuring instrument for vocational interests
s the *Strong Vocational Interest Blank.* This inventory is not intended for
ıse below the senior-high-school and college levels because of the transitory
ıature of interests in vocations at lower age levels. In common with many
·ther interest inventories, the Strong blank has separate forms for men
ınd women in order to provide for the types of sex differences usually
·ound to exist in interests.

Persons taking the Strong blank are asked to respond to items dealing
vith the following: (1) occupations, (2) school subjects, (3) amusements,
(4) activities, (5) peculiarities of people, (6) order of preference of activ-
·ties, (7) comparison of interest between two items, and (8) rating of
ʼresent abilities and characteristics. They designate their interests on a
:hree-point scale for most of the items to indicate their degree of liking.
The samples of the accompanying illustration show the nature of differ-
ɔnces in the men's and women's occupations items, the identical nature of
:tems on present abilities and characteristics in the men's and women's
·orms, and two of the methods of responding to the items.

The second excerpt used here to illustrate techniques of vocational
interest measurement is one from the *Picture Interest Inventory.* In each
group of three pictures, the pupil is asked to mark the two showing activities he most likes (L) and most dislikes (D), regardless of whether he
very positively likes or dislikes any of the three activities represented.
This excerpt is of the forced-choice variety used in several other interest
and adjustment inventories also. Furthermore, it reduces the emphasis
on reading ability to zero.

Pupil avocational interests in objects and activities are so easy to determine that classroom teachers can readily devise very informal procedures
or slightly more formal check lists for this type of measurement. Among
the fields in which such methods are appropriate, and for which educational journals often suggest promising techniques, are reading interests in

EXCERPTS FROM *Strong Vocational Interest Blanks* [8]

Occupations. Indicate after each occupation listed below whether you would like that kind of work or not. Disregard considerations of salary, social standing, future advancement, etc. Consider only whether or not you would like to do what is involved in the occupation. You are not asked if you would take up the occupation permanently, but merely whether or not you would enjoy that kind of work, regardless of any necessary skills, abilities, or training which you may or may not possess.

Draw a circle around L if you like that kind of work

Draw a circle around I if you are indifferent to that kind of work

Draw a circle around D if you dislike that kind of work

Work rapidly. Your first impressions are desired here. Answer all the items. Many of the seemingly trivial and irrelevant items are very useful in diagnosing your real attitude.

1 Actor (not movie)	L	I	D		1 Actress (movie)	L	I	D
2 Advertiser	L	I	D		2 Actress (stage)	L	I	D
3 Architect	L	I	D		3 Accountant	L	I	D
4 Army Officer	L	I	D		4 Advertiser	L	I	D
5 Artist	L	I	D					
					5 Architect	L	I	D
6 Astronomer	L	I	D		6 Artist	L	I	D
7 Athletic Director	L	I	D		7 Artist's Model	L	I	D
8 Auctioneer	L	I	D		8 Athletic Director	L	I	D

Rating of Present Abilities and Characteristics. Indicate below what kind of a person you are right now and what you have done. Check in the first column ("Yes") if the item really describes you, in the third column ("No") if the item does not describe you, and in the second column (?) if you are not sure. (Be frank in pointing out your weak points, for selection of a vocation must be made in terms of them as well as your strong points.)

	YES	?	NO
342 Usually start activities of my group	( )	( )	( )
343 Usually drive myself steadily (do not work by fits and starts)	( )	( )	( )
344 Win friends easily	( )	( )	( )
345 Usually get other people to do what I want done	( )	( )	( )

[8] Edward K. Strong, Jr., (1) *Vocational Interest Blank for Men*, Revised, and (2) *Vocational Interest Blank for Women*. Stanford University Press, Stanford, Calif., 1938 and 1933.

books, magazines, and newspapers, interests in the movies, radio, and TV, recreational interests, and interests in school subjects. The teacher can have the pupils write about their interests or list them without discussion.

EXCERPT FROM *Picture Interest Inventory* [9]

Again, he can prepare and distribute to the pupils a list of books, of magazines, of recreational activities, or of any one of a number of other types of objects and activities and then ask the pupils to check those in which they are interested. In any of these procedures, it is wise to limit the investigation of interests to one area rather than to attempt a complete inventory of pupil interests at one time.

The accompanying excerpt from *"What I Like To Do,"* an interest inventory for children, gives two sample items each from the art, active

[9] Kurt P. Weingarten, *Picture Interest Inventory*, Grades 7 to Adult. California Test Bureau, Monterey, Calif., 1958.

play, and home arts sections. The instrument also provides scores o
interests in five other areas—music, social studies, quiet play, manua
arts, and sciences.

EXCERPT FROM *"What I Like To Do"* [10]

Would you like to . . .

		NO	?	YES
1.	Make pictures with crayons.............................	□	□	☐
2.	Carve things out of wood..............................	□	□	☐
104.	Play baseball..	□	□	☐
105.	Go hunting	□	□	☐
203.	Pick out new wallpaper or paint for your room............	□	□	☐
204.	Help plan meals for the family.........................	□	□	☐

4. MEASUREMENT OF ADJUSTMENT

Every individual faces the problem of adjusting himself to a none-too
benign environment. Persons who are successful in adapting themselve
to their environments are well adjusted; those who fail in this adaptatio
become maladjusted. The school must go beyond learning in the classroom
sense and attempt to bring about the best possible form of adjustmen
between the individual and his environment in terms of his total per
sonality.

The measurement of adjustment is an extremely comprehensive task
In its broad sense such measurement implies the use of all types of device
that will furnish information concerning the child and his background
of heredity and environment. The discussion of adjustment in this sectio
applies primarily to emotional adjustment. Although this is a fundaentally important issue, because of the fact that maladjustment seem
to have consequences of great importance in the emotional life of the
individual, the measurement of emotional maladjustment should not be
regarded as the sole approach to this problem. The discussion in certair
portions of Chapter 12 deals with adjustment in a somewhat more genera
sense than the treatment given in this section.

[10] Louis P. Thorpe, Charles E. Meyers, and Marcella R. Sea, *"What I Like To Do:*
An Inventory of Children's Interests, Grades 4 to 7. Science Research Associates, Inc.
Chicago, 1954.

ature of Adjustment

Adjustment has been defined as "a condition of harmonious relation
) the environment wherein one is able to attain satisfaction for most of
ne's needs and to meet fairly well the demands, physical and social, put
pon one." [11] This makes it clear that adjustment occurs in an environ-
iental frame of reference. However, adjustment should not desirably be
iewed as passive acceptance and complete adaptation to the environment.
uch an emphasis would result in a static social order in which progress
'ould be sacrificed for conformance. Man's history demonstrates adjust-
ient in two ways—adaptation of man to the forces of nature and adapta-
on of nature by man so that it will better fulfill his needs and wants.
.djustment should therefore be considered as an optimum balance be-
ween adaptation to the environment as one finds it and further adaptation
f the environment for the attainment of desirable social, as contrasted
'ith selfish, ends.

Two types of adjustment can be distinguished—social adjustment and
elf-adjustment. The first involves acceptance of and usually assimilation
ito at least some aspects of the man-made society of the home, the school,
he boys' gang, the teen-age heterosexual crowd, and many other formal
nd informal groups of persons. The other depends on such things as
nowing and understanding one's own strengths and weaknesses, the
ealistic setting of one's own life goals in conformance with abilities and
alents, and what is sometimes described as ability to live with oneself.

Maladjustment may arise when an individual is frustrated in the satis-
iction of his fundamentally important aims, motives, or goals. It is the
esult of a lack of balance between the difficulties the individual encoun-
ers in his environment and his ability to meet the difficulties successfully.
'he underlying causes may be of many types, and frequently they are
ery elusive. Frustration itself is a result, not a cause. The effects, or
esults, are much more readily determined than are the causes. Symptoms
f maladjustment may fairly readily be observed by the teacher who has
isight into pupil behavior, but the determination of causes underlying
ialadjustment is often a task for the clinical psychologist. Although some
lleviation of maladjustment may be accomplished without knowledge of
ts causes, effective remediation depends upon a knowledge of and ability
o cope successfully with the true causal factors.

[11] Horace B. English and Ava C. English, *A Comprehensive Dictionary of Psychological
nd Psychoanalytical Terms.* Longmans, Green and Co., New York, 1958. p. 13.

Adjustment Inventories and Scales

The importance of an awareness by the teacher of existent emotion maladjustments in his pupils should be apparent from the preceding di cussion. Such recognition of maladjustments should be accompanied k evidence concerning their nature, and, if possible, their causes. Adjus ment inventories serve the first two purposes of pointing out the existen of and nature of existing maladjustments reasonably well in many ii stances, but they probably do not accomplish the third purpose, of di covering the causes of maladjustments. They sometimes, however, furnis evidence that will greatly facilitate further study of maladjusted pupi in the attempt to determine causes and then to eliminate them.

Three general procedures are probably most often used in the measur ment of adjustment—personal report blanks, rating scales, and projecti techniques. The first two of these methods are discussed briefly and illu trated by a few representative instruments in the following pages. Tl third is dealt with in the following section of this chapter, however.

Personal-report blanks. By far the majority of adjustment inventorie make use of the personal-report method, by which pupils are asked to giv answers to a variety of questions. The considerable quantity of adjus ment inventories and the wide variety of response methods they us precludes any more comprehensive treatment here than brief description and illustrations of a few of them.

The *Behavior Preference Record* consists of such groups of items a those shown in an accompanying excerpt for use with pupils in Grades to 12. The pupil is asked to read each problem and then encircle a capit letter in response to the question, "What would you do?" Finally, he expected to encircle as many of the small letters as are necessary in givir reasons for his choice. Responses are scored in such manner as to provic ratings on these characteristics of democratic behavior: cooperatioi friendliness, integrity, leadership, and responsibility.

Items in groups are also employed in the *Gordon Personal Profile,* illu trated here by three sets of items. Each unit consists of four descripti statements that apply to human beings. The pupil is asked to find tl two items in each group that give descriptions "most like you" and "lea like you" and to mark them under M and L respectively. This is a force choice type of situation in which the pupil is to give the answer that mo nearly applies to him, even though he may not think any of the descri tions in a group is strongly like, or strongly unlike, him. This instrumer is scored so as to give ratings on ascendancy, responsibility, emotion stability, sociability, and a total or over-all self-evaluation of adjustmer

EXCERPT FROM *Behavior Preference Record* [12]

. You are about to play baseball on a vacant lot with the neighborhood gang. Your mother asks you to take your little brother or little sister along while she goes shopping. You know that the gang will laugh.

What would you do?

A. Do it anyway.
B. Stay at home.
C. Explain why you don't want to do it.

Because:

a. It wouldn't do any good to explain.
b. You don't like to be laughed at.
c. "Kidding" doesn't bother you.
d. You do not wish to go that badly.
e. Mother would understand and would not make you do it.
f. A child might get hurt.
g. One is a good sport if he can stand some "kidding."

20. Jim has accidentally spilled some paint on a drawing you are making. You will need to do it over. He says that he is sorry.

What would you do?

A. Tell him it is all right.
B. Tell him to be more careful next time.
C. Be angry with him.
D. Tell the teacher.

Because:

a. He didn't mean to do it.
b. You do not want to do the picture over.
c. He should have been more careful.
d. It wouldn't help to get angry.
e. He should be punished for spoiling your work.
f. You do not want him to be angry with you.
g. You do not want it to happen again.

EXCERPT FROM *Gordon Personal Profile* [13]

	M	L
assured in relationships with others.....................	∷	∷
feelings are rather easily hurt.........................	∷	∷
follows well-developed work habits.....................	∷	∷
would rather keep to a small group of friends............	∷	∷

	M	L
becomes irritated somewhat readily.....................	∷	∷
capable of handling any situation......................	∷	∷
does not like to converse with strangers.................	∷	∷
thorough in any work performed.......................	∷	∷

	M	L
prefers not to argue with other people..................	∷	∷
unable to keep to a fixed schedule.....................	∷	∷
a calm and unexcitable person.........................	∷	∷
inclined to be highly sociable.........................	∷	∷

[12] Hugh B. Wood, *Behavior Preference Record: "What Would You Do?"* California est Bureau, Monterey, Calif., 1953.

[13] Leonard V. Gordon, *Gordon Personal Profile.* Copyright 1953 by Harcourt, Brace and World, Inc., New York. All rights reserved. Quoted by special permission.

EXCERPT FROM *Mooney Problem Check List* [14]

[DIRECTIONS: Read the list slowly, and as you come to a problem which]
troubles you, draw a line under it.

1. Often have headaches	36. Too short for my age
2. Don't get enough sleep	37. Too tall for my age
3. Have trouble with my teeth	38. Having poor posture
4. Not as healthy as I should be	39. Poor complexion or skin trouble
5. Not getting outdoors enough	40. Not good looking
6. Getting low grades in school	41. Afraid of failing in school work
7. Afraid of tests	42. Trouble with arithmetic
8. Being a grade behind in school	43. Trouble with spelling or grammar
9. Don't like to study	44. Slow in reading
10. Not interested in books	45. Trouble with writing

The *Mooney Problem Check List,* from which an excerpt is shown i
an accompanying illustration, differs from many personal-report form
in that it makes no provision for formal pupil scores and no norms ar
provided. Since its major uses are in counseling, surveying pupil problem:
and research, the use of indicated problems, simple counts of problems b
areas, and summaries of problems for groups of pupils constitute th
recommended bases for interpretation of results. Local norms are cor
sidered to be of greater significance than national norms. Therefore, it i
suggested by the publisher that they be derived as desired.

Rating scales. One rating scale that is of major use in locating mal
adjusted pupils is briefly commented upon and illustrated here. Althoug
rating scales have the same general purposes as the personal-report blank

EXCERPT FROM *Haggerty-Olson-Wickman Behavior Rating Schedules* [1]

25. Is he even-tempered or moody?   *Score*

Stolid, Rare changes of mood (3)	Generally very even-tempered (1)	Is happy or depressed as conditions warrant (2)	Strong and frequent changes of mood (4)	Has periods of extreme elations or depressions (5)

26. Is he easily discouraged or is he persistent?

Melts before slight obstacles or objections (5)	Gives up before adequate trial (3)	Gives everything a fair trial (1)	Persists until convinced of mistake (2)	Never gives in, Obstinate (4)

7. Is he generally depressed or cheerful?

Dejected, Melancholic, In the dumps (3)	Generally dispirited (4)	Usually in good humor (1)	Cheerful, Animated, Chirping (2)	Hilarious (5)

[14] Ross L. Mooney, *Mooney Problem Check List,* Junior High School Form, 1950 Rev
sion. Psychological Corporation, New York, 1950.
[15] M. E. Haggerty, E. C. Olson, and E. K. Wickman, *Haggerty-Olson-Wickman Behavi
Rating Schedules.* Copyright 1930 by Harcourt, Brace and World, Inc., New York. A
rights reserved. Quoted by special permission.

discussed above, the two types of adjustment measures differ greatly in method.

The *Haggerty-Olson-Wickman Behavior Rating Schedules* are illustrated by the few accompanying items. Although this scale is similar in general appearance to the more common graphic rating scale, it differs in that the two extremes do not necessarily represent the most and the least desirable situations. Instead, the numbers 1 to 5, variously spaced for different items, indicate in descending order the relative desirability of the stated condition.

5. MEASUREMENT OF TOTAL PERSONALITY

The major instruments discussed above for use in the measurement of personality are paper-and-pencil scales and inventories. They have come to be known as structured inventories because persons filling them out respond to the content of the instruments. In contrast are the unstructured techniques for evaluating personality. Although the various projective methods are most commonly referred to as unstructured, certain other evaluation techniques also permit free responses by the pupil. The unstructured techniques differ from the structured inventories in their direct concern with overt behavior of the whole child rather than with verbalized responses to specific situations. The two types of unstructured techniques dealt with below are used in the evaluation of individual pupils and the dynamics of group behavior.

Evaluation of Individual Behavior

Three evaluative techniques useful in the study of individual pupils are considered briefly below. The anecdotal record and the case study are appropriately used by classroom teachers, but projective techniques should be employed only by psychological examiners, school psychologists, clinical psychologists, or other persons with technical training in their use.

Anecdotal method. Teachers have doubtless for generations used the anecdotal method in their spare-time discussions about pupils. However, its first use as an evaluative technique was probably not more than a few decades ago. The anecdotal record is an objective description by the teacher of a significant occurrence or episode in the life of the pupil. Such a record must be carefully, although not laboriously, prepared if it is to be of value. The anecdote is a highly objective brief of what occurred in a situation in which a pupil behaved in a sufficiently unusual manner to make the incident meaningful. It may consist of an objective narrative of the incident only or it may consist of the narrative, an impartial interpretation of the occurrence, and, as a possible third stage, even a recommendation for guidance of the pupil concerned. If interpretations and recommendations are given, however, they should be distinguished from the original description so that their nature is clearly apparent to a person reading the anecdotal record. The anecdotal record has great value only when it is made cumulative by the addition of new anecdotes as meaningful situations arise and are observed and recorded by the teacher or some other school officer.

Case study. The case study is a broad and comprehensive approach to the problems of pupil behavior. It should include extensive information about the present status of the pupil as well as about his past experiences and his family background. In fact, the case study may well draw upon many or even all of the types of information contained in adequate cumulative pupil records.

Usually there is a specific reason for making a case study. Such an approach may be used to gain a better understanding of a failing pupil, or a pupil who is poorly adjusted in one or another of many possible ways.

Projective techniques. A simple characterization of projective techniques is that they attempt to induce the pupil to reveal his personality through his free responses to situations that can be observed by the psychologist. Bell stated that the "purpose of projective techniques is to gain insight into the individual personality," and that their method is "to reveal the total personality, or aspects of the personality in their framework of the whole." [16] Techniques classified as projective differ widely in the materials used, the methods of presentation to the pupil, and the methods of interpreting the pupil's behavior, but all are intended to bring forth behavior representative of the inner personality and to permit the psychologist to draw inferences concerning intrinsic motives.

Doubtless most widely used of the projective techniques are the *Rorschach* [17] and the *Thematic Apperception Test.*[18] The *Rorschach* makes use of pupil interpretations of inkblots and the *TAT* employs a wide variety of pictures as the basis for pupil responses. Some of the other projective methods involve drawing or painting, play, completion of pictures, dramatic productions, and even handwriting.

As only a trained psychologist should attempt to employ these projective techniques, this brief discussion is intended to familiarize the student with the general nature of a few of the most widely used projective methods. Teachers occasionally may encounter situations in which mal-

[16] John E. Bell, *Projective Techniques: A Dynamic Approach to the Study of the Personality.* Longmans, Green and Co., New York, 1948. p. 4.
[17] Distributed by Grune and Stratton, Inc., New York.
[18] Published by Harvard University Press, Cambridge, Mass.

adjusted pupils are studied by the use of these techniques, so they should
be sufficiently familiar with the general procedures involved to be intelligent users in subsequent pupil guidance of the interpretations made by
the examining psychologists.

Evaluation of Group Dynamics

Two methods are now used quite widely in studying the behavior of
the whole child in settings involving interactions among members of social
groups. Information is thereby obtained concerning the place of the individual within the group and concerning group behavior as influenced by
the contributions of the individual members. The methods briefly discussed below involve the use of the sociometric method and of analyses
of social relations. Both have been influenced considerably by developments in the field of sociology.

Sociometric test. When groups of individuals are thrown together, as in
a grade group of pupils in the elementary school or a homeroom group or
class in the high school, some type of social relationship inevitably exists
between each pupil and every other pupil individually. The possible range
of relationships is from that involved in very close friendships to that of
rejection. However, the variety of social situations is so wide that a pupil
who is rejected by another in a particular social situation may be sought
out in a second, and quite different, social framework. For example, a boy
preferred by a certain teammate as captain of the football team might be
rejected by the same teammate as a member of a debating team.

The sociometric test which leads to the production of a sociogram as the
end product is quite simple to apply. Most typically each pupil in the
group is asked to name his first, second, and perhaps third choices among
other members of the group in several significant and pertinent types of
social settings. Questions asking for the expression of individual preferences for class president, the occupant of an adjacent seat in the homeroom, or a member of a committee merely illustrate the wide range of
possibilities.

The sociogram is used to represent the results graphically. Prior to its
preparation, the results in response to a certain question are analyzed by
any one of several methods, ranging from the use of a tally sheet to the
employment of cards or slips of paper that can be sorted.[19] When these
results, showing first, second, and third choices, have been organized and
the pupils ranked from highest to lowest in frequencies of choice, the
sociogram can be constructed. Usually the pupils most often chosen are

[19] Helen H. Jennings, *Sociometry in Group Relations: A Manual for Teachers,* Second
edition. American Council on Education, Washington, D. C., 1959. p. 20-24.

represented near the center of the sociogram and those rejected or least often chosen are spotted near the margins. Mutual choices, i.e., pupils choosing each other, should be represented by closely adjacent figures. The

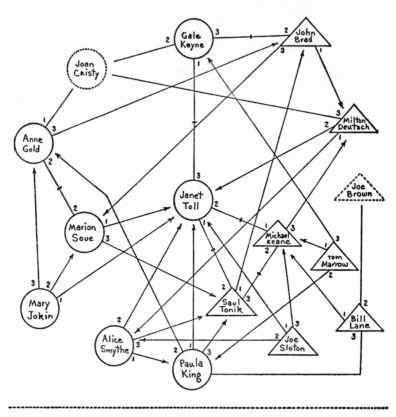

LEGEND

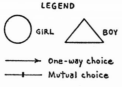

○ GIRL △ BOY

——➤ One-way choice

——|—— Mutual choice

l, 2, or 3 = order of choice

Note.—For an absent boy or girl, use the respective symbol dashed, leaving any choice line open-ended (see the case of Joe Brown in the above sociogram).

If rejections are obtained, the choice line may be made in dashes or in a different color.

Whenever a direct line from chooser to chosen cannot be drawn without crossing through the symbol for another individual, the line should be drawn with an elbow, as in the case of Bill Lane to Paula King.

FIGURE 3. Sample Sociogram [20]

lines showing choices should be as short as reasonably possible and inter-crossing of lines should be kept at a minimum. First, second, and third choices should be designated by numbers or by different types of lines.

[20] *Ibid.* p. 25.

Boys are often distinguished from girls by the use of figures, such as triangles and circles. The symbols should contain pupils' names or initials for ready identification. The application of these principles is shown in Figure 3, which represents the social interactions of a group of elementary-school pupils.

Social relations scale. The second approach to measurement of group dynamics dealt with here is represented by the *Syracuse Scale of Social Relations,* illustrated in Figure 4. The figure is a reproduction of the sample presented to the pupils and discussed with them before they are asked to fill out two copies of this basic form to show their patterns of social relationships in two specified types of situations.

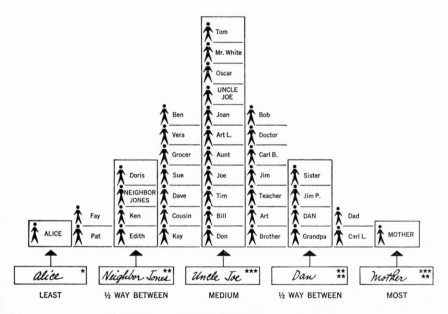

FIGURE 4. Sample from *Syracuse Scales of Social Relations* [21]

In this sample, names given in the various cells indicate the persons on whom a hypothetical boy, John Smith, felt he could depend in varying degree if he were very unhappy and wished to talk over his troubles with some kind, sympathetic person. He felt that his mother would be most satisfactory and that a friend, Alice, would be least effective for help and counsel in this type of situation. His friend Dan, his Uncle Joe, and Neigh-

[21] Eric F. Gardner and George C. Thompson, *Syracuse Scales of Social Relations,* Elementary level. Copyright 1959 by Harcourt, Brace and World, Inc., New York. All rights reserved. Quoted by special permission.

bor Jones were his choices to represent persons at indicated positions between the two extremes. Names of other friends, relatives, neighbors, and persons known to him are listed in the columns of the diagram to show how he rated them for possible help.

After the pupils have filled out blank copies of this form to indicate their patterns of social relations, the results are analyzed by the use of a scoring guide and are then coverted into ratings and numerical values that in themselves have meaning and that can be given further meaning by the use of percentile norms for grade groups. This technique differs from the sociometric test, usually restricted to a pupil's classmates or peers, primarily in the extension of social relations to all persons the pupil has ever known.

6. CLASSROOM USES OF PERSONALITY INVENTORIES
   AND TECHNIQUES

Wide differences among personality inventories and techniques in the aspects of behavior they attempt to evaluate, and consequently in the wide variety of scores resulting from their employment in testing, make any significant discussion of how to use such instruments and their results unusually difficult. Moreover, many of the results from personality measurement are more appropriately used by counselors and guidance officers, and even in some instances by psychological examiners and clinical psychologists, than by classroom teachers. This distinction is particularly true for personality measurement and evaluation as contrasted with mental ability or achievement measurement. Consequently, the brief discussion here is concerned primarily with those uses of personality evaluation devices that are quite clearly within the province of classroom teachers.

Results from all three types of attitude scales discussed in a preceding section of this chapter—scientific, social, and health—are typically presented in such form that classroom teachers can easily interpret them. Percentile norms for age groups, for grade levels, and even for boys and girls separately are often provided. However, the absence of any standards by means of which results can appropriately be rated as desirable or undesirable complicates the problem of using them directly in dealing with pupils. Furthermore, the degree to which attitudes expressed on personal-report forms, such as attitude scales, are borne out in related behavior cannot safely be inferred from the results. For these and other reasons, scores on attitude scales should probably be used by the teacher much more for gaining insights into one aspect of pupil tastes and preferences and in supporting or confirming other evidence about pupil characteristics than as a basis for direct action of any type.

In the discussion of interest measurement earlier in this chapter, two types, vocational and avocational, are distinguished. Results from the measurement of vocational interests are used mainly by counselors and other guidance workers in advising high-school pupils. Avocational interests, however, are measurable in nontechnical ways, by the teacher himself if he wishes, and results from such measurement are directly useful in the adaptation of instruction and other aspects of teacher-pupil relations to the interests and preferences of individual pupils.

Inventories or personal-report blanks and projective techniques are known respectively as structured and unstructured approaches to the measurement of adjustments. Each is sufficiently lacking in reliability and validity under many circumstances to require great discernment and care in the use of results. The personal-report inventories filled out by pupils are likely to yield inaccurate results to the extent that pupils falsify their answers, particularly to items dealing with areas of personality in which they individually are on the defensive. The reliability of results from even the most widely used projective techniques has not been demonstrably high. These two reasons, buttressed by others of more technical varieties, justify the belief that results from the measurement of pupil adjustment by these two most common approaches should seldom if ever be used by classroom teachers directly in the classroom. Rather, they should be used primarily by persons whose special preparation qualifies them for counseling pupils about their personality problems.

Finally, the classroom teacher can be and should be a major, if not the central, participant in the evaluation of group dynamics or of interpersonal relations within his class, his homeroom, or some other small and integrated group of pupils for which he is responsible. The sociometric test in education typically deals with the status of each of the individuals within such a group. The results of the sociometric test and of some other sociometric procedures for evaluating interactions are of greatest significance while the group is intact. Furthermore, because of the dynamic nature of the relationships measured, sociometric test results tend to be most useful soon after they are obtained and analyzed. As a result, the classroom teacher or the homeroom teacher is in far the best position to interpret results meaningfully and to employ them understandingly in the attempt to aid individual pupils to effect desirable social adjustments.

SUGGESTED ACTIVITIES

1. Read a review of an adjustment inventory in one of the Buros *Mental Measurements Yearbooks* and note what the author wrote about the degree to which results may be invalid because of "faking" by pupils.

2. Arrange if possible to observe unobtrusively a small group of children or adolescents in some natural and unsupervised setting for a period of twenty or thirty minutes and note how much, or how little, you can learn about their individual personality characteristics.

TOPICS FOR DISCUSSION

1. In what way is a knowledge of personality measurement procedures valuable to the teacher?
2. What is meant by personality? How do psychologists and laymen differ in their conceptions of personality?
3. How are personal reports used in personality measurement?
4. What is the nature of graphic rating scales?
5. Indicate the nature of observational procedures for the evaluation of personality.
6. Briefly characterize two association methods of evaluating behavior.
7. Briefly indicate the nature of attitudes. Of what concern are they to the teacher?
8. Indicate the nature of one or two attitude scales for use in the elementary or secondary school.
9. What is the nature of interests? How are pupil interests of significance to the teacher?
10. Discuss the two major procedures used in the measurement of interests.
11. What are some of the causes and symptoms of emotional maladjustment? Which are easier to recognize? Why?
12. Indicate some of the methods by which pupil adjustment is measured.
13. What are three major methods of evaluating individual behavior?
14. How should the teacher expect to be involved in the administration and use of results from projective techniques?
15. What are some of the modern methods for evaluating group dynamics?
16. In what ways can the classroom teacher appropriately use sociograms?
17. What are a few guiding principles for use of personality measurement results in the classroom?

SELECTED REFERENCES

ALLEN, ROBERT M. *Personality Assessment Procedures: Psychometric, Projective, and Other Approaches.* New York: Harper and Brothers, 1958.

ANASTASI, ANNE. *Psychological Testing.* Second edition. New York: Macmillan Co., 1961. Part 4.

ANDERSON, HAROLD H., AND ANDERSON, GLADYS L., editors. *An Introduction to Projective Techniques.* New York: Prentice-Hall, Inc., 1951.

BELL, JOHN E. *Projective Techniques: A Dynamic Approach to the Study of the Personality.* New York: Longmans, Green and Co., 1948. Chapters 2-24.

BONNEY, MERL E. "Sociometric Methods." *Encyclopedia of Educational Research.* Third edition. New York: Macmillan Co., 1960. p. 1319-24.

BUROS, OSCAR K., editor. *The Fifth Mental Measurements Yearbook.* Highland Park, N. J.: Gryphon Press, 1959. p. 86-324.

BUROS, OSCAR K., editor. *The Fourth Mental Measurements Yearbook.* Highland Park, N. J.: Gryphon Press, 1953. p. 67-293, 726-51.

BUROS, OSCAR K., editor. *The Third Mental Measurements Yearbook.* New Brunswick, N. J.: Rutgers University Press, 1949. p. 51-218.

CRONBACH, LEE J. *Essentials of Psychological Testing.* Second edition. New York: Harper and Brothers, 1960. Part 3.

DEHAAN, ROBERT F., AND KOUGH, JACK. *Identifying Students with Special Needs.* Teacher's Guidance Handbook, Vol. I, Secondary School Edition. Chicago: Science Research Associates, Inc., 1956. Section 3.

EDWARDS, ALLEN L. *Techniques of Attitude Scale Construction.* New York: Appleton-Century-Crofts, Inc., 1957.

FERGUSON, LEONARD W. *Personality Measurement.* New York: McGraw-Hill Book Co., Inc., 1952.

FORLANO, GEORGE, AND WRIGHTSTONE, J. WAYNE. "Measuring the Quality of Social Acceptability within a Class." *Educational and Psychological Measurement,* 15:127-36; Summer 1955.

FREEMAN, FRANK S. *Theory and Practice of Psychological Testing.* Revised edition. New York: Henry Holt and Co., 1955. Chapters 17-21.

FROEHLICH, CLIFFORD P., AND HOYT, KENNETH B. *Guidance Testing.* Revised edition. Chicago: Science Research Associates, Inc., 1959. Chapters 9-10, 19.

FRYER, DOUGLAS. *The Measurement of Interests.* New York: Henry Holt and Co., 1931.

GREENE, HARRY A., JORGENSEN, ALBERT N., AND GERBERICH, J. RAYMOND. *Measurement and Evaluation in the Elementary School.* Second edition. New York: Longmans, Green and Co., 1953. Chapter 11.

GREENE, HARRY A., JORGENSEN, ALBERT N., AND GERBERICH, J. RAYMOND. *Measurement and Evaluation in the Secondary School.* Second edition. New York: Longmans, Green and Co., 1954. Chapter 11.

GRONLUND, NORMAN E. *Sociometry in the Classroom.* New York: Harper and Brothers, 1959.

HARSH, CHARLES M., AND SCHRICKEL, H. G. *Personality Development and Assessment.* New York: Ronald Press Co., 1950.

JARVIE, L. L., AND ELLINGSON, MARK. *A Handbook on the Anecdotal Behavior Journal.* Chicago: University of Chicago Press, 1940.

JENNINGS, HELEN H. *Sociometry in Group Relations.* Second edition. Washington, D. C.: American Council on Education, 1959.

KOUGH, JACK, AND DEHAAN, ROBERT F. *Identifying Children with Special Needs.* Teacher's Guidance Handbook, Vol. I, Elementary School Edition. Chicago: Science Research Associates, Inc., 1955. Section 3.

KRUGMAN, MORRIS. "Projective Techniques in the Assessment of Personality in Schools." *Educational and Psychological Measurement,* 14:272-76; Summer 1954.

LUEBKE, PAUL T. "Charting Sociometric Data." *National Elementary Principal,* 34:175-79; September 1954.

McGUIRE, CARSON. "Personality." *Encyclopedia of Educational Research.* Third edition. New York: Macmillan Co., 1960. p. 945-57.

McNEMAR, QUINN. "Opinion-Attitude Methodology." *Psychological Bulletin,* 43:289-374; July 1946.

NORTHWAY, MARY L. *A Primer of Sociometry.* Toronto, Canada: University of Toronto Press, 1952.

NORTHWAY, MARY L., AND WELD, LINDSAY. *Sociometric Testing: A Guide for Teachers.* Toronto, Canada: University of Toronto Press, 1957.

REMMERS, H. H. *Introduction to Opinion and Attitude Measurement.* New York: Harper and Brothers, 1954.

SARGENT, HELEN. "Projective Methods: Their Origin, Theory, and Application in Personality Research." *Psychological Bulletin,* 42:257-93; May 1945.

SELLS, SAUL B., AND TRITES, DAVID K. "Attitudes." *Encyclopedia of Educational Research.* Third edition. New York: Macmillan Co., 1960. p. 102-15.

STERN, GEORGE C., STEIN, MORRIS I., AND BLOOM, BENJAMIN S. *Methods in Personality Assessment.* Glencoe, Ill.: Free Press, 1956.

SUPER, DONALD E. *Appraising Vocational Fitness by Means of Psychological Tests.* New York: Harper and Brothers, 1949. Chapters 16-19.

SUPER, DONALD E. "Interests." *Encyclopedia of Educational Research.* Third edition. New York: Macmillan Co., 1960. p. 728-33.

SYMONDS, PERCIVAL M. *Diagnosing Personality and Conduct.* New York: D. Appleton-Century Co., Inc., 1931.

TORGERSON, THEODORE L. *Studying Children.* New York: Dryden Press, 1947. Chapters 3-4, 9.

VERNON, PHILIP E. *Personality Tests and Assessments.* New York: Henry Holt and Co., 1953.

8

ACHIEVEMENT TESTS

The following problems in the construction and use of standardized achievement tests are considered in this chapter:

A. How standardized achievement tests are planned.
B. How achievement tests are standardized.
C. Selecting standardized achievement tests for classroom use.
D. Administering and scoring standardized tests.
E. Varieties of norms and derived scores.
F. Reporting test results to pupils and their parents.
G. Major uses of achievement test results.

A teacher who needs an achievement test for fulfilling a certain purpose in one of his classes has two alternatives—he can select a test from those already in existence or he can construct a new test. If he decides on the first alternative, he nearly always turns to standardized tests. If he decides on the second, he normally proceeds to construct his own test. The account in this chapter of how standardized achievement tests are built and used is designed to supply some knowledges and understandings of these instruments as aids to the student in making discriminative selections and in the appropriate use of test results. Construction of tests by teachers for use in their classes is the theme of Part 3 of this volume.

Standardized and teacher-made tests, especially when both are of the objective type and when both are results of well-planned and careful workmanship, differ more in certain mechanical features and in the availability of accessory materials than in the fundamental characteristics and even the content of the test themselves. Although the makers of a standardized achievement test follow procedures that are typically far more

153

complex and technical and also more extensive than those employed by teachers in constructing tests for use in their own classes, the techniques are quite similar in many important respects. Therefore, this chapter should not only aid the reader in attaining understanding of these tests but should also facilitate his study of the informal objective tests that are treated in Chapter 10.

1. ACHIEVEMENT AND ITS MEASUREMENT

Teachers and pupils particularly, but many other school officials and the parents of school children also, are concerned with the achievement of pupils in the school. Although most of these interested parties would doubtless describe achievement in general terms as proficiency in some performance, as attainment of some end or goal, or as a level of success in some area of learning, not many of them would be able to characterize achievement in ways that would be useful to makers of standardized achievement tests. Consequently, the nature of achievement and the most widely used types of standardized achievement tests are briefly discussed here as an introduction to the construction and use of these instruments.

Nature of Achievement

Because of the significance of pupil achievement in a book dealing with educational measurement and evaluation, a section of Chapter 1 of this volume is given over to a brief introductory treatment of educational objectives and to the pupil behaviors that become possible when the objectives are achieved. It can be said, therefore, that the attainment of educational objectives is achievement. Pupils who learn, then, acquire new or modified ways of behaving that are known as learning outcomes. When they learn directly as a result of instruction, they acquire instructional outcomes.

Seven of the types of learning outcomes distinguished by Gerberich [1] as particularly applicable in achievement measurement are described in Chapter 1 of this book. Examples of these seven and of two other outcomes that in their technical aspects are usually considered to be in the area of personality measurement are illustrated below as a further indication of what the terms can be taken to mean. Descriptive statements in the parentheses following the illustrations specify the nature of the learning outcomes in somewhat greater detail.

[1] J. Raymond Gerberich, *Specimen Objective Test Items: A Guide to Achievement Test Construction.* Longmans, Green and Co., New York, 1956. p. 16-21.

Skills: Writing the word "achievement" (Communication)
  Multiplying 20 by 8 (Computation)
  Driving a nail through a board (Manipulation)
Knowledges: The state in which Chicago is located (Place)
  The law of gravitation (Law)
  When to wear sports clothes (Custom)
Concepts: Green as a color (Qualitative)
  An inch as a distance (Quantitative)
Understandings: How to compute interest (Principle)
  What causes lightning (Cause and effect)
  How to drive an automobile (Procedure)
Applications: Planning a picnic (Mental)
  Baking a cake (Physical)
Activities: Reading a book (Mental)
  Jumping rope (Physical)
  Playing in a band (Directed)
  Building a model airplane (Spontaneous)
Appreciations: The colors in a sunset (Natural)
  An orchestral performance (Man-made)
Attitudes: Predisposition toward language as a school subject (Social)
Interests: Liking to collect and study rocks (Avocational)

These examples of behaviors in nine relatively distinct, although certainly not mutually exclusive, outcome areas are indicative of some of the kinds of learning variously dealt with in standardized achievement tests. Skills and knowledges, the most tangible outcomes, are represented most widely and activities, appreciations, attitudes, and interests least frequently in most subject matter tests. However, many of the better standardized tests of achievement measure the less tangible concepts, understandings, and applications in significant degree. Much depends on the nature of the test, of course; a test of arithmetic computation or of reading comprehension does not include factual knowledges as such nor does a test in English mechanics include items measuring computational skills and appreciations.

Major Types of Standardized Achievement Tests

Standardized achievement tests can be classified somewhat in terms of origin and use, as is true of the categories set apart in pages 38 to 45 of this volume, or in the broader terms that seem more useful here—by content or subject matter. Considered in this manner, achievement tests can be divided into three groups: (1) general achievement tests, covering a number of fields of subject matter, (2) tests in subject areas, such as reading, mathematics, or the social studies, and (3) tests in specific subjects, such as American history, French, or biology. Although the construction and use of standardized achievement tests as dealt with in this chapter seem to be most effectively based on these distinctions, a consideration of these tests in all of their ramifications should include the types of distinctions referred to above, as found in Chapter 2, and the further adaptations involved in the subject-centered chapters of Part 5.

2. STANDARDIZATION OF ACHIEVEMENT TESTS

Procedures involved in the construction of standardized achievement tests depend not only on the nature of the test to be constructed but also on the number and characteristics of the persons involved in the standardization process. One person can construct and standardize a test. More commonly, however, several authors or a committee consisting of several persons are active participants in the process. Two types of talents, those found in persons who are familiar with the subject and those found in the test specialist, are necessary if a test is to be well constructed. Sometimes the two types of talent are combined in one person. Much more often, however, the differing abilities and points of view of at least three or four persons, one or more of them sometimes in the capacity of a coordinator or editor, are involved in the process.

Six steps of procedure are briefly set out here to give a general idea of how standardized tests of achievement are typically constructed: (1) planning the test, (2) writing the test items, (3) trying out the items experimentally, (4) assembling the final test, (5) preparing the accessory materials, and (6) developing norms for the test.[2] These steps are deemed to be significant in terms of the understandings they afford of achievement test construction and not with the thought that the classroom teacher himself is likely at any time to be personally involved in such a procedure. The steps that have the most pertinence in informal objective test construction are dealt with very briefly here because their significance in the construction of objective classroom tests warrants the more extensive treatment they receive in Chapter 10.

It is assumed that certain decisions have been made before starting the test construction process. These include primarily such matters as the selection of the general types of outcomes to be measured, specification of the types of pupils or other persons expected to take the test, and uses to which the test results are to be put. These questions, together with the authorship and type of test desired, e.g., paper-and-pencil rather than performance, must be answered in advance.

[2] For brief and lengthy accounts of this process, differently organized, see: (1) Educational Testing Service, *ETS Builds a Test*. Educational Testing Service, Princeton, N. J., 1959; and (2) E. F. Lindquist, editor, *Educational Measurement*. American Council on Education, Washington, D. C., 1951. Chapters 6-11.

Planning the Test

Standardized test makers must first answer the question of what to measure, of what content to put into the test. They typically must construct a test for pupils who come from vastly different socioeconomic and home backgrounds, who have been taught by different teachers, and who attend schools, large and small, in all parts of the fifty United States. Their problems are consequently quite different from those of a teacher who is planning a classroom test for pupils he teaches. In general, test planning involves three methods or a combination of them in deciding what content shall be used. These are primarily designed to insure that the test will have the type of curricular validity discussed in detail in Chapter 3.

Analysis of outcomes. Pupils acquire new or modified ways of behaving as a result of instruction or learning. These changes indicate the degree to which instructional objectives have been attained. The introductory treatment of objectives and outcomes in Chapter 1 and the discussion and illustrations of outcome types in a foregoing section of this chapter make clear why there should be a close relationship between instructional outcomes and content of standardized achievement tests. Although the techniques employed in making this type of analysis may sometimes be complex, it seems sufficient here to point out that different types of tests involve very different combinations of outcome types. Consequently, determination of the appropriate pattern of skills, knowledges, understandings, attitudes, and other outcome types is one way of deciding what content to include in a test.

Analysis of textbooks and courses of study. Standardized test makers sometimes analyze the content of eight to ten of the most widely used textbooks as a means of deciding upon test content. They may also analyze representative courses of study to supplement the evidence from textbooks. To the extent that the number of pages in such sources devoted to certain aspects of subject matter are representative of instructional emphases, and in turn of what pupils learn, this method can appropriately be used in deciding what content should go into a test.

Judgments of qualified persons. Opinions of persons whose backgrounds and experiences qualify them for consultation may be represented in two ways—by checking on their writings as individuals or as members of yearbook committees for any suggestions or recommendations to be obtained from such sources, and by involving such persons directly in the planning process as members of the committee responsible for the test or as consultants. Human judgment is inevitably the ultimate source, or court of final authority, in selection of valid content for tests. Dependence on human judgment is obvious here, but it is indirectly reflected in the analysis of outcomes and of textbooks and courses of study.

A final step of test planning involves in some manner interrelationships between instructional outcomes and subject-matter units or subdivisions. Decisions concerning appropriate degrees of emphasis on content areas and pupil behaviors to be measured can be depicted in the two-way form shown in Table 6. Certain other decisions concerning distribution of emphasis must also be made. Among them are the number of items of each objective type or variety to be used, the number of items at each of several levels of difficulty, and the number of items using verbal, numerical, graphical, and other forms of presentation. Such decisions as these, when combined with those represented in the two-way chart, provide the type of specifications or blueprint the standardized test maker often prepares before starting to construct the instrument.

TABLE 6

Two-Way Chart of Content in Health Inventory Battery [3]

Aspects of Test Content	Learning Outcomes						
	ACTIVITIES	INFORMATION	INTERESTS	ATTITUDES	ANALYZING PROBLEMS	JUDGING INFORMATION	ALL
Personal appearance	34	21	24	10			89
Diet and nutrition	46	27	21		18	5	117
General operation of body	30	18	36	10	11	6	111
Health hazards	30	25	26		34	7	122
Reproduction and heredity		19	22		11		52
Health practices or problems				10	17	10	37
Individual responsibility				10		6	16
Maintenance of health				10		6	16
Control by agencies				10			10
Published sources of information						13	13
Effect of climate						5	5
Totals	140	110	129	60	91	58	588

[3] Adapted from Cooperative Study in General Education, *Health Inventories: Manual of Directions*. Educational Testing Service, Princeton, N. J., 1950.

Writing the Items

After the two-way chart has been accepted as a guide for the second step of the standardization process, test items or integrated sets of items in the form of exercises are written by persons skilled in the art of item writing. The items or exercises are typically in several of the basic types or varieties—alternate-response and related scaled-choice, multiple-choice, matching, and completion-type or augmentation. Since a major section of Chapter 10 is given over to test item writing, and to illustrations of various types, it seems sufficient here to note that standardized test makers follow the same techniques as classroom teachers constructing their own objective tests. Any differences in type and quality of items are the result of different levels of technical skill rather than of different methods of item writing.

Whether the items are written by the author or authors, by members of a committee, or by test technicians assigned to the job depends on the original sponsorship or assignment of responsibilities. Whether the items are critically examined and in some instances modified by authors or a committee meeting together, or by consultants and specialists working individually, is also a matter of choice. However, a critical appraisal of all items and exercises, revision of those found deficient, and rejection of any decided upon as inadequate typically follow the original item writing. When many more items or exercises than the final test is expected to include have passed this critical examination, the second, or tryout, stage of obtaining valid items becomes appropriate.

Trying Out the Items

The items surviving the inspectional process are now ready for incorporation into a preliminary form of the test and for pretesting as a basis for effecting still further improvements in the test items and exercises. This preliminary test is usually constructed to be very similar in format and mode of administration to what is planned for the final product. It is then administered to a number of pupils chosen to represent the appropriate age or grade levels, subject backgrounds, types of schools, and sections of the country. The preliminary test papers are analyzed in the two major ways indicated here only briefly. These procedures for analyzing test results are more fully presented in Chapter 10.

Item difficulty. Responses to each item of the preliminary tests are analyzed and the total number of correct answers is converted into a percentage of the pupils who get the right answer. This percentage is called an *index of item difficulty*. Indices for the various items can then be used as one basis for selecting content to go into the final form of the test or for allotting items to different forms of the test if, as often happens, two or more forms are being constructed at one time. The indices clearly distinguish items on a scale ranging from easy to hard and consequently can be used in constructing a final test having the desired level of difficulty.

Item discriminative power. Item responses are also analyzed separately for pupils who attain quite high scores and for other pupils who make quite low scores on the preliminary test. First, numbers and percentages of pupils answering each item correctly are obtained for both groups. Then the percentage for the "low" group is subtracted from that for the "high" group to obtain the difference, or what is called an *index of item discrimination,* for each item. An additional refinement of item discrimination is found when the percentages of high-ranking and low-ranking pupils who choose each incorrect answer, or distractor, are determined. In rather technical ways that are not touched upon here, the standardized test maker often uses these two types of information as a basis for summarily rejecting a few items, for revising other items in minor degree, and for retaining still other items without change.

It is usually at this point that preliminary information on test reliability is obtained by the use of procedures such as those outlined in Chapter 14. Test validity has to some extent been established by the procedures employed in all three steps of the construction process developed up to this point. The index of discrimination and the index of difficulty now jointly become major items of information for estimating the quality or "goodness" of each test item in assembling the final test.

Assembling the Test

Items are selected for inclusion in the final test, or final test forms, in the light of their discriminative power, their difficulty, their contribution to attainment of the balance between subject content and behavioral outcome represented in a two-way chart of the type shown in Table 6, and perhaps a few other factors. Items having greatest discriminative power and tending to center around difficulty indices of 50 percent are favored by standardized test makers for inclusion in most tests, although special conditions sometimes warrant the use of other bases for item selection. It is these items that make the most effective contribution to a test that truly discriminates among pupils at different levels of achievement, i.e., on which the best pupils make the highest scores, the worst pupils make the lowest scores, and the pupils in between are distributed from high to low essentially in descending order of achievement.

After the items have tentatively been selected for inclusion in the final test and after they and the necessary general and special directions for pupils have been coordinated appropriately in the form of a test, the items are often once again subjected to a critical review by committee members, consultants, or specialists. Any changes deemed necessary as a result of this final review are then made. The authors, usually with the assistance of an editor, then attend to any necessary matters of detail involved in the preparation of test copy for the printer. The authors and an editor usually work together in making sure that the final copy is satisfactory in format, accuracy, and other characteristics.

Preparing the Accessory Materials

Various accessory materials, differing considerably according to the scope and type of test in question, must be prepared as aids to teachers and other school personnel and pupils and their parents in using the tests and in interpreting test results. These must include directions for administering and scoring the tests and the scoring keys themselves; they often include separate answer sheets, class record forms, pupil profile forms, and even other materials. Some of these may be prepared in temporary form at this time with the expectation that they will later be incorporated in the manual of directions that is usually not prepared until the type of normative information discussed in the next, and last, step of procedure is completed.

Interpreting the Test Results

Several of the most technical and at the same time fundamentally important procedures in the construction of standardized achievement tests cannot be carried out until the final form of the instrument is ready for use. When it is ready, consequently, it is administered to large numbers of pupils of the appropriate types and the scores for this standardization group are used in establishing norms and other materials necessary for giving meaning to test scores. These same scores are also used in the determination of reliability and validity coefficients of the types described in Chapter 3.

Tables of test norms and information on test reliability and validity are often presented in a manual to supplement general descriptive statements about the test, about how it was constructed and standardized, and about its administration and scoring. However, some of the most recently published tests are accompanied by two or perhaps even three separate accessory publications—directions for administering and scoring, manuals on interpretation of scores, and sometimes more technical reports on how the test was standardized and on its reliability and validity.[4]

It seems apparent that a teacher in the modern school needs some understanding of the process of test standardization and even of a few of the technical aspects if he is to contribute effectively to a program of measurement and evaluation. However, his most direct needs seem certain to center around procedures for administering and scoring the tests and methods for interpreting and using test scores. Consequently, test norms of the types most often used for interpreting the results from standardized achievement tests are discussed and in some instances illustrated in a following section of this chapter, together with the related derived scores, pupil profiles, and still other interpretative materials now often provided with the better tests and test batteries. Norms of the four most basic types only —age norms, grade norms, percentile norms, and standard-score norms— are considered. Brief attention is also given in a later section of the chapter to administering and scoring the tests.

It seems worthy of comment as a final point on the process of achievement test standardization that, increasingly during the last few years, a cooperatively prepared set of recommendations for writing and publishing educational tests [5] has come to serve as a general guide for authors and publishers of such instruments. These recommendations apply particularly to the technical aspects of tests that are commented upon above, although they are also concerned with administration and scoring of tests, the manual of directions, and a few other less technical phases of the kinds treated rather extensively in the foregoing pages and in later sections of this chapter.

3. SELECTION OF STANDARDIZED TESTS

Classroom teachers in some instances choose tests in specific subjects for use in their own classes and on other occasions they participate as committee members or members of a department or school faculty in selecting tests in such subject areas as reading, language, and arithmetic or general achievement test batteries for use with pupils in a number of grades and classes. In any event, test selection depends on the type of testing planned, for tests should be chosen that not only are within the proper subject

[4] For example, *Cooperative English Tests:* (1) *Directions for Administering and Scoring,* (2) *Manual for Interpreting Scores,* and (3) *Technical Report.* Educational Testing Service, Princeton, N. J., 1960.

[5] Committee on Test Standards, American Educational Research Association and National Council on Measurements Used in Education, *Technical Recommendations for Achievement Tests.* National Education Association, Washington, D. C., 1955.

area and at the appropriate level of advancement for the pupils but that also will serve the desired function.

It should be pointed out here that not all standardized tests are appropriately named and that too much dependence can be placed on a test title and on what authors and publishers say about it in catalogs and advertisements. The fact that a test is standardized does not justify its uncritical acceptance as valid for the type of use specified by its author and publisher. Even if statements about its validity are well founded, it may not be equally valid for the use to which a teacher may wish to put it.

To guard against the possibility that tests do not actually accomplish what is claimed for them and to make sure that they are valid for the specific purposes to be fulfilled in his classroom or school, the teacher, as well as the student, should know how to utilize critical standards in the selection of standardized achievement tests. Two of the ways of approaching test selection in this critical manner are discussed here.[6]

Published Sources of Information

Valuable sources of information about standardized achievement tests, and in fact about all types of standardized tests discussed in this volume, are the *Mental Measurements Yearbooks*,[7] brought up to date by issuance of a new edition every few years. These yearbooks contain carefully edited descriptions and critical reviews of tests by subject and test specialists with which to supplement information about tests furnished by their authors and publishers.

Rating Scales

In the discussion of the criteria of a good examination in Chapter 3, no attempt is made to evaluate the relative importance of the various characteristics that affect test quality. However, rating devices that weight the various characteristics roughly in order of their importance are available. One that is designed to parallel the classification of examination characteristics, or criteria, appearing in Chapter 3 is illustrated here. The assignment of point values to the different features of a test is, of course, largely a subjective procedure. It is obvious that two different individuals using

[6] See also Educational Testing Service, *Selecting an Achievement Test: Principles and Procedures.* Evaluation and Advisory Service Series, No. 3. Educational Testing Service, Princeton, N. J., 1958.

[7] Oscar K. Buros, editor, (1) *The Third Mental Measurements Yearbook.* Rutgers University Press, New Brunswick, N. J., 1949; (2) *The Fourth Mental Measurements Yearbook.* Gryphon Press, Highland Park, N. J., 1953; and (3) *The Fifth Mental Measurements Yearbook.* Gryphon Press, Highland Park, N. J., 1959.

such a rating scale could not be expected to agree closely on the numerical rating assigned to a particular test. However, in spite of these limitations, a rating scale is of very real value in part because of the definite way in which attention is called to the important characteristics of a good test.

Standardized Achievement Test Rating Scale

Characteristics	Maxi-mum Rat-ings	Test: _____		Test: _____	
		Rat-ings	Reasons	Rat-ings	Reasons
1. Validity	20				
2. Reliability	10				
3. Adequacy	10				
4. Objectivity	10				
5. Practicality	5				
a. Administrability	10				
b. Scorability	10				
c. Economy	5				
6. Comparability	15				
7. Utility	5				
Totals	100				

Summary statement of major reasons for preference

The accompanying rating scale is valuable when two or more standardized achievement tests are being considered for use in a situation where the purpose is well defined and the pupils to be tested have been decided upon in advance. If the tests are rated by the same person, the resulting total scores should be influenced by such similar factors that their comparison should lead to the selection of the test that will best serve the purpose. The weights assigned to the various characteristics are thought to represent their relative significance in the determination of total test validity.

A supplementary check list for use before the rating scale is filled out appears in another accompanying illustration. Provided with spaces for recording significant information about a test, the check list should be used separately for each test under consideration. Such sources of information about each test as the publisher's catalog, the test manual and other accessory materials, the test booklet, and even the *Mental Measurements Yearbooks* and other unbiased sources might well be consulted in filling out such a check list.

Standardized Achievement Test Check List

Title _____Copyright_____

Author(s) _____ Publisher_____

1. Validity (Measures what it *attempts* to measure; Proper purpose and level)
   Analysis of _____
   Recommendations of _____
   Validity coefficients:
   Type_____: ____ on_____ cases in Grade_____ or on_____
   Type_____: ____ on_____ cases in Grade_____ or on_____

2. Reliability (Measures what it *does* measure; Consistency)
   Reliability coefficients:
   Type_____: ____ on_____ cases in Grade_____ or on_____
   Type_____: ____ on_____ cases in Grade_____ or on_____
   Type_____: ____ on_____ cases in Grade_____ or on_____

3. Adequacy (Wide sampling of items in outcome(s) measured
   No. of booklet pages_____; No. of items_____; Testing time_____
   Types of outcomes measured _____

4. Objectivity (Absence of subjectivity or bias in correct answers)
   Types and numbers of items:
   Selection: Alternate-response _____; Multiple-choice _____;
       Matching _____.
   Supplementation: Simple recall _____; Completion _____.
   Miscellaneous _____

5. Practicality (Practical considerations; Feasibility)
   a. Administrability (Ease of administering)
      Working time on Part(s): I ____; II ____; III ____; IV ____;
          V ____; VI ____.
      Directions____; Preparation for giving ____; Pupil instructions ____.
      Materials needed: Booklets ____; Answer sheets ____; Special pencils ____; Manual of directions ____; Other _____
      Administered by: Teacher ____; Specialist ____; Psychologist ____.

b. Scorability (Ease of scoring)
Scoring key _____; Scoring directions _____; No. of separate scores _____.
Scored by: Clerk _____; Teacher _____; Psychologist _____; Machine _____.
c. Economy (Cost in money and time)
Booklets reusable _____; Separate answer sheets _____.
Cost: Booklet _____; Answer sheet _____; Special materials_____.

6. Comparability (Bases for interpreting results)
Norms: Age _____; Grade _____; Percentile _____; Other _____.
Raw or derived scores _____; No. of duplicate forms _____.
Norms based on _____ cases from _____

7. Utility (Use to be made of results)
Need to be served _____
To be used in Grade(s) _____ or with _____
Planned use of results _____
Class record _____; Pupil profiles _____; Diagnostic aids _____; Instructional aids _____; Other special materials _____

4. ADMINISTRATION AND SCORING OF STANDARDIZED TESTS

Procedures for administering and scoring standardized tests differ considerably according to subject area, grade level, and type of instrument but the differences are greater in mechanics and details than in important aspects. Most of the tests published during the last ten or fifteen years and many of their predecessors provide clear and specific instructions in manuals of directions or in special manuals on administration and scoring of the instrument. Consequently, only a brief treatment of these phases of the testing process is given here. Even though the primary concern of this chapter is standardized achievement tests, much of the discussion of this section applies almost equally well to standardized tests of mental ability and personality.

Administering the Tests

Standardized achievement tests ranging from extensive batteries to tests in specific subjects are administered by teachers in their homerooms or the classrooms of many modern schools. When large numbers of pupils are assembled in a cafeteria or auditorium for taking tests or when a public address system is used in test administration, however, teachers more commonly serve as proctors. In either case, it is a responsibility of the teacher to be conversant with the procedures and to be an effective participant in test administration upon request.

A few of the many details to consider in test administration are enumerated below under headings arranged essentially in order of occurrence. The suggestions are intended as general guides for the teacher who is responsible for scheduling and administering a standardized test and who has available all necessary testing materials for pupil use and for his own use. If these suggestions go contrary to specifications in a test manual in any detail, the procedure recommended in the manual should be followed.

(1) Preparing for Testing Session—schedule test for definite time and place; guard against any interruptions that can be anticipated; read or study standardized directions for test administration; examine samples of booklet, answer sheet, any other testing materials; count out and arrange testing materials; have extra booklets, answer sheets, pencils, and any other materials used by pupils; be sure you have a stop watch, watch with second hand, or interval timer, a copy of examiner's directions, a complete set of testing materials, and a pencil for your own use.

(2) Setting the Scene—seat pupils in alternate sidearm chairs, at desks, or widely spaced at tables; be sure that writing surfaces are free of books or papers.

(3) Motivating Pupils—announce testing session, reason for it, and resulting values to pupils a few days in advance; adopt a businesslike but not severe manner during testing session.

(4) Distributing Test Materials—plan distribution procedure in advance for time saving and avoidance of confusion (good sequence is special pencils, answer sheets, booklets if all are needed); have materials counted out in separate piles for rows of seats or sections of room; distribute materials quickly but without strain; check to make sure every pupil is supplied with all necessary materials.

(5) Giving Preliminary Oral Directions—read preliminary instructions slowly and clearly; have pupils supply necessary personal information on answer sheets, test booklets, or other testing materials as needed; proceed to test or first test part without unnecessary delay.

(6) Answering Pupils' Questions—answer appropriate questions adequately but briefly; adhere closely to intent of standardized directions on scoring procedures and in all other respects.

(7) Timing Test or Test Parts—when starting signal is given, start timing device or, using a watch: (a) record hour, minute, and second, (b) add time allowed for test or test part, and (c) record hour, minute, and second at which test or test part ends; have pupils stop work promptly at end of time allowance for test or test part.

(8) Proctoring Test—circulate around room to make sure pupils are following directions in recording answers and are working on appropriate part or section of test; unobtrusively guard against copying or reference to notes, books, or other aids; have extra pencils in hand for distribution as needed.

(9) Giving Oral Directions during and at End of Test—make announcements at points specified in directions concerning such details as (a) working time remaining, (b) end of test or test part, (c) start of new test part, (d) working back to preceding parts, and (e) method of returning materials at end of session.

(10) Handling Special Situations—make plans in advance for handling interruptions in testing continuity, requests to leave room, and minor illness in pupils; be prepared for even more serious emergencies.

(11) Collecting Test Materials—plan collection procedure in advance for time saving and avoidance of confusion (good sequence is booklets, answer sheets, special pencils if all were used); collect materials quickly but without strain.

(12) Accounting for Testing Materials—sort and account for all testing materials, usually booklets first and then answer sheets, pencils, and any other materials used.

Prior to the development of electric and electronic scoring machines, separate answer sheets for hand-scoring were used quite widely with teacher-made tests. The perfection of scoring machines in recent years has stimulated the use of separate answer sheets with many of the modern standardized tests. Many different types of separate answer sheets have been developed for use with a wide variety of tests. The three samples of provision for answers on standardized tests pictured in Figure 7, page 172, show two fragments from answer sheets scorable on two quite different types of machines and an answer card scorable on still a third kind of machine. Brief comments about the various types of scoring machines appear in the next section of this chapter.

Scoring the Test Results

It is less easily possible to make generalized statements about standardized test scoring procedures than about methods of administration, primarily because of wide differences among modern tests in types of hand-scoring keys and in the persons or the machines doing the scoring. Although the major emphasis here is upon the use of hand-scoring keys by teachers, brief attention is given to the strong trend of recent years toward dependence of elementary and secondary schools on centralized testing agencies in city school systems, state universities and colleges, state departments of education, and regional centers for machine-scoring services. The time of classroom teachers is made available for more significant aspects of testing, most notably in the interpretation and use of test results, to the extent that these agencies assume the scoring task that otherwise might fall upon teachers.

Although most present-day standardized achievement tests are scorable by rather routine clerical or machine procedures, a high degree of accuracy, attention to a number of important details, and even some degree of discretion are essential if the resulting scores are to be reliable. Teachers can most effectively attain the essential accuracy in any hand-scoring they may do by strict conformance to methods outlined by test publishers, by the use of systematic procedures, by careful attention to the details of the process, and by checking their own work or by checking one another for accuracy.

Hand-scoring methods. Several types of keys for use in the hand-scoring of tests have been evolved. Some of these provide for scoring pupil answers recorded in test booklets but at least one of the most widely used varieties is designed primarily for scoring pupil responses recorded on separate answer sheets. Whether these answer sheets are of the machine-scorable type or are devised solely for local use is not important. Many modern tests provide both hand-scoring keys for use by teachers or clerks and machine-scoring keys.

Scoring devices variously referred to as fan or accordion keys and as strip keys are best used when answers are recorded in test booklets in columnar arrangement. Figure 5 shows a portion of such a key for a test that is available both for hand-scoring and machine-scoring. This type of device can be used as a fan or accordion key by folding on the vertical lines and changing the folds so that successive columns of correct answers are exposed in the process of scoring a booklet. A more convenient form of strip key can be made by cutting the key into strips and pasting them on a cardboard.

A transparent key is especially suitable when answers are scattered over the pages of a test booklet or even an answer sheet. Such a key is used by superimposing it over a booklet or answer-sheet page so that the keyed answers appear over or adjacent to the pupil's answers. The scorer is not able to record his scoring marks directly on the test, however. A cutout key having apertures immediately over the positions where pupil answers appear when it is superimposed over a booklet page or answer sheet is used in similar manner. Correct answers either are represented by the marking positions the scorer can see through the apertures or are printed on the key, as in the case of a completion type of test, immediately above or adjacent to the apertures. The sample portion of a cutout key shown in

SCORING KEY

FOR USE WITH FORMS W, X, Y

CALIFORNIA MATHEMATICS TEST ADVANCED (W X Y Z SERIES)

DIRECTIONS FOR SCORING

1. This key is intended for scoring answers *written in the test booklet only* and is for use with the above-named test whether it appears as part of an achievement battery or as an individual test booklet. It applies to the forms of the test listed above.
2. Fold the key along the vertical lines separating the columns and line up the answers on the key with the corresponding ones on the booklet. Make sure that you have the correct test section (as marked in the column headings) before starting to score a page.
3. Use the method of marking that you prefer (marking either wrongs and omissions or rights). A colored pencil may provide helpful contrast. Note that each item is to be considered either right or wrong. No partial credits are given for partial answers. Credit any clear method of indicating a response. Consider the intention of the student if it can be determined. If in doubt, consider the answer wrong. If two or more answers are given, count the item wrong unless the student has attempted to erase or cross out the incorrect answer.
4. The score for each section is the number right. If you mark wrongs, subtract them (counting omissions as wrongs) from the total possible score given in the box at the end of each section on the key. Record the number correct in the boxes provided at the end of each section in the test booklet.

NOTE: A test booklet may be marked with the correct answers and used in place of the key as an aid in scoring, if desired.

TEST 3—SECTION A		TEST 3—SECTION B		TEST 3—SEC. B (Cont.)		TEST 3 SECTION C	TEST 3 SECTION C (Cont.)
Column 1	Column 2	Column 1	Column 2	Column 1	Column 2	SECTION C	(Cont.)
							54. a
		21. c	26. d			46. d	
				36. c	41. e (6)		
		22. c	27. 1			47. e ($.89)	55. d
1. c	8. b						
	9. c	23. e (7)	28. 3	37. d	42. a	48. c	56. c
2. e (18,004)	10. d						
		24. d	29. 4			49. c	57. a
3. d	11. c			38. a	43. d		
	12. b						
4. b	13. a	25. a	30. 2			50. a	
	14. a						58. b
	15. b			39. b	44. d		
5. a	16. c					51. b	
	17. b						59. d
		31. 2				52. d	
6. c	18. a	32. 5					
	19. c	33. 1		40. c	45. c		60. d
7. c	20. a	34. 6				53. a	
		35. 4					
Possible Score: 20				Possible Score: 25			Possible Score: 15

Published by
CALIFORNIA TEST BUREAU
5916 Hollywood Boulevard
Los Angeles 28, California

FIGURE 5. Sample Scoring Key for *California Mathematics Test* [8]

[8] Ernest W. Tiegs and Willis W. Clark, *California Mathematics Test, Advanced.* California Test Bureau, Monterey, Calif., 1957.

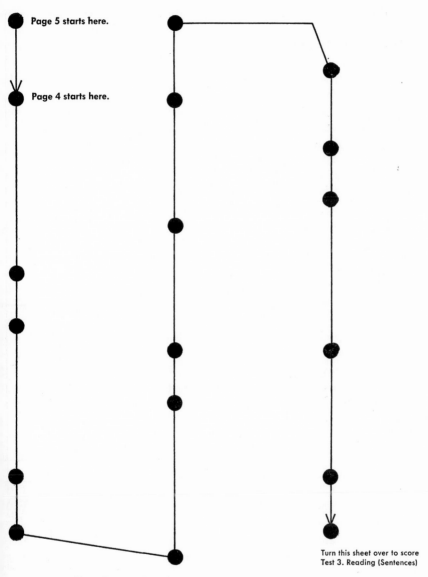

Page 5 starts here.

Page 4 starts here.

Turn this sheet over to score
Test 3. Reading (Sentences)

FIGURE 6. Sample Scoring Key for *Metropolitan Achievement Tests* [9]

[9] *Metropolitan Achievement Tests: Test 2, Word Discrimination.* Primary II Battery. Copyright 1959 by Harcourt, Brace and World, Inc., New York. All rights reserved. Quoted by special permission.

Figure 6 represents the type in which only correct answers can be seen through the holes.

Answer booklets provided with some standardized achievement tests make use of carbon or wax transfer paper so placed that the pupil's answers to test items are impressed on the back of the sheet on which he marks them. Each four-page booklet, kept sealed while the pupil takes the test, is opened for scoring. Correct answers appear in the spaces designated on the back of the sheet for ready counting, while incorrect answers appear outside of the designated positions. Scoring by this procedure amounts to very much the same thing as using a cutout key of the type shown in Figure 6.

Machine-scoring services. At least five types of electrical, electronic, or mechanical test scoring machines are now used in the scoring of objective tests, whether standardized or informal and whether of achievement, mental ability, or personality types. Of the four types of machines commented upon below, the first, which was introduced more than twenty years ago is now used in many school systems and testing centers throughout the country. The other four, which were first put into use not more than five years ago, provide services through several publishers of standardized tests, primarily for their own tests, or directly from a centralized testing agency by special arrangements. Samples of three distinct types of machine-scorable answer forms are pictured and identified in Figure 7.

The best known and most widely used of these, the *International Test Scoring Machine,*[10] is an electrical machine that enables an efficient operator to score several hundred per hour of the special answer sheets represented by a sample fragment in Figure 7. Special answer sheets are provided and directly adapted for use with many standardized tests, while standard answer sheets in a variety of styles are available for use by teachers or schools wishing to adapt their locally constructed tests to machine-scoring.

A second machine, the *IBM Electronic Scoring Punch 9002,* was developed by the same company for the rapid and automatic scoring of IBM answer cards of the type also partially represented in Figure 7. These cards, of the same size as those used with IBM punched-card equipment have so far been adapted for use with a limited number of standardized tests.[11]

Two electronic test scoring machines and several allied IBM machines became available several years ago for a series of automatic operations—scoring, memorizing, statistically analyzing, printing, and card punching—

[10] Produced by International Business Machines Corporation, New York.
[11] Published by California Test Bureau, Monterey, Calif., from which scoring service also available.

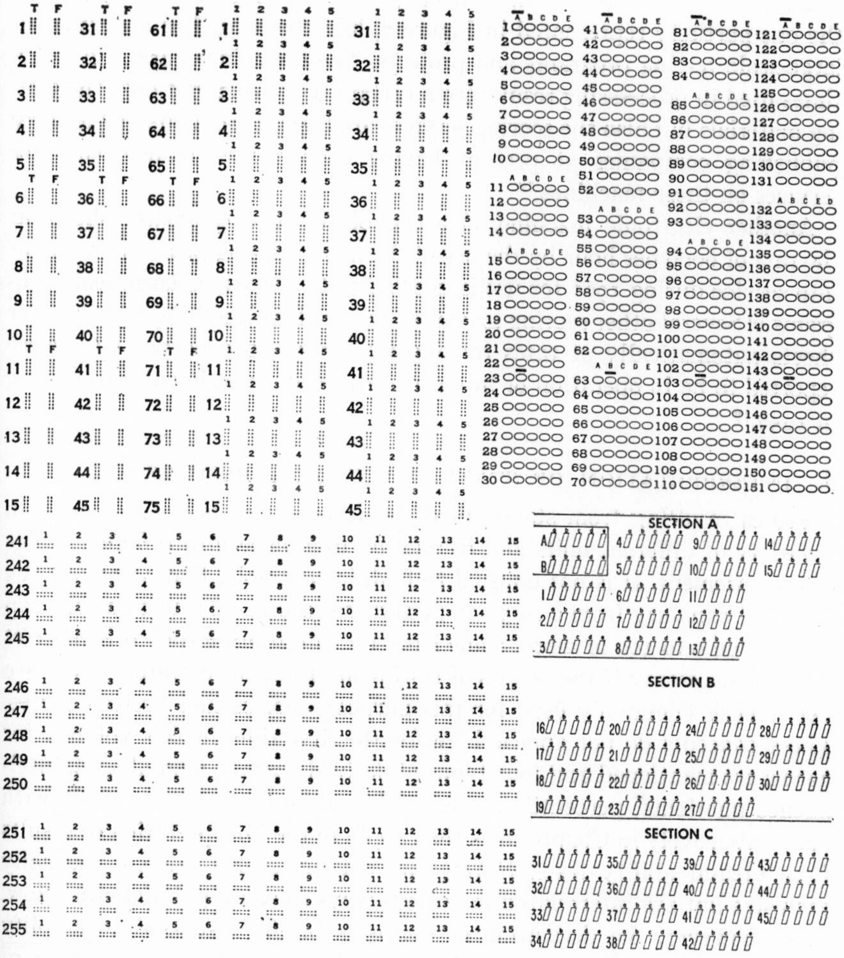

FIGURE 7. Samples of Machine-Scorable Answer Forms [12]

[12] Left—Scorable on IBM Electric Test Scoring Machines, International Business Machines Corporation; Upper Right—Scorable on Electronic Test Scoring Machines, Measurement Research Center, Inc.; Lower Right—Scorable on IBM Electronic Scoring Punch 9002, California Test Bureau.

at rates up to 6,000 test answer sheets per hour.[13] Answer sheets, such as the one partially represented in Figure 7, have been used in a number of large-scale testing programs and projects. These machines are also sometimes used in processsing results from certain tests when not only the testing materials but also the scoring services are bought from one of the three publishing companies at present having cooperative arrangements for services on these machines.[14]

Another electronic machine, also capable of scoring answer sheets at the rate of 6000 per hour by the use of the mark-sensing principle, was put into service during 1960 for use in scoring tests of various large-scale programs.[15] Several other scoring machines designed for handling IBM answer sheets automatically at rates ranging from 1200 to 2000 per hour were reported to be in operation or in various stages of experimental trials late in 1959.[16]

5. INTERPRETATION OF STANDARDIZED TEST RESULTS

Scores resulting from standardized achievement tests are expressed in a variety of different units and in relation to a variety of different scales of measurement. It is not unusual to find, for example, that scores on one such test can vary from 0 to 50 or 75 and that scores on a test battery can range from 0 to 300 or more. Some basis for interpreting such original test scores is necessary if the results of testing are to be meaningful. There are two devices commonly used for this purpose—norms and derived scores. These concepts do not appear here for the first time in this volume, for norms are mentioned and four types of derived scores—mental ages, intelligence quotients, percentile scores, and standard scores—are dealt with more extensively in Chapter 6 as they apply to the interpretation of results from mental ability tests. Norms and derived scores are not mutually exclusive but are interrelated in various ways that are pointed out below. First, however, the derivation of norms is briefly discussed to amplify slightly the brief comments made about them in a foregoing section of this chapter.

The standardized test for which norms are to be prepared is administered in its final form to large numbers of pupils in the same grades and of the same types as will take the test after its formal publication and after tables of norms are available. The resulting scores are then used by the test authors and publisher in the construction of norm tables in rather

---

[13] Machines and special services available at Measurement Research Center, Inc., Iowa City, Iowa.

[14] Houghton Mifflin Co., Boston, Science Research Associates, Inc., Chicago, and Harcourt, Brace and World, New York.

[15] By Educational Testing Service, Princeton, N. J.

[16] By the Psychological Corporation, New York.

complex and sometimes technical ways that need not concern the teacher except in very general terms. To the extent that the sampling used in obtaining the norms is distributed over a large number of pupils in typical school situations and that the standardized conditions under which the tests are to be administered are rigidly followed by the persons using the tests subsequently, the norms furnish a reliable and useful basis for interpretation of scores.

Norms

Some users of achievement tests have tended to confuse norms with standards, perhaps in part because of uncritical acceptance of the idea that standardized tests should provide standards. If the tests dealt with in this chapter had originally been called normalized tests, this confusion might have been avoided. The major concern here is with norms, or levels of achievement actually attained by pupils, rather than standards or goals of attainment. A standard probably occupies a position somewhere between a norm and an ideal; as such it may, if well conceived, be a goal or objective that can be attained by some if not by all pupils under some but not all conditions.

Two illustrations of standards can be considered to differ widely, and perhaps to be contrasted in the degree of objectivity involved. One type can be represented by the handwriting quality and speed considered adequate in pupils for the typical demands of postschool life. A widely accepted criterion or measure of the attainment of this standard is a quality of 60 on the Ayres *Scale for Measuring the Quality of Handwriting of School Children* [17] at the rate of 70 letters per minute. These levels represent the norm for pupils completing the sixth grade. Consequently, half of the pupils in a typical school reach this level before they enter Grade 7, some attain it a year or so earlier, and a few never do attain it. The other type can be illustrated by the expectations or goals set up for their pupils by teachers and principals. Sometimes these are definitely formulated but more often they are only vaguely conceived goals. Certainly such standards differ from school to school, from teacher to teacher, and even, as his ideas and pupil groups change, from year to year for the same teacher.

The form in which the norms are provided depends to a large degree upon the level in the school system at which the test is used. The norms are also conditioned somewhat by the nature of the test itself. Tests that are designed for use in the elementary-school grades are usually accompanied by age norms and grade norms and sometimes percentile norms

[17] Published by Russell Sage Foundation, New York.

based on grade placement. Tests intended for use in the secondary school are more frequently provided with percentile and grade norms only. Age norms do not seem to be particularly useful at the high-school level, since so many factors other than age operate to affect achievement.

Brief discussions of age norms, grade norms, percentile norms, and standard-score norms are given below. The brief illustration of how such norms are derived indicates roughly the procedure used by test makers in establishing norms for a test.

Age norms. At the elementary-school level, age norms of one type or another appear to provide a more adequate basis for the interpretation of individual pupil accomplishment than is possible with grade norms or percentile-grade norms alone. In its simplest form the preparation of age norms involves the grouping of all pupils into chronological age groups regardless of grade location or school progress. The test scores of these chronological age groups are then tabulated, and the means or medians computed. These results are then used as the basis for setting up tables of the scores corresponding to the several age groups.

The accompanying norm table for the vocabulary section of the *Gates Reading Survey* is used here to illustrate age norms. The reading age of a pupil in years and months can be obtained directly by entering the table with his test score and reading across to the third column. For example, the reading age of a child whose score on the vocabulary test is 19 is found to be 9-6. This indicates that his reading age in vocabulary is estimated to be approximately the same as that of the average or typical child whose chronological age is nine years and six months. This pupil may be an eight-year-old who is advanced for his age in vocabulary or an eleven-year-old who is retarded to about the same extent in vocabulary level.

Grade norms. The grade norms established for most of the commonly used achievement tests are based on the median scores obtained by giving the tests to large groups of pupils within each grade. In the derivation of grade norms, the scores of pupils are grouped by their levels of school advancement as represented by grade placement. The means or medians of the scores at each grade level are then computed and used in constructing tables of scores expected for pupils at each level of grade placement. Grade norms thus provide a convenient means of expressing the approximate progress of the pupil through the grades by turning his raw score into a grade-equivalent score.

Grade norms, as well as age norms, are presented for the vocabulary section of the *Gates Reading Survey* in the table referred to above. If the table is again entered with a pupil score of 19, the corresponding grade level for vocabulary is found to be 4.3. This indicates that the pupil has a vocabulary that is estimated to be about equal to that of the average or typical pupil who has been in Grade 4 for three months. This pupil could be one of the brighter and probably younger children in Grade 3 or one of the older and possibly duller pupils in Grade 5 or Grade 6.

Percentile norms. Relative accomplishment of individual pupils within a grade or who are taking a certain course may also be shown clearly by turning raw scores into percentile scores. This is done by computing the percentile values from the frequency tables for each grade or course distri-

TABLE 7

Grade and Age Norms for *Gates Reading Vocabulary Test* [18]

Raw Score	Reading Grade	Reading Age	Raw Score	Reading Grade	Reading Age
0	2.0	7-2	35	7.0	12-3
1	2.1	7-3	36	7.2	12-6
2	2.2	7-4	37	7.4	12-8
3	2.3	7-6	38	7.7	13-0
4	2.4	7-7	39	8.0	13-4
5-6	2.5	7-8	40	8.2	13-6
7	2.6	7-10	41	8.5	13-9
8-9	2.7	7-11	42	8.8	14-0
			43	9.2	14-5
10	2.8	8-0	44	9.6	14-11
11	2.9	8-1			
12	3.1	8-3	45	10.0	15-4
13	3.3	8-6	46	10.3	15-7
			47	10.4	15-8
14	3.4	8-7	48	10.6	16-0
15	3.6	8-9	49	10.7	16-1
16	3.8	9-0			
17	4.0	9-2	50	10.8	16-2
18	4.2	9-4	51	10.9	16-4
19	4.3	9-6	52	11.0	16-5
			53	11.1	16-6
20	4.4	9-7	54	11.2	16-7
21	4.5	9-8			
22	4.7	9-10	55	11.3	16-8
23	4.8	10-0	56	11.4	16-9
24	5.0	10-2	57	11.5	16-10
			58	11.6	16-11
25	5.2	10-4	59	11.7	17-0
26	5.4	10-6			
27	5.5	10-7	60	11.9	17-2
28	5.6	10-8	61	12.0	17-4
29	5.8	10-10	62	12.2	17-6
			63	12.4	17-9
30	6.0	11-2	64	12.6	18-0
31	6.2	11-5			
32	6.4	11-8	65	12.8	18-2
33	6.6	11-10			
34	6.8	12-1			

[18] Arthur I. Gates, *Manual for the Gates Reading Survey*. Bureau of Publications, Teachers College, Columbia University, New York, 1958. p. 5.

bution and assigning percentile equivalents for each score. Percentile norm tables show for a wide sampling of pupils in a certain grade or course either the percentage of pupils exceeding each score or the score below which certain percentages of pupils fall. Although percentile norms are customarily presented by one or the other of these methods, there is a great variety in the form of such tables. Percentile scores corresponding to specific raw scores may be reported by grades or by test parts and totals, or only the raw-score equivalents for specified percentiles, quartiles, and deciles may be shown in more compact tables.

An illustration of percentile norms by grades, also called percentile-grade or percentile-within-grade norms, appears in Table 8 for scores on the *Spitzer Study Skills Test*. It is possible to determine directly from the table that the raw score of 32 for a senior is equivalent to 62 in the percentile column. Inasmuch as neither the percentile column nor the four score columns include every possible number from lowest to highest, interpolation sometimes becomes necessary in using it. It requires only rather simple interpolation, however, to find the percentile equivalent, or percentile rank of 80, for a freshman whose raw score is 29.

TABLE 8

Percentile and Standard Score Norms for *Spitzer Study Skills Test* [19]

%-ILE	STAND. SCORE	GRADE				%-ILE	STAND. SCORE	GRADE			
		9	10	11	12			9	10	11	12
99	136	39	41	42	42	33	100	15	19	20	22
97	130	37	39	41	41	27	98	13	17	18	21
94	126	35	38	40	40	22	96	12	15	17	19
92	124	34	37	39		18	94	11	14	15	17
89	122	32	36	38	39	14	92	10	12	14	16
86	120	31	35	37	38	11	90	9	11	12	15
82	118	30	34	36	37	8	88	8	10	11	14
78	116	28	32	34	36	6	86	7	9	10	12
73	114	26	31	33	35	5	84	6	8	9	11
68	112	24	30	32	33	3	82	5	7	8	10
62	110	22	28	30	32	2	80		6	7	9
56	108	21	26	29	30	2	78	4	5	6	8
50	106	19	24	27	28	1	76	3	4	5	6
43	104	17	22	24	27	1	72	2	3	4	5
38	102	16	20	22	25	1−	68	1	2	3	4

[19] Herbert F. Spitzer, *Spitzer Study Skills Test: Manual of Directions*. Copyright 1954 by Harcourt, Brace and World, Inc., New York. p. 7. All rights reserved. Quoted by special permission.

Standard-score norms. Norms in the form of standard scores are determined by using the arithmetic mean and standard deviation of raw scores in certain rather technical ways. The simplest and basic procedure used in this process is presented briefly in Chapter 14.

Table 8 gives standard-score norms as well as percentile norms for the *Spitzer Study Skills Test.* Interpolation is necessary when entering the table with raw scores that do not appear in the score column being used. Again using the raw score of 32 for a senior, it can easily be seen that the standard-score equivalent is 110. The Grade 9 pupil whose raw score is listed above as 29 is found by interpolation to have a standard score of 117.

Derived Scores and Measures

As is mentioned above, a raw score obtained from a test typically has no meaning beyond what is shown by relating it to other scores on the same test. One of the necessary and final steps in standardizing an achievement test is the derivation of the appropriate types of derived scores as well as norms. Original test scores are variously converted into some types of derived score at three distinguishable times in the process of giving meaning to test results.

(1) As a direct part of the scoring process itself, when raw scores on some achievement tests, particularly those that are machine-scorable, are converted to standard scores having more meaning than the raw scores. In such instances, these derived scores in turn are often translated by the use of norms tables into a second series of derived scores, most commonly percentile ranks, that has still more meaning in this special situation.

(2) As a result of using tables of norms in converting from raw scores to some type of derived scores or even from one type of derived scores to another. The conversions from raw scores to age equivalents, grade equivalents, percentile ranks, and standard scores that are shown immediately above illustrate this procedure.

(3) As a result of relating some type of derived scores to another type, usually by division, to obtain quotients that are also derived scores, or, more properly, derived measures. The intelligence quotient, shown in Chapter 6 to be derived from mental age—one type of derived score— and chronological age is one illustration. Other illustrations are the educational quotient and achievement quotient that are treated later in this section of the chapter.

These three illustrations of how derived scores are obtained differ in another respect that has some meaning. A derived score of the first type is obtained from the one-step scoring process, one of the second type involves a two-step process of obtaining a score and of using a norm table to obtain a second type of score, and one of the third type requires a three-step process of obtaining a score, of using a norm table to obtain a second type of score, and of using simple arithmetic to obtain a quotient. Although the one-step process may actually amount to the telescoping of two steps into one and quotients are sometimes derived from special tables, these distinctions apply to most situations where raw scores are converted to derived scores or measures.

Derived scores and measures can be distinguished in another and perhaps more significant way—in terms of the types of numerical or statistical concepts underlying them. Consequently, distinctions are here made among those that are (1) based on a typical performance, (2) based on differences or variability in performance, and (3) obtained as quotients. The third type is dealt with fully here but for the first two the applicational aspects treated at this point are supplemented by brief consideration of the statistical aspects in Chapter 14.

Derived scores based on average performance. The two types of derived scores based on average or median performance are the age equivalent and the grade equivalent. These are directly dependent upon tables of norms, for it is only by entering norm tables with raw scores or some other type of scores that they can be determined.

Age equivalents occur both in a broad and in a narrow sense. The mental age (MA), discussed at some length in Chapter 6, and the educational age (EA), of particular pertinence in this chapter, are the most common illustrations of the broad usage. The reading age (RA), referred to previously in this chapter, and some other derived scores for subject areas, such as the arithmetic age (AA) or language age (LA), represent the less common narrow usage. In each of these instances, the age equivalent of a pupil represents his level of maturity in terms of the average chronological age of many other pupils whose performance is at the same level as his. His age equivalent can be thought of also as an indication of how far he has climbed up a growth ladder based on the performance of average or typical children. Such ages are commonly stated in hyphenated form, the first number indicating years and the second number months of age. Thus, to illustrate again the type of interpretation given in the foregoing discussion of norms, an EA of 11-10 indicates that in broad educational achievement as measured by a general achievement test a pupil is at the same level as average children eleven years and ten months of age.

Although this chapter is most directly concerned with the types of age equivalents noted above, the same technique is applied to the measurement of other aspects of child growth and performance. For example, anatomical age, physiological age, and social age are comparable terms that are employed with varying degrees of exactness in meaning.

Grade equivalents indicate position on a grade scale of growth similar in some respects to an age scale. A pupil's level of educational maturity is here stated in terms of the grade and months of attendance in that grade for which his test performance is typical. If, for example, to illustrate again what is presented in the preceding discussion of norms, a pupil has a grade equivalent of 6.8, he has attained the level of advancement educationally that is found in large numbers of pupils who have attended Grade 6 for eight months. Grades and months are typically listed as a number and decimal respectively. Grade equivalents are usually based on scores from general achievement test batteries; more specialized grade equivalents in reading, for example, are based on reading tests.

Derived scores based on differences in performance. Variability or differences in performance enter directly into the determination of percentile ranks and standard scores. The latter are sometimes obtainable as a direct outcome of the scoring process, as is mentioned above, but the former typically involve the use of norm tables.

Percentile ranks are used to express the relative standing of a pupil in a distribution of scores for large numbers of pupils in his school grade, in a certain course he is taking, such as algebra, or who have studied a certain subject, such as French, the same number of semesters as he has. This is accomplished by dividing the distribution of scores into 100 equal parts in such manner that each of the parts contains one one-hundredth of the total group of pupils. The parts are then labeled 99 to 0 from highest to lowest. A pupil in the tenth group from the top would thereby be assigned a percentile rank (P) of 90, and would have a score higher than 90 percent of the scores used in establishing the norms. Again, a pupil having a percentile rank of 63, or falling in the thirty-seventh group from the top, would have a score higher than those attained by 63 percent of the normative group.

Standard scores have the arithmetic mean and standard deviation of a large group of pupils as foundations for their derivation. Equated scores, scaled scores, normalized standard scores, and converted scores are terms used in various standardized achievement tests with very similar meanings. A simple illustration will perhaps suffice here to indicate the general meaning of standard scores. A score 1.0 standard deviation above the arithmetic mean of the master distribution would have a standard score value of 60 $[50 + (1.0 \times 10)] = 50 + 10 = 60$, and a score 1.3 standard deviations below the mean of the normative group of pupils would have a standard score equivalent of 37 $[50 - (1.3 \times 10)] = 50 - 13 = 37$. Thus, the original distribution of scores is converted to a standard-score distribution having an arithmetic mean and standard deviation set for convenience at 50 and 10 respectively.

Quotients as derived measures. The three types of quotients used in educational measurement are the intelligence quotient (IQ), dealt with extensively in Chapter 6, the educational quotient (EQ) and several related subject quotients, and the achievement quotient (AQ), quite different in type from the others. Educational, subject, and achievement quotients, sometimes of direct value in the interpretation of standardized achievement test results, are considered briefly here and intelligence quotients are reintroduced because of their relation to achievement quotients.

An *educational quotient* (EQ) or a subject quotient indicates a pupil's achievement level in comparison with the average achievement level of a large number of pupils of his chronological age when both measures are based on standardized achievement test results. Thus, a pupil who has an EQ of 110 is further advanced in educational growth than typical pupils of his age and a child who has an EQ of 83 is markedly retarded educationally in comparison with his age peers. Subject quotients differ only in the substitution of growth in a subject area, such as reading, for the broader concept of educational growth. The formulas for these quotients are

$$EQ = 100\,\frac{EA}{CA} \quad \text{and} \quad RQ = 100\,\frac{RA}{CA}.$$

These quotients are based on the idea that on the average a child grows in all ways more nearly in conformance with his chronological age than with any other measures, and also upon the recognition that deviations from that pattern of growth result from individual differences and are meaningful in the guidance of the child.

Computation of the quotients listed above is illustrated for a pupil who has a chronological age (CA) of 8-4, an educational age (EA) of 9-2, and a reading age (RA) of 9-4. The last two ages would be determined in the manner indicated in the above section from his scores on a general achievement test and a reading test. The quotients are based on computations in which each age is reduced to months, and ratios are multiplied by 100 to eliminate the use of decimals in the results.

For the child whose various age levels or age equivalents are given above, his educational quotient (EQ) would be

$$EQ = 100\,\frac{EA}{CA} = 100\,\frac{9\text{-}2}{8\text{-}4} = 100\,\frac{110\ (\text{months})}{100\ (\text{months})} = 110,$$

and his reading quotient (RQ) would be

$$RQ = 100\,\frac{RA}{CA} = 100\,\frac{9\text{-}4}{8\text{-}4} = 100\,\frac{112\ (\text{months})}{100\ (\text{months})} = 112.$$

An *achievement quotient* (AQ), or the ratio between a pupil's educational age and mental age, is based on the idea that mental age may be a better criterion for judging educational growth than is chronological age. The assumption underlying this relationship is that the pupil's educational age represents his accomplishment level, that the mental age represents his capacity for school work, and hence that the ratio between the two indicates how well he is living up to his capacities. The formula for this quotient in several adaptations is

$$AQ = 100\,\frac{EA}{MA} = 100\,\frac{EQ}{IQ} = 100\,\frac{\dfrac{EA}{CA}}{\dfrac{MA}{CA}}.$$

For a pupil who has a mental age (MA) of 10-0 and an educational age (EA) of 9-0, the achievement quotient (AQ) would be

$$AQ = 100\,\frac{9\text{-}0}{10\text{-}0} = 100\,\frac{108\ (\text{months})}{120\ (\text{months})} = 90.$$

The implication of this finding is that the pupil is not working up to his capacity.

The achievement quotient is briefly discussed and presented above because the concepts of underachievement and, unrealistically, of overachievement are widely used and because educators seem to be reluctant to abandon the idea represented by the AQ. Even so, the quotient has several technical defects that render it so unsuitable for accomplishing its original purpose that it is seldom used today.[20] Certainly it is not suitable for use with individual pupils and its use even with groups of pupils is not recommended.

Final Reports of Test Results

The norms and derived scores discussed in the foregoing sections of this chapter are variously used in the preparation of final reports of test results. Needs of the school and also of the pupils and their parents for systematic information about test results are satisfied in this manner. Accessory testing materials of several types for accomplishing this purpose variously accompany most of the modern standardized achievement tests.

Test reports within the school. Perhaps three types of records for immediate use within the school are most commonly provided with standardized batteries of general achievement tests in present-day practice: (1) pupil

[20] Anne Anastasi, *Psychological Testing.* Macmillan Co., New York, 1954. p. 463.

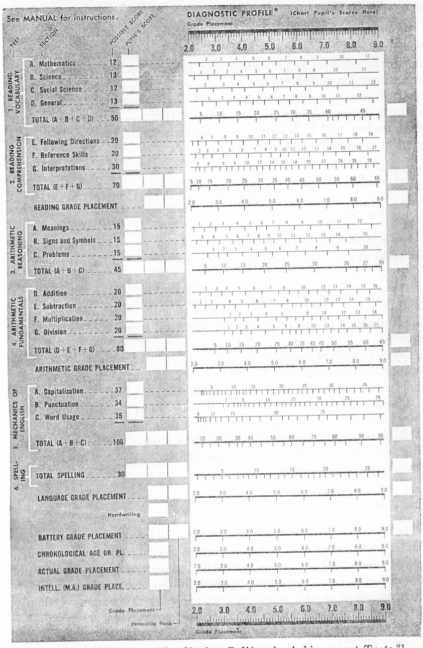

FIGURE 8. Diagnostic Profile for *California Achievement Tests* [21]

21 Ernest W. Tiegs and Willis W. Clark, *California Achievement Tests: Diagnostic Profile,* Elementary. California Test Bureau, Monterey, Calif., 1957.

profiles, (2) class lists, and (3) score distribution or class analysis forms. Tests designed for use in specific subjects or subject areas usually provide one or more but not necessarily all of these aids to interpretation and use of results.

Profile charts appear variously on covers of test booklets, on machine-scorable answer sheets, or as separate forms. A major purpose in each instance is to facilitate use of test results in various ways, some of which are suggested in a subsequent section of this chapter, and to provide forms for filing in pupil cumulative records. Two samples of such profiles are shown in Figures 8 and 9 to indicate general characteristics of such forms.

The first illustration, a diagnostic profile for the elementary level of the *California Achievement Tests*, represents the comprehensive type of report provided for by materials accompanying some of the general achievement test batteries. Spaces are designated for recording raw scores on the 18 sections, six tests, and three subject areas and for inserting the two types of derived scores—grade equivalents and percentile ranks—for tests, areas, and the total battery. A detailed profile scaled to grade equivalents can be constructed easily.

The second sample, from the *Iowa Tests of Educational Development*, provides spaces for recording percentile ranks on the eight basic tests, one supplementary test, and a composite of Tests 1 to 8. The ranks can easily be translated into a profile that permits a comparison of each pupil with norms based on large numbers of pupils in the same high-school grade and semester.

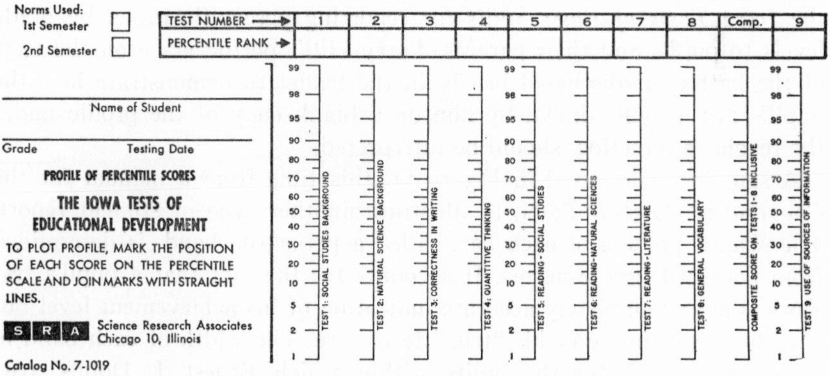

FIGURE 9. Profile of Percentile Scores for *Iowa Tests of Educational Development* [22]

[22] *Iowa Tests of Educational Development*, Pupil Profile Card. Science Research Associates, Inc., Chicago.

Class lists provide forms on which pupil names and the pertinent types of scores can be recorded for use by teachers and for permanent filing in the central office. Since such forms differ more in details than in significant respects, they seem to warrant only passing mention here.

Score distributions and class analysis forms are provided with some modern tests for use by the teacher in summarizing and analyzing test results for his class groups. The score distributions usually consist of tabulation forms and instructions for their use in summarizing test results so that group characteristics as well as individual pupil standings within the group become apparent. At least one of them is accompanied by an outline of procedures for an important further step in giving meaning to test results—construction of local test norms. These relatively simple procedures are outlined in Chapter 14, where other statistical procedures used in the interpretation of test results are presented. A few tests are accompanied by class analysis forms that provide in some manner for summarization, sometimes even by some sort of graphical representation, of results for a class or school. Such forms or charts are also useful in bringing out group as well as individual pupil achievement levels analytically.

Test reports for pupils and parents. Provisions are made by the authors and publishers of several batteries of general achievement tests and tests in broad subject areas for reporting test results to pupils and their parents. These usually take the form of a leaflet containing a profile of the individual pupil's test results and nontechnical statements about the nature of the test and how to interpret the results depicted.

The pupil profile shown in Figure 10 appears in a leaflet provided with the *Iowa Tests of Basic Skills* for reporting percentile ranks by grade levels to pupils and their parents. Larry Hill's performance on the tests of the battery is discussed briefly in the leaflet to demonstrate how the pupil's own profile, drawn by him on a blank copy of the profile under the teacher's direction, should be interpreted.

A sample is also used in Figure 11, this time from a manual for the *Cooperative English Tests,* to illustrate another type of student report. The shaded portion of each bar, called a percentile band, is determined from percentile-grade norms. It accounts for the fact that a pupil's test score is not a completely accurate indication of his achievement level but is rather an estimate of his "true" test score. The width of each band in this sample indicates the limits within which Ernest J. Dobbs' true score is likely to fall. When the bands overlap, as do all three of those for the reading test, it is not certain that the performance levels really differ. However, since there is no overlap between the English expression and reading comprehension bands, it is probable that the level of reading comprehension is higher than the English expression level. The statements about the number of students in ten scoring lower than and higher than Ernest can easily be verified by counting the silhouettes of the pupils to the left and right of the shaded percentile band.

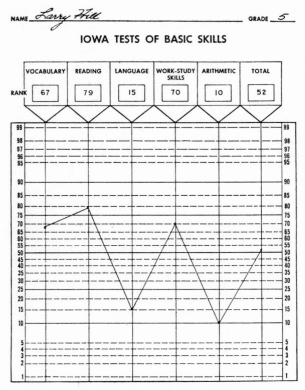

FIGURE 10. Example of Pupil Profile Chart for
Iowa Tests of Basic Skills [23]

6. PRACTICAL USES OF STANDARDIZED TESTS

The value of the educational test is directly proportional to the extent to which the results from its use are translated into improved practices in the school. If these practices bring about improvement in the conditions under which teachers teach and children learn, the primary functions of the tests will have been realized. While the problems of securing these results in the most effective and economical manner are treated in this

[23] *Iowa Tests of Basic Skills: "How Are Your Skills?"* Houghton Mifflin Co., Boston, 1955.

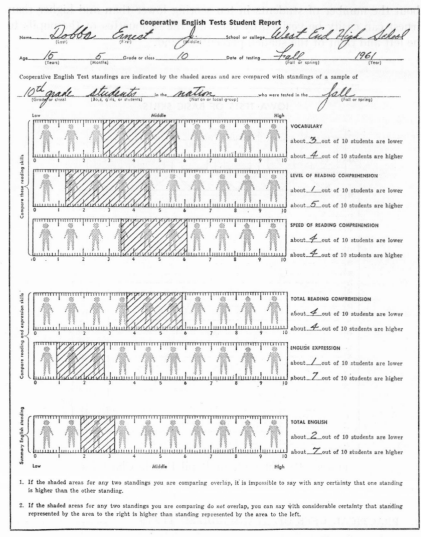

FIGURE 11. Example of Student Report for
Cooperative English Tests [24]

[24] *Cooperative English Tests: Manual for Interpreting Scores.* Educational Testing Service, Princeton, N. J., 1960. p. 15.

chapter primarily in terms of the test as an instructional device, the guidance, supervisory, and administrative uses of these instruments must not be slighted.

Many of the better standardized achievement tests and test batteries rather clearly depict appropriate uses in the accompanying test manuals and even sometimes in their titles, although such guides are not infallible indications. Even so, achievement tests can appropriately be used in a wide variety of special situations. Consequently, the brief consideration here of classroom uses and the even briefer mention of administrative uses are intended as general guides rather than as comprehensive treatments. The chapters of Part 5, on measuring and evaluating in subject areas, supplement this treatment in various specific ways. Moreover, the ingenious teacher may well discover other appropriate uses for certain types of standardized achievement tests.

Classroom Uses

The value of standardized tests for guidance, supervisory, administrative, and research purposes has been emphasized so generally that very often the classroom teacher overlooks their real value in the solution of his own instructional problems. Yet this is where the most vital and important uses of such tests are probably to be found. The modern conception of standardized tests implies their continuous use as instruction progresses. This means a continuous testing program, for experience indicates that only through continuous testing will standardized tests ever come to function at their highest efficiency as instructional instruments in the classroom.

Determination of status and progress. Very often a teacher, at the beginning of a school term, wishes to obtain advance information concerning the proficiency of his classes and individual pupils in certain subjects and their general preparation for the work. It is essential for him to know their weaknesses and their strengths in some detail in order so to direct their activities that the best results will be obtained. He needs to know the background of his pupils for the work they will encounter during the ensuing year.

Ability to read silently is the basis of proficiency in so many subjects that the teacher should secure a picture of the reading level of the class. The results should indicate whether the class as a whole and the individual members are able to interpret the printed page with facility, and so carry on their work without great assistance. It is also desirable to test for other general qualities, as well as for knowledge and other important outcomes. With this background, it is possible for the teacher to adapt class instruction to an appropriate level of advancement and, on occasion, particularly in the lower grades, to use within-class grouping so as to provide for individual differences within a class.

Not only is this preliminary survey of great value to the teacher, but it has also been found desirable and valuable to check progress or advancement from time to time by means of objective tests. Tests of achievement will reveal whether the class as a group is moving together, or whether there are more or less well-defined subgroups that seem to need special attention.

Diagnosis of deficiencies. Educational diagnosis implies the use of more or less technical procedures designed to locate specific learning and instructional difficulties, and if possible to determine their causes. Diagnosis has many of the same implications for the teacher as for the physican, but much of the exactness, objectivity, and precision of the medical diagnostician's instruments still appear to be missing in the teacher's equipment. Even today not many objective measuring instruments capable of rendering reasonably precise diagnosis are available to the educational diagnostician. Deficiencies of a general nature are often brought to light by general survey tests. Specific weaknesses, and to a certain extent causes of weaknesses, are less frequently identified by the use of properly selected diagnostic tests.

Good diagnosis must parallel the processes of good teaching. Effective diagnostic materials in any school subject can be prepared only after the skills contributing to success in this field have been isolated and identified. Diagnosis must be more exact than broad statements of general functions. Remedial work, accordingly, can function only when the point at which pupil mastery breaks down has been located. The exact nature of a pupil's handicap must be revealed before it is possible to undertake a remedial program. The more specific the diagnostic information revealed, the more exactly the remedial material can be made to fit the need.

Accurate diagnosis of class and individual pupil difficulties, coupled with application of specific remedy, underlies effective methods of teaching. The success of the remedial or corrective teaching depends upon the accuracy and detail with which the specific skills involved in successful achievement in the subject are identified and isolated in the test.

Unquestionably, one of the basic purposes of diagnosis is the location of weaknesses and the determination of their causes, but there is nothing in the method that precludes its use in the prevention of weaknesses through anticipation of their causes. Out of the knowledge gained through the use of diagnostic procedures should come the basis for preventive work of all types. The existence of a weakness implies a failure at some point in the program. The discovery of it should not be marked as important merely because it is then possible to correct it. The real importance in the discovery should lie rather in the prevention of its reappearance elsewhere under similar conditions.

Self-appraisal by teachers. Such test uses as are cited above are of great value in themselves, but equally important is the determination of ways and means by which the act of teaching itself may be improved. Ambitious teachers everywhere are looking for the best methods of instruction in their fields. Teaching methods, which in the last analysis should be studied in the classroom by the classroom teacher, can be evaluated effectively by means of standardized tests. Instructional units within the course of study should also be evaluated. The measurement of the effect of certain types of drill exercises and the determination of the specific strengths or weaknesses of groups or classes illustrate the uncounted opportunities for use of these valuable instructional devices.

Marking and reporting to parents. Results from standardized achievement tests are not appropriately used as a sole or even a major basis for course marks, since they can never be expected to reflect precisely the instructional outcomes sought by teachers in particular courses. The best they can be expected to do is to supplement the teacher-made tests and the many other appraisals of pupil achievement made by teachers in the course of a semester or school year. They can, however, particularly for college-preparatory pupils in the high school, supply information about how pupils compare in level of achievement with high-school pupils in general or even in some instances with others taking academic or college-preparatory courses.

Guidance Uses

In a very broad sense, any educational practice that affects the school child directly, or even indirectly, can be considered as guidance. In the more immediate sense, however, a guidance use is considered as one in which a counselor or teacher directs, or aids in directing, some of the pupil's activities. Two indications only of guidance uses are commented upon here. Standardized achievement tests are supplemented by other types of standardized tests in both instances.

Determination of expectancy levels. By the use of procedures dealt with in Chapter 14, it is possible to obtain an index showing the relationship between a pupil's educational attainments and his potentialities for educational growth. Although comparisons of the type needed for this purpose —between achievement test results and mental ability test results—can easily be misinterpreted or overemphasized, their values in classroom and sometimes in other and broader ways are great. In any event, pupils who surpass expectation are sometimes, incongruously, referred to as over-achievers and pupils who fail to come up to expectation are often, more soundly, called underachievers. The two groups need and definitely should receive different forms of guidance in the classroom and in other super-vised activities.

Educational and vocational counseling. A pupil's status as measured by standardized achievement tests constitutes one of the several types of evidence used in his guidance. Results from such tests serve as general indications of how well pupils will perform on similar and higher-level tests taken on later occasions and also of their scholastic success as meas-ured by course marks. Scores on such tests are often used to aid in the selection of courses and in charting the educational futures of junior-high-school pupils when combined with the measures of general or special mental ability discussed in Chapter 6. Pupils in the senior high school are often counseled as to their subsequent educational and vocational careers on the basis of results from standardized tests of achievement and of the multifactor mental ability tests treated in Chapter 6 and the interest tests dealt with in Chapter 7.

Administrative Uses

Modern school administration demands that the most objective and reliable evaluative instruments available be used to provide the answers to the problems continually arising in connection with the operation of a school system. Often, however, it is impossible to separate the administra-tive use of a test from an instructional use.

Pupil gradation and placement. Administrators, supervisors, and teach-ers find the problem of pupil placement one of the most difficult situations they have to face. The indefinite lines of division between the grades and the wide overlapping of ability between grades reveal that the typical tech-niques of pupil classification now in use are extremely crude. This could scarcely be otherwise in view of the methods commonly used. The proper grade placement of pupils implies that insofar as possible individuals who are normal for their group should be placed together. This means that pupils who are approximately alike in their chronological age, their edu-cational achievement, and their physiological, mental, social, and moral development should, where possible, be placed together for instructional purposes. Not all of these qualities lend themselves readily to objective measurement, but a number of them do, and within these limits the results of objective measurements should be used in deciding upon the pupil's placement in his group.

Group comparisons. Since the earliest beginnings of group instruction, administrators as well as classroom teachers have wished to know how their pupils compared in attainment with other similar pupils and classes. Until standardized tests were developed, it was practically impossible to secure this information. Now the giving of standardized tests makes fairly easy a comparison of the results for a school or class with the norms established for the subject and grade.

Comparisons with other classes within the system and within the same building, even between different sections of classes, can be made on a basis of objective norms derived for various tests. Another comparison that is even more useful is that between the attainment of a class at the beginning and the end of a year's work.

SUGGESTED ACTIVITIES

1. Read a review of a standardized test, either of general achievement or of achievement in a subject area of interest to you, and note what the author wrote about the degree to which the test satisfies the characteristics or criteria of a good examination.
2. Obtain educational quotients and achievement quotients for the two pupils whose chronological, mental, and educational ages are given below, and discuss the broad implications of the extent to which they seem to be learning in accordance with their potentialities for learning.

> Peter CA = 8-4; MA = 10-10; EA = 9-6
> Paul CA = 8-4; MA = 7-6; EA = 7-6

TOPICS FOR DISCUSSION

1. What are some major kinds of human behavior variously measured by standardized tests?
2. How do makers of standardized achievement tests decide upon the content of their tests?
3. By what procedures do persons who construct standardized tests of achievement sometimes plan in advance for a certain balance of test content and of learning outcomes measured?
4. How do the difficulty and discriminative power of test items affect the quality of an achievement test?
5. By what procedures can a teacher or school select standardized achievement tests that are most likely to serve the intended purposes?
6. What are a few general principles that should be observed in administering standardized tests?
7. Discuss the major types of test norms and illustrate each.
8. What factors appear to be involved in deciding upon the type of norms that should be provided for a standardized achievement test?

9. What are the major types of derived scores and how are they used?
10. How are derived scores related to norms?
11. What cautions should be observed in the interpretation of achievement quotients?
12. In what way are results from standardized achievement tests often reported to teachers for their classroom use?
13. In what way are results from standardized achievement tests often reported to pupils and their parents?
14. What should be the teacher's responsibility for the use of standardized tests in the classroom?
15. In what major ways are results from standardized tests of achievement useful to the classroom teacher?

SELECTED REFERENCES

ADAMS, GEORGIA S., AND TORGERSON, THEODORE L. *Measurement and Evaluation for the Secondary-School Teacher.* New York: Dryden Press, 1956. Chapters 11, 24, 26.

AHMANN, J. STANLEY, AND GLOCK, MARVIN D. *Evaluating Pupil Growth.* Boston: Allyn and Bacon, Inc., 1959. Chapters 6, 12, 16.

BARON, DENIS, AND BERNARD, HAROLD W. *Evaluation Techniques for Classroom Teachers.* New York: McGraw-Hill Book Co., Inc., 1958. Chapter 6.

BRADFIELD, JAMES M., AND MOREDOCK, H. STEWART. *Measurement and Evaluation in Education.* New York: Macmillan Co., 1957. Chapter 16.

BUROS, OSCAR K., editor. *The Fifth Mental Measurements Yearbook.* Highland Park, N. J.: Gryphon Press, 1959. p. 324-615, 721-870.

BUROS, OSCAR K., editor. *The Fourth Mental Measurements Yearbook.* Highland Park, N. J.: Gryphon Press, 1953. p. 294-527, 567-673.

BUROS, OSCAR K., editor. *The Third Mental Measurements Yearbook.* New Brunswick, N. J.: Rutgers University Press, 1949. p. 218-442, 501-626.

BUROS, OSCAR K., editor. *Tests in Print: A Comprehensive Bibliography of Tests for Use in Education, Psychology, and Industry.* Highland Park, N. J.: Gryphon Press, 1961.

COLLEGE ENTRANCE EXAMINATION BOARD. *Advanced Placement Program.* Princeton, N. J.: The Board, 1956.

CONRAD, HERBERT S. "The Experimental Tryout of Test Materials." *Educational Measurement.* Washington, D. C.: American Council on Education, 1951. Chapter 8.

COOK, WALTER W. "Achievement Tests." *Encyclopedia of Educational Research.* Revised edition. New York: Macmillan Co., 1950. p. 1461-78.

COOK, WALTER W., AND OTHERS. "The Functions of Measurement in Education." *Educational Measurement.* Washington, D. C.: American Council on Education, 1951. Part I.

CROOK, FRANCES E. "Elementary School Testing Programs: Problems and Practices." *Teachers College Record,* 61:76-85; November 1959.

DOWNIE, N. M. *Fundamentals of Measurement: Techniques and Practices.* New York: Oxford University Press, 1958. Chapter 6.

EBEL, ROBERT L., AND DAMRIN, DORA E. "Tests and Examinations." *Encyclopedia of Educational Research.* Third edition. New York: Macmillan Co., 1960. p. 1502-17.

EDUCATIONAL TESTING SERVICE. *ETS Builds a Test.* Princeton, N. J.: Educational Testing Service, 1959.
EDUCATIONAL TESTING SERVICE. *Selecting an Achievement Test: Principles and Procedures.* Evaluation and Advisory Series, No. 3. Princeton, N. J.: Educational Testing Service, 1958.
FINDLEY, WARREN G. "Progress in the Measurement of Achievement." *Educational and Psychological Measurement,* 14:255-60; Summer 1954.
GARRETT, HENRY E. *Testing for Teachers.* New York: American Book Co., 1959. Chapter 5.
GREENE, HARRY A., JORGENSEN, ALBERT N., AND GERBERICH, J. RAYMOND. *Measurement and Evaluation in the Elementary School.* Second edition. New York: Longmans, Green and Co., 1953. Chapter 5.
GREENE, HARRY A., JORGENSEN, ALBERT N., AND GERBERICH, J. RAYMOND. *Measurement and Evaluation in the Secondary School.* Second edition, New York: Longmans, Green and Co., 1954. Chapter 5.
HALL, E. C. "The Proper Use of Test Results." *Elementary School Journal,* 54:450-55; April 1954.
McLAUGHLIN, KENNETH F. "How Is a Test Built?" *School Life,* 42:6-9; September 1959.
NOLL, VICTOR H. *Introduction to Educational Measurement.* Boston: Houghton Mifflin Co., 1957. Chapters 13-14.
REMMERS, H. H., AND GAGE, N. L. *Educational Measurement and Evaluation.* Revised edition. New York: Harper and Brothers, 1955. Chapters 2-3.
REMMERS, H. H., GAGE, N. L., AND RUMMEL, J. FRANCIS. *A Practical Introduction to Measurement and Evaluation.* New York: Harper and Brothers, 1960. Chapters 4-6.
ROSS, C. C., AND STANLEY, JULIAN C. *Measurement in Today's Schools.* Third edition. New York: Prentice-Hall, Inc., 1954. Chapters 8, 10.
SCHWARTZ, ALFRED, AND TIEDEMAN, STUART C. *Evaluating Student Progress in the Secondary School.* New York: Longmans, Green and Co., 1957. Chapter 13.
SYMPOSIUM. "Future Progress in Educational and Psychological Measurement." *Educational and Psychological Measurement,* 14:245-82; Summer 1954.
THOMAS, R. MURRAY. *Judging Student Progress.* New York: Longmans, Green and Co., 1954. Chapter 4.
THORNDIKE, ROBERT L., AND HAGEN, ELIZABETH. *Measurement and Evaluation in Psychology and Education.* Second edition. New York: John Wiley and Sons, Inc., 1961. Chapter 11.
THUT, I. N., AND GERBERICH, J. RAYMOND. *Foundations of Method for Secondary Schools.* New York: McGraw-Hill Book Co., Inc., 1949. Chapters 8, 11, 14.
TORGERSON, THEODORE L., AND ADAMS, GEORGIA S. *Measurement and Evaluation for the Elementary-School Teacher.* New York: Dryden Press, 1954. Chapter 9.
TRAXLER, ARTHUR E. "Administering and Scoring the Objective Test." *Educational Measurement.* Washington, D. C.: American Council on Education, 1951. Chapter 10.
TRAXLER, ARTHUR E. "Standardized Tests." *NEA Journal,* 48:18-20; November 1959.
VAUGHN, K. W. "Planning the Objective Test." *Educational Measurement.* Washington, D. C.: American Council on Education, 1951. Chapter 6.

Constructing and Using
Classroom Tests and Techniques

Primary if not sole responsibility for what is here called classroom testing usually rests upon the classroom teacher. He, better than anyone else, knows the textbooks and supplementary materials he has used in teaching and what instructional outcomes he has sought to develop in his pupils. He, better than anyone else, is in a position to know the backgrounds and present positions, the strengths and weaknesses, the needs and goals of his pupils. Cooperative planning or prescription from the office of the principal, supervisor or guidance director may specify what tests of educational achievement are to be given and may also provide plans and instructions to teachers for such other matters as the administration and scoring of such tests. However, the classroom teacher is normally accorded major responsibility for measuring the specialized achievements of pupils in the classes he teaches.

Classroom tests and techniques vary considerably in a number of ways —types, values, uses, subject areas of greatest applicability, varieties of outcomes effectively measured, and many others. They range from the traditional oral and essay examination to the informal objective and the evaluative test. They include performance tests and various nontest tools and techniques that may but do not necessarily involve paper-and-pencil use. It is with such tests and techniques, each having its appropriate uses and none providing a satisfactory single approach to classroom testing, that Part 3 is concerned.

9

ORAL, ESSAY, AND SHORT-ANSWER TESTS

Methods of using the oral, essay, and related short-answer examinations and the characteristics of these traditional types of tests mentioned below are the basis for the discussion of this chapter:

A. Traditional measurement practices.
B. Types of oral and essay examinations.
C. Limitations and advantages of traditional examinations.
D. Preparation and use of oral questions.
E. Constructing essay and short-answer questions.
F. Reading and scoring essay test results.
G. Analyzing and recording results from essay and short-answer tests.

Every teacher is faced with constantly recurring problems of achievement measurement and evaluation in the classroom. Not all of these problems are best solved by using the types of standardized achievement tests discussed in Chapter 8. Addition of the informal objective and other types of teacher-made tests and techniques treated in Chapters 10 to 12 may still not fulfill all of the measurement needs envisioned by many teachers. It is here that the oral, essay, and short-answer tests can, when carefully devised and used, satisfactorily fill an important classroom need.

1. TRADITIONAL TEACHER-MADE TESTS

Of the several types of teacher-made or classroom tests needed to round out a testing program, the oral and essay-type examinations received first attention historically. The short-answer test is an offshoot of the essay test and as such can be put in the same class as the two more widely known traditional types. Although all three are commonly termed subjective tests, as indeed they usually are to a very great degree, the influences of personal opinion and prejudice on the part of the teacher can be reduced significantly when they are carefully prepared and their results are carefully evaluated.

Traditional Measurement Practices

It is probable that results from the use of these traditional tests have sometimes been misleading and unsatisfactory because of failure to attain the levels of reliability, validity, and other examination characteristics discussed in Chapter 3 as necessary for effective measurement and evaluation. This may come about because of a too-casual and uncritical use of familiar and widely known test types. It seems important that the dangers of using these traditional tests casually and unsystematically be recognized and that appropriate steps be taken to avoid them. If such procedures as are outlined in this chapter are properly put into practice and if these traditional tests are used only in situations for which their characteristics render them suitable, the oral and essay tests can contribute meaningfully to classroom testing.

Major Types of Oral and Essay Tests

Both oral and essay examinations have two quite distinct but seldom recognized aspects that are represented in the distinguishable types of situations in which they are most appropriately used. When the teacher uses either type of test for measuring knowledges and understandings, as he can in almost any subject area, he is interested, or at least should be interested, primarily in the content of the pupil responses. When he uses either of the test types for such more specialized purposes as measuring effectiveness of expressing ideas, he is interested in the manner in which the response is given. Since this distinction is made more fully later in this chapter, it seems sufficient at this point to indicate that the first, or more general, usage is of direct concern in this chapter but that the more specialized purpose receives attention in the appropriate chapters of Part 5.

2. ORAL EXAMINATIONS

In the evolution of mankind, the oral examination was obviously used before any form of written examination could have been conceived. In individual growth and development, a person is typically subjected to oral questioning not only before he can be expected to respond specifically but also at the time in his early life when such questioning can aid him in acquiring knowledges, concepts, and understandings about the world in which he finds himself. Consequently, the child usually enters school with a background of experience in responding orally to orally stated questions. Furthermore, children and adults probably learn more in daily living by the use of oral questioning than through any less personalized form of listening or through reading.

Varieties of Oral Examinations

Several rather distinctive types of behavior and of underlying purposes are involved when oral responses in examination situations are given by a pupil who is alone with the teacher, by a pupil who is in class, or by a group consisting of at least several pupils. It is unimportant whether some common and even simple type of individual pupil achievement or a quite unusual and complex type of group achievement is being evaluated. The manner of presenting the questions or requests is also unimportant. They can be given orally or in printed or written form, although the most traditional and narrow conception of the oral test involves oral questions as well as oral answers. As the concern of this chapter is solely with achievement measurement, such oral responses as are involved in some test elements of individual intelligence scales and some approaches to personality measurement are disregarded in the types of situations described below.

When oral tests are considered in this broad sense, four quite distinct situations involving various types of oral performances and basic purposes can be set apart. Only the first of these has typically been treated as an oral examination.

Individual oral tests. In the most widely applicable type of situation, a pupil is asked, either in the presence of classmates or when he is alone with the teacher, to respond orally to a question when the teacher, who himself knows the correct answer, wishes to determine whether the pupil knows it or not. His evaluation of the pupil depends primarily if not solely on the *content* of the answer given—facts enumerated, procedures outlined, points made, ideas presented, and even more complex patterns of response. This represents a typical but unduly narrow concept of an oral examination.

In a second type of situation, a pupil is asked, either in the presence of classmates or when he is alone with the teacher, to respond orally to a question or request when the purpose is to elicit a certain rather special type of response. Evaluation of the pupil is based primarily if not solely on the *manner* in which he responds—pronunciation of words in a foreign language or English; proficiency in oral reading, in delivering a prepared speech, in giving a dramatic monolog, in singing a song; and competency in still other patterns of previously practiced or prepared responses. Some of the less specialized oral performances of these types are dealt with in later chapters of this volume on English, foreign languages, and fine arts.

Group oral tests. In one version of this test, a small group of pupils may be asked to respond orally but individually and variously to a broad question asked or proposition stated when the purpose is to evaluate the pupils' individual contributions. Evaluation of each pupil is based primarily on the *manner* in which he contributes. For example, such factors as poise, attentiveness, vocabulary, tact, flexibility, leadership, ingenuity, and judgment were evaluated in a group oral examination designed for use in the selection of adults for filling certain positions.[1] Although this conception of a group oral examination seems not to have been employed much in the schools and perhaps is not adaptable for classroom testing, some sociometric techniques of the type treated in Chapter 7 deal with the manner in which an individual takes part in and contributes to group activity.

In a second version of this sort of oral test, two or more pupils may be asked to respond orally in concert to a request or command when the purpose is to elicit a predetermined type of group response. Evaluation of the performance is also based primarily on the *manner* in which the group performs orally—as a chorus, glee club, quartette, duet, or choral-speaking group. Such oral-response situations occur primarily in the field of music and would properly be treated in Chapter 21 of this volume if they were not so highly specialized.

A brief summary of these two individual and two group testing situations is important. The first describes what has traditionally been called the oral examination, the third illustrates a type of group test that is neither widely known nor widely used, and the other two, in which either an individual pupil or a group of pupils responds orally to various examination questions or requests, are oral examinations of specialized types that are properly treated in Chapters 16, 20, and 21. As a result, only one type of oral examination, the one traditionally recognized and used, the only one of the four emphasizing *content* of the response, is appropriately treated in this chapter. Hence, most of the ensuing discussion applies only to the oral examination of one pupil at a time primarily if not solely on the content types of instructional outcomes.

[1] William Brody and Norman J. Powell, "A New Approach to Oral Testing." *Educational and Psychological Measurement,* 7:289-98; Summer 1947.

Limitations and Advantages of Oral Examinations

Perhaps familiarity with oral questioning in ordinary living contributed to an uncritical acceptance of the oral test as a measurement tool in the early schools. As is pointed out in Chapter 2, however, Horace Mann more than a century ago outlined several of its important defects for the testing of individual pupils in the classroom.[2] His six major ideas, reported here in summary form only, were that the oral examination (1) is not equally fair and just to all pupils, (2) does not test extensively or efficiently, (3) permits interference and favoritism, intentional or otherwise, by the teacher, (4) is unjustifiably time-consuming, (5) leaves no permanent objective record of pupil performance, and (6) does not permit an evaluation of the difficulty of questions.

It is very probable that the weaknesses of the traditional oral examination for measurement purposes have not been stated any more effectively at any time since Mann enunciated his ideas. Although it serves very imperfectly in the measurement of content, the oral test is still widely used for that purpose. Even when used in testing only one pupil at a time, it was found by Barnes and Pressey to be seriously lacking in reliability and validity as a measurement technique.[3] However, Kostick and Nixon,[4] in one of the few recent publications dealing with this type of test, listed eight advantages of the oral examination centering around its flexibility, its provision of opportunities for observing the pupil being examined, and its values in supplementing written examinations.

Construction and Use of Oral Examinations

In addition to pointing out certain advantages of the oral test, Kostick and Nixon [5] offered suggestions to the teacher for its use and proposed that a good question should (1) present a single, central problem, (2) be stated in positive form, (3) enable the informed pupil to show evidence of attainment, (4) deal with an important point, and (5) present an element of novelty if it seeks to measure high-level outcomes.

Oral examinations are properly used for purposes other than measurement. For example, oral questioning has teaching significance in the Socratic manner for leading pupils by astute questioning to the attainment

[2] Otis W. Caldwell and Stuart A. Courtis, *Then and Now in Education, 1845-1923.* World Book Co., Yonkers, N. Y., 1923. p. 37.
[3] Elinor J. Barnes and S. L. Pressey, "The Reliability and Validity of Oral Examinations." *School and Society*, 30:719-22; November 23, 1929.
[4] Max M. Kostick and Belle M. Nixon, "How to Improve Oral Questioning." *Peabody Journal of Education*, 30:209-17; January 1953.
[5] *Ibid.*

of new understandings. It can also be used as a method of fact finding, in the interview and elsewhere.

The oral examination or quiz does have some uses, however, in the evaluation and measurement of pupil performance, even though its values admittedly are not great when it is used in the classroom situation. It is one of the few possible methods of testing pupils in the primary grades. It can be used as a diagnostic tool with an individual pupil in probing his reasons for having responded as he did to certain questions on written examinations or on certain mathematical or scientific problems. It can perhaps be used in determining how well an individual pupil has integrated his knowledge, can apply it to various situations, and sees its implications.

Oral examinations can perhaps be used with individual pupils satisfactorily if proper advance preparations are made, if consistent procedures are followed in the question session, and if scoring and rating methods are systematically applied. However, this use of the oral examination is very time-consuming, which makes it impracticable for use with each pupil in a class for purposes of pupil comparisons.

In considering the above legitimate uses of oral questioning, it should be clearly noted that the conditions under which this method is properly used and the purposes it is appropriately expected to serve are very different from those operating when it is used with a group of pupils in the classroom.

3. ESSAY EXAMINATIONS

The traditional or essay examination continues to occupy an important place among the testing techniques used by the classroom teacher, although during the past few decades it has lost the dominant position it occupied at the turn of the century. It is now much more commonly used for achievement measurement in parallel with such other paper-and-pencil tests as the standardized and informal objective and also performance and evaluative testing procedures.

Nature of Essay Examinations

Essay tests have been so widely used for centuries and so widely accepted until comparatively recently that their characteristics have often seemed to be self-apparent. To describe them as tests to which pupils must respond in their own writing and in their own words is not sufficient, however. Stalnaker went further when he specified that the response to a question usually consists of one or more sentences, that there is no single correct response, and that the accuracy and quality of the response can be evaluated only by a person who knows the topic.[6]

Subject-matter versus composition tests. Ebel and Damrin, properly, pointed out that a distinction should be made between the essay test used to measure knowledge of subject matter and the essay test employed to measure skill in writing.[7] Only the first of these usages, as a subject-matter test, receives consideration here; the measurement of skill in written expression in the form of a composition test is dealt with briefly in the treatment of language and English in Chapter 16. The same distinction between content of a response and manner of giving a response is pertinent here as is made in the foregoing discussion of oral examinations.

Findley, participating in a symposium on the use of test results in the schools, had the traditional or content-measuring test in mind when he commented that the essay test is the only place in life where a person writes in order to prove to someone who already knows the answer that he knows it too.[8] A similar distinction is made about answers to oral questions in the preceding section of this chapter.

Types of essay tests. Questions of the essay type are quite commonly classified into three types: (1) simple-recall, (2) short-answer, and (3) discussion. The simple-recall questions, demanding a short response that can be accurately scored, require a name, a number, a date, a place, or an event in answer to *who, how many, when, where,* and *what* questions. However, such questions are often slightly adapted in format by many modern teachers so they can be used as completion-type objective items. The short-answer questions, demanding statement, phrase, or sentence responses that can be rated quite objectively, require answers to such key words as *define, identify, list, find,* and *state.* Such questions are sufficiently distinguishable from discussion-type questions to warrant brief separate treatment in a later section of this chapter. The discussion questions, requiring responses of such complexity that objectivity of scoring is difficult, request answers to such words as *explain, describe, interpret, compare, contrast,* and *outline.* This is the classic or traditional type of essay question most commonly considered in discussions of essay testing and dealt with almost exclusively in this section of the chapter. As most classroom teachers are well aware, some simple essay questions are so definite that responses can be evaluated quite objectively, but others are so general that responses can be rated with reasonable accuracy only with

---

[6] John M. Stalnaker, "The Essay Type of Examination." *Educational Measurement.* American Council on Education, Washington, D. C., 1951. p. 495.

[7] Robert L. Ebel and Dora E. Damrin, "Tests and Examinations." *Encyclopedia of Educational Research,* Third edition. Macmillan Co., New York, 1960. p. 1503.

[8] Robert L. Ebel and others, "Eight Critical Questions about the Use of Tests in Education." *Education,* 81:67-99; October 1960.

considerable difficulty. It is the latter type that is most widely used in practice and that creates need for this chapter.

Limitations and Advantages of Essay Examinations

The pros and cons of essay tests have received wide attention and un- usually detailed treatment over a period of many years. Many prejudiced and biased arguments have been used in the controversy. A few of the major weaknesses and merits are briefly outlined here as background for the subsequent discussion of construction and use of essay tests.

Limitations of essay tests. Two major and a number of minor limitations of essay examinations have been widely discussed. The weaknesses most frequently advanced are discussed briefly at this point.

Limited sampling of course content is a major deficiency of the essay examination. A test that consists of five or ten questions cannot hope to sample widely over any sizable area of content or activities, but can meas- ure only a few of the important areas in which pupil abilities should be tested. For example, 75 to 100 objective items can reasonably be answered by a group of pupils in the same amount of time they require for writing on five to ten essay questions. The objective items can be distributed widely and equitably over the desired range of content or activities, whereas the essay questions can at best cover a much smaller number of areas or aspects of the course. As in discussed in the treatment of examina- tion characteristics in Chapter 3, a test in order to be adequate must include an extensive rather than an intensive sample of the pupil behaviors, or in this case the instructional outcomes, to be measured. One result of the intensive sampling of the essay test is that a pupil is likely to be penalized more heavily for weakness in one or two of the several course areas covered by questions than is probable on a test covering course aspects more broadly or extensively.

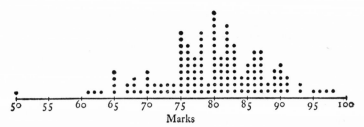

FIGURE 12. Marks Assigned to an English Examination by 142 Teachers [9]

[9] Daniel Starch and Edward C. Elliott, "Reliability of Grading High School Work in English." *School Review,* 20:442-57; September 1912.

Subjectivity of scoring is the second major weakness of the essay test. In one of the earliest studies on subjectivity, Starch and Elliott, who had 142 teachers score identical copies of an English examination paper, found that the scores based on 100 percent for perfection ranged from a low of 50 to a high of 98. Figure 12 shows the extreme range and variability of the marks assigned. In another type of study, Eells [10] had 61 teachers score an examination consisting of four essay questions in geography and history, and eleven weeks later had them score the same papers again. Wide differences in the two sets of scores assigned by the same persons led him to conclude that the same individuals vary from time to time in their judgments about as widely as different individuals vary. Stalnaker, on the basis of an extensive experiment in the evaluation of examination papers, concluded that the essay test as typically handled is not reliably graded and hence cannot be expected to stand alone as a good measuring instrument.[11] From these and other investigations, it becomes apparent that the scoring of the essay examination is a highly subjective process and that the resulting scores are typically quite inaccurate.

Among the minor, and actually extraneous, factors that also adversely affect the reliability of the essay test are the "halo" effect, which describes the tendency of the teacher to gain favorable impressions from the answers of pupils he generally rates as superior, and the opposite tendency, to react unfavorably to answers written by pupils generally considered to be weak, sometimes termed the "horn" effect.[12]

Pupils who do not know the answers to essay questions are prone to respond in terms calculated to cover up their lack of information, if not actually to mislead the teacher. Such responses, which tend to vary in plausibility directly in relation to the intelligence of the bluffer, may take the form of discussion concerning content closely related to that covered by the question, of very incomplete answers which by repetitious statements and copious illustration may give a sense of completeness, and various other devices. Whether bluffing is or is not desirable is not the issue. Certainly bluffing is resorted to in great or small degree by all persons on some, if not many, occasions. To the extent, however, that bluffing is actually successful on essay tests, the examination results are inaccurate measures of pupil achievement.

Still another type of factor affecting the objectivity of scoring of an essay test is found in the sometimes unrecognized but certain influence upon the reader of handwriting and general neatness of the paper; spelling,

[10] Walter C. Eells, "Reliability of Repeated Grading of Essay Type Questions." *Journal of Educational Psychology,* 21:48-52; January 1930.
[11] Stalnaker, *op. cit.* p. 499.
[12] Kostick and Nixon, *op. cit.*

punctuation, and grammar; organization of the paper; and even its length.

Other influences which in considerable degree enter into the marking of tests are evidences of pupil effort, improvement, attitude toward the teacher and the course, conformance, and a multitude of other indications of what the teacher might consider desirable behavior on the part of the pupil. Some teachers believe in assigning relatively higher marks to pupils who try but do poorly than to pupils who appear not to try but do well. Others assign good marks to pupils who conform to sometimes inconsequential and irrelevant demands and penalize pupils who do not conform.

It is now recognized that only a portion of the variability of marks assigned to an examination by different teachers, as in the Starch and Elliott and other studies, can be attributed to the unreliability of the examination itself. A comparable share of the variability can be charged to the lack of uniformity in the scoring procedures followed by the teachers. Whereas the different teachers used in such studies had very different educational aims and standards of excellence, the teacher who scores an entire set of papers attempts to apply the same set of standards to all papers, and has the benefit of experience with previous papers as a basis for doing so. Furthermore, the teachers in those studies used no scoring rules save those which they developed individually, but the teacher who scores a set of papers usually applies more or less tangible and consistent scoring procedures.

Advantages of essay tests. Various advantages have been claimed for the traditional examination. Some of these appear to depend on evidence that is not very conclusive. In many cases the decision depends as much on the philosophy of the individual teacher as on definite research findings, so that possible advantages cannot be claimed with certainty.

The freedom of response that the essay test question allows is considered by some students of examination methods as one of its fundamental characteristics. By the nature of the question the student is required to survey his own background of related information and to select the related facts and organize them for expression in his own words. It is important, however, that the freedom of selection, organization, and expression be suited to the measurable outcomes of the course.

Essay tests are commonly considered easy for teachers to prepare and to administer. Pupils feel that they know the nature of essay test questions and the traditional methods of answering them. However, essay tests prepared and administered with a minimum of effort are likely to have such resulting disadvantages that the saving of time and labor may well be at the expense of testing efficiency.

It is possible to use the essay examination for practically all subjects of the school curriculum, for the question and answer method is widely adaptable. Some types of outcomes, such as arithmetic skills, handwriting skills, reading ability, and others, cannot be tested directly by this device, but the factual backgrounds for them frequently can be so tested.

Advocates of the older type of examination insist that the discussion-type questions have values not possessed by the informal objective test in that they call for comparison, for interpretation of facts, for criticism, for defense of opinion, and for other types of higher mental activity. There is, however, little if any evidence to support this claim.

Some persons feel that students prepare for essay tests by reviewing broadly the important aspects of course content but that they review for objective tests by memorization of facts or exact wordings of the text-book. No one would deny the general desirability of the first rather than the second type of review. However, such opinions are usually based on observations of how a few groups of pupils say they prepare for examinations. Probably the type of examination is less important to the pupil in determining how he should review than the specific nature of the test, i.e., highly factual versus broadly emphasizing outcomes beyond the most tangible skill and knowledge types.

Planning and Constructing Essay Examination Questions

If essay examinations are to be used effectively, they need to be planned and constructed carefully in advance of their use in the classroom. In the planning stage, a two-way grid of the type shown in Chapter 8 can be used, although it need not be as elaborate as the one given on page 158. However, it should show major units of the school subject on one dimension and types of essay questions on the other. If such a chart is not used, care should be taken to distribute questions of various appropriate types among the different course units or major areas.

Monroe and Carter classified essay-type questions with respect to the mental activity each type is designed to elicit in the pupil, and presented both descriptive statements concerning, and examples of, the twenty varieties they distinguished.[13] The descriptive statements and illustrative questions below are from Odell's adaptation and supplementation[14] of the questions from Monroe and Carter's list.

1. Selective recall on a given basis. (Which three poets studied this year may properly be called poets of nature?)

[13] Walter S. Monroe and R. E. Carter, *The Use of Different Types of Thought Questions in Secondary Schools and Their Relative Difficulty for Students.* Bureau of Educational Research Bulletin, No. 14. University of Illinois, Urbana, 1923.
[14] C. W. Odell, *How to Improve Classroom Testing.* William C. Brown Co., Dubuque, Iowa, 1953. p. 32-33.

2. Evaluative recall on a given basis. (State the four rules as to a person's diet which you think are the most important.)

3. Comparison of two or more things on a given basis. (Compare the use of adjectives and of adverbs as to what they modify.)

4. Comparison of two or more things in general. (Compare and contrast the climate in Southern California with that in Florida.)

5. Decisions for or against. (Which is better wood to use for fence posts, cedar or maple? Why?)

6. Statements of causes or effects. (Why should a citizen vote at every election?)

7. Explanation of meanings or uses of words, phrases, or longer passages. (Explain what is meant by "Don Quixote" in the expression, "He was a modern Don Quixote.")

8. Summarization. (Summarize in not more than one page what you know about how a radio works.)

9. Analysis. (What are the traits in the writings of Jack London that make them popular?)

10. Statements of relationships. (What does baking powder or soda have to do with making good biscuits?)

11. Original illustration or exemplification of rules, principles, etc. (Illustrate the difference in the correct use of *expect* and *suspect* by using each correctly in a sentence.)

12. Classification. (To what group of animals do lions, tigers, and leopards belong?)

13. Application of rules, laws, and principles to new situations. (If living things like those on earth exist on any of the other planets, upon which one or ones are they most likely to be? Why?)

14. General discussion. (Discuss the place of music in life.)

15. Statement of aims of author in selection or organization of material. (Why does our history book include so many personal facts and anecdotes about persons often mentioned?)

16. Criticism as to adequacy, correctness, or relevance of words, etc. (Do you believe that Britain and its allies would have lost World War II if the United States had not helped them? Why?)

17. Outlining. (Outline, in not over one-half page, the life history of a butterfly.)

18. Reorganization of facts previously encountered in different arrangements. (Trace general changes in climate found in going from the Gulf of Mexico directly north to the Canadian border.)

19. Formulation of new questions and problems. (If you were asked to tell whether or not a particular uninhabited part of the Earth was a good place for people to settle, what are the four main things you would want to know about it?)

20. Suggestion of new methods of procedure. (How would you attempt to find out whether it would be more profitable for a certain farmer to raise beef cattle or to run a dairy?)

Preparing Essay Questions

Important safeguards against some of the typical causes of unreliability in the essay examination can be taken after the test has been planned and the questions have been written in tentative form. These safeguards should be exercised when the questions are placed in final form and the test is assembled. Stalnaker listed and discussed three such technical considerations [15] as (1) phrasing each question so that its intent and meaning will be clear to pupils, (2) wording each question so that its range or scope will be clear to pupils, and (3) restricting the coverage of each question so that pupils will have adequate time in which to answer it.

It should be evident that pupils cannot be expected to do themselves justice on an essay test if they do not know what the test questions mean, if they do not know the boundaries of content within which their answers should be drafted, and if they do not have sufficient time to write well planned and organized answers to the questions. Failure on the part of teachers to take such precautions has typically been responsible for a significant portion of essay test unreliability.

Stalnaker [16] also gave evidence to indicate that the use of optional questions is inadvisable because they reduce examination reliability and recommended that all pupils be asked to take the same examination.

Scoring Essay Examinations

Subjectivity of scoring is discussed previously in this chapter as one of the two major weaknesses of essay tests. The evidence presented there supports the belief that subjective factors loom large when essay tests are scored by teachers who possess typical rather than special skills in reading essay examinations and when no scoring rules are uniformly applied by the test readers. However, Stalnaker obtained reliability coefficients ranging from .84 to .99 for the scores assigned to essay examinations in a variety of high-school subjects by experienced teachers when scoring rules were used.[17] The reliability coefficients show a highly satisfactory degree of scoring accuracy, especially when it is considered that only the lowest coefficient was under .90. Other studies of the results obtained when the essay test was scored under closely controlled conditions substantiate the conclusion that the traditional examination can be scored reliably if proper precautions are taken.

[15] Stalnaker, *op. cit.* p. 520.
[16] *Ibid.* p. 505-6.
[17] John M. Stalnaker, "Essay Examinations Reliably Read." *School and Society,* 46:671-72; November 20, 1937.

Several suggestions have been made for improving the scoring process in the attempt to attain classroom results comparable to those reported by Stalnaker. In one of these, Sims proposed in detail a "whole" method of rating or classifying essay tests into several groups.[18] He suggested that the readers work out for themselves acceptable answers to the questions and then use the following procedures:

a. Quickly read through the papers and on the basis of your opinion of their worth sort them into five groups as follows: (*a*) very superior papers, (*b*) superior papers, (*c*) average papers, (*d*) inferior papers, (*e*) very inferior papers. (Remember that in a normal group you would expect to have approximately 10 per cent of *very superior* and 10 per cent of *very inferior* papers, 20 per cent of *superior* and 20 per cent of *inferior* papers, and 40 per cent of *average* papers. Do not, however, try to conform rigidly to this rule. Your group may not be a normal one.)
b. Re-read the papers in each group and shift any that you feel have been misplaced.
c. Make no attempt to give numerical grades or to evaluate each question. Place each paper on the basis of your general impression of the total.
d. Assign letter grades to each group; beginning with A for the very superior group, B for the superior group, etc.

Wrightstone, writing about use of an analytical method of scoring essay tests designed for measuring only one instructional objective at a time,[19] proposed that all scorers agree on a definition of the objectives and on certain standards of values, that an ideal answer be formulated and each part assigned a certain number of points, and that an 11-point scale from 0 to 10 be used for each test unit.

The following suggestions, by largely eliminating the personal judgment or bias of the person who reads test answers, have been found valuable for use in scoring essay-type responses:

1. Examinations should be scored by the one who makes out the questions. He should know what responses are desired, and should write out his answers to the questions in advance.
2. Each pupil taking the test should write his name on the back of the test paper and the scorer should disregard the name until the test is scored.
3. The scorer should not mark off for misspelled words or poor sentence structure, paragraphing, or handwriting. Similarly, he should not increase the score for excellence in these things.

---

[18] Verner M. Sims, "The Objectivity, Reliability, and Validity of an Essay Examination Graded by Rating." *Journal of Educational Research*, 24:216-23; October 1931.
[19] J. Wayne Wrightstone, "Are Essay Examinations Obsolete?" *Social Education*, 1:410-15; September 1937.

4. Each separate item should be scored in all of the papers consecutively.
5. Each question should be rated on a scale of five, ten, or at least a pre-determined small number of scoring points.
6. The total score should be obtained for each pupil by adding the scores on the different questions only after all of the scoring had been done.

Whatever rules are followed, they will necessarily be arbitrary and not always wholly defensible. The significant point in the use of rules is that they provide for reasonable uniformity in handling the papers of all the pupils and also furnish a guide for the control of irrelevant factors that may affect the objectivity of the scoring.

For many years the essay-type test has been subjected to intense criticism. In spite of these attacks, however, it is still in use in numerous classrooms and doubtless performs a worth-while function there. While it is true that when the essay test is subjected to a critical appraisal under research conditions many of the claims that have been advanced for it do not stand up well, it is also true that it performs certain functions in the classroom that other forms of tests fail to accomplish. Without doubt the essay-type test is firmly fixed in educational practice. It is a type of examination with which all teachers are familiar, and with all of its faults it undoubtedly possesses sufficient merit to warrant considerable attention to its improvement by the use of such methods as are outlined above.

4. SHORT-ANSWER TESTS

This third type of teacher-made traditional or subjective test is here considered to be midway between the essay examination and the informal objective test in format, degree to which responses are structured, objectivity, and several less important ways. The ordinary supplementation or completion-type of objective test item, particularly when it involves recall of facts, has sometimes loosely been referred to as a short-answer variety. As is indicated in the foregoing section of this chapter, the short-answer item is also sometimes classified as an essay-type question.

Nature of Short-Answer Tests

The authors adopt the view here that the short-answer item is a variety of traditional test question which differs sufficiently from completion-type objective items and from essay questions to deserve brief separate treatment. Responses are typically somewhat longer and less rigidly prescribed in form than are answers to recall-type objective items. On the other hand, they are normally much shorter and more rigidly prescribed in content than are answers to traditional essay questions. Gerberich distinguished the short-answer test question as "a compromise between the great breadth characteristic of essay examination questions and the structured specificity embodied in recall types of objective test items.[20]

Sample Short-Answer Test Questions

Seven samples of short-answer items are given below to illustrate some of the many possible varieties. The key words or phrases are similar to those employed to describe some of the twenty types of essay questions illustrated in a preceding section of this chapter. The terms used here in general call for more specifically factual, more narrowly structured, and much shorter answers than do those in the other list, however. These samples are representative only, for no attempt is made to illustrate types of questions broadly.

1. *Name or list* (Music) [21]

    Directions: Give all the terms or names called for or, if you cannot give all, as many as you can.

    3. Name in order the keys from no sharps to five sharps inclusive.

    _____

    _____

2. *Give examples of* (Sewing) [22]

    Directions: On the four blank lines immediately after and below each item in the following list write the names of four varieties or examples thereof.

    4. woolen cloth used for suits and coats   _____

    _____   _____   _____

3. *Give differences between* (Biology) [23]

    Directions: State as briefly and well as possible what the difference be-tween each pair of terms is.

    1. animal and plant   _____

    _____

---

[20] J. Raymond Gerberich, *Specimen Objective Test Items: A Guide to Achievement Test Construction.* Longmans, Green and Co., New York, 1956. p. 375.

[21] C. W. Odell, *Traditional Examinations and New-Type Tests.* Century Co., New York, 1928. p. 274-75.

[22] *Ibid.* p. 272-73.

[23] *Ibid.* p. 404.

4. *Define* (History) [24]

   Directions: Define carefully each of the following terms:

   1. Social control _____

   _____

5. *Illustrate* (English) [25]

   Directions: Write a sentence including and illustrating the correct use of each of the following words.

   1. eager _____
   2. mild _____

6. *Give cause of* (History) [26]

   Directions: State what you consider the most important cause of each of the following events.

   1. Victory of the North in the Civil War _____

   _____

7. *Give reason for* (Science) [27]

   Directions: Answer each question below by stating, in just one sentence, the reason called for.

   1. Why is milk pasteurized? _____

   _____

5. ANALYZING AND RECORDING TEST RESULTS

Improvement in oral, essay, and short-answer tests can be accomplished by use of procedures similar to those discussed for the standardized achievement test in Chapter 8 and even more closely comparable to those developed for informal objective tests in Chapter 10. Since the methods that are applicable in this chapter are much less technical than those presented in these adjacent chapters and since they vary considerably according to the variety of oral, essay, or short-answer test under consideration, they are discussed only briefly here.

---

[24] G. M. Ruch and G. A. Rice, *Specimen Objective Examinations.* Scott, Foresman and Co., Chicago, 1930. p. 79-80.
[25] C. W. Odell, *How to Improve Classroom Testing.* William C. Brown Co., Dubuque, Iowa, 1953. p. 37.
[26] *Ibid.* p. 37.
[27] *Ibid.* p. 37.

Analyzing Responses to Questions

When essay tests are scored by the analytical method outlined in a fore-going section of this chapter, and especially when each element of an answer has a specified number of score points assigned to it, pupil answers lend themselves to simple analysis. Responses to short-answer questions are specific enough to be analyzed quite easily. According to Kostick and Nixon,[28] answers to oral test questions can be recorded and analyzed by very similar methods over a period of years.

The two aspects of answers that afford evidence on the basis of which questions can be revised and improved for subsequent use are indices of difficulty and of discriminative power. Procedures for making the item counts or analyses and for converting the results into percentages indicating difficulty of question parts or even whole questions and into indices of discriminative power for the same parts or wholes are so similar to those outlined in Chapter 10 for the informal objective test that they are not discussed separately here. The reader can apply the procedures described in the following chapter to the essay and short-answer tests with only minor changes.

Maintaining a Record of Questions and Responses

It is a simple matter to maintain a card file of questions used in essay, short-answer, and even oral tests and to classify them according to subject areas or aspects and types of questions. When results from the type of question analysis discussed above are recorded on the cards and when the questions are revised from time to time as seems desirable, these traditional types of tests can be markedly improved in their effectiveness as classroom measuring tools.

SUGGESTED ACTIVITIES

1. Select some unit or phase of a school subject of interest to you and construct one essay question each to represent any five of the twenty types of questions for which illustrations were taken from Odell.
2. Select one of the broader questions written for the activity suggested above, draft a complete and satisfactory answer to the question, prepare an outline of the facts or ideas you gave in your answer, and decide on the number and distribution of the points you think should be allotted to the question in the scoring process.

[28] Kostick and Nixon, *op. cit.*

TOPICS FOR DISCUSSION

1. Indicate why there is need for improvement in classroom testing.
2. What are some of the major weaknesses of the oral examination for testing purposes?
3. What uses should the oral quiz be expected to serve in the school?
4. Discuss the manner in which limited sampling reduces the reliability of the essay examination.
5. List and discuss several factors that contribute to subjectivity of scoring the typical essay examination.
6. Comment upon some of the minor weaknesses of the essay test.
7. List and evaluate the advantages that have been attributed to the traditional examination.
8. What are your conclusions concerning the proper place of the essay test in classroom measurement?
9. Identify some of the types of essay questions and indicate key words by which they are introduced.
10. Suggest several specific devices or procedures for increasing the objectivity of scoring essay-type tests.
11. Outline testing procedures by which the essay-type test may be made more effective as a classroom testing technique.

SELECTED REFERENCES

DRESSEL, PAUL L., AND MAYHEW, LEWIS B. *Handbook for Theme Analysis.* Dubuque, Iowa: William C. Brown Co., 1954.

DUNWIDDIE, WILLIAM. "How to Give Oral Examinations." *Social Education,* 17:123, 134; March 1953.

EBEL, ROBERT L., AND DAMRIN, DORA E. "Tests and Examinations." *Encyclopedia of Educational Research.* Third edition. New York: Macmillan Co., 1960. p. 1502-17.

ENGELHART, MAX D. "Examinations." *Encyclopedia of Educational Research.* Revised edition. New York: Macmillan Co., 1950. p. 407-14.

GERBERICH, J. RAYMOND. *Specimen Objective Test Items: A Guide to Achievement Test Construction.* New York: Longmans, Green and Co., 1956. p. 381-82.

GREENE, HARRY A., JORGENSEN, ALBERT N., AND GERBERICH, J. RAYMOND. *Measurement and Evaluation in the Elementary School.* Second edition. New York: Longmans, Green and Co., 1953. Chapter 6.

GREENE, HARRY A., JORGENSEN, ALBERT N., AND GERBERICH, J. RAYMOND. *Measurement and Evaluation in the Secondary School.* Second edition. New York: Longmans, Green and Co., 1954. Chapter 6.

KEESEY, R. M. "How Useful Are Essay Tests?" *Social Studies,* 42:13-16; January 1951.

KOSTICK, MAX M., AND NIXON, BELLE M. "How to Improve Oral Questioning." *Peabody Journal of Education,* 30:209-17; January 1953.

MEYER, GEORGE. "The Choice of Questions on Essay Examinations." *Journal of Educational Psychology,* 30:161-71; March 1939.

ODELL, CHARLES W. *How to Improve Classroom Testing.* Dubuque, Iowa: William C. Brown Co., 1953. Chapter 5-6.

OSBORN, WORTH J. "Testing Thinking." *Journal of Educational Research,* 27:401-11; February 1934.

SIMS, VERNER M. "Essay Examination Questions Classified on the Basis of Objectivity." *School and Society,* 35:100-2; January 16, 1932.

SIMS, VERNER M. "Improving the Measuring Qualities of an Essay Examination." *Journal of Educational Research,* 27:20-31; September 1933.

STALNAKER, JOHN M. "The Essay Type of Examination." *Educational Measurement.* Washington, D. C.: American Council on Education, 1951. Chap. 13.

STALNAKER, JOHN M. "Should Optional Questions Be Used in Examinations?" *School and Society,* 42:644-47; November 9, 1935.

STALNAKER, JOHN M. "A Study of Optional Questions on Examinations." *School and Society,* 44:829-32; December 19, 1936.

TRIMBLE, OTIS C. "The Oral Examination: Its Validity and Reliability." *School and Society,* 39:550-52; April 28, 1934.

VALLANCE, THEODORE R. "A Comparison of Essay and Objective Eaxminations as Learning Experiences." *Journal of Educational Research,* 41:279-88; December 1947.

WEIDEMANN, CHARLES C. "Further Studies of the Essay Test." *Journal of Higher Education,* 12:437-39; November 1941.

WEIDEMANN, CHARLES C. "Review of Essay Test Studies." *Journal of Higher Education,* 12:41-44; January 1941.

10

INFORMAL OBJECTIVE TESTS

This chapter deals with the following points concerning the construction and classroom use of informal objective tests:

A. Informal objective and standardized achievement tests.
B. Major types and varieties of objective test items.
C. Major characteristics of objective test items.
D. Limitations and advantages of teacher-made objective tests.
E. Suggestions for constructing objective test items and exercises.
F. Planning an informal objective test.
G. Constructing an informal objective test.
H. Providing for subsequent use of objective test materials.

Developments in the measurement and appraisal of pupil achievement have largely followed two main lines—introduction and improvement of standardized tests and improvement of teacher-made or classroom tests. The more subjective and traditional types of classroom tests are treated in Chapter 9. It is in the objective, teacher-made, paper-and-pencil tests dealt with in this chapter that the major improvements in classroom achievement testing have occurred.

1. TEACHER-MADE OBJECTIVE TESTS

Achievement tests constructed by a teacher for use primarily in his classes are commonly referred to as teacher-made or classroom tests. When they consist of objective types of items rather than of the question types discussed in Chapter 9 and when they are also of a paper-and-pencil variety, they are called teacher-made objective tests or objective classroom tests. It is only during the last forty years that classroom tests of this sort have been known, and they have attained their widest acceptance and recognition primarily during the last twenty years.

Teacher-Made and Standardized Objective Tests

Standardized achievement tests are structurally not very different from informal objective tests in their basic elements. In fact, standardized achievement tests are in format essentially little more than improved and refined informal objective examinations. Both types include in their content only a sampling of the materials that could appropriately be included. Both make use of objective-type items. Both provide scores to represent the attainments of pupils.

Although properly constructed standardized achievement tests may be superior in certain respects to teacher-made examinations, they should never displace teacher-made tests as a means of measuring pupil attainments. The teacher frequently has need for a measuring instrument adapted to a particular course of study or to the instructional emphasis he has given to the subject in the teaching of a particular class. The informal objective examination constructed by the teacher is the obvious answer.

In contrast with their similarities from a structural point of view, the functions of the standardized test and the informal objective examination in the same classroom are quite distinct. The standardized test, because it is intended for use in many different school systems and in connection with many different types of courses of study, must be general as to content. The maker of a standardized test cannot be sure that its content will actually parallel the instructional emphasis given the subject in the course offered by any individual teacher. Accordingly, the standardized test is useful mainly for general comparisons of school with school, class with class, or city with city. It is not designed for use in evaluating the accomplishment of pupils in a class under a particular instructor with a specialized instructional emphasis. By the same reasoning, the standardized test certainly should not be used as a major basis for the assignment of course marks in any subject.

The informal objective examination, constructed in accordance with well-recognized principles and incorporating extensive samplings of the content actually taught by the teacher and the activities of his pupils, is, on the other hand, a suitable major basis for the assignment of course marks. It is quite probable that even though two objective tests, one standardized and one informal, could be made equal in objectivity, length, and reliability of measurement, their functional values in the classroom would still be quite unlike because of unavoidable differences in their content. Thus, in general, standardized and informal objective tests must be considered as having quite distinct and separate functions.

Significance of Learning Outcomes

Learning outcomes are as significant for the construction of informal objective tests as for all achievement tests and techniques treated in this volume. The ten types of behavioral changes brought about in pupils by instruction and learning are listed and briefly discussed in Chapter 1, and the meanings of those that are most pertinent in achievement measurement are further clarified by illustrations in Chapter 9. They are, consequently, commented upon only briefly here.

The outcomes, whether resulting from school or out-of-school learning, are listed as (1) skills, (2) knowledges, (3) concepts, (4) understandings, (5) applications, (6) activities, (7) appreciations, (8) attitudes, (9) interests, and (10) adjustments. Since adjustments are not specifically taught in the school, but rather may be considered as a broad resultant of learning and living, only nine of the outcomes are rated as significant for classroom achievement testing. Of the nine, skills and knowledges are in general the most tangible, the most easily measurable, and, in fact, the most widely measured by teachers. Concepts, understandings, and applications can be measured by the exercise of care in selection of ideas for test items and in the subsequent item writing. The four remaining outcomes of the nine—activities, appreciations, attitudes, and nonvocational types of interests—can be measured with varying degrees of success but in general the results are less specific and less meaningful than are those obtained for the more tangible outcomes.

2. MAJOR TYPES AND VARIETIES OF TEST ITEMS

Objective item types used in achievement measurement are dealt with in this volume according to several of the many ways in which they can be classified. They are treated in this chapter primarily in terms of their form or structure, although their suitability for the measurement of different learning outcomes and other characteristics are also considered briefly. They are, moreover, accorded some attention in the treatment of measurement and evaluation by school subjects in Part 5 of this book.

An over-all distinction between two sorts of items warrants brief mention here. Selection items are easily and meaningfully distinguished from supplementation items by the type of demand made on the pupil. In selection items, also called recognition items, the pupil is expected to choose an answer from the material placed before him. In supplementation items, sometimes too narrowly termed recall items, the pupil is expected to recall or by any of several other methods to obtain and then to supply an answer that he devises or originates. The distinction, then, is between a situation in which the pupil selects an answer from material appearing on the test but does not create it himself and a situation in which the pupil supplies an answer by some form of addition to what appears on the test.

The method arrived at by Gerberich for classification of item types according to their format [1] is employed here. He distinguished thirteen major varieties and many more subvarieties of four commonly recognized types: (1) alternate-response and related scaled-choice, (2) multiple-choice, (3) matching, and (4) completion-type or augmentation. With minor adaptations, these four types are treated separately in the following pages.

Samples of a number of item varieties are shown below and discussed briefly here as background for the treatment of item writing and test construction in a later section of this chapter. Some of the sample items and exercises used to illustrate these major varieties are taken from standardized achievement tests, since informal objective tests can include any of the item varieties found in the more formal instruments.

Alternate-Response and Scaled-Choice Varieties [2]

Alternate-response items, particularly the true-false variety, are widely used in classroom testing. However, some of the other varieties of this item type can be used in situations where the true-false is not appropriate. Moreover, the scaled-choice version, similar to the alternate-response in some usages but providing from three to five possible answers, has characteristics that permit of uses beyond those possible for two-alternative items.

Alternate-response items. The true-false is by far the best-known and most widely used alternate-response variety. Practically all versions of alternate-response items were for many years referred to categorically, if erroneously, as true-false. Actually there are many paired terms, usually having opposite meanings, that are commonly employed in this item type, however. A few of the most widely used are *true–false, plus–minus, yes–no,* and *same–different.*

A. Alternate-Response Type: True–False Variety. An accompanying excerpt from a test of functional thinking in mathematics is representative

[1] J. Raymond Gerberich, *Specimen Objective Test Items: A Guide to Achievement Test Construction.* Longmans, Green and Co., New York, 1956. Chapter 14.
[2] *Ibid.* p. 237-45.

of the most basic and widely used alternate-response variety. The test title indicates that the instrument is designed to measure the type of learning outcome referred to in this volume as applications by means of items involving mathematical and quantitative relationships.

EXCERPT FROM *Foust-Schorling Test of Functional Thinking in Mathematics* [3]

DIRECTIONS. *In the parentheses after each of the following statements, write T if the statement is true and F if the statement is false.*

21. As Mr. A and Mr. B grow older, the difference between their ages will decrease..................( )

22. The greater the distance you travel at a constant rate, the longer will be the time required...........( )

23. If the number of hours which a man works per day is increased, the number of minutes per hour will also be increased..( )

24. If the number of months taken to pay for a refrigerator bought on installments is decreased, the size of the monthly payments will be decreased...( )

B. Alternate-Response Type: Better–Poorer Variety. A second excerpt, illustrating a rather unusual item variety, asks the student to evaluate two short selections of poetry appearing in parallel columns and to select and indicate the one he believes to be of superior quality. One of the samples is taken directly from the work of a master poet whereas the other, of inferior quality, either deals with a similar theme or is a modified version of the original. The purpose is to measure appreciation of poetical form.

EXCERPT FROM *Rigg Poetry Judgment Test* [4]

Directions: Below you will find selections of poetry arranged in pairs. Examine each pair carefully and decide which selection you regard as the better poetry. If the selection you choose is the left one of the pair, make a cross ($\times$) in the circle under *Left* in the answer spaces at the right. If the selection at the right is the better poetry, make the $\times$ in the circle under *Right* in the answer spaces.

Left Right

Who misses, or who wins the prize—	Not every man can win the goal	
I Go, lose or conquer as you can;	That he may pursue	1. ◯ ◯
But if you fail, or if you rise,	But all of us can be polite	
Be each, pray God, a gentleman.	In all that we may do.	

[3] Judson W. Foust and Raleigh Schorling, *Foust-Schorling Test of Functional Thinking in Mathematics.* Form A. Copyright 1942 by Harcourt, Brace and World, Inc., New York. All rights reserved. Quoted by special permission.
[4] Melvin G. Rigg, *Rigg Poetry Judgment Test.* Form I. Bureau of Educational Research and Service, University of Iowa, Iowa City, 1942.

C. Alternate-Response Type: More Interested–Less Interested Variety. The third excerpt in alternate-response form is most applicable to the measurement of interests. In the entire test, each of the recreational interests involved is compared with each of the other interests in a separate item of the sort illustrated here. It is possible to list a pupil's recreational interests in order from strongest to weakest when his answers are tabulated.

SAMPLE TEST ITEMS ON Recreational Interests [5]

Place a check mark in the parentheses following the activity in each pair in which you are more interested.

  1. Go to the movies .... a( )
     Go swimming .... b( )

  2. Go to a dance .... f( )
     Go swimming .... b( )

  3. Read a book .... k( )
     Go to a dance .... f( )

Of the many alternate-response item versions, only three of which are illustrated here, the true–false is widely applicable in all subject fields. Its apparent ease of construction has resulted in somewhat wider use than has been attained by any other item form. However, its simplicity is delusive, for the elimination of ambiguities is sometimes difficult to accomplish. Since this weakness seems to be inherent in the item itself, test technicians are tending to use it less and less. However, this weakness does not necessarily apply to some alternate-response varieties that involve other than the true versus false or right versus wrong differences, especially when they are used in measuring some of the most functional types of learning outcomes. Despite their susceptibility to ambiguity, true–false items can be used satisfactorily in many situations if they are carefully constructed. They are especially useful for situations in which the difficulty of finding enough plausible distractors makes the use of a multiple-choice item impracticable.

Alternate-response item forms have the advantage of affording coverage of many individual points in a short period of time, since the time requirements are less than for most item types. On the other hand, guessing is more of a problem for this than for any other item variety. Alternate-response items are highly objective and are readily understood by pupils. This item type is scorable by mechanical methods in all of its common varieties.

5 Vivian Weeden, "A Technique for Determining Interest." Educational Research Bulletin, 13:191-97, 231-34; November 14 and December 12, 1934.

Scaled-choice items. These items occur in many varieties that are often closely related to comparable alternate-response versions. For example, *true–indeterminate–false* and *true–probably true–indeterminate–probably false–false* items are basically true-false variations having three and five optional answers. Similarly, an *agree–uncertain–disagree* item closely resembles the parent, two-option agree–disagree variety.

If, therefore, an item represents merely an extension of a two-point continuum, such as true–false or agree–disagree, to a scale having three, four, or five stages that may in general be considered as equally spaced along a scale from one extreme to the other, it is classified in this volume as a scaled-choice variety even though it is multiple-choice in its format. Multiple-choice items having three, four, or five alternatives are distinguishable from these scaled-choice items by the fact that their options are often of varied types and do not represent points on a scale or continuum.

D. Scaled-Choice Type: Never–Sometimes–Often Variety. Items from an inventory designed to measure leisure-time reading activities are shown in an accompanying sample. Newspapers, magazines, and books are represented respectively by items in the top row, middle row, and bottom row. Both the type and frequency of a pupil's reading activities are disclosed by his answers to scaled-choice items of this type.

SAMPLE ITEMS FROM *Inventory of Leisure Reading* [6]

In order to understand how to teach the ways and values of good reading, it is necessary to know what kinds of leisure-time reading students do. You are asked to indicate your answers to some questions so that this information may be obtained. . . .

Next to each question are three letters: N, S and O. If you never read the part or do not know it, circle N (never). If you sometimes read the part, circle S (sometimes). If you often read the part, circle O (often).

Comics	N S O	Current events	N S O
Crime and accidents	N S O	Book reviews	N S O
Romance monthlies	N S O	Adventure monthlies	N S O
Pictorials	N S O	Humor	N S O
Ardent romance	N S O	Plays	N S O
Sport	N S O	Mystery	N S O

E. Scaled-Choice Type: Yes–Uncertain–No Variety. The second scaled-choice excerpt shown here illustrates provision for instances in which neither of the categorical answers is considered by the pupil to be appro-

[6] Frederick L. Pond, "A Simplified Method of Scoring an Inventory of Reading Experiences." *Journal of Educational Research,* 45:585-97; April 1952.

priate. Adjustments of several types are evaluated by the inventory from which the excerpt is taken.

EXCERPT FROM *The Adjustment Inventory* [7]

DIRECTIONS

Are you interested in knowing more about your own personality? If you will answer *honestly* and *thoughtfully* all of the questions on the pages that follow, it will be possible for you to obtain a better understanding of yourself.

There are *no right* or *wrong* answers. Indicate your answer to each question by drawing a circle around the "Yes," the "No," or the "?". Use the question mark only when you are certain that you cannot answer "Yes" or "No." There is no time limit, but work rapidly.

If you have *not* been living with your parents, answer certain of the questions with regard to the people with whom you have been living.

1a	Yes	No	? Do you day-dream frequently?
1b	Yes	No	? Do you take cold rather easily from other people?
1c	Yes	No	? Do you enjoy social gatherings just to be with people?
4d	Yes	No	? Does it frighten you when you have to see a doctor about some illness?
1e	Yes	No	? At a reception or tea do you seek to meet the important person present?
4b	Yes	No	? Are your eyes very sensitive to light?
7a	Yes	No	? . Did you ever have a strong desire to run away from home?

F. Scaled-Choice Type: Special Variety. An item designed for use in evaluating general outcomes from an art course is shown here to illustrate a variety in which the five scaled choices are dependent upon a setting or foundation of some sort. The five possible answers appear to evidence attitudes toward historic and contemporary art in a manner very similar to that used in the multiple-option variety shown in *H* below. The main distinction lies in the fact that in *H* the options or choices are not scaled whereas here they are.

SAMPLE TEST ITEM ON Attitudes toward Art [8]

Suppose that you are going to make a two months' trip through Germany and, unfortunately, there is not time enough to see everything of importance. Germany is well known for its historic castles, old cities, and collections of historic paintings. There are also significant contemporary buildings, crafts, and paintings. How would you divide your time?

_____ a. Spend all of my time seeing the historic art products.
_____ b. Spend most of my time seeing the historic art products.
_____ c. Divide my time equally between the two.
_____ d. Spend most of my time seeing the contemporary art.
_____ e. Spend all of my time seeing the contemporary products.

[7] Hugh M. Bell, *The Adjustment Inventory,* Student Form. With the permission of the author and of the publishers, Stanford University Press, Stanford, Calif. Copyright 1934 by the Board of Trustees of Leland Stanford Junior University.

[8] Ray Faulkner, "Evaluation in a General Art Course." *Journal of Educational Psychology,* 31:481-506; October 1940.

Scaled-choice items of these and other varieties are useful in measuring some rather intangible instructional outcomes, among which are those generally referred to as tastes and preferences, and also for use in situations where the state of knowledge does not justify categorical answers concerning truth or falsity. Problems involved in their construction and appropriate use are not great in many of their applications, although the extension of a true-false variety to one involving a three-point or five-point scale, for example, involves some quite technical considerations.

Multiple-Choice Varieties [9]

Multiple-choice items have long been the most popular form for standardized testing and are increasingly coming into wide use for informal objective testing as well. The pupil is typically expected to choose the option, or occasionally even the options, that correctly or best completes the meaning from the several possibilities put before him. As from three to five possible answers or options are typically used, the choice is multiple. The scaled-choice items and exercises dealt with in the preceding section of this chapter are actually in multiple-choice form. However, their fundamental characteristics and nature are much more like those of alternate-response than of basic multiple-choice varieties. The options available to the pupil as possible answers for an item of the type dealt with here are unscaled and sometimes differ so widely from one another that they are not parallel or strictly comparable, whereas options for a scaled-choice item appear on a scale or continuum and are presumed to be evenly distributed from one end of that scale to the other. The item varieties illustrated below are referred to as multiple-option and multiple-response.

Multiple-option items. When an item provides several possible answers from which the pupil selects or chooses the one he will give, it is here called a multiple-option item. The term is perhaps not completely definitive, for choices and options have similar meanings. However, a multiple-option item is considered to be a basic type of multiple-choice item having multiple options, choices, or possible answers but only one correct, or one best, answer. A multiple-option item can be delimited, then, to a single-answer, multiple-choice item type.

G. Multiple-Option Type: Stem-and-Options Variety. The most widely used variety of multiple-option item is illustrated by an excerpt from a primary-grade test of word meaning. In this variety, a stem, or introduction, is followed by the options from which the pupil is asked to choose the best or, in some instances, the only correct answer. These items appear to measure the outcome types considered in this volume to be concepts.

[9] Gerberich, *op. cit.* p. 245-55.

EXCERPT FROM *Stanford Achievement Test* [10]

DIRECTIONS: Draw a line under the one word
that makes the sentence true, as shown in
the first sample. Look at all four words
and choose the best one.

SAMPLES:

A cat can

    paint   bark   read   **jump**

The name of a color is

    farm   milk   red   pet

1 A bird can

    study   write   bark   fly

2 We get eggs from

    cattle   hens   horses   pigs

H. Multiple-Option Type: Setting-and-Options Variety. An item from
a prognostic test of mechanical abilities and involving use of a ruler by
the pupil is shown here to illustrate a multiple-option variety in which the
optional responses are dependent upon a setting or foundation of some
sort. In this item type, the setting can consist of a graphical representation, as here, or of a sentence, paragraph, picture, equation, or some other
form of representation.

EXCERPT FROM *Prognostic Test of Mechanical Abilities* [11]

66-80. DIRECTIONS: Use the ruler given to you by the examiner to check the measurements as called for
in each statement below. Write the letter that appears before the correct answer on the line to the right.

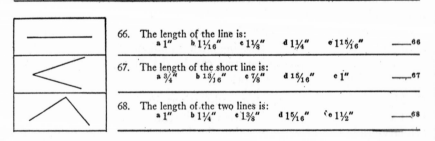

66. The length of the line is:
    a 1″   b 1$\frac{1}{16}$″   c 1$\frac{1}{8}$″   d 1$\frac{1}{4}$″   e 1$\frac{15}{16}$″   ____66

67. The length of the short line is:
    a $\frac{3}{4}$″   b 1$\frac{3}{16}$″   c $\frac{7}{8}$″   d 1$\frac{5}{16}$″   e 1″   ____67

68. The length of the two lines is:
    a 1″   b 1$\frac{1}{4}$″   c 1$\frac{3}{8}$″   d 1$\frac{5}{16}$″   e 1$\frac{1}{2}$″   ____68

[10] Truman L. Kelley and others, *Stanford Achievement Test: Test 2, Word Meaning,*
Primary. Form J. Copyright 1953 by Harcourt, Brace and World, Inc., New York. All
rights reserved. Quoted by special permission.

[11] J. Wayne Wrightstone and Charles E. O'Toole, *Prognostic Test of Mechanical Abilities.* Form A. California Test Bureau, Monterey, Calif., 1946.

I. Multiple-Option Type: Grouped-Term Variety. The items from a high-school chemistry test illustrated in an accompanying excerpt consist of groups of words or terms in which one does not logically belong in the same list as the other four. Positive forms of discrimination are used more frequently in this variety than the negative or "does not belong" sort used here for measuring understandings. The groups of from three to five terms commonly employed in items of this variety often consist of words or phrases but they sometimes are composed of letters, sentences, paragraphs, pictures, or representations in still other forms.

EXCERPT FROM *Anderson Chemistry Test* [12]

Each of questions 53 through 58 consists of five terms, one of which does NOT belong with the other four. You are to select the term which does NOT belong. Mark its number in the proper space on your answer sheet.

53.   **1.** nitrogen
       2. magnesium
       3. tin
       4. antimony
       5. bismuth

54.   **6.** boiling point
       7. inert
       8. solubility
       9. specific gravity
     10. density

J. Multiple-Option Type: Structured-Response Variety. The accompanying science test items measuring understandings illustrate how the structured responses D (directly), I (indirectly), and N (in no way) are used by the pupil in determining causality of relationship between the two halves of each item. This item variety imposes on the pupil the necessity of choosing answers to all items in a particular test exercise from the same constant and prescribed list of from three to five terms.

K. Multiple-Option Type: Contained-Options Variety. The fifth and last variety of multiple-option item distinguished in this volume is represented by an excerpt from a spelling test. Here the pupil, in a test designed to measure knowledges, is asked to choose the correct spelling from the three options given for each item or, if a correct spelling is not given, as in Item 26, to respond by the NG, for "not given," which appears on the

[12] Kenneth E. Anderson, *Anderson Chemistry Test*. Form A. Copyright 1950 by Harcourt, Brace and World, Inc., New York. All rights reserved. Quoted by special permission.

answer sheet where he records his answers. Contained options can consist of words, phrases, or errors in sentences or in paragraph-form exercises.

SAMPLE OF Test Items in Science [13]

DIRECTIONS

Each question in this exercise has two parts. Your job will be to judge how closely they are tied together. Both parts are true statements. They are separated from each other by a // mark.

If the first part *directly* causes the second part, draw a circle around the letter D.

If the first part *indirectly* causes the second part, draw a circle around the letter I.

If the first part is in *no way* a cause of the second part, draw a circle around the letter N.

D   I   N   1. An iron bar is held in a strong flame for ten minutes. // The iron bar gets red hot.

D   I   N   2. A shooting star falls to earth. // The stars in the sky twinkle.

D   I   N   3. A cow eats grass. // The cow gives milk.

The multiple-option item is unquestionably the most valuable and the most widely used objective type. It is readily, although not necessarily easily, adaptable to the measurement of practically all types of instructional outcomes. It is not difficult for pupils to understand and use. It can be readily scored either by hand or by machine.

Multiple-option items are not so easily constructed as are some other objective test forms, for there are various technical problems that require

EXCERPT FROM *Stanford Achievement Test* [14]

23 My aunt has one
      1 nephue.
      2 nephew. 23
      3 nefue.

24 We have a
      4 television
      5 telavision set. 24
      6 tellevision

25 Don't
      1 touch
      2 tutch the paint. 25
      3 tuch

26 The
      4 berres
      5 berrys are ripe. 26
      6 beries

27 Only one child was
      1 nauty.
      2 noughty. 27
      3 naughty.

[13] William B. Reiner, "Evaluating Ability to Recognize Degrees of Cause and Effect Relationships." *Science Education*, 34:15-28; February 1950.

[14] Truman L. Kelley and others, *Stanford Achievement Test: Test 3, Spelling,* Intermediate Partial Battery. Form JM. Copyright 1953 by Harcourt, Brace and World, Inc., New York. All rights reserved. Quoted by special permission.

great care in their drafting. The incorrect answers pupils give to simple recall items often serve as excellent incorrect alternatives if the item is converted to multiple-option form. However, the necessity for finding at least two and in many cases as many as four plausible responses to go with the correct completion somewhat limits the applicability of the item form in some subject fields. Ingenuity on the part of the test maker and the results of practice in item construction make the item variety very widely applicable to the content of various instructional areas, however.

A common use of multiple-option forms is in testing various types of reading ability, as, for example, ability to comprehend the meaning of a paragraph, by basing a single item or several items on a passage of reading material in English or a foreign language. Somewhat similarly, multiple-option items can singly or by groups be based on a map, chart, diagram, or table, and require the pupil to interpret the data presented as a basis for answering.

Multiple-response items. When an item provides several possible answers and asks the pupil to respond by indicating all correct answers, it is commonly termed a multiple-response item. The number of correct answers in such items may range from none to all of the possible answers put before the pupil. If the pupil fails to find what he thinks is a correct answer among the options, he is usually expected to indicate that judgment in some prescribed manner. If he thinks that only one option is correct, he indicates which one by a single answer. If, however, he believes that two or more options are correct, he gives a double or a multiple response. Therefore, a multiple-response item is one providing several answers or options and at least on occasion requiring a multiple response by the pupil who answers correctly.

L. Multiple-Response Type. The only illustration of this item type shown here is from an American history test. Understandings are measured in this instance by a multiple-response item in multiple-option format. Several combinations of options (1) to (5), represented by the answer-options **a** to **e,** are presented to the pupil as possible answers. As not all possible combinations of the (1) to (5) options are provided for in the five lettered answers, the sample item is more structured than the basic multiple-response types for which any possible combination of options can be chosen by the pupil in his response or responses.

When the multiple-response item form is used in its simplest version, in which case the pupil is expected to mark more than one answer if he thinks there are at least two correct ones, problems arise in deciding upon an equitable method of scoring. In the type of illustration used here, however, the item is scored in the same manner as are more typical multiple-option varieties even though it in fact requires the pupil to use at least three of the five possible options in his answer. This item variety is less flexible and much less widely useful than is the more common multiple-option form.

EXCERPT FROM Crary American History Test [15]

DIRECTIONS. *In questions 88 through 90, read the question and the possible answers which are numbered 1, 2, 3, 4, 5, 6. Any, all, or none of these answers may be right. Decide which of the responses, a, b, c, d, e, give ALL the numbers of the correct answers and mark the corresponding space on your answer sheet.*

88. What conditions contributed to the economic depression of the early 1930's?

    (1) The lack of farm prosperity in the 1920's.
    (2) The decline of foreign markets after World War I.
    (3) The lack of purchasing power of low-income groups.
    (4) The large military budgets of the 1920's.
    (5) The lack of industrial capacity and natural resources.

        a. 1, 2, 3
        b. 1, 2, 4
        c. 2, 3, 5
        d. 1, 4, 5
        e. all of the above

Matching Varieties [16]

Matching exercises are in their simplest form combinations of multiple-choice items in such a manner that the choices are compound in number. Matching exercises differ from all of the other objective forms in the fact that they must occur in groups. There is really no such thing as a matching test item, unless a correct pairing pulled from a group of which it is a part might be so designated. Matching tests are by nature, then, multiple in type, and the number of scoring points is ordinarily determined by the number of responses required of the pupil.

A matching exercise or set usually consists of two lists of related material between which a constant type of relationship exists throughout. The pupil's responses are expected so to pair items in the two lists as to indicate their proper relationships. If all terms on both sides are properly used in the matching process, the exercise has no distractors and is said to be balanced. If, however, one list is longer than the other and includes terms that are not involved in a pattern of correct answers, the exercise has distractors and is said to be unbalanced.

[15] Ryland W. Crary, *Crary American History Test*. Form A. Copyright 1950 by Harcourt, Brace and World, Inc., New York. All rights reserved. Quoted by special permission.
[16] Gerberich, *op. cit.* p. 255-60.

Balanced matching exercises. These exercises provide two or occasionally even three sets of paralleling items requiring the use of every item in each set by the pupil who gives correct answers throughout. The exercise is considered to be without distractors and also to be balanced if, for example, ten items in one list are paired in a one-to-one, nonoverlapping manner with the ten items in the other list.

M. Balanced Matching Type: Interrelation Variety. An illustration of the basic and most widely used type of balanced matching exercise from an arithmetic test is shown in an accompanying excerpt. Here the five problems are to be matched by the pupil in a one-to-one relationship with the five appropriate rules and formulas in the measurement of knowledges. Matching exercises of this variety entail the pairing of interrelated terms in two, or even occasionally in three, columns or separate lists. The relationship can be of many kinds, such as words and their meanings, foreign words and their English equivalents, book titles and authors, events and dates, and words and pictures.

EXCERPT FROM *California Achievement Tests* [17]

DIRECTIONS: Some rules and formulas used in measurement, numbered 1, 2, 3, 4, and 5, are given to the right below. Some problems that can be worked with them are given on the left, numbered 26, 27, 28, 29, and 30. Mark the number of the rule or formula on the right which is used to find the answer to each problem on the left.

Problems	Rule or Formula	Rules and Formulas Used in Measurement
26. Area of a triangle	___26	1. $6s^2$
27. Diameter of a circle	___27	2. Obtain the square root of the sum of the squares of the two sides.
28. Area of a parallelogram	___28	
29. Area of a cube	___29	3. $\frac{c}{\pi}$
30. Hypotenuse of a right triangle	___30	4. Multiply base by height.
		5. $\frac{1}{2}$ hb

N. Balanced Matching Type: Classification Variety. The accompanying excerpt from a language test measures knowledges concerning parts of speech by asking the pupil to classify each specified word used in context according to whether it is a noun, verb, adjective, or pronoun or to indicate that he does not know the answer. Exercises of this type entail the sorting of words or other types of material into their appropriate classes or categories. The lists of terms and categories may be of the same length, but more often each of the terms appropriately belongs in one of the smaller

[17] Ernest W. Tiegs and Willis W. Clark, *California Achievement Tests: Test 3, Arithmetic,* Complete Battery, Junior High School Level. Form W. California Test Bureau, Monterey, Calif., 1957.

number of classes. Since all terms are properly classifiable and since no classes are appropriately listed unless they have pertinence, such exercises normally have no distractors.

EXCERPT FROM *Metropolitan Achievement Tests* [18]

Part B Parts of Speech **DIRECTIONS**	In each of the sentences below, one word has been underlined and is written in heavy black letters. Decide whether this word is a *noun*, a *verb*, an *adjective*, or a *pronoun*. Then put a cross in the box under the answer you have chosen. If you do not know the answer, put a cross in the box under DK (for don't know).

	noun	verb	adjective	pronoun	DK
36 Most of the children have gone home.	[ ]	[ ]	[ ]	[ ]	[ ] 36
37 I fell down right in the middle of the street.	[ ]	[ ]	[ ]	[ ]	[ ] 37
38 These men want to become policemen.	[ ]	[ ]	[ ]	[ ]	[ ] 38
39 Henry and I took his father to the meeting.	[ ]	[ ]	[ ]	[ ]	[ ] 39
40 The man just stood there motionless.	[ ]	[ ]	[ ]	[ ]	[ ] 40

O. Balanced Matching Type: Rearrangement Variety. The excerpt of this variety shown here measures knowledges concerning the order in which four historical events occurred. This item asks the pupil for one answer that indicates the appropriate order for four events rather than to have him, for example, number the four events from 1 to 4 in historical sequence. In so doing, it becomes a rearrangement exercise presented in the form of a multiple-option item. Rearrangement exercises typically require a chronological, sequential, preferential, or some other ordering of terms and hence involve the pairing of terms with numbered or otherwise quantified sequences. Distractors are seldom used because all terms are ordinarily employed in the process of arrangement.

SAMPLE OF *Test Item in History* [19]

Directions: Which is the order in which the following events occurred:
(1)   A C D B   (2)   A C B D   (3)   D A B C   (4)   D A C B?
A. The steam engine was invented
B. People began to ride on trains
C. Robert Fulton made his first voyage by steamboat
D. The first telegraph message was sent

[18] Harold H. Bixler and others, *Metropolitan Achievement Tests: Test 4, Language,* Intermediate Battery. Form A. Copyright 1958 by Harcourt, Brace and World, Inc., New York. All rights reserved. Quoted by special permission.
[19] Howard R. Anderson, Elaine Forsyth, and Horace T. Morse, "The Measurement of Understanding in the Social Studies." *The Measurement of Understanding,* Forty-Fifth Yearbook of the National Society for the Study of Education, Part I. University of Chicago Press, Chicago, 1946. p. 81.

Unbalanced matching exercises. Exercises of this sort differ from those having no distractors primarily in their provision on one side or in one of the halves of the exercise of more terms than can properly be paired with the smaller number of items on the other side or in the other half. Such exercises are obviously unbalanced. The extra items are distractors in the same sense that incorrect answers in multiple-option items are distractors.

P. Unbalanced Matching Type: Interrelation Variety. The accompanying excerpt from a primary-grade reading test shows how knowledges can be measured by use of an unbalanced matching exercise. A pupil who gives the correct answers draws one line from the first sentence to the picture of the airplane, two lines from the second sentence to the picture of the barn, and three lines from the third sentence to the representation of a spider in his web. The three unused and inappropriate pictures in this item are the distractors characteristic of unbalanced matching exercises.

EXCERPT FROM *Gates Primary Reading Test* [20]

This is an airplane. I

This is a barn. II

This is a spider. III

Matching exercises are likely to be rather highly factual in nature, and to make use of the *who, what, when,* and *where* types of relationships and of identifying or naming abilities. They are rather easy to construct, and are perhaps for that reason more widely used than their characteristics warrant. They are likely to include clues to the correct responses unless there is rigid adherence to uniform categories of items in a matching set, and this restriction, desirable though it is, limits at least one side of the test unit to numbers, words, or at least short phrases. This restriction in turn tends to limit use of the item form mainly to factual types of subject matter.

The matching exercise is economical of space and of construction time. It is useful for matching terms and definitions, names and events, events and dates, books and authors, causes and effects, generalizations and applications, words and symbols, English and foreign words, and many other

[20] Arthur I. Gates, *Gates Primary Reading Test: Sentence Reading,* Grades 1 and 2. Form 3. Bureau of Publications, Teachers College, Columbia University, New York, 1958.

pairs of related items by use of verbal lists. It is also useful with numbered maps, charts, or pictorial representations for matching places and names, places and events, trends and dates, or objects and names in great variety.

Completion-Type or Augmentation Varieties [21]

The last of the four basic item forms distinguished in this volume is the only one classified broadly as being of the supplementation or augmentation type. Alternate-response and scaled-choice, multiple-choice, and matching forms are of the selection or recognition kind, for the pupil in answering these forms typically reacts to information, or in some instances misinformation, put before him rather than depending on his own memory or initiative for the responses he gives. In responding to completion items or exercises, however, the pupil must depend on his own initiative for recalling, computing, evolving, or otherwise creating the answers. Completion item types range from items testing the pupil's recall or knowledge of facts and skill in completing arithmetical computations, both testing the most tangible instructional outcomes, to items measuring the less tangible concepts, understandings, and applications and even on rare occasions to items evaluating intangible outcomes of learning.

EXCERPT FROM *Metropolitan Achievement Tests* [22]

10 On the day the circus opened in our town, 407 children's tickets and 278 adults' tickets were sold. How many tickets were sold that day?

_____

11 Richard had 65 newspapers to distribute. He has delivered only 17. How many more papers must he deliver?

_____

21 Gerberich, *op. cit.* p. 260-67.
22 Harold H. Bixler and others, *Metropolitan Achievement Tests: Test 7, Arithmetic Problem Solving and Concepts,* Elementary Battery. Form B. Copyright 1959 by Harcourt, Brace and World, Inc., New York. All rights reserved. Quoted by special permission.

Q. Augmentation Type: Completion Variety. The accompanying illustration of two items from an arithmetic problem-solving test shows how the simple and most widely used supplementation item type can be employed in measuring applications. Items of this sort place responsibility on the pupil for extending or adding to what appears on the test by writing words, phrases, numbers, or symbols in the places provided for his answers or by making marks in some specified manner.

R. Augmentation Type: Correction Variety. A second supplementation or augmentation variety is illustrated here by an excerpt from the part of a language test designed to measure punctuation skills. The pupil is here asked to correct the sentences appearing in the test by writing the appropriate capital letters and punctuation marks to show where errors occur. Correction items usually ask the pupil to respond by inserting or superimposing marks or symbols or otherwise to revise and improve material appearing in the test.

EXCERPT FROM *Metropolitan Achievement Tests* [23]

Part B
Punctuation and
Capitalization

DIRECTIONS

Look at each of the sentences below. There are one or more circles above each sentence. The arrow on each of these circles points to a certain place in the sentence where a capital letter or some punctuation mark may be needed. Look at each of these places. If the arrow points to a letter which should be a capital letter, write the capital letter inside the circle. If the arrow points to a space where some punctuation mark is needed, write that mark inside the circle. If no capital letter or punctuation mark is needed, put a ✔ in the circle. (✔) means *all right as it is — no change needed.* The sample below is marked correctly.

SAMPLE Ⓗis teacher is absent today(✔)(•)

25 Thanksgiving is the last thursday in november.

26 Edward T. Fiske is the coach of the football team.

27 Tex and i both go to franklin school.

28 Isnt your aunts house located on Cherry street

S. Augmentation Type: Construction Variety. A version of a seldom-used variety of supplementation item is illustrated here by an excerpt from a plane geometry test. The sample items measure concepts by asking the pupil to construct lines in freehand style on the geometric figures appear-

[23] Harold H. Bixler and others, *Metropolitan Achievement Tests: Test 5, Language,* Elementary Battery. Form B. Copyright 1959 by Harcourt, Brace and World, Inc., New York. All rights reserved. Quoted by special permission.

ing in the test. The pupil is often given considerable freedom in the form and manner of presenting his responses to construction varieties of items.

EXCERPTS FROM *Breslich Plane Geometry Survey Test* [24]

In each of the following four problems, make a careful freehand sketch of the required locus.

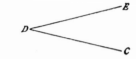

1. The locus of points equidistant from *A* and *B*.

2. The locus of points equidistant from lines *DC* and *DE*.

The completion-type or augmentation item is best adapted to the measurement of rather highly factual knowledges of the *who, what, when, where* types, and is widely adaptable to different subject matter in such uses. It can be used to test the ability to identify things described or pictured, in which form it has rather wide range. In identification exercises, it is perhaps best adapted for use with maps and charts in the social studies and representations of biological structures in the natural sciences. It is valuable in computational problem situations in arithmetic and the physical sciences.

One of the major characteristics of the simple completion item is its apparent ease of construction, which tends to encourage wider use than is perhaps justified. Because of its tendency to measure factual knowledges rather than understandings, there is danger of overweighting tests with factual materials if a verbal type of recall item is too widely employed.

The simple recall item is difficult to score because of its tendency to be quite low in objectivity, even though responses may be provided for in terminal and aligned form. Its use in the modern classroom is further limited by the fact that it is not directly adaptable to machine methods of scoring.

3. CHARACTERISTICS OF INFORMAL OBJECTIVE TESTS

Informal objective tests and test items are described and illustrated in the preceding sections of this chapter in some ways that constitute background for actual test construction. There are at least several further respects in which meaning can be given to objective items and objective

[24] E. R. Breslich, *Breslich Plane Geometry Survey Test,* Second Semester. Form A. Public School Publishing Co., Bloomington, Ill., 1931.

tests used informally by the teacher in measuring the achievement of his pupils, however. Important among them are the four aspects presented below: (1) types of pupil behavior measured by the tests, (2) sorts of stimuli to which pupils respond in taking the tests, (3) kinds of mental activity pupils employ in taking the tests, and (4) limitations and advantages of the tests.

Outcomes Measured by Various Item Types

Some of the nine outcomes of instruction mentioned in a foregoing section of this chapter and discussed in greater detail in Chapters 1 and 8 are more easily measured by certain objective item varieties than by others. Several of the outcomes can be measured satisfactorily by most if not all of the major varieties of items. Only a few of the most important relationships between outcomes and item varieties are mentioned here.

Highly tangible outcomes. Skills and knowledges, the most highly tangible instructional and learning outcomes, can be measured by widely varying item types of both the selection and the supplementation kinds. The most popular item types for testing skills are the multiple-option, completion, correction, and alternate-response, with matching types receiving little attention. Knowledges appear to be measurable most typically by alternate-response, completion, multiple-option, correction, and interrelation types occurring in all four basic forms.

Outcomes intermediate in tangibility. Of the four outcome types listed in this category, understandings are measurable by the greatest range of item types. Multiple-option, completion, and alternate-response types are widely represented in the measurement of concepts, but only completion varieties have much value for measuring applications. Activities are most often measured by alternate-response and scaled-choice techniques.

Intangible outcomes. The three intangible outcomes of learning and instruction of concern here appear to be measured most suitably by items or exercises other than the completion and matching forms. In fact, most of the items or exercises employed in measuring appreciations, attitudes, and nonvocational interests are of alternate-response and related scaled-choice varieties, with multiple-option types next in frequency of representation.

Types of Stimuli Presented to Pupils

Informal objective tests employ several types of stimuli in presenting items to pupils for their reactions. The stimuli are of two sorts that can most simply be distinguished as internal and external.[25]

[25] Gerberich, *op. cit.* p. 274-79.

Internal stimuli. The stimuli appearing most frequently as an integral part of the test itself are the mimeographed or printed words that are often called verbal stimuli. Some of the sample item varieties shown in the preceding section of this chapter also make use of numerical, graphical, and symbolical materials. Pictorial stimuli, or actual pictures, are not infrequently used in printed tests. All five of these types of stimuli variously appear on the pages of test booklets put into the hands of pupils.

External stimuli. Certain other stimuli are presented in other ways. In a listening test, for example, the examiner's voice provides an oral stimulus. In music tests, on occasion, a piano is used in providing an instrumental stimulus. The specimens of wood sometimes presented to pupils in object tests for manual arts courses are material stimuli. Finally, the girl who appears before a home economics class so that the pupils can evaluate the suitability of her clothes and makeup can be referred to as a corporeal stimulus. These four types of external stimuli have all been used in achievement testing by having pupils record their answers on regular paper-and-pencil tests.

It can be seen from this brief account that the teacher constructing informal objective tests for use in his classes is by no means restricted to printed words in presenting test material to pupils. The ingenious teacher can make significant use both of internal and external stimuli in ways that are illustrated by the sample items and exercises shown in a foregoing section of this chapter and at frequent points in the ten chapters of Part 5 that deal with measurement in various subject areas. Although many of these samples are from standardized achievement tests in printed format, their counterparts can in most instances be produced by clever use of a mimeograph or even a gelatin-plate process for reproducing copy.

Types of Pupil Mental Activity in Taking Tests

The type of mental activity required of the pupil as he takes an informal objective test is important, especially because the scope and level of the intellectual demands made upon him are closely related to both the purposes and the quality of any test of achievement. Five types of mental activity, as distinguished by Gerberich,[26] are considered here.

Dealing with errors. Achievement tests frequently ask pupils to deal with errors in one of two ways: (1) detecting errors and (2) correcting errors. In the simpler version, the pupil is asked to recognize and indicate errors. The more complex version makes the additional demand on the pupil of correcting the errors. Sample R in a preceding section of this chapter illustrates one in which this type of mental activity can be elicited.

[26] *Ibid.* p. 280-85.

Handling data. Four stages or levels can be distinguished in the handling of data, whether the data are in the form of numbers, as seems to be implied in common usage, or in the equally acceptable form of graphs, symbols, words, or pictures. The levels are (1) identifying data, (2) interpreting data, (3) organizing data, and (4) representing data. It seems unlikely that a pupil can interpret data unless he can recognize them, that he can organize them without identifying and interpreting them, and that he can represent them unless he is able to handle them at all three of the lower and less complex levels. The data to be dealt with variously appear in the form of graphs, charts, tables, and drawings, and also as sentences, paragraphs, and in still other forms. They may be presented in the items themselves, in the test but apart from the items, or even separately and apart from the test. Excerpts *L* and *N* of those shown above illustrate items dealing with the interpretation and organization of verbal data.

Extending meanings. This category, less well delimited than the other four, includes: (1) completing meanings, (2) selecting usage, and (3) solving problems. Meanings are completed in a wide variety of test items, but the other two varieties are more specific. Of the items and exercises illustrated above, excerpts *G* and *Q* are of this type.

Indicating activities and issues. The two types of mental performance appropriate here are (1) specifying practices and (2) specifying activities. Although these overlap with the outcome types designated as activities and adjustments previously in this volume, they are by no means commensurate. Excerpts *D* and *E* of the item types shown earlier in this chapter illustrate this variety.

Indicating tastes and preferences. Three distinguishable varieties of mental activity often influenced by emotional reactions are (1) expressing beliefs and opinions, (2) expressing likes-dislikes, and (3) judging characteristics. Although the most obvious representations of these three varieties are the learning outcomes discussed previously in this volume as attitudes, interests, and appreciations, the two sets of terms are not identical. Excerpts *B* and *C* among the illustrations of item types given above ask the pupil to indicate his tastes and preferences.

Limitations and Advantages of Informal Objective Tests

As is mentioned in the introduction to Part 3, there is no good reason to balance one type of teacher-made classroom test against another and thereby to conclude, to suggest, or even to imply unintentionally that one is preferable to the other. Therefore, the fact that some of the strengths of the informal objective test discussed below are in areas of weakness for the most prominent type of traditional test treated in Chapter 9 should be accepted as evidence of their different values and appropriate uses rather than of the over-all superiority of one test type over the other for all uses.

Limitations of teacher-made objective tests. A number of rather important criticisms of informal objective examinations have been brought forward by teachers and critics. The paragraphs in this section present evaluations of a few of the most significant of these objections. The criticism that the objective examination overemphasizes factual knowledge disregards the fact that there is nothing in the objective form which makes impossible the construction of items that stimulate critical and constructive thought. Many teacher-made tests do not contain such thought-provoking items, but that does not mean that they cannot be made to do so when teachers become adept in using objective techniques and learn to think deeply enough into the validation of their tests. The informal objective examination can be used in the measurement of various instructional outcomes of significance far beyond the acquisition of facts and of basic skills.

Some teachers and critics believe that there is a tendency for the objective test to encourage guessing to an undue extent. The objective examination form admittedly permits, but does not necessarily encourage, guessing. In fact, it may tend to discourage guessing through its emphasis upon exact knowledges and correct applications and interpretations of factual data, and in its use of correction-for-guessing formulae in scoring test results. Furthermore, it is probable that few guesses on objective tests are based on pure chance. Rather they are based on slight balances of evidence on one side of an issue on which the pupil is uncertain. Many life activities, as a matter of fact, are based on chances, considerably less than certain, of a given outcome. Therefore, it seems that guessing in the sense of weighing available evidence and making the best decision possible is neither injurious to the pupil nor a bad influence upon examination results.

The criticism that informal objective tests are difficult to prepare is frequently made. It is true that they may be difficult to prepare but they are certainly easy to score. When the advantages accruing to the use of objective tests are balanced against the difficulty of preparing them, the conclusion seems favorable rather than otherwise to this type of teacher-made test.

Experience in the use of objective examinations indicates that they are most valuable when available for classroom use in mimeographed form. Unquestionably the mimeographing and paper costs are items of expense which in some school systems may be considerable. However, the cost of preparing objective examinations probably represents one of the very minor items of expense in the average school system when it is considered in terms of the real educational importance of such instruments.

Teachers sometimes feel that the informal objective test inadequately allows opportunity for the pupil to organize and express his thoughts. Some objective methods are available for testing the ability of the pupil to organize his thoughts, but no claim should be made that the objective test provides opportunity for the verbal expression of organized thought. Neither should the written examination be expected to serve this purpose. The opportunity for training the pupils in self-expression can and should be provided adequately elsewhere in the school program.

Advantages of teacher-made objective tests. Of the several merits of the informal objective test, the two most important are answers of the early objective testers to the two major criticisms of the essay examination discussed above—limited sampling and subjectivity of scoring.

Extensive sampling is one of these advantages. Although all tests measure only samples of pupil performance, the objective test by its nature samples so widely that the results obtained from its use closely approximate those that would be obtained if pupil performance in the subject in question could be measured completely. A test made up of a hundred or so short, well-selected questions or items will widely and hence quite adequately sample pupil achievement for many purposes. By contrast, a test composed of only a few items or questions will usually fail to obtain an extensive sample because the person devising it sacrifices the possibility of sampling widely and extensively when he decides to delve into a few areas intensively.

Objectivity of scoring is the second of the major advantages of informal objective tests. In an objective test the items are so stated that the answers are brief, and usually only one correct answer is possible. A highly objective test may be scored repeatedly by one person or it may be scored by a large number of different persons with practically no disagreement in the scores assigned. Thus in the well-constructed objective examination the responses can be evaluated on an impersonal basis, entirely independent of the personal judgment of the scorer.

The form in which the objective item is stated makes it possible for the pupil to record his response definitely and briefly. This in turn permits many specific reactions to be called for in a relatively brief period of working time. In this way a wide area of course content can be sampled in a given period, resulting in a high reliability of measurement per unit of working time. Because of the nature of the items, the amount of writing done by pupils in responding to objective tests is reduced to a minimum, however. This practically eliminates bluffing and the advantage that rapid and fluent writers have over those not so gifted in this respect.

4. CONSTRUCTION OF OBJECTIVE TEST ITEMS

This section of the chapter considers the general principles to be followed in the construction of various objective item types. Such questions as adaptation of item types to various subject matter and the construction and use of the test as a whole are dealt with in a later section of this chapter. Because of the multiplicity of item types, it is impossible to discuss all of them in detail. Therefore, the suggestions are intended mainly for the basic or most common forms of items, although in many instances they are equally well adapted to modified types of the basic forms.

General suggestions that seem to be equally applicable to all objective item types are given first. These should serve as the introductory portion of the lists of suggestions on later pages for the various common or basic forms of items. The student will find that frequent reference to the samples shown in a preceding section will be helpful in the study of methods for constructing the various item types. It should be apparent that common sense and personal experience must furnish the basis for recommendations on many issues discussed. Therefore, this section can be said to present the authors' views, based on objective evidence and opinions of others and on their own experience in test construction, on a variety of detailed points which must be considered if objective items are to be well constructed.

General Suggestions for Constructing Objective Items

A number of the suggestions given here apply equally well to all or most objective item forms. Attention is given in the subsequent pages to suggestions that apply to the major selection or recognition types and the augmentation types.

(1) *Observe rules governing good language expression.* Carelessly framed and ungrammatically worded items are easily susceptible to misinterpretation by pupils.

(2) *Use simple rather than unnecessarily difficult language.* Complex and unusual words having general meaning, as contrasted with technical language of the subject being tested, are likely to lead to misinterpretations and to penalize many pupils unjustifiably.

(3) *Employ original rather than textbook language.* Textbook statements used without modification may be too narrow and specific, may depend too much on the particular textbook and its author, and may favor pupils who have unusually good memories for details read.

(4) *Use quantitative rather than qualitative words when feasible.* Indefinite words often result in items that have approximate rather than precise meanings.

(5) *Avoid ambiguous wordings.* Ambiguities in item statements are likely to confuse and hence to penalize many pupils unjustifiably.

(6) *Avoid use of clues and suggestions.* Clues and suggestions afford irrelevant and hence undesirable evidence concerning correct answers.

(7) *Avoid use of "catch" words or intentionally misleading wordings.* Such irrelevant confusions may be overlooked by some pupils, may be misinterpreted by others, and may distract pupil attention from major purposes.

(8) *Avoid use of items so interrelated that the answer to one logically determines the answer to another.* An unwarranted premium is attached to giving the correct answer to the first item of such a pair.

(9) *Provide for answers in a highly objective form.* Failure to provide for precise, unambiguous, and easily readable answers contributes to subjectivity of scoring.

Suggestions for Constructing Alternate-Response and Scaled-Choice Items

Both the alternate-response and the scaled-choice item have potential values and uses for classroom testing that seem not to be widely recognized. For example, such alternate-response varieties as the *yes–no, right–wrong, same–different, agree–disagree, like–dislike, better–worse,* and even still other possibilities can appropriately be used in separate test parts to supplement and perhaps on occasion to replace the overworked *true–false* variety. Furthermore, several sets of terms can effectively be used in separate test parts to extend a two-option alternate-response type to flexible scaled-choice varieties providing three, four, or five choices. Among such terms are (1) *true–indeterminate–false, yes–uncertain–no, agree–uncertain–disagree,* and *like–indifferent–dislike;* (2) *true–probably true–probably false–false* and *strongly agree–agree–disagree–strongly disagree;* and (3) *true–probably true–indeterminate–probably false–false* and also *strongly agree–agree–uncertain–disagree–strongly disagree.* Several of these alternate-response and scaled-choice varieties are illustrated on pages 223 to 226.

Most of the specific suggestions apply to such alternate-response varieties as are listed above. The alternatives are sometimes referred to below as affirmative and negative in order to include the various sets of paired terms rather than to apply only to the more restrictive true and false. A few of the suggestions apply to the scaled-choice item or broadly to both types dealt with here.

(1) *Use sparingly and carefully such "specific determiners" as* (a) *"always" and "never,"* (b) *clauses giving causes of or reasons for,* (c) *comparisons, and* (d) *very long statements.* "Specific determiners" tend to predispose items variously toward affirmative or negative answers.

(2) *Avoid using statements containing double negatives.* Double negatives introduce irrelevant and confusing factors.

(3) *Avoid using statements that are partly in the affirmative and partly in the negative.* Internal inconsistencies in items are confusing to pupils and irrational.

(4) *Apportion correct answers in approximately equal numbers to the affirmative and negative alternatives.*[27] A preponderance of correct answers in either response position has possibilities of introducing irrelevant factors.

(5) *Randomize the occurrence of affirmative and negative statements from item to item.*[27] Any order other than chance has possibilities of introducing extraneous factors.

(6) *Use choices in scaled-choice items that logically represent a progression from one extreme to the other.* Failure to do so reduces the meaning and significance of results.

(7) *Use the concept of indeterminancy or uncertainty for the middle term in scaled-choice items having three or five choices.* Omission of such a term forces a choice upon pupils whether or not they are willing to make one.

(8) *Use antonyms for the terms at opposite ends of the continuum in scaled-choice items.* Failure to use opposite meanings where they are appropriate results in an unbalanced and incomplete scale of meaning.

(9) *Provide for marginal and preferably terminal responses.* Irregular spacing of response positions needlessly complicates scoring procedures.

Suggestions for Constructing Multiple-Choice Items

Multiple-choice items are widely useful in achievement measurement, especially in the more common multiple-option version but on occasion also in the multiple-response variation. The multiple-option item type is adaptable to a wide range of needs and situations by the ingenious teacher who wishes to realize the values of varieties other than the most common one of a stem followed by several options. The five multiple-option formats considered in this volume to be distinctive and variously useful are (1) stem-and-options, (2) setting-and-options, (3) grouped-term, (4) struc-

---

[27] Applicable only to items for which answers can appropriately be scored as right or wrong; does not apply to items used in measuring activities, appreciations, attitudes, and interests.

tured-response, and (5) contained-options. Multiple-response items, less widely useful in general, have values that can be realized by adapting the principle of a multiple response to the common and easily scorable stem- and-options variety of multiple-option item. Illustrations of all of these types are shown on pages 228 to 232.

The following suggestions apply primarily to the multiple-option item with one correct or one best answer, but mention is also made of the multiple-response item variety to which a good and complete answer may on occasion list the two or even more options that are correct.

(1) *Use parallel language structure for all options in an item.* Failure to provide for ready interchangeability may furnish clues or leads to the correct answer.

(2) *Use "the" or "a(n)," meaning either "a" or "an," if an article immediately precedes a group of options.* Either of the indefinite articles alone usually imposes an extraneous grammatical restriction on an acceptable response.

(3) *Place as much of the item content as possible in any setting or any item stem that may be employed.* Repetition of words in the various options is wasteful of space and valueless.

(4) *Choose distractors, or incorrect options, that will appear plausible to many pupils.* Failure to attain plausibility in all distractors increases chances of obtaining correct answers by a process of logical elimination or by guessing.

(5) *Use four or five options in general.* Fewer options, except for young children, enhance chances of guessing correct answers and increase chances of obtaining correct answers by a process of logical elimination.

(6) *Maintain a constant number of options in the items of a test part.* Any failure to do so results in differing chances of guessing correct answers from item to item.

(7) *Apportion correct answers in approximately equal numbers to the several answer positions.*[28] A preponderance of correct answers for any option or options has possibilities of introducing irrelevant factors.

(8) *Randomize the occurrence of correct answers among the several answer positions from item to item.*[28] Any order other than chance has possibilities of introducing extraneous factors.

(9) *Use not less than two and not more than three correct responses in multiple-response items having four or five choices.* Providing variously for too few or too many correct responses may be confusing to pupils.

(10) *Adapt multiple-response items to multiple-option format* (sample *L,* page 232). Multiple-response items in usual format are difficult

---

[28] Applicable only to items for which answers can appropriately be scored as right or wrong.

if not impossible to score with appropriate concern for possibilities of guessing.

(11) *Provide for marginal and preferably terminal responses.* Internal placement of response positions needlessly complicates scoring procedures.

Suggestions for Constructing Matching Exercises

Matching exercises are suitable for measuring not only in the widely used interrelation or list format but also in the form of the rarely used but valuable classification and rearrangement exercises. Some exercises of this type require pairing of terms in two, or even more, lists of equal length but others consist of lists differing in the number of terms included. The former are balanced and have no distractors; the latter are unbalanced and have distractors, or unused terms, in one list. By their nature, however, the other two varieties of matching exercises are always balanced. Rearrangement exercises, difficult to score in the most common format, can be simplified by adapting them to the widely used and easily scorable multiple-option stem-and-options variety. Illustrations of these item types are pictured on pages 232 to 235.

Most of the suggestions that follow are applicable to interrelation exercises but some of them are equally suitable, or even uniquely suitable, for classification and rearrangement exercises. Suggestions also appear for unbalanced as well as balanced sets of matching items.

(1) *Maintain consistency of grammatical form within each category.* Failure to attain correspondence in such matters as number, person, and parts of speech may provide extraneous clues to correct answers.

(2) *Maintain consistency of pattern within each category.* Failure to attain homogeneity in type of parallel listings may provide extraneous clues to correct answers.

(3) *Provide for one and only one correct answer in each response position.* Failure to establish mutually exclusive listings may variously lead to false starts, backtracking, confusion, and other undesirable outcomes.

(4) *Arrange listings in some logical order, e.g., alphabetical or chronological, unrelated to the relationships being tested.* Failure to randomize ideas may allow unintentional clues to operate.

(5) *Provide for a minimum of three and ordinarily for a maximum of ten to fifteen responses in a set of items.* Provision for only two responses is inadequate and provision for more than twelve or so responses promotes a waste of pupil time in locating correct answers.

(6) *Provide several distractors on one side of a short interrelation exercise.* Logical completion or judicious guessing can aid pupils in deciding upon the last few answers in short balanced exercises.

(7) *Choose distractors, or incorrect listings, that will appear plausible to many pupils.* Failure to attain plausibility in all distractors increases chances of obtaining correct answers by a process of logical elimination.

(8) *Provide for the appearance of an exercise entirely on one page of a test.* Splitting of a set of items between two pages is confusing to pupils and wasteful of their time.

(9) *Adapt rearrangement exercises to multiple-option format* (sample *O*, page 234). Rearrangement exercises in usual format are scorable either easily but inappropriately or in a very complicated but suitable manner.

(10) *Provide for response positions in a marginal column or a row.* Irregular spacing of response positions needlessly complicates scoring procedures.

Suggestions for Constructing Completion-Type Items and Exercises

Items and exercises variously referred to here as supplementation or augmentation types occur most commonly in the completion format as contrasted with the somewhat less widely used but significant correction variety and the seldom-used construction version. The range in general is from short and unitary items requiring a simple completion or correction to lengthy integrated exercises providing for a number of related responses of a completion, correction, or even construction type. The range in another sense is from items measuring recall of specific facts to items and exercises measuring some of the less tangible but often more significant outcomes of learning. Several samples of these completion-type test materials appear on pages 236 to 238.

The suggestions appearing below apply to completion somewhat more than to correction or construction types of items and exercises but several of them are more broadly applicable.

(1) *Provide for short, simple, and specific responses, such as a word, a date, or a number.* Failure to attain brevity and specificity in answers usually results in subjectivity of scoring.

(2) *Use "the" or "a(n)," meaning either "a" or "an," if an article immediately precedes a response position.* Either of the indefinite articles alone usually imposes an extraneous grammatical restriction on an acceptable response.

(3) *Use unified and well-organized thought units in paragraph-completion exercises.* Lack of unification and organization may distract from over-all meaningfulness and discriminate against some pupils.

(4) *Avoid requirement of too many responses in paragraph-completion exercises.* Provision for more response positions than the supporting con-

text adequately accounts for may force many pupils to guess at the intended meaning.

(5) *Give credit for any correct answer.* Insistence upon one particular correct answer to an item is unduly restrictive and is unfair to pupils.

(6) *Avoid penalizing pupils for spelling errors.*[29] Spelling accuracy is often extraneous to the outcome that is being measured.

(7) *Avoid penalizing pupils for poor handwriting or rewarding them for good handwriting.* Handwriting quality is usually extraneous to the outcome being measured.

(8) *Provide spaces for answers that are of constant and of adequate size.* Inconstancy and inadequacy in size may increase subjectivity of scoring by giving clues, erroneous or real, to length of correct responses.

(9) *Provide for marginal and preferably terminal responses.* Irregular spacing of response positions needlessly complicates scoring procedures.

5. CONSTRUCTION AND USE OF INFORMAL OBJECTIVE TESTS

The problems of constructing informal objective tests are discussed in this section of the chapter. Treated here are the general issues that should receive consideration from the time a test is in the planning stage to the time when its results are used in the validation of its individual items.

As is discussed in Chapter 8 above, standardized and informal objective tests of achievement are constructed by application of procedures that differ more in precision and technical level than in kind. Consequently, the treatments of procedures for constructing teacher-made objective tests here and of standardized tests in the second section of Chapter 8 are intended to complement rather than to duplicate one another. Aspects of the construction process of special concern to classroom teachers are emphasized in the discussion. The seven steps are (1) planning the test, (2) writing the items, (3) assembling the test, (4) reproducing the test, (5) administering and scoring the test, (6) interpreting the test results, and (7) anticipating future testing needs.

Planning the Test

Teachers planning their own objective tests face many of the same problems standardized test makers encounter in a more formal and crucial manner. They must somehow come to two decisions—what types of content to include in the test and what types of pupil behaviors, or instruc-

---

[29] Not applicable to spelling tests or to technical words in a subject being tested.

tional outcomes, to measure. They must then effect a balance between test content and types of pupil behaviors to be measured.

The three procedures discussed in Chapter 8 as aids in making these decisions are analysis of instructional outcomes, analysis of textbooks and courses of study, and judgments of qualified persons. All three are applicable here in modified form. The teacher, who is certainly qualified to supply the judgment for his own classroom tests, should analyze the textbook and other instructional materials he has used as major sources of test content and should examine his instructional objectives and their mode of realization in modified pupil behaviors for outcomes. A merger of test content and types of behavior to be measured can then be sketched out formally or informally in a two-way chart of the sort shown in Table 9 for a 40-item classroom test in arithmetic for an intermediate grade. Such a chart or a similar one relating test content to types and numbers of objective items is useful in the next step of test construction.

TABLE 9

Two-Way Chart of Items for an Arithmetic Test [30]

Types of Computations		Types of Situations		
	COMPUTATIONAL EXAMPLES	THOUGHT PROBLEMS BASED ON PROCEDURES		
		PREVIOUSLY TAUGHT	NOT PREVIOUSLY TAUGHT	ALL
Use of fractions	7	4	1	12
Multiplication	2	3	1	6
Division	3	4	1	8
Measurement	1	5	1	7
Use of decimals	3	3	1	7
Totals	16	19	5	40

The length of the test should also normally be planned in advance. Test length depends on many factors other than the nature of the test items and the amount of time available for testing, but these are basic issues to be considered in the preparation of a test. The test should be of such length that all or very nearly all of the pupils can complete it before the end of the testing period. A reasonable estimate may be reached by allowing one minute of working time for each two recall items, each two multiple-choice items, and each three alternate-response items. Such recommendations seem to have only very general significance, however, for the difficulty of the items and the age level of the pupils have much

[30] Adapted from Educational Testing Service, *Making the Classroom Test: A Guide for Teachers.* Evaluation and Advisory Service Series, No. 4. Educational Testing Service, Princeton, N. J., 1959. p. 6.

to do with time requirements, and teachers vary a great deal in the types of items they construct. The teacher will learn after brief experimentation how long a test should be for a given period of time.

Writing the Items

It is ordinarily desirable to use more than one type of objective item in the test, but, on the other hand, not to use too great a variety of item types. For ordinary classroom tests given during one period, two or three types may be used; for longer examinations, variety can be increased by using four or five types or modifications. It should be kept in mind that the subject matter itself is often a factor limiting the types of items used. Since supplementation items place a greater demand upon the pupil's memory of specific facts than is true of selection items, it may reasonably be expected that the pupil will recognize the accuracy of certain facts presented to him but not necessarily be able to recall the facts without clues. Therefore, completion-type items should be used only for important facts.

The test maker may find it advantageous first to construct items that fall into large groupings, such as matching exercises, and then to construct items having narrower scope. It is often desirable to construct multiple-choice items prior to alternate-response forms. This does not mean that all matching and multiple-choice items should be constructed before any completion or alternate-response items are made, but rather that first consideration should be given for a certain fact or relationship to the possibility of its use in an item form which is not so flexible and widely applicable as are the alternate-response and recall types. If a particular idea does not, for example, readily combine with other similar relationships into a matching exercise and does not furnish enough plausible alternative responses for use in multiple-choice form, it should immediately be set up in one of the simpler forms.

The teacher will find it advantageous, for reasons that are brought out clearly below, to write each item or each test unit on a filing card or slip. Alternate-response, multiple-choice, and completion and other items can well be put on separate cards. Matching exercises should be written on cards in their entirety, for such test units cannot be broken down by items for listing on separate cards. It is possible and desirable to code these cards in terms of the content they cover and also to keep records of the use of each item in the test and its validity. More is said about these last two points in a later section of this chapter.

Since item writing can be most effective when certain general principles and other details of construction are observed, a preceding section of this chapter is devoted entirely to specific suggestions in supplementation of the general ones given above.

Assembling the Test

After the test items have been constructed, they should be sorted by types and carefully evaluated in their new settings. There should be a minimum number of items which all pupils can answer correctly or for which no pupils can get the correct answers. A difficulty level averaging about 60 to 70 percent is usually recommended as most satisfactory. Items should therefore range from that point toward very hard and toward very easy. If there should be too few items of a certain type for a section of a test, those items should be redrafted to fit into one of the sections definitely decided upon.

Items should be arranged in parts or sections according to type in the final test. There is little agreement among test workers concerning the best arrangement of items for informal objective tests. Some prefer arrangement of items in each part by approximately an increasing order of difficulty. Other persons prefer to arrange material topically within each section of the test, and to consider item difficulty in the arrangement of content only by introducing the test by a few very easy items so that pupils will not become discouraged before they get well started. On the whole, the second order seems to be the more natural one for classroom tests.

Reproducing the Test

The examination should normally be prepared for use with the pupils by a mimeographing or other method of reproduction. Complete directions to the pupils should always be provided. This sometimes entails general instructions at the beginning and separate directions for each part of the test. If the item forms are difficult to understand or if pupils are taking objective tests for the first time, samples showing how they are to record their answers should be given with the directions. The samples should be so simple in content that they will be readily comprehended by all pupils. Illustrations of directions to pupils and of samples to demonstrate methods of answering test items are given with some of the sample items appearing in a foregoing section of this chapter.

Pupils should be told in the directions whether or not to guess, and should also be told how the test will be scored. The most common procedures and those usually recommended are to instruct the pupils not to guess and then to correct their scores for guessing on alternate-response items. On the other hand, pupils are usually told to attempt each item on a matching test.

Administering and Scoring the Test

Many of the points made in Chapter 8 about the administration and scoring of standardized achievement tests are equally applicable to the informal objective test, although scoring procedures are discussed here in terms of their suitability for use with major types of test items.

Administering the test. Little need be said here concerning the administration of the informal objective test except to point out that if the directions to pupils and any necessary sample items are carefully and well prepared the actual administration of the test is simple indeed. The safest procedure is to make certain that the pupils understand how to take the test by careful preparation of the directions, to make sure that individual test items require no explanations by framing them with care, and then to answer no questions about word meanings or interpretations to be placed on certain items while the test is in progress. Pupil questions concerning typographical errors they may encounter in the test should be investigated and the attention of the entire class should be called to any such errors that might within reason cause misinterpretations of items.

Scoring the test results. Scoring of the test should be by the predetermined method, and should vary with the type of objective item. Scoring keys can be prepared easily by using a copy of the test and cutting it into strip keys and cutout stencils as required. With such keys available, the actual mechanics of scoring the tests are very simple. Each correct answer should ordinarily be given one point of credit.

Chances of guessing the correct answers vary with different item forms. There is little if any chance of guessing, or at least of making a pure guess, on completion-type items. Obviously, the chance is 50-50 on an alternate-response item, but it is only one in five for a multiple-choice item with five alternatives. The correction-for-chance formula is

$$\text{Score} = \text{Rights} - \frac{\text{Wrongs}}{N - 1}, \text{ or } R - \frac{W}{N - 1},$$

where N represents the number of possible answers to an item. For the true-false item, this becomes $R - W$. For multiple-choice items of 3, 4, and 5 alternatives, the formula becomes respectively

$$R - \frac{W}{2}, R - \frac{W}{3}, \text{ and } R - \frac{W}{4}.$$

Correction for chance is ordinarily used with the true-false test and the multiple-choice test consisting of items that have as few as three alternatives. It need not necessarily be used wtih multiple-choice items having four or more alternatives, since the chance of making a correct guess is not great in such tests. Matching tests are not usually corrected for chance, since little opportunity for guessing exists if they are properly constructed.

There should be no attempt to weight individual items of a test differently according to their importance or difficulty. It may be desirable in some instances, however, to assign varying weights to the scores resulting from different parts of the test in order to account for differences in difficulty or average time required per item, in which case the most satisfactory procedure is probably to multiply by 2 or by 3 the scores from test parts that are thought to be deserving of extra weighting.

Interpreting the Test Results

Results from the use of standardized achievement tests are commonly given meaning by the use of norms tables and derived scores. Because of their informal nature and because they are typically designed for use in single classes, informal objective tests are not accompanied by tables of norms and do not directly or indirectly provide any derived scores. However, there are several ways by means of which the classroom teacher can give meaning to scores made by pupils on the objective tests he constructs for use in his own classes.

Standardized achievement tests commonly provide such methods for establishing comparability of results from test to test as age norms, grade norms, percentile norms, and standard-score norms. Similarly, they provide for several types of related derived scores—age equivalents, grade equivalents, percentile ranks, and standard scores—that are variously obtained and used in interpretation of results. Norms and derived scores of these types are discussed at some length and illustrated in Chapter 8.

The classroom teacher can give comparability of meaning to results from his various classroom tests by the use of derived scores or measures not very different from those named above. He can compute percentile ranks or the similar but less detailed decile ranks, for example. He can also classify results into what are called stanines, or nine groups of scores ranging from highest to lowest. Finally, he can give a type of constant meaning to such letter marks as A, B, C, D, and F or to other patterns of final marks typically assigned to pupils in various school subjects at the end of a semester or school year. Methods for computing such derived scores are presented in Chapter 14, together with several other rather simple statistical procedures useful in informal objective testing. The interpretation of informal objective test results is consequently given no further attention here.

Anticipating Future Testing Needs

For the teacher who repeats courses annually or more than once each year, concern with a particular informal objective test should not end with the final direct use of the results. Informal objective testing is not economical of teacher time if the teacher starts afresh in the construction of every test over a period of years. Construction of informal objéctive tests should be a cumulative and selective process resulting in constant improvement of the tests actually used in the classroom. If tests are to be evaluated and improved in the manner suggested below, test booklets should not be returned to the pupils permanently. However, they may well be distributed for review purposes after the test has been scored, and collected when the instructional purpose has been accomplished, or used with individual pupils in conferences concerning special points needing further emphasis in their work.

Validation of test items. As a means of determining the validities of individual items for future use, the method generally known as item counting is of great value. One of the simple item-counting methods is based on a division of the class into groups of above-average and below-average performance on the test, with half of the class in each group. The test papers or answer sheets should then be sorted into corresponding groups. The number of correct responses to each test item by the pupils in each group can then be determined by a routine clerical procedure. This ordinarily involves the use of squared paper on which the columns represent the items of the test and the rows are used for checking the items correctly answered by each pupil. A summation of the check marks in each column for each of the two pupil groups is then made. The sum of these two numbers and also the difference between them is then obtained for each test item.

If machine-scored tests are used, the most routine portion of this item-analysis procedure can be done on the machine. If tests are hand-scored and the teacher has no clerical assistance available but wishes to avoid the routine portion of item analysis, it is possible for him to take class time for this activity and to depend on a "show of hands" and counting method of obtaining this basic information from the pupils item by item.[31]

---

[31] Educational Testing Service, *Short-Cut Statistics for Teacher-Made Tests*. Evaluation and Advisory Service Series, No. 5. Educational Testing Service, Princeton, N. J., 1960. p. 2-10.

Item difficulty is usually expressed as the percentage of pupils in the above-average and below-average groups combined who answer the item correctly. Consequently, the number of correct answers to each item is divided by the total number of pupils in the entire group to obtain the index of item difficulty. The common practice in test construction is to attempt to prepare items covering a wide range of difficulty, from very easy to very hard. Items are not ordinarily suitable for inclusion in later tests if they are so easy that no pupil fails to respond correctly. The presence of such items merely serves to lengthen the test without adding to the reliability of its measurement. In a similar way, items that are so difficult that no pupil is able to respond correctly should not be included in the test a second time. In general, items ranging from 30 percent to 90 percent of correct responses with an average of perhaps 60 to 70 percent are considered acceptable in difficulty for objective classroom tests.[32]

Item discriminative power is most simply represented by the difference between the number of above-average and below-average pupils answering it correctly converted into a percentage of all pupils in the group. This percentage is the index of discriminative power for the item. Although standardized test makers often base their item analyses on the highest 27 percent and the lowest 27 percent of the scores made by large numbers of pupils, division into upper and lower halves is often preferred for informal objective tests because of its adaptability to small pupil groups and because of its simplicity. Items are usually rated as satisfactory individually when they have indices of discrimination of at least 10, but the average of such indices for all items in a test should probably be above 10 and preferably be on the order of 15.[33]

If a class of 30 pupils is divided into above-average and below-average groups of 15 pupils each on the basis of total scores made on a classroom test, and if procedures for item counting correct answers for the two groups are carried through as discussed above, results such as those shown in Table 10 might be obtained for a group of items. For example, 22 pupils answered Item 8 correctly and 6 more of the above-average than of the below-average pupils got it right. When the sum, 22, and the difference, 6, are converted into percentages through division by 30, the difficulty index of 73 and the discrimination index of 20 are found.

Table 10 shows that Item 1 was answered correctly by nearly all of the pupils. Although it contributes almost nothing to the quality of the test, it would usually be considered satisfactory in terms of the easy introduction of pupils to the test situation. However, Item 16, answered

[32] *Ibid.* p. 8.
[33] *Ibid.* p. 8-9.

correctly by only seven of the above-average and five of the below-average pupils, is rather difficult and has limited power to discriminate between the two ability groups. Item 32, however, is a very hard item that is correctly answered by a smaller number of superior pupils than of inferior pupils. This is shown directly by the negative discrimination index of −3. It is probable that this item is either at fault in some respect or that the wrong impression concerning its background was inadvertently given to pupils in instruction. Thus, Items 16 and 32 should probably either be revised prior to using the same ideas again or should be discarded. Items 8, 13, 21, and 39 are good enough to retain for future use, with Item 13 at what is perhaps a minimum level of acceptable discriminative power.

TABLE 10

Difficulty and Discriminative Power of Sample Test Items
for a Class of 30 Pupils

Item Number	UPPER HALF	LOWER HALF	UPPER-LOWER SUM	DIFFERENCE	DIFFICULTY	DISCRIMINATION
1	15	14	29	1	97	3
8	14	8	22	6	73	20
13	11	8	19	3	63	10
16	7	5	12	2	40	7
21	9	4	13	5	43	17
32	2	3	5	−1	17	−3
39	10	2	12	8	40	27

If the information concerning item validities thus obtained is recorded on cards, as was suggested in a foregoing section, the cards become a valuable file for use in the construction of future tests. Items that show the proper type of difficulty and discrimination can be retained, and those that discriminate in the wrong direction can be discarded or revised after critical examination reveals the source of their ambiguity or other weakness. Ultimately, the card file should include only test items that have been found satisfactory in actual classroom measurement. It is, of course, desirable to add to the file as course content changes and to withdraw items which, although valid, are no longer applicable because of changing course content and objectives.

Although this procedure for validating test content may on the surface appear to be lengthy and somewhat involved, the teacher will realize significant dividends in improved pupil measurement by the use of it or some similar procedure. After such a system of keeping a cumulative test item file is once established, the teacher will profit by the great saving in time and the increased testing efficiency that result.

Determination of test reliability. Quality, and consequently future usability, of test items depends not only on item difficulty and discriminative power but also on the accuracy of the pupil scores obtained on the test as a whole. The need for accuracy and consistency of pupil scores on tests is discussed at length in Chapter 3 of this volume in the section on test reliability. Procedures for estimating the coefficient of reliability are presented in such simple form in Chapter 14 that they can easily be employed by any teacher. The resulting reliability coefficient indicates the degree to which pupil scores can be accepted as accurate measures of individual pupil achievement levels. It is sufficient at this point to comment that reliability coefficients of not less than .60 and preferably rather close to or even above .80 are considered desirable for informal objective tests.[34]

6. USING RESULTS OF INFORMAL OBJECTIVE TESTS

Only brief mention is made here of the uses to which informal objective test scores can be put. In fact, the discussion here is intended to supplement rather than to overlap the section of Chapter 8 in which uses of standardized test results are discussed at length.

The evaluation of pupil and class achievement is potentially most effectively accomplished through the use of the informal objective test. No one so well as the teacher who has taught a class knows the course content and instructional emphases that should be taken into direct account in measuring pupil achievements in that class. Properly constructed objective examinations within certain limits aid the teacher in determining points at which instructional adjustments should be made. Pupils, likewise, may be led to discover their specific weaknesses in achievement. Informal objective test results have general value for diagnosing pupil strengths and weaknesses. Such tests can also be used for instructional as well as for measurement purposes, as in the informal objective drill and remedial devices that can be constructed by the alert teacher.

Pupils' scores from valid and reliable informal objective examinations afford the teacher's best single basis for measuring and rating pupil achievement in a given subject. The results of objective classroom examinations enable the teacher to improve the reliability of his marks if the tests themselves are valid and reliable measures of the course outcomes. Teachers can construct course examinations that will be more valid for measuring the outcomes of their particular courses than standardized tests

[34] *Ibid.* p. 10-11.

could ever be. The remaining step for the use of test results in marking is to convert scores to the particular type of marks desired. Because of the importance of this use of informal objective test scores, a widely used method of converting them to course marks is explained in Chapter 14.

SUGGESTED ACTIVITIES

1. Construct five test items in any combination of alternate-response and scaled-choice varieties you wish in a subject or pupil activity area of interest to you.
2. Construct five multiple-option items representing at least three major varieties in some subject or activity area in which you specialize.
3. Construct an interrelation variety of matching exercise requiring not fewer than five responses in some school subject or area of pupil activity.
4. Devise one multiple-response item and one rearrangement exercise in multiple-option format in a subject or area of activity that concerns you.

TOPICS FOR DISCUSSION

1. What are some major differences between informal objective tests and standardized achievement tests?
2. Do standardized, traditional, and informal objective tests of achievement conflict or supplement one another? Give your reasons.
3. Of what significance are instructional and learning outcomes to the teacher in constructing an informal objective test?
4. What is the place of content in informal objective test construction?
5. How is a two-way chart useful in planning an objective classroom test?
6. How do selection and supplementation types of objective items differ?
7. What major distinctions should be made between types of situations in which selection and supplementation item varieties are most appropriate?
8. How do alternate-response and scaled-choice items differ in form and function?
9. Distinguish between multiple-option and multiple-response varieties of multiple-choice items.
10. How do best-answer and only-correct-answer types of multiple-option items differ?
11. What are five major varieties of multiple-option test items?
12. What are three major varieties of matching exercises?
13. How do three major varieties of supplementation or completion-type items and exercises differ?
14. How can the advantages of multiple-response items and rearrangement exercises be retained without incurring the scoring complications inherent in their traditional formats?
15. How should the various objective item types ordinarily be scored?

16. What are some major suggestions for constructing objective test items?
17. What procedures are used in determining item difficulty and discriminative power?

SELECTED REFERENCES

ADAMS, GEORGIA S., AND TORGERSON, THEODORE L. *Measurement and Evaluation for the Secondary-School Teacher.* New York: Dryden Press, 1956. Chapter 10.
ADKINS, DOROTHY C., AND OTHERS. *Construction and Analysis of Achievement Tests.* Washington, D. C.: U. S. Government Printing Office, 1947.
BLOOM, BENJAMIN S., editor. *Taxonomy of Educational Objectives: Handbook I, Cognitive Domain.* New York: Longmans, Green and Co., 1956.
BROWNELL, WILLIAM A., chairman. *The Measurement of Understanding.* Forty-Fifth Yearbook of the National Society for the Study of Education, Part I. Chicago: University of Chicago Press, 1946.
CURETON, EDWARD E. "The Rearrangement Test." *Educational and Psychological Measurement,* 20:31-35; Spring 1960.
DAVIS, FREDERICK B. "Item Selection Techniques." *Educational Measurement.* Washington, D. C.: American Council on Education, 1951. Chapter 9.
DOLE, ARTHUR A., AND FLETCHER, FRANK M., JR. "Some Principles in the Construction of Incomplete Sentences." *Educational and Psychological Measurement,* 15:101-10; Summer 1955.
EBEL, ROBERT L. "Obtaining and Reporting Evidence on Content Validity." *Educational and Psychological Measurement,* 16:269-82; Autumn 1956.
EBEL, ROBERT L. "Procedures for the Analysis of Classroom Tests." *Educational and Psychological Measurement,* 14:352-64; Summer 1954.
EBEL, ROBERT L. "Writing the Test Item." *Educational Measurement.* Washington, D. C.: American Council on Education, 1951. Chapter 7.
EDUCATIONAL TESTING SERVICE. *Making the Classroom Test: A Guide for Teachers.* Evaluation and Advisory Service Series, No. 4. Princeton, N. J.: Educational Testing Service, 1959.
ENGELHART, MAX D. "How Teachers Can Improve Their Tests." *Educational and Psychological Measurement,* 4:109-24; Summer 1944.
ENGELHART, MAX D. "Unique Types of Achievement Test Exercises." *Psychometrika,* 7:103-15; June 1942.
FINDLEY, WARREN G. "A Rationale for Evaluation of Item Discriminative Statistics." *Educational and Psychological Measurement,* 16:175-80; Summer 1956.
FURST, EDWARD J. *Constructing Evaluation Instruments.* New York: Longmans, Green and Co., 1958.
GERBERICH, J. RAYMOND. *Specimen Objective Test Items: A Guide to Achievement Test Construction.* New York: Longmans, Green and Co., 1956.
GERBERICH, J. RAYMOND. "A Technique for Measuring the Ability to Evaluate Objective Test Items." *Journal of Educational Research,* 27:46-50; September 1933.
GLASER, ROBERT; DAMRIN, DORA E.; AND GARDNER, FLOYD M. "The Tab Item: A Technique for the Measurement of Proficiency in Diagnostic Problem Solving Tasks." *Educational and Psychological Measurement,* 14:283-93; Summer 1954.
GREENE, HARRY A., JORGENSEN, ALBERT N., AND GERBERICH, J. RAYMOND. *Measurement and Evaluation in the Elementary School.* Second edition. New York: Longmans, Green and Co., 1953. Chapter 7.

Measurement and Evaluation in the Modern School

GREENE, HARRY A., JORGENSEN, ALBERT N., AND GERBERICH, J. RAYMOND. *Measurement and Evaluation in the Secondary School.* Second edition. New York: Longmans, Green and Co., 1954. Chapter 7

HAWKES, HERBERT E., LINDQUIST, E. F., AND MANN, C. R., editors. *The Construction and Use of Achievement Examinations.* Boston: Houghton Mifflin Co., 1936.

HUDDLESTON, EDITH M. "Test Development on the Basis of Content Validity." *Educational and Psychological Measurement,* 16:283-93; Autumn 1956.

LINDQUIST, E. F., editor. *Educational Measurement.* Washington, D. C.: American Council on Education, 1951.

MICHEELS, WILLIAM J., AND KARNES, M. RAY. *Measuring Educational Achievement.* New York: McGraw-Hill Book Co., Inc., 1950. Chapters 5-10.

MOSIER, CHARLES I.; MYERS, M. CLAIRE; AND PRICE, HELEN G. "Suggestions for the Construction of Multiple-Choice Test Items." *Educational and Psychological Measurement,* 5:261-71; Autumn 1945.

ODELL, C. W. *How to Improve Classroom Testing.* Dubuque, Iowa: William C. Brown Co., 1953.

REMMERS, H. H., GAGE, N. L., AND RUMMEL, J. FRANCIS. *A Practical Introduction to Measurement and Evaluation.* New York: Harper and Brothers, 1960. Chapter 8.

STALNAKER, JOHN M., AND STALNAKER, RUTH C. "Open Book Examinations." *Journal of Higher Education,* 5:117-20; March 1934.

TORGERSON, THEODORE L., AND ADAMS, GEORGIA S. *Measurement and Evaluation for the Elementary-School Teacher.* New York: Dryden Press, 1954. Chapter 10.

TRAVERS, ROBERT M. W. *How to Make Achievement Tests.* New York: Odyssey Press, 1950. Chapters 2-6.

TUSSING, LYLE. "A Consideration of the Open-Book Examination." *Educational and Psychological Measurement,* 11:597-602; Winter 1951.

WEAVER, CARL H. "Sharpening the Measuring Instrument." *Clearing House,* 34:40-44; September 1959.

WEITZMAN, ELLIS, AND MCNAMARA, WALTER J. *Constructing Classroom Examinations.* Chicago: Science Research Associates, Inc., 1949. Chapters 2-4.

WOOD, DOROTHY ADKINS. *Test Construction: Development and Interpretation of Achievement Tests.* Columbus, Ohio: Charles E. Merrill Books, Inc., 1960.

11

PERFORMANCE TESTS

This chapter presents a brief treatment of the following points in the construction and use of performance tests:

A. Measurable characteristics of performance.
B. Object tests and their functions.
C. Methods of measuring performance.
D. Techniques for evaluating products.
E. Constructing performance tests.
F. Using performance test results.

Teachers and other users of educational achievement tests have long been aware that results from paper-and-pencil tests in an instructional field reveal only a part of the story of educational accomplishment. Admittedly such tests are easily given, are quickly scored, and are extremely useful in the classroom, but they are also limited to the degree that in many instructional areas results from written tests emphasizing knowledges and understandings are not highly correlated with actual performance. The recognition of this fact makes quite obvious the need for performance tests to supplement other measures of achievement.

In one form or another, performance tests are utilized in all three areas of measurement and evaluation treated in this volume—intelligence, personality, and achievement. Such tests are used in measuring general intelligence of illiterate persons and individuals having language handicaps of other types. They are also used in the measurement of aptitudes for various types of manual skills. Moreover, conduct or performance tests are extensively used in the evaluation of a wide variety of personality characteristics and traits. This chapter is primarily concerned with the measurement of those physical and motor reactions that represent important behavioral and skill outcomes of learning and that are, therefore, evidences of educational achievement.

1. PERFORMANCE AND ITS MEASUREMENT

Although performance tests were used by primitive peoples in their tests and ceremonies preceding the induction of youth into adult society and by the Greeks and Spartans in their athletic games, the objective written test came into use many years before objective performance tests received much attention. With an increasing realization on the part of psychologists and educators that knowledge of facts and principles is not necessarily accompanied by skills in its use and application, attention was directed, or perhaps redirected, to objective procedures for the measurement of skills in functional situations.

Nature of Performance Tests

Broadly speaking, every test is a performance test, whether the performance consists of oral responses to questions, written responses on an essay or an objective test, or the application of physical or motor skills in a certain test situation. However, paper-and-pencil tests of knowledges and other outcomes are not generally regarded as performance tests. Neither are oral and essay tests, for that matter, but to the degree that the pupil's skill in expression is evaluated they actually are performance tests even though manipulation as such is not involved. For the purposes of this chapter, however, performance tests are considered primarily as those requiring the use and often the manipulation of physical objects and the application of physical and motor skills in situations not restricted to oral and written responses.

Major Types of Performance Tests

A distinction of importance is found among the measurable characteristics in the field of performance testing. These instructional outcomes appear to be largely in the areas of knowledges, concepts, understandings, skills, and applications.

The knowledges, concepts, and understandings serving as necessary background for many types of skill performances are measured by what are variously called object tests, recognition tests, and identification tests. Recognition tests and identification tests do not necessarily imply the use of physical objects in the test situation but instead may involve photographic or drawn representations of the articles. These testing techniques most appropriately are considered in the treatment of objective written tests. Object tests, on the other hand, imply the presentation and use in the test situation of three-dimensional articles. Accordingly, they are dealt with in this chapter.

The skill and application outcomes are measurable in some instances by written tests and in others by measures of performance itself. Such skills and applications as those involved in reading comprehension, written expression, and arithmetic and mathematics are commonly evaluated by means of paper-and-pencil tests. So are some of the mathematical aspects of the sciences and even of the social studies. The aspects of performance testing for the direct measurement of skills and applications to be dealt with in this chapter are concerned with the procedures followed in performing a certain task and the product resulting from the completion of the task. Check lists and timing devices are the most widely used educational tools for evaluating the performance of the pupil, whereas quality scales, rating scales, score cards, and counting and measuring are commonly used in the evaluation of performance as it is evidenced in the completed product.

Tests of performance may be classified in several useful ways. The one chosen here divides the instruments and techniques for performance testing of educational achievement into (1) object tests, (2) performance measures, and (3) product evaluations.

2. OBJECT TESTS

Object tests measure knowledges, concepts, and understandings prerequisite to functional performances of certain skills but in themselves are concerned with quite tangible and sometimes formal types of instructional outcomes. They are sometimes called identification tests or recognition tests because the pupil is asked to identify or recognize an object, specimen, or selection presented to him in his capacity as an observer or as a listener. The pupil may be asked to identify geological, biological, or other specimens presented to him in actuality or in the form of photographs or line drawings. He may be asked to recognize musical selections played by a soloist or orchestra or reproduced by a phonograph.

Although the visual and auditory senses are the ones primarily involved in such situations, the sense of touch may also enter in the case of objects where knowledge concerning grain, texture, or other surface qualities might aid in identification. The other two of the five basic senses—taste and smell—may even be employed in some less usual situations in the practical arts and physical sciences where physical objects are to be identified. The object test is more functional than the comparable type of test in which only photographic or drawn representations of the objects are presented, for the object may variously be seen, felt, listened to, and even smelled or tasted, whereas a pictorial representation can be interpreted only in terms of its visual stimulus.

EXCERPT FROM *Prognostic Test of Mechanical Abilities* [1]

31-50. DIRECTIONS: Each of the following incomplete statements or questions is followed by five possible answers. For each item, select the answer that best completes the statement or answers the question, and write its number or letter on the line to the right.

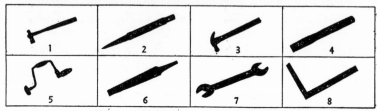

Statements 31-45 refer to pictures of tools above

31. A claw hammer is shown in picture   1   3   6   7   8   ____31

32. A chisel is shown in picture   2   4   5   6   7   ____32

33. A ball peen hammer is shown in picture   1   3   5   6   8   ____33

39 Tool No. 1 can be used to: a file metal   b polish metal   c drill holes   d take dents out of metal   e caulk metal   ____39

40. Tool No. 2 can be used to: a mark metal   b drive a screw   c file metal   d fasten a bolt   e lock a nut   ____40

41 Tool No. 3 can be used to.   a cut wood   b pull out a nail   c bend a rod   d drive a nut   e tighten a nut   ____41

The accompanying illustration from the *Prognostic Test of Mechanical Abilities* is used to represent an object test, although it actually involves the photographic presentation of objects and written responses by the pupils. However, if the student visualizes a setting in which the eight tools, appropriately numbered, are actually laid out on a table or bench and if he changes the first questions of the illustration so that they relate to the actual objects presented, he will obtain a clear idea concerning the setting and nature of an object test. The first three questions of the illustration are of the identification or recognition type and measure factual knowledges, but the last three questions go beyond formal knowledges in measuring concepts and understandings concerning the nature and appropriate uses of the tools.

Another illustration of an object test is drawn from the field of home

[1] J. Wayne Wrightstone and Charles E. O'Toole, *Prognostic Test of Mechanical Abilities*. Form A. California Test Bureau, Monterey, Calif., 1946.

economics. The accompanying illustration shows how pupils are asked to judge three samples each of shirts, ties, handkerchiefs, and socks displayed on a screen in demonstrating certain concepts and understandings concerning the significance of color in clothing selection.

SAMPLE OF Test in Clothing [2]

Assume that the articles displayed on Screen I are to be worn with a suit of dark-value gray, a top coat of middle-value gray, and middle-value pigskin gloves. Choose the most becoming shirt, tie, handkerchief, and socks for each man to wear with the gray suit, coat, and gloves. Write the number corresponding to your choice in the blank at the left of each item, and list no article more than once.

Articles of Clothing	Descriptions of Men
_____ 1. shirt	A. black hair, fair skin, and blue eyes
_____ 2. tie	
_____ 3. handkerchief	
_____ 4. socks	
_____ 5. shirt	B. medium brown hair, blue eyes, and somewhat
_____ 6. tie	sallow skin
_____ 7. handkerchief	
_____ 8. socks	
_____ 9. shirt	C. auburn (red) hair, brown eyes, and florid com-
_____ 10. tie	plexion
_____ 11. handkerchief	
_____ 12: socks	

3. PERFORMANCE MEASURES

The process by which a pupil produces some type of desired result in a test situation is appropriately observed and evaluated as to quality by use of check lists and as to quantity or time by use of timing devices. Performance measurement is often highly diagnostic in its significance, but it is time-consuming in those instances in which each pupil must be tested individually.

Check Lists

The processes involved in the performance of a complex skill are subject to measurement and evaluation by the use of observational techniques.

[2] Clara B. Arny, *Evaluation in Home Economics*. Appleton-Century-Crofts, Inc., New York, 1953. p. 143.

Although observation unaided by any objective instrument may often be effective when the observer is a qualified specialist in the skill in question, the use of check lists insures a more accurate and comprehensive record of the actual behavior of the individual observed. Such check lists have been evolved for a number of skill performances in industrial arts, home economics, and laboratory science.

Tyler illustrated procedures measurement in testing ability to use the microscope. The technique is necessarily used with only one person at a time because it requires full-time observation of the pupil by the examiner. The check list illustrated herewith includes a sequential listing of the appropriate and inappropriate steps of procedure in adjusting the instrument and finding a yeast cell or a blood cell on a slide, using a culture previously prepared by the examiner. As the student arranges the slide, endeavors to adjust the microscope, and attempts to locate a cell, the examiner records his operations by numbers in sequence at appropriate places on the check list. The result is a diagnostic version of the student's success or failure in the assigned task. The numbers in the illustration show the results of such a record for an actual performance by a student.

Supplementary portions of the check list provide for checking characteristics of student behavior, characteristics of the mount, and skills in which the student needs further training. When the student's performance is summarized and diagnosed by the use of these sections of the check list, the special type of remediation needed is ordinarily disclosed and serves as the basis for providing the necessary type of remedial instruction. The diagnostic significance of this type of summary is shown by the check marks in the illustration representing characteristics of and deficiencies in the student's performance.

As this individual technique is time-consuming, students can first be tested in a group situation where success or failure in a task common to all can be readily checked for each student by the quality of the adjustment he attains. It then becomes necessary to use the check list only with those individuals who do not succeed in the group test situation.

This illustration is representative of the work-sample tests employed both in procedures and product measurement. The use of a microscope in finding a yeast cell or a blood cell may be considered as a sample, or work sample, of the various ways in which a microscope is used in biological science.

Timing Devices

A stop watch or even an ordinary watch having a second hand is the only timing device the teacher ordinarily needs in performance testing, although some specialized types of performance may require the use of more precise timing instruments. In performances where speed is an important characteristic, the time required for the performance of the assigned task may constitute one measure, although in some instances

STUDENT'S ACTIONS	Sequence of Actions	STUDENT'S ACTIONS (*Continued*)	Sequence of Actions
a. Takes slide	*1*	ag. With eye away from eyepiece turns down fine adjustment a great distance	*15*
b. Wipes slide with lens paper	*2*	ah. Turns up fine adjustment screw a great distance	
c. Wipes slide with cloth		ai. Turns fine adjustment screw a few turns	
d. Wipes slide with finger		aj. Removes slide from stage	*16*
e. Moves bottle of culture along the table		ak. Wipes objective with lens paper	
f. Places drop or two of culture on slide	*3*	al. Wipes objective with cloth	
g. Adds more culture		am. Wipes objective with finger	*17*
h. Adds few drops of water		an. Wipes eyepiece with lens paper	
i. Hunts for cover glasses	*4*	ao. Wipes eyepiece with cloth	
j. Wipes cover glass with lens paper	*5*	ap. Wipes eyepiece with finger	*18*
k. Wipes cover with cloth		aq. Makes another mount	
l. Wipes cover with finger		ar. Takes another microscope	
m. Adjusts cover with finger		as. Finds object	
n. Wipes off surplus fluid		at. Pauses for an interval	
o. Places slide on stage	*6*	au. Asks, "What do you want me to do?"	
p. Looks through eyepiece with right eye		av. Asks whether to use high power	
q. Looks through eyepiece with left eye	*7*	aw. Says, "I'm satisfied"	
r. Turns to objective of lowest power	*9*	ax. Says that the mount is all right for his eye	
s. Turns to low-power objective	*21*	ay. Says he cannot do it	*19,24*
t. Turns to high-power objective		az. Told to start new mount	
u. Holds one eye closed	*8*	aaa. Directed to find object under low power	*20*
v. Looks for light		aab. Directed to find object under high power	
w. Adjusts concave mirror		NOTICEABLE CHARACTERISTICS OF STUDENT'S BEHAVIOR	
x. Adjusts plane mirror			
y. Adjusts diaphragm	*10*	a. Awkward in movements	
z. Does not touch diaphragm		b. Obviously dexterous in movements	
aa. With eye at eyepiece turns down coarse adjustment	*11*	c. Slow and deliberate	✓
ab. Breaks cover glass	*12*	d. Very rapid	
ac. Breaks slide		e. Fingers tremble	
ad. With eye away from eyepiece turns down coarse adjustment		f. Obviously perturbed	
ae. Turns up coarse adjustment a great distance	*13,22*	g. Obviously angry	
		h. Does not take work seriously	
af. With eye at eyepiece turns down fine adjustment a great distance	*14,23*	i. Unable to work without specific directions	✓
		j. Obviously satisfied with his unsuccessful efforts	✓

SKILLS IN WHICH STUDENT NEEDS FURTHER TRAINING	Sequence of Actions	CHARACTERIZATION OF THE STUDENT'S MOUNT	Sequence of Actions
a. In cleaning objective	✓	a. Poor light	✓
b. In cleaning eyepiece	✓	b. Poor focus	
c. In focusing low power	✓	c. Excellent mount	
d. In focusing high power	✓	d. Good mount	
e. In adjusting mirror	✓	e. Fair mount	
f. In using diaphragm	✓	f. Poor mount	
g. In keeping both eyes open	✓	g. Very poor mount	
h. In protecting slide and objective from breaking by careless focusing	✓	h. Nothing in view but a thread in his eyepiece	
		i. Something on objective	
		j. Smeared lens	
		k. Unable to find object	✓

FIGURE 13. Check List of Student Reactions in Finding an Object under a Microscope [3]

there may be other and even more important measures. In the measurement of speed and accuracy in clerical, typing, stenographic, and other types of performances where speed is an important factor, a watch becomes a tool for the measurement of educational achievement.

[3] Ralph W. Tyler, "A Test of Skill in Using a Microscope." *Educational Research Bulletin*, 9:493-96; November 19, 1930.

It is pointed out in Chapter 2 that speed may be measured in terms of the amount or quantity of production in a given period of time or in terms of the time required to complete a product of a certain quality or to perform a task of a certain level of difficulty. This second method is the one ordinarily applied in performance testing when the job is to produce a completed product, such as a planed and squared-up board in manual arts or a seam in home economics. In a skill such as typing, however, the time is usually held constant and the quantity, as well as the quality, of the production is measured.

4. PRODUCT EVALUATION

The quality of a skill performance can be evaluated in terms of the characteristics of the completed product as well as by the characteristics of the techniques used in its production. In assessing the characteristics of the product, quality scales, rating scales, score cards, and counting and measuring techniques are usually employed. There are occasions when it may be desirable to evaluate both the procedure and the product, but in many instances a good product depends so much upon effective procedures that product measurement alone may suffice. When such is the case, observation of each pupil separately during the performance ceases to be necessary. The resulting products can later be evaluated individually by the teacher.

Quality Scales

Although standardized quality scales have been devised and used at least to some extent for measuring a variety of skills in composition, fine arts, industrial arts, home economics, and handwriting, it is probably in the last-mentioned area that they have been used most. The handwriting scale of the *California Achievement Test* is shown in Figure 14 to illustrate the quality scale. The pupils taking this handwriting test write the words used as samples on the scale. Each pupil's handwriting quality is then evaluated by finding the scale sample most closely resembling his writing and assigning the appropriate grade or age equivalent.

Rating Scales and Score Cards

Rating scales and score cards are very similar devices for use in estimating the quality of the product made in a test situation. A numerical scale typically provides for separate ratings or evaluations on the various elements of skill required in the total performance. Such distinctive features

GRADE PLACEMENT	HANDWRITING SCALE	AGE EQUIV. (IN MONTHS)
5.0	The quick brown fox just came	123
5.5	over to greet the lazy poodle.	129
6.0	The quick brown fox just came	136
6.5	over to greet the lazy poodle.	142
7.0	The quick brown fox just came	148
7.5	over to greet the lazy poodle.	154
8.0	The quick brown fox just came	160
8.5	over to greet the lazy poodle.	166
9.0	The quick brown fox just came	172
9.5	over to greet the lazy poodle.	178
10.0	The quick brown fox just came	184
10.5	over to greet the lazy poodle.	190
11.0	The quick brown fox just came	196
	over to greet the lazy poodle.	

FIGURE 14. Handwriting Scale of the *California Achievement Tests* [4]

[4] Ernest W. Tiegs and Willis W. Clark, *California Achievement Test: Language* (*Handwriting Scale*). California Test Bureau, Monterey, Calif., 1957.

of the total performance may range from only a few to a large number, depending on the complexity of the skill performance and the degree of analysis desired in the evaluation. Numerical values representing various

(a) Nails:

(1) Straightness 1 2 3 4 5 6 7 8 9 10
Are nails driven straight, heads square with wood, no evidence of bending?

(2) Hammer marks 1 2 3 4 5 6 7 8 9 10
Is wood free of hammer marks around nails?

(3) Splitting 1 2 3 4 5 6 7 8 9 10
Is wood free of splits radiating from nail holes?

(4) Depth 1 2 3 4 5 6 7 8 9 10
Are depths of nails uniform and of pleasing appearance?

(5) Spacing 1 2 3 4 5 6 7 8 9 10
Are nails spaced too close or too far apart?

(6) Utility 1 2 3 4 5 6 7 8 9 10
Will the nails hold?

FIGURE 15. Sample from Rating Scale for Fastenings [5]

levels of quality usually range from three or four to ten. It is doubtful if more than ten degrees of quality can be distinguished reliably in evaluating qualitative performances.

WAFFLES   53

	1	2	3	Score
Appearance	1. Irregular shape	Regular shape	1.	
Color	2. Dark brown or pale	Uniform, golden brown	2.	
Moisture Content	3. Soggy interior or too dry	Slightly moist interior	3.	
Lightness	4. Heavy	Light	4.	
Tenderness	5. Tough or hard	Tender; crisp crust	5.	
Taste and Flavor	6. Too sweet or flat or taste of leavening agent or fat	Pleasing flavor	6.	

SCORE _____

FIGURE 16. Food Score Card for Waffles [6]

[5] Dorothy C. Adkins, *Construction and Analysis of Achievement Tests.* U. S. Government Printing Office, Washington, D. C., 1947. p. 231.
[6] Clara M. Brown, *Food Score Cards: Waffles,* No. 53. Published by University of Minnesota Press, Minneapolis, Minn., 1940. (Out of print)

Two samples are presented here to illustrate this method of product measurement. The first provides for a rather highly analytic rating of a fairly simple skill. The second shows how a more complex skill may be evaluated in a less highly analytic manner.

Counting and Measuring Techniques

Counting most often becomes a direct product measurement technique when the quantity of articles produced in a given time or the errors made in a certain piece of work are important to the total evaluation. Speed of production is usually not greatly stressed in the school classroom, although where boys and girls are receiving training for certain types of employment, as they often are in trade and industrial schools, speed of performance may assume considerable significance. The error count in typewriting is a direct measure of quality in the product, and it is often combined as a penalty with the number of words typed per minute to obtain an evaluation of the total product. This procedure in effect provides a combined quantitative and qualitative score.

Measuring instruments of various types are also used in evaluating the quality of a product. Such devices as rules, calipers, squares, scales, gauges, and other instruments may be used in determining how accurately the pupil has performed the assigned task. Special mechanical testing devices may even be devised by the teacher of a skill subject to serve certain specific purposes.

Newkirk and Greene illustrated a performance test in which the product is measured objectively to determine the quality of pupil workmanship on a test of accuracy in woodworking.[7] After each pupil has been assigned to a work bench, the examiner reads the following instructions aloud.

Directions to Pupil. This is a test to determine how accurately you can use woodworking tools. The wood and all necessary tools will be given to you. The surfaces of the block of wood are numbered 1, 2, 3, 4, 5, 6. You will be given specific directions for doing the job and a working drawing that gives all the necessary dimensions. Do this project as accurately as you can. Do not waste time, but do not work too fast to do your best work. The steps must be done in the order given. After you begin work do not ask unnecessary questions, but if you are in doubt about a step in the procedure or a dimension on the working drawing ask the examiner. Write your *name* and *grade* in school on surface *No. 6* of the test block. *Do not begin work until the examiner gives the signal.*

---

[7] Louis V. Newkirk and Harry A. Greene, *Tests and Measurements in Industrial Education.* John Wiley and Sons, Inc., New York, 1935. p. 147.

Procedure:

1. Select face No. 1. Plane it square and true and to the thickness indicated on the working drawing. When finished re-mark No. 1.

2. Select side No. 2. Plane it square and true to surface No. 1. When finished re-mark No. 2.

3. Select end No. 3. Plane it square and true to No. 1 and 2. When finished re-mark No. 3.

4. Measure from end No. 3 toward end No. 5, and square a sharp pencil line across the block to the length indicated in the working drawing. Saw off the waste material with a hack saw so that the stock will be as nearly the required length as you can make it. *Do not plane.* Re-mark end No. 5.

5. From edge No. 2 gauge a line the length of the block, allowing the exact width as indicated on the working drawing. Rip as nearly the exact width as possible. *Do not plane.*

6. On surface No. 1 lay out the center for the hole and bore.

7. When you have finished take your block to the examiner.

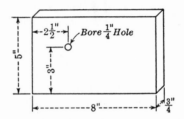

FIGURE 17. Working Drawing of a Wood Block [8]

The examiner then supplies a copy of the working drawing, reproduced in Figure 17, to each pupil and makes sure that he has the necessary tools and a piece of standard wood stock prepared in advance by the instructor. The directions to the examiner, given last here for purposes of simplicity of presentation but obviously familiar to the examiner in advance, serve to illustrate the remaining steps in test administration.[9]

Directions to Examiner: It is essential that the pupil shall understand the exact procedure, and that he be able to visualize how the block is to look when finished. The following directions are recommended:

1. Read aloud and distinctly the directions to the pupil while the class follows silently. Answer any questions about the directions at this point.

2. Show the pupils a completed test block, and if they care to, let them examine it.

3. When there are no further questions, say, "Get ready. Hold up the test block. Begin work."

[8] *Ibid.* p. 146.
[9] *Ibid.* p. 146-47.

4. During the examination answer any questions about the steps in the procedure by rereading the step in question with the pupil.

5. Observe the pupils as they work to make certain that they are doing all the steps in the correct order.

6. Make certain that the proper tool is used where indicated, but do not tell the pupil how to use the tool.

7. Help any pupil having difficulty in interpreting the working drawing, but do not make any measurement on the test block for the pupil. This test measures ability to measure to $\frac{1}{16}$ in. with a ruler, but it is not a measure of ability to read drawings.

8. Take in the test block when the pupil has finished. The time is not important, for this is a test of quality or accuracy as it applies to modifying wood with simple hand tools.

The authors specified the use of a try square, a $\frac{1}{4}$-inch dowel 3 inches long, and a scale graduated in sixty-fourths of an inch in evaluating the pupil products. They suggested that for each rated dimension 10 points be assigned for an exact measurement and 1 point be deducted for each $\frac{1}{16}$ inch of deviation from the specified dimension.[10] This final step illustrates the application of measuring instruments to the evaluation of the final product.

Arny illustrated a functional situation in which each home economics pupil is given a miniature dress pattern such as that shown in Figure 18, a piece of paper to represent cloth from which a dress might be made, and the other necessary tools and materials used in the actual process of cutting dress material from a pattern and preparing it for sewing. To simulate conditions in which a dress would actually be made, it was recommended that the paper used in lieu of dress fabric have a design on one side, to represent the right side of dress material, that its length be three times its width, to represent three yards of cloth 36 inches wide, and, of course, that it be appropriate in size to the miniature pattern. Each girl would be expected to "cut out the pieces of the pattern and pin them on the paper strip, and then to draw the outline of the other half of each piece of the pattern in its proper location." [11]

The resulting products could be evaluated by the teacher, using a rating scale or score card prepared specifically for this type of skill performance. This illustration of product measurement is of the simulated-conditions or miniature type. When it is not practicable to represent the real situation in which a certain functional skill is employed, it is sometimes possible,

[10] *Ibid.* p. 147-48.
[11] Arny, *op. cit.* p. 84.

as here, to simulate the conditions by the use of a miniature test representing the real situation quite accurately.

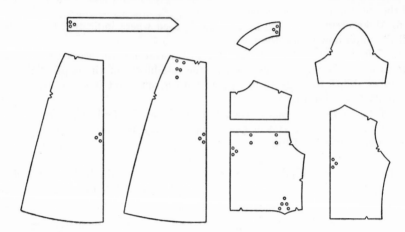

FIGURE 18.   Diagram of Pieces of a Dress Pattern [12]

5. CONSTRUCTING PERFORMANCE TESTS

While performance and other types of manipulative tests have been widely used in certain educational fields, such as the industrial arts and home economics, the practical reliability of many of these devices has not been very satisfactory. It is believed that a part of this difficulty arises from the fact that too many of the better-known paper-and-pencil testing techniques have been uncritically borrowed and used without the necessary technical and administrative modifications required for effective testing in the specialized field. It is not possible in this chapter to present examples of performance tests in many different areas of educational achievement, but a brief summary of certain general procedures that appear to be necessary in the construction of performance tests may be helpful.

The following summary of steps in preparing performance tests is taken with only minor modifications from a statement by Newkirk and Greene.[13] While these suggested steps were originally designed for use in classes in industrial education, there is little reason why they may not be expected to function equally well in other fields in which performance testing is desirable:

    1. Make a job analysis of the activities covered in the course of study to determine exactly what qualities may be tested.

---

[12] *Ibid.* p. 85.
[13] Newkirk and Greene, *op. cit.* p. 145.

2. Select the performance tasks that best represent the job.

3. Decide what tools, materials, and equipment are necessary for the testing situation.

4. Decide what elements in performance are to be evaluated: (a) performance in process or (b) product of performance.

5. Prepare a number of text exercises or make a composite exercise that will offer the pupil an opportunity to provide an adequate sample of his work with each tool or instrument and type of material it is desired to test.

6. Make a statement of procedure that tells the pupil exactly what to do in a vocabulary that is comprehensible at his grade level.

7. Prepare a set of general directions for the pupil before the test is administered.

8. Prepare directions for the examiner.

9. Devise methods of scoring the test or evaluating the product that will provide an adequate measure of the results of each tool or instrument.

10. Try out the test on a few students, and make the more obvious changes and corrections in its content or directions.

11. Make two or more approximately equal forms of the test.

12. Try out the test, and compute the reliability coefficient, standard deviation, and standard error of a score, along with the grade and percentile or other types of norms.

A simple illustration of the manner in which certain of these steps are used in the construction of a performance test is given on pages 273 to 275 of this chapter.

6. USING RESULTS OF PERFORMANCE TESTING

The problems of interpreting and using results from performance tests are similar in many respects to those involved in using results from the other types of tests discussed in Chapters 8 and 10. In fact, performance test results are important to the teacher primarily because they supplement other important tests of accomplishment or achievement. However, attention should be called to the fact that performance test results may be difficult to interpret, and hence to use with assurance, especially in those instances where two quite different types of achievement measures, such as speed and quality in handwriting, are necessary in measuring pupil performance.

For the standardized tests treated in Chapter 8 and the informal objective tests dealt with in Chapter 10, a single score in the form of a total or a composite can nearly always be obtained for the instrument as a whole, whether or not it is possible to obtain meaningful part scores. Furthermore, scores for such tests are based entirely on the products put on paper by the pupils and not at all on the procedures used by the pupils in taking the tests. By contrast, performance tests often involve one or even both of two quite different approaches to the appraisal of achievement, as embodied in the measurement of procedures and the evaluation of products. Somewhat similarly, they often result in two separate and negatively related measures of achievement, such as speed and quality, that can seldom be combined in a single score.

In the first of these problem areas, there is no certainty that what is generally accepted as a good performance will result in a good product or that a good product is produced only by a performance that is generally accepted as good. There are too many known instances in which excellent products result from the use of unorthodox procedures by persons highly skilled in applying them. There are also too many known instances in which what are good techniques for many people are ineffective for others who may seek to employ them. For this reason, a teacher should be careful not to overrate one at the possible expense of the other in measurement and should be sure that he appropriately allows for differences among pupils in the techniques that are most suitable for them as individuals.

In the second problem area, emphasis on speed of performance often results in a lowering of quality and emphasis on quality may well result in a reduction in speed. It is not easily possible to attain the most satisfactory level in one without sacrificing something in the other, to state the issue in another way. Therefore, the user of test results in instances where both speed and quality are important, as, for example, in handwriting and typewriting, should clearly recognize that effective performance involves both factors and that there are no standards or precise ways of obtaining a composite score that appropriately weights these dual characteristics. The user, consequently, often faces the need for balancing one measure against the other and for making judgments about total achievement in ways that are more complex than in the more usual situations where single indices of achievement are meaningful.

SUGGESTED ACTIVITIES

1. Set up a few general specifications for the construction of a performance test in some such field as laboratory science or physical education.
2. Devise at least a few items for inclusion in a simple rating scale or score card that could be used in evaluating some performance in manual arts or home economics.

TOPICS FOR DISCUSSION

1. Discuss way in which performance tests of achievement supplement paper-and-pencil achievement tests.
2. Justify the statement that in the broad sense every test is a performance test.
3. How do object tests differ from paper-and-pencil identification tests?
4. What are the major tools used in the measurement of performance in school subjects?
5. How can a check list be used advantageously with observational techniques in measuring certain types of performance?
6. By what tools and procedures can products be measured?
7. Show how quality scales, such as those for handwriting, drawing, and other industrial arts areas, are essential to the effective measurement of certain types of performance.
8. In what types of situations are rating scales useful in product evaluation?
9. Why is it sometimes difficult to know what values to assign to results from the measurement of procedures?
10. What difficulties are sometimes encountered in the interpretation, and hence the use, of results from the measurement of speed and quality of a performance?

SELECTED REFERENCES

ADKINS, DOROTHY C. *Construction and Analysis of Achievement Tests.* Washington, D. C.: U. S. Government Printing Office, 1947. Chapter 5.

ADKINS, DOROTHY C. "Principles Underlying Observational Techniques of Evaluation." *Educational and Psychological Measurement,* 11:29-51; Spring 1951.

ALLEN, MARION C. "Identification Card Test." *Industrial Arts and Vocational Education,* 42:354-55; December 1953.

ARNY, CLARA B. *Evaluation in Home Economics.* New York: Appleton-Century-Crofts, Inc., 1953. Chapter 7.

BLOOM, SAMUEL L. "Identification Tests." *Industrial Arts and Vocational Education,* 34:65-66; February 1945.

GREENE, EDWARD B. *Measurements of Human Behavior.* Revised edition. New York: Odyssey Press, 1952. Chapter 9.

GREENE, HARRY A., JORGENSEN, ALBERT N., AND GERBERICH, J. RAYMOND. *Measurement and Evaluation in the Elementary School.* Second edition. New York: Longmans, Green and Co., 1953. Chapter 8.

GREENE, HARRY A., JORGENSEN, ALBERT N., AND GERBERICH, J. RAYMOND. *Measurement and Evaluation in the Secondary School.* Second edition. New York: Longmans, Green and Co., 1954. Chapter 8.

MICHEELS, WILLIAM J., AND KARNES, M. RAY. *Measuring Educational Achievement.* New York: McGraw-Hill Book Co., Inc., 1950. Chapters 11-14.

NEWKIRK, LOUIS V., AND GREENE, HARRY A. *Tests and Measurements in Industrial Education.* New York: John Wiley and Sons, Inc., 1935. p. 116-23, 144-48.

REMMERS, H. H., AND GAGE, N. L. *Educational Measurement and Evaluation.* Revised edition. New York: Harper and Brothers, 1955. Chapter 6.

RYANS, DAVID G., AND FREDERICKSEN, NORMAN. "Performance Tests of Educational Achievement." *Educational Measurement.* Washington, D. C.: American Council on Education, 1951. Chapter 12.

SIRO, EINAR E. "Performance Tests and Objective Observation." *Industrial Arts and Vocational Education,* 32:162-65; April 1943.

TYLER, RALPH W. "A Test of Skill in Using a Microscope." *Educational Research Bulletin,* 9:493-96; November 19, 1930.

12

EVALUATIVE TOOLS AND TECHNIQUES

This chapter presents a treatment of the following aspects of evaluative tools and techniques:

A. The nature and characteristics of evaluation.
B. Tests of abilities to interpret.
C. Tests of practices and activities.
D. Cumulative records and reports to parents.
E. Questionnaires and participation schedules.
F. Observation of pupils and the interview.
G. Techniques involving pupil writing.
H. Using evaluation results in the classroom.

Evaluation is usually thought of as a broadly inclusive term. Accordingly, all types of tests, nontest tools, and techniques used in pupil appraisal may be considered evaluative. However, many of these instruments and techniques are treated elsewhere in this volume—achievement tests in Chapters 8 to 11, intelligence and aptitude tests in Chapter 6, and personality measures in Chapter 7. The line of demarcation between evaluative instruments and achievement tests on the one hand and evaluative techniques and personality measures on the other hand is not definite. The attempt is made in this chapter, therefore, to deal only with those tests, tools, and techniques not treated elsewhere in this volume but deemed most appropriate for use in evaluating and appraising pupil achievement.

1. MEANING OF EVALUATION

The concept of evaluation is still relatively new to education. The term has been used to include appraisal of the school program, curriculum, and instructional materials, appraisal of the teacher, and appraisal of the school child. Its methods run the gamut from observation and testing to elaborate research techniques. Evaluation as dealt with here is concerned in the direct sense only with characterizations of the school child through testing, measuring, and appraising.

Nature of Evaluation

Wrightstone in the following definition exemplified the point of view appropriate when the school child is the focus of evaluation.

Evaluation is a relatively new technical term, introduced to designate a more comprehensive concept of measurement than is implied in conventional tests and examinations . . . the emphasis in measurement is upon single aspects of subject-matter achievement or specific skills and abilities, but . . . the emphasis in evaluation is upon broad personality changes and major objectives of an educational program. These include not only subject-matter achievement but also attitudes, interests, ideals, ways of thinking, work habits, and personal and social adaptability.[1]

This definition supports the distinctions made in Chapter 1 among testing, measuring, and evaluating. The terms represent successively more inclusive and meaningful approaches to the appraisal of pupils. Evaluation thus includes not only the methods and tools appropriate in testing and measuring but also a variety of procedures and instruments of broader scope.

Characteristics of Evaluation

A somewhat more adequate understanding of evaluation can be obtained by considering its characteristics. Wrightstone characterized evaluation by stating its purposes and methods.

First, it attempts to measure a comprehensive range of objectives of the modern school curriculum rather than limited subject-matter achievement only. Second, modern evaluation uses a variety of techniques of appraisal such as achievement, attitude, personality and character tests . . . rating scales, questionnaires, judgment scales of products, interviews, controlled-observation techniques, sociometric techniques and anecdotal records. Third, evaluation includes integrating and interpreting the various indexes of behavior changes so as to construct an inclusive portrait of an individual. . . . For this purpose a comprehensive cumulative record is valuable.[2]

[1] J. Wayne Wrightstone, "Evaluation." *Encyclopedia of Educational Research,* Revised edition. Macmillan Co., New York, 1950. p. 403.
[2] J. Wayne Wrightstone, "Trends in Evaluation." *Educational Leadership,* 8:91-95; November 1950.

A somewhat more extensive characterization is that presented by Quillen and Hanna, who stated that

1. Evaluation includes all the means of collecting evidence on student behavior.
2. Evaluation is more concerned with the growth which the student has made than with his status in the group. . . .
3. Evaluation is continuous . . . an integral part of all teaching and learning.
4. Evaluation is descriptive as well as quantitative.
5. Evaluation is concerned with the total personality of the student and with gathering evidence on all aspects of personality development.
6. Evaluation is a cooperative process involving students, teachers, and parents.[3]

These characterizations of evaluation justify the concern here with evaluation as distinguished from testing and measuring. For that reason the treatment of this chapter should be considered particularly in relation to Chapters 8 to 12.

2. EVALUATIVE TESTS

The distinction between a test that measures and a test that evaluates is by no means exact. It is too much to demand that a test meet all of the characteristics outlined in the above section of this chapter, for testing techniques have not yet provided, and in fact may never provide, single instruments so broadly conceived. The tests considered here to be evaluative may in general be distinguished from tests that measure by their greater emphasis on the less tangible or even intangible types of instructional outcomes, on the types of outcomes resulting from broad and varied learning experiences, and on the ability of the pupil to apply and to use information in reasoning and problem solving. Such tests are here considered as of two types: (1) interpretive tests and (2) tests of practices and activities. The tests illustrated and discussed below are only in small degree representative. The wide variety of techniques used and the length of adequate illustrations preclude a wider sample.

Most of the tests of these types available in published form are for use in the high school or college. This is perhaps because to some extent they embody the philosophy of general education, so far considered most applicable to levels above the intermediate grades. A few such instruments are available for use in the junior high school and intermediate grades, however. Moreover, some of these tests are not provided with norms, since norms for tests of intangible outcomes appear to lack precise meaning.

[3] James Quillen and Lavone A. Hanna, *Education for Social Competence.* Copyright by Scott, Foresman and Co., Chicago, 1948. p. 343-46. Reprinted by permission.

Interpretive Tests

Tests measuring abilities to interpret are similar to reading comprehension tests in that both include not only the test items but also the material to which the test items refer. This material is usually in verbal form for reading tests and often consists of a paragraph or short selection on which

Excerpt from *Essential High School Content Battery* [4]

For questions 38 through 42, use your knowledge of scientific experiments, facts, laws, and principles as a basis, and decide for each statement which of the following five categories best describes the degree of truth or falsity of the belief. On the answer sheet, mark —

T — if it has been demonstrated clearly that the statement is *definitely true.*

PT — if the evidence indicates that the statement is *probably true,* but does not clearly demonstrate this.

I — if the statement is *indeterminate,* or if it is impossible to evaluate it from the available evidence.

PF — if the evidence indicates that the statement is *probably false,* but does not clearly demonstrate this.

F — if it has been demonstrated clearly that the statement is *definitely false.*

STATEMENTS

38. People born when certain planets are ascendant show the influence of the planets in their personalities.

39. One can tell the approximate age of a tree from the rings in the cross-section of its trunk.

40. Children of superior intelligence are more apt to be weak physically than are children of average intelligence.

41. The color red is more exciting to bulls than any other color.

42. Mothers know by intuition how to care for their children.

[4] David P. Harry and Walter N. Durost, *Essential High School Content Battery, Test 2, Science.* Form AM. Copyright 1950 by Harcourt, Brace and World, Inc., New York. All rights reserved. Quoted by special permission.

the test items are based. It may but often does not appear in verbal form for interpretive tests, since tabular and graphical materials are frequently the basis for the interpretations the pupils are asked to make. Furthermore, reading tests typically measure ability to answer questions of fact or to distinguish major ideas in the selection, whereas interpretive tests measure such complex abilities as are involved in the interpretation of data, application of scientific principles, logical reasoning, and critical thinking.

A development of rather recent date is that test exercises of the evaluative type are increasingly appearing in standardized achievement tests without any special designation and intermingled with items and exercises of more traditional types. One example is the accompanying excerpt in a *true–probably true–indeterminate–probably false–false* version from the science section of the *Essential High School Content Battery*. An accom-

EXCERPT FROM *Watson-Glaser Critical Thinking Appraisal* [5]

DIRECTIONS. In making decisions about important questions it is desirable to be able to distinguish between arguments that are *strong* and those which are *weak* in so far as the question at issue is concerned.

Strong arguments must be both important and directly related to the question.

Weak arguments may not be directly related to the question, even though they may be of great general importance; or they may be of minor importance; or they may be related to trivial aspects of the question.

Below is a series of questions. Each question is followed by three or four arguments. *For the purpose of this test you are to regard each argument as true.* The problem then is to decide whether it is a STRONG argument or a WEAK argument.

You are to answer by making a heavy mark on the Answer Sheet under "STRONG" if you think the argument is strong, or by making a heavy mark under "WEAK" on the Answer Sheet if you think the argument is weak. When evaluating an argument, judge it on its own merit; try not to let counter-arguments or your own attitude toward the question influence your judgment. Judge each argument separately. In some questions all the arguments may be STRONG; in others all may be WEAK.

Can rich and poor people who happen to oppose each other at law obtain approximately equal justice from the courts?

ARGUMENT
STRONG WEAK

86. No; a rich person can hire better lawyers and technical experts, pay for the time of more witnesses, and continue the fight in higher courts .... 86 ‖ ‖

87. No; rich people win the majority of their lawsuits against poor people .... 87 ‖ ‖

[5] Goodwin Watson and Edward M. Glaser, *Watson-Glaser Critical Thinking Appraisal, Test 5, Evaluation of Arguments.* Form AM. Copyright 1952 by Harcourt, Brace and World, Inc., New York. All rights reserved. Quoted by special permission. (Items discontinued in current editions; replaced by items of same general type.)

panying trend is that some of the specific evaluative tests published a decade or more ago have been allowed to go out of print.

Two excerpts from the *Watson-Glaser Critical Thinking Appraisal* are shown herewith. The first is designed to measure discrimination of argu· ments as strong or weak and the second, having items in alternate-response form, measures applied logical reasoning. This test also includes parts on inferences, recognition of assumptions, and interpretations.

EXCERPT FROM *Watson-Glaser Critical Thinking Appraisal* [6]

DIRECTIONS. Each exercise below consists of two statements (premises) followed by several proposed conclusions. For the purposes of this test, consider the two statements in each exercise as true without exception. Read the first conclusion beneath the statements, and if you think it *necessarily follows from the statements given,* answer by making a heavy black mark between the pair of dotted lines under "CONCLUSION FOLLOWS" in the corresponding blank on the Answer Sheet. If you think it is *not* a *necessary* conclusion from the given statements, then put a heavy black mark under "CONCLUSION DOES NOT FOLLOW," even though you may believe it to be true from your general knowledge.

Likewise read and judge each of the other conclusions. Try not to let your prejudices influence your judgment—just stick to the given statements and judge each conclusion as to whether it necessarily follows from them. Mark all your answers on the Answer Sheet.

All musicians are temperamental. Some musicians are not proud. Therefore—

	CONCLUSION FOLLOWS	DOES NOT FOLLOW
37. All temperamental people are musicians	37 ‖	‖
38. No proud people are temperamental	38 ‖	‖
39. Some proud people are musicians	39 ‖	‖

Tests of Practices and Activities

Paper-and-pencil tests of practices and activities must of necessity consist of verbalized statements or questions to which the pupils react instead of direct measurement. However, pupils' responses to tests of this type may well disclose information that can lead to inferences concerning their individual interests, personalities, and adjustment. In fact, such tests are similar in some respects to the adjustment inventories treated in Chapter 7.

One illustration only is given here of an instrument that seems to belong in this classification—an excerpt from a *Test of Social Insight* designed to determine what action a pupil says he would take in a specified social

[6] *Ibid. Test 3, Deduction.* Form AM. (Items discontinued in current editions; replaced by items of same general type.)

situation. At least one other instrument that in part appears to measure practices and activities is the *"What I Like To Do" Inventory,* from which an excerpt appears on page 138.

EXCERPT FROM *Test of Social Insight* [7]

15. You have forgotten to attend a party given by a close friend. You wanted very much to attend. What do you do?
   a. Call the friend and apologize; and request that you be invited to the next party he gives.
   b. Say you had an important meeting, and could not make his party.
   c. Do nothing.
   d. Insist that your friend was at fault for not calling to remind you.
   e. Avoid seeing your friend so that you will not have to explain.

16. While studying in a crowded library, you are disturbed by a loud talker. What do you do?
   a. Check out some books, and go home.
   b. Look for a quiet corner to study in.
   c. Ask the loud person to be quiet.
   d. Talk very loudly yourself.
   e. Call the librarian, and insist that the talking be stopped.

3. OTHER EVALUATIVE TOOLS

Evaluative tests of the types represented in the preceding section are of more recent origin than are most of the evaluative tools to receive consideration here. The significance of these tools lies much more in the broadened conceptions employed in their construction and use than in their uniqueness. These instruments can be distinguished according to whether teachers or pupils themselves supply the information recorded on them.

Instruments Prepared by Teachers

Teachers variously supply and record evaluative information about pupils on several types of records. Two types of such records—reports of test results for use within the school and the more recently developed re-

[7] Russell N. Cassel, *Test of Social Insight,* Youth edition. Martin M. Bruce, New Rochelle, N. Y., 1959.

ports of test results for pupils and their parents—are discussed and illustrated in the section of Chapter 8 devoted to the interpretation of standardized test results. They can be considered to supplement the evaluative tools discussed here.

Cumulative pupil records. An adequate system of cumulative pupil records is certainly essential if the program of the school is to be effective. Many modern schools have comprehensive and even elaborate systems of permanent records that provide for the recording of a wide variety of information concerning each pupil in a cumulative record folder.

No attempt is made here to catalog all of the types of information for which cumulative records should make provision. It is sufficient to indicate that the records should contain information about the pupil's family background and environment, personal history, health, personality, intelligence, special abilities, school progress, scholarship, achievement test performances, extracurricular activities, employment, educational plans, and vocational ambitions. Some record systems provide for the recording of data on all or most of these points on a record card or folder, and also for the filing of certain types of other data, such as test profiles and scores, anecdotal records, case studies, and reports of action taken on special problems, in the cumulative record folder.

The accompanying illustrations of both sides of the *Permanent Record Card of the National Association of Secondary School Principals* show a form on which a pupil's record may be kept over a period of years. No attempt is made here to discuss the types of evidence for which provision is made, but an examination of the samples will reveal that a very comprehensive picture of a pupil can be obtained from the types of data that can be recorded on such a form.

It is impossible here to discuss at all adequately the values and uses of the cumulative record in pupil guidance and adjustment. However, it should be apparent that the mere availability of such a variety of information for all pupils in a school as can be recorded on the pictured type of cumulative record is of great value. Such records are useful to administrators, to guidance workers, and to teachers as a basis for careful analyses in cases of maladjustment or disciplinary difficulties, and on others of the many occasions requiring or at least making desirable comprehensive information about individual pupils.

Reports to parents. Although the traditional report card may be considered to be an evaluative tool, the better modern report cards or report folders merit that designation much more definitely. The report to parents presents a series of evaluations of the pupil's scholastic success and frequently of other aspects of his school performance. Even though report

PERMANENT RECORD

School	City

Last Name	First Name	Middle Name	Sex	Race	Birthplace	Month	Day	Year
Entered from		Date	Age	Class	Curriculum		Adviser	
Parent or Guardian		Occupation	Nationality	Address			Telephone No.	

EXTRA CLASS ACTIVITIES

Date	Activity	Honors or Offices	Pts. Crs.

INTELLIGENCE-TEST RECORD

Date	Name of Test	Form	Score	%-ile Rank	MA	CA	IQ

ACHIEVEMENT-TEST RECORD

Date	Name of Test	Form	Score	Class Norm.	%-ile Rank	Subject Age

Was Graduated	Date		Rank	No. in Class	
Left	Date		Reason		

ATTENDANCE RECORD

Semester	1	2	3	4	5	6	7	8	9	10	Totals
Days Present											
Days Absent											
Times Tardy											

PERSONALITY RECORD

Symbols: (1) High; (2) Above Av.; (3) Av.; (4) Below Av.; (5) Low

	1st yr.	2nd yr.	3rd yr.	4th yr.	5th yr.	Summary
Motivation						
Industry						
Initiative						
Influence & Leadership						
Concern for Others						
Responsibility						
Integrity						
Emotional Stability						
General Health						
Significant Limitations						

Home conditions	Parents Living	No. Brothers	No. Sisters
Vocational Preferences			
College or Position		Date	
Credits Sent to		Date	

Name

SCHOLASTIC RECORD

Notes

Subject	Gr.	9	10	11	12	Extra	No. Wks.	Credits
	Yr.	19 1S 2S	19 1S 2S	19 1S 2S	19 1S 2S	19 1S 2S		

Specify laboratory periods, variations in time allowance for subjects, or any other information needed to interpret this record. Such other information as Regents grades, College Boards and record of a fifth year may be entered in the Extra column. If a school does not use marks, enter here an estimate of success achieved.

(Subject rows at left: English, Lang., Math., Science, Soc. Studies, Other Subjects)

FIGURE 19. Permanent Record Card of National Association of Secondary School Principals [8]

[8] National Association of Secondary School Principals, *Record Forms for Secondary Schools*. The Association, Washington, D. C. p. 6-7.

cards are widely known and their organization and content differ greatly, it seems desirable to illustrate this evaluative tool by one sample. Figure 20 shows excerpts from several parts of a report to parents designed for use in the junior high school. Academic progress is marked at three levels: S = satisfactory; IN = improvement needed; and I = improving.

ACHIEVEMENT			
READING			
Vocabulary			
Comprehension			
Independent Reading			
ARITHMETIC			
Knowledge of number facts			
Skill in using arithmetic to solve problems			
LANGUAGE ARTS			
Punctuation			
Capitals			
Oral Expression			
Spelling			
Penmanship			
Legibility			
Letter Formation			

PUPIL REPORT FORM   First Period

I am doing my best work in the following subjects:

I need to improve my work in

TEACHER'S COMMENTS

PARENT'S COMMENTS

FIGURE 20. Excerpts from Report of West Hartford Public Schools to Parents [9]

Pupil rating scales. A practice common in some schools and occasional in others requires that teachers fill out standardized or locally prepared rating scales for their pupils and submit them to central school offices. Such rating scales are usually so structured that check marks on numerically or otherwise calibrated scales of merit are required of the teacher.

Forms Completed by Pupils

At least three instruments classified here as evaluative tools are ordinarily selected or prepared by the teacher and reacted to by the pupils. These somewhat overlapping instruments are the questionnaire, the pupil record form, and the participation schedule.

[9] West Hartford Public Schools, West Hartford, Connecticut.

Questionnaires. The questionnaire is a data-gathering device consisting of questions to which the pupil reacts by checking or in some other manner briefly indicating his answers on the mimeographed or otherwise reproduced form placed in his hands. Questionnaires are usually prepared by the teacher or in the local school system with the aim of obtaining information on well-defined issues. As the instrument requires brief, to-the-point responses, it is structured or at least semistructured. It can be used for obtaining data on pupils' likes and dislikes, beliefs, wants, personal lives, and many other issues on which information is desired by the teacher.

Pupil record forms. The pupil record form is a structured or semistructured questionnaire to which pupils react by making check marks or writing brief answers. Obtainable in printed form or locally constructed to satisfy existing needs for information about pupils, these instruments deal with such issues as family history, health history, educational background, hobbies, and educational and vocational plans. The completed forms are usually placed in the pupils' cumulative record folders and they are frequently used later in counseling interviews with pupils.

Participation schedules. The participation schedule is actually still another type of specialized and structured or semistructured questionnaire filled out by pupils. It is typically prepared locally and adapted to local needs and conditions. As its name suggests, it deals with pupil likes and dislikes, attitudes, activities, felt needs, and other types of personal reactions to school affairs. In dealing primarily with pupil relationships in the school, the participation schedule differs from the pupil report form and from many other types of questionnaires.

4. EVALUATIVE TECHNIQUES

Evaluative techniques, as well as the nontest tools dealt with immediately above, can probably best be classified here in terms of the more active participant—teacher or pupil. Again the distinction is arbitrary rather than fundamental, for it is always the behavior of pupils, whether in response to directions from the teacher or self-initiated, that is measured or evaluated.

Techniques Used by Teachers

Evaluative techniques used directly by the teacher in appraisal of pupils variously involve observation of pupil behavior, interviews with and intensive studies of individual pupils, and records of class and individual pupil activities. These techniques are observation, the anecdotal method, the interview, the case study, and the teacher log. Since anecdotal methods and the case study are treated briefly in the section of Chapter 7 devoted to the measurement of total personality, they are not dealt with here.

Observation of pupils. Teacher observation and evaluation of pupils always occur as inherent characteristics of the teacher-pupil relationships. Planned observations in certain types of school settings, such as in the classroom or on the playground, are sometimes valuable. Controlled observations using time-sampling and other techniques are appropriate on occasion. Detailed records of observations should sometimes, but certainly not always, be kept. Observation of pupils is a broadly inclusive technique that supplies data for use particularly with such evaluative tools as the behavior record and rating scale. Moreover, the anecdotal method is a type of specialized observational technique.

Interviews. Interviews with individual pupils are often conducted by teachers informally and sometimes by prearrangement. Their purposes may range from an on-the-spot attempt to diagnose a pupil's difficulties with an arithmetic problem as a basis for remediation to a planned and even organized attempt to gain information pertinent to the causes of a pupil's maladjustment.

Teacher logs. Teacher logs are running accounts of day-by-day classroom procedures designed to aid the teacher later in assessing not only the pupils' reactions and learning but also his success in teaching. Such a technique, therefore, serves the dual purpose of evaluating pupils and evaluating instruction.

Techniques Dependent on Writing by Pupils

Three evaluative techniques place major responsibility on the pupil for providing desired types of information in written form. The first of these, the open question, is semistructured by the teacher but the others, the diary and autobiography, are of a free-response type.

Open questions. The open question is used to obtain from pupils indications of their beliefs, feelings, interests, ambitions, and various other types of reactions. The technique consists essentially of asking pupils to write a response to a rather general question that is designed to elicit information of the type in which the teacher is interested.

Diaries. Pupil diaries kept at the request of the teacher and made available to him provide sources of information about the varied school and out-of-school activities of the pupils. Such diaries are revealing not only of the pupil as an individual but also of his social interactions with members of his family, his fellow pupils, and others with whom he comes in contact.

Autobiographies. Autobiographies pupils write at the request of the teacher are sources of information in somewhat the same way as are pupil diaries. The autobiography, however, affords a broader understanding of the pupil's background by tracing his life span.

5. USING RESULTS FROM EVALUATIVE TOOLS
   AND TECHNIQUES

It should be apparent from the preceding discussion and illustrations that the equipment of the classroom teacher may well include evaluative tests, tools, and techniques as well as the more traditional types of measuring instruments and techniques. As is made quite clear in Chapters 10 and 11, the classroom teacher very properly may construct informal objective tests and performance tests to meet his particular needs and to supplement standardized achievement tests and scales. He can also participate in the cooperative planning and development of most of the evaluative instruments and techniques treated in this chapter. However, the development of some types of test units, such as those illustrated for the *Watson-Glaser Critical Thinking Appraisal* and the *Essential High School Content Battery,* involves principles of test construction going somewhat beyond those presented in Chapters 8 and 10 and entails a considerable amount of experience on the part of the test maker.

The interpretation of evaluation results demands more insight and understanding than is ordinarily required for handling results from more traditional objective tests, and as yet few guides other than those provided with the specific instruments themselves have been set up as aids to users. Moreover, the broad, integrative nature of evaluation and the wide variety of instruments and techniques preclude definite limitations on the use of results. Therefore, the considered judgment of the evaluator not only of the direct results of evaluation but also of all other sources of information about individual pupils should be exercised in drawing conclusions and in deciding upon any indicated courses of action.

SUGGESTED ACTIVITIES

1. Choose some area of pupil activity, such as reading, collecting, sports, or hobbies, and construct a few sample items or a short exercise that could be used in determining some of the specific types of this activity in which pupils engage.
2. Obtain samples of a few nontest evaluative forms, such as cumulative records, report cards, pupil rating scales, or report forms for test results from a school system or two, and evaluate them.

TOPICS FOR DISCUSSION

1. How are evaluative tests distinguishable from other paper-and-penc achievement tests?
2. For what grade levels are evaluative tests most often provided at present
3. How do interpretive tests differ from more traditional tests in purpose and testing techniques?
4. What are some major characteristics of tests of practices and activities?
5. For what types of information should a cumulative pupil record mak provision?
6. In what way is the questionnaire an evaluative instrument?
7. Briefly discuss observation of pupils and the interview as evaluative techniques.
8. What are some types of evaluative techniques involving writing by pupils?
9. How can the teacher make effective use of evaluative tests, tools, and techniques in the classroom?

SELECTED REFERENCES

ALEXANDER, WILLIAM M. "Reporting to Parents—Why? What? How?" *NEA Journal,* 48:15-28; December 1959.

BOLLENBACHER, JOAN. "Student Records and Reports—Elementary and Second-ary." *Encyclopedia of Educational Research.* Third edition. New York: Mac-millan Co., 1960. p. 1437-42.

BOYD, GERTRUDE A. "Sentence and Story Completions Offer Serviceable Infor-mation." *Personnel and Guidance Journal,* 37:504-8; March 1959.

CRUM, LEWIS R. "Evaluation of an Activities Program." *School Activities,* 26:243-47; April 1955.

DIEDERICH, PAUL B. "Design for a Comprehensive Evaluation Program." *School Review,* 58:225-32; April 1950.

DOWLEY, EDITH M. "Cues for Observing Children's Behavior." *Childhood Edu-cation,* 30:113-17; November 1953.

FINDLEY, WARREN G. "Educational Evaluation—Recent Developments." *Social Education,* 14:206-10; May 1950.

FINDLEY, WARREN G. "A Statistical Index of Participation in Discussion." *Journal of Educational Psychology,* 39:47-51; January 1948.

FROEHLICH, CLIFFORD P., AND DARLEY, JOHN G. *Studying Students: Guidance Methods of Individual Analysis.* Chicago: Science Research Associates, Inc., 1952. Chapters 4-8, 15.

FROEHLICH, CLIFFORD P., AND HOYT, KENNETH B. *Guidance Testing.* Chicago: Sci-ence Research Associates, Inc., 1959. Chapters 11-13, 15-17.

GREENE, HARRY A., JORGENSEN, ALBERT N., AND GERBERICH, J. RAYMOND. *Measurement and Evaluation in the Elementary School.* Second edition. New York: Longmans, Green and Co., 1953. Chapter 9.

GREENE, HARRY A., JORGENSEN, ALBERT N., AND GERBERICH, J. RAYMOND. *Measurement and Evaluation in the Secondary School.* Second edition. New York: Longmans, Green and Co., 1954. Chapter 9.

HAGEN, ELIZABETH P., AND THORNDIKE, ROBERT L. "Evaluation." *Encyclopedia of Educational Research*. Third edition. New York: Macmillan Co., 1960. p. 482-86.

HARTUNG, MAURICE L., AND OTHERS. "Aspects of Thinking." *Appraising and Recording Student Progress*. New York: Harper and Brothers, 1942. Chapter 2.

HORN, ALICE, AND LEWERENZ, ALFRED S. "Measuring the 'Intangibles' in Education." *California Journal of Educational Research*, 1:147-53; 195-206; September and November 1950.

MCCLEARY, LLOYD E. "A New Technique in Reporting Pupil Progress." *School Review*, 63:160-63; March 1955.

SCHWARTZ, ALFRED, AND TIEDEMAN, STUART C. *Evaluating Student Progress in the Secondary School*. New York: Longmans, Green and Co., 1957. Chapters 9-10, 18.

SMALLENBERG, HARRY. "Evaluating Pupil Progress." *Educational Leadership*, 2:290-93; April 1945.

SMITH, ANN Z., AND DOBBIN, JOHN E. "Marks and Marking Systems." *Encyclopedia of Educational Research*. Third edition. New York: Macmillan Co., 1960. p. 783-91.

SMITH, EUGENE R. "Recording for Guidance and Transfer." *Appraising and Recording Student Progress*. New York: Harper and Brothers, 1942. Part II.

SYMONDS, PERCIVAL M. "Pupil Evaluation and Self-Evaluation." *Teachers College Record*, 54:138-49; December 1952.

SYMPOSIUM. "Evaluation." *Journal of Educational Research*, 35:481-564; March 1942.

TABA, HILDA, AND OTHERS. *Diagnosing Human Relations Needs: Studies in Intergroup Relations*. Washington, D. C.: American Council on Education, 1951.

THOMAS, R. MURRAY. *Judging Student Progress*. New York: Longmans, Green and Co., 1954. Chapters 8, 10-13.

TRAXLER, ARTHUR E. "Cumulative Records: Their Nature and Uses." *Educational and Psychological Measurement*, 1:323-40; October 1941.

WRIGHTSTONE, J. WAYNE. "Evaluation." *Encyclopedia of Educational Research*. Revised edition. New York: Macmillan Co., 1950. p. 403-7.

WRIGHTSTONE, J. WAYNE. "Observational Techniques." *Encyclopedia of Educational Research*. Third edition. New York: Macmillan Co., 1960. p. 927-33.

WRINKLE, WILLIAM L. *Improving Marking and Reporting Practices*. New York: Rinehart and Co., Inc., 1947.

PART 4

Applying Statistical Procedures to Measurement and Evaluation Results

Today, more than at any time in the past, a teacher needs some knowledge and understanding of statistical methods in order to be a capable user of results from educational measurement and evaluation. This need results in part from the increasingly complex procedures used in test standardization and in reporting pupil test results. These, in turn, demand test manuals and interpretive materials that are sometimes quite technical and elaborate, particularly for achievement test batteries, for multiaptitude test batteries, and for personality inventories having a number of separate parts.

Construction of one's own classroom tests and the analysis and interpretation of resulting scores make a somewhat different type of demand for statistical proficiency on the part of the teacher. For the most effective construction and use of his own achievement tests, a teacher, in addition to the knowledge and understanding mentioned above, should desirably possess a few statistical skills that are neither complex nor unduly difficult to acquire. In fact, little more than a few elementary arithmetical skills are necessarily involved.

The purposes of Chapters 13 and 14 include provision of opportunity for the student to develop some fundamental statistical knowledge and understanding and to go further, as desired, in acquiring skills involved in the estimation or the computation of such basic statistical measures as arithmetic means, medians, standard deviations, quartile deviations, and correlation coefficients.

13

ANALYZING RESULTS OF MEASUREMENT

AND EVALUATION

The following points in the summarization and analysis of test results are considered in this chapter:

A. Statistical procedures in describing test scores.
B. Classification and tabulation of test scores.
C. Analysis of test scores arranged in rank order.
D. Analysis and representation of scores in frequency distributions.
E. Common measures of average or typical performance on tests.
F. Common measures of spread or variability of performance on tests.
G. Measures of relationship between two sets of test scores.

It is well known to all teachers that pupils in a typical class differ widely in the scores they make on tests as well as in the marks they receive in their courses. Since the human mind is not able to grasp and hold numerous isolated facts at the same time, accurate descriptions of test results and of other measurements of pupils depend on their summarization in some meaningful manner. Simple methods of describing and analyzing test scores of pupils are dealt with in this chapter. A few supplementary procedures useful in the validation of tests, in the assignment of marks, and in the derivation of the types of derived scores discussed in a preceding chapter are taken up in Chapter 14.

1. DESCRIPTION OF PUPIL SCORES ON TESTS

Scores made by pupils in a class group on any one of the various types of tests discussed in Chapters 6 to 12 need to be classified and organized in some logical order and then to be analyzed if the teacher is to use the results effectively in the classroom. The tools needed for accomplishing this purpose are those of descriptive statistics.

Basic Methods of Describing Test Scores

The most important and widely useful statistical techniques from the standpoint of the classroom teacher involve abilities to (1) classify and tabulate scores, (2) determine and apply the common measures of average or central tendency, (3) determine and apply the common measures of spread or variability, (4) represent scores graphically, and (5) apply correlational procedures in determining the relationships between two sets of scores. The discussion and explanation of these techniques constitute the major portions of this chapter.

Need for Giving Order to Test Scores

The very fact that people are unlike physically and mentally gives rise to the need for statistical methods in education and psychology. For example, it may be observed readily from Table 11 that there are great differences in the scores made by the 30 ninth-grade pupils who took a certain informal objective test of English usage. However, it requires rather careful scrutiny to determine that the highest and lowest scores are respectively 49 and 11, while very little further information can be obtained from these scores without rearranging them.

TABLE 11

Alphabetically Listed Scores of Pupils in a Ninth-Grade Class
on an Informal Objective Test of English Usage

Pupil	Test Score	Pupil	Test Score	Pupil	Test Score	Pupil	Test Score	Pupil	Test Score
LJA	37	LFD	27	REJ	25	ASN	21	RBS	33
JHB	28	GLF	24	JWK	27	RHP	14	INT	19
DB	25	FOF	16	CAK	30	DCP	39	NLW	36
HWC	43	WTG	31	CEL	49	JMS	28	CAW	34
WRC	30	HGH	32	LDM	31	GBS	11	VWW	32
WBC	29	WI	40	JM	28	ABS	30	RWY	22

Two methods of rearranging these scores are presented in the following sections of this chapter. The first, in order of scores from highest to lowest, can be used as a basis for analyzing the test results so simply and quickly that no teacher or student of education need be puzzled by complex procedures or difficult and laborious computations. The second, in the form of a frequency distribution, serves as the foundation for more technical but not difficult procedures for analyzing test results.

2. DEALING WITH TEST SCORES IN ORDER OF RANK

Rearrangement of test scores in order of rank is doubtless the simplest procedure for making them comprehensible. It also puts them in an order which lends itself to the ready computation of the types of measures needed for describing them adequately.

Classifying Scores in Rank Order

Table 12 reproduces the English usage test scores of the 30 ninth-grade pupils in descending order. It now is more easily apparent than from Table 11 that the highest and lowest scores are respectively 49 and 11, while it can also rather easily be determined that the two middle scores are 30 and 29. A more adequate description of these scores is necessary, however, if the teacher is to have a comprehensive basis for interpreting them.

TABLE 12

Ranked Scores of Pupils in a Ninth-Grade Class on an Informal Objective Test of English Usage

Pupil	Test Score	Pupil	Test Score	Pupil	Test Score	Pupil	Test Score	Pupil	Test Score
CEL	49	CAW	34	WRC	30	JMS	28	RWY	22
HWC	43	RBS	33	CAK	30	LFD	27	ASN	21
WI	40	HGH	32	ABS	30	JWK	27	INT	19
DCP	39	VWW	32	WBC	29	DB	25	FOF	16
LJA	37	WTG	31	JHB	28	REJ	25	RHP	14
NLW	36	LDM	31	JM	28	GLF	24	GBS	11

A different and still more meaningful arrangement of these 30 scores by order of rank is given in Table 13, where the scores are listed in a column in parallel with the numbers 1 to 30. It should be noted that the individual scores are not identified here, as they are in Tables 11 and 12, by the initials of pupils earning them. Furthermore, no distinction is made, and none is necessary here, for example, between the two scores of 32 or among the three scores of 30.

TABLE 13

Analysis of Ranked English Usage Test Scores of Ninth-Grade Pupils

Ranks	Test Scores			
1	49 ⎫			
2	43			
3	40 ⎬ 208			
4	39			
5	37 ⎭	Arithmetic	$=$	Sum of scores
6	36	Mean		Number of pupils
7	34 ⎫ 67			
8	33 ⎬		$= \dfrac{871}{30} = 29.03$	
9	32			
10	32		Sum of two middle scores	
11	31	Mid-Score $=$	$\dfrac{}{2}$	
12	31			
13	30		$= \dfrac{30 + 29}{2} = \dfrac{59}{2} = 29.50$	
14	30			
15	30 ⎱ 59			
16	29 ⎰			
17	28			
18	28			
19	28	Standard	$=$	Sum of high-sixth scores $-$ Sum of low-sixth scores
20	27	Deviation		Half the number of pupils
21	27			
22	25		$= \dfrac{208 - 81}{30 \div 2} = \dfrac{127}{15} = 8.47$	
23	25 ⎱ 49			
24	24 ⎰			
25	22	Quartile	$=$	Middle top-half score $-$ Middle bottom-half score
26	21 ⎫	Deviation		2
27	19			
28	16 ⎬ 81		$= \dfrac{(67 \div 2) - (49 \div 2)}{2} = \dfrac{33.50 - 24.50}{2} = \dfrac{9.00}{2} = 4.50$	
29	14			
30	11 ⎭			
30	871			

Analyzing Scores in Rank Order

Two sets of simple computations are shown in Table 13 to illustrate how measures of average or central tendency and of spread or variability can be obtained from scores listed by rank. The fact that the former are computed and that the latter are estimated is unimportant at this point, but the distinction is made for future reference.

Determination of the arithmetic mean and standard deviation. These two measures are unquestionably the most widely useful and important ones for describing test scores. The arithmetic mean provides an indication of average or central tendency that is employed more often than any other concept when a single fact is needed for describing performance or characteristics of a group of persons. The standard deviation supplements the arithmetic mean by giving an idea of the way in which scores are spread out above and below the arithmetic mean. Both of these measures are decribed more fully in the later section of this chapter where methods are presented for computing them from frequency distributions.

As is shown in Table 13, the sum, or total, of the 30 test scores is 871. When this total is divided by 30, the result, 29.03, is the arithmetic mean. Consequently, all that a teacher needs to do in obtaining the arithmetic mean of test scores for the pupils in one of his classes is to add the scores and to divide the total by the number of scores.

The standard deviation can be estimated by a simple procedure devised by W. L. Jenkins of Lehigh University and outlined by Diederich.[1] All that is necessary is to obtain the sum of two groups of scores, those in the highest sixth and the lowest sixth of the rank-order list, to subtract the smaller total from the larger, and to divide the result by half the number of pupils in the group. In Table 13, the five scores in the highest and lowest sixths respectively are shown to total 208 and 81.[2] When the difference between them, 127, is divided by 15, or half of 30, the result, 8.47, affords an estimate of the standard deviation. An estimate by this method is sufficiently accurate and stable for the classroom teacher to use in the ordinary course of events in the description of test scores attained by pupils in his classes. It obviously requires nothing beyond simple arithmetic and not more than three or four minutes of a teacher's time for computation.

Determination of the mid-score and quartile deviation. This pair of related measures supplies another set of terms used in describing groups of scores. The mid-score represents central tendency in terms of what is most typical and the quartile deviation is used to show the spread or variability of scores above and below this point. Meanings of these measures are brought out more fully in a subsequent section of this chapter.

The mid-score, as the term suggests, is the middle score in a rank-order list when the total is odd or the average of the two middle scores when the total is even. It is shown in Table 13 that the mid-score is 29.50, or halfway between the two middle scores of 30 and 29. Obtaining the mid-

[1] Educational Testing Service, *Short-Cut Statistics for Teacher-Made Tests*. Evaluation and Advisory Service Series, No. 5. Educational Testing Service, Princeton, N. J., 1960. p. 21-22.

[2] In the event that one-sixth of the total number of scores involves a fraction, a simple adaptation can be made. If there are 27 scores in a group, for example, one-sixth of the total is 4½. In such a case the four highest scores plus half of the fifth score and the four lowest scores plus half of the twenty-third score become the two totals to be used in the numerator of the fraction.

score for pupils in a class when scores are listed in descending order consequently requires only a simple procedure of counting and perhaps of averaging two scores.

The quartile deviation is estimated by obtaining half of the distance from the middle of the top half to the middle of the bottom half of the scores listed in order of rank. In Table 13, the scores of 34 and 33 are at the middle of the top half and the scores of 25 and 24 occupy this same position in the bottom half. When the two pairs of scores are averaged, in precisely the same manner as is done in obtaining the mid-score in this list, the resulting 33.50 and 24.50 divide each of the halves of the list into two equal parts. When the difference between these values, 9.00, is divided by 2, the result, 4.50, is a sufficiently accurate estimate of the quartile deviation for ordinary classroom uses. It is apparent that here again only very simple counting and arithmetic procedures are needed in obtaining significant evidence about a group of test scores.

One other point warrants mention here. When the two values used above in estimating the quartile deviation are combined with the mid-score in descending order, the three values, 33.50, 29.50, and 24.50, divide the distribution into four parts or quarters containing 7½ scores each. One-fourth of the scores lie above 33.50, one-fourth of them fall below 24.50, and the remainder are split into the two equal quarters between 33.50 and the mid-score and between the mid-score and 24.50.

3. DEALING WITH TEST SCORES IN FREQUENCY DISTRIBUTIONS

Statistical methods of a somewhat more involved nature than those outlined above but still not too complex for use by interested classroom teachers commonly provide for the classification of scores in frequency distributions. When test scores for large numbers of pupils in the same grade or course need to be described by the use of statistics, the persons in charge, more often guidance or administrative officers than classroom teachers, usually employ frequency distributions. The short-cut procedures dealt with in the preceding section become cumbersome when they are used with large groups of scores, in actuality.

A classroom teacher, however, can handle test scores for his own classes in simple rank-order arrangement or classified according to the more sophisticated method dependent on frequently distributions. Consequently, the procedures outlined here very briefly are for the guidance of teachers or future teachers who wish to apply the more precise and elaborate methods in their own classes or who may need to describe test results for rather large groups of pupils. References given at the end of this chapter can be consulted for more extensive treatments by any readers who wish to go more deeply into these procedures.

Tabulating Scores in Frequency Distributions

Five consistent ways in which the same 30 scores can be classified into a frequency distribution are shown in Table 14. The first illustration, in which the scores retain their individual identities, may be called a simple or ungrouped frequency distribution. The other four illustrations, in which the grouping of scores destroys the individual identities of most of them, are called grouped frequency distributions. The first distribution furnishes the basis for obtaining detailed information concerning these scores, but such information would be rather costly in the time required to derive it. The fourth and fifth illustrations furnish the basis for obtaining quick but quite unsatisfactory information, for the very rough grouping almost

TABLE 14

Grouped Scores of Pupils in a Ninth-Grade Class on an Informal Objective Test of English Usage

Interval of 1		*Interval of 1*		*Interval of 3*		*Interval of 5*	
TEST SCORE	FRE-QUENCY	TEST SCORE	FRE-QUENCY	TEST SCORES	FRE-QUENCY	TEST SCORES	FRE-QUENCY
49	1	29	1	47-49	1	48-52	1
48	0	28	3	44-46	0	43-47	1
47	0	27	2	41-43	1	38-42	2
46	0	26	0	38-40	2	33-37	4
45	0	25	2	35-37	2	28-32	11
44	0	24	1	32-34	4	23-27	5
43	1	23	0	29-31	6	18-22	3
42	0	22	1	26-28	5	13-17	2
41	0	21	1	23-25	3	8-12	1
40	1	20	0	20-22	2		

Interval of 7	
TEST SCORES	FRE-QUENCY

TEST SCORE	FRE-QUENCY	TEST SCORE	FRE-QUENCY	TEST SCORES	FRE-QUENCY	TEST SCORES	FRE-QUENCY
39	1	19	1	17-19	1	46-52	1
38	0	18	0	14-16	2	39-45	3
37	1	17	0	11-13	1	32-38	6
36	1	16	1			25-31	13
35	0	15	0			18-24	4
34	1	14	1			11-17	3
33	1	13	0				
32	2	12	0				
31	2	11	1				
30	3						

Interval of 15	
TEST SCORES	FRE-QUENCY
38-52	4
23-37	20
8-22	6

entirely sacrifices even the approximate identity of the individual scores. The second and third illustrations, neither of which demands an undue time expenditure in order to obtain accuracy nor sacrifices accuracy for a saving in time and labor, represent satisfactory practices midway between the two extreme methods. The second is somewhat preferable to the third for these scores.

TABLE 15

Frequency Distribution of English Usage Test Scores
of Ninth-Grade Pupils

Class Interval			Tabulation	Frequency (*f*)
INTEGRAL LIMITS	REAL LIMITS	MIDPOINT		
47-49	46.5-49.5	48	/	1
44-46	43.5-46.5	45		0
41-43	40.5-43.5	42	/	1
38-40	37.5-40.5	39	//	2
35-37	34.5-37.5	36	//	2
32-34	31.5-34.5	33	////	4
29-31	28.5-31.5	30	/////	6
26-28	25.5-28.5	27	////	5
23-25	22.5-25.5	24	///	3
20-22	19.5-22.5	21	//	2
17-19	16.5-19.5	18	/	1
14-16	13.5-16.5	15	//	2
11-13	10.5-13.5	12	/	1
				$N=30$

The steps of procedure presented in the following paragraphs are for the student's guidance in the preparation of grouped frequency distributions of test scores. The procedures are carried through in Table 15, which is designed to illustrate the tabulation of test scores in grouped frequency distributions. The table is also intended to serve as a point of reference for subsequent computations in which not only the integral or whole-number limits but also the real or actual limits or the midpoint of a class interval are involved.

(1) *Determine the range.* Find the highest score and the lowest score and obtain the difference between them. (Since the highest and lowest English usage test scores are 49 and 11, the range is 38.)

(2) *Determine the size of the class intervals.* If the result of step (1) is: 25 or less, use an interval of 1; 26 to 69, use an interval of 3; 70 to 125, use an interval of 5; 126 to 175, use an interval of 7; and 176 or more, use an interval of 15. (Since 38 is between 26 and 69, the

English usage test scores should preferably be grouped in intervals of three score units each.)

(3) *Set up the frequency table:*

    (a) Label three column headings *Class Interval, Tabulation,* and *Frequency (f),*

    (b) Determine the limits of the highest class interval so that its midpoint is divisible by, and the distance between its real limits is equal to, the size of the interval determined in step (2), and

    (c) Write the integral limits of the class intervals in the *Class Interval* column, starting at the top with the interval that contains the highest score and continuing downward consistently to include the interval that contains the lowest score.

(4) *Tabulate the scores.* Place a tally mark in the *Tabulation* column opposite the class interval that indicates the proper position for each score, carry across the total of the tally marks in each interval to the *Frequency* column, and add the frequencies in the *f* column to obtain the total number of cases (*N*).

Analyzing Scores in Frequency Distributions

Scores tabulated in grouped frequency distributions are widely used in computing such measures of central tendency as the arithmetic mean and median and such measures of spread or variability as the standard deviation and quartile deviation. All of these except the median are treated in the foregoing section of this chapter for the 30 English usage scores listed in rank order. The mid-score, obtained for the ranked scores, is replaced here by the closely comparable median in handling scores in frequency distributions.

Computation of the arithmetic mean. The steps outlined below summarize the procedures typically used in computing the arithmetic mean from a grouped frequency distribution. They assume that a frequency distribution of the type shown in Table 15 has been prepared and that columns for class intervals and frequencies have been extended by the addition of deviation and *fd* columns to the right of the *f* column. Columns 1 to 5 of Table 16 and the steps shown at the left immediately below the frequency distribution of that table illustrate computation of the arithmetic mean for the 30 English test scores.

(1) *Assume a value for the mean.* Choose the midpoint of an interval near the middle of the distribution.

(2) *Lay off the deviations from the assumed mean by intervals.* Write in the *Deviation (d)* column a value of 0 for the interval in which the assumed mean lies and write values for other intervals by counting upward (positive signs) and downward (negative signs) by units.

(3) *Obtain the products of the frequencies and deviations by intervals.* Multiply each frequency by its corresponding deviation, retaining negative signs for intervals below the assumed mean, and write the products in the *fd* column.

(4) *Obtain the algebraic sum of the fd column.* Algebraically add the values in the *fd* column and retain the appropriate sign.

(5) *Divide the algebraic sum of the fd column by N.* Divide the result of step (4) by the number of scores, retaining the appropriate sign.

(6) *Compute the correction to the assumed mean.* Multiply the result of step (5) by the size of the class interval, retaining the appropriate sign.

(7) *Obtain the arithmetic mean.* Algebraically add the correction of step (6) to the assumed mean of step (1) to obtain the Arithmetic Mean.

Computation of the standard deviation. Procedures are outlined below for computation of the standard deviation. They are also illustrated in Table 16, where they are applied to the same 30 scores dealt with previously in several settings. The frequency distribution used here differs from the one used in computing the arithmetic mean only by the addition of a column at the right labeled fd^2.

(1) *Carry out steps (1) to (5) for computation of the arithmetic mean.*

(2) *Square the algebraic sum of the fd column divided by N.* Square the result of step (5) from procedures for computation of the arithmetic mean.

(3) *Obtain the products of the frequencies and squared deviations by intervals.* Multiply each *d* by its corresponding *fd* and write the products in the fd^2 column.

(4) *Obtain the sum of the fd² column.* Add the values in the fd^2 column.

(5) *Divide the sum of the fd² column by N.* Divide the result of step (4) by the number of scores.

(6) *Subtract the result of step (2) from the result of step (5).*

(7) *Obtain the standard deviation in terms of class intervals.* Extract the square root of the result of step (6).

(8) *Obtain the standard deviation in terms of score values.* Multiply the result of step (7) by the size of the class interval.

Computation of the median. By definition, the mid-score and the median are quite similar, the main distinction being that the mid-score is designated as an actual score on a certain paper, or the average of the scores on the two middle papers, while the median is defined directly in terms of a point on the scale of the frequency table on which it is based. The median is a point on the scale such that 50 percent of the cases in the distribution are above it and 50 percent of the cases are below it.

TABLE 16

Analysis of a Frequency Distribution of English Usage Test Scores of Ninth-Grade Pupils—Arithmetic Mean and Standard Deviation

Class Interval		Frequency (f)	Deviation (d)	(fd)	(fd^2)
INTEGRAL LIMITS	MIDPOINT				
47-49	48	1	6	6	36
44-46	45	0	5	0	0
41-43	42	1	4	4	16
38-40	39	2	3	6	18
35-37	36	2	2	4	8
32-34	33	4	1	4	4
29-31	30	6	0	0	0
26-28	27	5	-1	-5	5
23-25	24	3	-2	-6	12
20-22	21	2	-3	-6	18
17-19	18	1	-4	-4	16
14-16	15	2	-5	-10	50
11-13	12	1	-6	-6	36
		30		-13	219

Arithmetic Mean

1. Assume a value for the mean.
   [30.00]
2. Lay off the deviations from the assumed mean by intervals.
   [Deviation (d) column]
3. Obtain the products of the frequencies and deviations by intervals.
   [fd column]
4. Obtain the algebraic sum of the fd column.
   [$-37 + 24 = -13$]
5. Divide the algebraic sum of the fd column by N.
   [$-13 \div 30 = -.43$]
6. Compute the correction to the assumed mean.
   [$-.43 \times 3 = -1.29$]
7. Obtain the arithmetic mean.
   [$30.00 - 1.29 = 28.71$]

Standard Deviation

1. Carry out steps (1) to (5) for computation of the arithmetic mean.
2. Square the algebraic sum of the fd column divided by N.
   [$-.43^2 = .18$]
3. Obtain the products of the frequencies and squared deviations by intervals.
   [fd^2 column]
4. Obtain the sum of the fd^2 column.
   [219]
5. Divide the sum of the fd^2 column by N.
   [$219 \div 30 = 7.30$]
6. Subtract the result of step (2) from the result of step (5).
   [$7.30 - .18 = 7.12$]
7. Obtain the standard deviation in terms of class intervals.
   [$\sqrt{7.12} = 2.67$]
8. Obtain the standard deviation in terms of score values.
   [$2.67 \times 3 = 8.01$]

The method of computing the median from a grouped frequency distribution is presented below and illustrated in Table 17 for the same group of test scores used previously in this chapter.

(1) *Obtain the half-sum.* Divide the number of scores by 2.
(2) *Obtain the subtotal.* Count upward into the distribution by adding successive frequencies until a number exactly equal to the half-sum or as closely approaching it as possible without exceeding it is reached.[3]
(3) *Determine the correction:*
    (a) *In terms of measures.* Subtract the subtotal from the half-sum.
    (b) *In terms of intervals.* Divide the result of step (3a) by the number of scores in the interval in which the median lies.
    (c) *In terms of scale distance.* Multiply the result of step (3b) by the size of the interval.
(4) *Obtain the median.* Add the correction of step (3c) to the lower real limit of the interval in which the median lies.

Computation of the quartile deviation. Shown below are the steps to be followed in computing this measure of variability for scores tabulated in a frequency distribution. An illustration of their application to the 30 English usage test scores appears in Table 17. Since the counting procedures involved here are almost identical to those used in obtaining the median, they are not restated here in the original degree of detail.

(1) *Compute Q_1* (twenty-fifth percentile):
    (a) *Obtain one-fourth of the number of scores.*
    (b) *Obtain Q_1 by carrying out steps (2) to (4) for computation of the median.* Substitute $N/4$ for $N/2$ and Q_1 for the median in this process.
(2) *Compute Q_3* (seventy-fifth percentile):
    (a) *Obtain three-fourths of the number of scores.*
    (b) *Obtain Q_3 by carrying out steps (2) to (4) for computation of the median.* Substitute $3N/4$ for $N/2$ and Q_3 for the median in this process.
(3) *Obtain the difference between Q_3 and Q_1.* Subtract Q_1 from Q_3.
(4) *Obtain the quartile deviation.* Divide $Q_3 - Q_1$ by 2.

Representing Scores in Frequency Polygons and Histograms

Graphical representations of scores frequently have value in the interpretation of results from educational measurement. Three types of

---

[3] If exactly the half-sum is reached, the median is usually the upper real limit of the interval the frequency of which was last added in the counting process. However, if the next higher interval should happen to have a zero frequency, the median is the midpoint of that interval.

TABLE 17

Analysis of a Frequency Distribution of English Usage Test Scores of Ninth-Grade Pupils—Median and Quartile Deviation

Class Interval		Frequency
INTEGRAL LIMITS	REAL LIMITS	(*f*)
47-49	46.5-49.5	1
44-46	43.5-46.5	0
41-43	40.5-43.5	1
38-40	37.5-40.5	2
35-37	34.5-37.5	2
32-34	31.5-34.5	4
29-31	28.5-31.5	6
26-28	25.5-28.5	5
23-25	22.5-25.5	3
20-22	19.5-22.5	2
17-19	16.5-19.5	1
14-16	13.5-16.5	2
11-13	10.5-13.5	1
		30

Median

1. Obtain the half-sum.
   [30 ÷ 2 = 15]
2. Obtain the subtotal.
   [1 + 2 + 1 + 2 + 3 + 5 = 14]
3. Determine the correction:
   a. In terms of measures.
      [15 − 14 = 1]
   b. In terms of intervals.
      [1 ÷ 6 = .17]
   c. In terms of scale distance.
      [.17 × 3 = .51]
4. Obtain the median.
   [28.50 + .51 = 29.01]

Quartile Deviation

1. Compute Q_1 (twenty-fifth percentile)
   a. Obtain one-fourth of the number of scores.
      [¼ × 30 = 7.5]
   b. Obtain Q_1 by carrying out steps (2) to (4) for computation of the median, except that $N/4$ is substituted for $N/2$ and Q_1 is substituted for the median.
      [1 + 2 + 1 + 2 = 6; 7.5 − 6 = 1.5; 1.5 ÷ 3 = .50; .50 × 3 = 1.50; 22.50 + 1.50 = 24.00 (Q_1)]
2. Compute Q_3 (seventy-fifth percentile)
   a. Obtain three-fourths of the number of scores.
      [¾ × 30 = 22.50]
   b. Obtain Q_3 by carrying out steps (2) to (4) for computation of the median, except that $3N/4$ is substituted for $N/2$ and Q_3 is substituted for the median.
      [1 + 2 + 1 + 2 + 3 + 5 + 6 = 20; 22.5 − 20 = 2.5; 2.5 ÷ 4 = .63; .63 × 3 = 1.89; 31.50 + 1.89 = 33.39 (Q_3)]
3. Obtain the difference between Q_3 and Q_1.
   [33.39 − 24.00 = 9.39]
4. Obtain the quartile deviation.
   [9.39 ÷ 2 = 4.70]

representations seem to be most widely useful in showing such results graphically: (1) the frequency polygon, (2) the histogram, and (3) the percentile curve. Since the third and probably least widely useful of these graphical methods is treated briefly in Chapter 14 and is illustrated in Figure 23, only the frequency polygon and the histogram receive attention at this point. Both of them are widely useful for showing individual differences in test scores among pupils in a class or school grade.

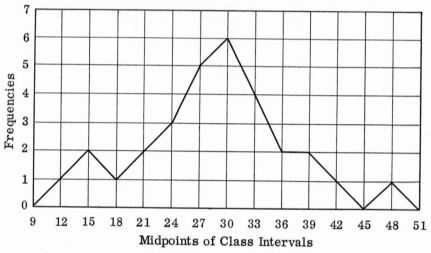

FIGURE 21.   Frequency Polygon for English Usage Test Scores
of Ninth-Grade Pupils

Construction of the frequency polygon. Figure 21 presents a frequency polygon for the same 30 test scores that are shown in Table 15. The vertical lines and the numerical values along the base line indicate the midpoints of class intervals. When the frequencies in successive class intervals are spotted above their respective midpoints in conformance with the scale of frequencies at the left and when the points so determined are joined successively by straight lines, the result is a frequency polygon. The frequency polygon always touches the base line to represent any zero frequency within the distribution, as at 45 for the interval 44-46 in this illustration. It always touches the base line at two other points as well— at the midpoints of the intervals next below the lowest one and next above the highest one in the distribution. Such points in this case are 9 for the zero in the interval 8-10 and 51 for the zero in the interval 50-52.

Construction of the histogram. Shown in Figure 22 is a histogram for the same 30 English usage test scores as are tabulated in a grouped frequency distribution in Table 15 and as are pictured graphically in Figure 21. The vertical lines here represent real limits of class intervals and the numerical values along the base line again, as in the frequency polygon shown above, indicate midpoints of intervals. When frequencies in successive class intervals are located above their respective intervals in accordance with the scale of frequencies at the left, in precisely the same way as for the frequency polygon, when horizontal lines are ruled through these points from the lower to the upper real limit of each interval, and when connecting vertical lines are drawn, the result is a histogram. The

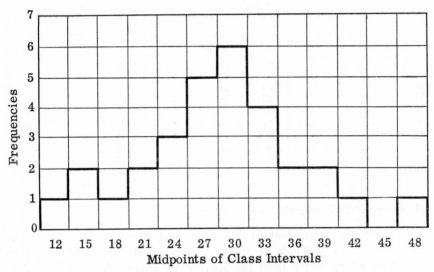

FIGURE 22. Histogram for English Usage Test Scores of Ninth-Grade Pupils

histogram always touches the base line at the lower real limit of the lowest interval and the higher real limit of the highest interval, as at 10.5 and 49.5 for this illustration. It also touches the base line at the lower and upper real limits of any class interval having a zero frequency. The vertical rulings at 43.5 and 46.5 are of this type, since the interval 44-46 has a zero frequency.

4. DEALING WITH PAIRED SCORES IN ORDER OF RANK

There remains for brief consideration the third basic type of statistical concept sometimes needed in analyzing the results of testing. This is the correlation coefficient, a measure of the relationship between two sets of paired scores. Reproduced in Table 18 are the same scores used in the computations of arithmetic means, mid-scores, and medians, and of standard deviations and quartile deviations, in the foregoing section of this chapter. The same 30 scores, originally obtained by administering an infor-

Measurement and Evaluation in the Modern School

mal objective test of English usage to ninth-grade pupils, are shown there in parallel with scores made by the same 30 pupils on a standardized test of English usage.

TABLE 18

Alphabetically Listed Scores of Pupils in a Ninth-Grade Class on Informal Objective and Standardized Tests of English Usage

Pupil	Test Scores		Pupil	Test Scores		Pupil	Test Scores	
	INFORMAL OBJECTIVE	STANDARD-IZED		INFORMAL OBJECTIVE	STANDARD-IZED		INFORMAL OBJECTIVE	STANDARD-IZED
LJA	37	76	HGH	32	60	DCP	39	59
JHB	28	54	WI	40	63	JMS	28	39
DB	25	49	REJ	25	41	GBS	11	17
HWC	43	83	JWK	27	54	ABS	30	71
WRC	30	47	CAK	30	66	RPS	33	81
WBC	29	50	CEL	49	75	INT	19	29
LFD	27	41	LDM	31	49	NLW	36	56
GLF	24	36	JM	28	67	CAW	34	69
FOF	16	24	ASN	21	32	VWW	32	52
WTG	31	73	RHP	14	35	RWY	22	44

Assigning Relative Ranks to Test Scores

Although the 30 original English usage test scores used above appear in order of rank in Table 13, the manner in which they are listed there differs in minor degree from the appropriate pattern for relative ranks. In that table, for example, two identical scores of 32 are ranked 9 and 10 and three identical scores of 30 are ranked 13, 14, and 15. For the purposes of the computations based on that table, such a method is satisfactory. In assigning the relative ranks needed at this point, however, identical scores must be assigned the same ranks and these must be at the average of the rank positions occupied by the two or more identical scores. For example, the two scores of 32 are both assigned the rank of 9.5 [(9 + 10) ÷ 2], and the three scores of 30 are similarly ranked 14 [(13 + 14 + 15) ÷ 3]. These and two other instances in which tied scores occur in the original group of 30 are shown in order of relative rank in the third column of Table 19. A section of Chapter 14, where various methods of interpreting test scores receive direct attention, outlines the process of assigning relative ranks in detail.

Analyzing Paired Scores in Rank Order

The scores listed by pairs in Table 19 are used in obtaining the tetrachoric *r*, which can be employed as an estimate of the Pearson product-moment correlation coefficient, and in computing the Spearman rank-order *rho*. Although the two measures differ somewhat in their significance as well as the methods by which they are typically obtained, they can be interpreted in the same manner for the types of classroom testing uses dealt with here. The methods outlined here are suitable only when pupil groups are rather small, perhaps not over 40 or 50, but the Pearson *r* can be computed, rather than estimated, for much larger numbers of pupils grouped in frequency distributions.

TABLE 19

Analysis of Informal Objective and Standardized English Usage
Test Scores for Ninth-Grade Pupils

Test Scores		Rank Positions		Difference	Square of Difference
INFORMAL OBJECTIVE	STANDARD- IZED	INFORMAL OBJECTIVE	STANDARD- IZED		
49	75	1	4	3	9.
43	83	2	1	1	1.
40	63	3	10	7	49.
39	59	4	12	8	64.
37	76	5	3	2	4.
36	56	6	13	7	49.
34	69	7	7	0	0.
33	81	8	2	6	36.
32	60	9.5	11	1.5	2.25
32	52	9.5	16	6.5	42.25
31	73	11.5	5	6.5	42.25
31	49	11.5	18.5	7	49.
30	47	14	20	6	36.
30	66	14	9	5	25.
30	71	14	6	8	64.
29	50	16	17	1	1.
28	54	18	14.5	3.5	12.25
28	67	18	8	10	100.
28	39	18	24	6	36.
27	41	20.5	22.5	2	4.
27	54	20.5	14.5	6	36.
25	49	22.5	18.5	4	16.
25	41	22.5	22.5	0	0.
24	36	24	25	1	1.
22	44	25	21	4	16.
21	32	26	27	1	1.
19	29	27	28	1	1.
16	24	28	29	1	1.
14	35	29	26	3	9.
11	17	30	30	0	0.
					707.00

(*continued on following page*)

Tetrachoric Correlation Coefficient	*Spearman Rank-Order Rho*
1. Determine the number of scores in the upper half of *both* distributions. [12]	1. Assign relative ranks separately to the scores in each set. [Rank Position columns]
2. Determine the percentage of scores in the upper half of *both* distributions. [12 ÷ 30 = .40]	2. Obtain the differences between pairs of ranks, disregarding signs. [Difference column]
3. Obtain the tetrachoric correlation coefficient from Table 20. [.40 = .81]	3. Square the differences between pairs of ranks. [Square of difference column]
	4. Obtain the sum of the squared differences between pairs of ranks. [707.00]
	5. Compute *rho.* Substitute the sum of the squared differences between pairs of ranks and the number of pairs of scores in the formula and obtain the Spearman rank-order *rho.* $$rho = 1 - \frac{6 \times 707.00}{30 \times 899}$$ $$= 1 - \frac{4242}{26970} = 1 - .16 = .84$$

Obtaining the tetrachoric correlation coefficient. Computation of the Pearson product-moment *r,* the most widely used and most important measure of relationship, involves rather complex procedures.[4] Consequently, a simple method of estimating it by use of the tetrachoric *r* is outlined below and illustrated in Table 19 for the 30 pairs of scores listed there. The resulting estimate can be used in approximating the degree of relationship existing between two sets of scores.

(1) *Determine the number of scores in the upper half of both distributions.* This can be done easily if one of the lists is arranged in descending order of scores and if the mid-scores of both distributions are known.

(2) *Determine the percentage of scores in the upper half of both distributions.* Divide the number obtained in step (1) by the number of pairs of scores to obtain this percentage.

(3) *Obtain the tetrachoric correlation coefficient.* Enter Table 20 with the percentage found in step (2) and read the corresponding estimate of the correlation coefficient.

Computing the Spearman rank-order rho. This measure of correlation can be obtained by using the steps of simple arithmetical procedures outlined below and illustrated in Table 19 for the 30 pairs of English usage

---

[4] A brief discussion and illustration of procedures for computing the Pearson product-moment *r* appear in Appendix A for use by those instructors and those students who wish to employ precise methods of computing this most reliable measure of relationship.

test scores. A work sheet having columns labeled according to the headings
of this table should be prepared in advance.

TABLE 20

Approximate Correlation Coefficients between Two Tests
Based on Percentages of Scores in Upper Half of Both Distributions [5]

Percent	r	Percent	r	Percent	r	Percent	r	Percent	r
45	.95	37	.68	29	.25	21	−.25	13	−.69
44	.93	36	.65	28	.19	20	−.31	12	−.73
43	.91	35	.60	27	.13	19	−.37	11	−.77
42	.88	34	.55	26	.07	18	−.43	10	−.81
41	.85	33	.49	25	.00	17	−.49	9	−.85
40	.81	32	.43	24	−.07	16	−.55	8	−.88
39	.77	31	.37	23	−.13	15	−.60	7	−.91
38	.73	30	.31	22	−.19	14	−.65	6	−.93

(1) *Assign relative ranks separately to the scores in each set.* Rank the scores
in each list from highest to lowest. When two or more identical scores
occur, assign the average value of the ranks they occupy to each of them.

(2) *Obtain the differences between pairs of ranks, disregarding signs.* Carry
all fractional values in the subtractions.

(3) *Square the differences between pairs of ranks.* Carry all fractional values
in the squaring process.

(4) *Obtain the sum of the squared differences between pairs of ranks.* Carry
all fractional values in the additive process.

(5) *Compute* rho. Substitute the sum of the squared differences between pairs
of ranks (ΣD^2) and the number of pairs of scores (N) in the following
formula and compute the *rho* coefficient:

$$rho = 1 - \frac{6 \, \Sigma D^2}{N(N^2 - 1)}$$

5. SIGNIFICANCE OF BASIC PROCEDURES
FOR ANALYZING TEST SCORES

Some of the underlying reasons for classifying and analyzing pupil
scores on tests systematically, and for that matter other types of information about pupils, are mentioned earlier in this chapter. The procedures
outlined above are useful not only for their direct significance in giving
meaning to the results of measurement but also as a foundation for the
interpretations dealt with in Chapter 14. It is important here to supple-

[5] Educational Testing Service, *op. cit.* p. 32.

ment the foregoing presentations of computational procedures by brief treatments of the three basic types of statistical measures: (1) measures of average or central tendency, (2) measures of spread or variability, and (3) measures of relationship.

As a preliminary to this discussion, however, what may on the surface appear to be discrepancies in the two sets of measures obtained in foregoing sections of this chapter warrant a brief explanation. Two sets of measures of central tendency and of variability are distinguished there—one set based on scores in order of rank and the other based on the same scores in a frequency distribution. Two types of correlation coefficients based on paired scores in rank order, one an estimate and the other obtained by computation, are also presented.

When results from application of the different procedures are compared, discrepancies are observable. These discrepancies occur in part as a result of the fact that original scores are used in obtaining some of the measures and that a grouped frequency distribution in which the identities, and even the precise values, of the original scores are lost is used in parallel situations. They result also in part from the use of estimates in some situations and of computations in others. Estimates tend to be less precise than computations and results based on grouped frequency distributions may differ in minor degree from those based on original scores. The differences in results reported previously in this chapter, consequently, do not indicate errors in computation. Furthermore, they are not of sufficient size to be of concern when results are to be used in typical classroom testing situations. For these reasons, it is appropriate for the teacher or prospective teacher to select those of the techniques presented in this chapter and in Appendix A that to him seem most in line with his mathematical backgrounds and his personal desires.

Measures of Average or Central Tendency

The grouping of test scores in frequency tables is the first step in the process of condensing them so that they can be analyzed and interpreted. However, a further step must be taken before it is possible to describe the scores. Some single term or value that is representative of the entire table must be found. Since these values most often occur near the center when the scores are arranged in order of size, they are commonly called measures of central tendency. The two most common measures of this type are the arithmetic mean and the median.

The *arithmetic mean* is the best known and the most widely used measure of central tendency. Practically everyone knows how to find and use the arithmetic mean. It is easily determined by dividing the sum of the scores by the number of pupils tested, but it can also be computed from a frequency distribution by using the procedures outlined above. The arithmetic mean can be described as the point on the scale above which and below which the sums of the deviations of scores are equal. Consequently, it is equally influenced by every score in the distribution.

The *median* and the *mid-score* are quite similar, the main distinction being that the latter is the actual middle score, or the average of the two middle scores, when they are arranged in order of size, whereas the former is the middle point in a frequency distribution of the scores. The median is the point in the distribution above which and below which 50 percent of the test scores lie. In this sense, it indicates the most typical score in the distribution, even though it is not directly influenced by the precise values of the scores definitely lying above or below this middle point in the distribution.

Measures of Spread or Variability

Measures of central tendency, represented by the widely useful arithmetic mean and median, are valuable statistical measures but they describe only one characteristic of the scores—the tendency for them to pile up near the middle of the distribution. Descriptions of test results based wholly on one or the other of these measures are, therefore, incomplete. A second type of measure showing how the scores are spread out above and below the mean or the median is needed if the scores are to be described adequately.

The *standard deviation* has many characteristics that make it a useful measure of variability. It is a sort of arithmetic mean of the squares of the deviations from the mean of the distribution. This measure of variability or dispersion is ordinarily employed as a unit of measurement above and below the mean. In a normal distribution, about two-thirds of the scores lie between a point one standard deviation above the mean and another point a like distance below the mean. All of the scores in a normal distribution typically deviate from the mean by less than three units of standard deviation.

The *quartile deviation* is related to the median in a manner not unlike that mentioned above for the standard deviation and arithmetic mean. This measure of variability, also called the semi-interquartile range, is half of the distance between Q_3 and Q_1, called the quartiles, or between the seventy-fifth and twenty-fifth percentiles. Half of the scores in a normal distribution lie within one quartile deviation of the median and all of the scores typically lie less than four quartile deviations from the median.

Measures of Relationship

In the selection, construction, and use of educational tests and other measuring instruments there are many situations in which a reasonably exact expression of relationship existing between two sets of measures is necessary. The basic procedure, called the method of correlation, is applied when two, or even more than two, measures of the same individuals are employed in determining the degree to which certain tested traits or abilities are related. In practical test construction this method is used in obtaining estimates of the validity, reliability, and objectivity of a test.

The *Pearson product-moment r* is a single numerical index that expresses the extent to which the pairs of corresponding measures of two variables tend to deviate similarly from their respective arithmetic means. The values of *r* may vary all the way from +1.oo, indicating perfect positive relationship, through all of the possible decimals to o.oo, indicating no relationship whatever, to −1.oo, indicating a perfect negative relationship. The Pearson *r* is by far the most common and, on the whole, the basic method used in correlations of educational test results, but it is complicated and difficult to compute because of the large number of different calculations to be made. That explains why it is presented in Appendix A for optional use rather than in a previous section of this chapter and why tetrachoric *r* is discussed as a device for estimating it.

The *Spearman rank-order rho,* however, can be computed for small groups of scores without difficulty. Its meaning is closely similar to, if not strictly comparable to, the meaning attributable to the Pearson *r* as mentioned above.

SUGGESTED ACTIVITIES

1. Obtain the scores made by a class or group of pupils on an informal objective test or a standardized achievement test and analyze the results when they are arranged in order of rank.
2. Obtain scores for the same pupils on an intelligence test or a second achievement test and estimate the Pearson product-moment *r* showing the degree of relationship between the paired scores on the two tests.

SELECTED REFERENCES

ADAMS, GEORGIA S., AND TORGERSON, THEODORE L. *Measurement and Evaluation for the Secondary-School Teacher.* New York: Dryden Press, 1956. Chapter 27.

BLOMMERS, PAUL, AND LINDQUIST, E. F. *Elementary Statistical Methods in Psychology and Education.* Boston: Houghton Mifflin Co., 1960. Chapters 2, 5-6, 13.

FRANZBLAU, ABRAHAM M. *A Primer of Statistics for Non-Statisticians.* New York: Harcourt, Brace, and Co., 1958. Chapters 3-5, 7-8.

GARRETT, HENRY E. *Elementary Statistics.* New York: Longmans, Green and Co., 1956. Chapters 2-4, 8.

GARRETT, HENRY E. *Statistics in Psychology and Education.* Fifth edition. New York: Longmans, Green and Co., 1958. Chapters 1-3, 6.

GREENE, HARRY A., JORGENSEN, ALBERT N., AND GERBERICH, J. RAYMOND. *Measurement and Evaluation in the Elementary School.* Second edition. New York: Longmans, Green and Co., 1953. Chapters 12, 14.

GREENE, HARRY A., JORGENSEN, ALBERT N., AND GERBERICH, J. RAYMOND. *Measurement and Evaluation in the Secondary School.* Second edition. New York: Longmans, Green and Co., 1954. Chapters 12, 14.

NOLL, VICTOR H. *Introduction to Educational Measurement.* Boston: Houghton Mifflin Co., 1957. Chapter 3, Appendix A.

TATE, MERLE W. *Statistics in Education.* New York: Macmillan Co., 1955. Chapters 2-4, 6.

TORGERSON, THEODORE L., AND ADAMS, GEORGIA S. *Measurement and Evaluation for the Elementary-School Teacher.* New York: Dryden Press, Inc., 1954. Chapter 19.

UNDERWOOD, BENTON J., AND OTHERS. *Elementary Statistics.* New York: Appleton-Century-Crofts, Inc., 1954. Chapters 2, 5-6, 10.

WALKER, HELEN M., AND LEV, JOSEPH. *Elementary Statistical Methods.* Revised edition. New York: Henry Holt and Co., 1958. Chapters 5, 7-8, 10.

14

INTERPRETING RESULTS

OF MEASUREMENT AND EVALUATION

This chapter gives consideration to the following points concerning the interpretation of results from measurement and evaluation:

A. Uses of statistics in describing tests and test scores.
B. Reliability and validity of tests.
C. Reliability of test scores.
D. Interpretation of test scores by rank-order methods.
E. Interpretation of test scores as deviations from an average.
F. Letter marks in expressing test results.
G. Composite measures of achievement.

The major techniques used in summarizing and analyzing sets of test scores are presented in Chapter 13. Various techniques and devices for attributing additional meaning to scores and distributions of scores are necessary, however, if optimum use of such results is to be attained. This chapter deals with the basic procedures and devices used in giving readily understandable meaning to the results of measurement and evaluation.

1. INTERPRETATION OF TESTS AND TEST SCORES

Statistical methods ranging from very simple to quite complex can be used in describing tests and in giving meaning to the scores pupils attain on tests. Only the simpler techniques that have their greatest values for use in classroom testing are treated in detail here. Readers who may be concerned with the more elaborate and technical procedures used by makers of standardized achievement tests can find treatments of them in some of the references listed at the end of this chapter.

Characteristics of Tests

A number of characteristics or criteria of a good examination are discussed at some length in Chapter 3. Statistical procedures can be used with several of these criteria, as is briefly noted in that chapter, to indicate the degree to which a test meets desired standards of quality. The two most important of these criteria, validity and reliability, are the ones for which statistical evidence is most widely useful. It is possible also to demonstrate the objectivity of a test by statistical means, but it is seldom necessary to prove by statistics that an objective test is indeed objective.

Reliability of tests. Several types of reliability coefficients, or correlation coefficients used for the special purpose of determining test reliability, are distinguished in Chapter 3. Mention is also made there of reliability coefficients reported for several standardized achievement tests. The three types set apart there are coefficients of (1) equivalence, (2) stability, and (3) internal consistency. The first two types are tools of the standardized test maker much more than of the teacher who uses objective tests in his classes. Consequently, only the two types of coefficients of internal consistency have much significance for use with teacher-made tests.

Validity of tests. Several types of validity coefficients, again special varieties of correlation coefficients, are useful in determining how well tests fulfill the purpose for which they are employed. These are outlined in Chapter 3 as coefficients of (1) concurrent validity, (2) predictive validity, and (3) construct validity. Since the values of the third are restricted mainly to formal as contrasted with informal or classroom tests, only the coefficients of concurrent and predictive validity are accorded direct attention in this chapter. However, predictive validity is also dealt with by the use of expectancy tables.

Meaning of Test Scores

Test scores are valuable to the classroom teacher to the extent that they can be interpreted. It is therefore important to know clearly what is meant by a test score. Simply stated, a test score is a numerical expression of performance on the part of an individual. Sometimes the score is merely the number of test items answered correctly. However, it can take a variety of other forms. But whatever its form, its function is to reveal in a quantitative way the performance of an individual as he responds to stimuli given under certain conditions.

One type of test result teachers typically encounter is represented by scores on standardized achievement tests. These scores can nearly always be interpreted in meaningful terms by using the norms and derived scores commonly provided with such tests. The age norms, grade norms, percentile norms, and standard-score norms most widely provided with standardized achievement tests are discussed at length and illustrated in Chapter 8.

Classroom teachers undoubtedly encounter results from informal teacher-made tests much more often, however. The results from these classroom tests are in turn of two types—the subjective scores assigned by teachers to pupils' responses to essay tests and scores resulting from informal objective examinations. While something can be done to improve the interpretation of the relatively unreliable marks assigned to the discussion-type exercise, much more is possible in the accurate interpretation of scores resulting from the use of objective examinations. There are no ready-made devices for giving meaning to classroom test results, despite the belief of some teachers that percentage scores can adequately serve this purpose. Meaning can be attributed to classroom testing results through the use of certain types of derived scores and even letter marks.

2. RELIABILITY OF TESTS

Classroom teachers may need on occasion to interpret the reliability coefficients reported by the authors and publishers of standardized tests, but they have direct responsibility for making sure that their own tests have adequate levels of reliability. They can do so either by estimating or by computing reliability coefficients of the internal consistency type. Internal consistency types of coefficients are based on the results of only one test, in contrast with the other varieties of coefficients that depend on two forms of a test or on two administrations of the same test to the same pupils, and are therefore suitable for use by teachers in evaluating their classroom tests.

Estimating Footrule Reliability

One method of estimating the reliability of a test by an adaptation of the Kuder-Richardson Footrule Formula 21 is provided in Table 21. Only three items of information are needed for using this table: (1) the arithmetic mean, (2) the standard deviation, and (3) the number of test items. An arithmetic mean of 29.03 and a standard deviation of 8.47 are shown in Table 13 of Chapter 13 for the scores on a 55-item informal objective test of English usage attained by 30 ninth-grade pupils. To estimate the reliability coefficient of the test by the use of Table 21, it is necessary to divide both the arithmetic mean and the standard deviation by the number of test items. These computations are:

Arithmetic mean ÷ Number of items = 29.03 ÷ 55 = .53
Standard deviation ÷ Number of items = 8.47 ÷ 55 = .15

The results show that the arithmetic mean is 53 percent of *n* and that the standard deviation is 15 percent of *n*. The desired estimate of the reliability coefficient is therefore found in the right-hand portion of the table in the column headed .15*n* and opposite an *n* of 55 in the left-hand column. By interpolating between 50 and 60 for values of *n*, an estimated reliability coefficient of .82 is obtained for the test.

TABLE 21

Approximate Reliability Coefficients of Tests Based on
Arithmetic Mean, Standard Deviation, and Number of Items [1]

Number of Items (*n*)	*When Arithmetic Mean of Scores Is*					
	70 to 90 Percent of n and When Standard Deviation Is			*50 to 70 Percent of n and When Standard Deviation Is*		
	.10*n*	.15*n*	.20*n*	.10*n*	.15*n*	.20*n*
20	.21	.68	.84	—	.49	.74
30	.48	.80	.90	.21	.67	.83
40	.62	.84	.92	.41	.75	.87
50	.69	.88	.94	.53	.80	.90
60	.75	.90	.95	.61	.84	.92
70	.78	.91	.96	.66	.86	.93
80	.81	.92	.96	.71	.88	.94
90	.83	.93	.97	.74	.89	.94
100	.85	.94	.97	.77	.90	.95

Estimating Chance-Half Reliability

This is a second method of estimating the reliability coefficient from the results of the administration of a single test to a pupil group. For this method the first step of procedure is to obtain two "half-scores" for each pupil on arbitrary halves of the test. The arbitrary halves of the test frequently consist of the odd-numbered and the even-numbered items. The second step is to obtain the coefficient of correlation between the sets of "half-scores" for the group of pupils. This coefficient represents the reliability of one-half of the test, but not of the entire test.

[1]Adapted from Educational Testing Service, *Short-Cut Statistics for Teacher-Made Tests.* Evaluation and Advisory Service Series, No. 5. Educational Testing Service, Princeton, N. J., 1960. p. 29.

The third and final step requires the use of the *Spearman-Brown Prophecy Formula* in estimating the reliability for the entire test by what is known as "stepping up" the correlation. A test increases in reliability as it is increased in length by additional test items comparable to those in the initial test; thus, the estimated reliability for the entire test is greater than for only half of the test. However, the increase in the coefficient is not directly proportional to the increase in test length. The Spearman-Brown formula is

$$r_{12} = \frac{2r_{\frac{1}{2}\frac{1}{2}}}{1 + r_{\frac{1}{2}\frac{1}{2}}},$$

where $r_{\frac{1}{2}\frac{1}{2}}$ is the correlation between scores on the "chance-halves" of the test and r_{12} is the estimated reliability coefficient for the entire test.

TABLE 22

Chance-Half and Total Scores of Pupils in a Ninth-Grade Class on an Informal Objective Test of English Usage

Pupil	Test Scores			Pupil	Test Scores		
	ODD	EVEN	TOTAL		ODD	EVEN	TOTAL
CEL	25	24	49	WBC	14	15	29
HWC	21	22	43	JHB	16	12	28
WI	18	22	40	JM	14	14	28
DCP	19	20	39	JMS	13	15	28
LJA	20	17	37	LFD	13	14	27
NLW	19	17	36	JWK	12	15	27
CAW	17	17	34	DB	12	13	25
RBS	15	18	33	REJ	11	14	25
HGH	17	15	32	GLF	13	11	24
VWW	16	16	32	RWY	11	11	22
WTG	14	17	31	ASN	9	12	21
LDM	18	13	31	INT	10	9	19
WRC	16	14	30	FOF	8	8	16
CAK	15	15	30	RHP	8	6	14
ABS	12	18	30	GBS	5	6	11

$$\text{Arithmetic Mean}_{\text{Odd}} = \frac{431}{30} = 14.37$$

$$\text{Arithmetic Mean}_{\text{Even}} = \frac{440}{30} = 14.67$$

Table 22 gives the scores made by the 30 ninth-grade pupils on the odd-numbered and even-numbered items of the English usage test used in several foregoing illustrations. The correlation between these "odd" and "even" scores can be estimated by the use of Table 20 of Chapter 13 and the accompanying discussion of how to use it. The arithmetic means of the "odd" and "even" scores are shown in Table 22 to be 14.37 and 14.67 respectively. Eleven of the 30 pupils are found by inspection to have *both* scores of 15 or above, i.e., above the arithmetic means. When 11 is divided by 30, or the total number of pupils, it is found that 37 percent of the pupils have *both* scores in the upper halves of their distributions. A Pearson product-moment *r* can easily be obtained as an estimate of the correlation between the "chance-halves" of the test by entering Table 20 on page 317 with this value of 37 percent. This *r* is found to be .68.

It is now possible to estimate the reliability coefficient for the entire 55-item test by applying the *Spearman-Brown Prophecy Formula*. Substituting .68 for the $r_{\frac{1}{2}\frac{1}{2}}$ of the formula given above,

$$r_{12} = \frac{2 \times .68}{1 + .68} = \frac{1.36}{1.68} = .81.$$

A reliability coefficient obtained by this process, involving as it does one estimate pyramided upon another, cannot be expected to give highly accurate results. However, this procedure combines a desirable degree of simplicity with a sufficiently high degree of reliability to make it appropriate for use by classroom teachers in checking on their own informal objective tests.

3. VALIDITY OF TESTS

Teachers often base the validity of their classroom tests largely on careful planning of content to be included and of learning outcomes to be measured. This type of content validity is not mentioned in the introductory section of this chapter because it cannot be demonstrated by the use of statistical techniques. However, teachers can obtain evidence by simple statistical procedures about the concurrent validity and even on occasion the predictive validity of their tests.

Estimating Concurrent Validity

An achievement test can sometimes be checked for validity by correlating scores on it with scores attained by the same pupils on a second test that is judged to be similar in purpose. To the extent that the informal objective and standardized tests of English usage dealt with in Chapter 13 can be compared in this manner, the correlation coefficients obtained between the sets of scores by two different methods can be accepted as coefficients of concurrent validity. It is shown in Table 19 on page 315 and the accompanying brief discussion that an estimated tetrachoric *r* and a computed Spearman rank-order *rho* between these sets of scores are respectively .81 and .84. These values can be accepted as evidence that the informal objective test has a quite high level of validity for measuring English usage of ninth-grade pupils because of the close agreement of scores on it and on the standardized test accepted as the criterion of quality.

Estimating Predictive Validity

When scores on an achievement test are related to some future outcome after a lapse of time, the result is a measure of the predictive validity of the test. Table 23 presents two kinds of evidence about the same 30 ninth-grade pupils that can be interpreted in this way—scores on the informal objective test of English usage previously reported and ratings on the essays written some months later in a local essay contest and rated by a panel of three English teachers. These scores and ratings can be related in two ways to show how well the test scores predicted the ratings assigned to the essays later in the school year.

TABLE 23

Standing of Pupils in a Ninth-Grade Class on an Informal
Objective Test of English Usage and an English Essay

Pupil	Test Score	Essay Rating *	Pupil	Test Score	Essay Rating *	Pupil	Test Score	Essay Rating *
CEL	49	G	WTG	31	F	JWK	27	F
HWC	43	E	LDM	31	G	DB	25	F
WI	40	G	WRC	30	G	REJ	25	F
DCP	39	G	CAK	30	F	GLF	24	P
LJA	37	G	ABS	30	F	RWY	22	F
NLW	36	G	WBC	29	G	ASN	21	F
CAW	34	F	JHB	28	E	INT	19	P
RBS	33	E	JM	28	G	FOF	16	G
HGH	32	G	JMS	28	F	RHP	14	F
VWW	32	G	LFD	27	G	GBS	11	P

* E = excellent; G = good; F = fair; P =poor.

Coefficient of predictive validity. It can be determined by inspection that 11 of the pupils whose test scores and essay ratings are shown in Table 23 have scores above the previously reported arithmetic mean of 29.03 and ratings of excellent or good. Although slightly more than half of the pupils, 16 out of 30, have these ratings, their acceptance as the upper half of the group in essay writing proficiency seems to be justifiable in approximating the correlation between scores and ratings by the use of Table 20 on page 317. Eleven is 37 percent of 30, and the table gives a Pearson product-moment r of .68 as an estimate of the degree of relationship between scores and ratings. The correlation of predictive validity can, therefore, be estimated as .68.

Constructing a probability table. It is a simple matter to construct a probability or expectancy table [2] to show the relationship between a set of test scores and a second and subsequently obtained measure of a related type of proficiency for the same pupils. An illustration appears in Table 24, where the test scores and theme ratings discussed immediately above are presented in a two-way chart similar to the "scatter diagram" of a correlation table. The test scores are grouped in four categories rather than in the greater number used previously because of the need here for a small number of cells for ease of interpreting expectancies when the number of cases is small.

The table presents results both in numbers, which are primarily means to an end, and in percentages. The probability aspect of the right half of the table can be illustrated by the broad generalizations, for example, that a pupil having a test score of 40 or above has a 33 percent chance of attaining a top rating on the theme but that a second pupil in the score range of 20 to 29 has only a 9 percent chance of doing likewise. This type of probability or expectancy statement on the one hand attests to the predictive validity of the test and on the other hand affords a basis for predicting similarly obtained theme ratings from scores on the same test for a new group of pupils on a later occasion. This predictive use is more reliable when larger numbers of pupils than the 30 of this illustration are used in constructing the expectancy table.

TABLE 24

Expectancy of Various Essay Ratings for Ninth-Grade Pupils as Predicted by Scores on an Informal Objective Test of English Usage

Essays Ratings in Numbers					Test Scores	Essay Ratings in Percentages				
TOTAL	POOR	FAIR	GOOD	EXCEL-LENT		POOR	FAIR	GOOD	EXCEL-LENT	TOTAL
3			2	1	40-49			67	33	100
12		4	7	1	30-39		33	59	8	100
11	1	6	3	1	20-29	9	55	27	9	100
4	2	1	1		10-19	50	25	25		100
30	3	11	13	3						

[2] Alexander G. Wesman, *Expectancy Tables—A Way of Interpreting Test Validity.* Test Service Bulletin, No. 38. Psychological Corporation, New York, December 1949.

4. RELIABILITY OF TEST SCORES

The fact that test scores are not absolutely accurate representations of pupil ability but rather are unreliable to some degree is brought out in Figure 11 on page 188 and the accompanying discussion. One of the percentile bands illustrated and described at that point in this volume represents the limits within which a pupil's "true" score, or the errorless score his obtained score is taken to approximate, is likely to fall. The reliability of test scores is here considered in its statistical aspects in order to aid teachers in this appropriate interpretation of pupil scores on classroom tests. Simple procedures rather than complex statistical computations are adequate for this purpose, however.

Estimating the Standard Error of a Score, or of Measurement

The standard error of a test score, or standard error of measurement, indicates the level of confidence that can justifiably be placed in an obtained score. As is pointed out in the section of Chapter 3 devoted to the reliability of tests, this measure is based on the reliability coefficient of a test but it supplies a more constant and invariable measure of consistency than does a reliability coefficient itself. It is also brought out in Chapter 3 that short tests tend to be lower in reliability than long tests. The reason is found in the fact that long tests sample the performances of pupils more widely, and hence more adequately and reliably, than do short tests.

In a statistical study, Lord found a strong tendency for tests of the same length to have the same standard error of measurement.[3] Diederich, referring to Lord's findings, stated that in general the standard error of measurement for a teacher-made test of up to 50 items is about three and the same measure of score reliability for a classroom test of around 100 items is likely to be about five. His estimates for tests of different lengths indicate that the standard error of a score is usually, in raw-score points, about—

2 on tests of less than 24 items,
3 on tests of 24 to 47 items,
4 on tests of 48 to 89 items,
5 on tests of 90 to 109 items,
6 on tests of 110 to 129 items, and
7 on tests of 130 to 150 items.[4]

[3] Frederic M. Lord, "Tests of the Same Length Do Have the Same Standard Error of Measurement." *Educational and Psychological Measurement,* 19:233-39; Summer 1959.
[4] Educational Testing Service, *op. cit.* p. 14.

If the standard error of a score is estimated by use of this list for the 55-item informal objective test of English usage, a value of 4 is obtained. If the same measure is computed by use of the appropriate statistical formula, employing the standard deviation and reliability coefficient computed for this set of 30 scores in Chapter 13 and a foregoing section of this chapter, the result is:

$$\text{Standard Error}_{\text{score}} = \text{Standard deviation} \sqrt{1 - \text{Reliability coefficient}}$$
$$= 8.01 \sqrt{1 - .81}$$
$$= 8.01 \sqrt{.19}$$
$$= 8.01 \times .44$$
$$= 3.52 \text{ or } 3.5$$

A comparison of the 3.5 of the computed value and the 4 of the estimated value shows a minor rather than a major difference. For highly precise work, the computational procedure is preferable to an estimate, but for ordinary classroom testing needs an estimate of the type obtained here is doubtless sufficiently accurate.

When the principle of the "bands" referred to previously in this section of the chapter is applied, as in the *Sequential Tests of Educational Progress,* one standard error of a score is measured off above and below an obtained score to find the points between which the chances are two out of three that the corresponding "true" score lies.[5] For example, when four score units are measured upward and downward from LJA's obtained score of 37, as shown in Table 23, the resulting 33 and 41 are the points between which the chances are two out of three that his "true" score lies.

Determining When Scores Are Really Different

Unless two scores on the same test differ by at least two standard errors of a score, it is not safe to conclude for typical classroom measurement purposes that they really differ in the pupil standings they represent.[6] For example, the scores of LJA ($37 \pm 4 = 33$ and 41) and of WBC ($29 \pm 4 = 24$ and 33) in Table 23 differ by eight score points or by two standard errors of a score, so that the lower limit of the "band" for LJA is the upper limit of WBC's "band." Although a more precise but more complicated measure called the standard error of a difference can be applied to this type of situation, it seems justifiable to use the simpler procedure of accepting twice the amount of the standard error of a score as representing a real difference between two scores for ordinary classroom uses.

[5] *Ibid.* p. 14.
[6] *Ibid.* p. 15.

5. INTERPRETATION OF TEST SCORES AS RANKS

There is frequent need, as is pointed out in the first section of this chapter, for giving meaning to test scores that in themselves have no inherent meaning. At least two methods of doing so involve the arrangement of scores in order of rank from high to low. One of these methods, illustrated in Table 19 of Chapter 13 but not discussed in detail at that point, involves the assignment of relative ranks. The other and more formal method, discussed in its application to standardized tests in Chapter 8, involves the assignment of percentile ranks. These two procedures are outlined below for the same English usage test scores of 30 ninth-grade pupils as are used in several preceding illustrations.

Assigning Relative Ranks

The scores of the 30 ninth-grade pupils are listed in Table 25 in descending order of size. As is shown in the *Relative Rank* column of the table, the first eight scores are ranked in descending order from 1 to 8. The next two scores are identical and hence must share the rank positions 9 and 10. Both scores are assigned a rank of 9.5, or the average of the two ranks $[(9 + 10) \div 2]$. The next two scores, also identical, must share the next two ranks. Consequently, each is assigned a rank of 11.5 $[(11 + 12) \div 2]$. Where three identical scores occur, as for 30 and 28, the same principle

TABLE 25

Interpretation of English Usage Test Scores of Ninth-Grade Pupils in Terms of Rank Order

Pupil	Test Score	Relative Rank	Rank Percentile	Pupil	Test Score	Relative Rank	Percentile Rank
CEL	49	1	99	WBC	29	16	50
HWC	43	2	96	JHB	28	18	44
WI	40	3	92	JM	28	18	44
DCP	39	4	90	JMS	28	18	44
LJA	37	5	86	LFD	27	20.5	39
NLW	36	6	84	JWK	27	20.5	39
CAW	34	7	78	DB	25	22.5	28
RBS	33	8	74	REJ	25	22.5	28
HGH	32	9.5	70	GLF	24	24	25
VWW	32	9.5	70	RWY	22	25	19
WTG	31	11.5	64	ASN	21	26	17
LDM	31	11.5	64	INT	19	27	13
WRC	30	14	58	FOF	16	28	9
CAK	30	14	58	RHP	14	29	4
ABS	30	14	58	GBS	11	30	1

applies. The first three are ranked 14 [(13 + 14 + 15) ÷ 3] and 18, which is the average of 17, 18, and 19.

The usefulness of this method is somewhat limited by the fact that it takes no account of the actual level at which the accomplishment takes place. A person ranking 28 in this group of 30 has a very low relative rank. However, if he ranked 28 in a group of 250, the significance of his accomplishment would be greatly changed.

Estimating Percentile Ranks

Percentile ranks, however, take the limitation noted above into account by reducing the ranking to a basis of 100 units. Similarly, decile ranks and quartile ranks accomplish the same purpose by reducing the number of separate groups to ten and four respectively.

Of the several available methods for obtaining percentile ranks, the one chosen for use here has the advantage of requiring very little computation.[7] The percentile ranks resulting from the application of this graphical method are sufficiently accurate to fulfill most classroom needs, however. Table 26 reproduces the same 30 English usage test scores used previously in a grouped frequency distribution similar to that of Table 17 in Chapter 13. Here, however, the table is extended by adding two columns for cumulative frequencies and for cumulative relative frequencies. In the first of these two new columns, the frequencies are added successively from bottom to top in such manner that each cumulative frequency represents the number of scores in and below the class interval to which it applies. The last column gives the results when the cumulative frequencies are divided by 30 to put them into percentages, or what are called relative frequencies.

Figure 23 shows a percentile curve for these same 30 scores. The horizontal lines represent the real limits separating adjacent class intervals and the numerical values at the left indicate midpoints of class intervals. When the percentages in the last column of Table 26 are spotted successively from bottom to top at the points representing upper real limits of class intervals and when the successive points are joined by straight lines, the result is a percentile curve that can be used directly in estimating the percentile ranks corresponding to the 30 original scores.

If the percentile rank equivalent of a score is desired and if a filing card or piece of paper with a square corner is used as a guide: (1) the guide

[7] A relatively simple computational procedure for developing local percentile norms adapted to use with 200 or more pupils in the same school group is described for the *STEP* tests in accompanying manuals, e.g., Educational Testing Service, *Sequential Tests of Educational Progress: Manual for Interpreting Scores—Reading.* Educational Testing Service, Princeton, N. J., 1957. p. 19-22.

TABLE 26

Cumulative Frequency Distribution of English Usage
Test Scores of Ninth-Grade Pupils

Integral Limits	Real Limits	Frequency (f)	Cumulative Frequency	Cumulative Relative Frequency
47-49	46.5-49.5	1	30	100
44-46	43.5-46.5	0	29	97
41-43	40.5-43.5	1	29	97
38-40	37.5-40.5	2	28	93
35-37	34.5-37.5	2	26	87
32-34	31.5-34.5	4	24	80
29-31	28.5-31.5	6	20	67
26-28	25.5-28.5	5	14	47
23-25	22.5-25.5	3	9	30
20-22	19.5-22.5	2	6	20
17-19	16.5-19.5	1	4	13
14-16	13.5-16.5	2	3	10
11-13	10.5-13.5	1	1	3

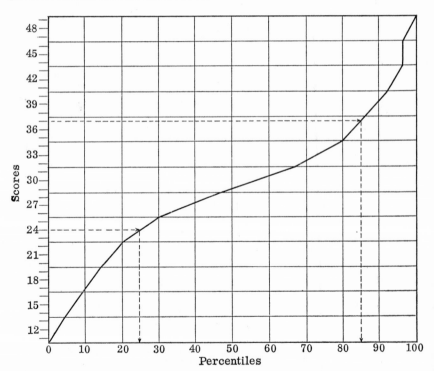

FIGURE 23. Percentile Curve for English Usage
Test Scores of Ninth-Grade Pupils

is placed at the specified point on the left-hand scale in a horizontal position, (2) the edge of the guide is followed to the point of intersection with the curve, (3) the end of the guide, properly positioned, is followed downward to the base line, and (4) the desired value is read from the percentile scale. For example, a score of 24 is shown by one set of dotted lines to be equivalent to a percentile rank of 25 and a percentile rank of 86 is shown by another set of dotted lines to correspond to a test score of 37. Any of the other percentile ranks estimated by this procedure in Table 25 can easily be checked by the same simple procedure.

6. INTERPRETATION OF TEST SCORES
AS DEVIATIONS FROM AN AVERAGE

Scores from teacher-made tests can be given comparability of meaning by a second set of procedures to supplement the rank-order methods outlined immediately above. These involve, as is indicated early in this chapter, consideration of the manner in which scores deviate from a measure of average. The measures used are frequently, although not of necessity, the standard deviation and the arithmetic mean. The three procedures involving this principle are discussed here for the 30 English usage test scores of ninth-grade pupils frequently used in the foregoing pages.

Assigning Letter Marks

Teachers often need to assign letter marks of the familiar A, B, C, D, F or some similar variety to pupils in their classes for use on report cards and in cumulative records. Consequently, they should be prepared to convert scores on their informal objective tests to the same types of letter marks. Although several methods of accomplishing this result are widely used, the most defensible seems to be the one based on the arithmetic mean and standard deviation of a set of scores.

Assigning marks to test scores. In Table 13 and the accompanying context, an arithmetic mean of 29.03 and a standard deviation of 8.47 are shown for the scores on an informal objective test of English usage made by 30 ninth-grade pupils. It is possible to establish comparability of meaning for scores on various tests by using these two basic measures of central tendency and variability in the manner outlined here.

After the mean and standard deviation have been obtained, the steps of procedure are to (1) obtain by multiplication and then by addition or subtraction four points that are 0.5 and 1.5 units of standard deviation above and 0.5 and 1.5 units of standard deviation below the arithmetic mean and (2) assign marks of C to scores between +0.5 and −0.5 standard deviations, marks of B and D respectively to scores between +0.5 and +1.5 and scores between −0.5 and −1.5 standard deviations, and marks of A and F respectively to scores more than +1.5 and scores more than −1.5 standard deviations from the arithmetic mean. When the steps are applied to the values given above for the 30 English usage test scores, the results are as follows:

$$29.03 + (0.5 \times 8.47) = 29.03 + 4.24 = 33.27,$$
$$29.03 - (0.5 \times 8.47) = 29.03 - 4.24 = 24.79,$$
$$29.03 + (1.5 \times 8.47) = 29.03 + 12.71 = 41.74, \text{ and}$$
$$29.03 - (1.5 \times 8.47) = 29.03 - 12.71 = 16.32.$$

These values when arranged in descending order indicate the following as score limits for the letter marks:

A   Above 41.74   or 42 and above,
B   Between 33.27 and 41.74   or 34 to 41,
C   Between 24.79 and 33.27   or 25 to 33,
D   Between 16.32 and 24.79   or 17 to 24, and
F   Below 16.32   or 16 and below.

The letter marks assigned by this method to the 30 ninth-grade pupils on the English usage test are shown in Table 27 in parallel with the test scores on which they are based.

TABLE 27

Interpretation of English Usage Test Scores of
Ninth-Grade Pupils in Terms of Deviation from an Average

Pupil	Test Score	Letter Mark	Standard Score	Stanine	Pupil	Test Score	Letter Mark	Standard Score	Stanine
CEL	49	A	74	9	WBC	29	C	50	5
HWC	43	A	67	8	JHB	28	C	49	5
WI	40	B	63	8	JM	28	C	49	5
DCP	39	B	62	7	JMS	28	C	49	5
LJA	37	B	59	7	LFD	27	C	48	4
NLW	36	B	58	7	JWK	27	C	48	4
CAW	34	B	56	7	DB	25	C	45	4
RBS	33	C	55	6	REJ	25	C	45	4
HGH	32	C	54	6	GLF	24	D	44	3
VWW	32	C	54	6	RWY	22	D	42	3
WTG	31	C	52	6	ASN	21	D	41	3
LDM	31	C	52	6	INT	19	D	38	3
WRC	30	C	51	5	FOF	16	F	35	2
CAK	30	C	51	5	RHP	14	F	32	2
ABS	30	C	51	5	GBS	11	F	29	1

It is readily apparent that practically no subjective factors are involved in the assignment of marks by this method. The score limits are determined by the standard deviation units and would be the same no matter who assigned the marks. This method of marking does not, however, take into account the absolute level of ability at which a particular class works. The superior pupil in an average or poor class receives an A by this method just as readily as does the superior pupil in a very superior class. This is probably less serious than it sounds, however, for most class groups large enough to warrant the application of this technique average out quite well in this respect.

Assigning course marks. Final marks summarizing test scores, and even including subjective marks such as those on themes, term papers, and notebooks, can be obtained quite readily for a marking period, semester, or school year. One of the best and simplest procedures involves the use of A, B, C, D, and F marks for stating results from each factor that is to receive consideration in determining the final marks. For valid and quite reliable measures, such as scores on carefully constructed objective tests, plus and minus marks in each letter category can be applied by a simple extension of the method outlined immediately above. For example, high C marks are rated C+, low C marks are assigned C−, and the intervening marks are designated as C. For less reliable ratings, such as marks on themes and term papers, the five-point scale consisting of A, B, C, D, and F is doubtless preferable.

It is possible not only to use more discrimination in weighting highly reliable and valid scores than is used for more subjective measures, as is illustrated above, but also to weight the various factors entering into the determination of final marks according to their estimated importance. This is accomplished by using a weighting of 1 for least significant results, a weighting of 2 for results of intermediate importance, and a weighting of 3 for measures judged to be most important. Higher weights can easily be obtained if desired by an extension of Table 28.

A simple illustration employing only three measures will suffice for showing how this method is applied. If a certain pupil has a B− on a mid-semester test, a C on his term paper, and a final examination mark of C+, and if the three measures are to be weighted 2, 1, and 3 respectively, his mid-semester test weighting is 20, his term paper weighting is 7, and his final examination weighting is 24. The sum of 20, 7, and 24, or 51, is his weighted composite score for total performance. When similar composites are obtained for the other pupils in the class, a distribution of the weighted composite scores can be made. It is then possible to assign final course marks by use of the method outlined above or by some modification of it. However, since no marking system should be rigidly defined, departures from any system of attaining objectivity should be made when conditions warrant.

TABLE 28

Suggested Weightings for Marks in Obtaining Composite Scores

Mark	Weighting of		
	1	2	3
A+	16	32	48
A	15	30	45
A−	14	28	42
B+	12	24	36
B	11	22	33
B−	10	20	30
C+	8	16	24
C	7	14	21
C−	6	12	18
D+	4	8	12
D	3	6	9
D−	2	4	6
F	0	0	0

Computing Standard Scores

Standard scores are at the same time among the more meaningful and among the computationally more difficult types of derived scores that can be used in interpreting test scores. They are widely used with standardized achievement tests, but letter marks and stanines are doubtless acceptable substitutes for the classroom teacher in giving meaning to informal objective test scores. Procedures involved in computing standard scores are outlined below, however, for use by any teachers who prefer them to more easily computed derived scores. The formula is:

$$\text{Standard Score} = 50 + \frac{10(\text{Score} - \text{Arithmetic mean})}{\text{Standard deviation}}$$

Using the arithmetic mean of 29.03 and the standard deviation of 8.47 originally shown in Table 13 of Chapter 13 for the 30 English usage test scores of ninth-grade pupils once again for purposes of illustration, the standard-score equivalents for representative test scores of 49, 29, and 25 are, respectively:

$$50 + \frac{10(49.00 - 29.03)}{8.47} = 50 + \frac{199.70}{8.47} = 50 + 23.6 = 50 + 24 = 74$$

$$50 + \frac{10(29.00 - 29.03)}{8.47} = 50 - \frac{0.30}{8.47} = 50 - 0.00 = 50 - 0 = 50$$

$$50 + \frac{10(25.00 - 29.03)}{8.47} = 50 - \frac{40.30}{8.47} = 50 - 4.8 = 50 - 5 = 45$$

These three standards scores and their equivalents for all other original scores in the series are given in Table 27.

Assigning Stanine Scores

A system of derived scores that is similar in some respects to the standard scores discussed immediately above but that can be put into practice with a minimum of difficulty is the one involving stanines. The word itself was coined as recently as World War II to represent a STAndard NINE-point scale. Although stanines can be obtained computationally, they can also be derived by a simple counting procedure after the number of scores to be allocated to each of the nine divisions has been determined. Stanines are less exact than are the standard scores previously discussed, but they are sufficiently precise for the majority of classroom uses. They distinguish nearly the same number of levels of achievement as do the deciles commented upon previously.

The percentages of scores that are expected to be classified in the nine stanines numbered from 9 to 1 and the approximate number of scores that should go into each stanine for groups of different sizes are shown in Table 29. For the 30 English usage test scores of ninth-grade pupils, it can easily be determined that the number of scores in the stanines from 1 to 9 should be approximately 1, 2, 4, 5, 6, 5, 4, 2, and 1. Working both upward and downward from the mid-score in a rank-order list, in this case 29.5, scores are allotted to the stanines in as close approximation to the numbers given above as is possible. Identical scores should always be assigned the same stanine ranks, of course. The stanines allotted to the 30 English usage test scores are shown in parallel with those scores in Table 28. It can readily be determined that the number of scores assigned to stanines in descending order from 9 to 1 are 1, 2, 4, 5, 7, 4, 4, 2, and 1. Only in two instances, for stanines 5 and 4, and then because of two identical scores, do these numbers differ from the list taken from the table.

7. SIGNIFICANCE OF BASIC PROCEDURES
   FOR INTERPRETING TEST SCORES

Educational tests are fallible instruments by the use of which fallible scores are obtained. Moreover, test scores must be interpreted in some meaningful manner before they can be used in educationally constructive ways. These statements are more significant for teacher-made than for standardized achievement tests and for achievement than for intelligence or personality tests. It is necessary for the teacher to provide means for demonstrating the quality of his own informal objective tests and for inter-

Measurement and Evaluation in the Modern School

preting the resulting scores, at least to his own satisfaction, but the user of standardized tests of all three major types usually finds that the authors and publishers have largely fulfilled these needs in advance as part of the standardization process. The three major types of statistical procedures often needed by classroom teachers in accomplishing these purposes are (1) measures of test reliability and validity, (2) measures of reliability

TABLE 29

Number of Scores in Each Stanine of a
Normalized Standard-Score Scale [8]

Number of Cases	Stanines								
	1 (4%)	2 (7%)	3 (12%)	4 (17%)	5 (20%)	6 (17%)	7 (12%)	8 (7%)	9 (4%)
20	1	1	2	4	4	4	2	1	1
21	1	1	2	4	5	4	2	1	1
22	1	2	2	4	4	4	2	2	1
23	1	2	2	4	5	4	2	2	1
24	1	2	3	4	4	4	3	2	1
25	1	2	3	4	5	4	3	2	1
26	1	2	3	4	6	4	3	2	1
27	1	2	3	5	5	5	3	2	1
28	1	2	3	5	6	5	3	2	1
29	1	2	4	5	5	5	4	2	1
30	1	2	4	5	6	5	4	2	1
31	1	2	4	5	7	5	4	2	1
32	1	2	4	6	6	6	4	2	1
33	1	2	4	6	7	6	4	2	1
34	1	3	4	6	6	6	4	3	1
35	1	3	4	6	7	6	4	3	1
36	1	3	4	6	8	6	4	3	1
37	2	3	4	6	7	6	4	3	2
38	1	3	5	6	8	6	5	3	1
39	1	3	5	7	7	7	5	3	1
40	1	3	5	7	8	7	5	3	1
41	1	3	5	7	9	7	5	3	1
42	2	3	5	7	8	7	5	3	2
43	2	3	5	7	9	7	5	3	2
44	2	3	5	8	8	8	5	3	2
45	2	3	5	8	9	8	5	3	2
46	2	3	5	8	10	8	5	3	2
47	2	3	6	8	9	8	6	3	2
48	2	3	6	8	10	8	6	3	2
49	2	4	6	8	9	8	6	4	2

[8] Adapted from Walter N. Durost, *The Characteristics, Use, and Computation of Stanines.* Test Service Notebook, No. 23. Division of Test Research and Service. Copyright 1959 by Harcourt, Brace and World, Inc., New York. All rights reserved. Quoted by special permission.

of test scores, and (3) derived measures for interpreting individual test scores.

Two sets of paralleling values are sometimes shown in the preceding sections of this chapter. One set is usually obtained by a method of estimation or very simple computation and the other set in some instances is based on more elaborate computations. Even though the parallel measures may not be in complete agreement, the minor differences are accountable for by the different procedures used in obtaining them. Since the methods of estimate are doubtless accurate enough for ordinary classroom testing needs, the teacher or student is encouraged to select them as alternatives to the somewhat more precise methods if they are most nearly in line with his abilities and needs.

Measures of Test Reliability and Validity

Statistical procedures are necessary in some form or other in checking tests of all types for the degree to which they are reliable and valid. Although coefficients of reliability and of validity are commonly employed in this manner, test validity can also be checked by a related but somewhat less technical procedure.

Reliability coefficients treated in this chapter are the two internal-consistency types that have direct meaning for teacher-made or classroom tests. Although precise standards for reliability coefficients cannot be established, a minimum level of acceptability probably lies somewhere between .60 and .70 and some of the better classroom tests can be expected to provide coefficients above .80 or .85.

Validity coefficients of two types are also pertinent in checking on the quality of classroom tests. No numerical standards can be established either for the concurrent or the predictive type. Two quite similar tests should be shown by coefficients of concurrent validity to be highly related. Coefficients of predictive validity are typically lower, especially when the performances that are being predicted are not measured until some time after the scores that are used in making the predictions are obtained. The second way shown in this chapter for demonstrating predictive validity is the expectancy chart, on the basis of which statements can be made in simple numerical or percentage terms about the probability of future outcomes.

Measures of Reliability of Test Scores

The fallibility of test scores mentioned in the foregoing section of this chapter must be recognized and allowed for in their interpretation. Since a score is only an approximation, even though sometimes a quite accurate one, of the "true" score it represents or stands for, it cannot properly be interpreted as absolute or fixed in value. Rather, it should be interpreted as accurate within certain limits above and below the stated value. These limits are best stated in terms of the standard error of a score, or the standard error of measurement.

For related reasons, it is not certain that the numerically larger of two closely similar scores on a test actually stands for a higher "true" score than does the smaller original or obtained score. If the larger should happen to be an overstatement and the smaller an understatement, for example, the opposite and more unlikely interpretation would be in order. Hence, one score is not correctly considered to represent a distinctly higher level of performance than a second score unless the difference between the scores is great enough in terms of either the standard error of a score or, more technically, the standard error of a difference between scores, to justify that interpretation.

Derived Measures for Interpreting Test Scores

Two sets of techniques are commonly employed in giving meaning, or comparability, to scores from different tests. The one set of procedures involves the assignment of ranks, either by a very simple counting process for relative ranks or by a graphical process of estimation for the more meaningful percentile ranks. The second set of procedures usually requires that the arithmetic mean and standard deviation, or at least a measure of central tendency and of variability, be used. Letter marks of the A, B, C, D, F variety, whether applied to test scores or to courses at the ends of prescribed marking periods, are the simplest to obtain. Standard scores, more precise and detailed, are obtained by similar but somewhat more complicated procedures. Stanines, somewhat similar to letter marks and standard scores, are also readily adaptable to many classroom testing situations.

SUGGESTED ACTIVITIES

1. Obtain the scores made by a class or group of pupils on an informal objective test or a standardized achievement test and estimate (a) the footrule reliability coefficient of the test and (b) the standard error of a test score.
2. Obtain the scores made by a class or group of pupils on an informal objective test and assign to each pupil (a) a letter mark of A, B, C, D, or F and (b) a stanine rank.

SELECTED REFERENCES

BLOMMERS, PAUL, AND LINDQUIST, E. F. *Elementary Statistical Methods in Psychology and Education.* Boston: Houghton Mifflin Co., 1960. Chapters 4, 7-8.

CONRAD, HERBERT S. "Comparable Measures." *Encyclopedia of Educational Research.* Revised edition. New York: Macmillan Co., 1950. p. 279-82.

EDUCATIONAL TESTING SERVICE. *Short-Cut Statistics for Teacher-Made Tests.* Evaluation and Advisory Service Series, No. 5. Princeton, N. J.: Educational Testing Service, 1960.

FLANAGAN, JOHN C. "Units, Scales, and Norms." *Educational Measurement.* Washington, D. C.: American Council on Education, 1951. Chapter 17.

FRANZBLAU, ABRAHAM M. *A Primer of Statistics for Non-Statisticians.* New York: Harcourt, Brace and Co., 1958. Chapter 6.

GARRETT, HENRY E. *Elementary Statistics.* New York: Longmans, Green and Co., 1956. Chapters 5-6, 10.

GARRETT, HENRY E. *Statistics in Psychology and Education.* Fifth edition. New York: Longmans, Green and Co., 1958. Chapters 4-5, 13.

GERBERICH, J. RAYMOND. "Conversion of Scores." *Encyclopedia of Modern Education.* New York: Philosophical Library, 1943. p. 715-16.

GERBERICH, J. RAYMOND, AND PETERS, CHARLES C. "Reliability." *Encyclopedia of Modern Education.* New York: Philosophical Library, 1943. p. 673-75.

GREENE, HARRY A., JORGENSEN, ALBERT N., AND GERBERICH, J. RAYMOND. *Measurement and Evaluation in the Elementary School.* Second edition. New York: Longmans, Green and Co., 1953. Chapter 13.

GREENE, HARRY A., JORGENSEN, ALBERT N., AND GERBERICH, J. RAYMOND. *Measurement and Evaluation in the Secondary School.* Second edition. New York: Longmans, Green and Co., 1954. Chapter 13.

TATE, MERLE. *Statistics in Education.* New York: Macmillan Co., 1955. Chapter 5.

UNDERWOOD, BENTON J., AND OTHERS. *Elementary Statistics.* New York: Appleton-Century-Crofts, Inc., 1954. Chapters 4, 7.

WALKER, HELEN M., AND LEV, JOSEPH. *Elementary Statistical Methods.* Revised edition. New York: Henry Holt and Co., 1958. Chapters 6, 12.

PART 5

Measuring and Evaluating in the School Subjects

Whether a teacher spends almost the entire school day teaching a class of third-grade pupils or whether he teaches English to several high-school classes daily, he needs to measure and evaluate the accomplishment of his important instructional objectives as revealed by changes in the behavior of his pupils. Standardized achievement test batteries nowadays administered every year or two in many schools may well measure some of the general outcomes such teachers are seeking to develop in their pupils, but these batteries do not definitely serve many of a teacher's specific needs. Furthermore, a teacher of art, of physical education, of home economics, or of speech would find little content from his instructional area in any standardized achievement test battery.

The chapters of Part 5 are designed to deal briefly with the appraisal of pupil learning in ten broad instructional areas and in general education. Instructional objectives and the related learning outcomes are employed in these chapters to indicate the types of pupil behavior the teacher should doubtless seek to measure in his subject area or areas of teaching. Attention is given to measurement problems from the primary grades to the senior high school. All types of tests and techniques having special significance for the school subjects are treated briefly—standardized and teacher-made paper-and-pencil tests, performance tests, evaluative tests and techniques, and even, on occasion, pertinent aptitude tests, attitude scales, and interest inventories.

Extensive coverage of measurement problems in each of these ten instructional areas is not possible in the limited space available here, but Chapters 15 to 25 are intended to present the major appraisal needs, possibilities, and methods, and to give selected bibliographies that should assist the interested student of education in his subsequent efforts to attain still higher proficiency in the special area of achievement measurement and evaluation.

15

READING, VOCABULARY, AND LISTENING

The following important points involved in the measurement and evaluation of reading and listening skills are summarized in this chapter:

A. Basic communication skills.
B. Significance and aims of receptive language.
C. Determination of readiness for reading.
D. Measurement of proficiency in oral reading.
E. Measurement of silent and work-study reading skills.
F. Measurement of vocabulary or of word knowledge.
G. Appraisal of listening skills.
H. Diagnosis and remediation in reading.

The receptive language arts consist primarily of reading and listening, but they also include study skills and vocabulary. They are distinguishable from the expressive language arts, which basically involve oral and written language but also include spelling and handwriting. These four basic skills—reading, listening, speaking, and writing—are often referred to as the communication skills because it is through their use that people are able to communicate with one another.

Both the receptive and expressive aspects of language are stressed in the elementary school. They are almost equally important phases of learning, if not always of direct instruction, in the secondary school. The receptive or assimilative aspects of language are dealt with in this chapter, while

347

the following chapter is concerned with the expressive forms of language. The treatments in both chapters are confined to the English language, whereas the foreign languages are the concern of Chapter 20.

1. SIGNIFICANCE AND OBJECTIVES
OF RECEPTIVE LANGUAGE

Reading is considered the indispensable means by which adults may keep abreast of current happenings, and familiarize themselves with current social, community, political, and national problems. The mass of printed matter which the typical adult should read and evaluate, even within the limits of his own fields of interest, is stupendous. This situation makes all the more imperative the development of a high degree of reading skill in the schools.

There is a growing conviction on the part of students of the language arts areas that, of the two language channels through which information is received, listening is seriously neglected in favor of reading. Reading has been analyzed, investigated, and evaluated perhaps more than any other school subject. Listening, on the other hand, still appears relatively infrequently in the literature.

Importance of Reading and Listening Skills

The solution of most classroom problems in the modern school requires the skillful use of books as sources of information. When considered from this point of view, reading as a school responsibility is something more than merely the rapid comprehension of printed symbols and the memory and organization of the materials read. It is also the ability to utilize books and libraries as efficient sources of information. This tendency to treat reading as a highly important tool of learning has resulted in establishing a very close relationship between reading and practically every other school activity. As a means of gaining information and pleasure it is essential in every content subject, such as history, geography, science, literature, and arithmetic.

Gray, in a recent survey of studies on the amount of time spent in reading,[1] reported that in 1952 adults with a background of high-school graduation averaged about 50 minutes a day reading newspapers and 15 minutes daily reading magazines, whereas in 1946 adults with the same educational background averaged 12 minutes a day in book reading. Asheim, also

[1] William S. Gray, "Sociology of Reading." *Encyclopedia of Educational Research,* Third edition. Macmillan Co., New York, 1960. p. 1091-92.

reporting on amount of reading done,[2] generalized that between 60 and 70 percent of adults read at least one magazine regularly, that 85 to 90 percent read a newspaper more or less regularly, and that not much more than one out of four reads even one book a month on the average. These estimates support a belief that typical adults average less than an hour and a half of reading activity per day and perhaps that many adults do almost no reading. Although these are not gratifying conclusions, they nevertheless attest to the importance of reading in the postschool lives of most adults.

Studies and observations dating back over a period of many years indidate that listening is without question one of the most frequently used language activities. Actually, the average adult spends much more time in listening than he does in reading. Since this is the case, there is ample reason for the growing belief that listening skills should be developed as a part of a systematic program of instruction in the language arts.

In a survey designed to discover (1) what percentage of the school day children are expected to listen, (2) whether teachers themselves are aware of the amount of listening children are expected to do, and (3) what relative importance teachers place upon the four phases of language education, Wilt [3] concluded, among other things, that pupils are expected to spend more time in listening than in any other single activity of the school. Teachers apparently are more concerned about the individual who is reading aloud or speaking than they are about the listeners. Almost fifteen hundred teachers estimated that children learn through reading approximately 110 minutes of the average school day, and through listening 78 minutes. Actually, the median amount of listening time was 158 minutes, 54 percent of which was spent in listening to the teacher, 31 percent in listening to the other children, and 15 percent in miscellaneous listening. While no comparable data on this problem are available at the high-school or college levels, it is quite probable that the relative importance of listening as a factor in learning at these levels is even more significant than in the elementary school.

Major Objectives and Outcomes of Reading and Listening

The extremely wide variety of school and life situations in which children and adults read or listen is indicated in the following list of reading

[2] Lester Asheim, "What Do Adults Read?" *Adult Reading,* Forty-Fifth Yearbook of the National Society for the Study of Education, Part II. University of Chicago Press, Chicago, 1956. p. 7-8.

[3] Miriam E. Wilt, "A Study of Teacher Awareness of Listening as a Factor in Elementary Education." *Journal of Educational Research,* 43:626-36; April 1950.

and listening objectives, attitudes, and abilities. The outline itself is an adaptation of material presented by Greene and Gray [4] in a discussion of the measurement of understanding in the language arts.

A Functional Analysis of Reading and Listening

I. Objectives and Illustrative Procedures
   A. Typical situations leading pupils to read or listen
      1. To find out what is going on
      2. To find one's way about
      3. To understand directions and assignments
      4. To verify spellings, pronunciations, meanings
      5. To secure answers to specific questions
      6. To gather information for fuller understanding
      7. To learn how to act in new situations
      8. To work out complicated problems
      9. To reach conclusions about guiding principles
      10. To identify and resolve propaganda
      11. To search for and discover the truth
   B. Typical recreational situations leading pupils to read or listen
      1. To relive everyday experiences
      2. To have fun or sheer enjoyment
      3. To escape from real life
      4. To satisfy curiosity about strange times and places
      5. To enjoy sensory imagery
      6. To enjoy ready-made emotional reactions
      7. To enjoy sentiments and ideals expressed by others
      8. To enjoy rhythm and quality of expression

II. Essential Knowledges, Attitudes, Skills, and Procedures
   A. Basic to securing meaning in reading and listening
      1. To respond to the motive, problem, or purpose
      2. To attend to the meaning of what is read
      3. To develop fluent, accurate perception of word forms
      4. To secure adequate understanding of what is read
      5. To react critically to what is read
      6. To integrate ideas acquired with previous experience
   B. Basic to securing meaning in silent reading
      1. To locate needed information
         a. To understand and use an index
         b. To use a table of contents
         c. To use the dictionary
         d. To use library card files
         e. To use reference books
         f. To use and interpret maps, graphs, and tables

---

[4] Harry A. Greene and William S. Gray, "The Measurement of Understanding in the Language Arts." *The Measurement of Understanding,* Forty-Fifth Yearbook of the National Society for the Study of Education, Part I. University of Chicago Press, Chicago, 1946. p. 189-200. Quoted by permission of the Society.

2. To recognize purposes to be achieved
   a. To find the central thought
   b. To follow a sequence of related events
   c. To identify important points and supporting details
   d. To solve a specific problem
   e. To compare the views of authorities
   f. To support a point of view or course of action
3. To apply fact-finding techniques
   a. To gain meaning from the title
   b. To make use of topic sentences and paragraphs
   c. To grasp the organization of ideas
4. To separate essential from nonessential information
5. To judge the significance of relative information
6. To organize information in terms of a purpose
7. To draw tentative conclusions

C. Basic in interpretive oral reading
1. To have a motive for reading to others
2. To sense the importance of the message for the listeners
3. To adjust speaking voice to purpose and to room size
4. To modulate the voice to make thought relationships clear
5. To adjust the voice to changes in character and mood
6. To use appropriate facial expressions and gestures
7. To control bodily movements and breathing
8. To be natural, sincere, convincing, free from tension

The foregoing outline of the major objectives of listening and reading affords a useful basis for the evaluation of present instructional emphasis in these two important acquisitive skill areas as well as a valuable source of criteria for the validation of analytical and corrective procedures in listening and reading.

2. MEASUREMENT OF READING READINESS

Readiness for learning is by no means restricted to reading in its educational significance. However, it is in this area particularly and to a minor degree in arithmetic that readiness tests as such are widely used. The belief that a pupil should be ready for the learning situations with which he is faced has long been accepted by teachers in all areas of instruction. Although many lists of factors involved in readiness have been brought forth, the three major ones listed by Blair and Jones can be accepted as representative: (1) maturation or development, (2) experience or practice, and (3) absence of disturbing emotional conditions.[5]

[5] Glenn M. Blair and R. Stewart Jones, "Readiness." *Encyclopedia of Educational Research,* Third edition. Macmillan Co., New York, 1960. p. 1082-84.

Nature of Reading Readiness

Reading readiness is dependent on a large number of characteristics. Harris listed the following as among the most important: (1) age, (2) sex, (3) general intelligence, (4) visual perception, (5) auditory perception, (6) physical health and maturity, (7) freedom from directional confusion, (8) background of experience, (9) comprehension and use of oral English, (10) emotional and social adjustment, and (11) interest in reading.[6] It is unsafe to assume that a child who enters school at the age of six is ready for reading. Some children have already learned to read, and are mentally much more mature than the average child of six, while others may have no more mental maturity than the average child of four, and may thus encounter considerable difficulty in learning to read.

Gates [7] recommended that "before the child actually begins to learn to read his status should be determined in the following respects: (1) intelligence or verbal aptitude, (2) vision, (3) color blindness, (4) hearing, (5) handedness, (6) speech, (7) health and vigor, and (8) emotional stability."

A reading readiness check list designed and tried out by Banham [8] has significance in affording an index of the maturity aspects of reading readiness. According to the author, it may also serve as a useful supplement to intelligence tests and reading readiness tests in obtaining a broad basis for judging when pupils are ready for reading. Scores on the 20-item check list of outdoor and indoor, physical and mental, activities pupils report they engage in are tentatively specified as representing minimum levels of maturity for success in reading.

Reading Readiness Tests

Reading readiness tests can best be classified as tests of specific intelligence, for their purpose is to measure the mental ability factors essential to success in reading. These factors are measured by tests that make use of visual and auditory abilities that are basic to reading. Reading readiness tests employ several testing devices. Among them are (1) distinguishing pictured objects that are named by the examiner, (2) matching one word of a group with its counterpart, which appears as a visual stimulus,

---

[6] Albert J. Harris, *How to Increase Reading Ability: A Guide to Developmental and Remedial Methods,* Fourth edition. Longmans, Green and Co., New York, 1961. p. 26.

[7] Arthur I. Gates, *The Improvement of Reading: A Program of Diagnostic and Remedial Methods,* Third edition. Macmillan Co., New York, 1947. p. 142.

[8] Katherine M. Banham, "Maturity Level for Reading Readiness: A Check List for the Use of Teachers and Parents as a Supplement to Reading Readiness Tests." *Educational and Psychological Measurement,* 18:371-75; Summer 1958.

(3) recognizing word similarities or differences, (4) recognizing rhyming words, and (5) reading numbers and letters. Only the last of these can perhaps be called a reading skill, although all of the types measure abilities on which later reading abilities depend. The major purpose of reading readiness tests is to locate those children who are not yet ready to start reading but for whom that activity should be delayed until their mental maturity and experience are adequate for such an undertaking.

EXCERPT FROM *Harrison-Stroud Reading Readiness Tests* [9]

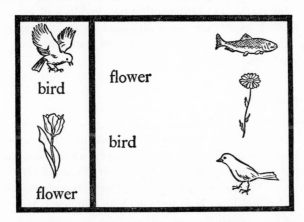

The accompanying illustration taken from the *Harrison-Stroud Reading Readiness Tests* is representative of testing methods for reading readiness. Instructions are given orally for all such tests. Readiness for reading is measured by six parts on (1) using symbols, (2) making visual discriminations, (3) using context, (4) making auditory discriminations, (5) using context and auditory clues, and (6) giving the names of letters.

Two other widely used tests of this variety are the *Gates Reading Readiness Test* [10] and the *Lee-Clark Reading Readiness Test.* [11] The five parts of the Gates test deal with (1) picture directions, (2) word matching, (3) word-card matching, (4) rhyming, and (5) letters and numbers. The Lee-Clark test, requiring less than 20 minutes for administration, measures (1) recognition of likenesses, (2) discrimination of differences, (3) experiential background, and (4) ability to discriminate among similar but different forms of letters and words.

[9] M. Lucille Harrison and James B. Stroud, *The Harrison-Stroud Reading Readiness Tests: Test 5, Using Symbols.* Houghton Mifflin Co., Boston, 1950.

[10] Arthur I. Gates, *Gates Reading Readiness Test.* Bureau of Publications, Teachers College, Columbia University, New York, 1939.

[11] J. Murray Lee and Willis W. Clark, *Lee-Clark Reading Readiness Test,* 1951 Edition. California Test Bureau, Los Angeles, 1951.

3. MEASUREMENT OF ORAL READING SKILLS

Whether oral reading should be considered as a receptive or an expressive language skill depends upon the manner in which it is used in the schoolroom. If it is conceived as a matter of communicating ideas and providing entertainment, its purpose is expressive. If it is considered as an adjunct to silent reading, it belongs to the area of receptive language. Since the second conception is commonly accepted, it is employed here. Two related types of oral reading measuring instruments are distinguished in the following pages: (1) oral reading paragraphs and (2) oral reading check tests. Both types are generally used as individual tests in the elementary grades, although they can be and sometimes are used in the intermediate grades.

Oral Reading Paragraph Tests

The *Gray Standardized Oral Reading Paragraphs* [12] consist of twelve paragraphs arranged in ascending order of difficulty. The tests are administered by having a pupil read the paragraphs under time control until a certain number of errors per paragraph occur. Types of errors detracting from an accuracy score are mispronunciations, omissions, substitutions, insertions, and repetitions. Five tests each at four levels covering Grades 1 to 8 provide for flexibility.

The *Gilmore Oral Reading Test* provides paragraph measures of accuracy of oral reading, comprehension of material read, and rate of reading. Vocabulary, sentence structure, and interest are carefully controlled as factors in the difficulty of the paragraphs. There are five comprehension exercises for each paragraph. Ten paragraphs, arranged in ascending order of difficulty, form a continuous story related to the same characters. A separately bound booklet contains the illustrations and the paragraphs for the use of the subject being tested. The type of material presented on the record booklet for the use of the examiner is illustrated by the accompanying samples, Paragraphs 3 and 4 from Form A of the test

Oral Reading Check Tests

The plan of recording the number and the kinds of errors made by the pupil in reading the *Gray Standardized Oral Reading Paragraphs* permits a type of diagnostic analysis of oral reading abilities. Much more concise

---

[12] William S. Gray, *Gray Standardized Oral Reading Paragraphs*. Public School Publishing Co., Bloomington, Ill., 1915.

information of this kind is made available, however, through the use of the *Gray Oral Reading Check Tests.*

EXCERPTS FROM *Gilmore Oral Reading Test* [13]

3. The name of the boy is Bob. The name of his sister is Jane. They live with their parents in a white house near the city. They are playing on the walk. The dog and cat are their pets. After Father has gone to work, the children will leave for school.

TIME _____Seconds

___1. What is the boy's name?
___2. What is his sister's name?
___3. Where is their house?
___4. What are their pets?
___5. When will the children leave for school?

NUMBER RIGHT _____

ERROR RECORD	Number
Substitutions	
Mispronunciations	
Words pronounced by examiner	
Disregard of punctuation	
Insertions	
Hesitations	
Repetitions	
Omissions	
Total Errors	

4. Mother waves good-by to Father each morning. She begins the housework soon after he leaves. Bob and Jane help her before they go to school. They dry the dishes and clean their own rooms. After Mother has finished the work indoors, she goes out to her pretty flower garden. She tends it nearly every day for about an hour. Mother does all her work with great care.

TIME _____Seconds

___1. What does Mother do as Father is leaving?
___2. What does Mother do after Father has gone?
___3. When do Bob and Jane help Mother?
___4. Where does Mother go after she has finished the work indoors?
___5. How long does she work in her garden each day?

NUMBER RIGHT _____

ERROR RECORD	Number
Substitutions	
Mispronunciations	
Words pronounced by examiner	
Disregard of punctuation	
Insertions	
Hesitations	
Repetitions	
Omissions	
Total Errors	

As in the oral reading paragraphs, these check tests are to be given individually. The errors made by the pupil are recorded by the teacher on a separate test sheet showing the types of errors made by the pupil which appear most frequently in oral reading. The following illustration may make clear the character of the errors and the method of recording them: [14]

The sun pierced into my large windows. It was the opening of October, and the sky was of a dazzling blue. I looked out of my window and down the street. The white houses of the long, straight street were almost painful to the eyes. The clear atmosphere allowed full play to the sun's brightness.

If a word is wholly mispronounced, underline it as in the case of "atmosphere." If a portion of a word is mispronounced, mark appropriately as indicated above: "pierced" pronounced in two syllables, sounding long *a* in "dazzling," omitting the *s* in "houses" or the *al* from "almost," or the *r* in "straight." Omitted words are marked as in the case of "of" and "and"; substitutions as in the case of "many" for "my"; insertions as in the case of "clear"; and repetitions as in the case of "to the sun's." Two or more words should be repeated to count as a repetition.

[13] John V. Gilmore, *Gilmore Oral Reading Test.* Form A. Copyright 1952 by Harcourt, Brace and World, Inc., New York. All rights reserved. Quoted by special permission.
[14] William S. Gray, *Gray Standardized Oral Reading Check Tests.* Public School Publishing Co., Cincinnati, Ohio, 1923.

The individual record sheet that accompanies the *Gray Oral Reading Check Tests* is useful in two important ways. It places before the teacher a carefully classified list of common errors in oral reading, and it provides space for the recording of successive repetitions of the test so that progress may be measured.

The analysis of the individual pupil's record gives a very concise picture of his oral reading difficulties. It should be noted that in these oral reading exercises no attention is paid to the degree of comprehension with which the material is read. The measurement of comprehension lies somewhat beyond the purpose of this test. Here the purpose is the determination of the efficiency with which words are recognized and pronounced in context, with little or no concern for the comprehension of the materials.

4. MEASUREMENT OF SILENT READING COMPREHENSION

Situations differing not only in nature and level but also according to the needs and purposes of the reader entail silent reading. A similar distinction can be made for tests of silent reading proficiency. The two major types dealt with here in a direct manner are work-study tests and vocabulary or word knowledge tests. Diagnostic silent reading tests are treated briefly in the last section of this chapter. Recreational varieties of silent reading tests, in direct contrast to work-study types, are dealt with in the section of Chapter 21 devoted to literature. It should be noted, however, that absolute distinctions cannot be made among types of reading skills or of tests. For example, a work-study test may frequently serve as a diagnostic tool and a test on recreational reading may sometimes be of a work-study variety for many pupils.

Tests of Work-Study Skills

The emphasis given to the work types of reading in the list of skills given on pages 350 and 351 indicates something of the importance of this type of reading in relation to the total reading field. Some pupils fail in arithmetic or science, for example, not necessarily because of ignorance of basic facts or lack of mental ability, but rather on account of sheer inability to read. In fact, one of the best ways to improve work in many other school subjects is to make a drive on the work type of reading ability. A recognition of this has caused makers of tests in reading to turn their attention in this direction over a period of some years. A number of reading tests which provide useful analytical information concerning a variety of work-study skills are available for use in the elementary and secondary school.

EXCERPTS FROM *Gates Primary Reading Tests* [15]

31.

minute   kitten

mitten   miller

15. Here are eight little ducks. Draw a line under the feet of three of these ducks.

EXCERPT FROM *Gates Basic Reading Test* [16]

9. Whenever election time draws near, pictures of elephants and donkeys are seen in the newspapers. These two____A____stand for the two____B____ parties.

A. monsters   animals   people   magazines   newspapers
B. birthday   religious   academic   New Year   political

10. Most trees could not live if their roots were covered with water. Cypress trees, however, love ____A____and are often found growing in____B____.

A. soil   drought   roots   water   sand
B. deserts   mid-ocean   swamps   oil   moss

[15] Arthur I. Gates, *Gates Primary Reading Tests: Word Recognition; Paragraph Reading.* Form 3, Grades 1 and 2 (First half). Bureau of Publications, Teachers College, Columbia University, New York, 1958.

[16] Arthur I. Gates, *Gates Basic Reading Test: Level of Comprehension.* Form 3, Grades 3 (Second half) through 8. Bureau of Publications, Teachers College, Columbia University, New York, 1958.

The *Gates Primary Reading Tests* and the *Gates Advanced Primary Reading Test* provide separate booklets for use in Grades 1 to 3. Tests of word recognition and paragraph reading, illustrated by an item each in an accompanying excerpt, occur at both levels, but the sentence reading test, an excerpt from which is shown on page 235, is provided only for the lower level. A third series, the *Gates Basic Reading Test,* for use in Grades 3 to 8, consists of five separate booklets designed to measure (1) Reading to Appreciate General Significance, (2) Reading to Understand Precise Directions, (3) Reading to Note Details, (4) Reading Vocabulary, and (5) Level of Comprehension. An accompanying excerpt shows two items from the last-named test.

The *Iowa Silent Reading Tests,*[17] available at two levels, are designed to provide a detailed and analytical measure of silent reading skills. The tests, available in several forms each for Grades 4 to 8 and Grades 9 to 13, cover a wide range of skills essential to effective reading of the work-study type. The following summary shows in parallel for the two levels the titles of the test parts and indications of the content used.

Elementary Level	*Test*	*Advanced Level*
Test 1 Sciences Social studies	Rate and Comprehension	Test 1 Sciences Social studies
Test 2 Sciences Social studies	Directed Reading	Test 2 Sciences
Test 3 General Sciences Mathematics Social sciences	Word Meaning	Test 4 Social sciences Sciences Mathematics English
Test 4	Paragraph Comprehension	Test 6
Test 5	Sentence Meaning	Test 5
Test 6 Alphabetizing Use of index	Location of Information	Test 7 Use of index Selection of key words
	Poetry Comprehension	Test 3

The *Kelley-Greene Reading Comprehension Test* measures certain elements of the student's ability to read, comprehend, and remember the type of material he encounters in connection with his high-school course

---

[17] (1) Harry A. Greene and Victor H. Kelley, *Iowa Silent Reading Tests,* New edition, Elementary. World Book Co., Yonkers, N. Y., 1943; (2) Harry A. Greene, Albert N. Jorgensen, and Victor H. Kelley, *Iowa Silent Reading Tests,* New edition, Advanced. World Book Co., Yonkers, N. Y., 1943.

work. Test 1 consists of nine specially prepared paragraphs dealing with many different types of content. The sentences in each paragraph are numbered. The five comprehension exercises accompanying each paragraph are to be answered by indicating on the separate answer sheet the numbers of the correct answers. The accompanying extract representing Paragraph V from Form AM of this test is presented here to illustrate the nature of these comprehension exercises.

EXCERPT FROM *Kelley-Greene Reading Comprehension Test* [18]

PARAGRAPH V

[1]When a piece of paper burns, it is completely changed. [2]A part of it is turned into a hot gas. [3]The ash that is left behind does not look like the original piece of paper. [4]When dull-red rust appears on a piece of tinware, it is quite different from the gleaming polished metal. [5]The tarnish that forms on silverware exposed to the air is a new substance unlike the silver itself. [6]Animal tissue is unlike the vegetable substances from which it is made. [7]A change in which the original substance is turned into a different substance is called a chemical change.

V

1. The best topic sentence for this paragraph is sentence—
    1. 4   2. 5   3. 7
2. Which key word or phrase tells best what this paragraph is about?
    1. transformation
    2. chemical changes
    3. new substances
3. Which is the best generalization from this paragraph?
    1. Any change is known as a chemical change.
    2. The growth of animal tissue is a physical change.
    3. Chemical change involves forming a new substance from the original.

The *Spitzer Study Skills Test,* because of its practical utility in many subject-matter fields and its use of a number of ingenious testing techniques, should attract the attention of high-school and college teachers. This instrument is designed to measure the student's knowledge of and his skill in using reference sources in the preparation of his course assignments. The five skill fields tested are: (1) Using the Dictionary, (2) Using the Index, (3) Knowledge of Sources of Information, (4) Understanding Graphs, Tables, and Maps, and (5) Organization of Facts in Note Taking. The accompanying excerpt from Test 1 is presented as an illustration of the manner in which dictionary skills may be tested.

A rich source of sample test items and exercises available for use by high-school teachers in constructing their own tests of study skills and

EXCERPT FROM *Spitzer Study Skills Test* [19]

Sample Dictionary

de·mur·rage (dǐ mûr′ǐj), *n.* *Com.* 1. the detention of a vessel, as in loading or unloading, beyond the time agreed upon. 2. the similar detention of a railroad car, etc. 3. a charge for such detention.

de·pot (dē′pō; *Mil. or Brit.* dĕp′ō), *n.* 1. *U.S.* a railroad station. 2. *Mil.* a. a place to which supplies and materials are shipped and stored for distribution. b. (formerly) a place where recruits receive their first training. 3. *Chiefly Brit.* a depository; storehouse. [t. F, g. L *dēpositum* DEPOSIT, n.] —Syn. 1. See station.

1. In the following statement which meaning of *demurrage* is used: "When the demurrage was added to the freight, the total cost for the car of wheat was $87.50"?

   1. first   2. second   3. third   4. not given

2. The *Com.* after *demurrage* means that the word is —

   5. in common usage   7. derived from command
   6. used in commerce   8. a completing word

3. The last syllable of *demurrage* rhymes with —

   1. gage   2. hodge   3. gig   4. ridge

4. Which pronunciation of *depot* is preferred by military men?

   5. dĕp′ō   6. dē′pō   7. dĕ′pō   8. dĕ pō′

KEY: b., blend of, blended; c., cognate with; d., dialect, dialectal; der., derived from; f., formed from; g., going back to; m., modification of; r., replacing; s., stem of; t., taken from; ?, perhaps.

KEY: ăct, āble, dâre, ärt; ĕbb, ēqual; ǐf, īce; hŏt, ōver, ôrder, oil, bŏŏk, ōōze, out; ŭp, ūse, ûrge; ə = a in alone; ch, chief; g, give; ng, ring; sh, shoe; th, thin; th, that; zh, vision.

[19] Herbert F. Spitzer, *Spitzer Study Skills Test, Test 1, Using the Dictionary.* Form AM. Copyright 1953 by Harcourt, Brace and World, Inc., New York. All rights reserved. Quoted by special permission.

closely related critical thinking is one of the bulletins of the National Council for the Social Studies.[20] Although the content is drawn from the social sciences much more than from the sciences or other content areas, the wide variety of skills tested and the placement of emphasis on study skills rather than on content itself make this source of test materials widely useful.

Teachers are free to take items and exercises directly from this source or to adapt them as desired for use in their classroom tests. An idea of the variety of materials can be obtained from the titles of the various bulletin sections: (1) Evaluating Sources of Information, (2) Distinguishing between Statements of Fact and Statements of Opinion, (3) Distinguishing between Sources and Secondary Accounts, (4) Discriminating between Statements of Fact and Statements of Motive, (5) Exercises on Acquiring Information, (6) Exercise on Open-Mindedness, (7) Determining Difficulty of Proof, (8) Determining Relative Length of Historical Periods, (9) Reading and Interpreting Graphs, Charts, and Tables, (10) Constructing and Reading Line Graphs, (11) Interpreting Tabular Data, (12) Recognizing and Interpreting Trends Revealed by Statistical Data, (13) Exercise on Consistency, (14) Drawing Inferences, (15) Recognizing Biased Statements, (16) Recognizing Statements Which Support Generalizations, and (17) Insight into the Relative Significance of Questions. If the reader should note similarities between some of these listings and some of those dealt with under the heading of evaluative tests in Chapter 12, it evidences the fact, commented upon in that chapter, that evaluative types of skills are now included in a wide variety of test types.

The *Cooperative Reading Comprehension Test* [21] has recently been issued in a revised edition and a completely new format. The test consists of parts on vocabulary and reading, and is so scored as to result in meaningful scores on vocabulary, speed of comprehension, and level of comprehension as well as in a total score. It is possible also to obtain a total English score by combining results from this and the *Cooperative English Expression Test* that is illustrated in the following chapter. The two tests together are designated as the *Cooperative English Tests*.

Tests of Vocabulary or Word Knowledge

One of the major aims of instruction in all phases of English is the development of a rich and expressive vocabulary. While vocabulary tests

[20] Horace T. Morse and George H. McCune, *Selected Items for the Testing of Study Skills and Critical Thinking*. National Council for the Social Studies, Bulletin No. 15, Third edition. National Education Association, Washington, D. C., 1957.

[21] Educational Testing Service, *Cooperative Reading Comprehension Test*. Educational Testing Service, Princeton, N. J., 1960.

are not necessarily classified as reading tests, the two types of tests are related in nature and function. Furthermore, many reading tests include parts on vocabulary.

The *Durost-Center Word Mastery Test,* in addition to measuring the general vocabulary level of secondary-school pupils as a single aspect of reading comprehension, should provide a very useful supplement to other reading comprehension tests not sampling the vocabulary fields. In Part 1 of the test 100 carefully selected words are tested in multiple-choice form. Part 2 presents the same words in sentences with the same options as are given in the first part. A comparison of the two scores reveals the extent to which the student is able to acquire meanings of words from contextual situations. A few sample items from Part 2 are shown in an accompanying excerpt.

EXCERPT FROM *Durost-Center Word Mastery Test* [22]

DIRECTIONS. In Part 2 each of the words in black type in Part 1 has been used in a sentence. Study each sentence carefully and then record your answer on the separate answer sheet in the same way you did in Part 1.

SAMPLE. The work was hard, but the pay was excellent.
Work means — 1 play   2 rest   3 labor   4 leisure

---

1. The clamor of the mob lasted throughout the night.
Clamor means — 1 uproar   2 attraction
3 crowding   4 anxiety...................... **1**

2. Mud and other particles floating in water can be removed largely by filtering.
Filtering is the process of — 1 evaporating a liquid   2 condensing a liquid   3 freezing a liquid   4 straining a liquid through porous material **2**

The *Michigan Vocabulary Profile Test,*[23] which is standardized for use with secondary-school pupils and college freshmen, provides an extensive sampling into the following eight different technical vocabulary areas: Human Relations, Commerce, Government, Physical Sciences, Biological Sciences, Mathematics, Fine Arts, and Sports. The test consists of 240 items comprising a definition or description and four words or phrases,

[22] Walter N. Durost and Stella S. Center, *Durost-Center Word Mastery Test,* Part 2. Form A. Copyright 1950 by Harcourt, Brace and World, Inc., New York. All rights reserved. Quoted by special permission.
[23] Edward B. Greene, *Michigan Vocabulary Profile Test.* World Book Co., Yonkers, N. Y., 1949.

only one of which is completely and accurately defined or described. As a supplement to other general comprehension measures, this test should prove especially useful with high-school and college students.

One other illustration of vocabulary test items appears in this volume— the excerpt from the Word Meaning section of the primary-level *Stanford Achievement Test* on page 228.

5. MEASUREMENT OF LISTENING COMPREHENSION

Listening is educationally the most recently recognized although doubt-less chronologically the oldest of mankind's receptive language skills. Man certainly acquired ideas through his sense of hearing the spoken word long before he was able to do so by reading the written or printed word. It is consequently rather strange that only quite recently in educational history has listening, or auding,[24] received extended attention.

Measurable Characteristics of Listening

In an attempt to identify the basic measurable factors in listening com-prehension, Brown [25] concluded that the following skills are involved in the effective use of listening as a learning instrument:

1. Identification and recall of details presented orally
2. Ability to follow the sequence of details in the form of oral directions
3. Retention of details long enough to answer questions about them
4. Ability to listen reflectively for the purpose of identifying the central idea of the statement given orally
5. Ability to draw inferences from the supporting facts presented in the statement
6. Ability to distinguish relevant from irrelevant materials
7. Use of contextual clues to word meanings
8. Recognition of transitional elements in sentences

This list can be considered to supplement the listening comprehension portions of the analytical list of objectives and procedures given in the first section of this chapter.

Tests of Listening Comprehension

Tests for the measurement of the comprehension of orally presented materials are limited in number. In fact, only one such test at the second-

[24] John Caffrey, "Auding." *Review of Educational Research*, 25:121-38; April 1955.
[25] James I. Brown, "The Construction of a Diagnostic Test of Listening Comprehen-sion." *Journal of Experimental Education*, 18:139-46; December 1949.

ary level and one such series of tests for Grades 4 to 14 are known to the authors, although sections of a few other tests measure listening comprehension informally and even incidentally. The aural-oral tests in the foreign languages treated in Chapter 20 are also of this type.

The *Brown-Carlsen Listening Comprehension Test* is a carefully validated test standardized for use with high-school students and college freshmen. It appears to be a very useful supplementary instrument in connection with analytical and remedial work in many achievement areas.

EXCERPT FROM *Brown-Carlsen Listening Comprehension Test* [26]

Directions (Given orally by examiner)

"Directly [to the left of] the answer spaces for this part is a group of numbers and letters to which you will need to refer." (Point to proper place.) "The even numbers and the vowels have been underlined; the numbers 3 and 6 have been circled. Now look at the sample. Referring to the row of numbers [to the left of] the answer spaces for this part, subtract the smallest number from the largest number." (Pause.) "The correct answer is 7; so on your answer sheet the answer space under the 7 has been filled in."

"All the questions in this part will be answered in the same manner. You are *not* to do any figuring on the answer sheet; all work must be done mentally. Listen carefully; I shall read each question only once."

1 2 ③ 4 5 ⑥ 7 8

A B C D E F G H

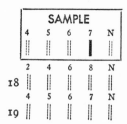

The test calls for pupil reactions to 76 test questions divided into five parts as follows: (1) Immediate Recall, (2) Following Directions, (3) Recognizing Transitions, (4) Recognizing Word Meanings, and (5) Lecture Comprehension. Part 5 is based on a 12-minute "lecture" read by the examiner. An illustration from this test, including the pertinent oral instructions, appears in an accompanying excerpt. After reading aloud the directions for taking the test that appear in the excerpt and making sure that they are understood, the examiner proceeds to the test questions. He pauses for approximately five seconds after each question to allow the pupils time for their answers. Questions for items 18 and 19 are, "The number above the second vowel is — ?" and "Multiply the next to the smallest number by the smallest number and add the smallest number to it. The answer is — ?" As the numerical manipulations are simple, the emphasis is on comprehension.

The *STEP Listening Test* at the lowest of the four levels—Grades 4 to 6 —is also illustrated here to represent emphasis on relatively long thought units. The selection quoted below and twelve others are included at Level 4, and the other three levels provide about the same number of selections. As preliminary steps, the examiner gives comprehensive directions to the pupils for taking the test and illustrates the procedures by reading a short selection and explaining how a sample question should be answered. Selection II, designed for reading in about 50 seconds, is shown here as an illustration.[27] After each selection has been read, the questions and the four options based on each are read in turn; the pupil has in his hands a test booklet containing the optional answers but not the questions and an answer sheet on which he records his responses.

> My business is buying and selling stamps. One day a perky old lady came into my office with a shoe box full of stamps from love letters written by her husband when he was a young seaman. He had posted the letters to her from many different countries. A friend had told her that one of the foreign stamps was worth $250, but she couldn't remember which stamp.
>
> "Will you find it please," she said, "and, when you do, don't you dare offer me less than $250 for it. I won't be cheated."
>
> I made a careful appraisal without finding one stamp worth anywhere near $250. But scads of them were worth from $1 to $100, and, in the end, I wrote the lady a check for $8,500. She was so surprised I thought she would faint.

6. DIAGNOSIS AND REMEDIATION IN RECEPTIVE LANGUAGE

The solution of the problem of the effective initial teaching of reading as well as the development of satisfactory remedial materials in reading is dependent to a large degree on the accurate identification of the specific

---

[27] Educational Testing Service, *Sequential Tests of Educational Progress: Listening— Directions for Administering and Scoring*, Level 4. Form A. Educational Testing Service, Princeton, N. J., 1957. p. 7.

causes of reading failure. Not only is it necessary to discover the child who in his later school experience is almost certain to encounter reading difficulties, but these reading difficulties must be identified definitely and accurately.

EXCERPT FROM STEP Listening Test [28]

9 **A** a dealer in antiques
     B a postman
     C a dealer in stamps
     D a coin collector

10 **E** she wanted to find out how much each one was worth
     F her friend had recommended him
     G she wanted to sell all the stamps to him
     H she wanted him to find one valuable stamp

11 **A** be polite to the old lady
     B see which ones he liked
     C see how much they were worth
     D see how many there were

Recent critical research in reading opens up new possibilities for analytical and corrective work. No longer need measurement in reading be confined to such vague and general qualities as rate and comprehension of word meanings. Although most of the existing reading tests do not provide the specific types of diagnosis required in the identification of reading disabilities, and although most of the commercially produced drill books and workbooks are still designed more for initial instruction than for remediation, considerable progress has recently been made in the analysis and identification of the causes of disability and also in the development of techniques for their remediation. A few of these techniques are outlined here to indicate some of the possibilities.

Identification of Reading Disabilities

Harris listed and discussed at length [29] the following causes of reading difficulties: (1) low intelligence, (2) visual defects, (3) auditory defects, (4) other physical conditions—illness, defects of muscular coordination

---

[28] Educational Testing Service, *Sequential Tests of Educational Progress: Listening,* Part 1, Level 4. Form A. Educational Testing Service, Princeton, N. J., 1957.
[29] Harris, *op. cit.* Chapters 9-10.

and speech, glandular disturbances, and neurological difficulties, (5) deficiencies in hemispherical dominance, (6) poor school record, (7) deficiencies in arithmetic, spelling, and handwriting, and (8) emotional and social problems. He pointed out,[30] however, that it is "impossible to determine the relative contribution of each handicap to the total picture of failure. ... From a practical standpoint, the aim of a thorough diagnosis is not to fix the blame for the child's difficulties, but to discover each of the many conditions that may require correction."

Many early investigators studying the problem of how to improve reading noted that there is a marked relationship between the rate and quality of reading and the control individuals have over their eye movements in reading. The meaning of eye movements may be readily understood by anyone who will take a position closely in front of and directly in the range of vision of a person engaged in reading. The observer can note that the reader's eyes do not move regularly and systematically forward as the reading progresses but that the movements are interspersed with pauses or fixation periods. It is during these pauses that the images of the words or groups of words are secured. Carefully conducted laboratory experiments reveal the fact that good readers make long sweeps with the eyes, take in large units of words, pause for very short periods, and rarely retrace material once covered. Gates [31] concluded that improper eye movements are probably the evidences of other types of reading disability that can be treated specifically.

Remediation of Reading Disabilities

An examination of one of the major aspects of remedial work in reading indicates that there are two angles from which it may be considered. In the first place, remedial instruction may be begun in the oral reading field. Gray and others have defended this point of attack on the problem on the ground that it enables the teacher to start with the child on a level at which he already has some mastery, that is, the oral language level. Others believe that on account of the large proportion of reading time spent in the work type of silent reading this field should receive the special remedial emphasis. There is merit on both sides of the question, undoubtedly, but emphasis on the pronunciation of words in oral reading should not be allowed to detract from attention to the development of meanings in silent reading.

[30] *Ibid.* p. 275.
[31] Gates, *op. cit.* p. 444.

Remediation in oral reading. Gray recognized the practical aspects of remedial instruction in reading and suggested a number of exercises designed to overcome specific difficulties in reading, many of which are indicated by the ineffectual eye movements of the pupil. One of these exercises is reproduced here in part to illustrate types of material adapted to remedying certain oral reading difficulties.

EXERCISE TO INCREASE ACCURACY OF RECOGNITION [32]

1. Words which a pupil failed to recognize accurately while reading were used in sentences at the end of each period, in order that he might associate them with their meaning. The words which repeatedly caused difficulty were then typewritten on cards and used in quick-perception drills, by presenting them as rapidly as they were recognized. Such words as *again, want, been, does,* and *heard* were frequently emphasized. As soon as a pupil was able to recognize a word readily, drill on it was discontinued. New words were added to the list as difficulties were encountered.

2. Words which a pupil confused because of their similarity in form were emphasized in drill exercises. These words included such groups as *thought, though,* and *through, there* and *where, then* and *when, now* and *how,* and *has, had,* and *have.* The words were used in sentences before they were presented in quick-perception drills. If unusual difficulties were encountered, words which were similar in form were presented together so that their differences could be studied.

By practice in the use of such informal reading devices as these and by training themselves in careful observation of their pupils, teachers should soon find that they can become proficient in the art of building drill exercises.

Remediation in silent and work-study reading. Possibly one reason for the rather marked instructional emphasis on the work-study type of reading to the exclusion of reading of the leisure types is that it is reasonable to expect a considerable carry-over of skills from work-type reading to the other type, because of the large number of common skills involved. For example, skill in recognition of word meaning, which functions in work-study reading, is probably similarly effective when the individual is reading solely for pleasure.

A few illustrations of remedial exercises suited for use in silent reading of the work-study types are presented here as a guide to teachers interested in the development of this kind of material.

A significant factor in the child's use of reading for work-study periods

[32] William S. Gray, *Remedial Cases in Reading: Their Diagnosis and Treatment.* Supplementary Educational Monograph No. 22. University of Chicago Press, Chicago, 1922.

is his ability to locate information in books. The following suggestions may prove helpful:

1. To develop in pupils an ability to use the index, children should: (a) be taught the alphabet; (b) be drilled in arranging words in alphabetical order; (c) be drilled in finding answers to questions by use of the index; (d) be asked to prepare indexes for books not provided with them.
2. To develop the ability to use a table of contents, pupils should: (a) be assigned lessons by topic or titles; (b) find the assigned lessons in the text by means of the table of contents; (c) find additional sources of information on the assignment in the library.

The ability to organize what is read is a necessary part of the equipment of everyone who expects to become a good student. Organization of reading materials calls for a superior type of judgment. The following suggestions should aid teachers in developing a variety of types of practice in organization:

1. Practice in deciding upon the main thought in the paragraph or topic.
2. Drill in outlining a study, an assignment, a reference reading, a poem.
3. Practice in analyzing the organization of selections.
4. Practice in restating the substance of a difficult passage to convey the same idea in simplified form.
5. Practice in selecting the most appropriate title for a selection.

SUGGESTED ACTIVITIES

1. Outline ten to fifteen of the specific skills you think a high-school senior should possess in some area such as using an index, using a table of contents, or using a card catalog.
2. Obtain copies of two or three work-study tests of silent reading at your level of educational interest and compare them as to content and types of skills measured.

TOPICS FOR DISCUSSION

1. State your idea of the relative importance of the receptive and expressive language arts skills.
2. In what specific ways does modern life place a particular burden on the ability to read rapidly and well?
3. What is the importance of pupil readiness as a basic principle of learning?
4. What are some of the major aspects of reading readiness?
5. By what techniques is reading readiness typically measured?
6. Summarize your position with respect to the relative placement of instructional emphasis on oral and silent reading.
7. What are the two major oral reading testing techniques?

8. What are some of the major work-study testing techniques?
9. In what respects do work-study tests differ for the elementary and secondary grades?
10. Evaluate the school importance of listening as a receptive language skill. Is listening as important socially as silent reading abilities or study skills?
11. Discuss the nature of listening tests in English.
12. Why would you expect reading disability to be reflected in classroom achievement?
13. Is there reason to assume that remedial practices that are helpful in improving oral reading defects may also be useful in correcting silent reading deficiencies?

SELECTED REFERENCES

BANHAM, KATHERINE M. "Maturity Level for Reading Readiness: A Check List for the Use of Teachers and Parents as a Supplement to Reading Readiness Tests." *Educational and Psychological Measurement*, 18:371-75; Summer 1958.

BETTS, EMMETT A. *Foundations of Reading Instruction.* New York: American Book Co., 1957. Chapters 13, 21.

BLAIR, GLENN M. *Diagnostic and Remedial Teaching: A Guide to Practice in Elementary and Secondary Schools.* New York: Macmillan Co., 1956. Chapter 2.

BOND, GUY L. "Identifying the Reading Attainments and Needs of Students." *Reading in the High School and College.* Forty-Seventh Yearbook of the National Society for the Study of Education, Part II. Chicago: University of Chicago Press, 1948. Chapter 5.

BOND, GUY L., AND WAGNER, EVA B. *Teaching the Child to Read.* Third edition. New York: Macmillan Co., 1960. Chapters 7, 16.

BROWN, JAMES I. "The Measurement of Listening Ability." *School and Society*, 71:69-71; February 4, 1950.

BUROS, OSCAR K., editor. *The Fifth Mental Measurements Yearbook.* Highland Park, N. J.: Gryphon Press, 1959. p. 650-55, 721-99.

BUROS, OSCAR K., editor. *The Fourth Mental Measurements Yearbook.* Highland Park, N. J.: Gryphon Press, 1953. p. 317-23, 333-35, 567-620.

BUROS, OSCAR K., editor. *The Third Mental Measurements Yearbook.* New Brunswick, N. J.: Rutgers University Press, 1949. p. 247-57, 501-71.

BURTON, WILLIAM H., AND OTHERS. *Reading in Child Development.* Indianapolis, Ind.: Bobbs-Merrill Co., Inc., 1956. Chapter 14.

COHEE, M. CATHERINE; MILLER, RUTH B.; AND WALLACE, MARIE E. "Developing Local Reading Tests for Citywide Use." *National Elementary Principal*, 17:601-7; July 1938.

CRONBACH, LEE J. "Measuring Knowledge of Precise Word Meaning." *Journal of Educational Research*, 36:528-34; March 1943.

DAVIS, FREDERICK B. "What Do Reading Tests Really Measure?" *English Journal*, 33:180-87; April 1944.

DOLCH, EDWARD W. "How to Diagnose Children's Reading Difficulties by Informal Classroom Techniques." *Reading Teacher*, 6:10-14; January 1953.

DOLCH, EDWARD W. "Testing Reading Comprehension with a Book." *Elementary English*, 28:124-25, 165; March 1951.

DOLCH, EDWARD W., AND LEEDS, DON. "Vocabulary Tests and Depth of Meaning." *Journal of Educational Research*, 47:181-89; November 1953.

GATES, ARTHUR I. *The Improvement of Reading: A Program of Diagnostic and Remedial Methods.* Third edition. New York: Macmillan Co., 1947. Chapter 3.

GERBERICH, J. RAYMOND. *Specimen Objective Test Items: A Guide to Achievement Test Construction.* New York: Longmans, Green and Co., 1956. p. 331-35.

GRAY, WILLIAM S. "Physiology and Psychology of Reading." *Encyclopedia of Educational Research.* Third edition. New York: Macmillan Co., 1960. p 1096-1114.

GRAY, WILLIAM S. "The Teaching of Reading." *Encyclopedia of Educational Research.* Third edition. New York: Macmillan Co., 1960. p. 1114-35.

GREENE, HARRY A., AND GRAY, WILLIAM S. "The Measurement of Understanding in the Language Arts." *The Measurement of Understanding.* Forty-Fifth Yearbook of the National Society for the Study of Education, Part I. Chicago: University of Chicago Press, 1946. p. 189-200.

GREENE, HARRY A., JORGENSEN, ALBERT N., AND GERBERICH, J. RAYMOND. *Measurement and Evaluation in the Elementary School.* Second edition. New York: Longmans, Green and Co., 1953. Chapter 15.

GREENE, HARRY A., JORGENSEN, ALBERT N., AND GERBERICH, J. RAYMOND. *Measurement and Evaluation in the Secondary School.* Second edition. New York: Longmans, Green and Co., 1954. Chapter 15.

HARRIS, ALBERT J. *How to Increase Reading Ability: A Guide to Developmental and Remedial Methods.* Fourth edition. New York: Longmans, Green and Co., 1961. Chapters 6-7.

KOTTMEYER, WILLIAM. *Teacher's Guide for Remedial Reading.* St. Louis, Mo.: Webster Publishing Co., 1959. Chapters 3-7.

LESTER, JOHN A., AND LINDQUIST, E. F. "Examinations in English." *The Construction and Use of Achievement Examinations.* Boston: Houghton Mifflin Co., 1936. p. 381-410.

McKIM, MARGARET G. *Guiding Growth in Reading in the Modern Elementary School.* New York: Macmillan Co., 1955. Chapter 13.

MECHEL, HENRY C. "Evaluating Growth in Reading." *Reading in the High School and College.* Forty-Seventh Yearbook of the National Society for the Study of Education, Part II. Chicago: University of Chicago Press, 1948. Chapter 12.

MORSE, HORACE T., AND McCUNE, GEORGE H. *Selected Items for the Testing of Study Skills and Critical Thinking.* National Council for the Social Studies, Bulletin No. 15. Third edition. Washington, D. C.: National Education Association, 1957.

NICHOLS, RALPH G. "Factors in Listening Comprehension." *Speech Monographs*, 15:154-63; 1948.

POND, FREDERICK L. "A Simplified Method of Scoring an Inventory of Reading Experiences." *Journal of Educational Research,* 45:585-97; April 1952.

RUSSELL, DAVID H. "Evaluation of Pupil Growth in and through Reading." *Reading in the Elementary School.* Forty-Eighth Yearbook of the National Society for the Study of Education, Part II. Chicago: University of Chicago Press, 1949. Chapter 14.

SPACHE, GEORGE. "The Construction and Validation of a Work-Type Auditory Comprehension Reading Test." *Educational and Psychological Measurement*, 10:249-53; Summer 1950.

STRANG, RUTH; McCULLOUGH, CONSTANCE M.; AND TRAXLER, ARTHUR E. *Problems in the Improvement of Reading.* Second edition. New York: McGraw-Hill Book Co., Inc., 1955. Chapters 12-13.

TRAXLER, ARTHUR E. "Measurement in the Field of Reading." *English Journal,* 38:143-49; March 1949.

WHEELER, LESTER R., AND SMITH, EDWIN H. "A Modification of the Informal Reading Inventory." *Elementary English,* 34:224-26; April 1957.

16

ENGLISH LANGUAGE,

SPELLING, AND HANDWRITING

This chapter presents a summary of the major points involved in measuring and evaluating the outcomes and products of instruction in English language and in subjects related to oral and written expression:

A. Social and educational significance of English language skills.
B. Specific aims, outcomes, and products of instruction in English.
C. Evaluation of oral and written language skills and products.
D. Diagnosis and analysis of mechanics of written composition.
E. Diagnosis and analysis of language usages.
F. Measurement and evaluation in spelling.
G. Measurement and evaluation in handwriting.

The language skills concerned primarily with expression and communication—English language, grammar and usage, speech, spelling, and handwriting—are discussed in this chapter. These, together with reading, listening, and the work-study skills treated in the preceding chapter, round out the English language arts subjects ordinarily stressed in the school program.

1. SCOPE, AIMS, AND OUTCOMES OF LANGUAGE

Mastery of the tools of expression and communication as represented by such specialized areas as composition, language usage, grammar, speech, spelling, and handwriting unquestionably constitutes the most fundamental of all school outcomes. The fact that instruction in each of these fields begins with the child's first days of school and in some form continues to receive needed emphasis throughout the individual's life may be taken as the best evidence of its educational and social importance. The fact that the individual rarely achieves adequate mastery over these important expressional skills demonstrates their great complexity and difficulty of learning. It is significant that English, which was one of the first subjects to be measured objectively, is one of the slowest areas to respond to analysis and to remedial treatment. This may be due in part to the formal methods of instruction followed by many teachers, but it is more likely to be due to the sheer complexity of the subject itself, and to the many specialized forms in which it expresses itself.

Social and Educational Significance of English

English is a distinctly social subject. The language skills function to make communication possible and pleasant. Accordingly, the activities of the English classroom must provide for social conditions under which communication can take place. The pupil must have something to transmit. He must write or speak to someone for a definite purpose. Whether he wishes to inform, to convince, to inspire, or merely to entertain, he must have a reasonable mastery of such tool skills of expression as sentence sense, language usage, mechanics of writing, and spelling.

Viewed in this way, English is much more than the specific language skills utilized in recording and transmitting ideas. It involves the skills required for the acquisition of ideas, either through the ear or through the eye. This is the aspect of language that is treated in Chapter 15. Thus, there are English skills that are definitely receptive and others that are as definitely productive or expressive. The latter, the language of expression, is the phase usually meant by the term "language ability," and is the phrase that receives special attention in the English classroom.

In this discussion, language skill is considered to mean facility in the use of the proper language habits and forms essential to effective intercommunication at a particular cultural level. Such a point of view makes reasonably clear the problems of the teacher of English. Language skills arise, as do other specific skills, through the proper exercise of the desired habits. Obviously, proper exercise is possible only when proper identification of the habits has taken place. Hence the habits upon which effective language expression depends must be identified and much carefully constructed instructional and drill material must be provided. This in itself serves two useful purposes. First, the use of good language drill material insures that the pupil will have experience in making the correct responses to language situations either with or without the assistance of formal grammar instruction. Second, the use of such material sets up in the pupil's mind an attitude toward language error.

Objectives and Outcomes of Language

The accompanying outline of language objectives and outcomes is a compilation and adaptation of material from several sources. It is believed that it will give the teacher and student helpful suggestions for the identification of important language skills.

LANGUAGE OBJECTIVES AND OUTCOMES

I. Oral Language
  A. General knowledge and skill outcomes
    1. To articulate and enunciate clearly
    2. To assume an appropriate posture when speaking
    3. To use common courtesy in social groups
    4. To speak with feeling and reflect meaning and thought
    5. To locate and give information
    6. To think while speaking
    7. To use sentence sense in stating ideas
    8. To pronounce words correctly
    9. To acquire new words
    10. To speak at a rate suitable to conditions
    11. To speak with suitable clarity and loudness
    12. To judge what is suitable to talk about
  B. Special knowledge and skill outcomes
    1. To relate anecdotes and incidents interestingly
    2. To make necessary announcements simply
    3. To participate in conversation easily
    4. To take part in arguments and debates
    5. To disagree or agree courteously
    6. To summarize and report activities, events, news items
    7. To react properly to social responsibilities
    8. To take part in dramatizations, plays
    9. To use the telephone properly

II. Written Language
  A. General knowledge and skill outcomes
    1. To answer letters promptly
    2. To choose content for friendly letters and letters of sympathy wisely
    3. To use correct form in business and social letters, invitations
    4. To fill in common forms, questionnaires, blanks
    5. To write notices, announcements, advertisements, telegrams
    6. To be skillful in creative writing
    7. To be skillful in making outlines from content material
    8. To record minutes of meetings, dictated material
    9. To organize class and lecture notes
    10. To prepare an acurate and comprehensive bibliography

B. Special knowledge and skill outcomes
  1. To write legibly and rapidly
  2. To spell socially useful forms correctly
  3. To utilize proper manuscript forms
  4. To use proper outline forms
  5. To punctuate correctly
  6. To capitalize correctly

III. Both Oral and Written Language
  A. General outcomes
    1. To desire to make correct use of language
    2. To be sensitive to errors in usage
    3. To use variety in sentence structure
    4. To identify sentence types by voice and punctuation
    5. To expand the meaning vocabulary
  B. Usage skills
    1. To use pronouns, verbs, subject-predicate relations correctly
    2. To avoid double negatives, vague antecedents, redundancy
  C. Rhetorical skills
    1. To avoid useless introductory words and phrases
    2. To avoid loose use of connectives
    3. To organize sentences so that they say precisely what is meant
    4. To organize ideas in a paragraph around a single topic
    5. To organize ideas in a paragraph in proper sequence
    6. To avoid use of overworked words
    7. To use accurate, suitable, colorful, and varied words
    8. To use contrasts, variety, simile-metaphor

Analysis of Language Skills

An accurate analysis of the underlying skills in language is necessary before any significant program of analytical and corrective work can be undertaken. In the past, certain general language abilities have been identified for measurement purposes, such as language usage, grammar, and composition. Recently, however, efforts have been made to reduce language in general to its more elementary or basic skills. Even so, the task of clarifying the purposes of English instruction and of analyzing and identifying the basic language skills and products is a difficult one.

Language as Process and as Product

The problems of measuring and evaluating the outcomes of instruction in English are peculiarly complicated by the fact that language expression is both a process and a product, and that both are important outcomes of the instructional program. Actually, it was the problems of appraising the quality of the language product that first attracted the attention of the early workers in educational measurement and prompted them to develop quality scales for the evaluation of the merit of such tangible products as handwriting and written composition. In the beginning it seemed natural to assume that a written or oral product of high quality was in itself direct evidence that the producer possessed superior mastery of the required expressional skills and that he uniformly utilized all of these skills at top efficiency. Later the subjective limitations involved in evaluating the products became apparent and gradually stimulated the development of objective measures of the special skills utilized in creative language expression. Many tests of language skills, such as punctuation, capitalization, usage, grammatical knowledge, sentence structure, organization of ideas, word choice and word meanings, and the like, appeared and for a time seemed to meet the requirements of the language classroom. Here again, however, a limitation on the validity of these instruments arose through the questionable assumption that the individual who is superior in knowledge and use of specific skills in a test situation will be equally superior in applying them to the production of superior expression. Examples of the failure of this assumption to work in practice are readily found in the experience of every classroom teacher or supervisor.

2. MEASUREMENT OF ORAL LANGUAGE SKILLS

Success in the use of oral language depends in the first place on the ability of the speaker to so choose, arrange, and enunciate his words as to affect his hearers as he intends. In order to guarantee success in the operation of these skills, the pupil must be given training and practice in thinking and talking under audience conditions. In this training, emphasis must be placed on the development of a pleasant speaking voice, a gracious attitude, a clear enunciation of words, an avoidance of common language errors, care in the selection of words, a careful selection and organization of ideas, and skill in the clothing of his thoughts in the proper words so that he may affect his hearers as he intends by leading their thinking along prescribed channels.

A thoughtful examination of the foregoing outline of general language outcomes makes it clear that oral language ability is made up of many highly interrelated skills. It also becomes equally obvious that from the standpoint of its social utility oral language is extremely important. Yet, in spite of its social importance and the long-time interest of teachers and research workers in the subject, evaluative instruments suitable for the reliable appraisal of the products or the oral language skills producing them are extremely limited. There are few standardized instruments for the measurement of oral expression that will stand inspection under

present-day criteria. Possibly the difficulties involved in securing adequate
samples of oral expression may also account for the limited use of measuring instruments in this skill area. Perhaps the encouraging results from
the experimental use of modern tape recorders may stimulate the development of oral scales and other types of measures of oral expression. In the
meantime the classroom teacher must depend chiefly upon informal devices for the appraisal of oral language skills and products.

Oral Language Objectives and Evaluative Techniques

The following abbreviated list of functional objectives of oral expression
with related samples of informal appraisal and evaluative techniques is
adapted from an extensive presentation of similar suggestions by Greene
and Gray.[1] These examples will undoubtedly suggest many other informal
procedures to the teacher or student who is seriously interested in the
evaluation of oral expressional skills and products.

ORAL LANGUAGE OBJECTIVES WITH SUGGESTED
EVALUATIVE PROCEDURES [2]

Objective: To greet others easily and courteously in social situations.
        Adequate social adjustment is best shown by the ease and courtesy
        of the individual in meeting others in all types of social situations.

Evaluation: a. Does he sense the relation of existing conditions to the suitability
        of the greeting?
        b. When strangers meet is he sensitive to the need for and the proper
        form of introduction?
        c. When entering or leaving a social group can he do so without unduly interrupting the conversation?

Objective: To tell a story or personal experience effectively
        The success of an oral story rests upon the audience appeal of the
        incident, the selection and arrangement of the details, and the animation of the narrator. Apply the following criteria in evaluating the
        pupil's presentation:

Evaluation: a. Standards for selecting a good topic for a story
        (1) Was the incident unusual, startling, or very amusing?
        (2) Did the narrator see it or take part in it himself?
        (3) Did he make the characters speak for themselves?

---

[1] Harry A. Greene and William S. Gray, "The Measurement of Understanding in the
Language Arts." *The Measurement of Understanding,* Forty-Fifth Yearbook of the National Society for the Study of Education, Part I. University of Chicago Press, Chicago,
1946. p. 175-80.
[2] Many more suggestions of evaluative techniques for both oral and written expression
are given in Harry A. Greene and Walter T. Petty, *Developing Language Skills in the
Elementary School.* Allyn and Bacon, Inc., Boston, 1959. Chapter 19.

      (4) Did the story have an interesting, surprising, satisfactory out-
come?
  b. Points for arranging the details of the story
     (1) When, where, and under what circumstances did the incident
take place?
     (2) Who were the characters? Did each have a distinctive part?
     (3) What fact or event started the incident?
     (4) What facts or events complicated the incident?
     (5) What did the incident lead to?
  c. Standards for judging the effective storyteller
     (1) He looked directly at his audience.
     (2) He spoke clearly and not too rapidly.
     (3) He avoided "and-uh" and other sounds between words and
sentences.
     (4) He chose colorful descriptive words.
     (5) He reflected his thoughts and interest in his face and general
attitude.
     (6) He used appropriate gestures.
     (7) He appeared relaxed and at ease.

Analysis and Remediation in Oral Language

Considerable progress in the identification of oral language disabilities
and in the development of sound and practical corrective procedures in
oral expression has been made by speech teachers and speech pathologists
in recent years. In spite of the fact that the typical classroom teacher
should not attempt corrective treatment for most of the identifiable speech
disorders except under medical or clinical direction, certain of these disorders have such immediate and serious effects upon the individual pupil
that it is important for the teacher to realize their nature and extent.
Baby talk, lisping, and nasal speech are quite readily recognized and
usually respond to simple treatment. Disorders arising from organic causes,
such as malformation of tongue, teeth, jaws, or palate, and emotional
disorders resulting in stammering or stuttering are extremely serious and
should be brought promptly to the attention of the speech pathologist.

Oral language activities in the classroom should avoid emphasis on the
artistic and technical aspects of speech since these specialized skills are
clearly outside the responsibility of the teacher of English. Aside from the
problems of oral language that are peculiarly identified with the field of
speech a large part of the oral language activity should be closely integrated with the work in written English and literature as well as with all
other content subjects. The teacher's primary aim should be to conduct
the work in such ways that the pupils will be equipped to meet effectively
the normal speech demands of everyday life.

3. MEASUREMENT OF WRITTEN LANGUAGE SKILLS

The problems involved in measuring the written language skills take a threefold form, although this is not entirely apparent from the list of outcomes given in the outline below. The first involves the formal or mechanical factors, primarily capitalization, punctuation, and general appearance. The second treats of certain grammatical factors, such as common usage in language form and sentence structure and form. The third is concerned with the more subtle elements of expression, the rhetorical components involving choice of words, qualities of interest innate in the material, and logical organization of the subject matter both within the sentence and the larger units. In the first two phases of the problem of written language, the elements are more generally uniform in their manner of affecting readers. However, there is greater difficulty in predicting the effect of the third phase on the reader. These mechanical and grammatical elements constitute in a way the raw material of written expression. The rhetorical components are the results of the manner in which these raw materials are put together. They are the factors that make for appeal, originality, style, and distinctiveness in written expression. The mechanical and grammatical elements are relatively tangible, objective, and measurable. The rhetorical factors are intangible, elusive, and extremely difficult to identify and to measure.

Skills Peculiar to Written Expression

The catalog of language outcomes presented on pages 375 and 376 is a reasonably satisfactory classification for the purpose of contrasting the two major types of verbal expression, but it seems inadequate when considered from the point of view of the complete identification and analysis of the specific underlying skills upon which verbal expression depends. For this more exacting purpose a classification based on such units of language form as the word, the sentence, the paragraph, and the composition unit, and on certain general mechanical factors, is superior. In order to present a more concrete idea of the types of abilities called into play at each of these levels of language skill, the accompanying detailed outline is given.

DIAGNOSTIC OUTLINE OF LANGUAGE SKILLS

A. Words—Skill in the spelling, choice, use, and definition
   1. Choice of words
     a. Same
     b. Opposite
     c. Exact word for meaning

       d. Variety
       e. Meaningful words
       f. Minimum number of words
       g. Semantic variations in meanings
   2. Correct usage
       a. Verbs
       b. Pronouns
       c. Modifiers
       d. Nouns

B. Sentences—Skill in the use, form, structure, and organization
   1. Form
       a. Complete, coherent, unified
       b. Variation in beginning
       c. Variation in length
   2. Kind
       a. Declarative
       b. Interrogative
       c. Exclamatory
   3. Structure
       a. Simple, compound, complex
       b. Subject and predicate
       c. Variety in structure
       d. Language usage—avoidance of slang, faulty expressions
   4. Organization
       a. Logical sequence of ideas
       b. Variety for interest

C. Paragraphs—Skill in the form, structure, and organization
   1. Form
       a. Indentation
       b. Initial and terminal line length
       c. Length
   2. Structure
       a. Unity
       b. Coherence
   3. Organization
       a. Outline
       b. Logical sequence of ideas
       c. Semantic variations in meanings
   4. Correct usage
       a. Verbs
       b. Pronouns
       c. Modifiers
       d. Nouns

D. General mechanical factors—Skill in control of
   1. Capitalization
       a. Initial words in sentences
       b. Proper nouns
       c. Proper adjectives

  d. Titles of honor and respect
  e. Important words in titles of stories, articles
 2. Punctuation
  a. End
  b. Series
  c. Quoted matter
  d. Special situations
 3. Margins
  a. Top, bottom, sides
  b. Indentation
 4. Abbreviations
  a. Titles
  b. Other situations
 5. Hyphenations
  a. Compound words
  b. Ends of lines

EXCERPTS FROM *Iowa Language Abilities Test* [3]

TEST 4. CAPITALIZATION

DIRECTIONS. In some of the following sentences, words which should begin with capital letters are written with small letters. All such words, and some of the others also, are numbered. Notice the number of each word you think should be capitalized. Then fill in the answer space under this number. There is not more than one error in any sentence. In some of the sentences, none of the numbered words should be capitalized. If a sentence contains no error, fill in the answer space under N.

1. the teacher asked me to help her. 1
2. Shall we go home now? 2
3. We expect to visit them at easter. 3
4. The man's name was John b. Ray. 4

TEST 5. PUNCTUATION

DIRECTIONS. In each of the following sentences, certain words are printed in type *like this*. This means that you are to look for some punctuation mark which may be needed before, within, or after this word. In some cases no punctuation is needed. Study each sentence and decide which punctuation mark, if any, is needed. In the answer spaces at the right, fill in the space under the correct punctuation mark to use in the sentence at the place indicated by the word. If you think that no punctuation is needed, fill in the answer space under N.

1. He will go *today* 1

2. That table is *theirs*. 2

3. We do not go to school during *June* July, and August. 3

4. The war began on *May 14* 1871. 4

[3] Harry A. Greene and H. L. Ballenger, *Iowa Language Abilities Test: Test 4, Capitalization; Test 5, Punctuation,* Elementary. Form A. Copyright 1948 by Harcourt, Brace and World, Inc., New York. All rights reserved. Quoted by special permission.

Measurement of English Mechanics

The first of the three important aspects of written expression mentioned above involves such elements as capitalization, punctuation, general appearance, and the two aspects of language—spelling and handwriting—treated in later sections of this chapter.

Two illustrations of test items designed to measure certain of these mechanics of English appear in accompanying excerpts. The first, from the *Iowa Language Abilities Test,* measures capitalization and punctuation skills separately. An excerpt from the language section of the *Metropolitan Achievement Tests* that is shown on page 237 illustrates another technique for measuring these two skills in combination. The second illustration shown here, from the *Cooperative English Expression Test,* measures these two skills in combination with spelling and usage.

EXCERPT FROM *Cooperative English Expression Test* [4]

Directions: Read each three-line sentence and decide whether there are errors in *usage, spelling, punctuation,* or *capitalization* in any of the three parts. If so, note the letter printed beside the part which contains the error or errors. Then mark the letter for that part next to the number of the question on your answer sheet. If there is no error in any part of the sentence, mark **0** on your answer sheet. No sentence has more than one part with errors, and some sentences do not have any errors.

13 **A** Fewer votes were cast than
  B had been perdicted by even
  C the most pessimistic of forecasters.

14 **E** He got a taxicab more quickly than he had anticipated,
  F thus he thought that he had plenty* of time to reach
  G the restaurant where the conference was to be held.

Measurement of Usage and Grammar

Methods used in measuring this second aspect of written language skill mentioned above vary from those emphasizing functional grammar or

[4] Educational Testing Service, *Cooperative English Expression Test: Part II, Mechanics.* Educational Testing Service, Princeton, N. J., 1960.

usage to those stressing the formal rules of grammar. Some tests even measure the functional and the formal aspects of language in combination.

Language usage. Two illustrations of techniques for usage testing are presented in this volume. The *Iowa Language Abilities Test* is represented by an accompanying excerpt that makes no direct demands on grammatical knowledges in asking pupils to distinguish a correct from an incorrect usage. The excerpt from the language section of the *Metropolitan Achievement Test* appearing on page 234, however, tests the ability of pupils to identify words used in context as nouns, pronouns, verbs, or adjectives.

EXCERPT FROM Iowa Language Abilities Test [5]

TEST 3. LANGUAGE USAGE: CORRECT WORD

DIRECTIONS. One of the two numbered words in each sentence below is the correct one to use in the sentence. Notice the number of the correct form. Then, in the column at the right, fill in the answer space which has the same number as the word which makes the sentence correct.

1. I think (1) them (2) those books are mine. 1

2. (1) Let (2) Leave me go, please. 2

3. (1) They (2) There is a package for you at home. 3

4. Did you (1) here (2) hear the bell? 4

Grammar. For those who believe that there is a formal as well as a functional aspect of usage, the *Kirby Grammar Test* [6] still meets the need for this type of test. This test measures the ability of the pupil to select the correct one of two usages in a sentence situation and to recognize the correct grammatical reason for his choice. The content of the usage exercises is based on a rather old study of the typical errors of children. Numerous comparisons of scores on usage and grammatical principles right on this test fail to show a significant positive relationship. Somewhat in contrast with this test, the *Iowa Grammar Information Test* [7] measures purely informational aspects of English grammar in 80 specific situations.

Measurement of English Effectiveness

This third and least tangible aspect of written expression mentioned above cannot be measured with the degree of precision possible for the mechanics and usage skills dealt with in the two immediately preceding

---

[5] Greene and Ballenger, *op. cit. Test 3, Language Usage.*

[6] T. J. Kirby, *Kirby Grammar Test.* Bureau of Educational Research and Service, State University of Iowa, Iowa City, 1920.

[7] Fred D. Cram and H. A. Greene, *Iowa Grammar Information Test.* Bureau of Educational Research and Service, State University of Iowa, Iowa City, 1935.

sections. The three approaches to measurement of these intangible outcomes treated here are (1) tests of English effectiveness, (2) English
composition scales, and (3) tests of specialized letter-writing skills.

Tests of English effectiveness. Certain aspects of rhetorical skills can
be measured by objective test items such as those shown in an accompanying excerpt from the *Cooperative English Expression Test.* The pupil is
asked in these items to select the one of four words or phrases that best
completes a certain sentence. Two levels of complexity seem to be represented—compound or complex sentences with single-word options from
which choices are to be made by pupils and simple sentences with pupil
responses to be selected from relatively long phrases or clauses.

EXCERPT FROM *Cooperative English Expression Test* [8]

Directions: In each question, decide which one of the
lettered choices would most suitably complete the
sentence if inserted in place of the (   ). Mark
the letter of that word or phrase opposite the
number of the question on your answer sheet.

8   Because literature was not considered an
    honorable calling, (   ) literary compositions
    were fairly common in the seventeenth century.

    E anonymous   **G** disguised
    F fictitious   **H** confidential

9   Holding his umbrella against the wind, (   ).

    A the old gentleman stubbornly pressed on to
          the park to feed the pigeons
    B the old gentleman pressed on to the park
          stubbornly to feed the pigeons
    C the old gentleman who had stubbornly
          pressed on to the park fed the pigeons
    D the pigeons received food from the old
          gentleman who was so stubborn that he
          pressed on to the park to feed them

English composition scales. Attempts to evaluate the general merit of
written expression, while dating well back into the history of educational
measurement, have not brought improvements in proportion to the attention given to the problem. This situation undoubtedly arises partly from
the complexity of the skills involved in producing written expression, and

[8] Educational Testing Service, *op. cit. Part I, Effectiveness.*

partly from the vagueness with which these skills have been recognized as contributing to quality in the product. Historically, the *Hillegas Composition Scale* was one of the first attempts to measure an educational product. Under the stimulation of Thorndike, Hillegas produced a scale [9] for the measurement of quality of children's written expression which provided the teacher with specimens arranged in order of merit according to assigned numerical values with which the written products of his class could be compared. Not only has this scale accomplished much good through the stimulation of teacher and research interest in the more accurate measurement of written expression, but, as later extended and standardized by Thorndike,[10] it is still considered by many to be a usable instrument.

Among the more useful of the currently available scales for the measurement of composition quality is the *Willing Scale for Measuring Written Composition*.[11] This scale is made up of eight specimens of composition all written on the topic, "An Exciting Experience." Through the definite recognition of the relation of form errors to the general quality of written work this scale increases its usefulness. Its value is also enhanced through the very clear directions for the collection of compositions for survey purposes. An excellent list of interesting topics is also suggested as the basis for the written work. The use of such standardized lists of topics and the control of conditions under which the writing takes place add distinctly to the reliability with which written composition abilities may be measured.

The *STEP Essay Tests,* developed by a large group of the publisher's staff members, cooperating advisors and readers, and test authors, represent an encouraging new approach for the evaluation of writing ability over a wide range of skills and interests.[12] The series consists of sixteen essay-writing tests in four alternate forms for use at four different ability levels ranging from the fourth grade to the sophomore year of college. Scoring the essays written on directed topics in the 30-minute writing time allowed is accomplished by matching students' papers with evaluated comparison essays on the same topics and assigning one of seven ratings (1—low to 7—high) to each test paper. Each rating is weighted 50 per-

[9] Milo B. Hillegas, *A Scale for the Measurement of Quality in English Composition by Young People.* Bureau of Publications, Teachers College, Columbia University, New York, 1912.

[10] Edward L. Thorndike, *Thorndike Extension of the Hillegas Scale for Measurement of Quality of English Composition by Young People.* Bureau of Publications, Teachers College, Columbia University, New York, 1914.

[11] M. H. Willing, *Willing Scale for Measuring Written Composition.* Public School Publishing Co., Bloomington, Ill., 1920.

[12] Educational Testing Service, *Sequential Tests of Educational Progress: Handbook for Essay Tests.* Educational Testing Service, Princeton, N. J., 1957.

cent for quality of thought and content, 30 percent for style, and 20 percent for mechanics of writing. By using tables appearing in the *Handbook*, these raw scores may be translated into converted scores and percentile ranks for comparison with national or locally derived norms.

While composition scales of the types described above have not generally been accepted with enthusiasm by English teachers, it appears certain that these scales, nevertheless, have accomplished much good through focusing teacher interest on the qualities capable of appraisal and the need for improved measures of written expression. In the actual use of these scales in the classroom, the pupil's written product is compared with each of the scaled specimens until a scaled sample is found that on the basis of the reader's best judgment reveals approximately the same elements of quality as the pupil's product. The scale value of the comparable scale specimen is then assigned to the pupil's sample.

Evaluating the quality of written products by using composition scales unfortunately is limited by at least two types of unreliability. The first of these results from the reader's subjective ratings; the second arises from the usually brief and inadequate samplings of written products on which the ratings are based. The teacher must realize that reliable evaluations of the written products of an individual pupil can be obtained only as a result of very extensive samplings of his written work, repeated ratings of the product by a qualified reader, many independent ratings by a number of expert judges, or a combination of all of these steps.

By constantly stressing the elements of quality in written expression and by collecting extensive samples of the written products of his pupils at the beginning and the conclusion of instruction, the teacher can evaluate class and individual improvements and at the same time determine whether or not his pupils are expressing themselves as well as they should at their present grade and maturity level. If the teacher avoids the error of thinking of these appraisals as having the accuracy of objective test scores, these measures of general merit of written expression can be extremely valuable aids in the language and English classroom.

Letter-writing tests. The evaluation of letter writing as effective language expression consists largely in the appraisal of the quality of the product itself in terms of content, form, and mechanics. From the start, the pupil usually learns about content from class discussions and about form and mechanics from models and from dictated letters which he copies. When more objective measures of letter-writing abilities and products are desired a copying test such as that comprising Part 8 of the *Iowa Primary Language Test* [13] may be used. This letter-writing test, standard-

[13] Lou A. Shepard and Harry A. Greene, *Iowa Primary Language Test.* Bureau of Educational Research and Service, State University of Iowa, Iowa City, 1936.

ized for use in the second and third grades, measures the child's ability to insert the correct punctuation marks, greeting, and signature in a printed letter form. Attention is called to certain omissions by reading the letter aloud to the class before the test is begun. The test is scored on the following ten points, allowing one point for each correct response: *comma after city, year* given correctly in date, *Dear* written correctly in salutation, *comma* after name in salutation, *period* after first sentence, *capital M* in Miss, *period* after last sentence, *comma* after sincerely, *whole name* written correctly, *name placed at right of paper* and below closing.

Teachers interested in an appraisal and guidance device for use with more mature pupils should examine the score sheet for evaluating friendly and informal letters given by Greene and Petty.[14] A total score of 100 points is possible on fifty elements of good letter form and content.

Analytical Measurement of Language Skills

When the currently available language tests are examined in the light of modern criteria for diagnostic measurement the majority of such instruments appear to fall short of being really diagnostic. Certain of these tests, however, do provide an analytical program in language of rather adequate breadth in grade and content coverage.

A reasonably accurate analytical appraisal of pupil accomplishment in Grades 1, 2, and 3 in eight different oral and written skill and product

INDIVIDUAL PUPIL'S TEST RECORD

Part	Test	Grade:	Perfect score		
			ONE	TWO	THREE
1.	Filling in forms		14	15	15
2.	Conversation		14	14	14
3.	Oral composition		12	12	12
4.	Telephone conversation		10	10	10
5.	Correct usage		40	40	40
6.	Recorded composition		6	6	6
7.	Miscellaneous social usage				
	A. Description		3	3	3
	B. Introductions		5	5	5
	C. Announcement, message, invitation		5	5	5
	D. Directions for finding a place		3	3	3
	E. Forms of courtesy		3	3	3
8.	Letter writing		..	10	10
Total			115	126	126

[14] Greene and Petty, *op. cit.* p. 454-55.

areas of language is provided by the *Iowa Primary Language Test*. The eight language areas sampled by the test with the number of points representing a perfect score at each grade level are indicated in the reproduction of the test record sheet appearing on page 388.[15]

The pupil reactions are simple and require little or no reading skill. The tests may be administered in groups of six or eight or even larger by the time the pupils have reached the maturity of the second half of the first grade. A special feature of the test is the comprehensive manual which presents a useful inventory of language skills ordinarily emphasized in these grades as well as a double-column set of directions which determine the form of the test being administered. Norms for the beginning, middle, and end of the school year are available.

The *Iowa Language Abilities Tests* [16] are analytical group batteries for use at two elementary-school levels. Both provide extensive samplings of important language skills and require long testing periods insuring reliable results. The elementary test booklet comprises five subtests on spelling, word meanings, language usage, capitalization, and punctuation, and is for use in Grades 4, 5, and 6 with optional use in Grade 7. In addition to these five tests, the intermediate booklet, designed for use in Grades 7, 8, and 9 with optional use in Grade 10, contains tests on grammatical form recognition and sentence sense.

The *Greene-Stapp Language Abilities Test* [17] is an attempt to extend the same types of analytical measurement into the high-school and college-freshman levels. The five test parts, covering capitalization, spelling, sentence structure and applied grammar, punctuation, and usage and applied grammar, require two class periods for administration. Tests 3 and 5 represent novel procedures in relating grammatical information to sentence structure and usage situations. The test uses separate answer sheets designed for hand- or machine-scoring.

Remedial Instruction in Written English

Remedial instruction in language will be effective only to the extent that pupils are made aware of the social importance of correct usage and are led to develop a desire to make use of the best forms of expression and to formulate correct habits of usage. Language tests of the analytic types should aid in the developing of a self-critical attitude on the part of the

[15] Shepard and Greene, *op. cit.*
[16] Greene and Ballenger, *op. cit.* Elementary and Intermediate.
[17] Harry A. Greene and Helen I. Stapp, *Greene-Stapp Language Abilities Test.* World Book Co., Yonkers, N. Y., 1952.

pupil, which naturally leads to the desire to acquire correct habits of expression.

Specimen types of remedial exercises in language are not presented here for two reasons. In the first place, there are countless excellent practice and drill books in the English field that provide adequate experience in the important skill areas. In the second place, the parallel between the desirable types of language drills and the types of exercises used in the tests to reveal the presence or absence of the skills is very close.

A number of diagnostic and remedial suggestions for the fields of capitalization, punctuation, language usage, sentence sense, and spelling were offered by Greene and Petty.[18]

4. MEASUREMENT OF PROFICIENCY IN SPELLING

The importance of correct spelling in the written communication of ideas is demonstrated repeatedly in ordinary social and business activities. Its social significance and its tool value in connection with later school progress are so great that most educators are unwilling to depend upon incidental learning for the development of the required skill. Spelling is an area in which the learning is specific. The child does not just learn spelling; he learns to spell specific words. He may master a definite method of learning certain words, but the words he learns to spell are acquired as a result of the definite application of effort and attention. Such factors as superior mental capacity, outstanding vividness of imagery, and an unusually retentive memory may all contribute to success in learning to spell. Being a good speller involves much more than merely being able to make a high score on a spelling test.

Nature of Spelling Ability

The good speller is one who recognizes the social importance of correct spelling in all of his written expression, endeavors at all times to spell correctly each word he writes, and equips himself to learn independently how to spell each new word he encounters. These attitudes, habits, and skills combine to produce in the individual what is known as the ability to spell.

The spelling ability of an individual may best be expressed in terms of his success in arranging correctly the letters comprising the specific words he is called upon to write. Words vary in difficulty of spelling just as individuals vary in their mastery of the skills required to spell the words. Word difficulty and pupil ability to spell the words thus appear to be much

[18] Greene and Petty, *op. cit.* p. 476-77, 481-84.

like the opposite ends of a teeter-totter; as word difficulty goes up, what is described as pupil ability goes down. On easy words, even the poor speller shows up favorably. At any given time the spelling ability of the individual child depends upon his capacity and his previous learning opportunity. Performance on a given spelling test varies in accordance with the testing conditions, and the difficulty of the words in the test, in addition to the factors mentioned above.

Measurable Qualities in Spelling

Ability to spell is usually revealed by the pupil's success in writing, in either list or context form, words that have been selected from some vocabulary list of social or school importance. For more mature pupils of high-school age, the ability to recognize the correct or incorrect spellings of words is a most desirable skill. This type of ability is most commonly measured by tests of the proofreading type, in which the pupil identifies the misspelled word and corrects it.

Early in the consideration of the problems of measurement in spelling, two aspects of the pupil's accomplishment in this subject should be pointed out. In the first place, there is the problem of determining the pupil's present spelling ability. The second aspect of the problem concerns the measurement of progress. This is expressed in terms of the improvement the pupil makes, under instruction, in the mastery of the specific spelling vocabulary on which he is at work. Thus the determination of the child's spelling ability should be undertaken prior to study on the specific list of words. At the end of the teaching process a second measure is taken. This affords an indication of how much the child has progressed in his mastery of the selected spelling vocabulary.

Systematic instruction in spelling is usually provided in the elementary school, but more often than not does not comprise a part of the high-school program of studies. Apparently it is assumed that the pupil has acquired a method of learning to spell as a part of his elementary-school training. Presumably also he has been brought into contact with fairly extensive vocabularies of socially useful words in these earlier school experiences. There is considerable evidence, however, that in many high schools specific emphasis on spelling might not be entirely wasted effort.

Systematic Sampling of Words

The introduction of scientific methods in education in recent years has resulted in many investigations into the scope and character of spelling lists. Studies such as those by Anderson, Ayres, Fitzgerald, O'Shea, Rinsland, Thorndike, and Horn seem to warrant the conclusion that between 4000 and 5000 carefully selected words would be an appropriate number for the basic spelling list. Furthermore, these studies have proved of great value in selecting the word lists to be included in spelling texts, tests, and scales. It is quite obvious that the words most commonly used in the written language activities of adults and children should receive the major emphasis in a spelling course of study. To teach pupils to spell words that they will very rarely be called upon to spell either in or outside of the school is clearly a waste of time. Such words are best left to incidental learning or to the responsibility of each person as the need for their use arises.

Constructing Objective Measures of Spelling

Because of the highly specific nature of spelling ability it is often difficult to guarantee the validity of a spelling test. The words selected for testing must not only be of high social importance but they must be chosen from words of suitable difficulty that have been previously presented for instruction to the pupils taking the test. This means that in many cases the most valuable measures of spelling are those constructed locally by the classroom teacher or supervisor.

In the construction of spelling tests the following four problems require careful consideration:

1. From what sources should the test words be selected?
2. At what levels of difficulty should the test words be selected?
3. How many words are required to secure reliable measures?
4. In what testing form should the words be presented?

Source of words. The values of spelling are almost entirely specific, and lie in the ability of the pupil to spell words that are certain to be widely used. It is important, therefore, that the content of a spelling test be sampled from words that are now and will be ultimately of greatest usefulness to the pupil. Among the word lists that have been widely used in the development of commercial spelling texts as well as spelling tests is the one by Anderson [19] used by Ashbaugh in constructing the *Iowa Spelling Scales,*[20] the Thorndike *Teacher's Word Book,*[21] the Horn *Basic Writing*

[19] W. N. Anderson, *Determination of a Spelling Vocabulary Based upon Written Correspondence.* University of Iowa Studies in Education, Vol. II, No. 1. University of Iowa, Iowa City, 1917.

[20] E. J. Ashbaugh, *The Iowa Spelling Scales.* Bureau of Educational Research and Service, State University of Iowa, Iowa City, 1945.

[21] E. L. Thorndike, *The Teacher's Word Book.* Bureau of Publications, Teachers College, Columbia University, New York, 1921.

Vocabulary,[22] and the Bixler *Standard Elementary Spelling Scale*.[23] The most recently developed source of socially evaluated and difficulty rated spelling material for this purpose is *The New Iowa Spelling Scale*.[24] The 5507 words were obtained by screening eight different vocabulary sources. The determination of the level of difficulty of the words was nation-wide, utilizing 230,000 pupils in almost 8800 classrooms in 645 different school systems. Since each pupil undertook to spell 100 words, over twenty-three million spellings comprise the basis for this scale. While this investigation was concerned primarily with results from Grade 2 through Grade 8, many of the more difficult words have definite utility at the high-school level.

Teachers who are using spelling texts made up of word lists of unknown social importance will find sources such as the above of great value in selecting valid content for their own tests. Words to comprise a spelling test should, of course, be among those comprising the vocabulary studied by the pupils. The most valid types of spelling words on which to test a pupil are also those words that have relatively high social usage. Thus a cross-check of the words common to the local spelling text and to *The New Iowa Spelling Scale,* or other similarly developed scales, will reveal the words of high social frequency the pupils have studied and will at the same time give the teacher a measure of the relative difficulty of the words from their ratings in the scale itself. Thus the teacher may construct his own valid test on words of known utility and difficulty.

A very satisfactory source of evaluated word lists for high-school testing and instructional purposes is the Simmons-Bixler *New Standard High School Spelling Scale*.[25] Intended for Grades 7 to 12, this list permits the construction of a large number of equivalent tests. The scales, containing words of relatively high social frequency from the *Commonwealth List,* consist of 2560 words for study purposes and 2910 alphabetically arranged words of given difficulty by grades for use in constructing spelling tests.

Difficulty of words. It is well known that some words are more frequently misspelled than others. If words are selected at random from any of the lists indicated above, some of them will be easy and some relatively difficult to spell. Words for a test should be selected in terms of their known spelling difficulties.[26]

[22] Ernest Horn, *A Basic Writing Vocabulary.* University of Iowa Monographs in Education, First Series, No. 4. University of Iowa, Iowa City, 1926.
[23] H. H. Bixler, *The Standard Elementary Spelling Scale.* Turner E. Smith and Co., Atlanta, Ga., 1940.
[24] Harry A. Greene, *The New Iowa Spelling Scale.* Bureau of Educational Research and Service, State University of Iowa, Iowa City, 1955.
[25] Ernest P. Simmons and Harold H. Bixler, *The New Standard High School Spelling Scale.* Turner E. Smith and Co., Atlanta, Ga., 1949.
[26] *Spelling difficulty* as used here is best represented by the percent of misspelling of a word in a given grade without regard to, or any information about, the previous oppor-

The words to be included in the test for any grade should be adapted to the ability of the group to be tested. Classes of average ability seem to respond best to words of average difficulty. On the other hand, if the test is to be given over a wide spread of ability, words ranging from 14 to 86 percent standard accuracy with a mean of 50 percent tend to give a distribution more closely approximating the normal frequency curve, with the pupils grouped more closely around the mean. In general, it is probably safe to say that the words to be included in a test for any grade should be those on which there are from 40 to 70 percent misspellings. Tests made up of such words will give a reliable measure of spelling ability, since the words will not be so easy that there will be many perfect scores or so difficult that there will be many low scores.

Number of words. The purpose the test is to serve will determine the number of words to use. For survey purposes a list of 25 words will probably be sufficient to determine the status of spelling efficiency for a school system. To be sure, the ability to spell one word is separate and distinct from the ability to spell other words. It would seem necessary, therefore, to subject a pupil to several hundred words in order to secure a reliable measure of his ability to spell the most commonly used words. However, the procedure of sampling applies to the testing of spelling as in all other testing. While 25 to 50 words are possibly a sufficient number for survey purposes, more are probably needed to reveal the spelling ability of individual pupils. On the whole it appears that a minimum of 100 words should probably be used for individual testing purposes in spelling.

Presentation of words. The form in which words should be presented for spelling testing purposes has been subjected to much debate and considerable experimental investigation with results that are not entirely conclusive. Except in school stimulated situations, spelling needs arise when the individual is engaged in writing connected discourse in which the words are chosen and written without special attention to correctness. Words are rarely spelled orally or in list or column forms. Because of these facts many educators prefer to teach and to test spelling in contextual form. They argue that this practice provides valuable training on important mechanical aspects of written expression in addition to spelling. On the other hand, reasonably conclusive experimental evidence indicates that the column method is fully as effective as the context method in the teaching of spelling, and also recognizes the pupil's need to spell words in context in his normal writing activities in other school subjects. This suggests that perhaps the best answer lies in a combination of list and content dictation

---

tunity the pupil may have had to learn it. The quality as defined here is really "persistence of error" and should not be confused with "learning difficulty" as such.

exercises as the most effective instrument for the measurement of spelling ability.

Horn [27] summarized the evidence on the form of the spelling test as follows:

Written tests are to be preferred to oral tests. . . . Recall tests are superior to and more difficult than recognition tests. The evidence indicates that the most valid and economical test is the modified sentence recall form, in which the person giving the test pronounces each word, uses it in an oral sentence, and pronounces it again. The word is then written by the students.

An illustration of a few items from the spelling section of the *Stanford Achievement Test* appearing on page 230 shows one common method for measuring the ability to recognize correct spellings.

Diagnosis and Remediation of Spelling Disabilities

Spelling tests and scales afford valuable sources of material that may be used to determine both the pupil's present status in spelling and his growth in accomplishment as a result of a period of instruction. If scales based on a sound philosophy of subject-matter content are used, they provide the most effective materials for the identification of the spelling difficulties of individual pupils. Samplings from scales used as tests give the teacher an objective basis for the study of these personal difficulties through the accumulation of individual lists of words that are sources of trouble.

To a large extent remedial procedures in spelling may be undertaken directly in connection with teaching. The words misspelled by pupils in their spelling lessons and tests are obviously the words to which they should give special attention. Each pupil should keep an individual list of such words and should be stimulated to master them. Occasional spelling periods should be set aside for studying and testing these individual lists. If such lists are properly utilized, each pupil will come to regard his "demon" list as an effective means for eliminating spelling deficiencies.

Written work in all subjects should be carefully checked for spelling errors. A list of such misspellings should be kept by every pupil, and he should realize that he is to be held responsible for the mastery of these troublesome words. The important thing is that the learning situation be so manipulated that the pupil will want to learn to spell and to feel the need for learning the meaning and spelling of words that are pertinent to his written work.

[27] Ernest Horn, "Spelling." *Encyclopedia of Educational Research,* Third edition. Macmillan Co., New York, 1960, p. 1350.

Individual pupil diagnosis. The discovery that a pupil is below the norm in spelling ability may be of considerable value, but it falls far short of its real function unless it reveals to the pupil the particular weaknesses that resulted in his low score. The following items of information procurable through observation and measurement are invaluable in diagnosing individual pupil disabilities and should be used as much as possible in connection with the analysis of the pupils' spelling habits: (1) intelligence quotients, (2) spelling marks, (3) reading marks, (4) writing marks, (5) attendance data, (6) visual-defects data, (7) auditory-defects data, (8) speech data, (9) general health data, and (10) personality characteristics—industry, aggressiveness, independence, attentiveness, exactness.

The following procedures in diagnosing and treating problem cases in spelling have been found to be helpful:

1. Give a standard spelling test to discover the amount of deficiency. Compare with achievement in other subjects.
2. Give an intelligence test to discover general mental capacity.
3. Test for defects of hearing and vision.
4. Give reading test.
5. Give test of spelling consciousness to show whether mistakes are due to carelessness or ignorance of the word.
6. Collect misspellings from spelling tests and written work, and classify them according to types of errors.
7. Get as much information as possible about the pupil's pedagogical history, especially methods of beginning reading; knowledge of meanings of words; knowledge of phonics; pronunciation and articulation; motor coordination in writing; and emotional attitude toward spelling.
8. From above, assemble probable causes of difficulty in spelling, and adopt appropriate remedial measures, such as the following:

    (*a*) Systematic word study.
    (*b*) Exercises in visualization.
    (*c*) Drill upon particular types of spelling errors.
    (*d*) Phonics drills.
    (*e*) Removal of physical defects.
    (*f*) Develop confidence through successful effort.

Remedial procedures. Poor spelling is due to faulty or inadequately formed associations. Basically, all spellers, good or bad, learn in the same way—through association. The main difference between the able and the poor speller lies in the study technique used, his personality characteristics, and the emphasis he gives to the subject.

Many investigators of spelling disabilities have abandoned the procedure of deducing the causes of spelling difficulties from an analysis of errors and are now devoting their time and energies to studying the work habits of pupils by means of careful observation and tests.

5. MEASUREMENT OF PROFICIENCY IN HANDWRITING

In spite of the widespread use of mechanical means for writing, both in school and out, there is little likelihood that handwriting will be displaced as the major means of written communication. If handwriting is to serve its important function as a tool of communication, it must be neat and pleasing of appearance, easy to read, and of such form that it can be produced rapidly under normal conditions.

Measurable Characteristics of Handwriting

It thus becomes a major objective of instruction in handwriting to develop the special skills enabling the individual to write with sufficient ease, legibility, and speed to meet his present and ultimate social demands for all forms of written communication. Handwriting skills involve a large number of highly complex visual-muscular coordinations which mature slowly through exercise and use. If the written product is to possess the desired legibility, general aesthetic qualities, and speed of production, a highly effective level of these skills must be developed. The close dependence of quality of written language expression upon handwriting legibility, speed, and appearance makes it important that an active emphasis on handwriting be coordinated with language and English instruction throughout the school.

Exact appraisal of certain elements of good handwriting from the point of view of analysis and diagnosis has encountered considerable difficulty. The available writing scales, however, have done much to establish for the pupil and the teacher rather definite standards of what constitutes acceptable written products as well as to make both more and more sensitive to common handwriting faults and needs. Two factors constitute the chief approaches to the measurement of handwriting. These are (1) quality, or degree of legibility, and (2) speed, or the quantity of writing produced in a given unit of time.

Quality or legibility. Handwriting quality is usually determined by comparing the specimens to be evaluated with samples of known merit. In the days when the child's writing was compared with a copybook model, the emphasis was on the shape, size, and shading of the letters rather than upon legibility and rate of writing. With the appearance of scales for evaluating quality and legibility, the teaching emphasis moved away from writing as a decorative art to writing as an effective tool of written communication. A number of scales for the measurement of handwriting quality are discussed in a later section of this chapter. One such scale, from the *California Achievement Tests,* is illustrated in Figure 14 of Chapter 11.

Rate or speed. The ability to write rapidly at an acceptable level of legibility unquestionably affords the individual an important advantage in most school and life situations. This advantage may be very real in note taking and in written examinations, provided the ideas come to the individual as rapidly as he is able to transcribe them.

The measurement of rate of writing is easily accomplished by having pupils write for a specified period selections from standardized copy which they have previously read and memorized. If the pupils all write from the same selection and they have previously memorized it, the number of letters each pupil writes in the allotted time may properly be used to express his rate score.

Securing Handwriting Samples

Measurement of the quality of handwriting and the rate at which it is produced is accomplished by the evaluation of handwriting specimens secured under standard conditions. Accordingly, the first step in the process of measuring handwriting is that of securing these specimens under controlled conditions. The usefulness of handwriting specimens for evaluation purposes is affected by three factors which must be considered when they are being collected. The first of these is the suitability of the copy the children are asked to write. Whatever copy is used should be simple enough that the pupils will not be disturbed by spelling or vocabulary difficulties. Sentences from Lincoln's Gettysburg Address may be of suitable difficulty for the fifth grade and above, but children in the lower grades are frightened by such unusual words as *fourscore, forefathers,* or *continent.* Simple sentences which the children may have memorized or used on some previous occasion, such as "Mary had a little lamb," are suitable. The sentence, "The quick brown fox jumps over the lazy dog," is simple, contains only 35 letters, and has the merit of using at least once all of the letters of the alphabet. The copy should be written on the blackboard several days prior to the test, where it can be studied and where it can be seen during the writing test itself. If the specimens are to be used for survey purposes, standard copy such as the Gettysburg Address should be used.

A second factor is the care with which the writing test is given. The manner of giving the test and the wording of the directions may easily influence the quality and the rate of the children's writing. The following directions are suggested: "When I say 'Begin,' start to write as well as you can and at your usual speed the copy you have read and memorized from the blackboard. Write the copy over and over until I say 'Stop.' When I say 'Stop,' you are to stop writing at once even though you are in the middle of a letter."

The third factor to be carefully controlled is the time allowed for the writing test. In the standardization of his scale, Ayres used the first four sentences of the Gettysburg speech and allowed each pupil a two-minute period for the writing of the samples.

Obtaining Quality and Rate Scores

The quality of the handwriting specimen being measured is determined by moving it along a scale such as that shown in Figure 14 until a specimen is found that closely matches it in quality. The quality value of the scale sample is then assigned as the quality of the sample of the pupil's handwriting. As the scorer gains experience intermediate values may be estimated. Skill in the evaluation of handwriting specimens requires a thorough understanding of the scale to be used and considerable training in its use. It is desirable, therefore, for the teacher, prior to any attempt to use the scale for the measurement of handwriting quality, to study carefully the scale itself, the directions for its use, the norms, and the specific functions which the particular scale is expected to perform. The accurate and reasonably objective rating of handwriting samples on a scale requires considerable skill, which experience shows can be developed through practice. For this purpose standard sets of writing samples of known quality are very useful.

Rate of handwriting is usually expressed in terms of the number of letters written per minute. This is determined by counting the total number of letters written by each pupil and dividing this by the number of minutes the pupils were allowed to write.

Using Handwriting Norms and Standards

Since each handwriting scale generally differs from each other one in its approach, in the type of copy used, the number of elements of quality measured, and in the values assigned the different levels of quality, it is difficult to compare the results secured from one scale with those secured from another. Norms of quality and rate, therefore, must be developed to meet the requirements of each specific scale. Grade norms for quality and rate scores on the Ayres scale based on the median performance of large numbers of school children are given in Table 30. These results do not agree exactly with those accompanying the Ayres scale. Perhaps the Ayres data may properly be considered as norms, while the quality and rate values proposed by West and Freeman may more nearly represent standards.

TABLE 30

Handwriting Quality and Speed Standards [28]

Grades	2	3	4	5	6	7	8
Quality on Ayres Scale	44	47	50	55	59	64	70
Rate in Letters per Minute	36	48	56	65	72	80	90

Surveys of the quality of adult writing and of the opinions of qualified adults concerning socially acceptable quality of handwriting lead to the conclusion that there is little reason to require pupils to learn to write at a quality better than 60 on the Ayres scale. Possibly most pupils, regardless of their vocational intentions, should not find it a hardship to learn to write at this quality. According to Table 30, pupils at the end of the sixth grade may be expected to write quality 59 at a rate of 72 letters per minute.

Scales for Measuring Handwriting Quality

The currently available instruments for evaluating handwriting may be divided into two groups in accordance with the purpose each serves: (1) general merit scales and (2) analytical and diagnostic charts and scales. Four scales for the measurement of general merit of cursive writing, one scale for the use of teachers of manuscript writing, and two analytical and diagnostic charts and scales are sufficiently widely used to justify description here.

Interest in the evaluation of handwriting was indicated early in the history of educational measurements by the publication of the *Thorndike Scale for Measuring the Handwriting of Children.*[29] The scale itself consists of fifteen specimens of handwriting in ascending order of merit from a low scale value of 4 units above a defined zero to a high of 18. The unit of measurement used in this scale was based upon the composite judgments of a large number of persons thought to be qualified by training and experience to identify small differences in handwriting

[28] Paul V. West and Frank N. Freeman, "Handwriting," *Encyclopedia of Educational Research,* Revised edition. Macmillan Co., New York, 1950. p. 524.
[29] Edward L. Thorndike, *Thorndike Scale for Measuring the Handwriting of Children.* Bureau of Publications, Teachers College, Columbia University, New York, 1912.

quality. Hundreds of judges independently examined thousands of handwriting samples and arranged them in order of merit from very poor to superior. A complicated statistical treatment of these judgments enabled the author to define a unit of quality and to select a series of specimens differing from each other by the defined unit of quality. These specimens were arranged in order from poorest to best to constitute the rough scale. The poorest specimen was arbitrarily assigned a quality value of four judgment units above zero, zero representing just no handwriting quality whatever. The next specimen, approximately one judgment unit better, was assigned a scale value of 5. Additional specimens were selected and assigned scale values until a suitable range of handwriting quality was covered by the fifteen specimens approximately one scale unit apart.

The *Ayres Handwriting Scale* [30] was based upon legibility alone. Ayres believed that the judgment unit used by Thorndike introduced many undesirable subjective elements and proposed to measure legibility in terms of the speed and ease with which the samples of handwriting were read by a number of trained and competent judges. The first edition of this scale contained eight scaled specimens in three different slant styles of handwriting, but after trying it out with teachers the three-slant specimens were discarded in favor of the more popular moderate-slant style. This scale, known generally as the *Gettysburg Edition* because the specimens were based upon the first four sentences of Lincoln's famous address, has been one of the most widely used handwriting scales.

The widespread practice of introducing the first-grade child to writing through the use of print script or manuscript writing has not stimulated the expected development of scales for the evaluation of this type of product. Only one instrument, the *Conard Manuscript Writing Standards*,[31] composed of two scales, has had extensive use. The scale for pencil-written forms contains twelve specimens ranging from the undecipherable scrawl of the beginner to excellent manuscript writing at the fourth-grade level. The scale for scoring pen-written forms is comprised of ten specimens ranging from beginning third-grade ink work to excellent quality pen and ink writing produced by the sixth-grade child.

Diagnosis and Remediation in Handwriting

For the purpose of locating specific faults in handwriting, interest today centers almost entirely on such analytical charts as the *Freeman Chart*

---

[30] Leonard P. Ayres, *A Scale for Measuring the Quality of Handwriting of School Children*. Russell Sage Foundation, New York, 1912.

[31] Edith U. Conard, *Conard Manuscript Writing Standards*. Bureau of Publications, Teachers College, Columbia University, New York, 1929.

for Diagnosing Faults in Handwriting or the Zaner-Bloser chart, *Handwriting Faults and How to Correct Them.*[32] The Freeman chart is actually three scales in one, each designed to reveal whether or not the pupil's writing specimen violates one or more of the following essential qualities of good handwriting: (1) uniformity of slant, (2) uniformity of alignment, (3) quality of line, (4) letter formation, and (5) spacing. Three readily identifiable levels of quality—excellent, mediocre, and poor—are shown for each trait.

The Zaner-Bloser chart is essentially a revision and improvement of Freeman's chart. In addition to the useful features of the original chart it contains suggestions on ways to test handwriting copy for such elements as legibility, slant, spacing, alignment, size of letters, and quality of line. The particular usefulness of this chart lies in the fact that it enables the pupil as well as the teacher to discover for himself the specific handwriting weaknesses that are in need of corrective treatment and gives excellent suggestions for remedying the defects.

Improvement in handwriting instruction depends to a large degree on the teacher's knowledge of the elements that make for quality in the product, and the use of instruments that are adequate to reveal significant differences in quality. Inferior products of handwriting instruction may be due to lack of skill or mastery in many different phases of the writing act. The diagnostic charts described above meet this need for securing separate measures of the several aspects of handwriting performance. They may be used to measure the whole class, but they are most effective when used to diagnose the writing of pupils who rank conspicuously below the grade norm as revealed through use of some general merit scale.

Physical conditions and materials. Prominent among the physical factors affecting the pupil's handwriting is his desk. The pupil's desk should be adjusted to his height so that when he is seated normally his thigh is at right angles to the lower part of his leg and his feet are flat on the floor. In accordance with most modern methods of writing, the pupil's body, when he is writing, should face the middle of the desk squarely and bend slightly forward at the hips. For right-handed writers, both forearms should be well up on the desk, the left holding the paper, the right wrist raised and inclined slightly to the right. It is necessary that the pupil be taught to move the paper upward and to the left as the writing progresses. The shifting is done with the left hand, while the right arm is held in the correct position. There is some difference of opinion about the best position of the writing arm. It is generally agreed, however, that

---

[32] Frank N. Freeman and the Zaner-Bloser Staff, (1) *Handwriting Faults and How to Correct Them.* Zaner-Bloser Co., Columbus, Ohio; (2) *Evaluation Scales for Guiding Growth in Handwriting.* Zaner-Bloser Co., Columbus, Ohio, 1958.

the writing hand should be supported on the third and fourth fingers and that the wrist should not be tilted more than 45 degrees. The right forearm should be at a right angle to the line of writing. The pen should be grasped lightly and in such a way that the forefinger is below the thumb and about an inch above the point of the pen.

Experiment and observation show that modern writing is a combination of whole arm, forearm, wrist, and finger movements. It is not possible or even desirable to eliminate finger movement entirely, even in so-called "muscular movement writing." The following list of handwriting defects and their causes should be useful to the classroom teacher.

ANALYSIS OF DEFECTS IN HANDWRITING AND THEIR CAUSES

Defect	*Causes*
1. Too much slant	(1) Writing arm too near body
	(2) Thumb too stiff
	(3) Point of pen too far from fingers
	(4) Paper in wrong position
	(5) Stroke in wrong direction
2. Writing too straight	(1) Arm too far from body
	(2) Fingers too near point of pen
	(3) Index finger alone guiding pen
	(4) Incorrect position of paper
3. Writing too heavy	(1) Index finger pressing too heavily
	(2) Using wrong type of pen
	(3) Barrel of pen too small
4. Writing too light	(1) Pen held too obliquely or too straight
	(2) Barrel of pen too large
5. Writing too angular	(1) Thumb too stiff
	(2) Pen gripped too loosely
	(3) Movement too slow
6. Writing too irregular	(1) Lack of freedom of movement
	(2) Movement of hand too slow
	(3) Pen gripped too tightly
	(4) Incorrect or uncomfortable position
7. Spacing too wide	(1) Pen progresses too fast to right
	(2) Too much lateral movement

Psychological conditions. Next in importance in preparing the way for effective elimination of writing faults is the provision of desirable psychological conditions. The establishment of a desire for improvement on the part of the pupil is essential. One plan that has been proved to be quite effective involves the pupils' use of handwriting scales for the appraisal of their own writing. A copy of some good general merit scale should be conveniently placed in every classroom to encourage and train pupils in its use as a means of facilitating comparisons and evaluation of personal products.

Another means of motivation is the exemption from further penmanship drill of all pupils who have attained an acceptable standard of speed and quality. The standard of 60 for speed and quality is the one generally accepted. Evidence seems to indicate that from 50 to 75 percent of the pupils in the upper grades can easily reach this standard. If these pupils are exempt from further drill, the teacher is able to devote more time to those who have failed to meet the standard.

For improving the rate of slow writers, the writing of some simple sentence, such as "The quick brown fox jumps over the lazy dog," is recommended. Instruction in the making of different letters may be required by some children. Pupils are greatly helped by special practice on the letters and strokes that have given them trouble as a means of enabling them to attain accepted standards of speed and quality.

Handedness. In addition to the physical and psychological conditions discussed in the preceding paragraphs, there is the very important factor of the pupil's handedness. The general considerations of method and remedial procedures in handwriting appear to assume right-handedness in the child. Yet left-handedness is common enough in the classroom to represent a significant problem to the teacher, and one worthy of some consideration here. Naturally enough the pursuit of methods of instruction and remedy suitable for the right-handed pupil results in the formation of atrocious writing habits for the left-handed pupil. Any attempts to force him to conform to common right-handed practices usually forces him to write backwards, i.e., toward the left. In order to correct for the resultant reversal of the image, the pupil frequently twists his left wrist around in such a way that the pencil or pen point is directed toward him, with the result that he works awkwardly and under a most severe muscular maladjustment. For these and for other reasons that appear to be related to the speech and language functions, the teacher should probably not attempt to change the pupil's handedness. It is almost certainly better to accept the tendency to left-handedness which is well developed by the time the child enters the first grade and to aid him in making the best possible adjustments and adaptations in his mastery of handwriting than it is to run the risk of confusing him and possibly causing serious emotional disturbances at a later time. There is little or no evidence that the child at birth has any predispositions to use one hand rather than the other. Since this is a predominantly right-handed world in which it is easier to conform than not to conform, parents may profitably give some serious attention to the problem during the child's early formative years. The proper time to affect the child's handedness without danger of harmful reactions would seem to be in the period from his first active moment until he reaches school age.

SUGGESTED ACTIVITIES

1. Outline a dozen or so of the essential skills involved in some specific area of written language, such as friendly letter writing or making notes to be used in presenting a committee report.
2. Collect three or four samples of handwriting from children at several age or grade levels and rate their quality by using the handwriting scale shown in Figure 14 of Chapter 11.

TOPICS FOR DISCUSSION

1. What are the major situations in life in which language is used?
2. Evaluate the relative demands made by life situations on the oral and written aspects of language.
3. What are some common signs of oral language disabilities?
4. Discuss and illustrate a few of the problems of measurement of oral language abilities.
5. How is ability in written composition measured?
6. Discuss the status of analytical testing of written language abilities.
7. Suggest some remedial drill materials of value in language instruction.
8. What appears to be the most acceptable fundamental assumption upon which the spelling vocabulary suitable for elementary-school instruction should be based?
9. Show how a spelling test can be made from a standard spelling scale.
10. How can a spelling test made up of socially useful words be validated for use in a classroom in which a textbook in spelling based on a vocabulary of unknown social significance is in use?
11. What range of difficulty in words would you select for the purpose of measuring a class of unusually poor spelling ability?
12. Which of the objectives or outcomes of instruction in handwriting are most defensible from a social utility point of view?
13. What is the relationship between handwriting speed and quality?
14. Describe some of the methods of diagnosing handwriting ability.
15. Discuss the implications of parental responsibility for left-handedness and the relation of handedness to handwriting, language, and speech.

SELECTED REFERENCES

Auston, John T. "Methods and Levels of Measurement in Speech." *Educational and Psychological Measurement,* 13:228-47; Summer 1953.

BUROS, OSCAR K., editor. *The Fifth Mental Measurements Yearbook.* Highland Park, N. J.: Gryphon Press, 1959. p. 324-63, 367-73.

BUROS, OSCAR K., editor. *The Fourth Mental Measurements Yearbook.* Highland Park, N. J.: Gryphon Press, 1953. p. 294-317, 323-32, 541-43.

BUROS, OSCAR K., editor. *The Third Mental Measurements Yearbook.* New Brunswick, N. J.: Rutgers University Press, 1949. p. 218-47.

COLLEGE ENTRANCE EXAMINATION BOARD. *English Composition: A Description of the English Composition Test of the College Entrance Examination Board.* Princeton, N. J.: The Board, June 1954.

DAWSON, MILDRED. *Teaching Language in the Grades.* Yonkers, N. Y.: World Book Co., 1951. Chapter 15.

DIEDERICH, PAUL B. "Making and Using Tests." *English Journal.* 44:135-40, 151; March 1955.

DIEDERICH, PAUL B. "The Measurement of Skill in Writing." *School Review,* 54:584-92; December 1946.

GERBERICH, J. RAYMOND. *Specimen Objective Test Items: A Guide to Achievement Test Construction.* New York: Longmans, Green and Co., 1956. p. 308-10.

GREENE, HARRY A. "English—Language, Grammar, and Composition." *Encyclopedia of Educational Research.* Revised edition. New York: Macmillan Co., 1950. p. 383-96.

GREENE, HARRY A., AND GRAY, WILLIAM S. "The Measurement of Understanding in the Language Arts." *The Measurement of Understanding.* Forty-Fifth Yearbook of the National Society for the Study of Education, Part I. Chicago: University of Chicago Press, 1946. p. 176-89.

GREENE, HARRY A., JORGENSEN, ALBERT N., AND GERBERICH, J. RAYMOND. *Measurement and Evaluation in the Elementary School.* Second edition. New York: Longmans, Green and Co., 1953. Chapter 16.

GREENE, HARRY A., JORGENSEN, ALBERT N., AND GERBERICH, J. RAYMOND. *Measurement and Evaluation in the Secondary School.* Second edition. New York: Longmans, Green and Co., 1954. Chapter 16.

GREENE, HARRY A., AND PETTY, WALTER T. *Developing Language Skills in the Elementary School.* Boston: Allyn and Bacon, Inc., 1959. Chapters 18-19.

GUILFOYLE, ELIZABETH, AND MACKINTOSH, HELEN K., cochairmen. *Language Arts for Today's Children.* Commission on the English Curriculum, National Council of Teachers of English, Curriculum Series, Vol. II. New York: Appleton-Century-Crofts, Inc., 1954. Chapter 13.

HARRIS, THEODORE L. "Handwriting." *Encyclopedia of Educational Research.* Third edition. New York: Macmillan Co., 1960. p. 616-24.

HATCHETT, ETHEL L., AND HUGHES, DONALD H. *Teaching Language Arts in the Elementary Schools.* New York: Ronald Press Co., 1956. Chapter 15.

HILDRETH, GERTRUDE. *Teaching Spelling.* New York: Henry Holt and Co., 1955. Chapter 11.

HORN, ERNEST. "Spelling." *Encyclopedia of Educational Research.* Third edition. Macmillan Co., 1960. p. 1337-54.

KNOWER, FRANKLIN H. "Speech." *Encyclopedia of Educational Research.* Third edition. New York: Macmillan Co., 1960. p. 1330-37.

MONROE, ALAN H. "Testing Speech Performance." *Bulletin of the National Association of Secondary School Principals,* 29:156-64; November 1945.

POOLEY, ROBERT C. *Teaching English Grammar.* New York: Appleton-Century-Crofts, Inc., 1957. Chapter 14.

ROBINSON, KARL F. *Teaching Speech in the Secondary School.* New York: Longmans, Green and Co., 1954. Chapter 10.

SEARLES, JOHN R., AND CARLSEN, G. ROBERT. "English Language, Grammar, and Composition." *Encyclopedia of Educational Research.* Third edition. New York: Macmillan Co. 1960. p. 454-70.

SMITH, DORA V., director. *The English Language Arts.* Commission on the English Curriculum, National Council of Teachers of English, Curriculum Series, Vol. I. New York: Appleton-Century-Crofts, Inc., 1952. Chapter 18.

STEWART, MARIETTA. "A Scale for Measuring the Quality of Conventional News Stories in High-School Journalism." *English Journal,* 23:209-15; March 1934.

SWEARINGEN, MILDRED E. "Evaluation in the Language Arts Program." *Children and the Language Arts.* Englewood Cliffs, N. J.: Prentice-Hall, Inc., 1955. Chapter 20.

THOMAS, MACKLIN. "Construction Shift Exercises in Objective Form." *Educational and Psychological Measurement,* 16:181-86; Summer 1956.

THOMPSON, ANTON. "Measurement of Pupil Progress in Learning to Spell Selected Words." *California Journal of Educational Research,* 2:104-10; May 1951.

TORGERSON, THEODORE L., AND ADAMS, GEORGIA S. *Measurement and Evaluation for the Elementary-School Teacher.* New York: Dryden Press, 1954. Chapter 12.

TRAVERS, ROBERT M. W. "A Review of Procedures for the Evaluation of the Outcomes of Teaching English." *Journal of Experimental Education,* 17:325-33; December 1948.

WEST, PAUL V., AND FREEMAN, FRANK N. "Handwriting." *Encyclopedia of Educational Research.* Revised edition. New York: Macmillan Co., 1950. p. 524-29.

17

ARITHMETIC AND MATHEMATICS

The following important points involved in the measurement and evaluation of achievement in arithmetic and in high-school mathematics are summarized in this chapter:

A. General and social significance of mathematics.
B. Basic skills and instructional outcomes of arithmetic.
C. Present status and current trends in mathematics for Grades 7 to 12.
D. Measurement, diagnosis, and remediation in arithmetic.
E. Arithmetic readiness tests.
F. Mathematics aptitude and prognostic tests.
G. Measurement in high-school mathematics courses.

Arithmetic and succeeding courses in mathematics constitute the intellectual background of exact thinking in the sciences and in the solution of many problems of modern society. For this reason arithmetic has long been recognized as a most important tool subject. Many think that failure to develop numerical concepts in high-school pupils and to acquaint them with the rudiments of higher mathematics is to neglect a most important educational responsibility. Whatever may be the individual's background or inclinations toward mathematics, civilization, and sciences, his modes of living and of thinking have a mathematical core that he cannot escape. Mathematics, therefore, has a justifiable place in the secondary-school curriculum. If properly taught and enriched, it has the possibility of providing a type of training that is essential to every individual. It is considered by some to be one of the permanent bases of both a practical and a liberal education.

1. PRESENT AND EMERGING SCOPE OF ARITHMETIC AND MATHEMATICS

Of the two levels treated in this chapter, arithmetic and mathematics, the higher is undergoing fundamentally and potentially great changes in its structure and methodology. The treatment in this section of backgrounds for measurement and evaluation in high-school mathematics courses, especially in the traditional college-preparatory subjects, is consequently less extensive and less definite than is the comparable treatment of presently less dynamic elementary-school arithmetic.

Social Significance of Mathematics

The content of elementary-school mathematics, which to most individuals means arithmetic, is not affected seriously by social and scientific changes, as is the case in certain other subjects. Mathematics is based upon a fixed system of numbers that bear definite relations to each other. However, definite as the facts of arithmetic may be, there are many evidences of changes in current beliefs about the importance of the subject, the best methods of developing skills in it, and the most effective ways of relating it to other equally important social objectives of education.

Within the past generation the emphasis on certain of the previously acceptable instructional objectives of elementary-school mathematics seems to have shifted significantly. While the earlier purpose of developing arithmetical skill to a point of computational efficiency still remains as one important objective, the modern elementary school is primarily concerned with securing real competence in the use of computational skills, not as an end in itself but as a means of understanding the quantitative aspects of the world.

Arithmetical Skills and Outcomes

Computational skills as factors in social efficiency may still be the desired but not very often realized goals of instruction in arithmetic. Critical students of elementary-school mathematics are seriously concerned with the development of understandings and competence in quantitative thinking that often involves little or no computational exactness. These practical objectives have in turn produced definite changes in the methods and materials of instruction in the subject. The basic facts upon which computational skill rests may be mostly unchanged, but many of the procedures and devices used to develop meanings and understandings on the part of the individual are new and in many ways quite different from those in use a decade or so ago.

Brownell summarized the meaning theory of arithmetic instruction, which has emerged during the past few decades, by stating that

within the meaning theory there is absolutely no place for the view of arithmetic as a heterogeneous mass of unrelated elements to be trained through repetition. The meaning theory conceives of arithmetic as a closely knit system of understandable ideas, principles, and processes. According to this theory, the test of learning is not mere mechanical facility in "figuring." The true test is an intelligent grasp upon number relations and the ability to deal with arithmetical situations with proper comprehension of their mathematical as well as their practical significance.[1]

The meaning approach does not abandon drill as a teaching device nor the results from psychological analyses of basic skills in the organization of instruction, but it attempts so to organize instruction that quantitative relationships become meaningful to the child. Spitzer, in a summary of theoretical and experimental considerations affecting learning in arithmetic, pointed out that "It is advantageous to the learner to see the reasons for the use or the application of the arithmetic that is being studied.... Drill on fundamental phases of arithmetic is essential if the needs of children are to be met.... To be effective, drill should follow understanding." [2]

Basic arithmetic skills. Arithmetic is one of the more definite tool subjects, and much of its content is suitably organized for teaching purposes. For years it has been recognized that success in addition depends on a mastery of the basic addition facts. The same may be said of each of the four fundamental processes with whole numbers. Teachers now recognize, however, that success in such work as long division is dependent on a great many more skills than are involved in the mastery of the basic division facts. Long division calls for the accurate use of skills in addition, multiplication, and subtraction, not to mention the skills that are usually recognized as belonging definitely to division. Multiplication itself may involve the basic multiplication facts, the addition and multiplication involved in carrying in multiplication, and addition itself. A partial catalog of arithmetical skills selected for teaching, testing, and remedial purposes is

---

[1] William A. Brownell, "Psychological Considerations in the Learning and the Teaching of Arithmetic." *The Teaching of Arithmetic,* Tenth Yearbook of the National Council of Teachers of Mathematics. Bureau of Publications, Teachers College, Columbia University, New York, 1935. p. 19.

[2] Herbert F. Spitzer, "Learning and Teaching Arithmetic." *The Teaching of Arithmetic,* Fiftieth Yearbook of the National Society for the Study of Education, Part II. University of Chicago Press, Chicago, 1951. p. 141-42.

presented here to illustrate the extent to which such an analysis may be carried as well as to furnish a broad basis upon which to build tests and diagnostic and remedial material.

BASIC ARITHMETIC SKILLS

A. Fundamental processes with whole numbers
   1. Basic addition facts
   2. Basic subtraction facts
   3. Basic multiplication facts
   4. Basic short division facts
   5. Higher decade addition
   6. Column addition
   7. Carrying in column addition
   8. Harder subtraction
   9. Borrowing or carrying in subtraction
   10. Addition used in harder multiplication
   11. Carrying in addition used in harder multiplication
   12. Complete process of multiplication
   13. Short division involving carrying
   14. Multiplication, addition, and subtraction used in long division
   15. Complete process of long division
B. Fundamental processes with fractions and whole numbers
   1. Changing fractions to equivalent forms
   2. Finding common denominators
   3. Reducing fractions
   4. Addition of fractions and mixed numbers
   5. Expressing mixed numbers as improper fractions
   6. Fundamentals of subtraction of fractions
   7. Reduction of mixed numbers
   8. Cancellation in the multiplication of fractions
   9. Multiplication of fractions
   10. Cancellation in division of fractions
   11. Changing from multiplication to division form
   12. Fundamentals of division of fractions
C. Fundamental processes with decimals
   1. Notation of decimals
   2. Changing fractions and mixed numbers to decimal form
   3. Changing decimals to fractions and mixed numbers
   4. Fundamentals of addition of decimals
   5. Fundamentals of subtraction of decimals
   6. Pointing off in multiplication of decimals
   7. Dividing decimals by pointing off
   8. Location of decimal points in division
   9. Changing remainders to decimal form
   10. Fundamentals of division of decimals
D. Fundamental processes with denominate numbers
   1. Reducing in denominate numbers
   2. Borrowing in denominate numbers
   3. Addition of denominate numbers

    4. Subtraction of denominate numbers
    5. Multiplication of denominate numbers
    6. Division of denominate numbers
E. Mensuration
    1. Mensuration of plane surfaces
    2. Mensuration of solids
    3. Finding areas and volumes
    4. Formulas used in mensuration
F. Percentage
    1. Fractional and percent relations
    2. Decimal and percent relations
    3. Expressing areas in percents
    4. Fundamentals of work in percentage
G. Interest
    1. Business forms
    2. Budgets
    3. Computation of interest
    4. Computation of discount
    5. Use of interest tables
H. Problem solving
    1. Comprehension of problem
    2. Knowledge of what is given
    3. Knowledge of what is called for
    4. Probable answer
    5. Knowledge of proper processes and proper order of processes
    6. Recognition of the correct solution

Outcomes of instruction in arithmetic. The list of arithmetical outcomes formulated by Brownell [3] can be accepted as a good representation of the behaviors instruction in arithmetic is expected to develop in pupils.

OUTCOMES OF INSTRUCTION IN ARITHMETIC IN THE
ELEMENTARY SCHOOL

1. Computational skill:
   Facility and accuracy in operations with whole numbers, common fractions, decimals, and per cents. (This group of outcomes is here separated from the second and third groups which follow because it *can* be isolated for measurement. In this separation much is lost, for computation without understanding *when* as well as *how* to compute is a rather empty skill. Actually computation is important only as it contributes to social ends.)
2. Mathematical understandings:
   a) Meaningful conceptions of quantity, of the number system, of whole numbers, of common fractions, of decimals, of per cents, of measures, etc.
   b) A meaningful vocabulary of the useful technical terms of arithmetic which designate quantitative ideas and the relationships between them.
   c) Grasp of important arithmetical generalizations.

[3] William A. Brownell, "The Evaluation of Learning in Arithmetic." *Arithmetic in General Education,* Sixteenth Yearbook of the National Council of Teachers of Mathematics. Bureau of Publications, Teachers College, Columbia University, New York, 1941. p. 231-32.

 d) Understanding of the meanings and mathematical functions of the fundamental operations.

 e) Understanding of the meanings of measures and of measurement as a process.

 f) Understanding of important arithmetical relationships, such as those which function in reasonably sound estimations and approximations, in accurate checking, and in ingenious and resourceful solutions.

 g) Some understanding of the rational principles which govern number relations and computational procedures.

3. Sensitiveness to number in social situations and the habit of using number effectively in such situations:

 a) Vocabulary of selected quantitative terms of common usage (such as kilowatt hour, miles per hour, decrease and increase, and terms important in insurance, investments, business practices, etc.).

 b) Knowledge of selected business practices and other economic applications of number.

 c) Ability to use and interpret graphs, simple statistics, and tabular presentations of quantitative data (as in study in school and in practical activities outside of school).

 d) Awareness of the usefulness of quantity and number in dealing with many aspects of life. Here belongs some understanding of social institutions in which the quantitative aspect is prominent, as well as some understanding of the important contribution of number in their evolution.

 e) Tendency to sense the quantitative as part of normal experience, including vicarious experience, as in reading, in observation, and in projected activity and imaginative thinking.

 f) Ability to make (and the habit of making) sound judgments with respect to practical, quantitative problems.

 g) Disposition to extend one's sensitiveness to the quantitative as this occurs socially and to improve and extend one's ability to deal effectively with the quantitative when so encountered or discovered.

Basic Competencies in Mathematics

Basic mathematical competencies underlie the 29 questions formulated by the National Council of Teachers of Mathematics for high-school pupils.[4] Although these questions, reproduced herewith, cannot be accepted as direct substitutes for objectives, they can well serve as broad but tangible guides to the high-school teacher in planning and constructing tests in some mathematical subjects.

THE CHECK LIST

1. Computation   Can you add, subtract, multiply, and divide effectively with whole numbers, common fractions, and decimals?

2. Percents   Can you use percents understandingly and accurately?

---

[4] National Council of Teachers of Mathematics, *Guidance Pamphlet in Mathematics for High School Students.* The Council, Washington, D. C., 1953.

3. Ratio — Do you have a clear understanding of ratio?

4. Estimating — Before you perform a computation, do you estimate the result for the purpose of checking your answer?

5. Rounding Numbers — Do you know the meaning of significant numbers? Can you round numbers properly?

6. Tables — Can you find correct values in tables; e.g., interest and income tax?

7. Graphs — Can you read ordinary graphs; bar, line, circle? The graph of a formula?

8. Statistics — Do you know how to collect and interpret data; can you use averages; can you draw and interpret a graph?

9. Nature of Measurement — Do you know the nature of a measurement, of a standard unit, or the largest permissible error, of tolerance, and of the statement that a measure is an approximation?

10. Use of Measuring Devices — Can you use a ruler, protractor, graph paper, tape, caliper, micrometer, and thermometer?

11. Square Root — Can you find the square root of a number by table or by division?

12. Angles — Can you estimate, read, and construct an angle?

13. Geometric Concepts — Do you have an understanding of point, line, angle, parallel lines, perpendicular lines, triangle, parallelogram, trapezoid, circle, regular polygon, prism, cylinder, cone, and sphere?

14. The 3-4-5 Relation — Can you use the Pythagorean relationship in a right triangle?

15. Constructions — Can you with ruler and compasses construct a circle, a square, and a rectangle, transfer a line segment and an angle, bisect a line segment and an angle, copy a triangle, divide a line segment into more than two parts, draw a tangent to a circle, and draw a geometric figure to scale?

16. Drawings — Can you read and interpret reasonably well, maps, floor plans, mechanical drawings, and blueprints? Can you find the distance between two points on a map?

17. Vectors — Do you understand the meaning of vector, and can you find the resultant of two forces?

18. Metric System — Do you know how to use the most important metric units?

19. Conversion — In measuring length, area, volume, weight, time, temperature, angle, and speed, can you shift from one commonly used standard unit to another widely used standard unit; e.g., do you know the relation between yard and foot, inch and centimeter, etc.?

| 20. Algebraic Symbolism | Do you understand the symbolism of algebra—do you know the meaning of exponent and coefficient? |

| 21. Formulas | Do you know the meaning of a formula? Can you write an arithmetic rule as a formula, and can you substitute given values in order to find the value for a required unknown? |

| 22. Signed Numbers | Do you understand signed numbers and can you use them? |

| 23. Using the Axioms | Do you understand what you are doing when you use the axioms to change the form of a formula or when you find the value of an unknown in a simple equation? |

| 24. Practical Formulas | Do you know from memory certain widely used formulas relating to areas, volumes, and interest, and to distance, rate, and time? |

| 25. Similar Triangles and Proportion | Do you understand the meaning of similar triangles, and do you know how to use the fact that in similar triangles the ratios of corresponding sides are equal? Can you manage a proportion? |

| 26. Trigonometry | Do you know the meaning of tangent, sine, cosine? Can you develop their meanings by means of scale drawings? |

| 27. Business Arithmetic | Have you a start in understanding the keeping of a simple account, making change, and the arithmetic that illustrates the most common problems of communications and everyday affairs? |

| 28. Stretching the Dollar | Do you have a basis for dealing intelligently with the main problems of the consumer; e.g., the cost of borrowing money, insurance to secure adequate protection against the numerous hazards of life, the wise management of money, and buying with a given income so as to get good values as regards both quantity and quality? |

| 29. Proceeding from Hypothesis to Conclusion | Can you analyze a statement and determine what is assumed, and whether the suggested conclusions really follow from the given facts and assumptions? |

A critical comparison of the foregoing check list and the content of the traditional four-year high-school course in mathematics indicates that most of these items occur in both places. Actually, many of the items are almost certain to be found in the newer types of courses in general mathematics and consumer mathematics.

Current Developments in Mathematics

Modern practices in arithmetic and mathematics often reflect changes in a dynamic world and new understandings about learning. Two of the most obvious of these that have pertinence here are the modern emphasis on developing meanings in elementary-school arithmetic and the present-day high-school courses in general or applied mathematics. Except for this second development, however, the "mathematics curriculum in many secondary schools today is little or no different from that of a century or more ago." [5] The typical pattern of algebra, geometry, and trigonometry has changed very little since this college-preparatory course sequence came into existence during the nineteenth century.

Urgent need for changes in the traditional college-preparatory curriculum in mathematics has recently been recognized by at least three groups—the College Entrance Examination Board's Commission on Mathematics, the University of Illinois Committee on School Mathematics, and the University of Maryland Project on Junior High School Mathematics. Concepts and areas previously in the domain of higher or specialized mathematics have recently been recommended for inclusion in the high-school program and many of them are receiving experimental tryouts. A few illustrations of these emerging concepts are variables, sets, complex numbers, and inequalities. Some of the proposals for new or largely new areas are coordinate geometry, probability, modern algebra, calculus, and analytic geometry.

The purpose here is not so much to describe the present rapid developments in mathematics as to recognize their likely impact upon problems of measurement and evaluation in the near future. No recognition of these imminent changes appears either in the treatment of mathematical competencies in the preceding section of this chapter or in the discussion of measurement techniques in the final section of the chapter. It is possible at this writing to deal with techniques of measurement and evaluation in college-preparatory mathematics courses only in terms of the traditional program, even though new adaptations and perhaps new techniques of measurement and evaluation will be needed in the more progressive schools as soon as the instructional program is modified.

2. MEASUREMENT OF ACHIEVEMENT IN ARITHMETIC

A comprehensive understanding of tests and their nature and use is best attained by an examination of sample tests and, if possible, such accompanying materials as manuals of directions, scoring keys, and pupil record forms, or, preferably, the actual use of one or more tests in the classroom. Therefore, the authors have chosen to present only a few sample items

[5] College Entrance Examination Board, *Program for College Preparatory Mathematics*. A Summary of the Report of the Commission on Mathematics. The Board, New York, 1959. p. 6.

from various tests to illustrate the application of different objective testing methods. To conserve space, directions to the pupils are not given for the sample items except in instances of unusually complex item forms.

It is believed that the presentation of sample items with brief comments will familiarize the student with procedures involved in standardized testing and with major item techniques in arithmetic and also will furnish suggestions concerning some of the methods he may very well apply in constructing tests for use with his own classes.

Tests of Computational Skills

Computational skills are most often tested by an item type of simple completion form, although multiple-choice items are sometimes used. Such item types can be used with any combination of the four fundamental operations—addition, subtraction, multiplication, and division—and the

EXCERPT FROM *Metropolitan Arithmetic Computation Test* [6]

24 Multiply	25 Multiply
4 × 5	3 × 2 3 = _____
28 Add	29 Subtract
8 4 6 9 7 6 5 4 6 8 0 7 +4 5 6 9	9 0 9 − 6 4 5
32 Divide	33 Divide
3)1 5	4)1 6

[6] Harold H. Bixler and others, *Metropolitan Achievement Tests: Test 6, Arithmetic Computation,* Elementary Battery. Form B. Copyright 1959 by Harcourt, Brace and World, Inc., New York. All rights reserved. Quoted by special permission.

four types of numbers—whole numbers, mixed numbers, fractions, and decimals. Some tests classify all items of a type together, while others use the "omnibus" arrangement of mixed order for the various operations and types of numbers.

When the items are of completion form, it is by means of performing certain calculations that a pupil obtains the answers. Directions are usually given to the pupil concerning the form of answer desired, e.g., mixed numbers reduced to whole numbers and fractions, fractions reduced to lowest terms. Definite rules are also usually provided in order to objectify the scoring of a type of performance that is often viewed by different teachers according to very different standards. Credit is ordinarily given only for answers that are entirely correct. The excerpt on page 417 shows several items of this type in the "omnibus" arrangement from the *Metropolitan Arithmetic Computation Test.*

Multiple-choice items require the pupil to perform the calculations in order to determine which is the correct answer, although there is usually no requirement that he put down the work by which he obtained the answer. Some pupils might obtain the answers by mental computation and others by putting down only a skeleton of their computations. An accompanying excerpt from the *California Arithmetic Fundamentals Test* illustrates the use of this item type for measuring column addition of whole numbers and addition of fractions.

EXCERPT FROM *California Arithmetic Fundamentals Test* [7]

(56)		(63)	
$2\ 6\ 4$ $+\ 3\ 2\ 3$	a 541 b 941 c 547 d 581 e None　(56)	$\dfrac{1}{4}$ $+\dfrac{1}{4}$	a 42 b $\dfrac{1}{16}$ c 0 d $\dfrac{1}{2}$ e None　(63)
(57)		(64)	
$4\ 0\ 6$ $+\ 2\ 3\ 0$	a 363 b 176 c 636 d 736 e None　(57)	$\dfrac{1}{5}$ $+\dfrac{1}{10}$	a $\dfrac{3}{10}$ b $\dfrac{2}{15}$ c $\dfrac{1}{3}$ d $\dfrac{1}{6}$ e None　(64)

Tests of Problem-Solving Skills

Problem solving in arithmetic is a complicated skill which is almost certainly highly related to general intelligence. Naturally, an attempt to

[7] Ernest W. Tiegs and Willis W. Clark, *California Achievement Tests: Test 4, Arithmetic Fundamentals,* Complete Battery, Junior High School Level. Form W. California Test Bureau, Monterey, Calif., 1957.

analyze and to identify the underlying skills meets with considerable difficulty. Thus far five fundamental steps in problem solving, closely paralleling steps in the thinking process, have been identified. Steps such as these afford practically the only workable basis for an attack upon evaluation of skills in problem solving in any comprehensive manner.

The first step in the solution of verbal problems demands a complete understanding of the elements and processes that are involved or implied. This is *comprehension.* This in itself involves many factors, such as rate of reading, vocabulary difficulties, reading of numerals, and problem organization, as well as complexity in terms of the number and order of the arithmetical processes involved. Underlying all of these is, of course, the ability of the pupil to hold the various facts and conditions in his mind long enough to analyze and organize them. This process of *selection* constitutes a second important step. The unnecessary facts or implications are discarded and only the significant data are retained. The third step in practice is actually a part of the second, for the *organization* involved is really a part of analysis or selection. From this the worker moves straight to the fourth step, *solution,* where he applies to a specific situation his knowledge of the fundamental tools of number. In his earlier practice he learned how to perform certain simple arithmetical computations. Now he learns when to apply them. The next and final step in the process is *verification,* which may be either a rough checking by the estimation of the probable answer to the problem or an actual recalculating and rechecking of the processes involved.

EXCERPT FROM *Metropolitan Arithmetic Problem Solving Test* [8]

20 If it takes Tom an hour and a half to wash and polish a car, how many cars could he wash and polish from 3:00 to 6:00 in the afternoon?

_____

21 John had 50 cents to spend at the church fair. He spent 15 cents for candy, 5 cents for punch and 10 cents for popcorn. How many cents did he have left?

_____

[8] Bixler and others, *op. cit. Test 7, Arithmetic Problem Solving and Concepts.*

Standardized tests in arithmetic problem solving are most frequently found either in completion or multiple-choice format. Completion items in this situation require solutions of problems, rather than any form of recall, in obtaining the answers. Scoring of responses is practically always on an all-or-none basis, for no credit is given unless an answer is correct. Only one illustration, from the *Metropolitan Arithmetic Problem Solving Test*, is shown here to represent this item type. A closely similar illustration from the same test appears on page 236.

The multiple-choice item in problem solving also usually requires the solution of the problem in order to determine which of the optional answers is the correct one. However, some items require only an indication of the information necessary in a problem situation. One item of each of these types appears in a nearby illustration from the *STEP Mathematics Test.*

EXCERPT FROM *STEP Mathematics Test* [9]

5 Jim said that in 1953 the speed record for a certain airplane was 750 miles per hour. About how many hours would it take this airplane to go the 2250 miles from Pittsburgh to Los Angeles at this speed?

A $\frac{1}{3}$
B   3
C   30
D 3,000

6 Sarah said that sound travels about 5 times as fast in water as in air. If you knew the speed of sound in water, how would you find the speed of sound in air?

E Divide by 5.
F Multiply by 5.
G Add 5.
H Subtract 5.

Finally, an illustration of an arithmetic test exercise in the area of problem solving appears on page 233 of Chapter 10 to illustrate an interrelation variety of matching exercise. Taken from the *California Arith-*

---

[9] Educational Testing Service, *Sequential Tests of Educational Progress: Mathematics,* Part 2, Level 4. Form A. Educational Testing Service, Princeton, N. J., 1957.

metic Test, the exercise asks pupils to match statements of problems with the rules or formulas needed in solving them.

3. DIAGNOSIS AND REMEDIATION IN ARITHMETIC

Tests as such are incapable of improving instruction directly. Existing conditions are merely revealed by them, and it is worthy of note that these conditions are revealed only within the limits of the validity and the reliability of the particular tests used. The importance of using tests that are themselves based upon a sufficiently detailed analysis of the skills required for successful achievement in the field to permit the application of definite remedial procedures can hardly be overemphasized. Remedial teaching is the result of deliberate instructional effort on the part of the teacher after the particular points of weakness of the pupils have been discovered. The accuracy with which these needs are revealed by the device used is the best measure of its value to the classroom teacher.

Diagnosis of Difficulties

It is not by chance that diagnostic tests have been developed in subject fields in which the aims are clean cut and the basic skills conditioning achievement have been analyzed carefully. Nor is it by chance that the blanket purposes of certain other subject fields, as expressed in courses of study and textbooks, have left the teacher groping vaguely for tangible goals and effective instructional methods. The order of development is clear: first, there must be a specific statement of aims lying back of the subject; second, a detailed analysis must be made of the basic skills upon which ultimate achievement depends; and third, material designed to give mastery of these skills must be prepared.

Diagnosing deficiencies in computation. Some progress has been made in the diagnosis of pupil defects in the computational aspects of arithmetic. This is possible because the aims of arithmetic are quite clearly stated, which in turn permits a rather detailed analysis of the underlying skills. As soon as it became known, for example, that the ability to do a certain type of column addition depends on the pupil's knowledge of certain higher-decade addition facts, it was possible not only to locate difficulties in teaching this material as such but also to furnish the teacher with specific aids in teaching it.

There are three currently useful diagnostic tests in arithmetic, each representing a rather specific point of view in diagnosis. Only one of these tests is of recent copyright, since not a great deal of work has been done during recent years on diagnostic testing in arithmetic. It is probable that no diagnostic test in any field is capable of indicating precisely why a skill breaks down, but there is not much greater certainty that the teacher's interpretation of why the pupils encountered difficulty will be more exact The list of skills enumerated in the outline on pages 411 and 412 gives a very definite idea of the wide range of ability that must be covered by such tests.

The *Compass Diagnostic Tests*[10] represent one of the earliest of the approaches to diagnosis. This series consists of 20 tests covering the fundamental processes with whole numbers, fractions, decimals, percentage, arithmetical definitions and concepts, business forms, mensuration, and problem analysis and problem solving. The tests are essentially analytical in structure, the total process in each case being broken down one step at a time as a basis for the identification of the causes of weakness. These tests are designed for group measurement and diagnosis.

The Buswell-John *Diagnostic Test for Fundamental Processes in Arithmetic*[11] is designed for individual diagnostic work. It consists of a diagnostic chart and a test sheet on which the pupil does his work aloud in the presence of the teacher. On the diagnostic chart, which is for the teacher's use, are listed the most frequent faulty habits of work and causes of error in the particular arithmetic process under diagnosis. The pupil is given the work sheet and instructed to work on each of the exercises. In this way the teacher is able to discover the pupil's method of work and check the major causes of his difficulty.

Most recent of the diagnostic tests, the *Diagnostic Tests and Self-Helps in Arithmetic*,[12] consist of four screening tests, 23 diagnostic tests, 23 corrective "self-help" exercises, and accompanying suggestions for analysis of results and remedial procedures. The screening tests are for whole numbers, fractions, decimals, and arithmetic in general, while diagnostic tests and the accompanying self-helps are provided for (1) basic facts—five; (2) fundamental operations with whole numbers—five; (3) fundamental operations with common fractions—seven; (4) fundamental operations with decimal fractions—four; (5) operations with percentages—one; and (6) operations with measures—one.

Every one of the 100 possible basic addition facts involving digits from 0 to 9 in pairs is presented in Test 1. Tests 2, 3, and 4 include all of the 100 comparable subtraction, multiplication, and division facts, whereas Tests 5 to 23 include samplings of possible items arranged in order from

[10] G. M. Ruch and others, *Compass Diagnostic Tests in Arithmetic*. Scott, Foresman and Co., Chicago, 1925.

[11] G. T. Buswell and Lenore John, *Diagnostic Test for Fundamental Processes in Arithmetic*. Public School Publishing Co., Bloomington, Ill., 1925.

[12] Leo J. Brueckner, *Diagnostic Tests and Self-Helps in Arithmetic*. California Test Bureau, Monterey, Calif., 1955.

easy to hard. A portion of one of the more complex tests, on common fractions, is shown in an accompanying excerpt to illustrate the diagnostic aspects of the materials.

EXCERPT FROM *Diagnostic Tests in Arithmetic* [13]

I. Regrouping Fractions in Addition   No. Correct

1. Write these numbers, expressing all fractions in lowest terms.   I.

 a $\frac{6}{8}=$ b $\frac{4}{6}=$ c $\frac{8}{12}=$ d $6\frac{4}{8}=$ e $5\frac{9}{12}=$ 1._____

2. Express the following fractions in simplest form.   2._____

 a $\frac{8}{8}=$ b $\frac{6}{4}=$ c $\frac{5}{2}=$ d $\frac{6}{3}=$ e $\frac{12}{5}=$ 3._____

                                                                              4._____
3. Express the following mixed numbers in simplest form.
                                                                              Total.____
 a $4\frac{2}{2}=$ b $6\frac{4}{3}=$ c $4\frac{6}{4}=$ d $3\frac{8}{4}=$ e $7\frac{5}{2}=$

4. Supply the missing numerators.

 a $\frac{1}{2}=\frac{}{8}$ b $\frac{3}{4}=\frac{}{8}$ c $\frac{2}{3}=\frac{}{12}$ d $1\frac{4}{5}=1\frac{}{20}$ e $3\frac{2}{3}=3\frac{}{6}$

II. Regrouping Fractions in Subtraction   II.

1. Express these numbers in lowest terms.   1._____

 a $\frac{4}{8}=$ b $\frac{0}{5}=$ c $3\frac{4}{6}=$ d $4\frac{10}{12}=$ 2._____

2. Supply the missing numerators.   3._____

 a $1=\frac{}{2}$ b $1=\frac{}{8}$ c $2=1\frac{}{4}$ d $3=2\frac{}{8}$ 4._____

3. Supply the missing numerators.   Total._____

 a $1\frac{1}{4}=\frac{}{4}$ b $1\frac{1}{8}=\frac{}{8}$ c $1\frac{3}{8}=\frac{}{8}$ d $1\frac{3}{5}=\frac{}{5}$

4. Supply the missing numerators.

 a $3\frac{1}{4}=2\frac{}{4}$ b $4\frac{3}{8}=3\frac{}{8}$ c $5\frac{2}{5}=4\frac{}{5}$

Diagnosing deficiencies in problem solving. Naturally, many children fail to proceed in the solution of problems in an orderly fashion, although it would ordinarily be economical for them to do so if possible. Sometimes imperfect work, even though finally successful, means using unnecessary steps and spending useless energy in doing essential steps in an ineffective order.

So far in the development of diagnostic instruments for the identification of the skills involved in problem solving only a rough sampling of these skills has been approximated, and these are found in tests of such ancient copyright dates that they are not reviewed here. It seems regrettable that up-to-date tests in this area have not been made available.

[13] *Ibid. Test 11, Diagnostic Test in Regrouping Fractions.*

Remediation of Deficiencies

Pupils do not fail in arithmetic computation in a vague, general sense, nor do they need remedial work of a vague and general type. Pupils' errors and failures are specific. The more exactly they can be located, the more promptly they can be removed. Diagnostic tests based upon a satisfactory analysis of the skills that are essential to pupil mastery are for the purpose of locating these specific breakdowns.

Remedial exercises incorporating most of the desirable characteristics of such material can be developed by the classroom teacher or can often be secured in commercial form. The preparation and use of such material to supplement available instructional devices should serve to increase the efficiency of teaching greatly. It should be remembered that the use of the tests without the accompanying remedial program is futile.

An examination of available practice and drill material in the field of arithmetic reveals two somewhat distinctive types and uses of such material. General practice exercises designed to simplify the first learning and to aid in maintaining a general mastery of skills are numerous and varied

TABLE 31

Diagnostic Tests and Classification of Computational Skills [14]

Area and Test Title	Computational Skills
A. Operations with Whole Numbers	
1. Addition Facts	
2. Subtraction Facts	
3. Multiplication Facts	
4. Division Facts	
5. Uneven Division Facts	Division by 2 to 5
	Division by 6 to 9
6. Addition of Whole Numbers	Addition of two numbers
	Addition by endings
	Column addition
7. Subtraction of Whole Numbers	No regrouping
	Regrouping
	Zero difficulties
	Other four-place numbers
8. Multiplication of Whole Numbers	One-place multipliers
	Two- and three-place multipliers
9. Division by One-Place Numbers	Even division
	Uneven division
	Zeros in division
10. Division by Two-Place Numbers	Finding quotients
	Multiplication and subtraction in division
	Two-place quotients (or more)

[14] *Ibid.* Adapted from Diagnostic Tests 1 to 23.

B. Operations with Fractions
    11. Regrouping Fractions

    12. Addition of Like Fractions

    13. Subtraction of Like Fractions

    14. Addition of Unlike Fractions

    15. Subtraction of Unlike Fractions

    16. Multiplication of Fractions

    17. Division of Fractions

C. Operations with Decimals
    18. Addition of Decimals

    19. Subtraction of Decimals

    20. Multiplication of Decimals

    21. Division of Decimals

D. Operations with Percentages
    22. Percents

E. Operations with Measures
    23. Measures

Regrouping in addition
Regrouping in subtraction
Regrouping in multiplication and division
No carrying
Carrying
No regrouping
Regrouping with whole numbers
Regrouping with mixed numbers
No carrying
More difficult fractions
No regrouping
Regrouping
Fractions and whole numbers
Mixed numbers
Division by fractions
Division by whole numbers

No carrying
Carrying in one or more places
Placement of numbers
No regrouping
Regrouping in one or more places
Zeros
Placement of numbers
Multiplying decimals by whole numbers
Multiplying whole numbers by decimals
Multiplying decimals by decimals
Zeros in products
Dividing decimals by whole numbers
Dividing whole numbers by decimals
Dividing decimals by decimals

Writing as percents
Writing as decimals
Writing as common fractions
Finding percents of given numbers
Finding percents numbers are of numbers
Finding wholes when percents are given

Adding and expressing in simplest form
Subtracting and expressing in simplest form
Multiplying and expressing in simplest form
Dividing and expressing in simplest form

in type. They range from practice cards designed for repeated use to cheap practice tablets and comprehensive workbooks designed for drill and maintenance purposes. The arithmetic drill devices that have been constructed particularly for remedial purposes are not so numerous.

Correcting deficiencies in computation. Some idea of the organization of remedial material within the computational aspects of arithmetic may be gained from the table shown above, in which the right-hand column lists specific trouble spots, and hence areas for remediation, in parallel with the names of the tests and paralleling self-helps referred to in the preceding section of this chapter. An illustration of remedial exercises from Unit 12, Addition of Like Fractions, is shown in an accompanying excerpt to represent the manner in which skills must be broken down into their basic elements for effective remediation.

EXCERPT FROM *Diagnostic Self-Helps in Arithmetic* [15]

The method of working the first example in each row is shown below. Study the explanation of the work of the examples for any row in which you had more than one incorrect answer. Then copy the examples in the test, and correct your errors. Your teacher will help you on hard spots.

I. No Carrying

1. $\frac{1}{3}$
   $\frac{1}{3}$
   $\frac{2}{3}$

Add the numerators, 1 and 1.
Write the sum over the denominator, 3.
Think: $\frac{1+1}{3}=\frac{2}{3}$.

2. $4\frac{1}{3}$
   $5\frac{1}{3}$
   $9\frac{2}{3}$

First, add the fractions, as in 1 above.
Then add 4 and 5.
The answer is $9\frac{2}{3}$.

3. $\frac{1}{4}$
   $\frac{1}{4}$
   $\frac{2}{4}=\frac{1}{2}$

First, add the fractions, as in 1 above.
Reduce $\frac{2}{4}$. $\frac{2\div2}{4\div2}=\frac{1}{2}$.
Use the drawing to show that $\frac{2}{4}=\frac{1}{2}$.

4. $4\frac{3}{8}$
   $3\frac{1}{8}$
   $7\frac{4}{8}=7\frac{1}{2}$

First, add $\frac{3}{8}$ and $\frac{1}{8}$. The sum is $\frac{4}{8}$.
Then add 4 and 3. The answer is $7\frac{4}{8}$.
Change $7\frac{4}{8}$ to $7\frac{1}{2}$ because $\frac{4}{8}=\frac{1}{2}$.
$\frac{4\div4}{8\div4}=\frac{1}{2}$.

The validity of any type of drill depends on the degree to which the sampling covers the fundamental skills and the degree to which the exercises themselves actually develop the skills they purport to develop. There are a number of places in which this complex chain may break. The task of diagnostic and remedial treatment is to locate and to repair quickly those links of the chain that have snapped under stress or have rusted out through lack of use.

Two further observations are important. First, while specific drill on some skill all by itself is often quite important, it must be accompanied by, if not preceded by, understanding of the total situation. Satisfactory performance on an isolated skill is not always matched by similar performance on the same skill when it operates in a more complex situation. Thus 9 + 4 may be an easy combination by itself, but it may not click at all

[15] *Ibid.* (Test 12) *Self-Helps in Addition of Like Fractions.*

when presented as $7 + 2 + 4$, where the 9 is unseen. From this it follows that after attention is paid to a specific breakdown the skill should also be practiced in the most complex situation in which it appears.

A second caution deals with a matter of policy. The need for remedial work of any kind and in any subject implies a failure at some point in the initial learning. Remedial work should be reduced as much as possible by making the first learning effective, by adequate review devices, and by the proper grade placement of pupils. A teacher should never be proud of the amount of remedial work he must do. However, he may be proud of his ability to direct it well when need for it arises. Obviously, preventive work based upon understanding is better teaching than remedial work.

Correcting deficiencies in problem solving. Skill in the solution of verbal problems is difficult to develop in pupils because of its psychological complexity and elusiveness. The remedial aspects of problem solving, as well as diagnostic aspects, consequently remain largely undeveloped. Pupils can reasonably be expected to solve types of problems with which they are familiar, i.e., varieties of problems they have specifically been taught to solve. However, the introduction of new elements or irrelevancies in problems seems to place more emphasis on pupil mental abilities than on direct results of instruction.

Table 32 lists the five steps in problem solving outlined in a preceding section of this chapter, in parallel with some of the skills that seem to be involved in solving arithmetical problems. Among them are reading

TABLE 32

Analysis of Steps in Solving Arithmetic Problems

Steps in Process	Underlying Factors
Comprehension	Reading or listening to the problem Comprehending the problem Determining the conditions of the problem
Selection	Selecting the pertinent elements Discarding the irrelevant elements Determining what is given Determining what is called for
Organization	Relating the elements to one another Selecting the processes Organizing the steps of procedure
Solution	Carrying out the computations
Verification	Estimating the form of the answer Estimating the magnitude of the answer Checking the answer

comprehension skills of types dealt with in Chapter 15 and arithmetic computation skills of types treated in foregoing portions of this chapter. Diagnosis and remediation are possible for both of these types. Among the skills listed in the table, however, are skills of critical thinking, of deduction, of induction, and of other higher mental processes that elude the best diagnostic and remedial techniques so far developed.

4. PREDICTION OF SUCCESS IN ARITHMETIC AND MATHEMATICS

Distinctions are made in Chapter 2 of this volume among readiness tests, aptitude tests, and prognostic tests. Since all three types are used in predicting future outcomes, they are dealt with in very similar terms here. Provision is made in one or another of these test types and in various tests for predicting success at three distinct levels: (1) arithmetic in Grade 2, (2) algebra and geometry in Grades 9 and 10, and (3) college mathematics courses in Grade 13. Determining when, or how completely, a child is ready for direct contact with computational work is a major purpose of readiness tests in arithmetic. Aptitude tests, or even the closely similar prognostic tests, are used at both of the higher levels in somewhat similar ways.

Readiness Tests in Arithmetic

Tests of arithmetic readiness are less common than are reading readiness tests. Furthermore, readiness as a general rather than a specific concept is probably more often applied in arithmetic than in reading. However, at least one recently published test is designed to provide a measure of a child's readiness to move ahead to computational and arithmetic skills. Excerpts from this instrument, the *New York Test of Arithmetical Meanings,* are shown herewith to represent techniques for testing the pre-measurement and numerical concepts the child typically acquires before he enters school or at least while he is in Grade 1. The instructions, given orally by the examiner, ask the child for the four items pictured to mark the flowerpot in which Johnny planted seeds *last,* the mat which took Alice the *longest* time to make, the *number* of umbrellas a mother bought for her twin girls, and the glass (*second*) from which Tom drank his milk.

Tests of Aptitude for High-School Mathematics

The growing tendency of high-school administrators and supervisors to utilize elementary-school records and test results as preregistration infor-

EXCERPTS FROM *New York Test of Arithmetical Meanings* [16]

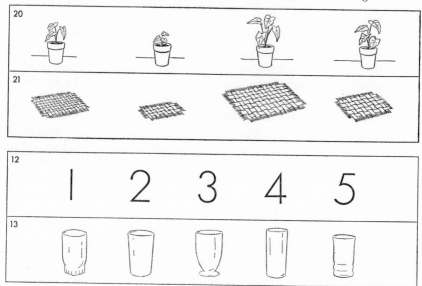

mation justifies some attention at this point to the problem of predicting success in secondary-school mathematics. The excessive difficulty which pupils encounter in first-year algebra has long impressed parents, teachers, and supervisors. In general, these difficulties are revealed in the high percentage of pupil failure in the subject and in the large amount of outside assistance required by pupils if failure is to be avoided.

Two somewhat different procedures have been followed as a basis for prognosis in mathematics beyond the elementary school. These are (1) the learning technique, in which the aptitude of the pupil for the subject is measured in terms of the speed and accuracy with which he is able to acquire skills and information in the new field and respond to objective tests over the newly learned material, and (2) the inventory technique, in which he reveals his aptitude in terms of reactions to specific exercises sampling into underlying skills upon which success in the subject depends.

The *Orleans Algebra Prognosis Test* [17] is of the former type. It gives a basis for predicting the pupil's success in the subject by measuring the speed and accuracy with which he is able to learn novel material of the

[16] J. Wayne Wrightstone and others, *New York Test of Arithmetical Meanings,* Level 1, Tests 1 and 2. Copyright 1956 by Harcourt, Brace and World, Inc., New York. All rights reserved. Quoted by special permission.

[17] Joseph B. Orleans, *Orleans Algebra Prognosis Test,* Revised edition. World Book Co., Yonkers, N. Y., 1950.

sort encountered in algebra. The test contains eleven simple lessons with a test on each covering fundamental principles and essential skills in learning algebra. An arithmetic and a summary test are also included.

The *Iowa Algebra Aptitude Test*,[18] of the more common inventory type, makes use of four basic skills selected from the large number of possible factors that have been demonstrated to be highly related to achievement in first-year algebra. These skills, none of which involves algebraic ability as such, deal with (1) arithmetic computations, (2) computations involving abstract concepts, (3) manipulation of numerical series, and (4) solution of problems involving dependence and variation. Pupils who score below the twentieth percentile of the test norms are almost certain to fail the course, or must practically be carried through the course by the teacher if they succeed in passing. Such pupils probably should be diverted into courses in general or applied mathematics or into other fields of study where they are more likely to succeed.

Prognostic and aptitude tests in plane geometry are similar to those in algebra with respect to their major types. The *Orleans Geometry Prognosis Test* [19] is similar to the algebra test by the same author in using the learning procedure as the basis for prediction. The *Iowa Plane Geometry Aptitude Test*,[20] however, as is true of its counterpart in algebra, approaches the problem by means of the inventory method. The four skills chosen for measurement deal with (1) reading of geometry content, (2) algebraic computations, (3) arithmetical and algebraic reasoning, and (4) visualization. The tests are useful guidance and supervisory tools in the same manner as is indicated above for aptitude and prognostic tests in first-year algebra.

Tests of Aptitude for College Mathematics

Although prediction of success in college courses is not of significance for elementary-school teachers, it may have some meaning for high-school teachers who are interested in advancing the interests of their college-bound students. For such teachers, the *IPE Mathematics Aptitude Test*,[21]

[18] Harry A. Greene and A. H. Piper, *Iowa Algebra Aptitude Test,* Revised edition. Bureau of Educational Research and Service, State University of Iowa, Iowa City, 1942.

[19] Joseph B. Orleans, *Orleans Geometry Prognosis Test,* Revised edition. World Book Co., Yonkers, N. Y., 1950.

[20] Harry A. Greene and H. W. Bruce, *Iowa Plane Geometry Aptitude Test,* Revised edition. Bureau of Educational Research and Service, State University of Iowa, Iowa City, 1942.

[21] George D. Stoddard, L. W. Miller, and E. W. Chittenden, *Iowa Placement Examinations: Mathematics Aptitude,* New Series MA-2, Revised. Bureau of Educational Research and Service, State University of Iowa, Iowa City, 1942.

also of the inventory variety previously discussed, can be used for estimating the success of high-school seniors in college mathematics courses or in the college-level courses that are now offered in some high schools to their outstandingly able advanced students. The four parts of the test measure (1) ability to extend number-series exercises, (2) ability to solve verbal problems, (3) ability to read and comprehend mathematical paragraphs, and (4) range of information in mathematics.

5. MEASUREMENT OF ACHIEVEMENT IN GENERAL MATHEMATICS

A distinction should be made between measuring general achievement in mathematics and measuring achievement in general mathematics. The primary source of difference is that the purpose of general achievement tests in mathematics is to measure the cumulative effect on pupils of courses, whether in arithmetic, in mathematics, or in a combination of the two, over a period of years, whereas the purpose of tests in general mathematics is to measure pupil achievement in a specific general mathematics course at the high-school level.

Tests of General Achievement in Mathematics

General achievement tests typically provide parts or sections on arithmetic in the elementary grades and on a limited number of skills from higher mathematics at the secondary-school level. Since general achievement tests are dealt with in Chapter 25 of this volume, no further attention is given here to the use of test batteries for the measurement of general achievement in mathematics. However, the *Davis Test of Functional Competence in Mathematics* [22] is one example of a specific instrument designed to fulfill this purpose. The content of this test is based on the essentials for functional competence in mathematics as recommended by the Commission on Post-War Plans of the National Council of Teachers of Mathematics. The two parts and four sections measure the following areas:

Part I. Section A. Consumer Problems (24 items)
         Section B. Graphs and Tables (9 items)
Part II. Section A. Symbolism, Equations (24 items)
         Section B. Ratio, Tolerance (23 items)

[22] David J. Davis, *Davis Test of Functional Competence in Mathematics.* World Book Co., Yonkers, N. Y., 1951.

Tests of Achievement in General Mathematics

Two important factors have been operating in recent years to promote interest in courses in general mathematics. The first of these is the general reduction in the number of units of secondary-school mathematics required for college entrance. Perhaps this is closely related also to the fact that student failure in mathematics has been exceedingly high in the secondary schools. Analysis of guidance information indicates that courses in first-year algebra and plane geometry are too specialized for the abilities and interests of many high-school pupils. The development and wide use of aptitude and prognostic instruments in the secondary-school mathematics areas has demonstrated that many pupils lack the abilities required for success in algebra and geometry courses. However, they are able to do entirely satisfactory work in properly organized general mathematics courses. Some training in mathematics beyond elementary-school arithmetic is undoubtedly desirable. General mathematics courses should meet this need.

The objectives of the course in general mathematics determine the nature and the content of standardized objective tests in the subject. General mathematics courses are primarily of two types: (1) those designed for the nonmathematically inclined pupil with emphasis on the practical applications of mathematics and (2) those that sample their content from the fields of arithmetic, algebra, geometry, and trigonometry. The *Snader General Mathematics Test,* one of the most recent tests in this area, is representative of the second type. The accompanying excerpts from this test illustrate items for measuring arithmetic and informal geometrical skills. Items on graphic representation, algebra, and numerical trigonometry are also included to round out the measurement of achievement in general mathematics.

EXCERPTS FROM *Snader General Mathematics Test* [23]

57. If baseball bats listed at twenty-one dollars per dozen are sold to schools at a discount of 20 per cent, how much do they cost the schools per dozen?
   a. $4.20
   b. $16.80
   c. $20.80
   d. $25.20
   e. none of the above

[23] Daniel W. Snader, *Snader General Mathematics Test,* Part C. Form AM. Copyright 1950 by Harcourt, Brace and World, Inc., New York. All rights reserved. Quoted by special permission.

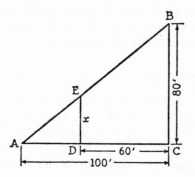

64. In the figure above, triangles *ACB* and *ADE* are
    similar triangles.   What is the length of side *DE*?
    f. 30 ft.
    g. 32 ft.
    h. 48 ft.
    i. 50 ft.
    j. none of the above.

6. MEASUREMENT OF ACHIEVEMENT IN ALGEBRA,
   GEOMETRY, AND TRIGONOMETRY

   Much attention has been given of recent years to a restatement of
objectives and a reorganization of mathematical subjects for the junior
and senior high schools, as is brought out in the introductory section of
this chapter. New methods and new patterns of content are being tried out
experimentally or are being introduced gradually in many of the more
progressive schools. Meanwhile, many schools are continuing to emphasize
the traditional academic sequence of algebra, geometry, and trigonometry
in Grades 9 to 12. In any event, new tests and testing techniques for use
with the emerging instructional programs are neither well enough developed nor widely enough useful in most present-day schools to warrant
any attempt at presenting them here.
   Standardized achievement tests in mathematics presently available at
the high-school level predominantly deal with college-preparatory algebra,
plane geometry, solid geometry, and trigonometry. These tests are based
largely on obsolescent statements of objectives and instructional outcomes.
Rather than to contribute to any perpetuation of traditional ideas by
restatements of these aims and outcomes, the authors of this volume prefer to present achievement tests designed for use in academic high-school
courses in mathematics without direct consideration of the objectives and

outcomes that lie behind them. It seems likely that new patterns of standardized achievement tests for the mathematics courses of Grades 7 to 12 will begin to emerge in the near future.

Tests of Achievement in Algebra

Two types of approach are noted among the more recently developed standardized tests in first-year algebra. One point of view, illustrated by the *Seattle Algebra Test* and the *Lankton First-Year Algebra Test*,

EXCERPTS FROM *Seattle Algebra Test* [24]

Part A. Vocabulary

1. In $3\ a^2c$, the c is
   1. a term.
   2. a binominal.
   3. an exponent.
   4. a factor.
   5. a numerical coefficient.

Part B. Fundamental Processes

10. $(-2)\ (-2)\ (-2)$ equals
    a. -8
    b. -6
    c. $+6$
    d. $+8$
    e. none of the above

Part C. Equations

31. If $\dfrac{x}{2} = 6$, then x equals
    a. 3
    b. 4
    c. 8
    d. 12
    e. none of the above

Part D. Algebraic Representation and Problems

DIRECTIONS. *In the following questions, read each problem and decide which of the five given algebraic expressions or equations is correct. Do not solve the equations.*

40. If n represents an odd number, the next higher consecutive odd number is
    a. $2\ n$
    b. $n + 1$
    c. $n + 2$
    d. $n + 3$
    e. n^2

---

[24] Harold B. Jeffery and others, *Seattle Algebra Test, Parts A, B, C, and D*. Form AM. Copyright 1951 by Harcourt, Brace and World, Inc., New York. All rights reserved. Quoted by special permission.

is based on the belief that single and relatively brief end-of-semester and end-of-course tests represent adequate measures for the evaluation of accomplishment in the subject. The second type assumes that unit-type tests standardized at the time of the completion of instruction afford the most effective measures of accomplishment. The *Larson-Greene Unit Tests in First-Year Algebra* are presented here as illustrations of this approach.

The first of the tests mentioned above consists of items covering vocabulary, fundamental processes, equations, and algebraic representations and problems. This test is designed for use at the end of the first half year of algebra. The accompanying excerpt shows sample items representative of each of the four parts of this test.

The *Lankton First-Year Algebra Test* is an end-of-course test consisting of items on vocabulary of algebra, meaning and use of symbols, fundamental operations, formulas, equations, simple algebraic fractions, radicals, ratios, proportions, variations, graphs, trigonometric functions, and

EXCERPT FROM *Lankton First-Year Algebra Test* [25]

42. **Which of the following graphs shows the same relationship between C and d as that expressed by the formula $C = \pi d$?**

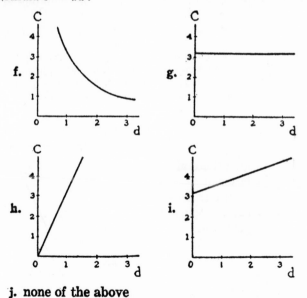

j. none of the above

the solution of problems by the use of algebra. An illustration of an item from this test that is designed to measure the application of knowledge to graphical representation appears in an accompanying excerpt.

The *Larson-Greene Unit Tests in First-Year Algebra* [26] comprise six tests in a 24-page booklet designed to cover the basic phases of first-year algebra. Separate quick-scorable answer sheets are provided. The tests are standardized for periodic use in any order through the school term following the completion of instruction on the specific subject-matter units. Tests 1, 2, and 3 cover the work normally taught in the first semester. Tests 4, 5, and 6 cover the second semester's work. No one of the tests is intended to be used as a semester final or end-of-course examination. For the teacher the primary advantage of a unit test is the fact that results from the various parts become available in time for remedial work to be undertaken.

Tests of Achievement in Geometry

As in the case of first-year algebra, there are two typical approaches to standardized testing in plane geometry—end-of-course achievement tests and unit tests adjustable to the order of presentation of the subject-

EXCERPT FROM *Shaycoft Plane Geometry Test* [27]

DIRECTIONS. *In questions 23 to 25, look at each figure at the right; then decide which of the terms at the left applies to it, and mark the corresponding space (a, b, c, d, or e) on your answer sheet. (The same answer may be chosen for more than one figure.)*

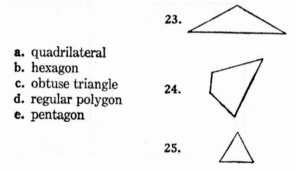

a. quadrilateral
b. hexagon
c. obtuse triangle
d. regular polygon
e. pentagon

23.

24.

25.

[26] Robert Larson and Harry A. Greene, *Larson-Greene Unit Tests in First-Year Algebra.* Bureau of Educational Research and Service, State University of Iowa, Iowa City, 1947.
[27] Marion F. Shaycoft, *Shaycoft Plane Geometry Test,* Part A. Form AM. Copyright 1950 by Harcourt, Brace and World, Inc., New York. All rights reserved. Quoted by special permission.

matter units. The *Seattle Plane Geometry Test* and the *Shaycoft Plane Geometry Test* are two recent examples of the first type. The *Lane-Greene Unit Tests in Plane Geometry* are representative of the second approach. The first-named test [28] consists of items designed to cover the first half of the course in a manner closely similar to that employed in the comparable test in algebra. The *Shaycoft Plane Geometry Test,* covering the objectives of the typical one-year course in plane geometry, has sections on fundamental concepts, lines and rectilinear figures, the circle, proportions, polygons, and geometric reasoning. Two exercises, both of useful but

EXCERPT FROM *Shaycoft Plane Geometry Test* [29]

DIRECTIONS. *Each of the questions below (44 to 48) consists of a set of measurements applying to a triangle (△ABC). You are to decide whether it is possible to construct a triangle with these measurements. For each of the questions choose from the following phrases the one which applies, and mark the corresponding answer space. For instance, if a triangle with these measurements is impossible, mark answer space "a"; otherwise mark "b," "c," "d," or "e" — whichever is descriptive of triangles with the given measurements.*

a. No such triangle exists.
b. All such triangles are congruent.
c. All such triangles are similar, but not necessarily congruent.
d. Exactly two distinct triangles (*neither congruent nor similar*) can be constructed with these characteristics.
e. More than two distinct triangles (*neither congruent nor similar*) can be constructed with these characteristics.

44. $\angle A = 30°$, $\angle B = 60°$, $\angle C = 30°$

45. $\angle A = 30°$, $\angle B = 60°$, $\angle C = 90°$

46. $AB = AC = BC = 6$ in., $\angle C = 90°$

47. $AC = BC = 10$ in., $\angle A = \angle B = 30°$

48. $AB = 6$ in., $\angle A = 150°$

[28] Harold B. Jeffery and others, *Seattle Plane Geometry Test*. World Book Co., Yonkers, N. Y., 1951.
[29] Shaycoft, *op. cit.* Part B.

rather unusual techniques, are pictured in accompanying excerpts. One further illustration of a plane geometry test item, one involving a simple construction by the pupil, is also shown on page 238 of Chapter 10.

The *Lane-Greene Unit Tests in Plane Geometry* [30] consist of six tests standardized for use in any desired order immediately following the completion of the teaching of each unit. In general, Tests 1, 2, and 3 comprise the usual coverage of the first semester and Tests 4, 5, and 6 the units normally taught in the second semester. Several novel testing techniques are utilized. No one of the tests is designed to serve as a semester final or end-of-course final test. As in the case of the unit tests in algebra, the advantage of these unit tests lies in the fact that the results become available to the pupil and the teacher before the completion of the entire course and in time for supplementary instruction to be undertaken if necessary. The six parts of the test are: (1) Fundamental Ideas of Geometry, (2) Parallel Lines and Triangles, (3) Rectilinear Figures, (4) The Circle, (5) Proportion and Similar Polygons, and (6) Areas of Polygons.

Tests of Achievement in Trigonometry

Measurement in trigonometry is presently concerned with (1) understanding of the fundamental propositions of trigonometry, (2) familiarity with the fundamental relations among the ratios, and (3) ability to solve problems involving the applications of such understandings. Trigonometry is usually offered as an elective subject in the junior or senior year of high school, and ordinarily is taken only by those pupils whose interests lie in the field of higher mathematics.

The extremely limited number of standardized tests for trigonometry make use primarily of the multiple-choice form of item in various ones of the modifications used for algebra and geometry in the preceding sections of this chapter. Because of the similarity in item form, no examples for this subject are given here.

SUGGESTED ACTIVITIES

1. Arrange the following randomly listed illustrations of additions of fractions in what seem to you to be an increasing order of difficulty from simple to complex: $\frac{1}{5} + \frac{2}{5}$; $\frac{1}{3} + \frac{1}{4}$; $\frac{2}{3} + \frac{3}{4}$; $\frac{2}{5} + \frac{4}{5}$; $\frac{3}{5} + \frac{2}{5}$; $\frac{1}{3} + \frac{1}{3}$; $\frac{1}{2} + \frac{1}{4}$.
2. Select some area of arithmetic or mathematics, such as addition of fractions or simple algebraic equations, and construct from seven to ten test items for measuring computational skills in that area.

[30] Ruth O. Lane and Harry A. Greene, *Lane-Greene Unit Tests in Plane Geometry.* Bureau of Educational Research and Service, State University of Iowa, Iowa City, 1944.

TOPICS FOR DISCUSSION

1. What are some of the basic skills and instructional outcomes of arithmetic?
2. Which of the 29 questions in the check list appearing in this chapter would be met adequately by courses in advanced arithmetic and general mathematics?
3. What accounts for the fact that the field of arithmetic has been subjected to rather extensive analysis and intensive measurement?
4. Identify some of the more important arithmetic skills that lend themselves to measurement and to diagnosis and remediation.
5. Illustrate some of the testing techniques that have been used in the measurement of computational skills and problem solving in arithmetic.
6. Show how the basic steps in problem solving are related to steps involved in the thinking process.
7. Describe the techniques proposed for the analysis of problem-solving skills.
8. Distinguish among readiness, aptitude, and prognostic tests. Where is each type appropriately used?
9. Outline a plan by which eighth-grade pupils could be given guidance concerning their selection of high-school mathematics courses.
10. What are the two types of techniques that are used in predicting success in high-school algebra and plane geometry?
11. How does general achievement in mathematics differ from achievement in general mathematics?
12. What are the comparative values of end-of-course tests and unit tests in algebra and plane geometry?
13. Comment on the origins and probable future of the algebra, geometry, trigonometry sequence in college-preparatory mathematics.

SELECTED REFERENCES

BLAIR, GLENN M. *Diagnostic and Remedial Teaching: A Guide to Practice in Elementary and Secondary Schools.* New York: Macmillan Co., 1956. p. 215-27.

BROMLEY, ANN, AND CARTER, GERALD C. "Predictability of Success in Mathematics." *Journal of Educational Research,* 44:148-50; October 1950.

BROWN, CLAUDE H. *The Teaching of Secondary Mathematics.* New York: Harper and Brothers, 1953. Chapter 11.

BROWNELL, WILLIAM A. "The Evaluation of Learning in Arithmetic." *Arithmetic in General Education.* Sixteenth Yearbook of the National Council of Teachers of Mathematics. New York: Bureau of Publications, Teachers College, Columbia University, 1941. Chapter 10.

BUROS, OSCAR K., editor. *The Fifth Mental Measurements Yearbook.* Highland Park, N. J.: Gryphon Press, 1959. p. 561-615.

BUROS, OSCAR K., editor. *The Fourth Mental Measurements Yearbook.* Highland Park, N. J.: Gryphon Press, 1953. p. 504-18.

BUROS, OSCAR K., editor. *The Third Mental Measurements Yearbook.* New Brunswick, N. J.: Rutgers University Press, 1949. p. 419-38.

BUSWELL, GUY T. "Arithmetic." *Encyclopedia of Educational Research.* Third edition. New York: Macmillan Co., 1960. p. 63-77.

CLARK, JOHN R., editor. *Emerging Practices in Mathematics Education.* Twenty-Second Yearbook of the National Council of Teachers of Mathematics. Washington, D. C.: The Council, 1954. Part 5.

COLLEGE ENTRANCE EXAMINATION BOARD. *Mathematics: A Description of the College Board Tests in Intermediate and Advanced Mathematics.* Princeton, N. J.: The Board, 1954.

DUTTON, WILBUR H. "Attitudes of Junior High School Pupils toward Arithmetic." *School Review,* 64:18-22; January 1956.

EPSTEIN, MARION, AND MYERS, SHELDON. "How a Mathematics Test Is Born." *Mathematics Teacher,* 51:299-302; April 1958.

GERBERICH, J. RAYMOND. *Specimen Objective Test Items: A Guide to Achievement Test Construction.* New York: Longmans, Green and Co., 1956. p. 321-24.

GIBB, E. GLENADINE; MAYOR, JOHN R.; AND TRUENFELS, EDITH. "Mathematics." *Encyclopedia of Educational Research.* Third edition. New York: Macmillan Co., 1960. p. 796-807.

GREENE, HARRY A., JORGENSEN, ALBERT N., AND GERBERICH, J. RAYMOND. *Measurement and Evaluation in the Elementary School.* Second edition. New York: Longmans, Green and Co., 1953. Chapter 18.

GREENE, HARRY A., JORGENSEN, ALBERT N., AND GERBERICH, J. RAYMOND. *Measurement and Evaluation in the Secondary School.* Second edition. New York: Longmans, Green and Co., 1954. Chapter 19.

HARTUNG, MAURICE L. "A Forward Look at Evaluation." *Mathematics Teacher,* 42:29-33; January 1949.

HARTUNG, MAURICE L., AND FAWCETT, HAROLD P. "The Measurement of Understanding in Secondary-School Mathematics." *The Measurement of Understanding.* Forty-Fifth Yearbook of the National Society for the Study of Education, Part I. Chicago: University of Chicago Press, 1946. Chapter 8.

KINNEY, LUCIEN B., AND PURDY, C. RICHARD. *Teaching Mathematics in the Secondary School.* New York: Rinehart and Co., Inc., 1952. Chapter 15.

LONG, JOHN A., LUNDHOLM, HAROLD T., AND SMITH, EUGENE R. "Examinations in Mathematics." *The Construction and Use of Achievement Examinations.* Boston: Houghton Mifflin Co., 1936. Chapter 7.

MACLATCHEY, JOSEPHINE H. "A Test on the Pre-School Child's Familiarity with Measurement." *Educational Research Bulletin,* 29:207-8, 222-23; November 15, 1950.

MALONE, WILLIAM H., AND FREEL, EUGENE L. "A Preliminary Study of the Group Attitudes of Junior and Senior High School Students toward Mathematics." *Journal of Educational Research,* 47:599-608; April 1954.

MORTON, ROBERT L. *Teaching Children Arithmetic.* New York: Silver Burdett Co., 1953. Chapter 12.

ROSSKOPF, M. F. "The Present State of Evaluation of Critical Thinking in Algebra and Geometry." *Mathematics Teacher,* 43:143-48; October 1950.

SCHAAF, WILLIAM L. "Testing the Clarity of Mathematical Concepts." *School Science and Mathematics,* 39:651-56; October 1939.

SPACHE, GEORGE. "A Test of Abilities in Arithmetic Reasoning." *Elementary School Journal,* 47:442-45; April 1947.

SPITZER, HERBERT F. "Procedures and Techniques for Evaluating the Outcomes of Instruction in Arithmetic." *Elementary School Journal,* 49:21-31; September 1948.

SPITZER, HERBERT F. "Testing Instruments and Practices in Relation to Present Concepts of Teaching Arithmetic." *The Teaching of Arithmetic.* Fiftieth Yearbook of the National Society for the Study of Education, Part II. Chicago: University of Chicago Press, 1951. Chapter 10.

SUELTZ, BEN A. "The Evaluation of Arithmetic Learnings." *National Elementary Principal,* 30:24-33; October 1950.

SUELTZ, BEN A. "The Measurement of Understandings and Judgments in Elementary-School Mathematics." *Mathematics Teacher,* 40:279-84; October 1947.

SUELTZ, BEN A. "Measuring the Newer Aspects of Functional Arithmetic." *Elementary School Journal,* 47:323-30; February 1947.

SUELTZ, BEN A.; BOYNTON, HOLMES; AND SAUBLE, IRENE. "The Measurement of Understanding in Elementary-School Mathematics." *The Measurement of Understanding.* Forty-Fifth Yearbook of the National Society for the Study of Education, Part I. Chicago: University of Chicago Press, 1946. Chapter 7.

THAYER, V. T., chairman. *Mathematics in General Education.* Report of Committee on the Function of Mathematics in General Education, Commission on Secondary School Curriculum, Progressive Education Association. New York: D. Appleton-Century Co., Inc., 1940. Chapter 13.

ULLSVICK, BJARNE R. "An Attempt to Measure Critical Judgment." *School Science and Mathematics,* 49:445-52; June 1949.

WILSON, GUY M. "Arithmetic." *Encyclopedia of Educational Research.* Revised edition. New York: Macmillan Co., 1950. p. 44-58.

WREN, F LYNWOOD. "Mathematics, Secondary." *Encyclopedia of Educational Research.* Revised edition. New York: Macmillan Co., 1950. p. 717-25.

18

BIOLOGICAL AND PHYSICAL SCIENCES

This chapter presents a discussion of the following points involved in the measurement of instructional outcomes in the biological and physical sciences:

A. Relation of science to the social environment.
B. Important principles of science.
C. Objectives and measurable outcomes of science instruction.
D. Measurement of scientific aptitude.
E. Measurement of achievement in science.
F. Evaluation of complex and intangible outcomes of science instruction.
G. Diagnosis and remediation in science.

This and the following chapter, on the social studies, discuss the problems of measurement in the major content subjects. The particular subjects dealt with here—elementary science, general science, biology, physics, and chemistry—follow the pattern accepted in most present-day schools. It would be difficult to overemphasize the importance of science in the age of atomic physics, of new chemical elements, of electronics, and of automation, for example, and the impact of these and many other scientific developments upon daily living. There is reason to think that progress in the selection and organization of content for science courses, in the suitability of the learning activities in which science pupils engage, and in the clear statement and measurement of instructional outcomes of science courses has failed to keep pace with these developments.

1. SIGNIFICANCE AND MAJOR OBJECTIVES OF SCIENCE

Science education is increasingly looked upon today in terms of its contribution to national survival. In the attempt to serve the needs of the learner in his interaction with his social environment, the methods of science are employed (1) in solving the problems of social living and (2) as a basis for developing an understanding of social problems.[1] In practice, however, the emphasis in many of the background materials of direct significance to the person interested in pupil evaluation is more on subject matter than on the applicational values of content.

Important Principles and Generalizations of Science

Specialists in science education place great emphasis on principles of science to supplement, or even to replace, objectives. The importance of these concepts in science education can be indicated by Martin's criteria [2] that a principle or comprehensive generalization should (1) be stated positively and definitely, (2) be true with but rare exceptions, (3) deal with a dynamic process or interaction, (4) be demonstrable experimentally, (5) not be included as part of a larger principle, (6) not be merely a definition, and (7) be widely applicable.

The Committee on the Teaching of Science suggested the following principles and generalizations which it considered of value for guidance in selecting and organizing content for science teaching.[3]

1. The sun is the chief source of energy for the earth.
2. Through interdependence of species and the struggle for existence a balance tends to be maintained among the many forms of life.
3. The earth's position in relation to the sun and moon is a determining factor of life on earth.
4. All life comes from life and produces its own kind of living organism.
5. Matter and energy cannot be created or destroyed, but may be changed from one form to another.
6. Species have survived because of adaptations and adjustments which have fitted them to the conditions under which they live.
7. The energy of solar radiation is continually working changes in the surface of the earth.
8. There have been profound changes in the climate, not only of certain regions, but also of the earth as a whole.
9. The evolution of the earth has come as a result of natural forces.

[1] Herbert A. Smith and Kenneth E. Anderson, "Science." *Encyclopedia of Educational Research,* Third edition. Macmillan Co., New York, 1960. p. 1217-18.

[2] W. Edgar Martin, "A Chronological Survey of Research Studies on Principles as Objectives of Instruction in Science." *Science Education,* 29:46-52; February 1945.

[3] S. Ralph Powers, chairman, "The Objectives of Science Teaching in Relation to the Aim of Education." *A Program for Science Teaching,* Thirty-First Yearbook of the National Society or the Study of Education, Part I. Public School Publishing Co., Bloomington, Ill., 1932. p. 53-55.

10. Units of time are defined by the earth's movements in relation to the sun.
11. All life has evolved from simple forms.
12. The earth seems very old when its age is measured in the ordinary units of time.
13. Distances in space seem extremely vast when compared with distances on earth.
14. The physical environment has great influence on the structural forms of life and on plant and animal habitats.
15. Man can modify the nature of plant and animal forms through application of his knowledge of the laws of heredity.
16. There is a great variety in the size, structure, and habits of living things.
17. There are processes that go on within an organism that are vital to its continued existence.
18. Chemical and physical changes are manifestations of energy changes.
19. There are fewer than one hundred chemical elements.
20. Every substance is one of the following: (a) a chemical element, (b) a chemical compound, (c) a mechanical mixture.
21. Certain material substances and certain physical conditions are limiting factors to life.
22. Light is a limiting factor to life.
23. Sound is caused by waves which are produced by a vibrating body and which can affect the auditory nerves of the ear.
24. Gravitation is the attractive force that influences or governs the movements of astronomical bodies.
25. Machines are devices for accomplishing useful transformations of energy.
26. Any machine, no matter how complicated, may be analyzed into a few simple types.
27. The properties of the different elements depend on the number and arrangement of the electrons and protons contained in their atoms.
28. All matter is probably electrical in structure.
29. The applications of electricity and magnetism in the home and in industry have revolutionized the methods of living of many people.
30. Heredity determines the differences between parents and offspring as well as the resemblances.
31. The kinetic energy of the molecules determines the physical states of matter.
32. The gravitational attraction between the earth and a mass of unconfined gas or liquid causes the pressure of the liquid or gas on the surface of the earth.
33. Liquid or gas pressure is exerted equally in all directions.
34. Chemical changes are accompanied by energy changes.
35. A change in rate or direction of motion of an object requires the application of an external force.

36. Radiant energy travels in straight lines through a uniform medium.
37. Electricity is a form of energy that results from disturbing the position or the regular paths of electrons.
38. In a chemical change a quantitative relationship exists between the amounts of substances reacting and the amounts of the substances that are the products of the reaction.

This list of principles and generalizations gives clues to some major objectives of science instruction and can also serve as a general source of ideas for the teacher in construction of classroom tests.

Objectives of Science Instruction

The following list for science in general includes eight types of objectives but in each instance provides only a few of the illustrations given in the original source to show how the objectives can be attained.[4]

A. *Functional information* or *facts* about such matters as:
  1. Our universe—earth, sun, moon, stars, weather, and climate.
  2. Living things—plants and animals.
  3. The human body—structure, functions, and care.
  4. Energy—sources, types of energy, machines.
B. *Functional concepts,* such as:
  1. Space is vast.
  2. The earth is very old.
  3. All life has evolved from simpler forms.
C. *Functional understanding* of principles, such as:
  1. All living things reproduce their kind.
  2. Energy can be changed from one form to another.
  3. All matter is composed of single elements or combinations of elements.
D. *Instrumental skills,* such as:
  1. Read science content with understanding and satisfaction.
  2. Perform fundamental operations with reasonable accuracy.
  3. Read maps, graphs, charts, and tables and interpret them.
  4. Make accurate measurements, readings, titrations, etc.
E. *Problem-solving skills,* such as ability to:
  1. Sense a problem.
  2. Define the problem.
  3. Select the most likely hypothesis.
  4. Test the hypothesis by experimental or other means.
  5. Draw conclusions.

[4] Victor H. Noll, chairman, "The Objectives of Science Instruction." *Science Education in American Schools,* Forty-Sixth Yearbook of the National Society for the Study of Education, Part I. University of Chicago Press, Chicago, 1947. p. 28-29.

F. *Attitudes,* such as:
1. Open-mindedness—willingness to consider new facts.
2. Intellectual honesty—scientific integrity, unwillingness to compromise with truth as known.
G. *Appreciations,* such as:
1. Appreciation of the contributions of scientists.
2. Appreciation of basic cause-and-effect relationships.
H. *Interests,* such as:
1. Interest in some phase of science as a recreational activity or hobby.
2. Interest in science as a field for a vocation.

Measurable Outcomes of Science Instruction

The literature of science education seems to deal more with the objectives of instruction, especially as they are reflected in scientific principles, than with instructional outcomes stated directly in terms of pupil behavior, although the illustrative points in the preceding list reflect the end products and in some instances the functional outcomes of learning. Moreover, Powers dealt with outcomes in very general terms when he pointed out that educational values of real significance will be attained if pupils acquire (1) the ability to use the scientific findings that apply in their experiences, (2) the ability to interpret natural phenomena in their environments, and (3) an appreciation of scientific attitude through understanding of and ability to use some of the methods of study that have been employed by scientists.[5]

At least nine of the ten types of instructional or learning outcomes discussed in Chapter 1 doubtless occur in the science subjects. However, only the seven to which science instruction contributes most directly and which at the same time can be measured with reasonable effectiveness are dealt with here.

Knowledges. Tests in science often tend to overemphasize information and knowledge as the goal of study. It is often assumed that knowledge is a positive index of satisfactory modes of adjustment. This assumption, of course, is only partially defensible. Merely to know is no assurance of subsequent proper reaction. But insofar as knowledge is essential to adjustment, its proper worth should not be discounted. Accordingly, measurement of the pupil's knowledge of scientific facts is to that extent valid and defensible.

Skills. Although laboratory and other science skills are not as much involved in the elementary-school as in the secondary-school sciences, the

[5] S. Ralph Powers, "The Plan of the Public Schools and the Program of Science Teaching." *A Program of Science Teaching,* Thirty-First Yearbook of the National Society for the Study of Education, Part I. Public School Publishing Co., Bloomington, Ill., 1932. p. 10.

degree to which pupils attain the desired skills can be measured readily at both levels. Performance rather than paper-and-pencil tests are often demanded in such situations. Since performance tests are treated in Chapter 11, the measurement of skill outcomes in the sciences receives little attention in this chapter.

Concepts and understandings. Facts in science are the vehicles for thought. The understanding of the relationships of facts and of generalized ideas is deemed most important. Tests should, therefore, measure the relational aspects of science.

Applications. Problem-solving tests in science call for the application of knowledge and may demand one or more types of scientific thinking. Similarly, test items that involve the interpretation of new situations demand more than mere recall and, thus, are measures of ability to use scientific knowledge or judgment. Such test items should find an extensive place in testing procedures.

Attitudes and interests. Some progress has been made in the measurement of pupils' attitudes toward and interests in science material and phenomena. Unscientific attitudes are reflected in superstitions and unfounded beliefs, in naïve reactions to propaganda, in stereotyped modes of responses to some problem situations, and doubtless in many other ways. Some of these attitudinal outcomes can be evaluated by use of such tools and techniques as are dealt with in Chapters 7 and 12. Scientific interests, both vocational and general, can be measured by methods outlined in Chapter 7 and elsewhere in this volume.

2. MEASUREMENT OF SCIENTIFIC APTITUDE

As is pointed out in the preceding chapter for mathematics aptitude tests at the highest level, aptitude tests in science are used primarily for senior pupils in high school or for college freshmen in obtaining a basis for sectioning of classes and in various types of educational guidance. These aptitude tests presuppose little or no study of the subject, but attempt to measure those specific intellectual abilities and those skills resulting from general training which make for success or failure in college courses in the subject.

The *Iowa Placement Examinations* in chemistry[6] and in physics[7] are designed to predict success in first-year college courses in their respective

[6] George D. Stoddard, Jacob Cornog, and L. W. Miller, *Iowa Placement Examinations, Chemistry Aptitude,* New Series CA-2, Revised. Bureau of Educational Research and Service, State University of Iowa, Iowa City, 1942.

[7] George D. Stoddard and C. J. Lapp, *Iowa Placement Examinations: Physics Aptitude,* New Series PA-2, Revised. Bureau of Educational Research and Service, State University of Iowa, Iowa City, 1941.

areas. Consequently they may be of interest to high-school teachers of science who advise and aid pupils in planning their college careers. Both tests are of the inventory type, since they measure mathematical backgrounds and reading comprehension skills deemed necessary for success in the subject, ability to interpret science materials, and general information in the subject area.

Another instrument for use in the same manner and at the same level is the *Engineering and Physical Science Aptitude Test*,[8] although it is designed to predict success in several related areas of college science rather than in one subject area only. It includes parts on mathematics, handling formulas, arithmetic reasoning, and comprehension of physical science, verbal, and mechanical materials.

3. MEASUREMENT OF ACHIEVEMENT IN ELEMENTARY SCIENCE

The construction of science tests should apparently be relatively simple, since the content of science is quite specific. However, problems of a degree no less marked than in the other content subjects are encountered. There is the same lack of high agreement on course content and organization that is found in the social sciences. Controversies about the importance of facts as contrasted with emphasis on relationships and problem solving are still somewhat in evidence in science teaching, although teachers have increasingly of late given attention to the more intangible outcomes of instruction. In fact, some of the major evidences of accomplishment in the sciences are probably found in such intangible outcomes as pupil attitudes, interests, appreciations, and activities. The problem consists more in deciding what particular behaviors to test and in what the test results signify than in how to measure the outcomes finally chosen for inclusion in the tests.

Measurable Aspects of Elementary Science

The elementary sciences must be viewed from two rather specific points of view—for their immediate educational values and for the background of preparation they afford for the later and more specialized study of the sciences at advanced levels. Although the first of these values is naturally of foremost concern at the elementary-school level and continues to be dominant for many high-school pupils, the second need must be fulfilled

[8] Bruce V. Moore, C. J. Lapp, and Charles H. Griffin, *Engineering and Physical Science Aptitude Test*, Revised. Psychological Corporation, New York, 1951.

for college-preparatory and perhaps for some other groups of pupils in the secondary school.

Biological and earth sciences. One of the major aspects of elementary science is found in the study of nature. Biological knowledge about how plants and animals serve human needs involves the earth sciences—soils, climatic conditions and effects, tillage, control of pests, plant and animal foods—and means of preserving plant and animal products. There is also much need for knowledge of the physical sciences in connection with food, clothing, shelter, transportation, and other everyday problems. The appreciative aspects of nature as revealed in plant and animal forms, in land and water formations, and earth and sky by day and night are also important outcomes in this area.

Physiology and hygiene. The aspects of science directly related to human welfare are also of great concern. The development of proper habits in nourishing and caring for the body requires some knowledge of the structure and use of its parts. The general structure of the teeth, the skin, the nails and hair, the eyes, the ears, the nose, the throat, and the mouth should be known for the contribution such knowledge makes toward keeping them all in a healthful condition. A general knowledge of the digestive organs, lungs, circulatory system, organs of excretion and sex, and the nervous system is useful in keeping these organs healthfully at work.

Tests of Achievement in Elementary Science

The number and variety of standardized tests in elementary science is not great. Tests for the intermediate grades are found mainly as sections of achievement test batteries, and these parts are seldom available as

EXCERPT FROM *California Elementary Science Test* [9]

81. Dandelion seeds are carried by the wind.   T   **F** 81

82. All birds fly south during the cold weather.   T   **F** 82

83. The moon shines because it reflects the light of the sun.   T   **F** 83

84. Squirrels have pouches in their cheeks in which they carry food. T   **F** 84

85. Plants drink the water they need through their leaves.   T   **F** 85

[9] Georgia S. Adams and John A. Sexson, *California Tests in Social and Related Sciences: Test 6, Elementary Science,* Elementary. Form AA. California Test Bureau, Monterey, Calif., 1953.

separate booklets. Since general achievement tests are treated directly in Chapter 25 of this volume, this source of science tests is not dealt with at this point. A few items illustrative of the manner in which various objective item forms are used in elementary science testing are presented here. The student should utilize the sample items and the bibliography at the end of the chapter for information concerning informal objective testing techniques appropriate for use at this level of science instruction.

EXCERPT FROM *California Health and Safety Test* [10]

18. If one does not have much money to spend for food, one can obtain the greatest health value by spending that money on

   a potatoes, bread, and inexpensive sweets.
   b meat, eggs, vegetables, ice cream.
   c milk, cereals, cheaper vegetables, and fruits.
   d potatoes, meat, bread, pie. ——18

19. Which one of the following foods contains the most protein?

   e lettuce   f lean meat
      g oranges   h cookies ——19

Illustrations of item types from the science portions of the *California Tests in Social and Related Sciences* are presented in two accompanying excerpts. The first employs *true–false* items in measuring knowledge about plant and animal life. The second consists of multiple-choice items dealing with the health values of certain foods.

A third excerpt, from the *Cooperative Science Test for Grades 7, 8, and 9,* illustrates a descriptive paragraph, or setting, dealing with earth science and one of the dependent multiple-choice items involving an interpretation of the paragraph.

4. MEASUREMENT OF ACHIEVEMENT
IN HIGH-SCHOOL SCIENCE

Measurement of instructional outcomes in secondary-school science subjects is held back by some of the same factors that are mentioned in

[10] *Ibid. Test 5, Health and Safety.*

EXCERPT FROM *Cooperative Science Test for Grades 7, 8, and 9* [11]

Water takes up oxygen from the air in varying amounts. Cold water will take up small quantities of oxygen while warm water takes up almost none. Running water will dissolve (that is, take up) more oxygen than standing water. Water in which plants are growing contains much oxygen because the green plants give off oxygen in the process of photosynthesis. When there is not enough light for plants to manufacture food, they do not give off oxygen but consume it in respiration. Water animals also use oxygen in respiration so that the amount of oxygen found in water is always changing. The oxygen content of an aquarium changes from day to day and from hour to hour and is different even at different levels in the aquarium.

13. Standing water takes up

    13–1 more oxygen than running water.
    13–2 as much oxygen as running water.
    13–3 less oxygen than running water.
    13–4 a great deal of oxygen.
    13–5 no oxygen. ....13(   )

the preceding section of this chapter as rather common to the content subject areas in the elementary school. What facts are of greatest importance, or what knowledge is of greatest worth, and how factual knowledge is related to applications are no more satisfactorily answered at this level than for the elementary grades, although the traditional academic curriculum may resolve this problem somewhat arbitrarily for the science subjects most typically taken by college-preparatory pupils. Laboratory skills, more common to the high school than the grades, are measured most satisfactorily by performance tests of the types dealt with in Chapter 11, although only the check list shown in Figure 13 on page 269 has any direct significance for measurement of laboratory skills in the science subjects.

Measurable Aspects of Secondary-School Science

Although both the terminal and the preparatory values are still represented in the sciences usually taught in the high school, the typical curriculum for college-preparatory pupils in the junior and senior years is distinctly intended as background for further study at the college level.

General science. Most intelligent adjustments, as distinguished from those that are purely accidental, impulsive, or habitual, are dependent upon scientific procedures. Everyone is called upon to make such responses in connection with his home, his neighborhood, his vocation, his civic duties, and his leisure. He is frequently confronted with a need for some

[11] John G. Zimmerman and Richard E. Watson, *Cooperative Science Test for Grades 7, 8, and 9.* Form R. Educational Testing Service, Princeton, N. J., 1941.

special knowledge of health control, mechanics, chemistry, physics, biology, or plant and animal life. At almost every hour of the day the individual is in the midst of the influence of mechanical and scientific appliances. For their operation, maintenance, adjustment, and repair, and as a protection from their dangers, he needs information and first-hand experience of the type obtained in general science.

Biology. Typically following general science in the high-school course of study, biology is concerned with the physical and mental health and the environments of pupils. In so doing, it emphasizes the maintenance of life, interrelationships among forms of life, dependence of man on his physical environment, and man's ability to control his environment. Some of the direct concerns of this course typically are health education, sanitation, physiology, sex education, first aid, the mechanics of heredity, cultivation of plants, behavior and control of animals, and conservation of natural resources.

Physics and chemistry. These two advanced and relatively specialized courses deal more with inorganic than organic matter. Physics deals with the transformation and conservation of energy, with heat, light, mechanics, and electronics, and with fundamentals of atomic energy. Chemistry treats the elements, their valences, and the periodic table, chemical compounds and their formation, chemical symbolism, and equations and their balancing. Both stress a large number of laboratory and mathematical competencies.

Tests of Achievement in High-School Science

There is considerable variety among the standardized tests in the secondary-school sciences. Although the majority of tests are for general science, biology, physics, and chemistry, several tests for the junior high school and at least one or two for the senior high school cover the science field broadly and without reference to particular courses. Most of the tests concentrate rather heavily on the content aspects of their respective science fields. A few samples illustrative of the manner in which various objective item types are used in secondary-school science testing are presented here for the four typical course areas.

A number of tests are available for the general science course typically given in the ninth grade. The *Read General Science Test* is representative of end-of-course instruments in this area. It includes items on light, sound, heat, mechanics, electricity, chemistry, weather, astronomy, nutrition, genetics, disease and health, conservation, and geology. A sample from this test appears in an accompanying excerpt as an illustration of graphical options in a multiple-choice item. An excerpt from the *Cooperative General*

Science Test, also used for end-of-course testing, shows an unusual modification of a multiple-option item.

EXCERPT FROM *Read General Science Test* [12]

49. If a 500-pound weight is placed at the arrow, which lever will lift the 60-pound weight W the highest?

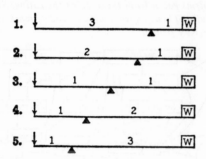

EXCERPT FROM *Cooperative General Science Test* [13]

2. In what way are the following alike?
 a. A gallon of gasoline
 b. A loaf of bread
 c. A mountain lake
 d. The sun

2–1 They are all used as sources of energy.
2–2 They are all combustible materials.
2–3 They are all carbohydrates.
2–4 They are all made up of identical percentages of the same elements.
2–5 They were all at one time composed of living materials. . . . . .2( )

The majority of tests in biology deal largely with the measurement of facts, information, and principles. However, the *Nelson Biology Test* is an end-of-course instrument measuring knowledge and understanding of facts, concepts, and principles; ability to identify cause and effect relationships; and ability to apply knowledge to lifelike situations. The accompanying excerpt from it shows a complex exercise that requests the pupil to interpret graphical data in deciding upon his answers to the three-option items. A second excerpt dealing with this subject, from the *Cooperative*

[12] John G. Read, *Read General Science Test.* Form AM. Copyright 1950 by Harcourt, Brace and World, Inc., New York. All rights reserved. Quoted by special permission.
[13] Carl A. Pearson, *Cooperative General Science Test,* Part I. Form Z. Educational Testing Service, Princeton, N. J., 1950.

Biology Test, illustrates an unusual variety of matching exercise used in testing knowledge outcomes.

EXCERPT FROM *Nelson Biology Test* [14]

Questions 52 through 54 are based on the chart below. This chart represents some of the food relations to be found in a deciduous forest community of organisms. The arrows point to the organisms eaten from those doing the eating. Study the chart and read each question carefully. Then, on your answer sheet, mark the number of your answer according to the KEY below.

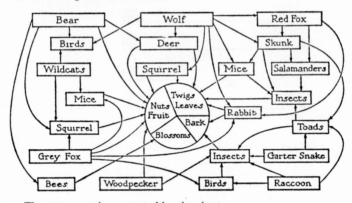

KEY
1. The statement is warranted by the chart.
2. The statement is contradicted by the chart.
3. The statement goes beyond the chart.

52. Toads are detrimental to man's interests and should be killed whenever possible.

53. Man's greatest loss of food supply can be attributed to parasitic organisms.

54. Plants constitute the foundation links in the various chains shown here.

It is not difficult to measure the factual and informational aspects of physics. Understandings of the relationships among facts or of generalized ideas are also capable of measurement, but this is much more difficult than merely testing for memory of facts. The accompanying excerpt from the *Dunning Physics Test* illustrates the use of ordinary multiple-option items in testing outcomes of instruction in physics.

Measurement in chemistry, the second major college-preparatory area, presents problems many of which are similar to those encountered in physics, but such skills as are involved in balancing and handling chemical equations do not occur in that area. Representative of tests in chemistry is the *Anderson Chemistry Test,* standardized for use in end-of-course

EXCERPT FROM *Cooperative Biology Test* [15]

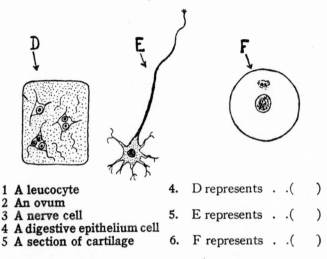

1 A leucocyte
2 An ovum
3 A nerve cell
4 A digestive epithelium cell
5 A section of cartilage

4. D represents . .(   )

5. E represents . .(   )

6. F represents . .(   )

EXCERPT FROM *Dunning Physics Test* [16]

23. The sun appears to rise earlier than it actually does. This is due to the earth's atmosphere causing the light waves to be—
    1. diffused.
    2. reflected.
    3. dispersed.
    4. polarized.
    5. refracted.

24. The phenomenon that best supports the hypothesis that light is a form of transverse wave motion is called—
    6. polarization.
    7. refraction.
    8. interference.
    9. reflection.
    10. dispersion.

testing. The test has parts measuring (1) factual information, (2) understanding of principles and their practical applications, (3) elements of the scientific method, together with its associated attitudes in chemical situations, and (4) ability to use formulas and to solve problems. An accompanying excerpt shows two multiple-option items in sequence from the section measuring understanding of chemical principles and their practical

[15] F. L. Fitzpatrick, *Cooperative Biology Test.* Form Q. Educational Testing Service, Princeton, N. J., 1940.
[16] Gordon M. Dunning, *Dunning Physics Test.* Form AM. Copyright 1950 by Harcourt, Brace and World, Inc., New York. All rights reserved. Quoted by special permission.

applications. A second excerpt from this test appears on page 229 of Chapter 10 to represent the multiple-choice item in which the pupil is asked to select the discordant or irrelevant option, the one that does not belong with others, for his response.

EXCERPT FROM *Anderson Chemistry Test* [17]

45. A boy placed some zinc in a flask with some dilute hydro-chloric acid. What happened?

    1. Hydrogen was given off.
    2. Chlorine was given off.
    3. Oxygen was given off.
    4. Zinc chloride was precipitated.
    5. Nothing happened.

46. Which one of the following statements gives the principle that best explains the answer to question 45?

    6. Metals replace hydrogen from all acids.
    7. Gases are produced by simple replacement reactions.
    8. Elements are able to replace those below them in the electrochemical series.
    9. Chemical opposites, such as a metal and an acid, usually unite.
    10. Zinc is a very inactive metal.

5. EVALUATION OF COMPLEX AND INTANGIBLE SCIENCE OUTCOMES

Objective items of the types illustrated in the two preceding sections of this chapter have been quite widely used by informal objective test makers in the evaluation of tangible outcomes of science instruction. Futhermore, rather involved adaptations of the common item forms have also been used in evaluating the more complex and even intangible outcomes. There seems excellent reason to believe, in fact, that much of the most significant testing in science has been done by such informal objective testing methods.

Space does not permit many illustrations here of the more complex and broadly conceived types of approach to the measurement of scientific outcomes classified as relatively intangible or intangible. Although all of the illustrations given below are for use in the junior or the senior high schools, it does not necessarily follow that these techniques are applicable

[17] Kenneth E. Anderson, *Anderson Chemistry Test,* Part B. Form AM. Copyright 1950 by Harcourt, Brace and World, Inc., New York. All rights reserved. Quoted by special permission.

only to instructional outcomes beyond those typical of the elementary school. It may mean that the rather complex and sometimes higher-level mental processes required of pupils are found more often at the secondary-school and college levels than in the elementary grades. However, the same techniques can be, and in a few cases have been, adapted to testing in the intermediate grades.

Measurement of Complex Outcomes

Test exercises or groups of items can be devised for measuring such relatively complex applications as are involved in handling cause and effect relationships, in interpreting scientific data, in generalizing and drawing inferences from scientific facts, and in numerous other ways. Such test materials are similar to some of these discussed and illustrated in the treatment of evaluative tests in Chapter 12. The excerpt from the science section of the *Essential High School Content Battery* on page 284, for example, shows a type of evaluative exercise that has been used quite widely in recently published standardized tests.

The accompanying illustration of test items based on a briefly stated background and answerable in terms of three possible cause-and-effect patterns shows how items in clusters can be used to measure pupil ability to apply scientific principles in everyday situations. A somewhat similar but less complex sample of science test items devised by the same author is shown on page 230 of Chapter 10.

SAMPLE OF Test Items in Science [18]

In the following examples, the first part is followed by *several* OTHER parts. Your job is to find out if the first part is a direct cause or an indirect cause or if it is not a cause of the other parts that follow it.

If the first part *directly* causes the second (numbered) part, draw a circle around the letter D.

If the first part *indirectly* causes the second (numbered) part, draw a circle around the letter I.

If the first part is in *no way* a cause of the second (numbered) part, draw a circle around the letter N.

A girl chews a cracker. //

D   I   N   64. The cracker is broken into smaller pieces.

D   I   N   65. The starch in the cracker changes into sugar.

D   I   N   66. The girl gains energy from the cracker.

D   I   N   67. The cracker is salty.

---

[18] William B. Reiner, "Evaluating Ability to Recognize Degrees of Cause and Effect Relationships." *Science Education*, 34:15-28; February 1950.

An informal, semiobjective test for teaching as much as for testing purposes was devised by Davis [19] for use in eighth- or ninth-grade science courses in the measurement of other than largely factual instructional outcomes. The following reproduction of the instructions to pupils and of the first paragraph of the selection to be read and evaluated by the pupils serves to show the nature of the instrument.

To the Pupil

Here is a test which I think you will find quite different from any you have ever taken. It is a story about Johnny Jones. He was quite an active boy, but sometimes he was a poor scientist. Some of his friends and the members of his family may not have been good scientists either. Whenever you find something in the story which does not agree with what you think good science means, put a pair of parentheses ( ) around the sentence or part of a sentence where you find this. Next, at the border of the paper beside the error write in the correct letter from the following list:

S means that Johnny or some one else was superstitious.
D means that what was being done or had been done was dangerous.
O means that statements are being taken or have been taken for truth without any proof being offered.
J means something unscientific for reasons other than S, D or O. If you use the letter J be prepared to tell the class what was wrong with the story at the point where you use this letter.

Now go on with the story.

Johnny's Day

Johnny Jones woke from a sound sleep one morning and noticed that the sun was already shining in his window. Without looking where he was going he jumped to the floor and started gathering up his articles of clothing to put them on. Suddenly he stopped and said, "Shucks, it's Saturday, no need for me to hurry. But it might just as well be a school day," he went on as he looked out of the window, "it's sure to rain today. Old man Smith said this was a wet moon."

The remaining parts of the selection, running to perhaps 1100 words, include many additional evidences of behavior or reasoning illustrative of the types of situations covered by the S, D, O, and J methods of marking the selection. One point of credit was assigned for each pair of parentheses placed approximately in the correct position and an additional point of credit was assigned for each pair of parentheses accompanied by the proper identifying letter in this semiobjective test.

[19] Warren M. Davis, "A Science Test Designed to Teach and Measure Outcomes Other Than Memorization of Factual Information." *Science Education,* 23:371-72; December 1939.

Measurement of Scientific Attitudes

Attitudes toward science and its laws and principles are subject to evaluation. Scientific attitude is represented in the behavior of a person who knows and understands scientific laws and principles and who employs the scientific method in attacking problems in the physical, biological, or social sciences. Failure to demonstrate scientific attitude results in what are usually called unfounded beliefs or, more narrowly, superstitious beliefs. Scientific attitudes, as distinguished from social attitudes, can be classed as right or wrong, or at least can be assigned a reasonably accurate degree of rightness or wrongness. Superstitious beliefs contradict known laws or principles of science. They consequently have a high degree of tangibility in the sense that definite standards can be employed in interpreting the results of their measurement. Unfounded beliefs are perhaps slightly less tangible, for sometimes they can neither be supported nor rejected with a high degree of assurance. Scientific attitudes, however, can be measured with greater likelihood of rightness or wrongness than seems possible for social attitudes.

Noll listed the following six abilities as essential to the scientific attitude: (1) accuracy in all operations—calculation, observation, and report, (2) intellectual honesty, (3) open-mindedness, (4) the habit of looking for natural causes, (5) the habit of suspended judgment, and (6) the habit of criticism.[20] Although he admitted that other habits might be included in such a list, he stated that a person who met all of the conditions listed above would possess the scientific attitude and would also be highly unique even in this scientific era.

Test items for measuring scientific attitudes. Suggestions concerning how each of these six essentials of scientific attitude can be measured informally were also presented by Noll.[21] Some of his illustrations are reproduced to show techniques useful in measuring scientific attitude.

(1) Accuracy in calculation—arithmetic examples.
   Accuracy of observation and report—questioning a pupil concerning the characteristics of an animal picture, plant, or diagram.

(2) Intellectual honesty.
   T F When a pupil makes a poor mark in an examination it is usually because he is not well or he was up late the night before.
   T F It is perfectly justifiable not to pay one's fare on a bus or street car if the conductor doesn't come around to collect it.

[20] Victor H. Noll, *The Teaching of Science in Elementary and Secondary Schools.* Longmans, Green and Co., New York, 1939. p. 25-26.
[21] *Ibid.* p. 34-37.

(3) Open-mindedness.
  T   F   All Indians are dirty.
  T   F   College professors as a rule would be failures in any line of
          work but teaching.

(4) Cause and effect relationships.
  T   F   Finding a horseshoe means that one will have good luck.
  T   F   Giraffes have such long necks because through many generations
          they have been stretched a little longer each time.

(5) Suspended judgment.
  T   F   My neighbor is away from home most of the time. He must be
          a traveling salesman.
  T   F   Mr. Jones bought a new car last week. He must have had an
          increase in salary.

(6) Criticism.
  T   F   One can always accept as true what is printed in a book.
  T   F   If my science teacher says a thing is so, it must be so.

Observation in evaluating superstitious beliefs. Zapf presented a technique for measuring the manner in which pupils actually behave in situations to which well-known superstitious beliefs apply.[22] Pupils were placed in a closed room, where they opened boxes in which were found directions for their subsequent action asking that they go contrary to widely held superstitious beliefs. The extent to which they performed the actions was taken as an indication of the degree to which they were not governed in their behavior by these beliefs. Such situations as breaking a mirror, walking under a ladder, and opening an umbrella indoors were among the twelve used in the test. Although all 32 pupils tested in these situations had previously indicated that they did not believe in the superstitions, only two pupils went contrary to all twelve superstitions and two pupils acted superstitiously in five of the twelve situations.

6. DIAGNOSIS AND REMEDIATION IN SCIENCE

Diagnostic procedures and remedial work in the field of science instruction are not highly developed. While certain of the available tests may show pupils to be deficient in some specific phase of science information, the majority of such tests do not point out the causes of the deficiencies. Practically all that can be done by way of diagnosis is in connection with certain skills that appear to be basic to the study of science.

The study of science involves the comprehension of a language peculiar

[22] Rosalind M. Zapf, "Superstitious Beliefs." *School Science and Mathematics,* 39:54-62; January 1939.

to the subject. Reading of scientific content is apt to be difficult. Thus, poor reading ability may form the basis of poor accomplishment in the subject. Diagnosis of reading abilities of the work-study type, accompanied by remedial instruction designed to overcome the weaknesses revealed, is one of the prerequisites to satisfactory progress in the study of the sciences. Laboratory work may call for many new abilities and techniques, as well as for considerable manual dexterity.

There is considerable promise for the future of diagnosis and remediation in the sciences through further development of the evaluation techniques illustrated in the preceding section of this chapter. The attempt so far has been more upon the construction of valid evaluation procedures for the less tangible outcomes of instruction than upon diagnostic values of the techniques.

SUGGESTED ACTIVITIES

1. List for some special area of science instruction at either the elementary-school or high-school level what you think are some of the major outcomes of instruction that should be developed in pupils.
2. Devise from seven to ten test items for the informal measurement of scientific attitudes.

TOPICS FOR DISCUSSION

1. What are some of the major principles of science in each of the common subject areas?
2. Evaluate the idea that the principles of science can be accepted as representations of instructional objectives.
3. What are some of the measurable outcomes of science instruction?
4. By what type of test, and at what educational level, is scientific aptitude measured?
5. What are the most important measurable outcomes of instruction in elementary science?
6. What are some of the most important measurable instructional outcomes in general science and biology?
7. How do the instructional outcomes of physics and chemistry differ from those of elementary science?
8. What are the most important types of instructional outcomes in college-preparatory science courses?
9. What are the advantages of the different objective item types for use in measuring instructional outcomes in science?
10. How can performance tests be adapted to the measurement of laboratory skills in science?
11. Discuss and evaluate the informal objective test approaches to the measurement of complex and intangible instructional outcomes in science.

12. How can scientific attitudes be measured informally?
13. In what way are superstitious beliefs indicative that science education has been ineffective?

SELECTED REFERENCES

ANGELL, GEORGE W., JR. "The Philosophy of Test Construction in Science." *Science Teacher*, 23:175-78, 202-3; May 1956.

BACHELDER, MYRTLE C. "A Diagnostic Test on the Mastery of Chemical Calculations for Eleventh and Twelfth Grade Students." *Journal of Chemical Education*, 25:217-18; April 1948.

BURNETT, R. WILL. *Teaching Science in the Secondary School*. New York: Rinehart and Co., Inc., 1957. Chapter 10.

BUROS, OSCAR K., editor. *The Fifth Mental Measurements Yearbook*. Highland Park, N. J.: Gryphon Press, 1959. p. 799-831.

BUROS, OSCAR K., editor. *The Fourth Mental Measurements Yearbook*. Highland Park, N. J.: Gryphon Press, 1953. p. 621-46.

BUROS, OSCAR K., editor. *The Third Mental Measurements Yearbook*. New Brunswick, N. J.: Rutgers University Press, 1949. p. 572-604.

COLLEGE ENTRANCE EXAMINATION BOARD. *Science: A Description of the College Board Tests in Biology, Chemistry, and Physics*. Princeton, N. J.: The Board, September 1954.

EDWARDS, T. BENTLEY. "Measurement of Some Aspects of Critical Thinking." *Journal of Experimental Education*, 18:263-78; March 1950.

ENGELHART, MAX D. "Evaluation of Achievement in Chemistry." *Journal of Chemical Education*, 28:373-79; July 1951.

ENGELHART, MAX D., AND LEWIS, HUGH B. "An Attempt to Measure Scientific Thinking." *Educational and Psychological Measurement*, 1:289-94; July 1941.

FRUTCHEY, FRED P., AND TYLER, RALPH W. "Examinations in the Natural Sciences." *The Construction and Use of Achievement Examinations*. Boston: Houghton Mifflin Co., 1936. Chapter 5.

GERBERICH, J. RAYMOND. *Specimen Objective Test Items: A Guide to Achievement Test Construction*. New York: Longmans, Green and Co., 1956. p. 335-39.

GRANT, CHARLOTTE L., AND MEDER, ELSA M. "Some Evaluation Instruments for Biology Students." *Science Education*, 28:106-10; March 1944.

GREENE, HARRY A., JORGENSEN, ALBERT N., AND GERBERICH, J. RAYMOND. *Measurement and Evaluation in the Elementary School*. Second edition. New York: Longmans, Green and Co., 1953. Chapter 19.

GREENE, HARRY A., JORGENSEN, ALBERT N., AND GERBERICH, J. RAYMOND. *Measurement and Evaluation in the Secondary School*. Second edition. New York: Longmans, Green and Co., 1954. Chapter 20.

HEIL, LOUIS M., AND OTHERS. "The Measurement of Understanding in Science." *The Measurement of Understanding*. Forty-Fifth Yearbook of the National Society for the Study of Education, Part I. Chicago: University of Chicago Press, 1946. Chapter 6.

HENDRICKS, B. CLIFFORD. "Laboratory Performance Tests in Chemistry." *Journal of Chemical Education*, 27:309-11; June 1950.

HENDRICKS, B. CLIFFORD. "Paper-and-Pencil Tests for the Laboratory." *Journal of Chemical Education*, 22:543-46; November 1945.

LEVY, BEATRICE. "Testing the Outcomes of Chemical Education." *Journal of Chemical Education,* 28:43-46; January 1951.

LUCOW, WILLIAM H. "The Whole Truth and Nothing but the Truth Examinations." *Science Education,* 41:99-103; March 1957.

MALLER, J. B. "Superstition and Education." *Encyclopedia of Educational Research.* Revised edition. New York: Macmillan Co., 1950. p. 1367-71.

NELSON, CLARENCE H. *Let's Build Quality into Our Science Tests.* Washington, D. C.: National Science Teachers Association, 1958.

NEUHOF, MARK. "Integrated Interpretation of Data Tests." *Science Education,* 26:21-26; January 1942.

NOLL, VICTOR H., chairman. *Science Education in American Schools.* Forty-Sixth Yearbook of the National Society for the Study of Education, Part I. Chicago: University of Chicago Press, 1947. Chapters 8, 15.

POWERS, SAMUEL R. "Science Education." *Encyclopedia of Educational Research.* Revised edition. New York: Macmillan Co., 1950. p. 1133-45.

RALYA, LYNN L. "A Study of Some Concepts and Beliefs in Chemistry and Physics." *Journal of Chemical Education,* 18:364-67; August 1941.

READ, JOHN G. "A Non-Verbal Test of the Ability to Use the Scientific Method as a Pattern for Thinking." *Science Education,* 33:361-66; December 1949.

REINER, WILLIAM B. "Evaluating Ability to Recognize Degrees of Cause and Effect Relationships." *Science Education,* 33:329-33; 34:15-28; December 1949 and February 1950.

REINER, WILLIAM B. "Evaluation and Testing in Science Education." *Education,* 80:28-31; September 1959.

REINER, WILLIAM B. "Testing and Evaluation in the Teaching of Science." *Science Teacher,* 25:324-27; October 1958.

RICHARDSON, JOHN S. *Science Teaching in Secondary Schools.* Englewood Cliffs, N. J.: Prentice-Hall, Inc., 1957. Chapter 7.

SMITH, HERBERT A., AND ANDERSON, KENNETH E. "Science." *Encyclopedia of Educational Research.* Third edition. New York: Macmillan Co., 1960. p. 1216-32.

TELLER, JAMES B. "Some Newer Forms of the Recognition Test." *School Science and Mathematics,* 44:859-63; December 1944.

TER KEUST, ARTHUR J. "The Acceptance of Superstitious Beliefs among Secondary School Pupils." *Journal of Educational Research,* 32:673-85; May 1939.

THURBER, WALTER A., AND COLLETTE, ALFRED T. *Teaching Science in Today's Secondary Schools.* Boston: Allyn and Bacon, Inc., 1959. Chapter 11.

ULLSVIK, BJARNE R. "An Attempt to Measure Critical Judgment." *School Science and Mathematics,* 49:445-52; June 1949.

VERDUIN, JACOB. "An Open-Book Objective Examination for Science Courses." *School Science and Mathematics,* 50:213-21; March 1950.

WEBB, SAM C. "A Generalized Scale for Measuring Interest in Science Subjects." *Educational and Psychological Measurement,* 11:456-69; Autumn 1951.

WRIGHT, WILLIAM A. E. "The Modified True-False Item Applied to Testing in Chemistry." *School Science and Mathematics,* 44:637-39; October 1944.

YOTHERS, LEE R. "The Practicum for Testing Science Learning." *Science Education,* 33:124-25; March 1949.

YOUNG, DORIS. "Some Techniques for Identifying Children's Science Interests." *School Science and Mathematics,* 57:462-64; June 1957.

19

HISTORY, GEOGRAPHY, AND CIVICS

This chapter presents a summary of the following points in the improvement of measurement and evaluation in the social studies:

A. Nature and organization of the social studies.
B. Objectives and outcomes of the social studies.
C. Measurement of achievement in elementary history and geography.
D. Measurement of achievement in high-school history and civics.
E. Evaluation of social attitudes.
F. Evaluation of complex social studies outcomes.
G. Diagnosis and remediation in the social studies.

The social studies deal primarily with past and current problems of human relationships and with the interactions of human beings as they associate with one another in varied political, economic, and social activities. Such school subjects as history, geography, civics, sociology, and economics are included in this area. Carr and Wesley stated that the social sciences "are those bodies of scholarly materials which deal with human relationships," and that the social studies "are those portions of the social sciences which have been selected for instructional purposes." [1]

Two other terms in the area of the social sciences have recently come into use. Social learning is conceived by Moffatt and Howell to be broader than the social studies and to include "the social growth and development of the child as achieved through his total experiences," whereas they indicated that social education, sometimes used as a synonym for social

[1] Edwin R. Carr and Edgar B. Wesley, "Social Studies." *Encyclopedia of Educational Research,* Revised edition. Macmillan Co., New York, 1950. p. 1214.

studies, "applies to all those activities that contribute to the child's social learning." [2] The broadened concept of the social studies embodied in these statements is reflected in portions of this chapter.

1. SCOPE, AIMS, AND OUTCOMES OF SOCIAL STUDIES

Instructional objectives and outcomes constitute important backgrounds for achievement test construction, standardized or informal objective, as is pointed out in Chapters 8 and 10 and exemplified in the preceding chapters on the language arts, mathematics, and science. Test construction is also closely dependent on the organization of instruction. Consequently, the organization of social studies instruction and then its aims and expected outcomes are dealt with here as background for the later sections of this chapter.

Organization of the Social Studies

The question of whether to organize the social studies according to the traditional subject divisions, to integrate the various specific subjects into a unified course, or even to integrate the social studies and other areas of knowledge into a core curriculum has received much attention from students in this field. Unified courses are based on the theory that the best way to prepare children to meet the problems they must face in life is to disregard subject divisions and to assemble materials from all sources possible. The core curriculum goes still farther in that it completely ignores traditional subject boundaries.

Believers in the unified course ignore history, geography, and civics as separate subjects and embody material from all of them in a single course. The core curriculum embodies the concept of social education and emphasizes social learning in attaining its goal. There has been a strong tendency toward an integration of the social studies, especially in the elementary grades, and the tendency has even extended in some degree to the high-school grades. Although there is a trend toward unification of the social studies in the secondary school, and the course in problems of democracy represents a partial integration of content in this area, many schools continue to teach subject matter as traditionally organized. Since testing necessarily lags behind the development of the curriculum, there is a real need for standardized tests and other evaluative devices in the newly organized instruction in this field to keep pace with changing classroom practices.

[2] Maurice P. Moffatt and Hazel W. Howell, *Elementary Social Studies Instruction.* Longmans, Green and Co., New York, 1952. p. 12.

Objectives of the Social Studies

The formulation of definite objectives in the social studies is a major problem, for research techniques useful in the establishment of objectives in such skill areas as arithmetic, reading, language, and spelling are difficult to apply in this area. There are, in fact, probably no scientifically established objectives for the social studies, which remain, in contrast to the areas emphasizing skills, a field in which content occupies a central position. This is still true even though modern social studies instruction places much more emphasis upon social skills than do more traditional methods.

General social studies objectives. Carr and Wesley included both individual and social purposes in a list of general objectives they formulated [3] after analyzing many statements of aims and purposes, since they felt that the trend toward statements in social terms is a modern recognition that the individual must function in a social setting. Their list included these fourteen commonly accepted points:

1. To respect the rights and opinions of others
2. To be skillful in securing, sifting, evaluating, organizing, and presenting information
3. To assume social and civic responsibility
4. To act in accord with democratic principles and values
5. To become a judicious consumer
6. To understand principal economic, social, and political problems
7. To learn about vocational activities and opportunities
8. To understand the interdependence of peoples and groups
9. To become a happy member of a home
10. To make intelligent adjustment to change
11. To get along with individuals and groups
12. To use basic social studies skills
13. To exercise critical judgment
14. To understand and promote social progress

Specific social studies objectives. Such objectives as those in the list given above can well serve as general directives for planning and thinking, but more definite objectives and objectives stated rather specifically in terms of anticipated pupil behavior are necessary supplements. Consequently, the detailed list given below is reproduced in order to illustrate the types of understandings, attitudes, and skills that social studies instruction should develop in pupils.[4]

[3] Carr and Wesley, *op. cit.* p. 1219.
[4] *Scope and Sequence of the Social Studies Program.* Wisconsin Cooperative Education Planning Program, Bulletin No. 14. State Department of Public Instruction, Madison, Wis., November 1947. p. 6-7.

1. Understandings
    a. Of the democratic faith and its meaning for human welfare and happiness
    b. Of the application of democratic faith in the development of the American heritage
    c. Of the forces which have made for world interdependence and the need for world organization
    d. Of the historical and geographic reasons for the behavior of regional and national groups
    e. Of the local community and its problems, and the need for wide participation in community concerns by all citizens
    f. Of the significance in social problems of the mental health and emotional balance of individual human beings
2. Attitudes
    a. That all human beings regardless of race, national origin, color, or any matter over which they may have no control are entitled to equal rights to life, liberty, and the pursuit of happiness
    b. That we concern ourselves with achieving and improving human welfare and democratic liberties everywhere in the world
    c. That all citizens should participate actively in working toward the solution of community problems for social betterment
    d. That reflective group thinking can serve as an approach toward the solution of social problems
3. Skills and/or abilities
    a. The ability to take part in group discussion
    b. The ability to take part in group planning
    c. The ability to think reflectively on social problems
    d. The ability to search out and use valid and adequate sources of information
    e. The ability to evaluate ideas and opinions on controversial problems offered by and through radio, movies, newspapers, periodicals, books

The student should note that these objectives are listed as understandings, attitudes, skills, and abilities. The best modern thinking in the social studies results in objectives of this definite type rather than in the indefinite and vague objectives that are sometimes listed even today.

Instructional Outcomes of the Social Studies

It is important that instructional objectives be restated as outcomes in terms of the behaviors developed in pupils. The teacher is better able to measure and evaluate pupil growth in a subject area as complex as the social studies through an understanding of such outcomes than through an understanding of instructional objectives alone. Furthermore, outcomes must be made specific and recognizable to the teacher in terms of definite pupil behavior. The classification outlined below is by Anderson, Forsyth, and Morse.[5]

A. Acquiring Functional Information.
   1. Understanding special vocabulary.
   2. Understanding chronological relationships.
   3. Understanding maps.
   4. Understanding graphs and tables.
B. Analyzing Social Problems.
   1. Knowledge of important concepts, generalizations, and findings.
   2. Locating, selecting, organizing, and evaluating information.
   3. Drawing conclusions and stating them effectively.
   4. Applying social facts, generalizations, and value principles to new problems.
C. Practicing Desirable Social Relationships
   1. Understanding and developing values consistent with the democratic ways of life.
   2. Understanding the social implications of specific facts and types of behavior.
   3. Applying democratic values ... in judging the desirability of policies and courses of action.
   4. Understanding the importance of social action to further the solution of social problems, and being willing to take such action.

Although the authors of these outcomes outlined methods of measuring and evaluating such behaviors,[6] space in this volume permits only a listing of the outcomes and illustrations of tests and techniques designed to measure some characteristics of these and closely similar types.

2. MEASUREMENT OF ACHIEVEMENT IN THE SOCIAL STUDIES

Measurement of achievement in the social studies is beset by various problems. Its major techniques vary somewhat according to level and course and greatly according to type of outcome under consideration. The following discussion of these issues and the samples of test items and exercises that are given to illustrate some major testing techniques are intended to indicate the present status of social studies measurement.

[5] Howard R. Anderson, Elaine Forsyth, and Horace T. Morse, "The Measurement of Understanding in the Social Studies." *The Measurement of Understanding,* Forty-Fifth Yearbook of the National Society for the Study of Education, Part I. University of Chicago Press, Chicago, 1946. p. 72-80.
[6] *Ibid.* p. 80-101.

Problems of Measurement in the Social Studies

The difficulty of measuring the outcomes of the social studies is great. Thus far, apparently, there has been too little careful analysis of the several subjects into the desired knowledges, skills, concepts, understandings, interests, and attitudes to permit exacting curriculum and test construction. Two crucial problems relating to this deficiency are discussed briefly here.

What facts to measure. The importance of factual knowledges in the social studies is still undecided. The modern emphasis upon the development of skills involved in social living and upon the development of work-study skills by the use of which pupils can locate factual knowledges as needed has in part resolved the conflict. Modern schools tend to emphasize carefully selected, functional facts directly useful in the solution of common social problems and to stress concepts, understandings, and abilities to apply facts in problem solving rather than to teach large numbers of facts indiscriminately. The selection of the facts to teach and which ones to teach as exact and as approximate knowledges continues to be a major problem, however. Consequently, the particular facts to test and the degree of knowledge to be expected of pupils continue to be measurement problems.

The available body of facts in geography, history, and civics is large and the rapid pace of events today results in constant and great increases in the content of these fields. It is not so much the need for knowledge of the array of facts as it is the determination of those likely to last long enough in a rapidly changing world to deserve special emphasis in instruction and in testing that complicates the problem. In their efforts to meet the problem of which facts to teach and test, most workers in these fields have made their courses of study and their tests more and more comprehensive, hoping thereby to satisfy the ideas of all concerning the basic items. Too often this has led both teacher and pupils to emphasize mere memorization of extensive catalogs of facts. As a result, these facts are too frequently learned in isolation and not for the purpose of giving the pupil a better understanding of life and human relationships.

How to measure social skills. A further problem exists in the area of the skills necessary for effective social living. Many of them cannot be measured directly in the behavior of the school child because the pertinent behaviors are not often evidenced in the school. They are often revealed in the pupils' out-of-school life and are therefore not subject to direct measurement. They may even be of types for which only the adult behavior of the present school child is the true criterion. Consequently, the problem of measurement and evaluation involves the degree to which present school behavior is representative of out-of-school and even adult behavior and the degree to which results from social attitude tests accurately represent social actions. These questions have not as yet been answered satisfactorily.

Major Types of Tests in the Social Studies

Three general groups of tests in the social studies may be identified: (1) tests of facts and information, (2) tests of ability to solve social problems, and (3) tests of civic, social, and economic attitudes.

Factual tests. Tests of facts and information are by far the most numerous of the tests in the social studies. This is to be expected, for the pupil's knowledge of certain facts or items of information is quite easily discovered. Furthermore, teachers of the social studies have tended to emphasize the acquisition of facts and information much more than other desirable general outcomes of instruction. Factual tests are of limited value for analytical purposes. They fail to reveal why pupils do not know the facts if they have not been acquired. The factual tests do not aid the teacher very significantly in discovering the ability of pupils to use facts in their thinking in the social science fields.

Problem-solving tests. The development of the ability to utilize facts and basic principles in the attack on a novel social situation is one of the basic outcomes of teaching in the social studies. This type of problem solving duplicates the steps in the ordinary process of thought. As in arithmetic, problem solving in the social studies involves reading the problem to comprehend it, picking out the facts that are pertinent to the problem, choosing a method of solution, solving the problem, and testing the results for accuracy and probability.

It is well recognized that knowledge of the facts necessary for the solution of a problem is no guarantee that the problem will be solved, nor can a problem be solved unless the necessary facts are available. However, availability of facts in this day of widely available library facilities does not depend only upon a knowledge of them by their prospective user. Many of the tests for various types of problem-solving abilities present the necessary facts to the pupils in the test so that the result will depend upon their abilities so to use the facts that they are able to solve the problems.

Attitude scales. Since actions depend to such a large degree upon attitudes and emotional reactions, the measurement of attitudes resulting from instruction in the social sciences is as greatly needed as are tests of ability to solve problems. As a matter of fact, much attention is now being given in school to the development of the desirable traits of citizenship which are so much needed in later adult life. The attitude inventories available are in the main much better adapted to the secondary-school than to the elementary-school level.

Standardized Tests in Social Studies Course Areas

Most of the currently available standardized tests in history, geography, and civics and government were published some years ago. It is largely in the form of a few tests for general social studies and the social studies parts of achievement test batteries that new standardized tests have appeared for this field, although several new tests for certain high-school courses have been published recently.

History. Standardized history tests for the elementary grades and junior high school are entirely for American history, in order to conform to the course offerings below the high-school level, but tests in world history, medieval history, modern European history, and even ancient history are also available at the high-school level. The major emphasis of most tests is upon factual knowledges, although a few of the tests satisfactorily measure some of the more complex and significant results of instruction requiring various applications and interpretations of factual data.

Geography. Many tests are available in geography, but most of these are of the formal factual type. Few of the tests take into account the problem-solving aspects of social studies instruction. Many standardized tests in geography attack the subject as a study of places and their characteristics, whereas the modern approach to the study of geography has come largely to be founded upon the manner in which geographical factors influence human beings and the societies they establish.

Civics and government. Standardized tests in civics and government are limited in number. In general, measurement here is as satisfactory as can be expected under the changing conditions now existing in the social studies. However, there is need for tests that attack important citizenship problems in a more positive and realistic manner than do most of the standardized tests in civics now available.

Tests of Achievement in the Elementary Social Studies

Makers of standardized tests have recently been developing tests in the social studies for the junior high school and even at the elementary-school level to meet the needs of schools that are offering the unified type of social studies course discussed in a preceding section of this chapter. These tests include material from history, from civics and government, and from geography, but subject-matter lines are broken down. Some of them include content from related sciences as well as from the social studies.

Many of the numerous tests that appear as parts of general achievement test batteries are not dealt with here, since test batteries are the subject of Chapter 25.

EXCERPT FROM *California American Heritage Test* [7]

23. Many of the pioneers built small houses or shelters on their flat boats.   **T F** 23

24. Many of the log cabins built by the pioneers were two-story houses with stairways leading to the second floor.   **T F** 24

25. The pioneers of the Great Plains had little difficulty with the Indians.   **T F** 25

26. Cattle used to be driven hundreds of miles to be shipped on the first cross-country railroad.   **T F** 26

EXCERPT FROM *California Geography Test* [8]

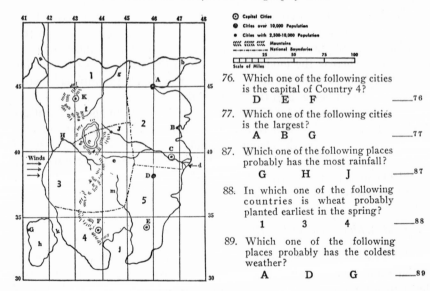

76. Which one of the following cities is the capital of Country 4?
D   E   F   ____76

77. Which one of the following cities is the largest?
A   B   G   ____77

87. Which one of the following places probably has the most rainfall?
G   H   J   ____87

88. In which one of the following countries is wheat probably planted earliest in the spring?
1   3   4   ____88

89. Which one of the following places probably has the coldest weather?
A   D   G   ____89

[7] Georgia S. Adams and John A. Sexson, *California Tests in Social and Related Sciences: Test 1, The American Heritage,* Elementary. Form AA. California Test Bureau, Monterey, Calif., 1953.
[8] *Ibid. Test 3, Geography.*

Tests that measure broadly over the social studies must almost of necessity avoid some of the weaknesses of tests in particular subjects because of their lack of concern for divisions within the field. Furthermore, the few tests of this type are relatively new, and consequently have the advantage of being constructed with regard for recent thinking and experimentation with tests. Factual knowledges are less stressed and greater emphasis is placed upon relationships, applications, interpretations, and other reasoned uses of facts than is true on the average of standardized tests for particular courses.

EXCERPT FROM *Cooperative Social Studies Test* [9]

70. What was the principal work done on a medieval manor?
   70-1 Defending the castle against attack.
   70-2 Buying from and selling to caravans.
   70-3 Manufacturing shoes and cloth.
   70-4 Farming.
   70-5 Copying ancient manuscripts. ....70(　)

71. The Greek city-states never united, largely because of
   71-1 geographic barriers.
   71-2 different languages spoken in different cities.
   71-3 religious differences.
   71-4 conflicting forms of government.
   71-5 opposition from Persia. ....71(　)

Four test excerpts only are reproduced here to illustrate item varieties useful in social studies testing in the elementary grades, but most of the illustrations for high-school subjects in the next section of this chapter can be adapted to the elementary-school level very easily. Two illustrations are taken from the *California Tests in Social and Related Sciences*—a true-false item variety in American history and, in geography, multiple-choice item varieties based on a map of a fictitious country. The first two multiple-choice items measure simple map-reading skills, whereas the other three measure applications of fundamental knowledges and understandings to hypothetical situations. A third excerpt, also of a standard variety of multiple-choice item, is from the *Cooperative Social Studies Test for Grades 7, 8, and 9.* The last of the four excerpts, from the *Metropolitan History and Civics Test,* shows a classification variety of matching exer-

[9] Harry D. Berg and Elaine Forsyth, *Cooperative Social Studies Test for Grades 7, 8, and 9.* Form X. Educational Testing Service, Princeton, N. J., 1947.

cise that ranks second only to the multiple-choice form for usefulness in social studies testing.

The typical emphasis in the elementary school on general tests rather than tests in specific subjects is represented by these excerpts. The first two are from a three-booklet test battery in the social and closely related sciences, the third is from a general social studies test, and the last is from one of the social studies parts of a general achievement test.

EXCERPT FROM *Metropolitan History and Civics Test* [10]

DIRECTIONS. After each event in the list below put the number —

1 if it happened before the *Settling of Jamestown* in 1607.
2 if it happened between the *Settling of Jamestown* and the *Adoption of the Constitution* in 1787.
3 if it happened between the *Adoption of the Constitution* and the *Civil War* in 1861–65.
4 if it happened between the *Civil War* and the *Spanish-American War* in 1898.
5 if it happened since the *Spanish-American War*.

For example, you should write the number *1* after "Columbus discovered America," because it happened before the *Settling of Jamestown*.

SAMPLE. Columbus discovered America . . . .(   )

42. The Stamp Act. . . . .(   ) 42
43. The South Pole was discovered . . . .(   ) 43
44. Eli Whitney's cotton gin was perfected . . . .(   ) 44
45. The first trip around the world was completed . . . .(   ) 45
46. Daniel Boone guided settlers across the Appalachians . . . .(   ) 46

Tests of Achievement in High-School Social Studies

Tests at this level, except for those that appear as parts of general achievement test batteries, occur almost entirely in subject areas. In addition to the three areas represented by accompanying excerpts below, standardized tests are available for American government, ancient history, modern European history, and even a few other less common course areas.

A nearby illustration from the *Cummings World History Test* shows a variety of short matching exercise of the interrelation sort to supplement the classification variety of matching exercise shown in the preceding section of this chapter. The sample from the *Crary American History Test* also involves matching, although the items, dependent on the map, are in multiple-choice format. Finally, an unusual alternate-response variety

[10] Richard D. Allen and others, *Metropolitan Achievement Tests: Test 7, Social Studies —History and Civics,* Advanced. Copyright 1946 by Harcourt, Brace and World, Inc., New York. All rights reserved. Quoted by special permission.

is illustrated by a group of items from the *Dimond-Pflieger Problems of Democracy Test.*

EXCERPT FROM *Cummings World History Test* [11]

19. He established the practice of using chemicals to destroy bacterial infections.   a. Koch
                                                                                        b. Lister
20. He directed the study which discovered the cause of yellow fever.   c. Pasteur
                                                                                        d. Pavlov
21. He discovered and developed a treatment for rabies.   e. Reed

31. An illegal seizure of power in a country.   a. Coup d'état
                                                                                        b. Entente Cordiale
32. An alliance between France, Great Britain, and Russia.   c. Plebiscite
                                                                                        d. Propaganda
33. A vote in a country or region to decide who is to govern in the region or country.   e. Sabotage

EXCERPT FROM *Crary American History Test* [12]

DIRECTIONS: *Questions 51 through 58 are based on the map above. For each question there are five possible answers. You are to decide which answer is correct; then mark the corresponding space on your answer sheet.*

51. The western terminal of the Erie Canal is represented on the map by—
   a. 1   b. 2   c. 6
   d. 12   e. none of the above

52. America's leading seaport is represented on the map by—
   a. 2   b. 3   c. 7
   d. 12   e. none of the above

[11] Howard H. Cummings, *Cummings World History Test.* Copyright 1950 by Harcourt, Brace and World, Inc., New York. All rights reserved. Quoted by special permission.
[12] Ryland W. Crary, *Crary American History Test.* Form AM. Copyright 1950 by Harcourt, Brace and World, Inc., New York. All rights reserved. Quoted by special permission.

EXCERPT FROM *Dimond-Pflieger Problems of Democracy Test* [13]

Questions 76 through 80 are descriptive of some governments. On your answer sheet, mark the number of your answer according to the KEY below.

KEY {
1. If it describes a *democratic* form of government.
2. If it describes a *totalitarian* form of government.
}

76. State is supreme
77. Freedom of speech
78. Censorship of press
79. One political party
80. Respect for rights of minorities

Two other illustrations of item varieties for use in social studies testing appear in Chapter 10. One of them, on page 234, measures knowledge of the chronological order in which certain events occurred, and the other, on page 232, tests knowledge concerning which ones of five factors contributed to a specified historical outcome. An unusual variation of a multiple-choice item is illustrated in each of these excerpts.

One other major aid to high-school teachers of American history, world history, American government, and economics should be mentioned. For each of these four subjects, a monograph, published by the National Council for the Social Studies, consists of a brief introductory section and then of several hundred classified test items and exercises for use in measuring various specified aspects of the respective subjects.[14] The test items can be taken bodily from the monographs or adapted as desired by teachers for use in their own classroom tests.

3. EVALUATION OF SOCIAL ATTITUDES

A wide variety of social attitudes can be evaluated. Among them are attitudes toward individuals and toward racial, religious, and other groups, toward such practices as birth control and capital punishment, toward such productions as plays, movies, and books, and toward such institutions of society as the Church, the public school, and the family. Attitudes toward vocations, school subjects, and a wide variety of activities and actions are

[13] Stanley E. Dimond and Elmer F. Pflieger, *Dimond-Pflieger Problems of Democracy Test.* Form AM. Copyright 1952 by Harcourt, Brace and World, Inc., New York. All rights reserved. Quoted by special permission.

[14] Howard R. Anderson, E. F. Lindquist, and others; (1) *Selected Test Items in American History,* Bulletin No. 6, Fourth edition, 1957; (2) *Selected Test Items in World History,* Bulletin No. 9, Revised, 1947; (3) *Selected Test Items in American Government,* Bulletin No. 13, Revised edition, 1950; and (4) *Selected Test Items in Economics,* Bulletin No. 11, 1939. National Council for the Social Studies, National Education Association, Washington, D. C.

other possibilities. A common factor in such attitudes is their concern with human beings in their interrelationships and in the results of their labors. Social attitudes cannot ordinarily be distinguished as right and wrong; differences in attitudes are properly to be considered as of degree rather than of kind.

Measurement of Specific Attitudes

Social attitudes result not only as indirect outcomes of instruction in some, although probably not all, social studies courses but also as by-products or secondary outcomes of instruction in many other subject areas and as indirect results of the many and varied out-of-school influences to which the pupil is exposed. Although social attitudes are typically not subject centered, the accompanying excerpt from the *Peltier-Durost Civics and Citizenship Test* shows items on which the instructional influence of a typical civics course even in a democratic society would doubtless be in an easily recognized direction. The "right" answers used in scoring responses to these and the other attitude items of this test agree with recommendations of a special Committee on Citizenship of the National Council for the Social Studies. Even so, the last statement in the direction to the pupils, as shown in the excerpt, and the presentation of separate norms for the attitude section of the test represent the intangibility of attitudes and the indirect rather than specific influence of instruction in their formation.

EXCERPT FROM *Peltier-Durost Civics and Citizenship Test* [15]

DIRECTIONS. *The following statements express attitudes toward important social and civic issues, many of which you have been studying. Read each statement carefully. If you agree with the statement, mark the answer space under "A" for "agree"; if you disagree with the statement, mark the answer space under "D."*

If under some circumstances you would agree, while under others you would disagree, mark the answer space under the "?". If you don't know enough about the situation to have an honest opinion, mark the answer space under "DK." If you just don't understand the statement, mark the answer space under "DU."

Be sure you answer just as you really feel. This section is not like the rest of the test, where there are definitely right or wrong answers. These statements are matters of opinion on which people may have different ideas.

1. A good citizen tries to obey the law at all times, even when no one is watching him.
2. Every man is, and should be, equal in the eyes of the law. No man should expect special favors because he has influence or "pull."

[15] Charles L. Peltier and Walter N. Durost, *Peltier-Durost Civics and Citizenship Test.* Form AM. Copyright 1958 by Harcourt, Brace and World, Inc., New York. All rights reserved. Quoted by special permission.

Thurstone was the editor and a major author of some thirty-five social attitude scales [16] designed for measuring attitudes toward a wide variety of practices, productions, organizations, institutions, and racial groups. A few illustrations, to give a general idea of the areas covered, are scales for measuring attitudes toward capital punishment, toward war, toward communism, toward evolution, toward public ownership, toward birth control, toward the Church, and toward the Chinese.

Generalized Measurement of Attitudes

Another series of scales for the measurement of attitudes [17] consists of about a dozen generalized scales that are designed for broader uses than are the individual Thurstone scales. The Remmers scales that have the greatest significance for the social studies, for example, are generalized to the extent of measuring attitudes toward any institution of society, any practice of society, any proposed social action, and any racial or national group.

One specific instrument that provides measures in several related areas of social significance is illustrated by an excerpt on page 134 of Chapter 7. This *Survey of Attitudes and Beliefs* provides separate scores on attitudes toward society, toward education and work, and toward sex, marriage, and the family.

4. EVALUATION OF COMPLEX SOCIAL STUDIES OUTCOMES

The situation for the testing of complex outcomes in the social studies is similar to that discussed for the sciences in the preceding chapter. Standard varieties of objective test items are used in both subject areas, sometimes in unusual adaptations and other times in basic item forms, for the measurement of some of the complex outcomes that differ in degree if not in kind from the most tangible knowledge and skill outcomes of instruction.

The types of tests discussed and illustrated in Chapter 12 as interpretive in nature are more widely available for the senior high school than for the elementary grades and junior high school. They are not dealt with extensively in this and other chapters on measurement and evaluation in subject

[16] L. L. Thurstone, editor, *Scales for the Measurement of Social Attitudes*. University of Chicago Press, Chicago, 1929 to 1934.

[17] H. H. Remmers, editor: (1) *Studies in Attitudes*. Studies in Higher Education, No. 26. Purdue University, Lafayette, Ind., 1934; (2) *Further Studies in Attitudes, Series II*. Studies in Higher Education, No. 31. Purdue University, Lafayette, Ind., 1936; and (3) *Further Studies in Attitudes, Series III*. Studies in Higher Education, No. 34. Purdue University, Lafayette, Ind., 1938.

areas because the authors classify them among the evaluation instruments, tools, and techniques to which Chapter 12 is devoted. Such tests typically cut across the lines of demarcation between subject areas, so that a teacher interested in the measurement of direct outcomes from a course in American history or from a unified course in the social studies would not find them valid for his purposes. However, they measure broad functional outcomes of a type often sought by teachers of social studies and therefore warrant the careful attention of teachers of this subject field.

An evaluation instrument that purports to measure several aspects of social adaptation by means of reports by pupils concerning what they would do in certain social situations is the *Test of Social Insight.* Two illustrations from the test appear in this volume—one in an accompanying excerpt and one on page 287 of Chapter 12. The fact that the results are differentially scored to give ratings on five social traits—withdrawal, passivity, cooperativeness, competitiveness, and aggressiveness—as well as a total score indicates that responses to items such as those shown in the excerpts are not, and as a general rule doubtless should not be, scored arbitrarily as either right or wrong.

EXCERPT FROM *Test of Social Insight* [18]

27. A friend tells you about a surprise party that is being planned for you by a second friend. What do you do?

   a. Tell off your informing friend, and show you are very angry with him.

   b. Indicate that you knew about the party before he told you.

   c. Walk away, and avoid the informing person in the future.

   d. Do nothing, and act natural.

   e. Tell him it is not fair of him to tell about surprise parties; they are fun.

As is pointed out in Chapter 9, the essay test can be used satisfactorily for certain classroom testing purposes even though it is not likely to be highly reliable. Osborn outlined procedures for improving the reliability of the essay examination [19] as a tool for testing thinking, however. He illustrated his proposals by giving eleven sample questions from elementary

[18] Russell N. Cassel, *Test of Social Insight,* Youth edition. Martin M. Bruce, New Rochelle, N. Y., 1959.

[19] Worth J. Osborn, "Testing Thinking." *Journal of Educational Research,* 27:401-11; February 1934.

history of the United States, by outlining scoring procedures, and by giving a detailed scoring key.

5. DIAGNOSIS AND REMEDIATION IN THE SOCIAL STUDIES

Diagnosis in the social studies is difficult because (1) the knowledges, skills, and understandings pupils should acquire are not clearly identified and (2) it would be impossible, even if they were well identified, to determine whether or not the pupil responded in his social relationships in a desirable manner because of his possession of the informational elements tested. Diagnosis and remedy are often needed in those skills that are basic to successful work in the social studies. Instruction in these subjects requires much reading of the work-study type. Therefore, pupils, in order to achieve at acceptable levels, must possess many of the following work-study reading skills:

1. Knowledge of technical vocabularies employed in the social studies.
2. Reading comprehension adequate for interpretation of social science content.
3. Ability to locate material readily—use of the index, library files, table of contents, maps, charts.
4. Ability to outline.
5. Ability to summarize.

These skills are discussed in sufficient detail in Chapter 15, along with other ways and means for corrective work in these important acquisitive skills.

SUGGESTED ACTIVITIES

1. Select some reasonably short segment of a social studies course at either the elementary-school or high-school level and set up a two-way chart of the type discussed in Chapter 10 to show your idea of a proper balance between course content and instructional outcomes.
2. Construct from seven to ten objective test items on some aspect or aspects of the course covered by the two-way chart of the preceding suggestion.

TOPICS FOR DISCUSSION

1. Describe the field of the social studies in such a way as to clarify the meaning of the term.
2. Discuss the pros and cons of a unified social studies curriculum as contrasted with the traditional organization of content by subjects.
3. State several of the major general objectives of instruction in the social studies.

4. What are some of the types of specific social studies objectives?
5. In what behavioral terms are instructional outcomes of the social studies best expressed?
6. What are some of the sources of difficulty in constructing tests of problem solving?
7. What are some of the weaknesses of attitude scales as measures of functional behavior?
8. Discuss the use of various objective item forms in social studies tests.
9. Comment on some of the types of evaluative tests used in measuring complex instructional outcomes of the social studies.

SELECTED REFERENCES

ANDERSON, HOWARD R. "Examinations in the Social Studies." *The Construction and Use of Achievement Examinations.* Boston: Houghton Mifflin Co., 1936. Chapter 4.

ANDERSON, HOWARD R.; FORSYTH, ELAINE; AND MORSE, HORACE T. "The Measurement of Understanding in the Social Studies." *The Measurement of Understanding.* Forty-Fifth Yearbook of the National Society for the Study of Education, Part I. Chicago: University of Chicago Press, 1946. Chapter 5.

ANDERSON, HOWARD R., AND LINDQUIST, E. F. *Selected Test Items in Economics.* National Council for the Social Studies, Bulletin No. 11. Washington, D. C.: National Education Association, 1939.

ANDERSON, HOWARD R., LINDQUIST, E. F., AND BERG, HARRY D. *Selected Test Items in American Government.* National Council for the Social Studies, Bulletin No. 13. Revised edition. Washington D. C.: National Education Association, April 1950.

ANDERSON, HOWARD R., LINDQUIST, E. F., AND STULL, HARRIET. *Selected Test Items in American History.* National Council for the Social Studies, Bulletin No. 6. Fourth edition. Washington, D. C.: National Education Association, October 1957.

ANDERSON, HOWARD R., LINDQUIST, E. F., AND STUTZ, FREDERICK H. *Selected Test Items in World History.* National Council for the Social Studies, Bulletin No. 9. Revised. Washington, D. C.: National Education Association, 1947.

ARNOLD, DWIGHT L. "Social Studies Evaluation in the Intermediate Grades." *Social Education,* 7:117-20; March 1943.

BINING, ARTHUR C., AND BINING, DAVID H. *Teaching the Social Studies in Secondary Schools.* Third edition. New York: McGraw-Hill Book Co., Inc., 1952. Chapter 17.

BOODISH, H. M. "Short Answer Tests in American History." *Social Studies,* 41:260, 269-73, 297-301, 350-57; October to December 1950.

BRANOM, MENDEL E. "Objective Diagnostic Testing Illustrations from the St. Louis Area." *Journal of Geography,* 44:239-45; September 1945.

BROCKMYER, IRENE. "Testing with Pictures." *Journal of Geography,* 50:54-57; February 1951.

BUROS, OSCAR K., editor. *The Fifth Mental Measurements Yearbook.* Highland Park, N. J.: Gryphon Press, 1959. p. 841-70.

BUROS, OSCAR K., editor. *The Fourth Mental Measurements Yearbook.* Highland Park, N. J.: Gryphon Press, 1953. p. 657-73.

BUROS, OSCAR K., editor. *The Third Mental Measurements Yearbook.* New Brunswick, N. J.: Rutgers University Press, 1949. p. 604-26.

CAMPBELL, DONALD T. "The Indirect Assessment of Social Attitudes." *Psychological Bulletin,* 47:15-38; January 1950.

CARR, EDWIN R., AND WESLEY, EDGAR B. "Social Studies." *Encyclopedia of Educational Research.* Revised edition. New York: Macmillan Co., 1950. p. 1213-38.

COLLEGE ENTRANCE EXAMINATION BOARD. *Social Studies: A Description of the Social Studies Tests of the College Entrance Examination Board.* Princeton, N. J.: The Board, 1953.

EBEL, ROBERT L. "The Problem of Evaluation in the Social Studies." *Social Education,* 24:6-10; January 1960.

GERBERICH, J. RAYMOND. *Specimen Objective Test Items: A Guide to Achievement Test Construction.* New York: Longmans, Green and Co., 1956. p. 340-47.

GREENE, HARRY A., JORGENSEN, ALBERT N., AND GERBERICH, J. RAYMOND. *Measurement and Evaluation in the Elementary School.* Second edition. New York: Longmans, Green and Co., 1953. Chapter 17.

GREENE, HARRY A., JORGENSEN, ALBERT N., AND GERBERICH, J. RAYMOND. *Measurement and Evaluation in the Secondary School.* Second edition. New York: Longmans, Green and Co., 1954. Chapter 18.

GROSS, RICHARD E., AND BADGER, WILLIAM V. "Social Studies." *Encyclopedia of Educational Research.* Third edition. New York: Macmillan Co., 1960. p. 1296-1319.

HANNA, LAVONE. "An Evaluation Program for American History." *California Journal of Secondary Education,* 20:209-16; April 1945.

HARRIS, DALE B. "A Scale for Measuring Attitudes of Social Responsibility in Children." *Journal of Abnormal and Social Psychology,* 55:322-26; November 1957.

JAROLIMEK, JOHN. *Social Studies in Elementary Education.* New York: Macmillan Co., 1959. Chapter 16.

KOHN, CLYDE F. "Geography." *Encyclopedia of Educational Research.* Revised edition. New York: Macmillan Co., 1950. p. 501-3.

MOFFATT, MAURICE P. *Social Studies Instruction.* Second edition. New York: Prentice-Hall, Inc., 1954. Chapter 18.

MORSE, HORACE T., editor. "Evaluation and Tests in American History." *The Study and Teaching of American History.* Seventeenth Yearbook of the National Council for the Social Studies. Washington, D. C.: The Council, 1947. Section 6.

PACE, ETHEL. "Some Tests for First Grade Geography." *Journal of Geography,* 53:11-14; January 1954.

SAMFORD, CLARENCE D., AND COTTLE, EUGENE. *Social Studies in the Secondary School.* New York: McGraw-Hill Book Co., Inc., 1952. Chapter 14.

"Selected Test Items in American Government." *Journal of the National Education Association,* 39:445-46; September 1950.

STUTZ, FREDERICK H. "United Nations Test for Junior Highschools." *Journal of the National Education Association,* 39:192-93; March 1950.

TABA, HILDA, AND MCGUIRE, CHRISTINE. "Evaluation of Social Sensitivity." *Appraising and Recording Student Progress.* New York: Harper and Brothers, 1942. Chapter 3.

THAYER, V. T., chairman. *The Social Studies in General Education.* Report of Committee on the Function of Social Studies in General Education, Commission on Secondary School Curriculum, Progressive Education Association. New York: D. Appleton-Century Co., Inc., 1940. Chapter 9.

WAGNER, LOUISE D. "Measuring the Map-Reading Ability of Sixth-Grade Children." *Elementary School Journal*, 53:338-44; February 1953.

WESLEY, EDGAR B. *Teaching Social Studies in High Schools*. Third edition. Boston: D. C. Heath and Co., 1950. Chapters 30-31.

WESLEY, EDGAR B., AND ADAMS, MARY A. *Teaching Social Studies in the Elementary School*. Boston: D. C. Heath and Co., 1946. Part VII.

WOOD, HUGH B. "The Measurement of Social Values." *Social Education*, 17:76-77; February 1953.

20

FOREIGN LANGUAGES

The purpose of this chapter is to present a summary of the following points involved in measurement and evaluation in the foreign languages:

A. Needs and trends in the modern foreign languages.
B. Objectives and outcomes of foreign language instruction.
C. Aptitude and prognostic tests in the foreign languages.
D. Measuring achievement in the modern foreign languages.
E. Measuring achievement in Latin.
F. Diagnosis and remediation in the foreign languages.

The third language arts area at the high-school level is the foreign languages. Both the modern and the classical foreign languages involve receptive as well as expressive language arts. They also naturally involve a second language for the pupil. Hence, the measurement problems pointed out in Chapters 15 and 16 for the English language carry over to the foreign languages and are further complicated by the fact that the beginner is acquiring certain aspects of a second language in terms of his native tongue. This holds true despite the fact that the aims and objectives of foreign language study do not necessarily parallel those appropriate for the pupil's native language. About one in five high-school pupils was studying a foreign language in 1955—two-thirds of them were taking a modern language and one-third were in Latin courses.[1]

---

[1] Emma M. Birkmaier, "Modern Languages." *Encyclopedia of Educational Research,* Third edition. Macmillan Co., New York, 1960. p. 863.

1. SOCIAL SIGNIFICANCE AND TRENDS
IN MODERN FOREIGN LANGUAGES

The complexity of the problem of communication is made apparent when it is recognized that there are some 2800 different languages spoken in the modern world, although probably under one hundred of these are of major importance culturally and economically and only about twenty are so widely used that their importance is paramount.[2] Only three— French, German, and Spanish—have been studied by significant percentages of pupils in American schools. Of these three, German was by far the most popular in 1915, French was studied most widely in 1934, and Spanish was the leader in 1949 and 1955.[3] The influences of World Wars I and II are doubtless reflected in these changes.

Need for Proficiency in the Modern Foreign Languages

The need for more foreign language instruction, both in quantity and in variety, and for new instructional emphases in the foreign languages has become increasingly clear during the last twenty years. This need appears to be an outgrowth of three developments: (1) the demand during World War II for military and civilian personnel qualified to handle a large number of foreign languages, (2) the demand for more widespread foreign language proficiency as increasingly rapid facilities of transportation and communication brought the people of the world closer together, and (3) the demand for effective communication by means of foreign language skills in furtherance of the Good Neighbor Policy and emphasis by the United Nations on improved understanding among the peoples of the world.

Present Trends in the Modern Foreign Languages

The influences commented upon above have led to numerous changes in modern foreign language teaching and to demands for new tests and new techniques of measurement and evaluation. A few of the most significant trends that have recently brought such demands or seem likely to do so in the near future are presented here as background for the subsequent direct treatment of measurement and evaluation of instructional outcomes of the foreign languages.

[2] Jack Cohn, "The Implications of the Current World Situation for Foreign Language Instruction." *Modern Language Journal,* 36:402-4; December 1952.
[3] Birkmaier, *op. cit.* p. 863.

English as a foreign language. The concept of English as a foreign language has only recently received much attention in America. The Good Neighbor Policy, entailing the teaching of English widely in the Western Hemisphere, and the increasing number of displaced persons coming to America from various European countries with facility only in their native tongues have given rise to the concept in this country. Non-English speaking children in New York and the Southwest constitute the largest group of regular school pupils needing this type of program. Lado [4] constructed what possibly still is the only published test of English as a foreign language.

The *Cooperative Inter-American Tests* [5] deserve mention here, although they are not designed for use in foreign language courses and are not, in fact, used solely in the measurement of achievement. The series of tests printed in parallel English and Spanish editions was prepared under the auspices of the Committee on Modern Languages of the American Council on Education. Parallelism of forms in the two languages makes possible the use of these tests in bilingual situations and for the classification of pupils of foreign parentage or backgrounds. They are also useful in a single language when comparisons across linguistic borders are not desired. Two broad tests, for general ability and reading, and specialized tests in language, natural sciences, and social studies are variously available at three levels covering Grades 1 to 13.

Foreign language in the elementary school. The teaching of a second language in the elementary school, a common practice in many foreign countries, has been introduced in a number of American communities during the last few years. This is particularly true of certain southern states where there are many school children of Mexican parentage, but the movement is by no means restricted to such communities. Birkmaier reported an increase in enrollments in elementary-school foreign language classes from less than 5000 pupils before 1950 to 271,617 pupils enrolled in FLES (Foreign Languages in the Elementary School) and an additional 156,000 pupils in Catholic elementary schools in the fall of 1955. [6] She also reported that these pupils were attending nearly 2500 different schools in more than 350 cities located in at least 44 states and that Spanish, French, and German ranked first, second, and third in enrollments.

Pupils typically start foreign language study in FLES in Grade 3 or

[4] Robert Lado, *English Language Test for Foreign Students.* George Wahr Publishing Co., Ann Arbor, Mich., 1951.

[5] Herschel T. Manuel, editor, *Cooperative Inter-American Tests of:* (1) *General Ability;* (2) *Reading;* (3) *Language Usage;* (4) *Natural Sciences;* and (5) *Social Studies;* English and Spanish editions. Educational Testing Service, Princeton, N. J., 1950.

[6] Birkmaier, *op. cit.* p. 870.

Grade 4. The emphasis at first is entirely on hearing and speaking the language, but reading and writing are sometimes introduced in the intermediate grades. Although no tests specifically designed for use in this program have apparently been published up to this time, the need for evaluation instruments and techniques to measure the hearing and speaking outcomes in the elementary grades is great.

Aural-oral objectives. Agard and Dunkel,[7] with whose point of view many writers in the area of modern foreign languages have expressed agreement, supported the belief that the speaking and understanding, or oral-aural, objectives are of primary significance today and that they are superseding the reading objective in that position. This applies not only to the FLES program discussed immediately above but also to instruction at the high-school and college levels. Among the important accompaniments of this trend are the increasing use of tape recordings and other audio-visual aids in special language laboratories and the emergence, in limited degree so far, of listening tests in the foreign languages. These tests are similar to some of the aural-oral tests in French and German published about thirty years ago, although they make use of modern equipment and testing techniques. They also employ some techniques similar to those represented in Chapter 15 for listening tests in English.

2. APTITUDE AND PROGNOSTIC TESTS IN THE FOREIGN LANGUAGES

The distinction between the closely similar aptitude and prognostic tests was pointed out in Chapter 2. Aptitude tests are essentially tests of specific intelligence, or of intellectual abilities influenced only slightly by training, which apply to the particular subject or performance for which aptitude is being measured. Prognostic tests are achievement measures that draw largely upon the abilities essential for success in a particular subject and that admittedly deal with abilities the pupil may have learned specifically or acquired incidentally. As the two types of tests may be employed in the determination of a pupil's readiness for the study of a particular subject, they are both considered in this section of the chapter.

It is probable that a large proportion of high-school failures in foreign languages could be avoided if an adequate system of guidance were employed to direct pupils out of the field when the essential aptitudes are missing. A few tests capable of yielding the necessary type of prognostic information for giving accurate guidance in the study of the foreign languages are now available. In common with most other prognostic tests,

[7] Frederick B. Agard and Harold B. Dunkel, *An Investigation of Second-Language Teaching.* Ginn and Co., Boston, 1948. p. 17-38.

they are most successful in pointing out those who should not study the subject. The negative aspect of prognostic measurement is one of its most discouraging features.

Aptitude Tests

The newest and most broadly conceived instrument of this type is the *Modern Language Aptitude Test*.[8] It consists of five parts: I, Number Learning, designed to measure a memory component and perhaps an auditory alertness factor; II, Phonetic Script, intended to measure ability to associate speech sounds and orthographic symbols and also perhaps memory for speech sounds; III, Spelling Clues, measuring sound-symbol association ability, with some dependence on knowledge of English vocabulary; IV, Words in Sentences, intended to measure sensitivity to grammatical structure; and V, Paired Associates, measuring rote memory. The test can be given either in a short form that can be administered in about thirty minutes or as a complete test requiring from sixty to seventy minutes of time. It can also be given either with or without a tape recorder.

Instead of being designed for use primarily at one educational level and for one language or several related languages, the *Modern Language Aptitude Test* can be used in the high school or the college and it has been validated[9] in terms of how well it predicts high-school and college course marks and final examination marks in Latin, as well as in French, Spanish, German, Russian, and even, with groups taking intensive courses, such unusual languages as Mandarin Chinese and two groups of Indo-European languages. Part scores on the test also have some diagnostic value subsequently in accounting for particular types of difficulties in the actual study of a language.

The *Foreign Language Aptitude Examination* of the *Iowa Placement Examinations*,[10] primarily for predicting success at the college level, undertakes to furnish a prognostic measure by sampling into four types of skills found to be highly related to success in the study of the foreign languages. A unique feature of this test is the use of Esperanto as the unfamiliar situation in which to test the student's ability to acquire new language skills.

[8] John B. Carroll and Stanley M. Sapon, *Modern Language Aptitude Test*. Psychological Corporation, New York, 1958.

[9] John B. Carroll and Stanley M. Sapon, *Modern Language Aptitude Test: Manual,* 1959 Edition. Psychological Corporation, New York, 1959. p. 12-17.

[10] George D. Stoddard, *Iowa Placement Examinations: Foreign Language Aptitude,* New Series FA-2, Revised. Bureau of Educational Research and Service, State University of Iowa, Iowa City, 1941.

Prognostic Tests

The *Luria-Orleans Modern Language Prognosis Test* [11] is designed to measure the ability of pupils to learn French, Spanish, or Italian. It is intended to be used before study of the language is begun. The results are useful as a basis for advising pupils whether to begin a foreign language, as a guide in classifying students, and as an aid in determining the effectiveness of instruction. The test contains a number of simple lessons with a test on each, covering certain fundamental principles and skills involved in learning a romance language. The *Orleans-Solomon Latin Prognosis Test* [12] is similarly used for predicting success in Latin.

3. MEASUREMENT OF PROFICIENCY IN MODERN FOREIGN LANGUAGES

The modern foreign languages are ordinarily considered to consist primarily of Spanish, French, and German. Birkmaier reported that, in 1955, high-school enrollments in Spanish were about a third larger than those in French and that only about one in sixteen pupils in these three languages was enrolled in German.[13]

Outcomes of Instruction in the Modern Foreign Languages

Some problems encountered in defining aims and objectives for the English language arts and the foreign languages are similar, but there is no tendency to uphold the same objectives or the same levels of skill and proficiency for the pupil in a foreign language as may be widely accepted for his native tongue. The two sets of objectives are, on the contrary, distinctly different. The modern and the classical foreign languages also differ so widely in their present-day values and uses that separate sets of general objectives again are necessary.

Although the literature on the modern foreign languages is replete with articles treating instructional objectives and outcomes, most of the articles deal only with aspects of the broad issue or treat objectives and outcomes for single languages rather than for the modern languages in general. The authors believe that the following list summarizing the discussion of instructional outcomes by Kaulfers [14] is representative:

[11] Max A. Luria and Jacob S. Orleans, *Luria-Orleans Modern Language Prognosis Test.* World Book Co., Yonkers, N. Y., 1930.

[12] Jacob S. Orleans and Michael Solomon, *Orleans-Solomon Latin Prognosis Test.* World Book Co., Yonkers, N. Y., 1926.

[13] Birkmaier, *op. cit.* p. 863.

[14] Walter V. Kaulfers, *Modern Languages for Modern Schools.* McGraw-Hill Book Co., Inc., New York, 1942. p. 349-56. By permission.

1. Direct outcomes
   a. Reading
   b. Writing
   c. Speaking
   d. Translating
2. Concomitant outcomes, such as
   a. Mental discipline
   b. Habits of neatness in written work
   c. Habits of attention to . . . language mechanics . . .
   d. Critical attitude toward correct usage in language . . .
   e. Insights into the mechanical structure of language
   f. Habits of consulting the dictionary
   g. Better speech habits, pronunciation, and diction
3. Associate outcomes, contributive to
   a. Worthy use of leisure
   b. Ability to understand, adjust to, and cooperatively improve the social environment
   c. Ability to understand, appreciate, adjust to, and improve the physical environment
   d. Building of desirable physical and mental health
   e. Increased vocational and prevocational efficiency

Kaulfers distinguished the direct outcomes as subject to control by the teacher in his selection of methods, classroom activities, and course content. He classed under concomitant outcomes those values resulting from experiences of the pupil in the process of acquiring the direct outcomes and under associate outcomes the values accruing primarily from the content used in the attainment of the direct outcomes.

Agard and Dunkel [15] classified objectives as basic skills and as those resulting from the acquisition of basic skills:

1. Basic linguistic skills objectives
   a. Reading
   b. Writing
   c. Speaking
   d. Aural comprehension
2. Objectives for which the language skills serve as means, such as
   a. Disciplinary training in neatness, accuracy, and logical thought
   b. Increased understanding of . . . language as a means of communication and as a tool of thought
   c. Better command of one's native language
   d. Knowledge of the foreign people's history, culture, and civilization . . .
   e. Increased international understanding and good will
   f. Development of historical and cultural perspective

[15] Agard and Dunkel, *op. cit.* p. 15-16.

Tests of Achievement in the Modern Foreign Languages

The four immediate objectives of instruction in the foreign languages—the development of the ability to speak, to understand, to read, and to write the language—are of significance to the test maker in this field. They primarily determine the character of the tests to be used in the classroom. If these general abilities are to be measured effectively, the tests must be broken into several parts, each capable of measuring specific elements.

Measurement of achievement in the modern foreign languages typically employs techniques quite similar to those used in many tests of English language. The emphasis in French, Spanish, and German is definitely upon testing the pupil's familiarity with vocabulary, his comprehension of various types of written material, his skill in functional grammar, occasionally his knowledge of customs and culture, and in a few instances his listening comprehension. There are very few new tests in these languages, and some tests published prior to 1930 are still in demand. In fact, it is mainly in the older tests and in informal objective tests that such item forms as objective varieties of the completion type and variations of the alternate-response type are found. The more recent tests use several varieties of multiple-choice items almost exclusively.

Tests in French. Two excerpts are shown here to represent tests of reading comprehension. Measurement of sentence comprehension is illustrated by samples from the advanced level of the *Cooperative French Test* and

EXCERPT FROM *Cooperative French Test* [16]

22. Les routes sont toute couvertes de poussière, à cause
22-1   des arbres.
22-2   du manque de pluie.
22-3   du manque de soleil.
22-4   des inondations.
22-5   des fleurs. . . . . 22(   )

23. Jean va au cinéma ce soir, de sorte que nous ne le verrons que
23-1   ce matin.
23-2   l'année passée.
23-3   demain.
23-4   hier.
23-5   avant-hier. . . . . 23(   )

[16] Geraldine Spaulding and Paule Vaillant, *Cooperative French Test*, Part I, Advanced. Form Q. Educational Testing Service, Princeton, N. J., 1940.

from the *Columbia Research Bureau French Test*. The first employs a typical multiple-choice item type but the second uses a *plus-zero* version of an alternate-response variety that, despite its suitability for such situations as this, is almost never found in recently published tests.

EXCERPT FROM *Columbia Research Bureau French Test* [17]

a. Le temps passe et ne revient pas. ....(+)
b. Il est plus facile d'écrire une langue que de la lire. ....(0)
c. Tous les chevaux sont blancs. ....(0)

---

1. Le dimanche est un jour de travail aux États-Unis mais le lundi on se repose. .(   )
2. Ordinairement on travaille le jour et on se repose la nuit. ....(   )
3. Les pères et les mères des soldats et des généraux sont heureux pendant une bataille. ....(   )
4. Les parents sont joyeux et fiers du succès de leurs enfants. ....(   )
5. L'homme riche dont la bourse est fermée aux malheureux est un être qu'on n'admire pas souvent. ....(   )

Vocabulary testing is represented by an excerpt picturing items of a simple multiple-choice variety from the elementary level of the *Cooperative French Test*. A completion variety of item seldom used in tests having recent copyright dates is shown in the accompanying excerpt from the *American Council Beta French Test* in its application to the measurement of grammar.

EXCERPT FROM *Cooperative French Test* [18]

    5. **vert**
        5–1 poetry
        5–2 towards
        5–3 green
        5–4 voice
        5–5 view . . . . .5(   )
    6. **heureux**
        6–1 honor
        6–2 early
        6–3 horrible
        6–4 heaven
        6–5 happy . . . . .6(   )

---

[17] A. A. Meras, Suzanne Roth, and Ben D. Wood, *Columbia Research Bureau French Test, Part II, Comprehension.* Form A. Copyright 1926 by Harcourt, Brace and World, Inc., New York. All rights reserved. Quoted by special permission.

[18] Jacob Greenberg and Geraldine Spaulding, *Cooperative French Test,* Part II, Elementary. Form Q. Educational Testing Service, Princeton, N. J., 1940.

EXCERPT FROM *American Council Beta French Test* [19]

10. How many books have you?
(___) **livres avez-vous?**...................(_____)

11. It is half-past six.
Il est (___) **et demie**....................(_____)

12. Is John at home?
Jean, est-t-il (___)**?**....................(_____)

Tests in German. Three item varieties for the measurement of vocabulary in German are illustrated in an accompanying set of samples. The first sample shows a *plus-minus* variety of alternate-response item applied to similarities and differences in the meanings of paired words. In the second sample, pupils are asked to choose the two out of five terms that are opposite in meaning, or antonyms. The variety of three-option multiple-choice item shown last illustrates another method of measuring vocabulary by means of words having related meanings.

SAMPLES OF Test Items in German [20]

In the proper spaces, write plus (+) if the words have essentially the same meaning and minus (−) if they have the opposite meaning:

( ) 1. der Arzt—der Doktor
( ) 2. Hunger haben—hungrig sein
( ) 3. fleissig—träge
( ) 4. am Morgen—am Abend

Underline the two words in each group that have essentially the *opposite meaning* (antonyms):

1. alt, hoch, breit, niedrig, klein
2. braun, lang, gut, kurz, schwarz
3. offnet, scheint, schreibt, unterrichet, schliesst
4. spielen, verkaufen, tanzen, kaufen, besitzen

Underline the *word* most closely related in thought to each group at the left:

die Nase ⎫
die Augen ⎬das Gesicht, das Gewebe, das Gerede
der Bart ⎭

der See ⎫
der Fluss ⎬backen, baden, bauen
das Meer ⎭

[19] Jacob Greenberg and Ben D. Wood, *American Council Beta French Test, Part III, French Grammar Completion.* Form A. Copyright 1926 by Harcourt, Brace and World, Inc., New York. All rights reserved. Quoted by special permission.
[20] Raymond P. Maronpot, "Let's Teach and Test Vocabulary on a One-Language Basis." *German Quarterly,* 25:26-32; January 1952.

Tests in Spanish. The two accompanying excerpts from the elementary and advanced levels of the *Cooperative Spanish Test* are item types similar to those shown for French in preceding excerpts for use in measuring reading comprehension and functional grammar respectively. The third illustration for Spanish is the only one shown in this chapter for the measurement of listening skills. After the examiner presents the background orally for the skeleton item shown in the excerpt by reading the paired statements, *"Es* muy buen tiempo hoy," and *"Hace* muy buen tiempo hoy," the pupil is expected to indicate in alternate-response form whether he thinks the first (a) or the second (b) is a correct statement.

EXCERPT FROM *Cooperative Spanish Test* [21]

33. Este verano no podré hacer el viaje a
    España por falta de
    33–1   dinero.
    33–2   humo.
    33–3   naranjas.
    33–4   miedo.
    33–5   preguntas. . . . . .33(   )

34. Se parece Vd. mucho a su hermano
    aunque
    34–1   él es más joven.
    34–2   no le he visto.
    34–3   es Vd. el hijo único.
    34–4   hoy es lunes.
    34–5   Vd. no hace nada. . . . . . .34(   )

EXCERPT FROM *Cooperative Spanish Test* [22]

22. **They were on a wide path.**
    22–1   Estaban en un senda ancha.
    22–2   Estaban en un senda ancho.
    22–3   Estaban en una senda ancha.
    22–4   Estaban en un ancha senda.
    22–5   Estaban en una ancho senda. . 22(   )

23. **Tell them to me.**
    23–1   Dígalas a me.
    23–2   Dígamelas.
    23–3   Dígame ellas.
    23–4   Me las diga.
    23–5   Me dígalas. . . . . .23(   )

[21] Jacob Greenberg, Robert H. Williams, and Geraldine Spaulding, *Cooperative Spanish Test,* Part I, Elementary. Form P. Educational Testing Service, Princeton, N. J., 1939.
[22] E. Herman Hespelt, Robert H. Williams, and Geraldine Spaulding, *Cooperative Spanish Test,* Part III, Advanced. Form P. Educational Testing Service, Princeton, N. J., 1939.

SAMPLE ITEM FROM Aural Spanish Test [23]

The examiner will make a statement in two different ways, a right way and a wrong way. As soon as the examiner has finished speaking, put an X in the box before the number of the exercise that shows whether the first way (labeled a) or the second way (labeled b) is the correct one.

☐ a.
☐ b.

4. MEASUREMENT OF PROFICIENCY IN LATIN

Latin is the only classical language dealt with here, since Greek, second in importance among the ancient languages, is taught primarily at the college and university level.

Objectives of Instruction in Latin

The objectives of instruction in Latin naturally differ considerably from those in the modern foreign languages. The *Classical Investigation* stated the immediate objective as the progressive development of the power to read and understand Latin through an increasing mastery of vocabulary, forms, and syntax. Ultimate objectives stated in this report included: [24]

1. Development of an increased understanding of those elements in English which are related to Latin
2. Development of an increased ability to read, speak, and write English
3. Development of an increased ability to learn other foreign languages
4. Development of correct mental habits
5. Development of an historical and cultural background
6. Development of right attitudes toward social situations
7. Development of literary appreciation
8. Development of an elementary knowledge of the simpler general principles of language structure
9. Development of improved literary quality of written English

More recently, the objectives of high-school Latin teaching were restated for a course sequence by a Committee on *Educational Policies of the Classical Association of the Middle West and South*. The report, dealt with in a symposium later the same year,[25] was restricted to a two-year program. Else [26] stated the objectives for the two-year course sequence as follows:

---

[23] Walter V. Kaulfers, "Wartime Development in Modern-Language Achievement Testing." *Modern Language Journal* 28:136-50; February 1944.

[24] American Classical League, *The Classical Investigation, Part I, General Report*. Princeton University Press, Princeton, N. J., 1924.

[25] Symposium, "Toward Improvement of the High-School Latin Curriculum." *Classical Journal*, 43:67-90; November 1947.

[26] Gerald F. Else, "Objectives and Overview." *Ibid*. p. 74-75.

I. The developing high-school student should gain added proficiency in language through
  A. Increased awareness of the structure of language as a skeleton of speech and thought
  B. An improved ability to understand and use English words of Latin derivation
  C. A knowledge of actual Latin words and phrases commonly used in English
II. The developing student ... needs to become more keenly aware of the roots of our culture. He should be conscious of the role played by classical culture in shaping not only our American tradition but the Western tradition as a whole. Such an understanding is not merely desirable but vitally necessary if Americans are to become citizens of the world.

It is clear that the general pattern of the *Classical Investigation* is followed in the more modern list of objectives. In fact, the differences between the earlier and later formulations lie primarily in the selection of materials and instructional emphases. The 1947 program recommended "a functional approach to the teaching of grammar, new reading material for the first year, the reading of Virgil's *Aeneid* during the second year, and the selection of a vocabulary which will take into consideration its usefulness as a source for building English words of Latin derivation." [27] Dunkel indicated that this two-year program is designed primarily to serve the needs of the 80 to 90 percent of pupils who are not likely to study the subject more than two years, to limit the methods used to the job at hand by simplification in the treatment of grammar, and to "discover and emphasize those objectives which promise to make the most sense to the greatest number of this diverse group of students we have." [28]

Tests of Achievement in Latin

Measurement in Latin has thus far been restricted mainly to the immediate objectives of the subject. Effective measurement in Latin, as in every other field of learning, is dependent upon the exact identification of the specific elements that comprise the desired outcomes of instruction. To attempt to measure all of the objectives of instruction in Latin would lead to confusion and almost certain failure. Many of these objectives emphasize cultural and disciplinary values which at present are not measurable and some of which perhaps do not exist.

The analysis of achievement in Latin indicates that the accomplishment of the immediate objectives in the subject is dependent upon a variety

[27] Fred S. Dunham, "Introduction." *Ibid.* p. 67.
[28] Harold B. Dunkel, "Changing Latin in a Changing World." *Ibid.* p. 71-73.

of specific abilities, many of which are measurable. Among these are such factors as the acquisition of vocabulary and the oral and silent reading skills.

EXCERPT FROM *Cooperative Latin Test* [29]

10. **biduum**
   - 10–1 fowl
   - 10–2 invitation
   - 10–3 two days
   - 10–4 wait
   - 10–5 having two teeth. 10(   )

11. **cupidus**
   - 11–1 eager
   - 11–2 lovely
   - 11–3 captured
   - 11–4 spear
   - 11–5 zeal . . . . . . .11(   )

EXCERPT FROM *Cooperative Latin Test* [30]

15. **The lieutenant will lead his men out of camp.**
   Lēgātus suōs (——) ēdūcet.
   - 15–1 ex castrā
   - 15–2 ex castribus
   - 15–3 ex castrīs
   - 15–4 ex castrō
   - 15–5 ob castrīs . . . . .15(   )

16. **A man is larger than a boy.**
   Vir est (——) quam puer.
   - 16–1 magnior
   - 16–2 plus magnus
   - 16–3 maior
   - 16–4 maius
   - 16–5 maiōrus. . . . . .16(   )

Several tests designed to measure the elements involved in the accomplishment of the more immediate objectives of instruction in Latin are now available. They are intended to measure general achievement rather than specific factors underlying achievement. Many parallel quite closely the testing techniques developed in the field of English. Reading, vocabu-

---

[29] George A. Land, *Cooperative Latin Test,* Part II, Elementary. Form R. Educational Testing Service, Princeton, N. J., 1949.
[30] *Ibid.* Part III.

lary, and grammar are for Latin, as well as for the modern foreign languages, the aspects of proficiency most often set apart.

Objective item forms used in standardized tests are very similar in all of the foreign languages. Many of the illustrations given in a preceding section of this chapter for the modern languages could equally well apply to Latin. Therefore, only three illustrations are given here as examples of measurement techniques in Latin. The first two excerpts, from the elementary level of the *Cooperative Latin Test*, illustrate the measurement

EXCERPT FROM *Cooperative Latin Test* [31]

Ipse inter primos dextram sub moenia tendit
Aeneas, magnaque incusat voce Latinum,
Testaturque deos iterum se ad proelia cogi,
Bis iam Italos hostis, haec iam altera foedera rumpi.

21. In this passage Aeneas is
    21-1   under the wall.
    21-2   inside the city.
    21-3   to the right of the leaders.
    21-4   among the leaders.
    21-5   in the house of Latinus. . . . . . 21(   )

22. Aeneas is angry because
    22-1   Latinus has accused him.
    22-2   another treaty has been broken.
    22-3   he is prevented from fighting.
    22-4   the city has been taken.
    22-5   the gods have turned against him. . 22(   )

of vocabulary and grammar, while the third, from the advanced level of the same test, illustrates the measurement of reading skill by basing items on a short selection. Three different modifications of the multiple-choice item appear in these samples.

5. DIAGNOSIS AND REMEDIATION
   IN THE FOREIGN LANGUAGES

The problems of diagnosis and remedy in the modern foreign languages and Latin are essentially the same. Reading, pronunciation (accent), vocabulary (idiom), and grammar constitute the major remedial areas. Naturally, a careful diagnosis of possible causes of difficulty must be made. The results of intelligence tests are helpful in locating general causes of trouble. Prognostic and aptitude tests are also useful in identify-

[31] George A. Land, *Cooperative Latin Test*, Part I, Advanced. Form R. Educational Testing Service, Princeton, N. J., 1941.

ing students who apparently lack the special abilities upon which success-ful work in the foreign languages depends.

Reading tests of the work-study type do much to reveal reading de-ficiencies. Such reading tests are of much the same character as those for silent reading in English. Such tests should be analytical within the limits of the subject, measuring such qualities as reading comprehension at the word level, comprehension in sentences and in larger units, reading rate, use of books, and methods of study. Informal objective tests in vocabulary, grammar, composition, and reading and comprehension are also useful.

The analysis of causes of pupil failure is indispensable to remedial work. The results of such an analysis may readily provide the basis for preventive work designed to reduce the number of failures. Low mentality, bad health conditions, poor study conditions, ineffective methods of study, lack of cooperation between teacher and pupil, and classes that are too large or too heterogeneous are certainly some of the factors that necessitate an effective remedial program.

SUGGESTED ACTIVITIES

1. Outline in detail for a specific type of instructional outcome in a modern foreign language or Latin the types of pupil behavior you would accept as indicating that the desired outcomes had been attained.
2. Construct from seven to ten objective test items for the measurement of achievement in some aspect of one of the modern languages or Latin.

TOPICS FOR DISCUSSION

1. What important changes of emphasis have taken place recently in the objectives of modern foreign language teaching?
2. What are some of the recent developments that have contributed to changes in the objectives of the modern foreign languages?
3. Of what significance is the study of English as a foreign language?
4. What is the place of modern foreign language teaching in the secondary school? In the elementary school?
5. What is the value of prognostic testing in the foreign languages?
6. How do the foreign languages differ from the English language arts as they are taught in American schools?
7. How do direct, concomitant, and associate outcomes differ from each other in the modern foreign languages?
8. Point out the differences in the types of measurement techniques that are used in the foreign languages and in English.
9. What is the place of aural-oral testing in the modern foreign languages?
10. What distinguishes immediate from ultimate objectives of instruction in Latin?

11. In what respects do the instructional objectives of the modern foreign languages and of Latin differ?
12. For what major reason have the objectives of instruction in Latin been modified recently?
13. In your judgment what are the greatest weaknesses of foreign language tests?

SELECTED REFERENCES

AGARD, FREDERICK B., AND DUNKEL, HAROLD B. *An Investigation of Second-Language Teaching.* Boston: Ginn and Co., 1948. Chapters 3-4.

ANDRUS, LAWRENCE. "A Composition Test for Foreign Languages." *Educational and Psychological Measurement,* 1:355-64; October 1941.

BIRKMAIER, EMMA M. "Modern Languages." *Encyclopedia of Educational Research.* Third edition. New York: Macmillan Co., 1960. p. 861-88.

BOTTKE, K. G., AND MILLIGAN, E. E. "Test of Aural and Oral Aptitude for Foreign Language Study." *Modern Language Journal,* 29:705-9; December 1945.

BUROS, OSCAR K., editor. *The Fifth Mental Measurements Yearbook.* Highland Park, N. J.: Gryphon Press, 1959, p. 388-415.

BUROS, OSCAR K., editor. *The Fourth Mental Measurements Yearbook.* Highland Park, N. J.: Gryphon Press, 1953. p. 348-71.

BUROS, OSCAR K., editor. *The Third Mental Measurements Yearbook.* New Brunswick, N. J.: Rutgers University Press, 1949. p. 265-93.

CARR, W. L., AND HUTCHINSON, MARK E. "Latin." *Encyclopedia of Educational Research.* Revised edition. New York: Macmillan Co., 1950. p. 654-62.

COLEMAN, ALGERNON. "Examinations in the Foreign Languages." *The Construction and Use of Achievement Examinations.* Boston: Houghton Mifflin Co., 1936. Chapter 6.

COLLEGE ENTRANCE EXAMINATION BOARD. *Foreign Languages: A Description of the College Board Tests in French, German, Latin, and Spanish.* Princeton, N. J.: The Board, April 1954.

DEWITT, NORMAN J. "Classical Languages." *Encyclopedia of Educational Research.* Third edition. New York: Macmillan Co., 1960. p. 211-21.

DUMMER, E. HAYSE. "A New Vocabulary Test." *Modern Language Journal,* 27:21-24; January 1943.

GERBERICH, J. RAYMOND. *Specimen Objective Test Items: A Guide to Achievement Test Construction.* New York: Longmans, Green and Co., 1956. p. 313-15.

GREENE, HARRY A., JORGENSEN, ALBERT N., AND GERBERICH, J. RAYMOND. *Measurement and Evaluation in the Secondary School.* Second edition. New York: Longmans, Green and Co., 1954. Chapter 17.

HALEY, SISTER MARIE P. "Evaluation in Oral French." *Modern Language Journal,* 25:390-93; February 1941.

KAULFERS, WALTER V. "General Language." *Encyclopedia of Educational Research.* Revised edition. New York: Macmillan Co., 1950. p. 500-1.

KAULFERS, WALTER V. "Objective Tests and Exercises in French Pronunciation." *Modern Language Journal,* 22:186-88; December 1937.

KAULFERS, WALTER V. "Wartime Developments in Modern-Language Achievement Testing." *Modern Language Journal,* 28:136-50; February 1944.

KAVETSKY, JOSEPH, AND MORRISON, J. CAYCE. "English as a Second Language." *Encyclopedia of Educational Research.* Third edition. New York: Macmillan Co., 1960. p. 478-82.

KERN, EDITH. "FLES Testing." *French Review,* 33:45-52; October 1959.

KURATH, WILLIAM. "A Testing Plan for First-Year German Classes." *Modern Language Journal,* 28:346-51; April 1944.

LADO, ROBERT. "Phonemics and Pronunciation Tests." *Modern Language Journal,* 35:531-42; November 1951.

MANUEL, HERSCHEL T. "The Use of Parallel Tests in the Study of Foreign Language Teaching." *Educational and Psychological Measurement,* 13:431-36; Autumn 1953.

MARONPOT, RAYMOND P. "Let's Teach and Test Vocabulary on a One-Language Basis." *German Quarterly,* 25:26-32; January 1952.

MARONPOT, RAYMOND P. "Teaching and Testing Vocabulary on a One-Language Basis." *Hispania,* 34:280-82; August 1951.

MILLER, MINNIE M. "Test on Spanish and Spanish-American Life and Culture." *Modern Language Journal,* 32:140-44; February 1948.

PRATT, NORMAN T., JR. "Some Objective Test Materials." *Classical Journal,* 43:179-81; December 1947.

RAYMOND, JOSEPH. "A Controlled Association Exercise in Spanish." *Modern Language Journal,* 35:280-91; April 1951.

SANDRI, LUIGI, AND KAULFERS, WALTER V. "An Oral-Fluency Rating Scale in Italian." *Italica,* 22:133-44; September 1945.

SCHAEFFER, RUDOLF F. "What Kind of Tests for Oral-Aural Courses." *German Quarterly,* 21:94-101; March 1948.

SYMPOSIUM. "Foreign Languages in the Elementary School: What Effect Does FLES Have on Later Language Learning." *NEA Journal,* 49:33-36; February 1960.

THARP, JAMES B. "A Test in French Civilization." *French Review,* 8:283-87; March 1935.

THARP, JAMES B.; COLEMAN, ALGERNON; AND KING, CLARA B. "Foreign Languages —Modern." *Encyclopedia of Educational Research.* Revised edition. New York: Macmillan Co., 1950. p. 464-85.

21

MUSIC, ART, AND LITERATURE

The following factors underlying the measurement of aptitudes and achievement in music, art, and literature are discussed in this chapter:

A. Social and educational significance of the fine arts.
B. Measurement of musical talent and aptitude.
C. Aims and outcomes of music education.
D. Measurement of accomplishment and appreciation in music.
E. Measurement of art judgment and aptitude.
F. Objectives and outcomes of art education.
G. Measurement of achievement in art.
H. Measurement of achievement in literature.

The objective measurement of aptitudes and achievement in the fine arts is a relatively recent accomplishment—so recent, in fact, that there is still an echo of protest from a small group of artists that artistic production does not lend itself to objective evaluation. In spite of this feeling, however, much progress has been made in these fields of measurement. This is as it should be, for certainly in these cultural subjects is to be found much of the best that the educational program affords. With the trend of recent years in the direction of greater individual leisure for the cultural pursuits, the need for a better understanding of the content, aims, and methodology of these artistic subjects is greater than ever before.

1. MEASUREMENT OF MUSICAL TALENT

Measurement in music takes two major lines of approach. The first is the determination of basic aptitudes. Here, as in other subjects, the techniques and instruments used are psychological. Such instruments are mentioned previously in this volume as tests of special intelligence, since they have to do with the determination of tendencies to respond in certain ways to specific types of musical stimuli. Accomplishment in music depends to such a large degree upon the existence of aptitude that this phase of measurement must be given primary emphasis. The mere existence of aptitude in music is in no sense an index to musical accomplishment, however. The second approach to the problem, the measurement of accomplishment, is dealt with in the next section of this chapter.

Tests of musical aptitude are designed to measure those largely innate musical capacities that constitute the individual's musical inheritance. Aside from the sheer physical endowment that certain types of musical expression demand, there are certain more or less psychological factors that determine an individual's musical talent. The identification of these factors calls for an unusually critical analysis. Two rather distinctive types of purposes are now served by tests of this type—measurement of musical talent or aptitude in general and assessment of aptitude or readiness for the study of instrumental music. The former has been accorded by far the greater amount of attention and research. Without doubt the most extensive of the research programs for the purpose of isolating the elements of talent in music was the one undertaken by Seashore and his students at the State University of Iowa.

Measurement of Talent for Music in General

The *Seashore Measures of Musical Talents* [1] consist of a battery of six tests on three records for phonographic reproduction in about an hour of testing time. The six tests are designed to measure (1) pitch, (2) loudness, (3) rhythm, (4) time, (5) timbre, and (6) memory. These are elemental abilities upon which responses to musical training appear to depend.

The testing situation involves careful and critical listening. In these tests the individual typically is asked to listen to two notes, sound patterns, or musical phrases, sometimes the same and sometimes different, and then to distinguish the nature and perhaps the type of difference, if any, between the two. The earliest age at which these group measures can be used effectively is at the fifth-grade level. The tests may be administered to groups depending in size somewhat on the acoustical qualities of the testing room. Naturally the stimulus must be heard clearly at all times. The *Kwalwasser Music Talent Test* [2] is available in Form B for pupils

---

[1] Carl E. Seashore, Don Lewis, and Joseph G. Saetveit, *Seashore Measures of Musical Talents*, Revised edition. Psychological Corporation, New York, 1939.
[2] Jacob Kwalwasser, *Kwalwasser Music Talent Test*. Mills Music, Inc., New York, 1953.

in Grades 4 to 6 and Form A for older pupils and adults. About 10 to 15 minutes of testing time are required for obtaining four measures of musical talent: (1) pitch, (2) rhythm, (3) loudness, and (4) time. In the forced-choice type of measurement situation, three tones are given first, three more tones are then given with a change in one, but only one, of these four characteristics, and the subject is then forced to indicate whether the change occurred in pitch, rhythm, loudness, or time.

The *Musical Aptitude Test* [3] by Whistler and Thorpe is designed to be administered from a piano keyboard by the pianist himself. Designed for use with pupils in Grades 4 to 10, the test has five parts: (1) rhythm recognition, (2) pitch recognition, (3) melody recognition, (4) pitch discrimination, and (5) advanced rhythm recognition. Results from the five parts are combined in such manner as to give separate scores on rhythm, pitch, and melody. For each of the five parts, the pianist-administrator illustrates the procedure to be followed and then, for each test item, plays two rhythms, two melodies, or two chords and asks the pupil to indicate whether they are the same or different and in two test parts to specify the nature or direction of any difference. Testing time for the series of tests in about 40 minutes.

The *Drake Musical Aptitude Tests* [4] consist of two parts—the equivalent of the older *Drake Musical Memory Test* for one and a new rhythm test for the other. The test is designed for persons of any age above seven whether or not they have had musical training. In the memory test, the subject listens to melodies played in their proper form or with variations in key, time, or notes. He records his responses to each of the trials on a special record sheet to show whether he recognizes the nature of the difference, if any, between the melody itself, which is played first, and the various versions of it which follow. The rhythm test measures the subject's ability to "keep time," or to retain a particular established beat over a period of time both without and with the distraction of a contrary beat.

Measurement of Talent for Instrumental Music

The *Farnum Music Notation Test* [5] is a test of readiness for the study of instrumental music and is designed primarily to aid in the selection of pupils in Grades 7 to 9 who will benefit most from instruction of this type. Administrable in from 20 to 25 minutes to groups of not over 30 pupils,

[3] Harvey S. Whistler and Louis P. Thorpe, *Musical Aptitude Test,* Series A. California Test Bureau, Los Angeles, 1950.

[4] Raleigh M. Drake, *Drake Musical Aptitude Tests.* Science Research Associates, Inc., Chicago, 1954.

[5] Stephen E. Farnum, *Farnum Music Notation Test.* Psychological Corporation, New York, 1953.

the test is based on a phonographic recording and a musical score in the hands of each pupil. As each of forty recorded melodies is played, the pupil is expected to decide which bar of each four-bar melody differs in pitch or rhythm from what appears in the score and to mark his answer sheet accordingly. Thus, the test actually consists of forty four-option multiple-choice items.

Another test having a similar purpose is the *Conrad Instrument-Talent Test*,[6] designed for use with pupils beyond the age of six years. A piano and an electric metronome are used in administering the three-part test consisting of five listening tests of musical aptitude, a questionnaire on scholastic and musical interests, and an assessment of the shape of the pupil's hands, lips, and jaws.

2. MEASUREMENT OF ACCOMPLISHMENT IN MUSIC

The second line of approach to music, going beyond the musical talents dealt with in the preceding section of this chapter, is the measurement of musical accomplishment. Achievement tests are used in this approach for the threefold purpose of measuring the knowledges, skills, and appreciations acquired as a result of training.

Major Aims and Outcomes of Music Education

A rather recent statement of the major goals of music is that presented by Brooks and Brown.[7] It is believed that this general summary of elementary-school music instructional goals also affords a useful basis for the validation of improved tests in the fields of music information, accomplishment, and aptitudes at the secondary-school level. Fifteen of these major goals are reproduced here and are summarized with minor modifications under the following seven practical categories:

1. In Song Singing
    Ability to ... use the voice to express and convey musical meaning in free, spontaneous, and beautiful song singing. ...
2. In Chorus
    Ability and disposition to associate with others ... in joint rendering of music in chorus singing. ...
3. In Appreciation and Its Background
    a. Discrimination and taste in music with evidence of preference for that which has excellence and worth.

[6] Jacques W. Conrad, *Conrad Instrument-Talent Test*. Mills Music, Inc., New York, 1941.

[7] B. Marian Brooks and Harry A. Brown, *Music Education in the Elementary School*. American Book Co., New York, 1946. p. 114-16.

b. Sensitiveness to ordered perfection of structure and design in music. ... and realization of aesthetic satisfaction in the beauty, appropriateness, and adequacy thus seen and expressed.

c. Integrated volitional structure in personality with reference to selection in music. . . .

d. Understanding of some phases of the development of music and some insight into the essential nature and meaning of music and the forces and influences that have produced it. . . .

4. In Instrumental Music

a. Ability to use instruments as a means of musical expression and with satisfaction in such experience.

b. Ability to handle with manipulative skill such musical instruments as are used.

5. In Creative Music

Ability to use individual originality and general initiative in interpreting, using, and creating music.

6. In Connection with the Musical Score

a. Ability to read musical meaning fluently from the printed score.

b. Ability to use musical notation to express or record musical meaning.

c. Understanding of selected phases of the theory of music ... as essentially a functional approach to music literature and as a means toward a broader interpretation. . . .

7. In Connection with More Than One Phase of Music Education

a. Complete freedom from inhibitions arising from focal attending to mechanical processes. . . .

b. Ability to sense and feel the movement resident in music and to express it in bodily motion in some appropriate manner. . . .

c. Growth toward possession of music as a social institution on a ... level of comprehension and participation. . . .

In addition to the above general goals these same authors listed eighty "subsidiary goals which are contributory to the major goals and which may serve as guides to the teacher in the attainment of the major goals." These goals must not "be considered as a course of study to be followed." They "are constituent elements of the larger objectives. A listing of them should be a great aid to the classroom teacher and the college student who is preparing to teach music or to be a supervisor in that field." [8]

Measurement of Musical Achievement

The knowledge, skill, and appreciative outcomes of music instruction are measured by a variety of tests of the pencil-and-paper type. The majority of these instruments appear to measure the knowledge and skill objec-

[8] *Ibid.* p. 116.

tives quite adequately, but they largely neglect the appreciative outcomes. This is not surprising, because of the fact that appreciations are very difficult to define and even more difficult to measure.

Tests of musical knowledge. Tests of musical knowledge are variously concerned with musical symbols and terms, time and key signatures, note and rest values, syllables, instrumentation of the orchestra, musical form, the history of music, and the biographies of musicians. Samples are given below to illustrate the measurement techniques rather commonly used.

The first of the accompanying excerpts, from the *Kwalwasser Test of Music Information and Appreciation,* shows several completion-type and several *true-false* items for measuring knowledge of composers and of

EXCERPTS FROM *Kwalwasser Test of Music Information and Appreciation* [9]

Directions: Below are the names of famous compositions. On the lines at the right you are to write the *name of the composer* of each. The sample is marked as it should be.

Sample: The Elijah......*Mendelssohn*......

1. March Slav ....
2. To a Wild Rose ....
3. The Unfinished Symphony ....
4. Liebestraum ....

1. (　) The viola is an alto horn.
2. (　) Violins are frequently employed in brass bands.
3. (　) The first violin section is seated to the left of the conductor.
4. (　) The harpsichord is one of the predecessors of the piano.

EXCERPT FROM *Diagnostic Tests of Achievement in Music* [10]

[9] Jacob Kwalwasser, *Kwalwasser Test of Music Information and Appreciation.* Bureau of Educational Research and Service, State University of Iowa, Iowa City, 1927.

[10] M. Lela Kotick and T. L. Torgerson, *Diagnostic Tests of Achievement in Music, Test 1A, Diatonic Syllable Names.* Form A. California Test Bureau, Monterey, Calif., 1950.

musical instruments. The second illustration, from the *Diagnostic Tests of Achievement in Music,* shows a section of the machine-scorable answer sheet. In answering the items, the pupil is asked to recall the syllable name of each note in the score and to mark the appropriately designated space in the column directly underneath the note. The sample shows, for example, that the first three notes are respectively *sol, mi,* and *do.*

EXCERPT FROM *Kwalwasser-Ruch Test of Musical Accomplishment* [11]

DIRECTIONS: The song "America" is written below. One measure has been crossed out because the melody is wrong. Five other measures are wrong. Hum over the melody to yourself and *cross out all five wrong measures.*

EXCERPT FROM *Knuth Achievement Test in Music* [12]

We shall hear a melody of four measures played on the piano. The first two measures are written in Part I. The last two measures occur in one of the four staves of Part II.

You are to recognize these last two measures. Listen carefully and place a cross in the square after the measures you hear played.

Mark only one of the four squares.

[11] Jacob Kwalwasser and G. M. Ruch, *Kwalwasser-Ruch Test of Musical Accomplishment.* Bureau of Educational Research and Service, State University of Iowa, Iowa City, 1924.

[12] William E. Knuth, *Knuth Achievement Test in Music,* Division 3. Form A. Educational Test Bureau, Minneapolis, Minn., 1936.

Tests of musical skills. Among the musical skills most commonly measured by various paper-and-pencil tests are detection of pitch and time
errors and recognition of melodies. An illustration of each is given above.
The first, from the *Kwalwasser-Ruch Test of Musical Accomplishment,*
asks the pupil in a strictly paper-and-pencil test to identify and cross out
the five bars of "America" that are written incorrectly in the score. This
is actually a *right–wrong* variety of alternate-response item, since each
measure appears either in correct or incorrect form. The second excerpt,
a single item from the *Knuth Achievement Test in Music,* is based on a
short melody played on the piano and the music symbolism appearing in
the test booklet. The pupil attempts to identify the correct set of third and
fourth measures in a four-option multiple-choice item by reacting to the
external instrumental stimulus.

Performance scales are also available for the measurement of functional
musical skills as evidenced on band instruments. The *Watkins-Farnum
Performance Scale* [13] consists of fourteen exercises in scaled order of difficulty adapted for use with various band instruments. As the pupil sight-
reads and plays, errors of eight different types are noted by the examiner.
The test is completed when the pupil fails to score in two consecutive
exercises that in their entirety range from very easy to very difficult.

Tests of music appreciation. Only one test purporting to measure music
appreciation, the *Kwalwasser Test of Music Information and Appreciation*
mentioned above, is known to the authors. Its approach is mainly through
the testing of knowledges, many of which unquestionably carry appreciative values with them. However, many critics are not convinced that appreciations are measured directly, if, indeed, they can be measured in that
manner. In view of the modern emphasis upon music appreciation for all
pupils, it is unfortunate that the appreciative types of outcomes are not
subject to more satisfactory measurement.

3. MEASUREMENT OF ART JUDGMENT AND APTITUDE

Two somewhat different approaches to the measurement of aptitude or
talent for art are embodied in tests intended to be used in the prediction
of success in this subject. One approach is by means of the pupil's ability
to make good judgments or discriminations between paired samples of
pictured art products. Tests of this type also measure appreciative aspects
that may reflect both an aptitude factor and effects of general training or
experience. The other approach, by means of what are typically designated

[13] John G. Watkins and Stephen E. Farnum, *Watkins-Farnum Performance Scale: A
Standardized Achievement Test for All Band Instruments.* Hal Leonard Music, Inc.,
Winona, Minn., 1954.

as art aptitude tests, involves the actual production by the subject of some pencil representations.

Tests of Art Judgment

In the *Meier Art Judgment Test,* which may be given as an individual or as a group test in Grades 7 to 12, the pupil is confronted with 100 pairs of artistic specimens adapted from many sources. One of each pair of specimens has been changed in some specific element from the original form. The exact feature changed is specified in the record sheet on which the pupil records his reactions. A consideration of the complete series of paired specimens insures a comprehensive sampling of the various elements that enter into esthetic judgment. According to the evidence obtained by the author, this test measures the sensitivity of the individual to the effect that the composition as a whole produces on the observer. In order to give a better idea of the exact nature of specimens and the accompanying

EXCERPT FROM *Meier Art Judgment Test* [14]

DIRECTIONS

In the accompanying booklet are pictures arranged in pairs, the two in each pair being very nearly alike. They differ only in one respect and you are told *what that is* in each case on pages 1, 2, and 3 of this blank.

You are to compare the two pictures in each pair, noting the unlike portion, and then decide which one is better (more pleasing, more artistic, more satisfying). Do not hurry. Study each pair carefully in turn.

Indicate your preference by making an X in the circle under *Left,* if you decide that the left-hand picture is better, or in the circle under *Right* if you believe that the right hand one is more desirable.

Examples of proper marking: (pictures not illustrated).
Left Right No.

⊗   ○   A Presence or absence of tree. *(This would mean that you prefer the left-hand picture)*

○   ⊗   B Treatment of waves. *(This would mean that you prefer the right-hand picture)*

Select the better one in every pair. Do not omit any. If unable to decide within a reasonable time mark the place and return to that one later.

49

14 Norman C. Meier, *The Meier Art Tests: I, Art Judgment.* Bureau of Educational Research and Service, State University of Iowa, Iowa City, 1940.

record sheets, a pair of the etchings is reproduced here together with directions from the Test Record Sheet. The pair of specimens reproduced here is used with item 49. In this item, the presence or absence of horns is the point for special consideration in making the judgment. The scoring key lists the drawing with horns as the one of greater merit.

The Graves *Design Judgment Test* [15] is similar to the *Meier Art Judgment Test* in many respects, although it consists of paired plates of designs, rather than pictures, in black, white, and gray. It is intended to measure certain aspects of aptitude considered to be important in the appreciation or the production of art structure in terms of the pupil's reactions to such principles of aesthetic order as unity, dominance, variety, balance, continuity, symmetry, proportion, and rhythm. The test is designed for use with pupils in Grade 7 or above and with adults.

Test of Art Aptitude

The *Horn Art Aptitude Inventory*,[16] for use in Grades 12 to 16 and also with adults, consists of two parts. The first is a "scribble and doodle" exercise in which the subject is asked to sketch a number of familiar objects under considerable time pressure and the other presents various semi-structured "springboards" for the subject to use in evolving compositions and designs under untimed conditions.

4. MEASUREMENT OF ACCOMPLISHMENT IN ART

The theory of art for art's sake, which dominated the field of art education for many years, has largely given way of late to the theory that all pupils should receive an opportunity in art courses to develop a sensitivity to beauty and critical taste in evaluating art objects. Hence, art is no longer thought of as a field only for the talented few. Creative self-expression, especially in the lower grades, and correlation of art with other activities of the school are important modern trends. These purposes involve the use of a wide variety of art materials in the classroom. Extension of the content of art education courses beyond the drawing and painting, which largely constituted the curriculum in the past, particularly to industrial arts is another trend worthy of note. Last, and perhaps most important, the appreciative aims of art education have increasingly come to the front.

[15] Maitland Graves, *Design Judgment Test.* Psychological Corporation, New York, 1946.
[16] Charles C. Horn, *Horn Art Aptitude Inventory.* C. H. Stoelting Co., Chicago, 1951.

Objectives and Outcomes of Art Education

Modern aims and purposes of art education in relation to current social needs are summarized effectively in the following statement: "Art in the modern school should aim both to stimulate in the child the experience of creating and to help him to improve the manner in which he expresses himself through creative processes; at the same time, it should aim to stimulate in him the experience of appreciating by acquainting him systematically with fine examples of the arts of various peoples, both of the present and of the past." [17]

General outcomes of art education. Three general outcomes of art education appear to be of major importance: (1) information, (2) appreciation, and (3) expression.[18] It is quite probable that art appreciation is not necessarily taught, although real appreciation may be considered to rest to a large degree upon the broader aspects of information and to some degree upon the ability to distinguish a truly artistic product. The third major objective might be better expressed as exploration. Not many potentially great artists are discovered in the elementary-school or high-school classroom, but practically all of the great artists have come up through this avenue. Not everyone can express himself effectively in artistic form, but everyone has a right to explore for himself the fields of human expression in the hope that his own hidden talent may be uncovered.

Outcomes of Art Instruction [19]

A. Fruitful knowledge
> Functional information
> Practical relation of art to everyday life (clothing, home, town, or city)
> Understanding of elements and principles of art and their adaptation to everyday use
> Knowledge of construction and industrial processes involved in art training
> Acquaintance with art of other countries

B. Attitudes, interests, and appreciations
> Civic consciousness (civic pride)
> Appreciation and understanding of beauty in modern products of all kinds
> Interest in art museums, travel, and further study
> Interest in the civic, domestic, and social service of art

C. Mental technique
> Good taste, discriminating judgment, ability to select and choose wisely
> Creative ability, originality, initiative, imagination, keen observation

[17] Leon L. Winslow, *The Integrated School Art Program.* McGraw-Hill Book Co., Inc., New York, 1949. p. 43.

[18] Walter H. Klar, Leon L. Winslow, and C. Valentine Kirby, *Art Education in Principle and Practice.* Milton Bradley Co., Springfield, Mass., 1933. p. 2.

[19] Adapted from W. G. Whitford, *An Introduction to Art Education.* Century Co., New York, 1929. p. 120-22.

Ability to analyze works of art and to understand the factors of beauty in production

Keener observation; beauty of nature and fine things of art

D. Right habits and skills

Constructive thinking and planning

Systematic organization

Practical technique

Coordination of mind, hand, and eye

Freedom and spontaneity

Order, neatness

Body and mind training

Self-activity

Worthy use of leisure time

Specific outcomes of art education. A detailed expression of outcomes of instruction in art is given in the accompanying outline adapted from a course of study covering the first six years of the elementary school. It can be noted that this course is organized around four groups of outcomes which are quite similar to the artistic experiences presented in the previous paragraph and which also reflect the point of view presented for instructional outcomes in Chapter 1.

The accomplishment of these specific outcomes of instruction in art in the elementary school provides an excellent basis for the general art course in the high school. The following statements of purposes of such a general art course apply to the secondary-school level.[20]

1. To develop appreciation (visual, mental, enjoymental), knowledge, and understanding of art quality so that
   (a) The pupils may more completely enjoy life and react to the beauties therein
   (b) The pupils may become intelligent consumers (of art)
   (c) The pupils, as adults, may build and furnish more beautiful homes and demand beauty in public buildings and structures
2. To give exercise in creating beauty (technique, motor) so that
   (a) The pupils may develop ability to choose and arrange fine (art) objects for specific uses
   (b) The pupils may develop ability to originate, design, and produce fine (art) objects
   (c) The pupils may develop initiative, imagination, and observation (in dealing with art)

Measurement of Achievement in Art

Two tests that purport to measure art abilities mainly the outcomes of art instruction are the Lewerenz *Tests in Fundamental Abilities of Visual*

20 *Ibid.* p. 162-63.

Art and the *Knauber Art Ability Test*. Their major values seem to be in the junior and senior high schools, although the first is designed for use as low as the third grade.

The Lewerenz *Tests in Fundamental Abilities of Visual Art* is designed to measure aspects of art ability in nine areas: (1) recognition of proportion, (2) originality of line drawings, (3) observation of light and shade, (4) knowledge of subject matter, (5) visual memory of proportion, (6) analysis of problems in cylindrical perspective, (7) analysis of problems in parallel perspective, (8) analysis of problems in angular perspective, and (9) recognition of color. A sample from the part on originality of line drawing is shown in an accompanying excerpt as an illustration of how the test attempts to measure creativity in the use of art abilities.

EXCERPT FROM *Test in Fundamental Abilities in Visual Art* [21]

DIRECTIONS: (*To be read aloud by examiner and silently by pupils*).
What interesting things can you draw in the ten sets of dots below? Perhaps they will be joyful, serious, tragic, humorous, entertaining or decorative. Draw some pleasing well proportioned shape in each of the spaces. Let each drawing include all dots in that particular space. You may use straight or curved lines. If you wish you may add lines to improve your drawing. Draw any object your imagination may suggest. With one word tell what you have drawn.
(*Time Limit: 20 minutes*)

The *Knauber Art Ability Test* [22] requires up to three hours of time for measuring a variety of responses—reproducing a design from memory, drawing a figure of Santa Claus, adapting or modifying designs, drawing objects in perspective, creating pictorial compositions, checking drawings for accuracy, and working out light and dark arrangements. It seems well adapted to the measurement of progress in art classes from the junior high school through the college years.

5. MEASUREMENT OF ACHIEVEMENT IN LITERATURE

The use of reading for the acquisition of facts and figures in the satisfaction of academic requirements represents only one small phase of its

[21] Alfred S. Lewerenz, *Tests in Fundamental Abilities of Visual Art: Part I, Test 2, Originality of Line Drawing*. California Test Bureau, Monterey, Calif., 1927.
[22] Alma J. Knauber, *Knauber Art Ability Test*. The Author, Cincinnati, Ohio, 1932.

function. The ability to read literature opens up rich avenues of enjoy-ment and pleasure which provide the mediums through which the individual can become acquainted with life, its meaning and significance. Reading reveals those aspects of life, its activities, ideas, ideals, and emotions, about which human interests cluster. But these are not freed for the individual unless he has acquired skill in reading and a desire to sample the right sort of experiences in his reading. Thus the teacher of high-school English faces the dual responsibility of developing new or reviving old reading skills and directing the reading interests of the individual into wholesome channels.

Tests of Literary Acquaintance

The measurement of outcomes in literature has quite largely been confined to the knowledges and skills resulting from instruction, since these objective features are easily observed and measured. Among the tests designed to serve this purpose are the *Center-Durost Literature Acquaintance Test* [23] and the Satterfield *Objective Tests in English*.[24] The former, for high-school juniors and seniors, uses three-response multiple-choice items entirely in measuring pupil acquaintance with quotations, excerpts, or episodes taken largely from widely taught prose selections but including also a liberal sprinkling of well-known poems. The latter consists of a series of some fifty separate tests for measuring the acquaintance of high-school pupils with important prose and poetry classics, plays, biographies, and orations and addresses. These tests are primarily concerned with the informational outcomes that should result from the study of secondary-school literature.

Tests of Literature Appreciation

Although ability to comprehend literature seems to be an essential prerequisite to literary appreciation, adequate comprehension is not necessarily accompanied by appreciation. However, it seems justifiable to conclude that the manner by which literary appreciation has been approached in most standardized tests in this field is mainly through a higher form of comprehension. The two major distinguishable varieties of tests are those in which the pupil is asked to (1) judge the relative literary quality of sample materials and (2) answer questions based on representative literary selections.

[23] Stella S. Center and Walter N. Durost, *Center-Durost Literature Acquaintance Test.* World Book Co., Yonkers, N. Y., 1953.
[24] Mable S. Satterfield and others, *Objective Tests in English.* Turner E. Smith and Co., Atlanta, Ga., 1926-41.

The Carroll *Prose Appreciation Tests* [25] and the *Rigg Poetry Judgment Test* [26] are of the first type. The pupil is asked to rank four short prose selections in order of literary merit from best to worst in each exercise of the Carroll tests. Separate forms are available for the junior and the senior high schools. In his test of poetry judgment, Rigg asks the high-school pupil to choose the better of two short selections, one of which is by a poet of established reputation and the other of which is an inferior parody. A sample item from this test appears on page 223 of Chapter 10.

Tests of the second and more common type are represented here by the Logasa-Wright *Tests for the Appreciation of Literature* [27] and the *Cooperative Literary Comprehension and Appreciation Test*.[28] The six tests of the Logasa-Wright set measure, in a sequence designed to recapitulate steps in the development of appreciation at the high-school level: (1) discovery of theme, (2) reader participation, (3) reaction to sensory images, (4) discrimination between good and poor comparisons, (5) appreciation of fresh as opposed to trite expressions, and (6) recognition of rhythm. The Cooperative test seeks to measure comprehension and appreciation in high-school pupils by testing their abilities to recognize literary devices, define the author's viewpoint or attitude, and identify verse patterns and meter.

SUGGESTED ACTIVITIES

1. Outline ten to twelve subsidiary or specific outcomes of music education for pupils of vocal or instrumental music at your level of educational specialization.
2. Devise from eight to ten test items for the measurement of acquaintance with one or several literary selections commonly taught at your level of educational interest.

TOPICS FOR DISCUSSION

1. Is there reason to assume that achievement in the fine arts cannot be measured objectively?
2. What sorts of abilities do musical talent tests measure?
3. How do musical aptitude tests differ in nature from musical talent tests?

[25] Herbert A. Carroll, *Prose Appreciation Tests*. Educational Test Bureau, Minneapolis, Minn., 1932.
[26] Melvin G. Rigg, *Rigg Poetry Judgment Test*. Bureau of Educational Research and Service, State University of Iowa, Iowa City, 1942.
[27] Hannah Logasa and Martha M. Wright, *Tests for the Appreciation of Literature*. Public School Publishing Co., Bloomington, Ill., 1926.
[28] Mary Willis and H. A. Domincovich, *Cooperative Literary Comprehension and Appreciation Test*. Educational Testing Service, Princeton, N. J., 1943.

4. What is the nature of tests measuring talent for instrumental music?
5. What are the major types of aims in music education?
6. Briefly discuss and illustrate the manner in which musical knowledge and musical skills are measured.
7. What is the status of standardized tests of musical appreciation?
8. What similarities in the basic problems of measurement do you see in the fields of music and art?
9. What are the major classes of general outcomes in art instruction?
10. Which of the art tests described here seem most adequately to measure the major features of accomplishment in art?
11. What are the general characteristics of literature acquaintance tests?
12. How well do you think literature appreciation tests accomplish their purpose?

SELECTED REFERENCES

ASHTON, LOIS. "An Art Quiz for Students of the Classics." *Classical Journal*, 39:551-54; June 1944.

BARNES, MELVIN W. "A Technique for Testing Understanding of the Visual Arts." *Educational and Psychological Measurement*, 2:349-52; October 1942.

BEITTEL, KENNETH R. "Art." *Encyclopedia of Educational Research*. Third edition. New York: Macmillan Co., 1960. p. 77-87.

BROOKS, B. MARIAN, AND BROWN, HARRY A. *Music Education in the Elementary School*. New York: American Book Co., 1946. Chapter 16.

BRYSON, LYMAN L. "American Opportunity in Art Education." *This Is Art Education*. 1952 Yearbook of the National Art Education Association. Kutztown, Pa.: The Association, 1952. p. 9-24.

BUROS, OSCAR K., editor. *The Fifth Mental Measurements Yearbook*. Highland Park, N. J.: Gryphon Press, 1959. p. 363-67, 376-87.

BUROS, OSCAR K., editor. *The Fourth Mental Measurements Yearbook*. Highland Park, N. J.: Gryphon Press, 1953. p. 317-23, 335-48.

BUROS, OSCAR K., editor. *The Third Mental Measurements Yearbook*. New Brunswick, N. J.: Rutgers University Press, 1949. p. 239-44, 257-64.

CAIN, THERON. "The Objective Measurement of Accuracy in Drawings." *American Journal of Psychology*, 56:32-53; January 1943.

COHEN, JOZEF B. "A Scale for the Measurement of Attitude toward the Aesthetic Value." *Journal of Psychology*, 12:75-79; July 1941.

EBERHART, WILFRED. "Evaluating the Leisure Reading of High-School Pupils." *School Review*, 47:257-69; April 1939.

EBERHART, WILFRED. "The Teaching of Literature: An Approach to Evaluation." *Educational Research Bulletin*, 17:1-6, 27-28; January 19, 1938.

FARNSWORTH, PAUL R. *Musical Taste: Its Measurement and Cultural Nature*. Education-Psychology Series, Vol. II, No. 1. Stanford, Calif.: Stanford University Press, 1950.

FARNSWORTH, PAUL R. "Rating Scales for Musical Interests." *Journal of Psychology*, 28:245-53; July 1949.

FAULKNER, RAY N. "Evaluation in Art." *Journal of Educational Research*, 35:544-54; March 1942.

FAULKNER, RAY N. "Standards of Value of Art." *Art in American Life and Education.* Fortieth Yearbook of the National Society for the Study of Education. Bloomington, Ill.: Public School Publishing Co., 1941. Chapter 27.

GERBERICH, J. RAYMOND. *Specimen Objective Test Items: A Guide to Achievement Test Construction.* New York: Longmans, Greeen and Co., 1956. p. 311-12, 332-33.

GILDERSLEEVE, GLENN. "Standards and the Evaluation and Measurement of Achievement in Music." *Music Education.* Thirty-Fifth Yearbook of the National Society for the Study of Education, Part II. Bloomington, Ill.: Public School Publishing Co., 1936. Chapter 19.

GORDON, DONALD A. "Methodology in the Study of Art Evaluation." *Journal of Aesthetics and Art Criticism,* 10:338-52; June 1952.

GREENE, HARRY A., JORGENSEN, ALBERT N., AND GERBERICH, J. RAYMOND. *Measurement and Evaluation in the Elementary School.* Second edition. New York: Longmans, Green and Co., 1953. Chapter 20.

GREENE, HARRY A., JORGENSEN, ALBERT N., AND GERBERICH, J. RAYMOND. *Measurement and Evaluation in the Secondary School.* Second edition. New York: Longmans, Green and Co., 1954. Chapter 21.

HARRIS, CHESTER W. "Measurement of Comprehension of Literature." *School Review,* 56:280-89, 332-42; May and June 1948.

HARRIS, CHESTER W.; BETTELHEIM, BRUNO; AND DIEDERICH, PAUL B. "Aspects of Appreciation." *Appraising and Recording Student Progress.* New York: Harper and Brothers, 1942. Chapter 4.

HENDRICKSON, GORDON. "Music." *Encyclopedia of Educational Research.* Third edition. New York: Macmillan Co., 1960. p. 905-16.

KINTER, MADALINE. *The Measurement of Artistic Abilities: A Survey of Scientific Studies in the Field of Graphic Arts.* New York: Psychological Corporation, 1933.

LARK-HOROVITZ, BETTY. "On Art Appreciation of Children: I. Preference of Picture Subjects in General; II. Portrait Preference Study; III. Textile-Pattern Preference Study." *Journal of Educational Research,* 31:118-37, 572-98; 33:7-35; October 1937, April 1938, and September 1939.

LEONHARD, CHARLES. "Evaluation in Music Education." *Basic Concepts in Music Education.* Fifty-Seventh Yearbook of the National Society for the Study of Education, Part I. Chicago: University of Chicago Press, 1958. Chapter 13.

LOBAN, WALTER. "Evaluating Growth in the Study of Literature." *English Journal,* 37:277-83; June 1948.

MEIER, NORMAN C. "Recent Research in the Psychology of Art." *Art in American Life and Education.* Fortieth Yearbook of the National Society for the Study of Education. Bloomington, Ill.: Public School Publishing Co., 1941. Chapter 26.

MUELLER, KATE H. "Studies in Music Appreciation—I. A Program of Testing; II. Measuring the Listener's Recognition of Formal Musical Structure." *Journal of Research in Music Education,* 4:3-17; Spring 1956.

MURSELL, JAMES L., AND OTHERS. "The Measurement of Understanding in the Fine Arts." *The Measurement of Understanding.* Forty-Fifth Yearbook of the National Society for the Study of Education, Part I. Chicago: University of Chicago Press, 1946. Chapter 10.

POOLEY, ROBERT C. "English—Literature." *Encyclopedia of Educational Research.* Third edition. New York: Macmillan Co., 1960. p. 470-78.

SCHULTZ, HAROLD A., ROOS, FRANK J., AND MOORE, J. E. "Art Education." *Encyclopedia of Educational Research.* Revised edition. New York: Macmillan Co., 1950. p. 64-72.

WATKINS, JOHN G. "Objective Measurement of Instrumental Performance." *Teachers College Record,* 44:376-77; February 1943.

WHITE, VERNA, AND ENOCHS, J. B. "Testing the Reading and Interpretation of Literature." *English Journal,* 33:171-77; April 1944.

WOODS, ROY C., AND MARTIN, LUREATA R. "Testing in Musical Education." *Educational and Psychological Measurement,* 3:29-42; Spring 1943.

22

INDUSTRIAL ARTS AND HOME ECONOMICS

The following aspects of measurement and evaluation in the industrial arts and home economics are treated in this chapter:

A. Scope of industrial education.
B. Purposes and aims of industrial arts.
C. Aptitude and prognostic tests in industrial arts.
D. Measurement of industrial arts achievement.
E. Sources of achievement tests in industrial arts.
F. Outcomes of instruction in home economics.
G. Standardized achievement tests in home economics.
H. Informal objective and performance testing in home economics.

The demand both for vocational education and practical arts education has grown rapidly during the past several decades. There seems to be no reason to expect that this demand will diminish in the years ahead. Industrial arts and home economics education have proved to be a profitable investment for society, since these subjects contribute to the making of citizens as well as to the education of industrial workers and homemakers. In the course of the development of a progressive social economy, it may become desirable for a large proportion of the population to acquire a certain amount of education in the practical arts.

1. SCOPE AND AIMS OF INDUSTRIAL ARTS

Formerly vocational courses were designed to prepare the individual for a more effective entrance into and pursuit of a particular kind of occupation. In the modern educational program courses of this type are relatively unimportant, however, because of the high state of specialization of the industrial system. Today, practically all industrial organizations employing any number of workers maintain their own training schools in which the workers are taught their specific tasks under factory conditions.

Scope of Industrial Education

These introductory remarks do not mean that industrial education is not receiving any emphasis in the general program of education. They merely show that the emphasis has changed. Specialization in the vocations and in manufacturing processes has made it more and more important that the school build up a rich prevocational background rather than technical skill. This the manual and industrial arts courses of the junior and senior high schools are now attempting to do. The manual arts courses have a place in the general program of education corresponding to their effectiveness in helping men to become socially efficient. Such courses contribute to social efficiency in different ways.

In the elementary grades, the individual pupil is best served by the manual arts courses that give him a broad foundation of firsthand contact with a large variety of materials and processes rather than specific vocational or technical training. Here the aim is not so much to teach techniques as it is to stimulate and guide the individual's natural constructive activity and to utilize the opportunities that naturally present themselves at this age for expression through concrete materials. In the junior-high-school grades it may be assumed that the child is ready, both mentally and physically, to form definite habits and to develop definite skills in the use of his hands. The end sought may be vocational, general, or both, but in any case the manual arts should be so correct in technique, should place such emphasis on fundamental processes, and should be so closely in harmony with industry that they will have distinctly vocational values.

A general summary of the industrial education courses is difficult to make because of the number and types of courses. Among those usually offered in the various junior and senior high schools are manual training, or woodworking and cabinetmaking; carpentry; aeronautics; plumbing; home mechanics; consumer education; automobile mechanics; mechanical drawing; and not only general shop but also electrical, machine, metal, and print shops.

Purposes of Industrial Arts Courses

Industrial arts courses must contribute in a very definite sense to the general educational objectives of the secondary school. The aims of industrial arts courses, while expressed in many different forms, may be briefly stated as follows:

I. To offer exploratory industrial activities to aid in revealing interests, aptitudes, and vocational possibilities; such exploratory values are noted in the following "self-finding" aims:
   1. To try out individual interests, inclinations, and abilities for industrial pursuits
   2. To provide for the industrial needs of pupils who would not remain for academic education alone
   3. To help pupils to choose future courses more wisely in secondary and higher education
II. To provide general manual arts experiences of common value to all pupils who elect such work; such common values are found in the following consumers' or utilizers' aims:
   1. To develop "handyman" abilities through repair and construction work for home, shop, and office
   2. To assist in better choice and use of industrial products and service
   3. To gain sympathetic attitudes toward other workers and their work
   4. To appreciate economic production by firsthand experience in production work
III. To offer opportunity for beginning specialized preparation for entrance into chosen industrial fields
   A. Such opportunity should provide guidance and limited training facilities of the types that are included in the following aims:
      1. To assist in the final selection of a promising career
      2. To extend the tryout activity to meet the preparatory-vocational needs of pupils who must leave school with a minimum of preparation
      3. To provide supplementary training through coordinated shop-work and related schoolwork in mathematics, science, and drawing
      4. To offer opportunities for commercial experiences through cooperation with outside industrial agencies
   B. The more intensive industrial courses to be formulated to serve two purposes:
      1. To meet the needs of boys with mechanical ability who might profit more by industrial work than by the regular courses of study
      2. To assist those who remain only a short time in school and who need short, intensive courses of training before entering industry

Aims of Instruction in Industrial Arts

Throughout all industrial arts education the solving of problems and the training of individuals to meet new and unexpected situations intelligently, or training in creative or constructive thinking, should be emphasized. The following summary statements of the teaching aims of industrial arts express these modern objectives quite concisely, and in a form that should be of real assistance to the student or teacher interested in the measurement of understandings in the industrial arts field.[1]

1. Ability to express one's self through planning and constructing projects, using common tools and a variety of construction materials, typical of industry.
2. Discovery of aptitudes and reactions contributing to the maturing of life interests, both of a vocational and of an avocational character.
3. Understanding of industry and its products and services, together with their influence in determining patterns of living in modern society.
4. Ability to read and make working drawings for planning and constructing useful projects typical of modern industry.
5. The ability to choose industrial products with reference to design, pleasing color combinations, and durability; and to maintain and service such products.
6. Growth in abilities and attitudes related to mathematics, science, and the language arts, and to work habits, safety practices, and cooperation with others.

2. APTITUDE AND PROGNOSTIC TESTS IN INDUSTRIAL ARTS

Mechanical aptitude is the special capacity of the individual to deal successfully with mechanical devices and to acquire knowledge essential to their selection and operation during the training process. Individuals with large measures of mechanical aptitude, other things being equal, readily respond to instruction along mechanical lines. On the other hand, individuals with low mechanical abilities are likely to react slowly regardless of the quality of instruction or the opportunities they are given to work with mechanical devices.

A large portion of the gainfully employed population in the United States is dependent in some measure for its economic success on the possession of mechanical ability. It thus becomes apparent that a knowledge of

---

[1] Maris M. Proffitt, E. E. Ericson, and Louis V. Newkirk, "The Measurement of Understanding in Industrial Arts." *The Measurement of Understanding,* Forty-Fifth Yearbook of the National Society for the Study of Education, Part I. University of Chicago Press, Chicago, 1946. p. 303-5.

the pupil's mechanical ability is important to the teacher from both the guidance and the instructional point of view. Knowledge of the fact that an individual has high or low mechanical aptitude provides an objective basis for guiding him into or out of vocations that involve high degrees of these abilities.

Mechanical Aptitude Tests

A wide variety of tests, some of them now out of print, have been constructed for the purpose of measuring mechanical aptitudes. These range from parts of the multiaptitude batteries discussed in Chapter 6 to separate tests or series of related tests. The samples shown on page 113 of Chapter 6 from the *Differential Aptitude Tests,* particularly the items from the space relations and mechanical reasoning parts, are quite representative of item types appearing in many of these tests.

One of the most widely used measures of mechanical aptitude is the *Revised Minnesota Paper Form Board Test,*[2] an adaptation of a pioneer instrument [3] of this type published in 1930. Each of the 64 multiple-choice items consists of a geometrical figure cut into several parts and five "assembled" geometrical figures. The success of the pupil from age nine upward in selecting the appropriate assembly is a measure of his ability to think spatially in two dimensions, or of his mechanical aptitude.

Three other related tests of this general type are designed to measure mechanical insight,[4] object visualization,[5] and space relations ability.[6] These tests, for use in Grade 9 and above, are variously intended to measure aptitude for solving problems encountered in mechanical work and to predict future success as draftsman, machinist, or mechanic, and even in architecture and engineering. The first two use items similar to the mechanical comprehension and space relations items pictured on page 113 and the third consists of items adapted from the techniques of the *Minnesota Paper Form Board Test.*

[2] Rensis Likert and William H. Quasha, *Revised Minnesota Paper Form Board Test,* Series MA. Psychological Corporation, New York, 1939.

[3] Donald G. Paterson and others, "Minnesota Paper Form Board Tests," *Minnesota Mechanical Ability Tests.* University of Minnesota Press, Minneapolis, Minn., 1930. p. 94-101.

[4] D. R. Miller, *Survey of Mechanical Insight,* Revised. California Test Bureau, Los Angeles, 1955.

[5] D. R. Miller, *Survey of Object Visualization,* Revised. California Test Bureau, Los Angeles, 1955.

[6] Harry W. Case and Floyd L. Ruch, *Survey of Space Relations Ability.* California Test Bureau, Los Angeles, 1944.

Prognostic Tests of Mechanical Abilities

Prognostic tests differ from aptitude tests primarily in their greater or at least their more obvious dependence on the acquired skills and abilities found to be prerequisite for success in subsequent activities, as is pointed out in Chapter 2. One test designated as prognostic and two related tests of mechanical comprehension are briefly described here to represent this second type of predictive test in the industrial and mechanical arts.

The *Prognostic Test of Mechanical Abilities* [7] is designed for use in Grades 7 to 12 for measuring abilities common to many mechanical occupations. It provides a total score and five part scores on (1) Arithmetic Computation Skills, (2) Reading Simple Drawings and Blueprints, (3) Knowledge and Use of Tools, (4) Spatial Relationships, and (5) Checking Measurements. An illustration from the part on reading drawings and blueprints appear on page 42 of Chapter 2.

Two tests of mechanical comprehension, one for boys in Grade 9 to 12 [8] and one for high-school girls and college women,[9] are designed for measuring ability to understand mechanical relationships that seem to be important in mechanical work and in technical and engineering training. Since these tests measure understanding, although not specific knowledge, of physical relationships and laws, they appear to belong in the category of prognostic tests.

3. MEASUREMENT OF ACHIEVEMENT IN INDUSTRIAL ARTS

Practically all of the rather numerous achievement tests of mechanical drawing and industrial arts published during the early history of standardized testing have gone out of print and even some of the more modern replacements of industrial arts tests are no longer listed in the catalogs of their publishers. One series of trade information tests constitutes practically all of the commercially available industrial arts and related vocational tests.

Testing in Industrial Arts

The student and teacher interested in measuring the achievement of pupils in industrial arts is practically forced to depend primarily on such

[7] J. Wayne Wrightstone and Charles E. O'Toole, *Prognostic Test of Mechanical Abilities.* California Test Bureau, Los Angeles, 1946.
[8] George K. Bennett, *Test of Mechanical Comprehension,* Form AA. Psychological Corporation, New York, 1940.
[9] George K. Bennett and Dinah E. Fry, *Test of Mechanical Comprehension,* Form W1. Psychological Corporation, New York, 1942.

resource materials as a yearbook of the National Society for the Study of Education,[10] the books by Newkirk and Greene [11] and Micheels and Karnes,[12] and a few bulletin and journal references listed at the end of this chapter for general guidance in this subject area.

Informal objective tests in industrial arts. Objective item forms useful in the area of industrial arts are varied in type. Several varieties of multiple-choice items are widely applicable. The rearrangement variety of matching item is well adapted to the measurement of knowledge concerning the sequence of steps in the performance of certain skill operations. Identification varieties, in which the pupil is asked to identify pictures or actual samples of woods or tools in simple recall items or matching exercises, are also very useful. An example of such a matching exercise appears on page 266 of this volume. This and the accompanying illustration of a classification variety of matching exercise on automobile maintenance show how two of the basic item forms can be used in industrial arts measurement.

SAMPLE TEST EXERCISE ON Automobile Maintenance [13]

DIRECTIONS: Listed below are several types of lubricants followed by automotive units that require one of these lubricants. You are to match each unit with the correct type of lubricant and place the identifying letter in the blank space provided. Use each letter (A, B, etc.) as many times as necessary. The first item is answered as an example.

A. engine oil
B. fibrous grease
C. gear oil

D. lubricant impregnated
E. penetrating dripless lubricant
F. pressure-gun lubricant

(C)	x. transmission		8. front-wheel bearings
	1. distributor		9. drag-link ends
	2. striker plate		10. spring pens
	3. universal joint		11. steering gear
	4. dovetail		12. carburetor air cleaner
	5. differential		13. spindle pin
	6. door hinges		14. drive-shaft center bearing
	7. generator		

Issues of *Industrial Arts and Vocational Education* carried many informal objective tests in their entirety and occasional accounts of performance

---

[10] Proffitt, Ericson, and Newkirk, *op. cit.* Chapter 16.

[11] Louis V. Newkirk and Harry A. Greene, *Tests and Measurements in Industrial Education.* John Wiley and Sons, Inc., New York, 1935.

[12] William J. Micheels and M. Ray Karnes, *Measuring Educational Achievement.* McGraw-Hill Book Co., Inc., New York, 1950.

[13] *Ibid.* p. 233.

tests over the period from 1935 to the early 1950s. Oldknow,[14] in fact, reported that 118 articles on testing appeared in this journal during the ten-year period from 1936 to 1945. Although many of the tests may well be helpful to industrial arts teachers, space limitations preclude more than their introduction in summary form in this volume. Table 33 indicates where 51 of the more recently published articles, classified by course areas, can be located. Gerberich [15] presented a bibliography of more than a hundred journal articles and other sources on testing in the industrial arts that lists many of the 51 and still other articles by author and title as well as by source.

Some idea of the variety of test samples to be found in the sources outlined in Table 33 can be obtained from the following listings of types of tests by subject areas.

(1) Aeronautics—aircraft sheet metal, fuel and oil systems, aerodynamics, and motors, propellors and carburetors

(2) Consumer education—metal and wood consumer goods

(3) Drawing—mechanical drawing, architectural and aircraft drafting, and orthographic projection and dimensioning

(4) Electrical shop—basic electricity, aircraft sources of electrical power, aircraft ignition systems, aircraft starters, and radar

(5) General shop—plastics, fasteners, and leatherworking

(6) Machine shop—basic skills and use of hand tools in automotive work

(7) Metal shop—general metal work and sheet metal work

(8) Print shop—basic printing skills and the platen press

(9) Woodworking shop—general woodworking and carpentry skills

Performance tests in industrial arts. Measurement of pupil attainments in industrial arts should give an important place to performance tests of both the product and the procedure variety. Such tests are necessary in measuring the skill outcomes, especially in such courses as shopwork and drawing. Industrial arts areas rank high among the school subjects in which pupils acquire skill in operations involving the construction and modification of materials. Consequently, Chapter 11, on performance testing, deals both indirectly and directly with methods and techniques that have wide significance for industrial arts teachers. The sample from a rating scale for fastenings that is shown on page 272 illustrates an analytical tool of product measurement. The discussion of counting and measuring techniques in that chapter and the illustration on pages 274 and 275 of how the latter can be used in evaluating the quality of workmanship

---

[14] J. T. Oldknow, "How to Improve Objective-Type Tests." *Industrial Arts and Vocational Education,* 33:49-51; February 1949.

[15] J. Raymond Gerberich, *Specimen Objective Test Items: A Guide to Achievement Test Construction.* Longmans, Green and Co., New York, 1956. p. 316-21.

TABLE 33

Sources of Informal Objective Tests in Industrial Arts Classified by Course Areas

Course Area	1946 [16]	1947 [17]					1948 [18]			1949 [19]	1950 [20]	1951 [21]	1953 [22]	ALL
	Jan.	Feb.	Mar.	Apr.	May	June	Feb.	Mar.	May	Feb.	Feb.	Feb.	Feb.	
Aeronautics									1	1	2	1	1	6
Consumer Education										2				2
Drawing		3	2	1	2	1	1			2	4			16
Shop: Electrical					1	1	1		1	3				7
General		2								1	1	1		5
Machine								2						2
Metal		2	1								1	1		5
Print		2										1	1	4
Woodworking	1						2				1			4
Totals	1	9	3	1	3	2	4	2	2	9	9	4	2	51

16 "Testing and Tests." *Industrial Arts and Vocational Education*, 35:19-23; January 1946.
17 "Testing and Tests." *Industrial Arts and Vocational Education*, 36: 56-77, 139ff., 163-65, 206-13, and 241-45; February, March, April, May, and June 1947.
18 "Testing and Tests." *Industrial Arts and Vocational Education*, 37:57-67, 18Aff., and 196-200; February, March, April, and May 1948.
19 "Testing and Tests." *Industrial Arts and Vocational Education*, 38:56-71; February 1949.
20 "Testing and Tests." *Industrial Arts and Vocational Education*, 39:44-59; February 1950.
21 "Testing and Tests." *Industrial Arts and Vocational Education*, 40:65-72; February 1951.
22 "Testing and Tests." *Industrial Arts and Vocational Education*, 42:34-46; February 1953.

in woodworking deal with a more comprehensive approach to product measurement.

Vocational and Trade Tests

Vocational and trade tests are designed to determine an individual's ability to perform the work of a specific occupation. Training or experience in the occupation are assumed, and the purpose is to measure the results of these or to find out what stage of progress the individual has achieved. This type of test, valuable as an aid in determining whether an individual should be recommended for a particular occupation requiring known standards of proficiency, has the advantage of being typical of occupational situations.

Standardized trade tests have not been widely used, although trade unions developed a few of them some years ago for use in many phases of trade work. Standardized tests of occupational proficiency suitable for use in rating those who pursue any kind of vocational preparatory training in public schools are not at all widely available at the present time. In fact, the authors are aware of only four such tests in industrial areas—for carpentry, welding, lathe operation, and sheetmetal work.[23]

4. NATURE AND OUTCOMES OF HOME ECONOMICS

The earliest concentration on cooking and sewing for girls in home economics was later supplanted by attention to such other, or broader, areas as food, clothing, textiles, furniture, equipment, and housing and to the growth, development, and relationships of all persons living in the home. Emphasis in modern home economics is placed on the home and in particular upon the persons who live in it.

Scope of Home Economics

Various dynamic aspects of the home and its occupants receive attention in home economics classes today. Among them are child development, nutrition, health, housing, home management, consumer education, social relations, use of leisure time, and personal development, as well as food preparation and clothing construction. Courses for boys tend less often to concentrate on cooking only and more often to include personal hygiene,

---

[23] Joseph Tiffin and others, *Purdue Trade Information Test:* (1) in *Carpentry,* (2) in *Engine Lathe Operation,* (3) in *Welding,* and (4) for *Sheetmetal Workers; Purdue Personnel Tests.* University Book Store, West Lafayette, Ind., 1951 to 1958.

selection and care of clothing, and other aspects of the boy's interactions with his home and the persons who live in it.

In the junior high school, home economics instruction emphasizes the role of helper and of home duties and responsibilities. A more responsible role is emphasized in the senior high school as a means of developing the learning outcomes necessary for effective participation in the life of a well-managed home.

Outcomes of Personal and Family Life Education

One of the useful statements of the outcomes of personal and family life education is that resulting from a study made by a joint committee of the American Home Economics Association and the American Council on Education, and reported by McGinnis and her colleagues [24] in a discussion of the measurement of understanding in home economics. The outline presented here is an adaptation and abbreviation of this highly detailed statement.

OUTCOMES OF EDUCATION FOR PERSONAL AND FAMILY LIFE

I. Personal Adjustment
   A. Health
      1. His own physical and mental health status
      2. Importance of seeking help and information on health
      3. Relations of health to personal, family, and community betterment
      4. First-aid and home nursing procedures
      5. Means of controlling communicable diseases and accidents
   B. Personal relations
      1. Means of achieving an attractive personal appearance
      2. Socially acceptable ways of behaving
      3. Ways of working well with people
      4. Desirability of sharing use and care of family possessions
      5. Importance of personal independence and friendly relationships
      6. Importance of wholesome attitude toward sex
      7. Ways of making friends of both sexes
   C. Vocational choice
      1. Demands of homemaking vocations in abilities and training
      2. Procedures for getting a job
      3. Relative values of payroll jobs and homemaking
II. Use of Time and Energy
      1. Methods of deciding what needs to be done
      2. Ways of comparing conflicting values and making choices
      3. Principles concerning the management of resources

[24] Esther McGinnis and others, "The Measurement of Understanding in Home Economics." *The Measurement of Understanding,* Forty-Fifth Yearbook of the National Society for the Study of Education, Part I. University of Chicago Press, Chicago, 1946. p. 254-57.

4. Ways of applying skill in maintaining standards of living
5. Ways of planning division of labor in the home

III. Use of Money
   1. Ways of anticipating and making plans for expenditures
   2. Methods of buying with optimum satisfaction
   3. Value of joint financial planning and records
   4. Banking procedures and use of credit
   5. Distribution and stability of income in the United States
   6. Effects of social and commercial pressures on buying habits
   7. Importance of insurance, annuities, savings, social security
   8. Relation of personal and family welfare to nation and world

IV. Family and Children
   A. Family
      1. Factors in courtship and successful marriage
      2. Biological aspects of marriage
      3. Importance of legal requirements and counseling services for marriage
      4. Kinds of family crises and ways of meeting them
      5. Adjustments among family members of different ages
      6. Importance of esthetic and cultural values in the home
      7. Ways of fostering and building traditions, ideals, values
      8. Acceptance of various racial, religious, and family patterns
      9. Ways of helping to maintain democracy in the home
   B. Children
      1. Reasons children behave as they do
      2. Constituents of normal growth—physical, mental, social, emotional
      3. Significance of children for the family and society
      4. Importance of careful guidance of play and selection of equipment
      5. Influence of environment on security and development

V. Foods and Nutrition
   1. Ways of ordering appropriate food in public places
   2. Importance of acceptable table manners
   3. Principles of food preservation
   4. Factors in planning of individual and family meals
   5. Cookery principles and ability to use them
   6. Methods of serving food attractively
   7. Methods of preparing and serving foods for the sick
   8. Purposes and effects of government regulations concerning foods
   9. Principles of child nutrition and feeding

VI. Clothing and Textiles
   1. Methods of harmonizing textures, colors, and styles
   2. Principles of selecting clothing and household fabrics
   3. Ways of constructing, repairing, and altering clothes, furnishings
   4. Principles of laundering clothes and fabrics
   5. Methods of using and maintaining a sewing machine

VII. The Home
   1. Need for cooperation in planning for housing
   2. Factors to consider in selection of family living quarters
   3. Principles of arranging furniture and furnishings
   4. Care of furnishings and equipment
   5. Principles of planning attractive home grounds

5. MEASUREMENT OF ACHIEVEMENT IN HOME ECONOMICS

Prior to 1930, standardized tests in home economics were almost entirely factual tests. Since that date, accompanying the increasing recognition of the fact that changes in behavior and attitudes must be measured, tests and scales appeared in this field for the measurement of various skills, applications, attitudes, and appreciations. Among such instruments were scales for measuring sewing ability, quality of foods prepared by the pupil, and attitudes toward homemaking activities, as well as tests in the areas of house design and furnishing, foods, and household management. Although a few of these instruments are still available, a number are now out of print. The result is that the teacher and student of home economics almost certainly must supplement standardized tests with informal objective tests and evaluation techniques in any well-rounded program of classroom achievement measurement.

Standardized Measures of Achievement in Home Economics

Standardized instruments for the measurement of achievement in home economics are considerably more adequate in the area of foods than in the other basic areas of clothing and household management, but even here they are neither numerous nor very recent in publication dates. Three types of instruments, one of which is not ordinarily classified as a tool of achievement measurement, can be distinguished: (1) achievement tests, (2) check lists and score cards, and (3) interest inventories.

Tests on foods and the home. The *Illinois Foods Test*,[25] originally prepared in 1924 by the test committee of the Illinois Home Economics Association, measures knowledge in fourteen important aspects of foods, their preparation and sanitation, and the etiquette of food service. The two-part *Unit Scales of Attainment in Foods and Household Management* [26] make use of multiple-choice, multiple-response, and occasional simple recall items in measuring the factual knowledge necessary for efficient performance in these two areas of home economics.

The *Minnesota House Design and House Furnishing Test* [27] measures the ability of the pupil to judge and discriminate between good and poor design in house and house furnishing samples presented to her in the

[25] Test Committee of the Illinois Home Economics Association, *Information Test on Foods: Illinois Foods Test*, Revised. Public School Publishing Co., Bloomington, Ill., 1939.

[26] Ethel B. Reeve and Clara M. Brown, *Unit Scales of Attainment in Foods and Household Management*. Educational Test Bureau, Minneapolis, Minn., 1933.

[27] Clara M. Brown, Nell White, and Muriel F. Puhr, *Minnesota House Design and House Furnishing Test*. University of Minnesota Press, Minneapolis, Minn., 1938.

form of photographs. The instrument is intended for the measurement of the degree to which study of related art results in improved taste on the part of pupils.

Check lists and score cards on foods. Two instruments worthy of note are the *Minnesota Check List for Food Preparation and Serving* [28] and the Brown *Food Score Cards.*[29] The check list provides a five-point scale for the teacher's use in rating fourteen aspects of food preparation and serving after having observed individual pupils or small groups of pupils in situations involving the opportunity to use the desirable techniques. The score cards, available for 53 items of food commonly prepared in the home economics laboratory, provide variously for different foods for ratings on such characteristics as appearance, color, consistency, flavor, lightness, moisture content, size, taste, tenderness, and texture. For example, bacon is rated on only four points, whereas nine of the ten characteristics are used in the rating of baking powder biscuit. An illustration of the score card for waffles is shown on page 272 of this volume.

Home economics interest inventory. One of the few interest inventories designed for use in a special area of instruction is found in home economics. The *Johnson Home Economics Interest Inventory,*[30] for use in Grade 12 and above, is designed to measure the specialized interests of girls who have studied the subject and who plan to continue in some aspect of it. The instrument makes no pretense of measuring aptitude or any of the other factors beyond interests that influence success in home economics activities. Differential scoring of responses to the 300-item inventory results in scores that can be used for predicting success in fourteen areas of specialization ranging from the designing to the merchandising of clothes, from the promotion of foods to the direction of food services, and from secondary-school teaching to working with young children.

Informal Objective Testing in Home Economics

Two extensive treatments of informal objective testing and evaluation in home economics written by Brown,[31] later Arny,[32] include many sample

---

[28] Clara M. Brown and others, *Minnesota Check List for Food Preparation and Serving,* Third edition. University of Minnesota Press, Minneapolis, Minn., 1951.

[29] Clara M. Brown and others, *Food Score Cards.* University of Minnesota Press, Minneapolis, Minn., 1940.

[30] Hildegarde Johnson, *Johnson Home Economics Interest Inventory.* Iowa State College, Ames, 1955.

[31] Clara M. Brown, *Evaluation and Investigation in Home Economics.* F. S. Crofts and Co., New York, 1941.

[32] Clara B. Arny, *Evaluation in Home Economics.* Appleton-Century-Crofts, Inc., New York, 1953.

items and exercises for use in measuring achievement in home economics. Although some materials are more suitable for college than for high-school courses, others are appropriate for use with high-school girls. Illustrations and accompanying discussions appear for foods and nutrition, dietetics, clothing, homemaking, household equipment, house planning and furnishing, child welfare, home nursing, and many other general and special aspects of the subject.

Paper-and-pencil testing in home economics. Only one group of sample items is presented here to illustrate possible paper-and-pencil testing techniques in home economics. The accompanying excerpt shows a group of matching items of the classification variety that is intended for the measurement of factual knowledge plus understanding. The sample is from the food portion of the home economics curriculum.

SAMPLE OF Test Exercise in Foods [33]

To which food group does each of the following descriptions apply?

Food Groups

1. Cereals
2. Fruits—citrus
3. Fruits—other
4. Milk and cheese

5. Potatoes and sweet potatoes
6. Vegetables—green and yellow
7. Vegetables—other
8. Sugars and sweets

Descriptions of Characteristics

_____1. Is the cheapest source of Vitamin A.
_____2. Is an inexpensive source of energy and protein.
_____3. Provides the highest percentage of riboflavin.
_____4. Is the poorest source of vitamins.
_____5. Supplies the American people with the largest amount of ascorbic acid.

Performance testing in home economics. Three other test exercises, all of the performance type, appear in this volume to illustrate achievement testing in clothing and textiles. The accompanying excerpt illustrates the use of samples of ten different dress fabrics to supplement the paper-and-pencil test items. A somewhat more complex but fundamentally similar sample is shown on page 267 of Chapter 11. Both of these are classified as object tests, since they combine the use of objects, or materials, with paper-and-pencil testing techniques. The other example, pictured and described on pages 275 and 276 of Chapter 11, illustrates a product variety of test in clothing construction sometimes called a miniature test because of the reduced size of the materials used by the girls as they take the test.

[33] *Ibid.* p. 115-16.

SAMPLE OF Test Exercise in Textiles [34]

Directions: In Envelope X are 10 fabrics (labeled A-J). In the blank in front of each description write the letter corresponding to the fabric to which it applies. More than one description may apply to the same fabric.

Descriptions

_____1. May be combined with sample B to form a monochromatic color harmony.

_____2. May be used as a belt on a dress made of sample G to form an analogous harmony.

_____3. May be used with sample A to form a striking complementary harmony.

_____4. May be used with sample D to form a subdued but pleasing complementary harmony.

_____5. May be combined with sample C to make an analogous harmony which would be more becoming to a person with warm coloring than with cool coloring.

SUGGESTED ACTIVITIES

1. List a number of representative instructional outcomes from some specific area of industrial arts or home economics, e.g., general shop or clothing.
2. Devise a short performance testing instrument, such as a check list or score card, for measuring achievement in some relatively simple and unitary type of skill in industrial arts or home economics.

TOPICS FOR DISCUSSION

1. In what ways are the demands made on industrial education today different from those of twenty years ago? Why?
2. What are some of the major purposes and aims of instruction in industrial arts?
3. How do aptitude tests differ from prognostic tests in industrial arts?
4. What is the present status of standardized testing in industrial arts?
5. What are the major sources of guidance for persons interested in industrial arts achievement testing?
6. What types of understandings desirably result from the study of home economics?
7. What do you consider to be the greatest weaknesses of the standardized tests now available in home economics?
8. In what way are interests in home economics properly to be considered as instructional outcomes?
9. What is the status of informal objective testing in home economics?
10. What are a few of the performance testing techniques useful in achievement measurement in home economics?

[34] *Ibid.* p. 63.

SELECTED REFERENCES

ARNY, CLARA B. *Evaluation in Home Economics.* New York: Appleton-Century-Crofts, Inc., 1953.

BECKLEY, DONALD K., AND SMITH, LEO F. "Constructing Achievement Tests." *Industrial Arts and Vocational Education,* 34:52-54; February 1945.

BECKLEY, DONALD K., AND SMITH, LEO F. "Test Forms for Use in Vocational Education." *Industrial Arts and Vocational Education,* 36:56-59; February 1947.

BENNETT, GEORGE K., AND CRUIKSHANK, RUTH M. *A Summary of Manual and Mechanical Ability Tests.* New York: Psychological Corporation, 1942.

BOWERS, VICTOR L. "Why Be Concerned with Testing?" *Industrial Arts and Vocational Education,* 36:241-42; June 1947.

BROWN, CLARA M. *Evaluation and Investigation in Home Economics.* New York: F. S. Crofts and Co., 1941.

BROWN, SARA ANN. "Home Economics." *Encyclopedia of Educational Research.* Third edition. New York: Macmillan Co., 1960. p. 668-75.

BUROS, OSCAR K., editor. *The Fifth Mental Measurements Yearbook.* Highland Park, N. J.: Gryphon Press, 1959. p. 648-50, 901-20.

BUROS, OSCAR K., editor. *The Fourth Mental Measurements Yearbook.* Highland Park, N. J.: Gryphon Press, 1953. p. 553-59, 751-68.

BUROS, OSCAR K., editor. *The Third Mental Measurements Yearbook.* New Brunswick, N. J.: Rutgers University Press, 1949. p. 481-83, 683-723.

CHADDERTON, HESTER. "Evaluation of Evidence in Measurement." *Practical Home Economics,* 13:363, 374-75; December 1935.

CHADDERTON, HESTER. "Home Economics Education." *Encyclopedia of Educational Research.* Revised edition. New York: Macmillan Co., 1950. p. 556-64.

CHADDERTON, HESTER. "Measurement in Home Economics Education." *Practical Home Economics,* 13:289, 308-9; October 1935.

CHADDERTON, HESTER. "Planning a Measurement Program." *Practical Home Economics,* 13:322, 341-42; November 1935.

ERICKSON, MARCUS E. "Examination in School-Shop Safety." *Industrial Arts and Vocational Education,* 44:134-36; April 1955.

ERICKSON, MARCUS E. "Evaluation of Student Progress in the Industrial Arts." *Industrial Arts and Vocational Education,* 35:441-43; December 1946.

GERBERICH, J. RAYMOND. *Specimen Objective Test Items: A Guide to Achievement Test Construction.* New York: Longmans, Green and Co., 1956. p. 315-21.

GREENE, HARRY A., JORGENSEN, ALBERT N., AND GERBERICH, J. RAYMOND. *Measurement and Evaluation in the Secondary School.* Second edition. New York: Longmans, Green and Co., 1954. Chapter 22.

HUSTON, HAZEL H. "Measuring Achievement in Home Economics." *Journal of Home Economics,* 29:19-22; January 1937.

HUTCHCROFT, C. ROBERT. "Industrial Arts." *Encyclopedia of Educational Research.* Third edition. New York: Macmillan Co., 1960. p. 688-96.

JARVIS, JOHN A. "Evaluation of Test Results." *Industrial Arts and Vocational Education,* 38:41-44; February 1949.

KARNES, M. RAY. "Concepts of Evaluation." *Problems and Issues in Industrial Arts Teacher Education.* Fifth Yearbook of the American Council on Industrial Arts Teacher Education. Manhasset, N. Y.: The Council, 1956. Chapter 6.

MAYS, A. B. "Industrial Education." *Encyclopedia of Educational Research.* Revised edition. New York: Macmillan Co., 1950. p. 571-88.

McGINNIS, ESTHER, AND OTHERS. "The Measurement of Understanding in Home Economics." *The Measurement of Understanding.* Forty-Fifth Yearbook of the National Society for the Study of Education, Part I. Chicago: University of Chicago Press, 1946. Chapter 13.

MICHEELS, WILLIAM J. "Educational Evaluation." *A Sourcebook of Readings in Education for Use in Industrial Arts Teacher Education.* Sixth Yearbook of the American Council on Industrial Arts Teacher Education. Manhasset, N. Y.: The Council, 1957. Chapter 7.

MICHEELS, WILLIAM J., AND KARNES, M. RAY. *Measuring Educational Achievement.* New York: McGraw-Hill Book Co., Inc., 1950. Chapters 11-14.

MURRY, J. L. "Unit Test on Automobile Radios." *Industrial Arts and Vocational Education,* 43:53-54; February 1954.

NEWKIRK, LOUIS V., AND GREENE, HARRY A. *Tests and Measurements in Industrial Education.* New York: John Wiley and Sons, Inc., 1935.

OLDKNOW, J. T. "How to Improve Objective-Type Tests." *Industrial Arts and Vocational Education,* 38:49-51; February 1949.

PENDERED, NORMAN C. "Test Items That Teach." *Industrial Arts and Vocational Education,* 45:4-6; January 1956.

PRICE, HAZEL H. "Measuring Ability to Make Wise Decisions." *Journal of Home Economics,* 35:349-52; June 1943.

PROFFITT, MARIS M., ERICSON, E. E., AND NEWKIRK, LOUIS V. "The Measurement of Understanding in Industrial Arts." *The Measurement of Understanding.* Forty-Fifth Yearbook of the National Society for the Study of Education, Part I. Chicago: University of Chicago Press, 1946. Chapter 16.

PUTNAM, FLORENCE E. "Improving the Teacher-Made Test." *Practical Home Economics,* 19:168-69; May 1941.

ROTHROCK, THURSTON M. "Checking the Student's Knowledge with a Camera." *Industrial Arts and Vocational Education,* 38:19-22; January 1949.

SCHWALM, R. A. "Industrial Arts Aptitude Test." *Industrial Arts and Vocational Education,* 35:321-24; September 1946.

SELLON, WILLIAM A. "The Importance of Constructing Good Tests." *Industrial Arts and Vocational Education,* 40:63-64; February 1951.

SIMNICHT, GEORGE L. "General Test for Girls' Home Mechanics." *Industrial Arts and Vocational Education,* 30:60-62; February 1941.

SIRO, EINAR E. "Performance Tests and Objective Observation." *Industrial Arts and Vocational Education,* 32:162-65; April 1943.

SMITH, EUGENIA. "Testing Can Be Teaching." *Practical Home Economics,* 34:10-11, 39; December 1955.

WILBER, GORDON O. *Industrial Arts in General Education.* Second edition. Scranton, Penn.: International Textbook Co., 1954. Chapter 19, Appendices I to III.

23

BUSINESS EDUCATION

The following aspects of business education related to measurement and evaluation are presented and discussed in this chapter:

A. Aims and objectives of business education.
B. Aptitude tests in typewriting and stenography.
C. Clerical and sales aptitude tests.
D. Content and skill subjects in business education.
E. Measurement of achievement in the content areas of business education.
F. Measurement of achievement in the skill areas of business education.
G. Achievement tests for entrance into business careers.

Business education is a field in which the emphases have changed materially during the last several decades. Originally planned only for pupils wishing training in office techniques for vocational use, the curriculum of business education during the early years of the century consisted largely of such courses as typewriting, shorthand, bookkeeping, and penmanship. The first three of these continue today to be the courses most commonly offered, but they have been supplemented by a wide variety of new courses.

1. AIMS AND OBJECTIVES OF BUSINESS EDUCATION

The major aspects of business education as outlined by Price and his colleagues [1] consist of (1) basic business education, with emphasis on consumer efficiency, (2) technical business education, stressing training for jobs, and (3) distributive education, concerned primarily with the

[1] Ray G. Price and others, "Business Education." *Encyclopedia of Educational Research,* Revised edition. Macmillan Co., New York, 1950. p. 115-26.

selling of goods and services. Consumer problems have received direct attention in business education only during the last twenty or so years, and distributive education has been increasingly emphasized of late. Programs of technical business education have been modified least. Even here, however, the traditional vocational objectives have been supplemented by personal-use values, particularly in typewriting, as the number and popularity of courses in personal typewriting increase.

Basic business education courses are best represented by such non-technical subjects as economic geography, consumer problems, bookkeeping, business law, and junior business training. Technical business education includes courses in typewriting, shorthand and transcription, general clerical training, and business arithmetic, but here the personal-use as well as the technical values receive direct attention. The variety of courses in distributive education is great, but merchandise information, salesmanship, retailing, store methods and systems, and occupational relations probably are the most widely offered.

Adjustment of the individual to his business environment is a primary aim of business education. Involved in this are the two following types of major aims, the first of which applies to nontechnical needs and the second of which applies to vocational needs.[2]

1. Training in those phases of business that concern every member of organized society
   a. Education of persons to be intelligent consumers of the services of business
   b. Education of persons to a clear understanding of the nation's economy
2. Training in technical or specific vocational skills and abilities
   a. Training in specific job skills
   b. Development of ability to use these skills in the environment of business

So rapidly has the shift of emphasis taken place recently that the first of these major aims, the provision of business education for the types of business activities met by all persons, has probably come to be the dominant purpose in business education at the secondary-school level.

2. APTITUDE AND PROGNOSTIC TESTS IN BUSINESS EDUCATION

Aptitude and prognostic tests in business education differ in the manner pointed out in Chapter 2 and also commented upon in several of the pre-

[2] Herbert A. Tonne, Estelle L. Popham, and M. Herbert Freeman, *Methods of Teaching Business Subjects.* Gregg Publishing Division, McGraw-Hill Book Co., Inc., New York, 1949. p. 8.

ceding chapters dealing with other school subjects. These types of predictive tests occur here primarily for typing, shorthand and stenography, and clerical work. Their values lie primarily in the use of results for the guidance of pupils into or away from business education curricula. The first type of test presupposes little or no previous experience with the business education subjects for which the tests are given, whereas the latter assumes a certain amount of experience, either specific or general, with the types of abilities necessary for the form of office work in question.

Typing Aptitude Tests

A test for the measurement of aptitude for typewriting and other keyboard tasks, *The Tapping Test,* involves a selective manual performance by the pupil that simulates motions involved in the operation of a typewriter. The accompanying illustration from the directions on the cover of the test booklet indicates the manner by which colored pads attached

EXCERPT FROM *The Tapping Test* [3]

[3] John C. Flanagan, *The Tapping Test.* The Author, Pittsburgh, Pa., 1959.

to the pupil's fingers are used by him in the attempt to put appropriately colored dots in appropriate circles. Pupils are expected to put the proper pattern of dots in as many of the 108 lines of circles in the entire test as they can in the time allowed in seven different short work periods. This speeded test is designed to measure two elements predictive of success in using the typewriter and other keyboard machines. These are abilities (1) to tap quickly and accurately with one finger at a time by controlling each finger separately and independently and (2) to respond with a particular finger on perceiving a certain letter.

Shorthand and Stenographic Aptitude Tests

Two similar tests of this type are the Bennett *Stenographic Aptitude Test* [4] and the *Turse Shorthand Aptitude Test*. The former includes a transcription test from numbers to symbols and back to numbers and a test in recognition of correct spellings of words. The latter consists of seven parts that test stroking, spelling, phonetic associations, symbol transcription, word discrimination, dictation, and word sense. Because of the unique method of measurement of transcription in these instruments, the accompanying illustration of the directions portion of the symbol transcription subtest from the *Turse Shorthand Aptitude Test* is presented here.

EXCERPT FROM *Turse Shorthand Aptitude Test* [5]

Directions. This is a test to determine how rapidly and how accurately you can decipher or transcribe the following shorthand sentences by using the alphabetic key which is provided below. Letters which are *not* pronounced are *not* written in the shorthand, but all missing letters must be supplied in every word in your answer. Study the sample given below. You will find that the word "mean" is written in shorthand "m-e-n" because the "a" is not pronounced. Each sentence is complete and grammatically correct. You will be allowed *ten* minutes.

Key

Letter: r a v s e t h i m n l o f d

Symbol: ∧ ° (∩ ° ⌣ - ⟨ | ∨) ⟩ — ꞌ

Sample   1. _____

Answer. He is a mean man

[4] George K. Bennett, *Stenographic Aptitude Test.* Psychological Corporation, New York, 1939.

[5] Paul L. Turse, *Turse Shorthand Aptitude Test.* Copyright 1940 by Harcourt, Brace and World, Inc., New York. All rights reserved. Quoted by special permission.

Measurement and Evaluation in the Modern School

Clerical Aptitude Tests

Somewhat different purposes are served by two types of clerical aptitude tests, even though the differences between the purpose and nature of the two varieties are not great. One kind of test is intended for school use but some tests of the other sort, intended primarily for use by business concerns, can also, in fact, be used in the schools.

Clerical aptitude tests for school use. Two tests that measure clerical aptitudes as a basis for classification and counseling purposes at the junior- and senior-high-school levels are the *Detroit Clerical Aptitudes Examination* [6] and the *Turse Clerical Aptitudes Test*. The eight parts of the Detroit test variously measure motor skills, visual imagery, and educational knowledges and skills that are basic to performance in clerical work. The Turse test consists of six parts that measure verbal and number skills, following written directions, clerical speed, classifying and sorting, and alphabetizing. An accompanying excerpt from this test illustrates a widely used item type for measuring speed and accuracy of clerical checking in which the pupil is expected to mark "S" or "D" to show whether the paired letter and number combinations are the same or different.

EXCERPT FROM *Turse Clerical Aptitudes Test* [7]

6. 9u8erC	9u8erC.........	S	D
7. StrSsb	StrsSb..........	S	D
8. 322332	322332.........	S	D
9. RmBmMa	RmBnMa.......	S	D
10. YtrEWQ	YtrEWQ.......	S	D

Trade tests of clerical aptitude. Tests of clerical aptitude are used frequently as trade tests by business concerns attempting to select employees who are best fitted to do their work satisfactorily. The aim may be to measure either general clerical aptitude by tests that are closely similar to verbal intelligence tests or aptitude for specific types of performances by tests that measure the unique traits thought to be essential for such skills as filing or stenography.

[6] Harry J. Baker and Paul H. Voelker, *Detroit Clerical Aptitudes Examination.* Public School Publishing Co., Bloomington, Ill., 1938.
[7] Paul L. Turse, *Turse Clerical Aptitudes Test: Test 4, Checking Speed.* Copyright 1953 by Harcourt, Brace and World, Inc., New York. All rights reserved. Quoted by special permission.

The *O'Rourke Clerical Aptitude Test, Junior Grade,*[8] consists of two subtests on clerical problems and on reasoning problems. The various parts measure abilities of several clerical types, information and factual knowledge important in office work, and reasoning ability with materials chosen from fields of business. Another test serving the same general purpose is the *Minnesota Clerical Test,*[9] called the *Minnesota Vocational Test for Clerical Workers* in an earlier edition. This test consists of pairs of numbers and pairs of names. The pupil is expected to compare the items of each pair and to check those pairs for which the items are identical in every respect. The *SRA Clerical Aptitude* [10] test measures three aspects of aptitude for clerical work—office vocabulary, office arithmetic, and, in a checking test, ability to see office details easily and quickly.

Sales Aptitude Tests

A *Test for Ability To Sell,*[11] one of the George Washington University Series, measures characteristics important to store salesmanship. The six parts of the test measure judgment in selling situations, memory for names and faces, observation of behavior, ability to learn selling points in merchandise, ability to follow store directions, and ability to solve selling problems. A second test in this area, the *Detroit Retail Selling Inventory,*[12] consists of four subtests on personality, intelligence, checking, and arithmetic. It is designed for use as an aptitude test with high-school pupils or as a selection test by business.

3. MEASUREMENT OF KNOWLEDGE OUTCOMES IN BUSINESS EDUCATION

Course offerings common to business curricula may be classified as content subjects and skill subjects. The content subjects, such as business English and law, economic geography, general business, and junior business training, place major emphasis upon the development of knowledges, attitudes, and abilities to apply information to practical situations.

[8] L. J. O'Rourke, *O'Rourke Clerical Aptitude Test, Junior Grade.* Psychological Institute, Lake Alfred, Fla., 1935, 1958.

[9] Dorothy M. Andrew, Donald G. Paterson, and Howard P. Longstaff, *Minnesota Clerical Test.* Psychological Corporation, New York, 1933, 1959.

[10] Richardson, Bellows, Henry and Co., Inc., *SRA Clerical Aptitude.* Science Research Associates, Inc., Chicago, 1947-50.

[11] Thelma Hunt, Robert George, and William Schnell, *Test for Ability to Sell: George Washington University Series,* Revised. Center for Psychological Service, George Washington University, Washington, D. C., 1950.

[12] Harry J. Baker and Paul H. Voelker, *Detroit Retail Selling Inventory.* Public School Publishing Co., Bloomington, Ill., 1940.

Measurement and Evaluation in the Modern School

Tests in the content subjects of business education differ little in type from those that are discussed and illustrated in Chapters 18 and 19 of this volume. However, there are only a few standardized achievement tests available for the content subjects in this area, and most of those that were available fifteen years or so ago are now out of print. As Hardaway and Maier pointed out,[13] the major sources of ready-made achievement tests in business education, and, it would seem, particularly in the content subjects, are a number of textbook publishers, four collegiate institutions in as many states, and four business education journals. Most of the tests available through these channels are unstandardized instruments designed for use with particular textbooks or constructed for use in a certain state-wide testing program. Two sources of classified bibliographies of such tests are available—one in Hardaway and Maier [14] and one of more recent publication date in a special issue of the journal, *American Business Education*.[15]

Two samples of test items in the content aspects of business education appear in accompanying illustrations. The first deals with a knowledge aspect of bookkeeping, a subject in which the predominantly skill outcomes are necessarily dependent on knowledge of such account classification principles as the sample items measure. The second sample, from business law, illustrates a type of true-false item providing a third option for use when a statement is neither true nor false.

SAMPLE OF Test Items in Bookkeeping [16]

Directions: The statement columns of a work sheet are shown below together with the account titles used. After each account title make a check mark (√) in the appropriate column to indicate in which column of the work sheet the balance will appear. For each account that will have no balance extended into these four columns, write a zero in all four columns.

	P. & L. Statement		Balance Sheet	
Account Titles	Dr.	Cr.	Dr.	Cr.
0. Accounts Payable				√
1. Accounts Receivable				
2. Cash				
3. Delivery Expense				
4. Expired Insurance				
5. Merchandise Inventory				

[13] Mathilde Hardaway and Thomas B. Maier, *Tests and Measurements in Business Education,* Second edition. South-Western Publishing Co., Cincinnati, Ohio, 1952. p. 239-41.
[14] *Ibid.* p. 244-56.
[15] Dean R. Malsbary, editor, "The High School Business Library." *American Business Education* (A Special Issue), 16:224, 242, 251, 269, 287-89, 301-3, 314; May 1960.
[16] Hardaway and Maier, *op. cit.* p. 121.

SAMPLE OF Test Items in Business Law [17]

Directions: After each statement below that is true, place a check mark in the column headed "True." After each statement that is false, place a check mark in the column headed "False." After each statement that is neither entirely true nor entirely false, place a check mark in the column headed "Neither." If you do not know the correct answer, skip the statement. *Do not guess!*

	True	False	Neither
1. The Federal Government has only those powers granted to it by the Constitution of the United States.	___	___	___
2. The Supreme Court is composed of twelve justices.	___	___	___
3. When a citizen of one state sues a citizen of another state, he does so in a United States court.	___	___	___
4. It is often impossible to enforce international law because there is no law-enforcing agency.	___	___	___

4. MEASUREMENT OF SKILL OUTCOMES IN BUSINESS EDUCATION

Skill subjects constitute the second basic type of course offerings in business education. Such subjects as bookkeeping, typewriting, shorthand, business arithmetic, machine calculation, and office practice, in which skills receive the major emphasis, subordinate the necessary basic knowledges to the ultimately important skills. Tests for the measurement of business skills are predominantly of the performance type, and it is of great importance that they closely approximate conditions under which the skills will be used in an office or in the personal life of the pupil. It is evident, therefore, that the measurement problems in business education relate to two rather distinct types of instruments—those predominantly paper-and-pencil tests for content subjects dealt with in the foregoing section and the primarily performance-type tests treated here for the skill subjects.

No attempt is made to distinguish tests for vocational objectives from tests for personal-use objectives in the discussions and illustrations that follow. The distinction is perhaps relatively unimportant, furthermore, because of the fact that sufficient overlaps in course content and method probably exist in several subjects to permit the use of one test for the measurement of both types of desired outcomes.

Tests in Typewriting

Testing practices in typewriting seem to be dominated quite largely by the types of tests set up by typewriter manufacturers in the contests they

[17] *Ibid.* p. 98-99.

have sponsored. Tests based solely on speed and accuracy over standardized material, as measured by a combination of credits for strokes per time unit and weighted deductions for errors, are therefore in the majority. Such tests seldom require use of the numbers and symbols keys of the typewriter, but select material for which mainly the letters are used. The present trend is toward the broadening of tested skills to include abilities in placing letters on a page, in use of the tabulation keys, and in typing rought drafts, and also toward a meaningful method of penalizing for errors in terms of their importance and correctibility.

One of the very few standardized tests in this area [18] makes provision for comparing pupil performance with standards used by employers in the selection of typists and stenographers. In taking the test, a pupil types a business letter containing about 225 words as often as he can during a ten-minute period on a special form and under prescribed conditions. His product is then scored by using International Typewriting Contest rules in order to obtain a conventional words-per-minute, or speed, score and an accuracy ratio to show the proportion of words typed without error.

Tests in Shorthand

Most of the achievement tests in stenography are limited to the measurement of ability to take dictation, to read shorthand, and to transcribe shorthand notes. In too few cases have such important stenographic abilities of a nonshorthand type as filing, telephoning, and meeting callers been considered.

The *Turse-Durost Shorthand Achievement Test* [19] is almost alone in the field of independently constructed and standardized achievement tests in shorthand. It measures language skills, shorthand penmanship, and shorthand principles by providing for the pupil to correct his own copy after he has made shorthand notes for the several short passages dictated to him under timed conditions by the examiner.

Tests and Testing in Bookkeeping

Tests in this area, whether standardized or teacher-made, involve not only skill objectives but also, as is indicated in the foregoing section of this chapter, certain basic content objectives. The *Breidenbaugh Book-*

[18] Marion W. Richardson and Ruth A. Pedersen, *SRA Typing Skills.* Science Research Associates, Inc., Chicago, 1947.
[19] Paul L. Turse and Walter N. Durost, *Turse-Durost Shorthand Achievement Test* (Gregg). World Book Co., Yonkers, N. Y., 1942.

keeping Tests [20] are designed for use in high-school courses where single-proprietor bookkeeping is taught. The four tests, spaced for use at different times during a course, cover journalizing, adjustments, closing entries, and the work sheet, balance sheet, and profit-and-loss statement. True-false and recall-type items are employed in measuring knowledge outcomes, and performance-type content in paper-and-pencil format is used in the measurement of skill outcomes.

Carlson suggested a procedure for testing bookkeeping skills that eliminates the subjectivity and tedium involved in scoring bookkeeping sets step by step, and that distinguishes between the training function of bookkeeping sets and the testing function of bookkeeping tests.[21] He recommended that informal objective items be constructed by the teacher and used periodically during the course. The accuracy of the pupil's work and his understanding of the set of books he is keeping can be measured by keying objective items to the set in such manner that the pupil obtains the answers by actual reference to his work in the books. Not only is the accuracy of the pupil's work tested by his answers to the objective items but his ability to use the set with understanding is tested by his ability to locate the answers.

Suggestions were also offered by Carlson for the use of problem-type tests in bookkeeping and business arithmetic that eliminate the all-or-none characteristic of lengthy problems scored on the sole basis of the final result.[22] He recommended, for example, that a favorite form of bookkeeping test, based upon the use of figures and actual computations on a working sheet, balance sheet, and statement of profit and loss, be replaced by a test of ability to place check marks in the proper places on a similar set of forms to indicate where the figures should be filled in.

5. NATIONAL BUSINESS ENTRANCE TESTS

The field of business education is unique among secondary-school areas of instruction in having developed for some of its important measurement needs a cooperative, comprehensive series of objective tests. The *National Clerical Ability Tests* were sponsored by the Eastern Commercial Teachers Association when they originated in 1937. They later became a joint enterprise of the National Council for Business Education and the New England Office Management Association. The present tests, known as the *National*

[20] V. E. Breidenbaugh, *Breidenbaugh Bookkeeping Tests.* Public School Publishing Co., Bloomington, Ill., 1936.

[21] Paul A. Carlson, *The Measurement of Business Education.* South-Western Publishing Company Monograph, No. 18. South-Western Publishing Co., Cincinnati, Ohio, 1932. p. 17.

[22] *Ibid.* p. 16.

Business Entrance Tests, are under the direction of the Joint Committee on Tests,[23] United Business Education Association, and result from the cooperation of business educators, school administrators, and office and personnel managers.

These achievement tests are consistent with recognized instructional objectives in business education and can be used for achievement measurement in courses using any textbooks or instructional materials. Two similar series of tests, revised periodically, are available: (1) a General Testing Series, available to schools and to business, and (2) an Official Testing Series, available solely, usually in April, May, or June of each year, in official testing centers. The first type only, often used by schools in preparing pupils for the Official Testing Series, is of direct concern here.

Tests of General Education

A general test is designed to measure educational outcomes acquired in school and also resulting from such out-of-school influences as radio, television, newspapers, and other sources. This *Business Fundamentals and General Information Test* measures educational outcomes in such areas as English mechanics, spelling, business vocabulary, and arithmetic.

Tests of Business Skills

Five tests in specific skill areas are designed to measure marketable productivity in five basic office jobs. They attempt as closely as possible to simulate actual working conditions in an office.

Bookkeeping test. This test includes the application of recording techniques, preparation of statements, locating and correcting inaccuracies, and other operations and knowledges common in bookkeeping.

General office clerical test. Skills of checking and classifying, ability in producing and interpreting business forms, and knowledge and speed in locating and filing business materials are measured by this general clerical test.

Machine calculation test. Pupil facility in using office machines is measured by this test in order to determine speed, accuracy, and stamina in computational work common to many offices.

Stenography test. This test of stenographic achievement measures pupil performance in taking ordinary dictation for a reasonable length of time and in transcribing the shorthand notes promptly in mailable form.

[23] Joint Committee on Tests, *National Business Entrance Tests.* United Business Education Association, Washington, D. C., 1938-57.

Typewriting test. Such office jobs as typing letters, filling in forms, setting up statistical material, addressing envelopes, and typing from rough drafts are among those measured by this typewriting test.

SUGGESTED ACTIVITIES

1. Outline major instructional outcomes in some such skill area as typewriting, shorthand and transcription, bookkeeping, machine calculation, business arithmetic, or clerical office practice.
2. Devise a short performance-type test to measure some aspects of performance in such a skill area as typewriting, shorthand, machine calculation, or clerical office practice.

TOPICS FOR DISCUSSION

1. What are the major functions served by business education in the modern school?
2. Distinguish between the content and skill subjects of business education and name several of each type.
3. What are the major aims and objectives of business education?
4. How can aptitude for the skill aspects of typewriting and operation of various keyboard machines be measured?
5. What is the nature of aptitude tests for shorthand?
6. By what different approaches is aptitude for clerical work measured?
7. What is the status of standardized achievement testing in business education subjects?
8. By what general procedures are instructional outcomes in the content subjects of business education measured?
9. What are some general characteristics of achievement tests for use in the skill subjects of business education?
10. What sources can be consulted for information about published but largely unstandardized achievement tests in business education?
11. What are the major purposes of the National Business Entrance Tests?
12. What are the major characteristics of the National Business Entrance Tests?

SELECTED REFERENCES

ANDRUSS, HARVEY A. "Appraising Achievement in Bookkeeping and Accounting." *American Business Education*, 6:135-44; March 1950.

BECKLEY, DONALD K. "Constructing Achievement Tests in Retailing." *Journal of Business Education*, 19:13-14; January 1944.

BECKLEY, DONALD K. "Constructing a Comprehensive Examination in Retailing." *Industrial Arts and Vocational Education*, 40:58-61; February 1951.

BECKLEY, DONALD K. "When To Use Multiple-Choice and True-False Questions in Tests." *Business Education World*, 30:29-32; September 1949.

BENNETT, GEORGE K., AND CRUIKSHANK, RUTH M. *A Summary of Clerical Tests.* New York: Psychological Corporation, 1949.

BUROS, OSCAR K., editor. *The Fifth Mental Measurements Yearbook.* Highland Park, N. J.: Gryphon Press, 1959. p. 615-27, 871-79.

BUROS, OSCAR K., editor. *The Fourth Mental Measurements Yearbook.* Highland Park, N. J.: Gryphon Press, 1953. p. 528-35, 711-26.

BUROS, OSCAR K., editor. *The Third Mental Measurements Yearbook.* New Brunswick, N. J.: Rutgers University Press, 1949. p. 442-63; 628-44.

DEUTCHMAN, BERNARD V. "The Good Typist—A Test." *Business Education World*, 21:306-7; December 1940.

EYSTER, ELVIN S. "Business Education." *Encyclopedia of Educational Research.* Third edition. New York: Macmillan Co., 1960. p. 173-84.

GERBERICH, J. RAYMOND. *Specimen Objective Test Items: A Guide to Achievement Test Construction.* New York: Longmans, Green and Co., 1956. p. 305-8.

GREENE, HARRY A., JORGENSEN, ALBERT N., AND GERBERICH, J. RAYMOND. *Measurement and Evaluation in the Secondary School.* Second edition. New York: Longmans, Green and Co., 1954. Chapter 23.

HARDAWAY, MATHILDE. "Tests in Business Education." *Business Education World*, 25:30-32; September 1944.

HARDAWAY, MATHILDE, AND MAIER, THOMAS B. *Tests and Measurements in Business Education.* Second edition. Cincinnati, Ohio: South-Western Publishing Co., 1952.

HOKE, MARGARET R. "Filing Tests." *Journal of Business Education*, 15:23-24; April 1940.

HUFFMAN, HARRY, editor. *The Clerical Program in Business Education.* American Business Education Yearbook, Vol. 16. (Eastern Business Teachers Association and National Business Teachers Association.) New York: New York University Bookstore, 1959. Chapters 23, 29.

LESLIE, LOUIS A. "Testing and Grading in Shorthand." *Business Education World*, 22:499-503, 603-8; February and March 1942.

MALSBARY, DEAN R. "Evaluation of Instruction." *Educating Youth for Economic Competence.* American Business Education Yearbook, Vol. 15. (Eastern Business Teachers Association and National Business Teachers Association.) New York: New York University Bookstore, 1958. Chapter 22.

MAYNE, F. BLAIR, editor. *Evaluating Competence for Business Occupations.* American Business Education Yearbook, Vol. 7. (Eastern Business Teachers Association and National Business Teachers Association.) New York: New York University Bookstore, 1950. Part 2.

MCFADZEN, J. A.; GRAHAM, JESSIE; AND GARDENHIRE, ERIN M. "A True-False Secretarial Test on Telephoning and Receiving Callers." *Business Education World*, 23:537-39; May 1943.

POPHAM, ESTELLE L., editor. *Evaluation of Pupil Progress in Business Education.* American Business Education Yearbook, Vol. 17. (Eastern Business Teachers Association and National Business Teachers Association.) New York: New York University Bookstore, 1960.

PRICE, RAY G., AND OTHERS. "Business Education." *Encyclopedia of Educational Research.* Revised edition. New York: Macmillan Co., 1950. p. 115-26.

Rowe, John L. "The Four Arts of Shorthand Teaching—Part 3: The Art of Testing." *Business Education World,* 40:27-29; January 1960.

Satlow, I. David. "Business Law Device: Quizzes and Tests." *Business Education World,* 30:186-87; December 1949.

Selby, P. O. "Measurement of Accuracy in Typewriting." *Journal of Business Education,* 21:23; April 1946.

Watson, Dorothy M. "Group Evaluation of Learning." *Enriched Learning in Business Education.* American Business Education Yearbook, Vol. 10. (Eastern Business Teachers Association and National Business Teachers Association.) New York: New York University Bookstore, 1953. Chapter 12.

24

PHYSICAL EDUCATION AND RECREATION

This chapter presents a brief summary of the following aspects of measurement in physical education and recreation education:

A. Aims and objectives of physical education.
B. Classification of pupils in physical education.
C. Standards of achievement in physical education.
D. Knowledge testing in physical education and sports.
E. Skill testing in physical education and sports.
F. Scope and purposes of recreation education.
G. Measuring recreational activities and interests.

The rather closely related fields of physical education and recreation are exceedingly important, although not even the former seems to be as much favored in the curricular setup in most schools as are the academic areas. However, physical education perhaps occupies a more important place in the schools of today than was true some years ago because of the modern need to counteract the effects of the physically inactive lives led by many persons. Moreover, recreation perhaps assumes a new meaning when it is recognized that leisure time increases as the work week decreases in length.

1. AIMS AND OBJECTIVES OF PHYSICAL EDUCATION

Physical education during the past several decades has come to be thought of as making an increasingly valuable contribution to the educational process, and its philosophy has consequently been dominated recently by broader aims than were generally held previously. The colleges and secondary schools have better-organized programs than do the elementary schools, as less attention has been devoted to physical education for elementary-school children than for high-school and college students. The statement of aims that follows represents the modern philosophy concerning the contribution physical education should make to the attainment of desirable educational outcomes in the pupil.

The nine general objectives of physical education listed by LaPorte [1] indicate the types of pupil outcomes to which a good physical education program should lead. LaPorte's tenth objective, for health education, is excluded because it applies to the health and physical fitness dealt with in Chapter 5 much more than to the content of this chapter.

1. The development of fundamental skills in aquatic, gymnastic, rhythmic, and athletic activities for immediate educational purposes—physical, mental, and social.
2. The development of useful and desirable skills in activities suitable as vocational interests for use during leisure time.
3. The development of essential safety skills and the ability to handle the body skillfully in a variety of situations for the protection of self and of others.
4. The development of a comprehensive knowledge of rules, techniques and strategies in the above activities suitably adapted to various age levels.
5. The development of acceptable social standards, appreciations and attitudes as the result of intensive participation in these activities in a good environment and under capable and inspired leadership.
6. The development of powers of observation, analysis, judgment, and decision through the medium of complex physical situations.
7. The development of the power of self-expression and reasonable self-confidence (physical and mental poise); by mastery of difficult physical-mental-social problems in supervised activities.
8. The development of leadership capacity by having each student within the limits of his ability, assume actual responsibility for certain activities under careful supervision.
9. The elimination of remediable defects and the improvement of postural mechanics insofar as these can be influenced by muscular activities and health advice.

2. MEASUREMENT OF PHYSICAL STATUS AND POTENTIAL

Human beings differ almost as widely in physical characteristics as in mental abilities and personality traits. Differences among pupils of the

---

[1] William R. LaPorte, "The Ten Major Objectives of Health and Physical Education." *California Physical Education, Health and Recreation Journal,* 5:5-6, 18; January 1936.

same age in size, maturity, and physical ability are so great that physical education and sports programs must take them into account. These differences are similar to the ones dealt with in the portion of Chapter 5 that is devoted to physical fitness, but the emphasis in that chapter is on the influences of physical fitness on behavior in general. Here, however, major attention is directed toward the influences of physical traits and characteristics on success in physical education activities.

Two related and overlapping approaches to the problem of how to provide for differences of these types in physical education programs can be distinguished: (1) use of physical classification indices and (2) use of achievement standards. Only a few of the most important and most easily measurable physical characteristics are widely used in these two procedures. The traits commonly used are age, height, and weight, in addition to sex.

Physical Classification Indices

The importance of tools to be used in the classification of pupils for physical education and particularly for competitive sports is obvious. Physical differences among pupils of the same age are so great that classification by chronological age is likely to result in injuries to the smaller and weaker children and usually deprives them of adequate opportunities for exercise. Indices useful for classification purposes in the elementary, junior high school, and secondary school have been validated.

McCloy developed a classification index for elementary-school children.[2] The formula is as follows:

$$\text{Classification Index} = 20A + 6H + W,$$

where A refers to age in years, H to height in inches, and W to weight in pounds. Another index making use of the same physical and age measures was derived for junior-high-school girls,[3] as follows:

$$\text{Classification Index} = 20A + 10H + 1.1W$$

Cozens, Trieb, and Neilson developed a third classification index for high-school boys,[4] in the belief that real differences exist between ele-

[2] C. H. McCloy, *The Measurement of Athletic Power*. A. S. Barnes and Co., New York, 1932. p. 95.

[3] Frederick W. Cozens, Hazel J. Cubberly, and Neils P. Neilson, *Achievement Scales in Physical Education Activities for Secondary School Girls and College Women*. A. S. Barnes and Co., New York, 1937. p. 113.

[4] Frederick W. Cozens, Martin H. Trieb, and Neils P. Neilson, *Physical Education Achievement Scales for Boys in Secondary Schools*. A. S. Barnes and Co., New York, 1936. p. 10-13.

mentary-school and secondary-school boys. The formula, again using the same meanings for symbols, is as follows:

$$\text{Classification Index} = 20A + 4.75H + 1.6W$$

Ashbrook, Espenschade, and Cozens stated that the factors of age, weight, and height when properly combined are probably almost as useful for classification purposes as are more complex measures and the simplicity of their use is of considerable importance.[5]

Achievement Standards

Several sets of achievement standards are available for use in estimating the physical performances of which pupils classified into groups are capable. The scales designed for this type of use show in the form of differentiated norms how pupils classified into several groups or categories differ in a wide variety of physical education and sports activities. The groups or categories are typically based on the same factors—age, height, weight, and sex—as are used in the classification indices presented above.

Neilson and Cozens evolved an elaborate set of scales [6] on the basis of test results for more than 79,000 boys and girls in elementary and junior high schools. They presented instructions for administering 33 tests to boys and 20 of the same tests to girls and paralleled each test with a scale having an arithmetic mean of 50 and a range, from 0 to 100, of six standard-deviation units. Thus, the scores on the tests, most of which involve specific skills from baseball, basketball, soccer, softball, and track, can be given constancy of meaning by converting them to these scale values. A few of the tests for boys, such as pull-ups and push-ups, measure aspects of physical strength.

A similar set of scales [7] was produced by Cozens, Trieb, and Neilson for use with high-school boys. The 45 tests and comparable scales are similar to those in the lower-level scale but they also include tests from field events, football, gymnastics, and walking.

The third set of scales [8] in this series, by Cozens, Cubberly, and Neilson, includes somewhat different tests and scales for girls at the two high-school

[5] Willard P. Ashbrook, Anna Espenschade, and Frederick W. Cozens, "Physical Education—Measurement." *Encyclopedia of Educational Research,* Revised edition. Macmillan Co., New York, 1950. p. 837.

[6] Neils P. Neilson and Frederick W. Cozens, *Achievement Scales in Physical Education Activities for Boys and Girls in Elementary and Junior High Schools.* A. S. Barnes and Co., New York, 1934.

[7] Cozens, Trieb, and Neilson, *op. cit.*

[8] Cozens, Cubberly, and Neilson, *op. cit.*

levels and for college women. The authors included tests in baseball, basketball, field hockey, soccer, speedball, swimming, and volleyball, and also in running, jumping, and hopping, for high-school girls.

3. MEASUREMENT OF KNOWLEDGE ABOUT PHYSICAL EDUCATION ACTIVITIES

Tests of knowledge outcomes in physical education differ little in form from similar tests in other subjects. Occurring mostly in sports areas, they deal primarily with such matters as rules governing the activity in question, strategy of the game, types of demands made upon the performers, characteristics of equipment and playing surface, and perhaps history of the activity. Knowledge tests in specific sports and comprehensively for physical activities in general have appeared in the physical education journals but have not been made available in the form of commercially published standardized tests.

Students and teachers who are interested in techniques of knowledge testing in physical education activities may well consult physical education journals both for general and for specialized treatments of this topic. Such articles often include paper-and-pencil tests in their entirety and in other instances they give illustrations of item types applied to various testing situations. Students can also refer to summaries of knowledge tests as they appear in a number of books on measurement and evaluation in physical education. Consequently, brief comments appear on the following pages concerning the nature of some major source materials of these types.

Summaries of Knowledge Tests in Physical Education Activities

A major source of knowledge tests for high-school boys is found in the report by Hemphill.[9] He presented tests in five areas that in a few respects go beyond the most common sports areas with which the remainder of this section deals. His tests are in the areas of (1) major sports—baseball, basketball, and football; (2) minor sports—handball, soccer, tennis, and volleyball; (3) health related to physical education; (4) self-defense—boxing and wrestling; and (5) recreational sports, including golf, horseshoes, and swimming.

French presented a summary [10] of knowledge testing in physical education up to 1942. Other summaries appear in books by Bovard, Cozens, and

---

[9] Fay Hemphill, "Information Tests in Health and Physical Education for High School Boys." *Research Quarterly*, 3:83-96; December 1932.

[10] Esther L. French, "The Construction of Knowledge Tests in Selected Professional Courses in Physical Education." *Research Quarterly*, 14:406-24; December 1943.

Hagman,[11] Clarke,[12] Larson and Yocom,[13] Mathews,[14] McCloy and Young,[15] and Scott and French.[16]

Knowledge Tests in Specific Sports

The small number of specialized references listed and commented upon here supplement the broader and generalized treatments referred to previously. These apply directly to the elementary grades and high school or to a beginner's level in activities that may be taught both in the secondary school and the college.

Basketball. Schwartz [17] constructed a knowledge test consisting of 50 true-false, 15 completion-type, 20 best-answer, and 15 pictorial questions on rules, fundamental techniques, positions and duties of players, and team play and strategy for high-school girls.

Field hockey. Deitz and Frech [18] devised a 77-item instrument for the teaching and informal testing of high-school girls on rules, techniques, and playing situations.

Playground baseball or softball. Rodgers and Heath [19] devised a 100-item true-false test on rules and strategy for use with both boys and girls in Grades 5 and 6. Rodgers [20] subsequently presented the test and discussed the procedures involved in its construction.

Soccer. Heath and Rodgers [21] constructed a 100-item test for boys and girls in Grades 5 and 6. The true-false items deal with elements of the

[11] John F. Bovard, Frederick W. Cozens, and E. Patricia Hagman, *Tests and Measurements in Physical Education,* Third edition. W. B. Saunders Co., Philadelphia, 1949. Chapter 11.

[12] H. Harrison Clarke, *Application of Measurement to Health and Physical Education,* Third edition. Prentice-Hall, Inc., Englewood Cliffs, N. J., 1959. Chapter 15.

[13] Leonard A. Larson and Rachael D. Yocom, *Measurement and Evaluation in Physical, Health, and Recreation Education.* C. V. Mosby Co., St. Louis, Mo., 1951. Chapter 11.

[14] Donald K. Mathews, *Measurement in Physical Education.* W. B. Saunders Co., Philadelphia, 1958. Chapter 12.

[15] Charles H. McCloy and Norma D. Young, *Tests and Measurements in Health and Physical Education,* Third edition. Appleton-Century-Crofts, Inc., New York, 1954. Chapter 24.

[16] M. Gladys Scott and Esther L. French, *Evaluation in Physical Education.* C. V. Mosby Co., St. Louis, Mo., 1950. Chapter 8.

[17] Helen Schwartz, "Knowledge and Achievement Tests in Girls' Basketball on the Senior High School Level." *Research Quarterly,* 8:143-56; March 1937.

[18] Dorothea Deitz and Beryl Frech, "Hockey Knowledge Test for Girls." *Journal of Health and Physical Education,* 11:366, 387-88; June 1940.

[19] Elizabeth G. Rodgers and Marjorie L. Heath, "An Experiment in the Use of Knowledge and Skill Tests in Playground Baseball." *Research Quarterly,* 2:113-31; December 1931.

[20] Elizabeth G. Rodgers, "The Standardization and Use of Objective Type Information Tests in Team Game Activities." *Research Quarterly,* 10:102-12; March 1939.

[21] Marjorie L. Heath and Elizabeth G. Rodgers, "A Study in the Use of Knowledge and Skill Tests in Soccer." *Research Quarterly,* 3:33-53; December 1932.

game, rules, and strategy. Knighton [22] constructed a test on soccer rules for beginners consisting of 35 true-false, multiple-choice, and completion-type items.

Tennis. Wagner [23] devised a multiple-choice test on rules, court positions, tactics, and strategy for use with beginners.

4. MEASUREMENT OF SKILL IN PHYSICAL EDUCATION ACTIVITIES

Measurement of the skills involved in physical education activities is accomplished by the use of performance tests similar in many respects to those illustrated in Chapter 11. As in other subjects where performance testing is important, both the performance itself and the tangible result produced by it are subject to measurement and evaluation. Consequently, the check lists and timing devices discussed in Chapter 11 as major approaches to measurement of the process itself and the quality scales, rating scales, score cards, and counting and measuring procedures dealt with there as being useful in evaluation of the product or result are of direct significance here.

Scores obtained by counting are used in measuring results in such performances as those involved in golf and archery. Measures of time, height, and distance are variously employed in measuring performance in track and field events. Rating scales are most suitable for evaluating performance in such activities as diving, dancing, and gymnastics. Check lists are variously applicable to measurement of success in basket shooting, goal kicking, and other individual performances in certain group sports. These illustrations are merely representative of the way in which both performance measurement and product evaluation can be applied to the skill outcomes of physical education.

Summaries of Skill Testing in Physical Education Activities

A summary of performance testing techniques applicable to special skills involved in several sports activities was prepared by Latchaw [24] for pupils in the intermediate grades. She outlined procedures for use with the pass

[22] Marian Knighton, "Soccer Questions." *Journal of Health and Physical Education,* 1:29, 60; October 1930.

[23] Miriam M. Wagner, "An Objective Method of Grading Beginners in Tennis." *Journal of Health and Physical Education,* 6:24-25, 79; March 1935.

[24] Marjorie Latchaw, "Measuring Selected Motor Skills in Fourth, Fifth, and Sixth Grades." *Research Quarterly,* 25:439-49; December 1954.

in basketball, the volley in soccer and volleyball, the throw in softball, and for vertical and broad jumps and a shuttle run. More extensive summaries of skill testing in various sports and other physical activities appear in the books by Bovard, Cozens, and Hagman,[25] Clarke,[26] Larson and Yocom,[27] Mathews,[28] McCloy and Young,[29] and Scott and French.[30]

Skill Testing in Specific Sports

Physical education journals abound in articles dealing with techniques for measuring sports skills ranging from the common to the unusual. The ones chosen for brief comment and notation here apply to physical education activities commonly included in the elementary-school and high-school programs of study.

Baseball. A check-list type of data sheet was evolved by De Groat [31] as an aid to baseball coaches in evaluating players, and Dean [32] designed a scale for use in rating pitchers.

Basketball. Schwartz [33] devised a high-school level test for girls and presented achievement scales based on 1000 sets of results. The five tests are: (1) bounce over a six-foot area, (2) pass and catch, (3) jump and reach, (4) throw for goal, and (5) pivot, bounce, and shoot. Dyer, Schurig, and Apgar [34] set up a performance test for high-school girls and college women that includes parts on (1) moving target, (2) ball handling, (3) bounce and shoot, and (4) free jump and reach. They devised scoring scales for three levels—junior and senior high school and college. Russell and Lange [35] devised a two-part test on (1) dribble for distance and (2) throw and catch. They gave scales to be used in interpreting results for girls in Grades 7 to 9.

[25] Bovard, Cozens, and Hagman, *op. cit.* Chapter 10.

[26] Clarke, *op. cit.* Chapter 14.

[27] Larson and Yocom, *op. cit.* Chapter 10.

[28] Mathews, *op. cit.* Chapter 7.

[29] McCloy and Young, *op. cit.* Chapter 20.

[30] Scott and French, *op. cit.* Chapter 4.

[31] H. S. De Groat, "Data That Will Aid the Baseball Coach." *Athletic Journal,* 18:20, 24, 26; March 1938.

[32] Everett S. Dean, "The Stanford Pitching Chart." *Athletic Journal,* 31:20, 44; 32:34, 36, 53-55; April 1951 and May 1952.

[33] Schwartz, *op. cit.*

[34] Joanna T. Dyer, Jennie C. Schurig, and Sara L. Apgar, "A Basketball Motor Ability Test for College Women and Secondary School Girls." *Research Quarterly,* 10:128-47; October 1939.

[35] Naomi Russell and Elizabeth Lange, "Studies Relating to Achievement Scales in Physical Education Activities." *Research Quarterly,* 9:43-56; December 1938.

Lehston's test [36] for high-school boys includes five parts: (1) dodging run, (2) 40-foot dash, (3) baskets per minute, (4) wall bounce, and (5) vertical jump. Edgren [37] discussed and presented a test having parts on (1) speed pass, (2) accuracy pass, (3) pivot and shoot, (4) dribble and shoot, (5) accuracy shooting, (6) opposition shooting, and (7) ball handling. Friermood's test [38] consists of four parts on (1) accuracy of passing, (2) efficiency and form in pivoting, (3) speed and control in dribbling, and (4) accuracy in shooting. Gibble [39] contributed a rating scale for use in evaluating individual players.

Football. Meyer [40] devised a performance test for use in rating backfield men and Geesman [41] brought out an evaluation chart for offensive linemen. Another rating scale, by Merrell,[42] is for use in rating individual players.

Playground baseball or softball. Rodgers and Heath [43] constructed a series of tests for boys and girls in Grades 5 and 6. The tests are for (1) throw for accuracy, (2) batting, (3) catching flyballs, (4) fielding grounders, and (5) hit and run. Fox and Young [44] in their performance test dealt only with skill in batting.

Soccer. Heath and Rodgers [45] devised a skill test for boys and girls and presented T-score norms based on 2500 cases. The test parts are: (1) dribble, (2) throw-in, (3) place kick for goal, and (4) kicking a rolling ball. Vanderhoof [46] analyzed soccer into ten elements in her test: (1) dribble, (2) trapping, (3) throw-in, (4) place kick, (5) drop ball, (6) volleying, (7) throw down, (8) tackling, (9) corner kick, and (10) goalkeeping.

Swimming. Parkhurst [47] devised a performance test and rating scale for evaluating the proficiency of swimmers at the beginning and also higher

[36] Nelson Lehston, "A Measure of Basketball Skills in High School Boys." *Physical Educator,* 5:103-9; December 1948.

[37] H. D. Edgren, "An Experiment in the Testing of Ability and Progress in Basketball." *Research Quarterly,* 3:159-71; March 1932.

[38] H. T. Friermood, "Basketball Progress Tests Adaptable to Class Use." *Journal of Health and Physical Education,* 5:45-47; January 1934.

[39] Alfred T. Gibble, "An Individual Basketball Rating Chart." *Athletic Journal,* 19:26, 28; October 1938.

[40] Kenneth L. Meyer, "A Backfield Ability Test." *Athletic Journal,* 27:9-10, 41-42; June 1947.

[41] Sterling Geesman, "Evaluation Chart for Offensive Linemen." *Athletic Journal,* 32: 52-53; September 1951.

[42] R. R. Merrell, "Individual Football Rating System." *Athletic Journal,* 19:13-14, 43-44; September 1938.

[43] Rodgers and Heath, *op. cit.*

[44] Margaret G. Fox and Olive G. Young, "A Test of Softball Batting Ability." *Research Quarterly,* 25:26-27; March 1954.

[45] Heath and Rodgers, *op. cit.*

[46] Mildred Vanderhoof, "Soccer Skill Tests." *Journal of Health and Physical Education,* 3:42, 54-56; October 1932.

[47] Mary G. Parkhurst, "Achievement Tests in Swimming." *Journal of Health and Physical Education,* 5:34-36, 58-59; May 1934.

levels. Hewitt [48] devised similar scales separately for high-school boys and girls.

Tennis. Wagner's test [49] for beginners in the game includes elements on (1) forehand drive, (2) backhand drive, (3) forehand drive with footwork, (4) backhand drive with footwork, and (5) service. The pupil is given the opportunity to stroke 50 balls in the entire series. Miller [50] worked out a chart for use in analyzing tennis strokes. Dyer [51] developed a backboard test of tennis ability involving a 30-second period of volleying a ball against a backboard.

Volleyball. French and Cooper [52] constructed a series of tests for high-school girls on (1) repeated volleys, (2) serving, (3) setup and pass, and (4) recovery from the net. Russell and Lange [53] experimented with the French-Cooper serving and volleying tests and provided scoring tables for girls in the junior high school. Bassett, Glassow, and Locke [54] cooperated in constructing a test on three aspects of serving and volleying: (1) getting the ball across the net, (2) placing the ball, and (3) serving a fast ball.

5. MEASUREMENT IN RECREATIONAL ACTIVITIES

Physical education is closely allied to recreation, but at least several other and perhaps all other instructional areas also make their contributions. Recreation can perhaps best be considered broadly as the types of activities in which people engage to refresh themselves mentally and physically. The pressures of modern living and the increase in leisure time resulting from the shorter work week contribute to the need for recreation and hence to the need for recreation education.

The wide diversity of human characteristics, aptitudes, interests, and many other traits leads to the belief that almost any type of human activity can be recreational for at least a few people. Consequently, it is feasible neither to prescribe limits for recreational activities nor to outline specific aims and objectives of recreation education.

[48] Jack E. Hewitt, "Achievement Scales for High School Swimming." *Research Quarterly,* 20:170-79; May 1949.

[49] Wagner, *op. cit.*

[50] Richard T. Miller, "A New System of Tennis Stroke Analysis." *Athletic Journal,* 32: 45-46, 75-77; March 1952.

[51] Joanna T. Dyer, "The Backboard Test of Tennis Ability." *Research Quarterly,* 6:62-74, Supplement; March 1935; and Joanna T. Dyer, "Revision of the Backboard Test of Tennis Ability." *Research Quarterly,* 9:25-31; March 1938.

[52] Esther L. French and Bernice I. Cooper, "Achievement Tests in Volleyball for High School Girls." *Research Quarterly,* 8:150-57; May 1937.

[53] Naomi Russell and Elizabeth Lange, "Achievement Tests in Volleyball for Junior High School Girls." *Research Quarterly,* 11:33-41; December 1940.

[54] Gladys Bassett, Ruth B. Glassow, and Mabel Locke, "Studies in Testing Volleyball Skill." *Research Quarterly,* 8:60-72; December 1937.

Scope of Recreation Education

Certainly the physical sports, especially those in which adults can participate as members of small groups or even alone, are recreational. Among the recreational sports, in contrast with team sports, are golf, tennis, swimming, badminton, bowling, shuffle board, riding, fishing, and sailing. Such social activities as dancing, playing cards, checkers, or chess, and taking part in dramatics and musical organizations are recreational. Hobbies, such as photography, collecting, engaging in arts and crafts, are recreational, as are talking, singing, and reading for other than vocational or educational purposes.

Recreation education usually implies activity rather than passivity, which ordinarily involves participation rather than observation. For this reason, and also because it does not seem necessary to give specific instruction in some types of diversions, recreation education does not ordinarily give direct attention to such activities as radio listening, television viewing, and movie viewing, for example.

Purposes of Recreation Education

One of the few formulations of purposes or aims of recreation education was presented by Clarke in his list and discussion of seven factors that should be kept in mind in planning for recreation education. His list [55] of important considerations, or criteria, includes:

1. Enjoyment—giving pleasure to the participant
2. Companionship—possible when activity is popular widely or at least among the participant's friends
3. Participants—in general few in numbers, perhaps not over four
4. Vigor—activity appropriate to the participant's age, sex, and physical condition
5. Skill—such as can be recognized and evaluated by the participant
6. Competition—in general but not necessarily involved in the activity
7. Facilities—available widely or at least in the participant's community

This list of points should serve to bring recreation education into focus for the purposes of this chapter even though no list of objectives, and certainly none of learning outcomes, can be presented here to parallel the lists given in most other chapters in this part of the volume.

[55] Clarke, *op. cit.* p. 317-18.

Measuring Recreational Activities and Interests

It is possible to obtain evidence about an individual's recreational activities and recreational interests. Techniques such as some of those discussed or commented upon in sections of Chapters 7, 11, and 12 are variously useful. Among them are observations, check lists, questionnaires, diaries, autobiographies, and other forms of personal reports.

SAMPLE ITEMS FROM Play Quiz [56]

What things have you been doing the past two weeks just because you wanted to?

Read the following list of activities and, as you read through the list, draw a circle around each number that stands in front of anything that you have been playing with during the past two weeks, or anything that you have been doing during the past two weeks just because you wanted to do it.

1. Football	26. Writing letters	48. Rowing or canoeing
6. Tennis	29. Dancing	60. Chess or checkers
10. Prisoner's base	34. Skating	69. Spinning tops
23. Listening to the radio	43. Cooking for fun	77. Playing house

SAMPLE ITEMS FROM Inventory of Collecting Activities [57]

We are anxious to see what you have been collecting. Listen and follow directions carefully.

Section I.—Draw a ring around the number in front of every item you have collected at any time in the past, but which you are not now collecting. . . .

Section II.—Now go back over the list and *underline* those items which you are now actively collecting with the idea of seeing how many and how many kinds you can get together.

1. Acorns	66. Earrings	125. Pencils
19. Books, story	76. Games	139. Riddles
30. Butterflies	86. Insects	153. Shells
50. Coins	100. Marbles	164. Stamps
56. Dolls	105. Minerals	181. Valentines

Recreational activities. Two examples of techniques for measuring recreational activities are shown in accompanying excerpts. The first, showing only a few of the 80 activities in the entire quiz, includes activities ranging from the sedentary to the violently active, from those of primary concern

---

[56] Paul Witty and David Kopel, "Diagnostic Child Study Record: Form III, Pupil Report of Interests and Activities." *Reading and the Educative Process.* Ginn and Co., Boston, 1939. Part 2, p. 319-20.

[57] Paul A. Witty and Harvey C. Lehman, "Further Studies of Children's Interest in Collecting." *Journal of Educational Psychology*, 21:112-27; February 1930.

for girls to those more likely to appeal to boys, and from those engaged in alone to those requiring teams or at least groups of participants. Each item presents a two-response possibility to the pupil. The second, showing a few sample listings from an inventory of collecting activities, seeks to determine both past and present practices by asking the pupil to react to each item in two different ways.

Brief comments and references both to knowledge tests and skill tests appear in the two preceding sections of this chapter for sports activities that are classified above as recreational. However, such sports as swimming and tennis also appear in the instructional or the extracurricular programs of many schools. Moreover, there are several other recreational sports or physical activities that seldom appear in school programs or that are typically college-level or adult activities. References for a few such areas are given and commented upon below.

Archery. Hyde [58] developed scales for measuring performance in the Columbia round, a standard event used in archery competition. A total of 72 arrows at three distances are shot by a person who is being rated by use of her test.

Badminton. Scott [59] reported on a skill test in badminton on the serve and clear and also presented an 80-item knowledge test consisting of true-false and two varieties of multiple-choice items.

Dancing. Waglow's test [60] of social dancing uses a transcription of waltz, tango, slow fox trot, jitterbug, rhumba, and samba music and ratings by an observer of the subject's ability to perform each of the steps.

Golf. Murphy [61] devised a knowledge test in golf consisting of 50 true-false items, 13 completion-type questions, and 30 statements for matching, and McKee [62] evolved a performance test for the full swinging shot in golf based on the use of a Number 5 iron and both hard and cotton balls.

Riding. A rating scale for group horseback riding based on the evaluation of individual riders making up the group was devised by Crabtree.[63]

[58] Edith I. Hyde, "An Achievement Scale in Archery." *Research Quarterly*, 8:109-16; May 1937; and Edith I. Hyde, "The Measurement of Achievement in Archery." *Journal of Educational Research*, 27:673-86; May 1934.

[59] M. Gladys Scott, "Achievement Examination in Badminton." *Research Quarterly*, 12:242-53; May 1941.

[60] I. F. Waglow, "An Experiment in Social Dance Testing." *Research Quarterly*, 24:97-101; March 1953.

[61] Mary A. Murphy, "Criteria for Judging a Golf Knowledge Test." *Research Quarterly*, 4:81-88; December 1933.

[62] Mary E. McKee, "A Test for the Full Swinging Shot in Golf." *Research Quarterly*, 21:40-46; March 1950.

[63] Helen K. Crabtree, "An Objective Test for Riding." *Journal of Health and Physical Education*, 14:419, 446; October 1943.

Skating. Rechnagel [64] devised a performance test of skill in figure skating for use with beginners.

Table tennis. Mott and Lockhart [65] devised a backboard test of table tennis or ping-pong patterned after the Dyer backboard test of tennis ability mentioned in the preceding section of this chapter.

Recreational interests. A sample from a recreational interests inventory is shown on page 224 of Chapter 10. The three items shown there illustrate a method of ranking a pupil's recreational interests by having him compare each recreation with all of the other recreations in separate inventory items.

SUGGESTED ACTIVITIES

1. Devise a short check list or performance test for use in measuring accuracy and technique in some such sports activity as serving in tennis or volleyball, kicking points after touchdown in football, throwing a softball for distance, or making free throws in basketball.
2. Devise a short check list or inventory for measuring participation or interest in some recreational activity such as collecting, reading, arts and crafts, or party games.

TOPICS FOR DISCUSSION

1. What are the major objectives of physical education?
2. What factors are important in the classification of pupils for physical education?
3. What is the nature of the indices used in the classification of pupils for physical education?
4. Of what value are achievement standards in physical education?
5. What is the nature of achievement scales in physical education?
6. What is the relative importance of standardized, informal objective, and performance tests in physical education?
7. What are some sources in which knowledge tests in physical education and sports may be found?
8. What techniques and tools are widely useful in measuring physical education and sports skills?
9. What are some of the sports skills that are subject to measurement?
10. What is the scope of recreation education?
11. How are recreational and sports activities different, in general?
12. How are participation and interests in recreational activities measured?

[64] Dorothy S. Rechnagel, "A Test for Beginners in Figure Skating." *Journal of Health and Physical Education,* 16:91-92; February 1945.

[65] Jane A. Mott and Aileene Lockhart, "Table Tennis Backboard Test." *Journal of Health and Physical Education,* 17:550-52; November 1946.

SELECTED REFERENCES

ASHBROOK, WILLARD P.; ESPENSCHADE, ANNA; AND COZENS, FREDERICK W. "Physical Education—Measurement." *Encyclopedia of Educational Research.* Revised edition. New York: Macmillan Co., 1950. p. 835-42.

BLANCHARD, B. E., JR. "A Behavior Frequency Rating Scale for the Measurement of Character and Personality in Physical Education Classroom Situations." *Research Quarterly,* 7:56-66; May 1936.

BOVARD, JOHN F., COZENS, FREDERICK W., AND HAGMAN, E. PATRICIA. *Tests and Measurements in Physical Education.* Third edition. Philadelphia: W. B. Saunders Co., 1949. Chapters 1-2, 5-6, 10-12.

BURLEY, LLOYD R. "Paper-and-Pencil Tests in Physical Education." *Education,* 75:134-36; October 1954.

BUROS, OSCAR K., editor. *The Fifth Mental Measurements Yearbook.* Highland Park, N. J.: Gryphon Press, 1959. p. 641-48, 661.

BUROS, OSCAR K., editor. *The Fourth Mental Measurements Yearbook.* Highland Park, N. J.: Gryphon Press, 1953. p. 543-53, 563-65.

BUROS, OSCAR K., editor. *The Third Mental Measurements Yearbook.* New Brunswick, N. J.: Rutgers University Press, 1949. p. 475-81, 486.

CLARKE, H. HARRISON. *Application of Measurement to Health and Physical Education.* Third edition. Englewood Cliffs, N. J.: Prentice-Hall, Inc., 1959. Parts 1, 4-5.

COWELL, CHARLES C. "Diary Analysis: A Suggested Technique for the Study of Children's Activities and Interests." *Research Quarterly,* 8:158-72; May 1937.

COWELL, CHARLES C. "Evaluation versus Measurement in Physical Education." *Journal of Health and Physical Education,* 12:499-501, 534-35; November 1941.

COZENS, FREDERICK W., TRIEB, MARTIN H., AND NEILSON, NEILS P. *Physical Education Achievement Scales for Boys in Secondary Schools.* New York: A. S. Barnes and Co., 1936.

COZENS, FREDERICK W., CUBBERLY, HAZEL J., AND NEILSON, NEILS P. *Achievement Scales in Physical Education Activities for Secondary School Girls and College Women.* New York: A. S. Barnes and Co., 1937.

CURETON, THOMAS K., AND OTHERS. "The Measurement of Understanding in Physical Education." *The Measurement of Understanding.* Forty-Fifth Yearbook of the National Society for the Study of Education, Part I. Chicago: University of Chicago Press, 1946. Chapter 12.

FRENCH, ESTHER L. "The Construction of Knowledge Tests in Selected Professional Courses in Physical Education." *Research Quarterly,* 14:406-24; December 1943.

GERBERICH, J. RAYMOND. *Specimen Objective Test Items: A Guide to Achievement Test Construction.* New York: Longmans, Green and Co., 1956. p. 324-31.

GLASSOW, RUTH B., AND BROER, MARION R. *Measuring Achievement in Physical Education.* Philadelphia: W. B. Saunders Co., 1938.

GLOSS, GEORGE M. "What People Do in Their Spare Time." *Research Quarterly,* 9:138-42; May 1938.

GREENE, HARRY A., JORGENSEN, ALBERT N., AND GERBERICH, J. RAYMOND. *Measurement and Evaluation in the Elementary School.* Second edition. New York: Longmans, Green and Co., 1953. Chapter 21.

GREENE, HARRY A., JORGENSEN, ALBERT N., AND GERBERICH, J. RAYMOND. *Measurement and Evaluation in the Secondary School.* Second edition. New York: Longmans, Green and Co., 1954. Chapter 24.

HEMPHILL, FAY. "Information Tests in Health and Physical Education for High School Boys." *Research Quarterly*, 3:83-96; December 1932.

HUTCHINS, H. CLIFTON. "Recreation." *Encyclopedia of Educational Research.* Third edition. New York: Macmillan Co., 1960. p. 1135-44.

HUTCHINSON, JOHN L., AND GLOSS, G. M. "Recreation." *Encyclopedia of Educational Research.* Revised edition. New York: Macmillan Co., 1950. p. 1005-16.

KNAPP, CLYDE. "Achievement Scales in Six Physical Education Activities for Secondary School Boys." *Research Quarterly*, 18:187-97; October 1947.

LARSON, LEONARD A., coordinator. *Measurement and Evaluation Materials in Health, Physical Education, and Recreation.* Washington, D. C.: American Association for Health, Physical Education, and Recreation, 1950. Chapters 6-9.

LARSON, LEONARD A., AND COX, WALTER A. "Tests and Measurements in Health and Physical Education." *Research Quarterly*, 12:483-89, Supplement; May 1941.

LARSON, LEONARD A., AND YOCOM, RACHAEL D. *Measurement and Evaluation in Physical, Health, and Recreation Education.* St. Louis, Mo.: C. V. Mosby Co., 1951. Parts 1, 4.

LATCHAW, MARJORIE. "Measuring Selected Motor Skills in Fourth, Fifth, and Sixth Grades." *Research Quarterly*, 25:439-49; December 1954.

LEHMAN, HARVEY C., AND WITTY, PAUL A. *The Psychology of Play Activities.* New York: A. S. Barnes and Co., 1927.

LOCKHART, AILEENE. "Testing Can Improve Teaching." *Journal of Health and Physical Education*, 19:590, 627-29; November 1948.

MATHEWS, DONALD K. *Measurement in Physical Education.* Philadelphia: W. B. Saunders Co., 1958. Chapters 1-3, 7, 12.

McCLOY, CHARLES H., AND YOUNG, NORMA D. *Tests and Measurements in Health and Physical Education.* Third edition. New York: Appleton-Century-Crofts, Inc., 1954. Chapters 1-7, 13, 16-17, 19-20, 22, 24-26.

NEILSON, NEILS P., AND COZENS, FREDERICK W. *Achievement Scales in Physical Education for Boys and Girls in Elementary and Junior High Schools.* New York: A. S. Barnes and Co., 1934.

RARICK, G. LAWRENCE. "Physical Education." *Encyclopedia of Educational Research.* Third edition. New York: Macmillan Co., 1960. p. 973-95.

SCOTT, M. GLADYS. "The Use of Skill Tests." *Journal of Health and Physical Education*, 9:364-66, 388-90; June 1938.

SCOTT, M. GLADYS, AND FRENCH, ESTHER L. *Evaluation in Physical Education.* St. Louis, Mo.: C. V. Mosby Co., 1950. Chapters 1-8.

25

GENERAL EDUCATIONAL ACHIEVEMENT

This chapter treats the following points in the measurement of general educational achievement:

A. Advantages of general achievement test batteries.
B. Limitations of general achievement test batteries.
C. Types of general achievement tests.
D. Batteries of general achievement tests.
E. Achievement test batteries in content areas.
F. Achievement test batteries in skill areas.

The emphasis throughout this volume is rather definitely on survey, analytic, and diagnostic testing and on evaluative techniques in subject and performance areas. A consideration of the practical problems of measurement and evaluation in the classroom leads to the conviction that there is a real service to be rendered by broad survey tests of general achievement. Accordingly, tests of that type are treated briefly here.

1. MEASUREMENT OF GENERAL ACHIEVEMENT

The battery type of general achievement test possesses certain types of possibilities for survey, analytic, and even general diagnostic testing and for the use of test results in educational guidance. Such a test affords a rather complete survey of the pupil's educational status. It presents a perspective of the aspects of his accomplishment measurable by paper-and-pencil tests.

Results from general achievement tests are of value in affording one basis for educational guidance of pupils. Evidence concerning the suitability for the individual pupil of certain subsequent courses or programs and even of certain vocations may often be obtained early in the pupil's school career. When cumulated over a period of years and when supplemented by other evidence, such test results can contribute significantly to pupil guidance.

A general survey test may also reveal weakness in a specific area or certain areas. To the critical teacher this may be a challenge to discover more exactly the factors underlying the deficiency. Accordingly, the pupils identified by the test as weak in certain areas should sometimes be subjected to a detailed analytic or diagnostic test in the subject for the purpose of locating specific difficulties and their causes. This is particularly true if the area is one of basic importance.

Advantages and Limitations of General Achievement Tests

Among the advantageous qualities of the battery-type tests of general achievement that have been given considerable emphasis by persons interested in the improvement of classroom measurement are the following:

Equivalency of measurement units. The use of a uniform unit of measurement in the scaling of battery tests constitutes a real advantage in the interpretation of the test results and in the comparisons of results from one subject field to another. While this is an important advantage, it does not at all mean that uniformity in units of measurement may not be secured in single tests in unrelated subjects.

Unity of population in standardization. The fact that the standardization of most comprehensive batteries is based upon results from the same pupils for each of the different subject tests insures a good picture of the relationships of achievement in these different subjects. The achievement of pupils of a certain grade in two subject areas can be compared only when tests are standardized under these conditions.

Simplicity of interpretation. The use of comparable units of measurement and similar testing techniques in the several tests comprising a general achievement battery simplifies the problems of comparing and interpreting the results. The test scores are readily turned into standard scores, educational ages, and grade equivalents. Modern graphic methods of summarizing test results make effective use of such derived scores. Profile charts of the type commonly provided with these tests add to the clearness with which test results may be interpreted. Naturally, such profiles are useful only in case test scores from a number of different tests are reducible to a common unit of measurement.

Simplicity of administration and scoring. The tendency of the authors of battery-type tests to utilize the same or similar types of testing techniques throughout the battery unquestionably tends to simplify the problems of administering it. The use of uniform methods of recording the pupil's responses also simplifies the problem of scoring. In general, such battery tests are usually so long that the time required to administer them and the labor involved in hand-scoring them become serious problems. However, many of these tests are now available for either hand- or machine-scoring above the primary grades.

Economy of cost. Any economy that results from the use of battery tests appears to be conditioned by the assumption that broadly diagnostic rather than specifically diagnostic or analytic measurement is desired. It is probably true that almost any one of the modern batteries of achievement tests will furnish a wider sampling into more subject fields at a lower cost per pupil than could be accomplished by the selection of single-subject tests for the purpose. There are numerous occasions, however, when it is of greater importance to measure more intensively a limited range of subjects. For this type of measurement the battery tests are usually not the most economical. In order to provide for this situation, the authors of most test batteries have prepared the tests for certain subjects in separate form. Indeed, several of the battery tests are available only in the form of separate coordinated test booklets.

Types of General Achievement Test Batteries

There are available today a number of general achievement batteries, several of which have very distinct merit. Most of the better-known and more widely used batteries are briefly described here. No attempt is made to illustrate their measurement techniques in this chapter, for the wide variety of outcomes tested makes that impracticable. Moreover, illustrations from some of these tests appear in preceding chapters of this volume. The tests discussed and summarized below are classified under four headings: (1) general achievement batteries for Grades 1 to 9, (2) general achievement batteries for Grades 4 to 12, (3) achievement batteries in content areas, and (4) achievement batteries in skill areas. A classified outline appearing in Table 34 for the tests described in the following pages gives test titles, levels at which they are available, and the grades provided for at each level.

2. GENERAL ACHIEVEMENT BATTERIES: GRADES 1 TO 9

Nearly half of the general achievement test batteries now available are designed for measuring outcomes in all of the major instructional areas

TABLE 34

Levels and Grade Coverage of General Achievement Test Batteries

Test and Level	Grade												
	1	2	3	4	5	6	7	8	9	10	11	12
General Achievement Batteries: Grades 1-9												
American School Achievement Tests												
Primary I	X											
Primary II		X	X									
Intermediate				X	X	X						
Advanced							X	X	X			
Coordinated Scales of Attainment												
Battery 1	X											
Battery 2		X										
Battery 3			X									
Battery 4				X								
Battery 5					X							
Battery 6						X						
Battery 7							X					
Battery 8								X				
Gray-Votaw-Rogers General Achievement Tests												
Primary	X	X	X									
Intermediate				X	X	X						
Advanced							X	X	X			
Master Achievement Tests												
Level 3			X									
Level 4				X								
Level 5					X							
Level 6						X						
Level 7							X					
Level 8								X				
Metropolitan Achievement Tests												
Primary I	X	X										
Primary II		X	X									
Elementary			X	X								
Intermediate					X	X						
Advanced							X	X	X			
National Achievement Tests												
Intermediate				X	X	X						
Advanced							X	X	X			
National Achievement Tests: Municipal Battery												
Grades 3-6			X	X	X	X						
Grades 6-8						X	X	X				
Stanford Achievement Tests												
Primary	X	X	X									
Elementary			X	X								
Intermediate					X	X						
Advanced							X	X	X			

continued on following page

Test and Level	1	2	3	4	5	6	7	8	9	10	11	12
General Achievement Batteries: Grades 4-12												
High School Fundamentals Evaluation Test									X	X	X	X
Iowa Tests of Educational Development									X	X	X	X
Myers-Ruch High School Progress Test									X	X	X	X
Sequential Tests of Educational Progress												
Level 4				X	X	X						
Level 3							X	X	X			
Level 2										X	X	X
Achievement Batteries in Content Areas												
California Tests of Social and Related Sciences												
Elementary				X	X	X	X	X				
Advanced									X	X	X	X
Cooperative General Achievement Tests												X
Essential High School Content Battery									X	X	X	X
Iowa High School Content Examination												X
Achievement Batteries in Skill Areas												
California Basic Skills Tests												
Elementary				X	X	X						
Intermediate							X	X	X			
California Achievement Tests												
Lower Primary	X	X										
Upper Primary			X	X								
Elementary				X	X	X						
Junior High School							X	X	X			
Advanced									X	X	X	X
Iowa Tests of Basic Skills			X	X	X	X	X	X	X			
Modern School Achievement Tests		X	X	X	X	X	X	X				
Scholastic Achievement Battery												
Pre-Primary	X	X										
Primary		X	X									
Elementary				X	X	X						
Advanced							X	X	X			
SRA Achievement Series												
Grades 1-2	X	X										
Grades 2-4		X	X	X								
Grades 4-6				X	X	X						
Grades 6-9						X	X	X	X			

appropriate for the grade levels in question. As instructional emphases in the primary grades are mainly upon skill in reading, arithmetic, and language, battery tests designed for use in the first three grades concentrate upon these skill areas almost entirely. Such content subjects as the social studies and elementary sciences commonly receive more attention in the intermediate and upper grades. For this reason, batteries designed for use above Grade 3 usually include parts in these subject areas and often on health and safety, as well as sections in the areas of receptive and expressive language and computational skills. Consequently, the number of separate parts and of resulting scores tends to be greater at the intermediate and upper grade levels than for the primary grades. There is a parallel tendency for time requirements in administration and scoring to be greater at the intermediate and upper grade levels than for the primary grades.

American School Achievement Tests

These tests have been extended both upward and outward since their first publication in 1941 by provision in the 1947 edition for pupils in Grades 7 to 9 and by inclusion of social studies and science tests in the current edition. The tests appear in four-page booklets—one for Primary I, two for Primary II, and four each for Intermediate and Advanced levels—in a self-marking format that reduces scoring to a process of counting the marks appearing in designated cells printed on the inside, and originally sealed, pages of the booklet.

TABLE 35

Organization of *American School Achievement Tests* [1]

		Level, Grades, and Timing			
		PRIMARY		INTER-MEDIATE	AD-VANCED
Area	Test	I	2-3	4-6	7-9
Reading	Word Recognition	5			
	Word Meaning	10			
	Sentence and Word Meaning		10	10	10
	Paragraph Meaning		15	15	20
Arithmetic	Numbers	5			
	Arithmetic Computation		12	30	35
	Arithmetic Problems		10	20	25
Language	Language		8	20	25
	Spelling		10	12	12
Social Studies	Social Studies			25	25
Science	Science			25	25

[1] Willis E. Pratt and others, *American School Achievement Tests,* Primary I and II, Intermediate, and Advanced. Public School Publishing Co., Bloomington, Ill., 1955, 1957.

Measurement and Evaluation in the Modern School

Titles of the tests in reading, arithmetic, language, and the two major content subjects and the pupil working time for each test at each level are shown in Table 35. Time requirements for pupils range from 20 minutes for Grade 1 to about three hours at the Advanced level. Grade and age norms are provided for all of the batteries.

Coordinated Scales of Attainment

These scales, successors to the *Unit Scales of Attainment,* are issued in eight separate single-booklet editions for Grades 1 to 8, as is shown in Table 36. Batteries for the primary grades entail the recording of answers in the booklets and must be scored manually. Pupils in Grades 4 to 8 record their answers on answer sheets which may be scored either by hand or by machine. Working times for pupils vary from approximately 100 minutes in the primary grades to 256 minutes for the intermediate and upper grades. Tests are available in separate booklets for the various subject areas. Norms are provided in the form of grade equivalents and age equivalents for major scores.

TABLE 36

Organization of *Coordinated Scales of Attainment* [2]

Area	Test	Battery and Grade							
		1	2	3	4	5	6	7	8
Reading	Picture-Word Association	10	10	10					
	Word-Picture Association	10	10	10					
	Vocabulary Recognition	10	10	10					
	Reading Comprehension	10	10	10					
	Reading				45	45	45	45	45
	Reading Experience—Literature				15	15	15	15	15
Arithmetic	Arithmetic Experience	10	10						
	Number Skills	10	10						
	Arithmetic Computation	15	15	20	45	45	45	45	45
	Arithmetic Problem Reasoning	15	15	20	30	30	30	30	30
Language	Spelling		20	20	40	40	40	40	40
	Punctuation				12	12	12	12	12
	Capitalization				12	12	12	12	12
	Usage				12	12	12	12	12
Social Studies	History				15	15	15	15	15
	Geography				15	15	15	15	15
Science	Elementary Science				15	15	15	15	15

[2] M. E. Branom and others, *Coordinated Scales of Attainment,* Grades 1, 2, 3, 4, 5, 6, 7, and 8. Educational Test Bureau, Minneapolis, Minn., 1946.

Gray-Votaw-Rogers General Achievement Tests

A revision of the *Gray-Votaw General Achievement Tests,* the present batteries[3] appear at the Primary, Intermediate, and Advanced levels and provide tests for Grade 1 to Grade 9. Pupil working time on the Primary battery is 62 minutes in Grades 1 and 2 and 50 minutes in Grade 3. Working time is 135 minutes each on the higher-level batteries. These batteries are hand-scorable, but an abbreviated edition for Grades 5 to 9 is accompanied by machine-scorable answer sheets that can also be scored manually. Grade and age norms are provided for each test and for a total score on each battery; percentile grade norms are given for the total battery score at each level. The part scores cover reading comprehension, vocabulary, arithmetic computation and reasoning, and spelling at all levels and, in addition, literature, language, social studies, elementary science, and health and safety at the two upper levels.

Master Achievement Tests

The six levels of this battery,[4] for use in Grades 3 to 8, are available in single booklets for each grade. The testing time in Grades 7 and 8 is about 140 minutes. In the four lower grades the time requirement is slightly longer. Grade norms, by means of which grade equivalents may be obtained, are provided for the various tests of the battery at each grade level. Test parts deal with reading and vocabulary, English and spelling, arithmetic, geography, history, and science and health.

Metropolitan Achievement Tests

The present batteries of these tests represent a third revision. The original edition was published in the 1920s, the first revision was issued in several forms during the period 1931 to 1937, and the second revision appeared in 1946. As is shown in Table 37, tests in the three common skill areas and two major content fields are supplemented by two tests of study skills at the higher levels. Only the skill areas are provided for in the Primary and Elementary batteries. Both hand-scoring and machine-scoring editions are available at the Intermediate and Advanced levels, but batteries for Grades 1 to 4 appear only in a hand-scoring format. Partial batteries consisting of tests in the skill areas of reading, arithmetic, and

[3] Hob Gray, David F. Votaw, and J. Lloyd Rogers, *Gray-Votaw-Rogers General Achievement Tests,* Primary, Intermediate, and Advanced. Steck Co., Austin, Tex., 1950-51.
[4] *Master Achievement Tests,* Grades 3, 4, 5, 6, 7, and 8. American Education Press, Columbus, Ohio, 1937.

language are provided for Grades 5 to 9 and separate booklets for four subject areas—reading, arithmetic, social studies, and science—can be had for Grade 3 and above.

A number of excerpts from various levels and tests of this battery appear in earlier chapters of this volume. Excerpts from the reading and language sections are shown on page 31 of Chapter 2 and on pages 234 and 237 of Chapter 10. Arithmetic test items from the Elementary level are reproduced on page 236 of Chapter 10 and pages 417 and 419 of the chapter on arithmetic and mathematics. Still another excerpt, from the Advanced test in history and civics, is given on page 474 of Chapter 19. Pupil working time on the batteries ranges from 92 minutes for Grade 1 to 267 minutes for the Advanced level. Grade equivalents, percentile grade norms, and stanine scores are provided for giving additional meaning to standard scores, which themselves express results on all subtests on all batteries in comparable terms.

TABLE 37

Organization of *Metropolitan Achievement Tests* [5]

Area	Test and Subtest	Level, Grades, and Timing				
		PRIMARY I	II	ELE-MENTARY	INTER-MEDIATE	AD-VANCED
		1-2	2-3	3-4	5-6	7-9
Reading	Words: Knowledge	20	22	18	14	14
	Discrimination	12	12	12		
	Reading: Sentences	12	10			
	Stories	25	25			
	General			25	25	25
Arithmetic	Concepts and Skills	23	25	8	12	12
	Problem Solving			22	25	25
	Computation			30	40	35
Language	Spelling		10	20	17	17
	Language Usage			10	15	10
	Punctuation and Capitalization			15	9	7
	Grammar				6	12
	Sentences					6
Social Studies	Information: Geography, etc.				17	17
	Study Skills: Reading Maps				15	25
	Reading Tables, etc.				15	25
Science	Science				17	17
Study Skills	Dictionary Skills				10	10
	Sources of Information				10	10

[5] Harold H. Bixler and others, *Metropolitan Achievement Tests,* Primary I and II, Elementary, Intermediate, and Advanced. World Book Co., Yonkers, N. Y., 1959.

National Achievement Tests

These tests [6] are issued in two batteries, for Grades 4 to 6 and 7 to 9, and in three subject areas—the language arts, including both reading and language; arithmetic, both in fundamentals and reasoning; and social studies, science, and health areas of content. The single-booklet batteries require about a hundred minutes of pupil working time. Provision is made for giving meaning to the three test scores at each level in terms of grade equivalents.

National Achievement Tests, Municipal Battery

A second series of *National Achievement Tests* [7] provides separate tests for reading comprehension and speed, literature, English, spelling, arithmetic fundamentals and reasoning, geography, history-civics, and health. The testing time is slightly over two hundred minutes at each level. Three sets of grade and age equivalents are furnished for each of the ten tests—for pupils having low, medium, and high intelligence quotients.

Stanford Achievement Tests

The original battery of these tests, published in 1923, did much to stimulate the improvement of educational measurement in general. After six years, the tests were revised in the form known as the *New Stanford Achievement Tests*. They have more recently been revised a second and a third time and are again known as the *Stanford Achievement Tests*.

In their present form the batteries consist of five primary tests for Grades 2 and 3, six elementary tests for Grades 3 and 4, nine intermediate tests for Grades 5 and 6, and nine advanced tests for Grades 7 to 9, as is shown in Table 38. The testing times are 85 minutes for the Primary battery, 145 minutes for the Elementary battery, and 232 and 227 minutes respectively for the Intermediate and Advanced batteries. At the two upper levels the tests are also available for machine-scoring in partial batteries. Norms are of two types—percentile norms by grades and modal-age norms, based only on those pupils in the standardization group who were at grade for their age. Two excerpts from this battery appear in Chapter 10 of this volume—one from the Primary test on word meaning on page 228 and one from the Intermediate spelling test on page 230.

[6] Lester D. Crow, Alice Crow, and William H. Bristow, *National Achievement Tests,* Intermediate and Advanced. Acorn Publishing Co., Rockville Centre, N. Y., 1955-58.

[7] Robert K. Speer and Samuel Smith, *National Achievement Tests,* Municipal Battery, Grades 3-6 and 6-8. Acorn Publishing Co., Rockville Centre, N. Y., 1938-58.

TABLE 38

Organization of *Stanford Achievement Tests* [8]

Area	Test and Subtest	Level, Grades, and Timing			
		PRIMARY 2-3	ELE-MENTARY 3-4	INTER-MEDIATE 5-6	AD-VANCED 7-9
Language Arts	Reading: Paragraph Meaning	25	30	30	30
	Word Meaning	10	10	12	12
	Spelling	15	20	15	15
	Language		25	20	20
Arithmetic	Arithmetic: Computation	18	30	40	40
	Reasoning	17	30	35	35
Social Studies	Social Studies			20	20
Science	Science			15	15
Study Skills	Study Skills			45	40

3. GENERAL ACHIEVEMENT BATTERIES: GRADES 4 TO 12

A second group of general achievement test batteries, less numerous than those described in the preceding section, provides in general for the grades from 4 to 12 and in particular for the high-school grades. All of these batteries include materials from one or more of the basic areas of content as well as from the three basic skill areas.

High School Fundamentals Evaluation Test

This survey-type test [9] for use in Grades 9 to 12 contains parts on reading vocabulary, reading comprehension, mathematics, science, and history and the social studies in a single booklet. Scaled scores can be converted to percentile ranks by grades on the five parts. Two hours of testing time are required for the hand- or machine-scorable instrument.

Iowa Tests of Educational Development

The *Iowa Tests of Educational Development* are the outgrowth of a state-wide testing program for secondary schools conducted over a period

---

[8] Truman L. Kelley and others, *Stanford Achievement Tests*, Primary, Elementary, Intermediate, and Advanced. World Book Co., Yonkers, N. Y., 1953.

[9] David F. Votaw, *High School Fundamentals Evaluation Test*. Steck Co., Austin, Tex., 1955.

of years by the State University of Iowa. A single answer sheet is used for this battery and the results are scored and reported to schools using the tests by the State University of Iowa through arrangements with the publisher. One form was also issued in 1951 in nine separate booklets with accompanying answer sheets subject to manual- or to machine-scoring.

This integrated battery of tests for Grades 9 to 13 is designed to yield a comprehensive description of each pupil not only in the sense that it measures all broad aspects of general educational development that are readily measurable but also in the more important sense that emphasis is placed on the ultimate outcomes of the educational program rather than on the outcomes in the separate school subjects or areas. The four general background tests in social studies, science, English, and mathematics are supplemented by functional tests of abilities to interpret reading materials in the first three of these areas and by tests of general vocabulary and use of sources of information, as is shown in Table 39.

TABLE 39

Organization of *Iowa Tests of Educational Development* [10]

Type	Test	Title	Timing
Background Tests	1	Understanding of Basic Social Concepts	55
	2	Background in the Natural Sciences	60
	3	Correctness and Appropriateness of Expression	60
	4	Ability To Do Quantitative Thinking	65
Reading Tests	5	Ability To Interpret in the Social Studies	60
	6	Ability To Interpret in the Natural Sciences	60
	7	Ability To Interpret Literary Materials	50
Vocabulary Test	8	General Vocabulary	22
Information Test	9	Uses of Sources of Information	27

Provision is made for the reporting of separate standard scores for each of the nine basic tests and for a composite of Tests 1 to 8 on pupil profile cards prepared in quadruplicate. The battery is designed for administration in three or four sessions and requires 459 minutes of pupil working time. Percentile-grade norms for pupil scores and also for school averages are available both on a nation-wide basis and for several regions of the country separately. A copy of the pupil profile card used in reporting results to teachers is reproduced on page 185 of Chapter 8.

[10] E. F. Lindquist, general editor, *Iowa Tests of Educational Development*. Science Research Associates, Inc., Chicago, 1942, 1951.

Myers-Ruch High School Progress Test

This single-booklet test for use in the high school and the first year of college [11] consists of four parts—one each in English, social studies, mathematics, and science. The back of the cover page is printed as an answer sheet for hand-scoring. Separate answer sheets are also available either for manual- or machine-scoring. The battery requires 60 minutes of testing time. Percentile-grade norms are provided for the four high-school classes.

Sequential Tests of Educational Progress

The *STEP* series provides tests at Levels 2 to 4 for use with pupils in Grades 4 to 12 and also, of no direct significance in this volume, at Level 1

TABLE 40

Organization of *Sequential Tests of Educational Progress* [12]

Test	Measures	Level, Grades, and Timing		
		LEVEL 4 4-6	LEVEL 3 7-9	LEVEL 2 10-12
Reading	Ability to read new material with comprehension, insight, and critical understanding	70	70	70
Listening	Comprehension, interpretation, and evaluation of what is heard as pronounced by examiner	70	70	70
Writing	Proficiency in selecting best versions of written material for effective expression of ideas	70	70	70
Essay	Ability to write short themes on assigned topics for which settings are given in short paragraphs	35	35	35
Mathematics	Attainment of broad mathematical objectives of general education	70	70	70
Science	Understanding of basic concepts; attainment of skills essential to applications and critical thinking	70	70	70
Social Studies	Attainment of abilities and understandings considered essential in development of effective citizens	70	70	70

[11] Charles E. Myers, Giles M. Ruch, and Graham C. Loofbourow, *Myers-Ruch High School Progress Test.* World Book Co., Yonkers, N. Y., 1936-38.

[12] Educational Testing Service, *Sequential Tests of Educational Progress,* Levels 2, 3, and 4. Educational Testing Service, Princeton, N. J., 1957.

for college freshmen and sophomores. Separate test booklets for reading, listening, writing, mathematics, social studies, and sciences are supplemented by a seventh test on essay writing at all levels. Brief descriptive statements about what each of the seven tests is designed to measure are given in Table 40. In addition, an account of the procedures used in evaluating essays appears on pages 386 and 387 of Chapter 16, and the battery is further represented by a few sample items each from the listening test and the arithmetic test of Level 4 on pages 366 and 420 respectively.

Separate answer sheets scorable either by hand or by machine are required for all except the essay test. Three-digit converted scores ranging from approximately 225 to about 350 are established by the publisher in such manner that they are comparable not only among the seven tests but also from level to level of the battery. Percentile norms by grades are provided for all tests and levels. Recognition that pupil scores afford estimates rather than absolutely accurate indications of pupil achievement is evidenced by use of percentile bands of the type discussed in Section 5 of Chapter 8 for giving approximate meaning to converted scores after they are translated into percentile ranks.

4. ACHIEVEMENT BATTERIES IN CONTENT AREAS

General achievement batteries dealing with the content aspects of subject areas are considerably less numerous than those in the basic skills areas. In fact, the authors know of only one instrument of this type for use below the high-school level that may properly be considered an achievement battery. The other three tests dealt with here apply only to the high-school grades or even to the senior year of high school.

California Tests in Social and Related Sciences

These tests in the two major content areas are outgrowths of the earlier *Progressive Tests in Social and Related Sciences*. However, the earlier edition appeared at one level only whereas the newer one provides Elementary and Advanced batteries for Grades 4 to 8 and Grades 9 to 12. Each of the three-booklet batteries consists of six tests, four in the social studies and two in the sciences, as is shown in Table 41. Pupil working times are 140 and 170 minutes respectively for the intermediate-grade and high-school batteries. Age, grade, and percentile-grade norms are provided for the six tests at each level and also for a number of subtests at each level.

Excerpts from four of the tests of the Elementary battery appear in Chapters 18 and 19 of this volume to illustrate techniques for testing in science and social studies. The illustrations of items in elementary science and in health and safety appear on pages 449 and 450. American history and geography are represented by two excerpts on page 472.

TABLE 41

Organization of *California Tests in Social and Related Sciences* [13]

Parts	Tests	Level, Grades, and Timing	
		ELEMENTARY 4-8	ADVANCED 9-12
Social Studies I	The American Heritage People of Other Lands and Times	50	
American History to 1865	Creating a New Nation Nationalism, Sectionalism, and Conflict		45
Social Studies II	Geography Basic Social Processes	50	
American History since 1865	The Emergence of Modern America The United States in Transition		45
Related Sciences	Health and Safety Elementary Science	40	
	Physical Science Biological Science		80

Cooperative General Achievement Tests

Suitable for use only in Grade 12 of the secondary school and during the first year of college, these tests [14] are available in three separate booklets for social studies, natural sciences, and mathematics. The current editions are revisions of editions published some years previously. Each 40-minute test provides three scores—a total score and part scores on terms and concepts and on comprehension and interpretation. The tests require use of separate answer sheets that can be scored either by hand or by machine. Percentile norms are provided for use in giving meaning to the scaled scores.

[13] Georgia S. Adams and John A. Sexson, *California Tests in Social and Related Sciences,* Elementary and Advanced. California Test Bureau, Los Angeles, 1953.

[14] Paul J. Burke, Jeanne M. Bradford, and others, *Cooperative General Achievement Tests: I, Social Studies; II, Natural Sciences; III, Mathematics.* Forms XX and YZ. Educational Testing Service, Princeton, N. J., 1951, 1953.

Essential High School Content Battery

This single-booklet battery [15] includes tests in mathematics, science, social studies, and English. The test provides for the recording of pupil responses on a separate answer sheet that is scorable either manually or by machine. The battery, requiring 225 minutes of working time, is designed for use with pupils in Grades 9 to 12 and with entering college freshmen. End-of-year percentile-grade norms for pupils in Grades 9 to 12 are provided for each of the four tests and a median of the four scores. The general norms for all pupils are supplemented by differential norms for pupils in academic and scientific courses and pupils in commercial and general courses. A few sample items from the science section of the battery are shown on page 41 of Chapter 2.

Iowa High School Content Examination

The original edition of this test, published in 1925, was followed in 1943 by the revised, quick-scoring edition. The present single-booklet edition [16] includes sections on the four major areas of secondary-school instruction for use in Grades 12 and 13. It is designed to measure primarily knowledge and skill outcomes in English, mathematics, science, and social studies. Two forms of special answer sheets, one for hand-scoring and the other for either manual- or machine-scoring, are available. The battery requires 75 minutes of testing time. Percentile-grade norms for April testing are provided for scores on each of the four sections and for a total score.

5. ACHIEVEMENT BATTERIES IN SKILL AREAS

A second group of test batteries is distinguishable from those discussed above by the fact that they are concerned with the skill areas to the exclusion of the content areas of instruction. These batteries are not restricted to the primary-grade level, where the instructional emphasis is mainly upon reading, language, and arithmetic skills, but variously provide tests for the intermediate and upper grades and for the entire range from primary grades to senior high school.

[15] David P. Harry and Walter N. Durost, *Essential High School Content Battery*. World Book Co., Yonkers, N. Y., 1950.

[16] D. B. Stuit, Harry A. Greene, and Giles M. Ruch, *Iowa High School Content Examination*, Revised. Bureau of Educational Research and Service, State University of Iowa, Iowa City, 1943.

California Basic Skills Tests

These basic skills tests in reading, arithmetic, and language consist of single-booklet reproductions of some of the levels and forms of the *California Achievement Tests,* 1950 edition. They are available in hand-scoring editions only and pupils record their answers in the test booklets. Two levels—Elementary for Grades 4 to 6 and Intermediate for Grades 7 to 9— are available. Six tests, two each in reading, arithmetic, and language, are included. As is shown in Table 42, all of the tests except spelling are made up of several subtests. Approximately two hours and two and a half hours of pupil working time respectively are required for pupils in the intermediate grades and junior high school.

TABLE 42

Organization of *California Basic Skills Tests* [17]

Area	Test and Subtest	Level, Grades, and Timing	
		ELEMENTARY 4-6	INTERMEDIATE 7-9
Reading	Vocabulary: Word Forms	3	
	Word Recognition	3	
	Meaning of Opposites	3	
	Meaning of Similarities	3	
	Mathematics		3
	Science		3
	Social Studies		3
	General		3
	Comprehension: Following Directions	5	8
	Reference Skills	6	5
	Interpretations	12	25
Arithmetic	Reasoning: Number Concepts	3	4
	Signs and Symbols	3	
	Symbols and Rules		5
	Numbers and Equations		5
	Problems	10	16
	Fundamentals: Addition	10	10
	Subtraction	10	10
	Multiplication	12	12
	Division	12	12
Language	Mechanics: Capitalization	3	3
	Punctuation	4	4
	Words and Sentences	5	5
	Parts of Speech		6
	Spelling	12	12

[17] Ernest W. Tiegs and Willis W. Clark, *California Basic Skills Tests,* Elementary and Intermediate. California Test Bureau, Los Angeles, 1954.

Grade and age equivalents and percentile-grade norms are provided for each of the six tests, for total achievement separately in reading, arithmetic, and language, and also for a total score on the complete battery. A supplementary handwriting test is provided for use if desired and a scale for interpreting quality in terms of grade placement appears in the manuals for the language test. However, age equivalents and percentile norms are not provided for handwriting, and this test is not an integral part of the battery.

California Achievement Tests

The *Progressive Achievement Tests* were retitled the *California Achievement Tests* in the 1950 editions. As is indicated immediately above, the *California Basic Skills Tests* were brought out in 1954 as a third stage in the sequence. Shortly thereafter the *California Achievement Tests* were issued in the 1957 edition. This current edition is similar in some of its parts to the 1950 edition, but it provides five levels to replace the four of its predecessor. As is shown in Table 43, the five levels from Lower Primary to Advanced cover all of the public school grades. The battery also provides for the first two years of college. The six tests are published in three separate booklets at each of the three higher levels, with one booklet each for reading, arithmetic or mathematics, and language. Single-booklet editions are available at all five levels to provide for Grade 1 to Grade 14.

Working time varies from about 70 minutes for the Lower Primary level to nearly three hours at the Advanced level. Hand-scoring of answers recorded in the booklets is necessary in the primary grades but possibilities at the three higher levels also include use of hand- or machine-scorable answer sheets, *CTB Scoreze* answer sheets for manual scoring, or *Cal-Cards* for scoring by the publisher. Since the statements about norms and about the supplementary handwriting test appearing in the preceding section for the *California Basic Skills Tests* apply equally well to this battery, there is no need for further mention of norms here. A reproduction of the diagnostic profile for the Elementary level on page 184 of this volume indicates the manner in which original scores, grade equivalents, and percentile ranks are reported and made available for use. Two excerpts from the junior-high-school test in arithmetic also appear in earlier chapters. A few sample items measuring arithmetic reasoning are shown on page 233 of Chapter 10 and several items used in testing fundamental skills or computation involving addition of whole numbers and fractions appear in Chapter 17 on page 418.

TABLE 43

Organization of *California Achievement Tests* [18]

Area	Test and Subtest	PRIMARY LOWER 1-2	PRIMARY UPPER 3-4	ELE-MENTARY 4-6	JUNIOR HIGH 7-9	AD-VANCED 9-14
Reading	Vocabulary:					
	Word Form	5				
	Word Recognition	3	4			
	Meaning of Opposites	3	5			
	Picture Association	4				
	Mathematics			4	4	4
	Science					
	Social Science			4	4	4
	General					
	Comprehension:					
	Reading	8				
	Following Directions		6	10	10	10
	Reference Skills		10	12	15	15
	Interpretations		15	20	35	35
Arithmetic	Reasoning:					
	Meanings	14	7	4	5	6
	Signs and Symbols	14	4	4		
	Symbols and Rules				10	10
	Problems		10	12	16	15
	Fundamentals:					
	Addition	6	6	12	10	9
	Subtraction	5	8	12	10	9
	Multiplication		9	12	12	10
	Division		10	14	15	13
Language	Mechanics:					
	Capitalization	5	5	10	6	8
	Punctuation	5	5	9	6	6
	Word Usage	7	10	7	8	12
	Spelling	10	10	12	10	10

Iowa Tests of Basic Skills

Growing out of the basic skills tests used in a state-wide testing program in Iowa over a period of years, the present multilevel edition of this battery for Grades 3 to 9 is published in a spiral-bound, reusable booklet. The five area tests, in vocabulary, reading comprehension, language skills, work-study skills, and arithmetic skills, require more than four and a half hours of pupil working time and are usually given in several sittings over a

[18] Ernest W. Tiegs and Willis W. Clark, *California Achievement Tests,* 1957 Edition, Lower and Upper Primary, Elementary, Junior High School, and Advanced. California Test Bureau, Los Angeles, 1957.

period of two or more days. The immediate forerunners of this battery, the machine-scorable *Iowa Every-Pupil Tests of Basic Skills*,[19] are also available in four separate booklets for use at the same grade levels.

The multilevel edition of this battery provides for having the pupils in each grade take tests that are appropriate in difficulty and content for their particular levels of advancement. Each test consists of one continuous series of items that serves at all grade levels, but the pupils in the various grades begin and stop at different points in the series. This principle is illustrated by the item numbers shown by grades in Table 44. In the Vocabulary Test, for example, some of the items taken by pupils in Grade 4 (11-48) are also taken by pupils in Grade 3 (1-31) and Grade 5 (24-66).

Either of two types of answer sheets, for scoring by electrical or by electronic machines, or even by hand, can be used with these tests. Both grade norms and percentile-grade norms are provided for use in interpreting part scores as well as scores on the five tests of the battery. Three sets of percentile-grade norms are available—for testing done near the beginning, toward the middle, and close to the end of the school year. Provision is made for reporting results in profile form both to teachers and to pupils and their parents. A reproduction of the latter form appears on page 187 of Chapter 8. The leaflet in which it appears carries the descriptive title, "How Are Your Skills?"

TABLE 44

Organization of *Iowa Tests of Basic Skills* [20]

Test	Part	Timing	Grades and Item Numbers					
			3	4	5	6	7	8-9
Vocabulary	Vocabulary	17	1-31	11-48	24-66	40-85	58-105	67-114
Reading	Comprehension	55	1-60	12-79	25-98	61-136	80-157	99-178
Language	Spelling	12	1-31	11-48	24-66	40-85	58-105	67-114
	Capitalization	15	1-38	10-48	19-58	39-80	49-91	59-102
	Punctuation	20	1-38	10-48	19-58	39-80	49-91	59-102
	Usage	20	1-32	12-43	23-54	33-64	44-75	55-86
Work-Study	Map Reading	30	1-27	6-37	12-47	28-67	38-78	48-89
	Reading Graphs	20	1-20	9-32	21-46	33-60	41-68	47-74
	Use of References	30	1-42	15-66	27-82	43-101	67-125	83-141
Arithmetic	Concepts	30	1-30	16-51	31-72	52-96	73-120	89-136
	Problem Solving	30	1-25	13-39	26-54	40-70	55-86	63-96

[19] E. F. Lindquist, editor, *Iowa Every-Pupil Tests of Basic Skills*, Elementary and Advanced. Houghton Mifflin Co., Boston, 1940-43.

[20] E. F. Lindquist and A. N. Hieronymus, *Iowa Tests of Basic Skills*, Multi-level edition. Houghton Mifflin Co., Boston, 1955.

Modern School Achievement Tests: Skills

This single-booklet battery,[21] the presently available curtailment of the more comprehensive *Modern School Achievement Tests,* includes five tests in three subject areas—reading comprehension, reading speed, arithmetic computation, arithmetic reasoning, and spelling. The content ranges in difficulty from material suitable for use in Grade 2 to that appropriate for pupils in Grade 8. The total testing time is about two hours. Age and grade norms are provided for each of the tests and a table is provided for the interpretation of percentage of accuracy scores on the reading speed and accuracy test in terms of grade equivalents.

Scholastic Achievement Battery

This recent addition to batteries for use in testing some major instructional skills is designed to meet the particular needs of a Catholic school curriculum. The battery, for which the organizational plan is shown in Table 45, provides tests in the major skill areas except for reading. Each of the four levels—Pre-Primary, Primary, Elementary, and Advanced—includes not only the language, spelling, and arithmetic content indicated in the table but also a content test in religion.

TABLE 45

Organization of *Scholastic Achievement Battery* [22]

Area	Test	PRE-PRIMARY 1-2	PRIMARY 2-3	ELE-MENTARY 4-6	AD-VANCED 7-9
English	Recognition of Nouns	6			
	Recognition of Pronouns	3			
	Recognition of Verbs	3			
	Punctuation and Capitalization		13	12	12
	Terms and Concepts of Grammar			15	15
	Correct Usage		7	7	7
	Oral and Written English			8	7
Spelling	Spelling	5	5	8	8
Arithmetic	Computation	20	20	28	28
	Reasoning	8	23	25	25

Levels, Grades, and Timing spans the four rightmost columns.

[21] Arthur I. Gates and others, *The Modern School Achievement Tests: Skills.* Bureau of Publications, Teachers College, Columbia University, New York, 1931.

[22] Oliver F. Anderhalter, R. Stephen Rawkoski, and John O'Brien, *Scholastic Achievement Battery,* Pre-Primary, Primary, Elementary, and Advanced. Scholastic Testing Service, Inc., Chicago, 1955.

Time requirements for the skills portion of the battery range from 45 minutes in Grades 1 and 2 to about 100 minutes in the junior high school. The booklets are designed for hand-scoring only. Grade norms and percentile-grade norms are provided for all tests and for language, spelling, and arithmetic totals. An individual pupil profile for use in giving meaning to the results appears on the back cover of the test booklets.

SRA Achievement Series

Basic skills tests in reading, arithmetic, language, and the work-study area are provided at four levels in this recently published battery, as is shown in Table 46. The two lower levels, for Grades 1 to 2 and 2 to 4, do not include a work-study test, but the Grades 4 to 6 and 6 to 9 levels do make provision for this area. Seven part scores at the two lower levels and ten for pupils in Grade 4 and above result from use of this battery. Pupil working time for the entire battery ranges from slightly under four hours at the lowest level to about five hours in Grades 6 to 9. Hand-scoring is possible at all levels and machine-scorable answer sheets can be used with pupils in the intermediate grades and junior high school.

Grade equivalents and skeleton-type percentile-grade norms for first and second semesters are available for use in interpreting results. Pupil profile and pupil progress forms for use within the school and a pupil profile chart for use in reporting results to pupils and their parents are provided.

TABLE 46

Organization of *SRA Achievement Series* [23]

Area	Test	Grades and Timing 1-2	2-4	4-6	6-9
Reading	Verbal-Pictorial Association	32			
	Language Perception	31			
	Comprehension	30	50	} 65	} 70
	Vocabulary	27	40		
Arithmetic	Reasoning (or Problem Solving)	50	45	60	45
	Concepts	20	10	} 60	25
	Computation	35	45		35
Language	(Grammatical) Usage		} 60	} 60	} 40
	Capitalization and Punctuation				
	Spelling		8	15	20
Work-Study	References			57	30
	Charts			35	40

[23] Louis P. Thorpe, D. Welty Lefever, and Robert A. Naslund, *SRA Achievement Series,* Grades 1-2, 2-4, 4-6, and 6-9. Science Research Associates, Inc., Chicago, 1958.

SUGGESTED ACTIVITIES

1. Obtain access to sample sets of two achievement test batteries, preferably of the same general type and grade coverage, and compare them by using such a rating scale as the one shown on page 164 of Chapter 8.
2. Read one or more of the reviews of general achievement test batteries appearing in one of the later editions, say the Fourth or Fifth, of the Buros *Mental Measurements Yearbook.*

TOPICS FOR DISCUSSION

1. What major functions are served by batteries of general achievement tests?
2. What are some of the advantages of general achievement test batteries?
3. What are some of the limitations of general achievement test batteries?
4. How do the functions of these test batteries and of analytic or diagnostic tests differ?
5. What are some of the instructional outcomes achievement test batteries fail to measure?
6. How may general achievement tests be used in the grade placement and sectioning of pupils in a school system?
7. Into what major types may achievement test batteries be classified?
8. How do tests of general educational achievement differ from other general achievement test batteries?
9. What are the advantages of the pupil profile charts provided with most achievement test batteries?
10. How can achievement test batteries and pupil profile charts be used in the measurement of the educational progress of pupils?

SELECTED REFERENCES

BUROS, OSCAR K., editor. *The Fifth Mental Measurements Yearbook.* Highland Park, N. J.: Gryphon Press, 1959. p. 1-85.

BUROS, OSCAR K., editor. *The Fourth Mental Measurements Yearbook.* Highland Park, N. J.: Gryphon Press, 1953. p. 1-66.

BUROS, OSCAR K., editor. *The Third Mental Measurements Yearbook.* New Brunswick, N. J.: Rutgers University Press, 1949. p. 1-50.

GREENE, HARRY A., JORGENSEN, ALBERT N., AND GERBERICH, J. RAYMOND. *Measurement and Evaluation in the Elementary School.* Second edition. New York: Longmans, Green and Co., 1953. Chapter 22.

GREENE, HARRY A., JORGENSEN, ALBERT N., AND GERBERICH, J. RAYMOND. *Measurement and Evaluation in the Secondary School.* Second edition. New York: Longmans, Green and Co., 1954. Chapter 25.

JORDAN, A. M. *Measurement in Education.* New York: McGraw-Hill Book Co., Inc., 1953. Chapter 4.

SMITH, JANET. "A Test of General Achievement for Children of Preschool Age." *Journal of Experimental Education,* 12:92-105; December 1943.

APPENDIX A

COMPUTING THE PEARSON PRODUCT-MOMENT

CORRELATION COEFFICIENT

A brief outline is given here of procedures involved in computing the Pearson product-moment coefficient of correlation. Some instructors may prefer to use the Pearson r with their classes in addition to, or even instead of, the tetrachoric r and the Spearman rho that are dealt with on pages 313 to 317 of Chapter 13. Moreover, some students and classroom teachers individually may wish to extend their understanding of correlation beyond what is covered in Chapter 13. The largely rule-of-thumb steps of procedure and the illustration appearing on the following pages are designed primarily to satisfy such desires.

The paired English usage test scores given in Table 18 on page 314 for 30 ninth-grade pupils and used in the treatment of correlation in Chapter 13 are again employed in the following illustration and discussion. Scores on the informal objective test and the standardized test here appear respectively on the Y axis and X axis of the double-entry table shown in Figure 24.

(1) Set up a double-entry table on cross-section paper or use a special correlation chart. Construct a frequency distribution at the left of the chart (Y axis) for one of the variables, using the procedure of steps (1) to (3), pages 306 and 307, for setting up a frequency distribution. Construct a second frequency distribution by the same procedure across the top of the chart (X axis) for the other variable, with the low scores at

the left and the high scores at the right. [The Y-axis variable of Figure 24 provides in class intervals of three, e.g., 29-31, for the informal objective test scores of English usage. The X-axis variable of the figure similarly provides in class intervals of five, e.g., 48-52, for the standardized test scores of the 30 ninth-grade pupils.]

(2) Tabulate the pairs of scores in the double-entry table. Place a tally mark in the cell of the table that correctly represents the paired scores of each individual on the Y-axis and X-axis variables. [The 30 sets of paired English usage test scores listed in Table 18 are represented by small tally marks in the lower left-hand corners of the appropriate cells in the correlation chart shown in Figure 24. The Y-axis score of 11 and the X-axis score of 17 made by GBS, for example, are both represented by the single tally mark in the lower left-hand cell of the tabulation portion of the chart. WBC's Y-axis score of 29 and X-axis score of 50 are similarly represented by one of the two tally marks in the central cell of the tabulation section of the chart.]

(3) Add the tally marks in each cell and write the appropriate total at the center of the cell. [All except three of the functional cells in Figure 24 are occupied by only one tally mark each; three cells near the center of the chart have frequencies of 2.]

(4) Add the cell frequencies in each row and record the totals in the f_y column; do likewise for the cell frequencies in each column and record the totals in the f_x row. Add the frequencies in the f_y column to obtain N and in the f_x row to obtain N again as a check on accuracy. [The sum of the f_y column and the sum of the f_x row are both shown to be 30 in Figure 24.]

(5) Assume values for the arithmetic means and count off the deviations for the two distributions. Assume a value for the mean on each axis and count off the deviations in the d column and row, using the procedure of steps (1) and (2), page 307, for computing the arithmetic mean. Deviations upward and to the right are positive; deviations downward and to the left are negative. [The means of the Y-axis and X-axis scores in Figure 24 are assumed to fall at the midpoints of the intervals 29-31 and 48-52 respectively; the d values for the Y-axis and X-axis scores consequently range from $+6$ to -6 and from -7 to $+7$ respectively.]

(6) Multiply each frequency in the f_y column and the f_x row by its corresponding d and record the products in the fd_y column and fd_x row. Add the values in the fd_y column and the fd_x row algebraically to obtain

X axis Standardized Test

Y axis Informal Objective Test

	13–17	18–22	23–27	28–32	33–37	38–42	43–47	48–52	53–57	58–62	63–67	68–72	73–77	78–82	83–87	f_y	d	fd_y	fd_y^2	x'y' +	x'y' −
49–47	-42	-36	-30	-24	-18	-12	-6		6	12	18	24	30 /	36	42	1	6	6	36	30	
46–44	-35	-30	-25	-20	-15	-10	-5		5	10	15	20	25	30	35	0	5	0	0		
43–41	-28	-24	-20	-16	-12	-8	-4		4	8	12	16	20	24	28 /	1	4	4	16	28	
40–38	-21	-18	-15	-12	-9	-6	-3		3	6 /	9 /	12	15	18	21	2	3	6	18	15	
37–35	-14	-12	-10	-8	-6	-4	-2		2 /	4	6	8	10 /	12	14	2	2	4	8	12	
34–32	-7	-6	-5	-4	-3	-2	-1	/	1	2 /	3	4 /	5	6 /	7	4	1	4	4	12	
31–29							/	2			/	/	/			6					
28–26	7	6	5	4	3	2 2	1		-1 2	-2	-3 /	-4	-5	-6	-7	5	-1	-5	5	4	5
25–23	14	12	10	8	6 /	4 /	2	/	-2	-4	-6	-8	-10	-12	-14	3	-2	-6	12	10	
22–20	21	18	15	12 /	9	6	3 /		-3	-6	-9	-12	-15	-18	-21	2	-3	-6	18	15	
19–17	28	24	20	16 /	12	8	4		-4	-8	-12	-16	-20	-24	-28	1	-4	-4	16	16	
16–14	35	30	25 /	20	15 /	10	5		-5	-10	-15	-20	-25	-30	-35	2	-5	-10	50	40	
13–11	42 /	36	30	24	18	12	6		-6	-12	-18	-24	-30	-36	-42	1	-6	-6	36	42	
f_x	1	0	1	2	2	3	2	4	3	2	3	2	3	1	1	N 30		Σfd_y	Σfd_y^2	$\Sigma x'y'$	$\Sigma x'y'$
d	-7	-6	-5	-4	-3	-2	-1		1	2	3	4	5	6	7			-13	219	+224	-5
fd_x	-7	0	-5	-8	-6	-6	-2		3	4	9	8	15	6	7	Σfd_x		18		$\Sigma x'y'$	
fd_x^2	49	0	25	32	18	12	2		3	8	27	32	75	36	49	Σfd_x^2		368		219	

FIGURE 24. Tabulation and Analysis of Paired Scores on Two English Usage Tests for Ninth-Grade Pupils

Σfd_y and Σfd_x respectively. [The Σfd_y and Σfd_x values for Figure 24 are respectively -13 $(-37 + 24)$ and 18 $(-34 + 52)$.]

(7) Multiply each value in the fd_y column and the fd_x row by its corresponding d and record the products in the $fd_y{}^2$ column and $fd_x{}^2$ row. Add the values in the $fd_y{}^2$ column and the $fd_x{}^2$ row to obtain $\Sigma fd_y{}^2$ and $\Sigma fd_x{}^2$ respectively. [The $\Sigma fd_y{}^2$ and $\Sigma fd_x{}^2$ values for Figure 24 are respectively 219 and 368.]

(8) Obtain the moment, i.e., the algebraic product of the deviations on the Y axis and X axis, for each cell, or in any event for each cell in which at least one tally mark appears, and write it in the upper right-hand corner of the cell. [In Figure 24, for example, the cell in the lower left-hand corner of the tabulation has a moment of 42 (-7×-6) and the cell in the 26-28 interval on the Y axis and the 63-67 interval on the X axis has a moment of -3 (-1×3).]

(9) Multiply the frequency in each cell by the moment in the upper right-hand corner of that cell, separately add the positive and the negative products in each row, and record the positive and negative sums appropriately in the two $x'y'$ columns. [For example, the topmost score on the chart in Figure 24 has a cell value of 30; the product of the frequency and moment (1×30) is recorded in the $+$ column as 30. Again, for the scores in the class interval 29-31 on the Y axis, the $x'y'$ value in the $+$ column is 4 (2×2) and the $x'y'$ value in the $-$ column is 5 $(2 \times -1) + (1 \times -3)$.]

(10) Add the values in the $x'y'$ columns algebraically to obtain $\Sigma x'y'$. [In Figure 24, $\Sigma x'y'$ is 219 $(224 - 5)$.]

(11) Divide $\Sigma fd_x{}^2$ by N and $\Sigma fd_y{}^2$ by N. [For the paired scores of Figure 24, the quotients are 12.27 and 7.30 respectively.]

$$\frac{\Sigma fd_x{}^2}{N} = \frac{368}{30} = 12.27 \qquad \frac{\Sigma fd_y{}^2}{N} = \frac{219}{30} = 7.30$$

(12) Divide Σfd_x by N and Σfd_y by N. [For the paired scores of Figure 24, the quotients are .60 and $-.43$ respectively.]

$$\frac{\Sigma fd_x}{N} = \frac{18}{30} = .60 \qquad \frac{\Sigma fd_y}{N} = \frac{-13}{30} = -.43$$

(13) Square the results of step (12) for the X-axis and for the Y-axis scores. [For the paired scores of Figure 24, the squares are .36 and .18 respectively.]

$$\left(\frac{\Sigma fd_x{}^2}{N}\right) = .60^2 = .36 \qquad \left(\frac{\Sigma fd_y{}^2}{N}\right) = -.43^2 = .18$$

(14) Subtract the result of step (13) from the result of step (11) for the X-axis and for the Y-axis scores. [For the paired scores of Figure 24, these subtractions result in 11.91 and 7.12 respectively.]

$$\frac{\Sigma f d_x^2}{N} - \left(\frac{\Sigma f d_x}{N}\right)^2 = 12.27 - .36 = 11.91$$

$$\frac{\Sigma f d_y^2}{N} - \left(\frac{\Sigma f d_y}{N}\right)^2 = 7.30 - .18 = 7.12$$

(15) Extract the square root of the results of step (14) to obtain the standard deviations in terms of class intervals for the X-axis and for the Y-axis scores. [For the paired scores of Figure 24, the square roots in deviation form are 3.45 and 2.67 respectively.]

$$\sigma_x = \sqrt{\frac{\Sigma f d_x^2}{N} - \left(\frac{\Sigma f d_x}{N}\right)^2} = \sqrt{11.91} = 3.45$$

$$\sigma_y = \sqrt{\frac{\Sigma f d_y^2}{N} - \left(\frac{\Sigma f d_y}{N}\right)^2} = \sqrt{7.12} = 2.67$$

(16) Divide the result of step (10) by N. [For the paired scores of Figure 24, the quotient is 7.30.]

$$\frac{\Sigma x'y'}{N} = \frac{219}{30} = 7.30$$

(17) Solve the equation for the Pearson product-moment correlation coefficient by using the result of step (16) and the two results of step (12) in the numerator and the two results of step (15) in the denominator. [For the paired scores of Figure 24, the Pearson product-moment r is .81.]

$$r = \frac{\dfrac{\Sigma x'y'}{N} - \left(\dfrac{\Sigma f d_x}{N}\right)\left(\dfrac{\Sigma f d_y}{N}\right)}{\sigma_x \times \sigma_y} = \frac{7.30 - (.60 \times -.43)}{3.45 \times 2.67}$$

$$= \frac{7.30 - (-.26)}{9.21} = \frac{7.30 + .26}{9.21} = \frac{7.56}{9.21} = .81$$

APPENDIX B

DIRECTORY OF TEST PUBLISHERS AND

EQUIPMENT MANUFACTURERS

Acorn Publishing Co., Inc., Rockville Centre, Long Island, N.Y.

American Child Health Association, 1201 Sixteenth St., N.W., Washington 6, D.C.

American Guidance Service, Inc., 720 Washington Ave., S.E., Minneapolis 14, Minn.

Bureau of Educational Measurements, Kansas State Teachers College, Emporia, Kans.

Bureau of Educational Research and Service, State University of Iowa, Iowa City, Iowa.

Bureau of Publications, Teachers College, Columbia University, New York 27, N.Y.

California Test Bureau, Del Monte Research Park, Monterey, Calif.

Center for Psychological Service, George Washington University, Washington, D.C.

Division of Educational Reference, Purdue University, Lafayette, Ind.

Educational Test Bureau, 720 Washington Ave., S.E., Minneapolis 14, Minn.

Educational Testing Service, 20 Nassau St., Princeton, N.J.

John C. Flanagan, 413 Morewood Ave., Pittsburgh 13, Pa.

Gregg Publishing Division, McGraw-Hill Book Co., Inc., 330 West 42nd St., New York 36, N.Y.

Grune and Stratton, Inc., 381 Fourth Ave., New York 16, N.Y.

Hal Leonard Music, Inc., 64 East Second St., Winona, Minn.

Harcourt, Brace and World, Inc., Tarrytown, N.Y.

Harvard University Press, 79 Garden St., Cambridge 38, Mass.

Houghton Mifflin Co., 2 Park St., Boston 7, Mass.

International Business Machines Corporation, 590 Madison Ave., New York 22, N.Y.

Iowa State College Press, Press Building, Ames, Iowa.

Joint Committee on Tests, United Business Education Association, 1201 Sixteenth St., N.W., Washington 6, D.C.

Keystone View Co., Meadville, Pa.

Alma J. Knauber, 6988 Warder Drive, Cincinnati 24, Ohio.

McKnight and McKnight, Bloomington, Ill.

Measurement Research Center, Inc., State University of Iowa, Iowa City, Iowa.

Mental Measurements Yearbooks, Rutgers University, New Brunswick, N.J.

Mills Music, Inc., 1619 Broadway, New York 19, N.Y.

National Society for the Prevention of Blindness, Inc., 1790 Broadway, New York 19, N.Y.

New York University Bookstore, 239 Greene St., New York 3, N.Y.

Ohio College Association, Ohio State University, Columbus, Ohio.

Personnel Press, Inc., 188 Nassau St., Princeton, N.J.

Psychological Corporation, 304 East 45th St., New York 17, N.Y.

Psychological Institute, P.O. Box 1118, Lake Alfred, Fla.

Purdue Research Foundation, Purdue University, Lafayette, Ind.

Russell Sage Foundation, 505 Park Ave., New York 22, N.Y.

Scholastic Magazines, Inc., 33 West 42nd St., New York 36, N.Y.

Scholastic Testing Service, Inc., 2056 West Devon Ave., Chicago 45, Ill.

Science Research Associates, Inc., 259 West Erie St., Chicago 11, Ill.

South-Western Publishing Co., 5101 Madison Road, Cincinnati 27, Ohio.

Stanford University Press, Stanford, Calif.

University Book Store, 360 State St., West Lafayette, Ind.

Western Psychological Services, 10655 Santa Monica Blvd., Los Angeles 25, Calif.

INDEX OF NAMES

INDEX OF SUBJECTS

Measurement (*Continued*)
  of mental ability, 100-14
  of musical talent, 502-5
  of occupational status, 75-76
  of oral language skills, 377-79
  of oral reading skills, 354-56
  of performance, 264-65, 267-70
  of personality, 129-32
  of physical status and potential, 553-56
  of pupil background and status, 6-8
  of readiness, 351-53, 428
  of reading comprehension, 356-63
  of reading readiness, 351-53
  of recreational actvities, 561-65
  of scientific aptitude, 447-48
  of scientific attitudes, 459-60
  of skill in business education, 545-47
  of skill in physical education, 558-61
  of social attitudes, 476-78
  of status characteristics, 76-78
  of total personality, 143-48
  of written language skills, 380-90
  prior to 1800, 20-21
  significance of educational, 13-15
  standard error of, 62, 330-31
Measures: of average or central tendency, 318-19
  of home status, 73-75
  of nutrition and body build, 92-93
  of occupational status, 75-76
  of physical maturity, 85-86
  of posture and body mechanics, 92
  of relationship, 320
  of reliability of test scores, 341-42
  of spread or variability, 319
  of strength, power, and endurance, 91
  of test reliability and validity, 341
Measuring, 4
  techniques, 273-76
Mechanical abilities, tests of, 42, 228, 266, 525
Mechanical aptitude tests, 524
Median: computation of, 308, 310-11
  meaning of, 319
Medical tests, 88-90
Meier Art Judgment Test, 510-11
Meier Art Tests, 510
Mental abilities: multifactor tests of, 112, 124
  tests of special, 108-11, 124
Mental ability: and socioeconomic status, 81
  general tests of, 102-8, 122-23
  measurable evidences of, 8
  multifactor tests of, 112, 124

performance tests of, 125
  special tests of, 108-11, 124
Mental ability testing, derived results of, 115-16
Mental age, 115
Mental testing: nineteenth century, 23-24
  present status of, 29
  since 1900, 24-26
Mental tests: common types of, 34-45
  special types of, 29-34
Mental traits, 5-6
Methods: anecdotal, 143-44
  observational, 131-32
  projective, 26, 144-45
Metropolitan Achievement Tests, 31, 171, 233-34, 236, 237, 383, 384, 417-18, 419-20, 473-74, 571, 575-76
Metropolitan Arithmetic Computation Test, 417-18
Metropolitan Arithmetic Problem Solving Test, 419-20
Metropolitan History and Civics Test, 473-74
Metropolitan Readiness Tests, 111
Michigan Vocabulary Profile Test, 362-63
Mid-score: determination of, 302-4
  meaning of, 319
Minnesota Check List for Food Preparation and Serving, 533
Minnesota Clerical Test, 543
Minnesota Home Status Index, 74
Minnesota House Design and House Furnishing Test, 532
Minnesota Paper Form Board Test, 524
Minnesota Vocational Test for Clerical Workers, 543
Modern foreign languages: measurement of achievement in, 489-95
  significance and trends in, 485-87
  tests in, 491-95
Modern Language Aptitude Test, 57, 61, 488
Modern School Achievement Tests, 572, 588
Mooney Problem Check List, 142
Motor fitness testing, 94
Multifactor tests of mental abilities, 112
  nature of, 36
  uses of, 124
Multiple-choice items: construction of, 246-48
  varieties of, 227-32
Multiple-option items, 227-31
Multiple-response items, 231-32
Music: measurement of accomplishment in, 505-9

Test results (*Continued*)
 interpretation of, 161-62, 174-87, 255-56
 recording, 215-16
 representation of, 310-13, 333-34
 use of, 259-60, 277-78, 293
Test scores: analysis of, 302-4, 307-10
 as deviations from an average, 335-39
 classification of, 301-4
 description of, 299-301
 distributions of, 186, 304-7
 giving order to, 300-1
 in double-entry tables, 591-93
 in frequency distributions, 304-13
 in rank order, 301-4, 332-35
 interpretation of, 323-24, 339-42
 nature of, 299-301
 paired, in rank order, 313-17
 representation of, 310-13, 333-34
 tabulation of, 305-7
Test standards, 175
Testing, 4
 in the nineteenth century, 21-24
 in present-day schools, 13-14
Testing program, planning a comprehensive, 45-49
Tests: achievement, 153-95
 administering, 166-68, 254
 analytic, 41-42
 aptitude, 25-26, 35-36, 109-10
 assembling, 161-62
 bifactor, 35
 cardiovascular, 90-91
 common types of, 34-36
 diagnostic, 41-42
 educational, 38-45
 essay, 33, 39, 204-13
 evaluative, 28, 283-87
 first educational, 21-23
 first mental, 23-24
 first personality, 24
 first standardized achievement, 27
 for archery, 564
 for badminton, 564
 for baseball, 557, 559, 560
 for basketball, 557, 559-60
 for dancing, 564
 for football, 560
 for golf, 564
 for hockey, 557
 for playground baseball, 557, 560
 for riding, 564
 for skating, 565
 for softball, 557, 560
 for soccer, 557-58, 560
 for swimming, 560-61

 for table tennis, 565
 for tennis, 558, 561, 565
 for volleyball, 561
 general achievement, 570-89
 general intelligence, 24-25, 34-35, 102-8, 122-23
 general mental ability, 102-8, 122-23
 group intelligence, 34-35, 105-8
 in algebra, 434-36
 in arithmetic, 233, 236, 416-21, 428
 in art, 226, 509-14
 in biology, 453-55
 in bookkeeping, 546-47, 548
 in business education, 539-49
 in chemistry, 229, 454-56
 in civics, 474
 in earth science, 449
 in elementary science, 449-50
 in elementary social studies, 471-74
 in English language, 234, 237, 383-89
 in expressive language, 234, 237, 383-89, 392-95
 in fine arts, 223, 226, 428-38, 502-16
 in foods, 532
 in foreign language, 487-98
 in French, 491-93
 in general mathematics, 432-33
 in general science, 453
 in geography, 472
 in geometry, 238, 436-38
 in German, 493
 in government, 476
 in history, 232, 234, 472-75
 in home economics, 267, 272, 275-76, 532-33
 in household management, 532
 in hygiene, 449
 in industrial arts, 42, 228, 266, 272-75, 523-25, 529
 in Latin, 497-98
 in literature, 223, 515-16
 in mathematics, 223, 428-38
 in modern foreign languages, 491-95
 in music, 502-9
 in physical education, 553-61
 in physics, 455
 in physiology, 449
 in reading, 225, 235, 352-63
 in receptive language, 352-65
 in recreation education, 224, 561-65
 in science, 41, 230, 269, 284, 447-56
 in secondary school science, 451-56
 in secondary school social studies, 474-76
 in social studies, 232, 234, 287, 471-80
 in Spanish, 494-95